Presented to

The Official Guide to American Historic Inns

Rated "Outstanding" by Morgan Rand.

Winner of Benjamin Franklin Award — Best Travel Guide

Comments from print media:

"Readers will find this book easy to use and handy to have. The Sakaches have conveyed their love of historic inns and have shared that feeling and information in an attractive and inviting guide. An excellent, well-organized and comprehensive reference for inngoers and innkeepers alike." **Inn Review**, Kankakee, Illinois.

" ... thoughtfully organized and look-ups are hassle free ... well-researched and accurate ... put together by people who know the field. There is no other publication available that covers this particular segment of the bed & breakfast industry — a segment that has been gaining popularity among travellers by leaps and bounds. The information included is valuable and well thought out." **Morgan Directory Reviews**

"This is the best bed and breakfast book out. It outshines them all!" Maggie Balitas, Rodale Book Clubs

"Most of us military families have lived all over the world, so it takes an unusual book, service or trip to excite us! As I began to look through ***The Official Guide to American Historic Bed & Breakfast Inns and Guesthouses*** *by Tim and Deborah Sakach, my heart beat faster as I envisioned what a good time our readers could have visiting some the very special historic bed and breakfast properties."* Ann Crawford, **Military Living**

"Delightful, succinct, detailed and well-organized. Easy to follow style ... " Don Wudke, **Los Angeles Times.**

"This is one of the best guidebooks of its kind. It's easy to use, accurate and the thumbnail sketches give the readers enough description to choose among the more than 1000 properties detailed and thousands others listed. " **Dallas Morning News**

" ... helps you find the very best hideways (many of the book's listings appear in the National Register of Historic Places.)" **Country Living**

"I love your book!" Lydia Moss, Travel Editor, **McCalls.**

Comments from radio:

"Absolutely beautiful!" KQIL talk show radio.

"This is a great book. It makes you want to card everything." KBRT Los Angeles radio talk show.

"All our lines were tied up. We received calls from every one of our 40 stations." Business Radio Network regarding inquiries about **The Official Guide to American Historic Inns.**

Comments from innkeepers:

"Your book is wonderful. I have been reading it as one does a novel." V. Kilpatrick, Olallieberry Inn, CA.

"We want to tell you how much we love your book. We have it out for guests to use. They love it, each featured inn stands out so well. Thank you for the privilege of being in your book." Maine innkeeper.

"When the new edition comes out, please send us a box of your beautiful guidebooks. Our guest love it and the local book store can't keep up with the orders. We'd like to have them right here at the inn." Wisconsin innkeeper.

"What a wonderful book! We love it and have been very pleased with the guests that have made reservations using your book." Vermont innkeeper.

Recommended by:

McCalls, Changing Times, Women's Day, USA Today, Library Journal, Publishers Weekly, Book-of-the-Month Club News, Los Angeles Times

The Official Guide to

American Historic Inns

Third Edition

Includes 5400 Bed & Breakfasts and Country Inns

Formerly called:

The Official Guide to

American Historic

Bed & Breakfast

Inns and Guesthouses

The Official Guide to

American Historic Inns

Third Edition

Includes 5400 Bed & Breakfasts and Country Inns

Formerly called:

The Official Guide to

American Historic

Bed & Breakfast

Inns and Guesthouses

Deborah Edwards Sakach

Timothy J. Sakach

Association of American Historic Inns

Dana Point, California

Distributed by

Rand McNally & Company

Skokie, Illinois

Published by:
The Association of American Historic Inns
P. O. Box 336
Dana Point, California 92629

Front cover:
Green Gables Inn, Pacific Grove, California

Photos by Timothy Sakach.

Every effort has been made to provide dependable reference material from information gathered from innkeepers and from the authors' own personal observations. This information is subject to change without notice. The authors and publisher make no representation that this book is complete and free from all errors. We recommend that you contact the inns and B&Bs to verify information herein prior to making reservations. Unfortunately, in spite of our best efforts, errors or omissions, whether typographical, clerical or otherwise, may sometimes occur. If such are brought to our attention, future editions will be changed accordingly.

Some of the drawings in this edition were done by artist Claire Read of San Juan Capistrano, California.

Publisher's Cataloging in Publication Data
Sakach, Timothy J & Deborah Edwards
The Official Guide to American Historic Inns
1. Bed & Breakfast Accommodations — United States, Directories, Guide Books.
2. Travel — Historic Inns, Directories, Guide Books.
3. Bed & Breakfast Accommodations — Historic Inns , Directories, Guide Books.
4. Hotel Accommodations — Bed & Breakfast Inns, Directories, Guide Books.
5. Hotel Accommodations — United States, Inns, Directories, Guide Books.
I Title . II Author. III American Historic Inns, The Official Guide
ISBN 0-9615481-1-8 Softcover
Library of Congress: ISSN 1043-1195 87-71501

647'.947

Printed in the United States of America

Contents

Our appreciation and thanks to each of the innkeepers who provided reams of historical information, brochures, drawings, copies of newspaper articles, photographs, and local folklore about their inns. Most of all we are grateful for their constant enthusiasm and support for the project all along the way.

We are grateful to our son Tim and daughter Suzanne for their ideas, advice and encouragement and to our son Stephen, for his journalistic experience and sharp editorial eye. A special thanks to our son David for the long hours spent sizing and preparing nearly 800 pen and ink drawings.

Our thanks also to Beth Baldwin, Pam Moffett and Sydney Mack for their assistance along the way.

A heartfelt thanks to Sandy Imre whose hard work and skill with a computer was crucial to making this edition possible.

Tim & Deborah Sakach

How to use this book

You hold in your hands the largest and most comprehensive book available in the United States on bed & breakfasts and country inns. This expanded third edition provides the inn connoisseur with a convenient reference for present and future travel needs. Only *historic* country inns and *historic* B&B inns are included here (by *historic* we mean those in buildings dating prior to 1940.) Some have recently opened. Others have been operating for hundreds of years and have a long and rich history. All have stories to tell.

We have not included homestays except in rare instances. All currently active homestays can be reached through the reservation services listed in the appendix of this book.

Cross references

Some inns desired to be listed under a nearby city or town. This is helpful to travelers who may not be familiar with the proximity of a lesser known town to a larger, better known city. This cross reference should be checked if you are considering a stay at the major city. Most of the cross references are within 30 minutes drive from the better known city.

Codes

We have kept the use of codes to a minimum and have used them only to refer to those things with which we are all very familiar.

Credit Cards

Visa .... Visa
MC .... Master Charge
AE .... American Express
CB .... Carte Blanche
DC .... Diner's Club
DS .... Discover Card

Beds

K .... King size bed
Q .... Queen-size bed
D .... Double size bed
T .... Twin beds
W .... Waterbed
C .... Crib available

Meals

Continental breakfast: coffee, juice, toast, or pastry.

Continental-plus breakfast: A continental breakfast plus a variety of breads, cheeses, fruit.

Full breakfast: Coffee, juice, breads and an egg or meat entree.

B&B: Breakfast (full or continental) included in the price of the room.

AP: American Plan. All three meals are included in the price of the room. Check to see if quoted for two people or per person.

MAP: Modified American Plan. Breakfast and dinner are included in the price of the room.

EP: European Plan. No meals are included.

"Seen in:"

If the inns provided us with excerpts from verifiable articles appearing in magazines or newspaper, or perhaps radio and TV shows, we have indicated the source in the listing. These articles may be available either from the source as reprints or through libraries.

Rates

Unless indicated with a "pp" (per person) all rates are double occupancy. Those marked with "❀" have made special offers to the readers of this book. These discount certificates can be found in the back of the book.

The symbol "⁕" indicates inns that can be booked either directly or through a reservation service or travel agent. If your travel agent is unfamiliar with the inn, show him or her a copy of **The Official Guide to American Historic Inns.**

All rates are listed as ranges. The range covers both off-season low rates and busy season high rates. When making reservations you should verify rates. Although rates were accurate at press time, they are always subject to change.

Smoking

The majority of country inns and B&Bs in the United States prohibit smoking, therefore if you are a smoker we advise you to call and specifically check with each inn to see if and how they accommodate smokers.

Comments

We have requested that innkeepers provide us with actual guest comments and with the names and addresses of the guests making the comment. If the names were not provided we did not use the comment.

INNspections

This book contains nearly 1200 major listings of historic inns plus a comprehensive directory of more than 5400 historic inns. Each year we travel across the country visiting hundreds of inns and often covering more than 20,000 miles per year. Since 1981 we have had a happy informal team of inn goers who report to us on a regular basis about new bed and breakfast discoveries and repeat visits to favorite inns.

However, "inspecting" inns is not the major focus of our travels. We visit as many as possible, photograph them, and get to know the innkeepers. There are inns that are models of fineness. And there are others that are rustic which we enjoyed and hated to leave. Many of the old buildings have warmth, charm and character and are managed by some of the finest people in the country. We cherish all these memories whether pristine or rustic. Only rarely have we come across a "bad" inn — poorly kept and poorly managed. These usually do not survive since much of an inn's success depends upon repeat business and word of mouth from satisfied customers.

Travel is an adventure into the unknown, full of surprises and rewards. One thing a seasoned traveler learns is that even after elaborate preparations and careful planning travel provides the new, the unexpected, the adventure. The traveler learns to live with uncertainty and considers it part of the adventure.

To the *tourist,* whether "accidental" or otherwise, however, such reality is always frustrating and disconcerting. Tourists want no surprises. They expect things to be exactly as they had envisioned them. To these we recommend staying in a hotel or motel chain where sameness from one locale to another is the rule.

Experienced inn-goers are travelers at heart. They know that America's intimate historic inns are all different. This uniqueness, a reflection of our individuality, is the magic that makes traveling from inn to inn the delightful experience it is.

If you wish to participate in evaluating your inn experiences, use the **Inn Evaluation Form** in the back of the book. You might want to make copies of this form prior to departing on your journey.

Minimum stay requirements

When traveling in peak seasons, expect two night minimums. In some areas two night minimums are required at all times on weekends.

Advance Reservations Required

For weekend travel and travel to resort areas during peak season, advance reservations are always required. Some inns fill up six to twelve weeks in advance.

What to do if all the inns you call are full

Ask the inn for recommendations. Perhaps a new inn has opened or there might be one a little off the beaten path.

Call a reservation service for that area. See **Reservation Services** in this book.

Call the local Chamber of Commerce in the town you hope to visit. They may know of inns that have recently opened.

Call or write to the state tourism bureau. See the **State Tourism Information** section.

Alabama

Mentone

Mentone Inn

Highway 117, PO Box 284
Mentone AL 35984
(205) 634-4836

Circa 1927. Mentone is a refreshing stop for those looking for the cool breezes and natural air-conditioning of the mountains. Here antique treasures mingle with modern-day conveniences. A sun deck and spa complete the experience. Sequoyah Caverns, Little River Canyon and DeSoto Falls are moments away. The inn has its own hiking trails.

Location: On Lookout Mountain in northeast Alabama.

*Rates: $35-$70. Season: April - Nov 1.

Amelia Kirk.

12 Rooms. 12 Private Baths. Guest phone available. TV available. Beds: QT. B&B. Gourmet meals. Jacuzzi. Conference room.

Seen in: *Birmingham News*.

Mobile

Vincent-Doan Home

1664 Springhill Ave
Mobile AL 36604
(205) 433-7121

Circa 1827. This is not only the oldest house in Mobile but also the last remaining example of French Creole architecture. The house has been restored and retains its original roof line, galleries and facade. Each bedroom has a fireplace and provides direct access to the gallery overlooking the garden.

Rates: $50-$70.

Betty Doan.

3 Rooms. 3 Private Baths. Guest phone in room. TV in room. Beds: DT. Full breakfast. CCs: MC VISA.

Alaska

Anchorage

Alaska Private Lodgings

PO Box 200047
Anchorage AK 99511
(907) 248-2292

Circa 1900. Mercy Dennis operates this bed and breakfast reservation service. She lists several historic properties including one with a charming downtown suite in one of the oldest buildings in town, a carriage house. Additional accommodations are available in apartments and private homes. Mercy is also knowlegeable about tours and sightseeing trips throughout Alaska.

Rates: $60-$75.

McCarthy Wilderness B&B

Box 111241
Anchorage AK 99511
(907) 277-6867

Circa 1917. This cabin, once occupied by the territorial commissioner, is in the National Register. Nearby is another cabin, once the mother lode powerhouse for copper mines, now closed, that are up McCarthy Creek. There is no electricity here so wood stoves provide the heat, kerosene lanterns the light.

Location: South Central Alaska.
Bob & Bobbie Jacobs.
6 Rooms. Beds: QT. B&B. Jacuzzi. Sauna. Conference room. Rafting, glacier trekking, horseback riding, ghost towns.

"Loved every minute. Just wish we could have stayed longer."

Homer

Driftwood Inn

135-T W Bunnell Ave
Homer AK 99603
(907) 235-8019

Circa 1920. Clean, comfortable and unpretentious, the Driftwood Inn is in a historic building on the shores of Kachemak Bay. The inn caters to families and sportsmen and all-you-can-eat breakfasts are a special feature. There are spectacular mountain and water views.

Location: On the beach with views of mountains, glaciers and the bay.
Rates: $45-$75.
Shonie Cordes.
8 Rooms. 7 Private Baths. Guest phone available. TV available. Full breakfast. Sauna. Moose watching, wildflower photography.

Talkeetna

Fairview Inn

PO Box 379
Talkeetna AK 99676
(907) 733-2423

Circa 1923. Built along the Alaska Railroad 100 miles north of Anchorage, the "View" as it is called locally, once hosted president Warren Harding. As gold and silver mining and fur trapping in the area increased, the inn gained in popularity and today it is a favorite

meeting place for local old timers. In the spring and summer, climbers hoping to reach the summit of Mt. McKinley, often stop by.

Rates: $25.
7 Rooms. Guest phone available. TV available. Beds: KDTC. CCs: MC VISA. Cross-country skiing, hiking, fishing, rafting, dog sled & snow machine trips.

Arizona

Bisbee

Park Place B&B

200 E Vista
Bisbee AZ 85603
(602) 432-5516 (602)990-0682

Circa 1919. Grant McGregor was a civil engineer and designed mines and mills throughout the world. One of Bisbee's pioneer homes, the McGregor house incorporates several styles including Spanish-Mediterranean, Greek Revival and Italian Villa. Graceful old sycamores and evergreens provide shady spaces, while peach, fig, pomegranate, and plum trees add seasonal splashes of color. Owners of a local bakery and a restaurant, Innkeepers Bob & Janet Watkins, serve a full breakfast on the terrace, or in the library.

*Rates: $50-$70.
Bob & Janet Watkins.
4 Rooms. 2 Private Baths. 2 Fireplaces. Guest phone available. TV available. Beds: QDT. B&B. Conference room. CCs: MC VISA. Tennis, golf, underground mine tour.

Flagstaff

Birch Tree Inn

824 W Birch Ave
Flagstaff AZ 86001
(602) 774-1042

Circa 1917. This midwestern style bungalow is surrounded by a wraparound veranda supported with Corinthian columns. Southwestern and antique decor is featured including shaker pine and white wicker. Nature lovers and ski enthusiasts will appreciate the Ponderosa Pine Forest nearby. Adjacent to the inn, cross-country ski trails are especially popular. For winter warm ups the innkeepers provide fresh baked bread and steaming homemade soup. In summer an afternoon tea is served.

Rates: $60-$75.
Donna & Rodger Pettinger, Sandy & Ed Znetko.
5 Rooms. 3 Private Baths. Guest phone available. TV available. Beds: KQT. Full breakfast. Game room. CCs: MC VISA. Horseback riding, cross-country & downhill skiing, telescope viewing.

"...charming hosts and wonderful food."

Phoenix

Westways "Private" Resort

PO 41624
Phoenix AZ 85080
(602) 582-3868

Circa 1939. This Spanish Mediterranean house originally constructed

in the Thirties, has been completely renovated and now reflects a contemporary southwestern tone. The inn is on an acre landscaped with plants from the various regions of Arizona. There are desert cactus, palm trees, grapefruit and orange trees, as well as semi-tropical plantings and mountain pines. A tranquil Mexican fountain is the centerpiece of the courtyard.

Location: Northwest Phoenix, adjacent to Arrowhead Country Club.
**Rates: $78-$105.
Darrell Trapp & Brian Curran.
6 Rooms. 5 Private Baths. Guest phone in room. TV in room. Beds: QD. B&B. Jacuzzi. Handicap access. Swimming pool. Conference room. CCs: MC VISA DS.
Seen in: *Los Angeles Times, TravelAge West.*

"Personalized service made our stay memorable."

Prescott

Marks House Inn

203 E Union
Prescott AZ 86303
(602) 778-4632

Circa 1894. In the 1890s four prominent residences dominated Nob Hill. One of them was the

Marks house. Built by Jake Marks, cattle rancher and mine owner it's now in the National Historic Register. This Victorian mansion provides a special setting in which to enjoy rare antiques, gracious breakfasts, and majestic sunsets. Fireplaces are in the living and dining rooms.

Location: Ninety miles north of Phoenix. One block from Courthouse Square.
*Rates: $75-$110.
Anita & Kristin Fetterly.
4 Rooms. 4 Private Baths. Guest phone available. Beds: KQD. B&B. Conference room. CCs: MC VISA. Hiking, art fairs,

antiquing. May Territorial Days. World's oldest rodeo, July.
Seen in: *Member of B&B in Arizona.*
"Exceptional!"

Prescott Pines Inn
901 White Spar Rd
Prescott AZ 86303
(602) 445-7270 (800)541-5374 US only

Circa 1902. Originally the Haymore Dairy, a white picket fence now beckons guests to the veranda

of this comfortably elegant country Victorian inn. Masses of fragrant pink roses, lavender and delphinium afford a gracious welcome. Stately ponderosa pines tower above the inn's four renovated cottages, once shelter for farm hands. Each guestroom reflects the rose, cream, and blue theme of the garden. An acre of grounds include a garden fountain and a romantic tree swing.
Location: One-and-a-third miles south of Courthouse Plaza.
Rates: $45-$145.
Jean Wil and Michael Acton.
13 Rooms. 13 Private Baths. 4 Fireplaces. Guest phone in room. TV in room. Beds: KQC. B&B. Gourmet meals. Handicap access. Conference room. CCs: MC VISA DS. Horseback riding, hiking, golf, tennis.
Seen in: *Sunset Magazine*
"The ONLY place to stay in Prescott!. Tremendous attention to detail, great flower garden and tree swing!"

Sedona

Saddle Rock Ranch
255 Rock Ridge Dr
Sedona AZ 86336
(602) 282-7640

Circa 1926. If you want an authentic Old West experience, stay at the Saddle Rock Ranch. Nipper, the RCA Victor dog, greets visitors at the front door. The house is con-

structed of native red rock, beamed ceilings and wood and flagstone floors. Guest suites feature fieldstone fireplaces and panoramic vistas of the surrounding red rocks. The house has often been featured in motion pictures depicting the Old West.
Location: On two acres of hillside.
Rates: $55-$98.
Fran & Dan Bruno.
3 Rooms. 3 Private Baths. 3 Fireplaces. Guest phone available. TV available. Beds: QT. Continental-plus breakfast. Jacuzzi. Exercise room. Swimming pool. Conference room. Horseback riding, hiking, fishing, archaeological and back-country jeep expeditions. Horseback riding nearby.
"Thank you for sharing your ranch with us...it has been the highlight of our trip."

Tucson

La Posada Del Valle
1640 N Campbell Ave
Tucson AZ 85719
(602) 795-3840

Circa 1929. The 18-inch thick walls of this southwest adobe wrap around to form a courtyard. Ornamental orange trees surround the property, across the street from the University Medical Center. All the rooms have outside entrances and open to the patio or overlook the courtyard and fountain. A Twenties decor includes a fainting couch. Afternoon tea is served.
Location: Walking distance to the University of Arizona.
*Rates: $60-$110. Season: Closed July.
Charles & Debbi Bryant.
5 Rooms. 5 Private Baths. Guest phone in room. TV available. Beds: KQT. B&B. Gourmet meals. CCs: MC VISA. Individual heating and cooling in each room. Turn-down service.
Seen in: *Gourmet.*
"Thank you so much for such a beautiful home, romantic room and warm hospitality."

The Peppertrees B&B
724 E University
Tucson AZ 85719
(602) 622-7167

Circa 1900. Two ancient peppertrees shade the yard of this red brick territorial house. Outside, a front porch overlooks the bay. Inside you'll find English antiques inherited from the innkeeper's native family. A patio filled with flowers and a fountain divide the main house from two newly built southwestern style guesthouses, each with a kitchen and laundry. Bluecorn pancakes with pecans are a house specialty. Special diets are accommodated. It's a two-block walk to the University of Arizona.
*Rates: $60-$100.
Marjorie C. Martin.
3 Rooms. Guest phone available. TV available. Beds: Q. EP.
Seen in: *Travel Age West.*

Arkansas

Brinkley

The Great Southern Hotel

127 West Cedar
Brinkley AR 72021
(501) 734-4955

Circa 1913. The Victorian-style Great Southern Hotel was built at

the cross roads of seven railroads. Now only one remains. The hotel is across from the Rock Island railroad tracks and adjacent to the Union passenger depot. Both the hotel and depot are in a national historic district. Recently restored, the inn has an elegant and serene atmosphere. There are two balconies and a wraparound veranda.

Location: Midway between Memphis and Little Rock.
*Rates: $40-$42.
Stanley & Dorcas Prince.
4 Rooms. 4 Private Baths. Guest phone available. TV in room. Beds: QD. Full breakfast. Restaurant. Sauna. Exercise room. Conference room. CCs: MC VISA AX DC CB DS. Fishing, duck and quail hunting.
Seen in: *Southern Living, Arkansas Times, Arkansas Gazette.*

"Absolutely terrific! Beautiful."
"A lovely, quaint place."

Eureka Springs

Brownstone Inn

75 Hillside, PO Box 409
Eureka Springs AR 72632
(501) 253-7505

Circa 1800. This native limestone block building served as the Ozark Water Company during the late 1800s. Water was piped from mineral springs in Mill Hollow, bottled here and transported by wagon and railroad around the country. Air-conditioned rooms are furnished in antiques and reproductions.

Rates: $55-$65. Season: March - Dec.
Virginia Rush & John Rakes.
3 Rooms. 3 Private Baths. Guest phone available. Beds: D. Full breakfast. Handicap access. CCs: MC VISA. Fishing, canoeing, boat trips, hiking, Country & Western music shows.
Seen in: *Arkansas Gazette.*

"...wonderful hospitality and delicious breakfast."

Dairy Hollow House

515 Spring St
Eureka Springs AR 72632
(501) 253-7444

Circa 1888. Dairy Hollow House, (the first of Eureka Springs' bed and breakfast inns) consists of a restored Ozark vernacular farm house and a 1940s bungalow style cottage, both in a national historic district. Stenciled walls set off a collection of Eastlake Victorian furnishings. Outstanding *"Nouveau'zarks"* cuisine is available by reservation. The innkeeper is the author of several books, including the award-winning *Dairy Hollow House Cookbook.*

Location: At the junction of Spring & Dairy Hollow Road.
*Rates: $95-$145. Season: March - Dec.
Ned Shank & Crescent Dragonwagon.
5 Rooms. 5 Private Baths. 5 Fireplaces. Guest phone available. Beds: D. Full breakfast. Restaurant. Gourmet meals. Jacuzzi. Handicap access. Conference room. CCs: MC VISA AX DC DS. Hiking, fishing, rafting.
Seen in: *Innsider, Christian Science Monitor, Los Angeles Times.*

"The height of unpretentious luxury."

Heart of the Hills Inn

5 Summit
Eureka Springs AR 72632
(501) 253-7468

Circa 1883. Three suites and a Victorian cottage comprise this antique-furnished homestead located just four blocks from downtown. The Victorian Room is furnished with a white iron bed, dresser, antique lamp and antique pedestal sink. Evening dessert is served. The village trolly stops at the inn.

Rates: $55-$70 Season: Feb - Dec.
Jan Jacobs Weber.
5 Rooms. 5 Private Baths. Guest phone available. TV in room. Beds: KQDTC. Full breakfast. CCs: MC VISA. Horseback riding, water skiing, fishing.
Seen in: *The Carroll County Tribune's Peddler.*

"It was delightful-the bed so comfortable, room gorgeous, food delicious and ohhh those chocolates."

The Heartstone Inn & Cottages

35 King's Hwy
Eureka Springs AR 72632
(501) 253-8916

Circa 1903. Described as a "pink and white confection", this handsome restored Victorian with its wraparound verandas is located in the historic district. The inn is filled

with antiques. Pink roses line the picket fence surrounding the inviting garden.
Location: Northwest Arkansas.
Rates: $55-$85.
Iris & Bill Simantel.
12 Rooms. 12 Private Baths. 1 Fireplace. Guest phone available. TV in room. Beds: KQDC. B&B. Conference room. CCs: MC VISA AX. Horseback riding, water sports, golf, country music shows, museums, galleries. Private cottages available.
Seen in: *Innsider Magazine, Arkansas Times, New York Times, Arkansas Gazette.*
"Extraordinary! Best breakfasts anywhere!"

Palace Hotel
135 Spring
Eureka Springs AR 72632
(501) 253-7474

Circa 1901. When the Palace Hotel and Bath House went through an

extensive renovation, the elegant lobby, the six-foot-long clawfoot tubs (now converted into whirlpools) and the original Eucalyptus steam barrels visitors used at the turn-of-the-century were preserved. Victorian furnishings throughout the hotel add to the opulence. Built on the edge of a cliff, the hotel's lower mineral bath level has a white tiled corridor with private alcoves providing dramatic views of the village below.
*Rates: $85-$100.
Steve & Francie Miller.
8 Rooms. 8 Fireplaces. Guest phone in room. TV in room. Beds: K. Continental-plus breakfast. Jacuzzi. CCs: MC VISA AX DS. Fishing, water & jet ski, horseback riding, hiking, golf.
Seen in: *New York Times, Oklahoma Home & Lifestyle.*

The Piedmont House
165 Spring St
Eureka Springs AR 72632
(501) 253-9258

Circa 1880. An original guest book from the inn's days as a tourist home is a cherished item here. The Piedmont offers the best views in town and is in the National Register.

Rates: $65-$75.
Rose & Larry Olivet.
8 Rooms. 8 Private Baths. Guest phone available. TV available. Beds: DT. Full breakfast. Handicap access. CCs: MC VISA AX. Walking distance to downtown shops and restaurants.
Seen in: *Arkansas Times.*
"Wonderful atmosphere and your personalities are exactly in sync with the surroundings."

Fayetteville

Heart of the Hills Inn
See: Eureka Springs, AR

Helena

Edwardian Inn
317 S Biscoe
Helena AR 72342
(501) 338-9155

Circa 1904. Mark Twain wrote in *Life on the Mississippi,* "Helena oc-

cupies one of the prettiest situations on the river." William Short, cotton broker and speculator, agreed and built his stately home here. The Edwardian Inn boasts a large rotunda and two verandas wrapping around both sides of the house. Inside, wood carpets, floor designs imported from Germany, are composed of 36 pieces of different woods arranged in octagon shapes. Polished-oak panelling and woodwork are set off with a Victorian era decor.
Rates: $50-$59.
Mrs. Jerri Steed.
12 Rooms. 12 Private Baths. Guest phone in room. TV in room. Beds: KD. Continental-plus breakfast. Handicap access. Conference room. CCs: MC VISA AX. Golf, tennis, fishing, duck hunting.
Seen in: *Arkansas Times Magazine, The Dallas Morning News.*
"The Edwardian Inn envelopes you with wonderful feelings, smells and thoughts of the Victorian Era."

Hot Springs

Williams House Inn
420 Quapaw St
Hot Springs AR 71901
(501) 624-4275

Circa 1890. Williams House is a brownstone and brick Victorian nestled among towering oaks and a

40-foot tulip tree. Light and airy rooms are filled with antiques and plants. The carriage house, hitching posts, and mounting blocks are still on the property and the inn is listed in the National Register of Historic Places. Eggs Benedict is popular for breakfast.
Location: Fifty miles southwest of Little Rock, three blocks off Hwy 7.
Rates: $50-$75.
Mary & Gary Riley.
6 Rooms. 4 Private Baths. Guest phone available. TV available. Beds: QDT. Full breakfast. CCs: MC VISA.

Hot Springs Natl Pk

Dogwood Manor B&B

906 Malvern Ave
Hot Springs Natl Pk AR 71901
(501) 624-0896

Circa 1884. This romantic Victorian manor was built by W.H. Moore,

lumber man and owner of the local hardware store. The exterior construction consists of cedar, planed and sawn at Mr. Mills sawmill. A veranda wraps around two sides of the house. Nine-foot pocket doors open to the parlor. There are Chippendale, Queen Anne, Art Deco, Jacobian and Eastlake furnishings throughout the inn. Each day fresh water from the mineral springs is delivered to the guest rooms. The bath houses of Hot Springs National Park have been restored so travellers may enjoy the natural hot springs.

*Rates: $60-$95.
Donna Meadows.
5 Rooms. 5 Private Baths. Guest phone available. TV available. Beds: QDT. Gourmet meals. Conference room. CCs: MC VISA. Horseback riding, water sports, antique heaven, National Park spa baths, natural hot springs, mineral springs.

Mountain View

The Commercial Hotel

PO Box 72,
Washington at Peabody St
Mountain View AR 72560
(501) 269-4383

Circa 1920. The inn's wraparound porches are a gathering place for local musicians who often play old-time music. If you rock long enough you're likely to see an impromptu hootenanny in the Courthouse Square across the street. Since there are no priceless antiques, children are welcome. However, you may have to watch them (and yourself),

because there's a tempting first-floor bakery that's always "fixin up" divinity cookies, macaroons and hot breads.

Location: In the Ozarks.
Rates: $34-$49.
Todd and Andrea Budy.
8 Rooms. 3 Private Baths. Guest phone available. Beds: QDC. B&B. CCs: MC. White water rafting, horseback riding, caverns. Gourmet bakery on site.
Seen in: *Midwest Living, New York Times, Dan Rather & CBS.*

"It's the kind of place you'll look forward to returning to."

"A restful and welcoming bed and breakfast."

California

Alameda

Garratt Mansion

900 Union St
Alameda CA 94501
(415) 521-4779

Circa 1893. This handsome 27-room Colonial Revival mansion was built for industrialist W.T. Garratt. It features outstandingly preserved walnut and oak panelling, crystal windows and ornate mantled fireplaces. The staircase rises three stories with hundreds of gleaming Jacobian-style turned balusters. A set of stained- glass windows encircle a bay at the stairwell landing. The elegance of the mansion is matched by the warmth of its proprietress, Betty Gladden. Often on weekends an authentic English tea is presented.
Rates: $65-$110.
Royce & Betty Gladden.
6 Rooms. 3 Private Baths. 1 Fireplace. Guest phone in room. Beds: QDT. B&B. Conference room. CCs: AX. Tennis, golf, wind surfing, bicycling, jogging, beach.
Seen in: *Alameda Times Star, The Denver Post.*

"I'm delighted that you haven't "commercialized."

Albion

Fensalden B&B

PO Box 99
Albion CA 95410
(707) 937-4042

Circa 1860. Originally a stagecoach station, Fensalden looks out over the Pacific Ocean as it has for more than one-hundred years. The Tavern Room has witnessed many a rowdy scene. If you look closely you can see bullet holes in the original red-

wood ceilings. The inn provides twenty acres for walks, whale-watching, viewing deer and bicycling.
Location: Seven miles south of Mendocino on Hwy 1.
Rates: $75-$125.
Scott & Frances Brazil.
7 Rooms. 7 Private Baths. Guest phone available. Beds: KQ. Full breakfast. CCs: MC VISA.

"...closest feeling to Heaven on Earth."

Altadena

Eye Openers

PO Box 694
Altadena CA 91003
(818) 797-2055 (213) 684-4428

Circa 1926. Eye Openers is a reservation service representing homes throughout Southern California. One of their listings, a French Normandy-style house, was built as a summer home for a railroad industrialist. It has a two-story living room where a former owner, an opera singer, sang to her guests from the half-balcony on the upper level.
Rates: $35-$135.
8 Rooms. 8 Private Baths. Continental-plus breakfast.

Seen in: *Los Angeles Times, Pasadena Star News.*

Anaheim

Anaheim Country Inn

856 South Walnut St
Anaheim CA 92802
(714) 778-0150

Circa 1910. An elegant Craftsman farmhouse built by Mayor John Cook, the inn with its circular

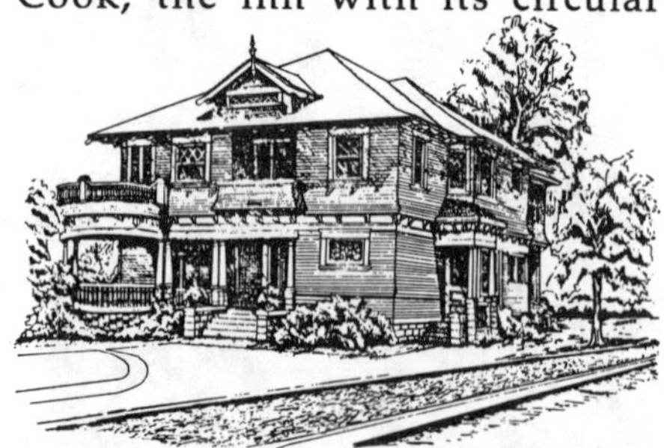

porch, is surrounded by nearly an acre of lawns, gardens and avocado trees. Detailed woodwork graces the entry and staircase, and beveled and leaded windows cast rainbows in the parlor and dining room. A

gazebo and spa are just steps from the honeymoon suite.
Location: One mile from Disneyland.
*Rates: $60-$85.
Lois Ramont & Marilyn Watson.
9 Rooms. 6 Private Baths. Guest phone available. TV available. Beds: QDT. Full breakfast. Jacuzzi. Conference room. CCs: MC VISA AX DS.

"My husband is still telling anyone who'll listen how good the breakfasts were."

Seal Beach Inn & Gardens
See: Seal Beach, CA

Aptos

Bayview Hotel B&B Inn
8041 Soquel Dr
Aptos CA 95003
(408) 688-8654

Circa 1878. This Victorian hotel was built by Joseph Arano, a French

immigrant who married Augusta, youngest daughter of General Rafael Castro, landowner of the sprawling 6,680-acre Rancho de Aptos. Lillian Russell and King Kalakaua were among the famous guests. Newly renovated, the hotel contains a restaurant on the first floor with lodging on the second and third. The hosts come from a family of British innkeepers.
*Rates: $75-$145.
Katja & James Duncan.
8 Rooms. 8 Private Baths. Beds: D. B&B. Restaurant. CCs: MC VISA. Hiking, bicycling, tennis, golf, fishing, boating, beaches.
Seen in: *Santa Cruz Sentinel.*

The Inn at Depot Hill
134 Hyannis Ct
Aptos CA 95003
(408) 462-DEPO

Circa 1901. Situated in a quaint beach town on Monterey Bay, reminiscent of a mediterranean fishing village, the Inn at Depot Hill is a converted Southern Pacific Railroad depot. The depot's Round Room still retains the old ticket window and there are 14-foot-high ceilings in the living and dining rooms. Guest rooms are named after railroad stations of the world and decorated accordingly (Stratford on Avon is Country English and Stazione de Milano has an Italian theme). The Railroad Barn Room resembles a plush, private pullman car. Jacuzzi tubs and featherbeds are features of some rooms.
*Rates: $115-$185.
Suzanne Lankes.
8 Rooms. 8 Private Baths. 8 Fireplaces. Guest phone in room. TV in room. Beds: KQ. Continental-plus breakfast. Handicap access. CCs: MC VISA AX DC DS. Beaches, state parks.
Seen in: *Santa Cruz Sentinel.*

Mangels House
570 Aptos Creek Rd, PO Box 302
Aptos CA 95001
(408) 688-7982

Circa 1886. Claus Mangels built this country house when he estab-

lished the California sugar beet industry with the famous Spreckels family. The inn, on four acres, is reminiscent of a southern mansion with its encircling veranda, lawns and orchards. Bounded by the Forest of Nisene Marks the property encompasses 10,000 acres of redwood trees, creeks, and trails. Monterey Bay is just three-quarters of a mile away.
Location: Central Coast.
*Rates: $90-$110.
Jacqueline & Ron Fisher.
5 Rooms. 3 Private Baths. 1 Fireplace. Guest phone available. Beds: QDT. B&B. Game room. Conference room. CCs: MC VISA. Horseback riding, golf, tennis, water sports, hiking.
Seen in: *Inn Serv, Innviews.*

"Compliments on the lovely atmosphere. We look forward to sharing our discovery with friends and returning with them."

Arcata

Plough & the Stars Country Inn
1800 27th St
Arcata CA 95521
(707) 822-8236

Circa 1860. After losing his ranch and all his possessions to the 1862

Indian raids, Isaac Minor, businessman and rancher, built this farm. It's surrounded on three sides by 100 acres of lillies. The house, of post & beam construction, supports ground floor joists of 12"x12" handhewn redwood beams. The Courtia Worth suite has an elegant Victorian atmosphere and features a woodstove. Guests are welcome to invite friends over for hors d'oeuvres or late evening snacks, for an additional charge.
Rates: $65-$95. Season: Feb. 15-Dec. 15
Bill & Melissa Hans.
5 Rooms. 2 Private Baths. 1 Fireplace. Guest phone available. TV available. Beds: QDT. B&B. Jacuzzi. Handicap access. Hiking, bicycling, canoeing, bird watching, golf, tennis, swimming, croquet & lawn bowling.

Arroyo Grande

Guest House
120 Hart Ln
Arroyo Grande CA 93420
(805) 481-9304

Circa 1850. Set among old-fashioned gardens, this New England Colonial was built by an eastern sea captain. The flavor of that period is kept alive with many family heirlooms and a colorful gar-

den terrace. It is located seventeen miles south of San Luis Obispo.
Location: In the village.
Rates: $60.
Mark V. Miller.
3 Rooms. Guest phone available. Beds: QD. Wineries, beaches, Hearst Castle and antique shops nearby.
"The charm of the home is only exceeded by that of the hosts."

Rose Victorian Inn
789 Valley Rd
Arroyo Grande CA 93420
(805) 481-5566

Circa 1885. Once the homestead for a large walnut farm, this pic-

turesque Victorian inn features a tower that rises four stories, providing a view of meadows, sand dunes and the ocean. Surrounded by a white picket fence, the inn is decorated with authentic Victorian furnishings. A 30-foot long rose arbor leads to a gazebo in the garden, a favorite setting for weddings. Rates include dinner at the inn's restaurant.
Location: Halfway between Los Angeles and San Francisco.
*Rates: $125-$160,MAP.
Ross & Diana Cox.
8 Rooms. 7 Private Baths. Guest phone available. Beds: KD. MAP. Restaurant. Handicap access. Conference room. CCs: MC VISA.
Seen in: *Los Angeles Times, Daughters of Painted Ladies. Sunset Magazine.*

Auburn

Power's Mansion Inn
164 Cleveland Ave
Auburn CA 95603
(916) 885-1166

Circa 1885. This Victorian mansion was built by Harold Power from the gold-mining millions he excavated from Auburn's richest mine. The house was always filled with children and according to a neighbor, there was always something happening over there, games and parties or going together to Clarke's Hole on the American River for swimming. Many prominent folk, such as engineer Herbert Hoover, visited in the Power's Mansion. Throughout the second floor halls of this elegantly restored mansion are notes and memorabilia that tell the history of the inn. The luxury and extravagance of the inn is typified by the heart-shaped tub and fireplace at the foot of a lacy bed in the honeymoon suite.
Location: In the heart of downtown.
*Rates: $70-$160.
Judith & Rene Vincent.
13 Rooms. 13 Private Baths. 2 Fireplaces. Guest phone in room. TV available. Beds: Q. B&B. Gourmet meals. Jacuzzi. Conference room. CCs: MC VISA AX. Water rafting, cross-country skiing, horseback riding, antiquing.
Seen in: *Sierra Heritage Magazine.*

Benicia

The Union Hotel
401 First St
Benicia CA 94510
(707) 746-0100

Circa 1882. Once a famed bordello, this old clapboard hotel has been

reformed and refurbished with whitewash, polished brass, and stained glass. The inn is set in a picturesque town that served as the capital of California for one year. Extra comfort is provided by whirlpool tubs available in all guest rooms. Some rooms feature water views of Carquinez Strait.
*Rates: $75-$125.
Stephen Lipworth.
12 Rooms. 12 Private Baths. Guest phone in room. TV in room. Beds: KQ. Continental breakfast. Restaurant. Jacuzzi. Handicap access. CCs: MC VISA AX DC DS. Marine World & Wine Country nearby. Sunday brunch, entertainment 5 nights a week, full service bar.
Seen in: *PG&E Progress.*

Big Bear Lake

Knickerbocker Mansion
869 S Knickerbocker Rd
Big Bear Lake CA 92315
(714) 866-8221

Circa 1917. The inn is one of the few vertically designed log struc-

tures in the area. Built of local lumber by Bill Knickerbocker, the first damkeeper of Big Bear, this grand old mansion is set against a backdrop of trees. Spacious front lawns provide seating for the annual summer "Astronomy Weekends" led by a Griffith Park Observatory astronomer.
Location: One-quarter mile south of Big Bear Village.
**Rates: $85-$150.
Phyllis Knight.
10 Rooms. 6 Private Baths. Guest phone available. Beds: KQT. Full breakfast. Jacuzzi. Handicap access. Conference room. Horseback riding, skiing, parasailing, water slide. Astronomy weekends, weddings.
Seen in: *Los Angeles Magazine, Yellow Brick Road.*

"Best breakfast I ever had. We especially enjoyed the hot tub with its terrific view."

Big Sur

Deetjen's Big Sur Inn

Hwy One
Big Sur CA 93920
(408) 667-2377

Circa 1938. Norwegians Helmut and Helen Deetjen built these casual, rustic rooms on several acres

of a redwood canyon. Today they are managed by a non-profit corporation and provide employment for local residents. Two rooms overlook a bubbling stream. Some have fireplaces and down comforters. The inn's restaurant is open daily. The adventurous will appreciate the setting and the whimsy, but due to the rustic nature of the accommodations this is not for everyone.

Location: Twenty-eight miles south of Carmel.
Rates: $50-$100.
Bettie Walters.
19 Rooms. 14 Private Baths. Beds: QDT. EP. Handicap access. Hiking trails and beaches nearby.
Seen in: *New York Times, California Magazine.*

"Like stepping back in time, so unique and charming."

Bishop

Chalfant House

213 Academy St
Bishop CA 93514
(619) 872-1790

Circa 1898. "It has been Earth's nearest touch of heaven above," wrote P.A. Chalfant of his Victorian home. As founder of the area's first newspaper, Mr. Chalfant enjoyed its village setting in full view of the surrounding mountains. For a time the house served as a hotel for area Tungsten miners, and in the 1920s was managed by Big Bertha. Now restored and decorated with antiques, collectibles, and quilts, each guest room has been named after Chalfant family members.

*Rates: $55.
Fred & Sally Manecke.
5 Rooms. 5 Private Baths. 2 Fireplaces. Guest phone available. TV available. Beds: QDT. Full breakfast. CCs: AX. Biking, fishing, boating, back packing, museums.
Seen in: *Inyo County Resister.*

"You set the standards for hospitality and quality in the B&B industry."

Rainbow Tarns

See: Crowley Lake, CA

Calistoga

Brannan Cottage Inn

109 Wapoo Ave
Calistoga CA 94515
(707) 942-4200

Circa 1860. This Greek Revival cottage was built as a guest house for the old Calistoga Hot Springs Resort. Behind a white picket fence towers the original palm tree planted by Sam Brannan and noted by Robert Louis Stevenson in his "Silverado Squatters." Five graceful arches, an intricate gingerbread gableboard, and unusual scalloped ridge cresting make this a charming holiday house. Hand-painted flower stencils of sweet peas, wild iris, violets, morning glories and wild roses are part of the fresh country Victorian decor.

Location: Napa Valley.
*Rates: $85-$135.
Jay & Dottie Richolson.
6 Rooms. 6 Private Baths. Beds: Q. Full breakfast. Handicap access. CCs: MC VISA. Ballooning, spas, hiking, biking, tennis, golf, hot springs, gliding, wine tasting.
Seen in: *New York Herald Tribune, Los Angeles Herald Examiner, Chicago Tribune, Orange County Register.*

"I think of you as the caretakers of romance in our busy world."

Calistoga's Wine Way Inn

1009 Foothill Blvd
Calistoga CA 94515
(707) 942-0680

Circa 1915. In the garden of this white Craftsman house is a gazebo

set on a lushly planted hillside, providing a spectacular view across Calistoga to the mountains beyond. Inside the inn are beamed ceilings, leaded glass cabinets and 19th-century English and American antiques. Innkeeper Allen Good's grandfather was humorist Chic Sale, and each guest room features Sale's books. *The Specialist,* for instance, is about a gentleman who specializes in building outhouses.

*Rates: $70-$105.
Allen & Dede Good.
6 Rooms. 6 Private Baths. 1 Fireplace. Guest phone available. Beds: QD. Full breakfast. CCs: MC VISA. Mudbaths in town, golf, tennis, horseback riding nearby. Air conditioning.
Seen in: *Los Angeles Times.*

"We loved being here and loved meeting Dede & Allen. Such personal service!"

The Pink Mansion

1415 Foothill Blvd
Calistoga CA 94515
(707) 942-0558

Circa 1875. Painted pink in the 1930s by the innkeeper's Aunt Alma, the Pink Mansion as it be-

came known, was originally built by William Fisher who established Calistoga's first stage line. Here he cleared the mountainside, established vineyards and dug wine

caves. Aunt Alma's collections of Victorian and Oriental items, including cherubs and angels, are placed throughout the inn. Views of woodlands and Mount St. Helena may be enjoyed from the guest rooms. There is an indoor pool.
*Rates: $75-$145.
Jeff Seyfried.
5 Rooms. 5 Private Baths. 1 Fireplace. Guest phone available. TV available. Beds: QT. B&B. Jacuzzi. Swimming pool. CCs: MC VISA. Golf, hiking, biking, tennis, fishing, wine tasting.

Scarlett's Country Inn
3918 Silverado Trail N
Calistoga CA 94515
(707) 942-6669

Circa 1890. Formerly the winter campground of the Wappo Indians,

the property now includes a restored farm house. There are green lawns and refreshing country vistas in a setting where woods and vineyards meet. Fruit trees abound, and guests are free to sample their wares. Breakfast is often taken beneath the apple trees or poolside.
Location: Napa Valley wine country.
*Rates: $85-$125.
Scarlett & Derek Dwyer.
3 Rooms. 3 Private Baths. 1 Fireplace. Guest phone in room. TV available. Beds: Q. Continental-plus breakfast. Swimming pool. CCs: MC VISA. Hiking, biking, fishing, water skiing, ballooning, gliding, mud baths.

"Wonderful, peaceful, serene."

Cambria

Olallieberry Inn
2476 Main St
Cambria CA 93428
(805) 927-3222

Circa 1873. This Greek Revival style home was built by a German pharmacist but has been influenced by other former owners, including dairy farmers and a Morro Bay

fisherman. Restored and recently refurbished, two downstairs rooms are accessible to the handicapped via an outside ramp. The blue honeymoon suite features a canopied bed and sunken tub. The cheery breakfast room faces a well-groomed lawn with a small fountain. Hearst Castle is seven miles up the coast.
*Rates: $75-$95.
Linda Boyers.
6 Rooms. 6 Private Baths. Guest phone available. TV available. Beds: KQD. Continental-plus breakfast. Handicap access. CCs: MC VISA. Private tennis, pool, bicycles. Fishing, hiking, beaches, wineries, Hearst Castle.
Seen in: *Los Angeles Times, Elmer Dills Radio Show.*

"Our retreat turned into relaxation, romance and pure Victorian delight."

Carmel

The Stonehouse Inn
Box 2517
Carmel CA 93921
(408) 624-4569

Circa 1905. This quaint Carmel country house boasts a stone exterior, made from beach rocks collected and hand shaped by local Indians at the turn of the century. The original owner, "Nana" Foster, was hostess to notable artists and writers from the San Francisco area, including Sinclair Lewis, Jack London and Lotta Crabtree. The romantic Jack London room features a dramatic gabled ceiling, a brass bed and a stunning view of the ocean. Conveniently located, the inn is a short walk from Carmel Beach and two blocks from the village.
*Rates: $80-$105.
Virginia Carey.
6 Rooms. 1 Fireplace. Guest phone available. Beds: KQDT. Full breakfast. Conference room. CCs: MC VISA. Tennis, golf.
Seen in: *Travel & Leisure, Country Living.*

"First time stay at B&B - GREAT!"

Vagabond's House Inn
Box 2747
Carmel CA 93921
(408) 624-7738

Circa 1940. Shaded by the intertwined branches of two California

live oaks, the stone-paved courtyard of the Vagabond's House sets the tone of this romantic retreat. The inn is comprised of a cluster of white-stucco cottages built into a slope. Some include kitchens, but all feature a fireplace and an antique clock. In the morning guests pick up breakfast trays in the lobby and choose a spot near the camelias or take it to the privacy of their rooms.

Location: 4th & Dolores.
*Rates: $79-$135.
Honey Jones & Dennis Levett.
11 Rooms. 11 Private Baths. 11 Fireplaces. Guest phone in room. TV in room. Beds: KQD. Continental breakfast. CCs: MC VISA AX. Golf, tennis, bicycling, hiking, fishing, kayaking.

"Charming & excellent accommodations and service. Very much in keeping with the character and ambiance of Carmel's historic setting."

Chico

Bullard House
256 E First Ave
Chico CA 95926
(916) 342-5912

Circa 1902. City fathers bestowed the Golden Rose Award for restoration excellence upon Bullard House, a country Victorian home. It was also selected as a "Decorator Dream House." The inn is centrally located for guests who want to be close to

Chico State College or historic Bidwell Mansion.
Rates: $50-$60.
Patricia & Patrick Macarthy.
4 Rooms. Guest phone available. Beds: DT. Continental breakfast. Hunting, fishing and boating.

Shallow Creek Farm
See: Orland, CA

Cloverdale

Abrams House Inn
314 N Main St
Cloverdale CA 95425
(707) 894-2412

Circa 1870. This restored Victorian inn is one of the oldest buildings in

Cloverdale. It was built by the Abrams family and stands adjacent to a brick building believed to have been the town's first jail. Ask for the suite with the four-poster bed and private porch.
Location: Sonoma County wine country.
*Rates: $45-$90.
Mary & David Hood.
4 Rooms. 1 Private Bath. Guest phone available. Beds: KQT. Full breakfast. Conference room. CCs: MC VISA. Bicycling, wine tasting, fishing, canoeing, boating.

"Although we have stayed in many fine inns, our family agrees that our stay at Abrams House was by far the best."

Vintage Towers Inn
302 N Main St
Cloverdale CA 95425
(707) 894-4535

Circa 1900. This gracious Victorian inn boasts three towers - square,

round and an octagon. Guests may try a different tower room each visit, but each one features an antique bedstead and interesting memorabilia. Bicycles may be borrowed to ride to several nearby vineyards.
Location: Six blocks from Russian River.
*Rates: $70-$110. Season: Feb. to Dec.
James Mees & Garrett Hall.
7 Rooms. 5 Private Baths. Guest phone available. TV available. Beds: KQD. Full breakfast. Conference room. CCs: MC VISA. Wineries, white water rafting, horseback riding, fishing. Special meals by prior arrangement.

Coloma

Coloma Country Inn
PO Box 502, #2 High St
Coloma CA 95613
(916) 622-6919

Circa 1852. Situated in the middle of 300-acre Gold Discovery State

Park, this inn is one of several buildings that will take you back to the days of the Gold Rush. Visit the blacksmith, tinsmith and one-room schoolhouse, as well as Sutter's Mill, site of California's first gold discovery. The inn was built by Hugh Miller, owner of Coloma's Fashion Billard Saloon. Antique beds, primitives, stenciling and country decor complement an idyllic five-acre setting, with duck pond and gazebo in the garden.
Location: Heart of the Gold Country, Coloma, where the Gold Rush began.
*Rates: $68-$75.
Alan & Cindi Ehrgott.
5 Rooms. 3 Private Baths. Guest phone available. Beds: D. Full breakfast. Hot air ballooning with host, white water rafting. Wine seminars.
Seen in: *Country Living, Los Angeles Times.*

Vineyard House
Cold Spring Rd, PO Box 176
Coloma CA 95613
(916) 622-2217

Circa 1878. Ulysses Grant is said to have made a speech from the bal-

cony of this 19-room house built by Robert Chalmers, winery owner. The parlor is decorated in a Victorian fashion with velvet-covered furniture and antiques. In the basement, a saloon occupies the house's former wine cellar. It is said that when Mr. Chalmers went insane as a result of syphilis, his wife had him chained in the basement. The house is rumored to be haunted but it doesn't seem to disturb the conviviality found in the dining room almost any evening.
Location: Off Highway 49.
*Rates: $60-$70.
Gary, Frank, Darlene Herrera. David Van Buskirk.
7 Rooms. Guest phone available. Beds: KQDT. B&B. Restaurant. Conference room. CCs: MC VISA. Hiking, whitewater rafting, ballooning. Old melodramas next door.
Seen in: *United Magazine, Sierra Heritage, Sacramento Union.*

Columbia

City Hotel
PO Box 1870, Main St
Columbia CA 95310
(209) 532-1479

Circa 1856. Only pedestrians and horses may pass the City Hotel fronting the wooden staircase of Main Street. This National Historic District celebrates the days when $87 million in gold was mined in Columbia. The two-story brick hotel has been preserved and filled with museum furnishings which include massive mahogany beds and marble-topped dressers. The inn's dining room is of note. Nearby shops maintained by the Park Service include a working blacksmith shop, a courthouse, and a carpenter shop. The old saloon still pours sarsaparilla, and the Matelot Gulch Mining Store still sells gold panning equipment.
*Rates: $65-$80.
Tom Bender.
9 Rooms. 9 Private Baths. Guest phone available. Beds: QDT. Continental-plus breakfast. Restaurant. Gourmet meals. Conference room. CCs: MC VISA AX. Horseback riding, swimming, fishing, tennis, gold panning.
Seen in: *Innsider, Bon Appetit, New York Times.*

"Excellent, by any standard."

Crowley Lake

Rainbow Tarns
PO Box 1097, Rt 1
Crowley Lake CA 93546
(619) 935-4556

Circa 1920. Just south of Mammoth Lakes, at an altitude of 7,000 feet,

you'll find this secluded retreat amid three acres of ponds, open meadows and hills. Country-style here includes luxury touches, such as a double jacuzzi and a skylight for star-gazing. In the Thirties, ponds on the property served as a "U-Catch-Em": folks rented fishing poles and paid 10 cents an inch for the fish they caught. Nearby Crowley Lake is still one of the best trout-fishing areas in California. Corrals are provided should you bring your horse for the inn's trails. A small charge is levied for feed.
Location: Eight-tenths of a mile north of Tom's Place.
Rates: $85-$125.
Lois Miles.
3 Rooms. 1 Private Bath. 1 Fireplace. Guest phone available. TV available. Beds: QDT. Full breakfast. Jacuzzi. Handicap access. Skiing, horseback riding, backpacking, fishing, hunting, hiking, bird watching.
Seen in: *Mammoth Magazine.*

"I love it! I'd rather stay here than go on to Tahoe!"

Davenport

New Davenport B&B
31 Davenport Ave
Davenport CA 95017
(408) 425-1818

Circa 1902. Captain John Davenport came here to harvest the gray whales that pass close to shore during migration. The oldest remaining original building is modest in appearance and was originally used as a public bath. It later became a bar, restaurant and dance hall before finally converted into a private home. Completely renovated, it now houses four of the inn's rooms.
Location: Halfway between Carmel and San Francisco on the coast.
*Rates: $60-$105.
Bruce & Marcia McDougal.
13 Rooms. 13 Private Baths. 1 Fireplace. Guest phone in room. Beds: KQD. Full breakfast. Restaurant. Handicap access. CCs: MC VISA AX. Whale watching, water skiing, surfing, elephant seal viewing, beach access.
Seen in: *Monterey Life, Travel & Leisure, Sacramento Bee, Peninsula Time Tribune.*

"We have been in California for over 25 years and never knew there was a Davenport! I cannot express the wonderful thrill at the first glimpse of our room with its lovely country appeal and garden."

Del Mar

Rock Haus B&B Inn
410 15th St
Del Mar CA 92014
(619) 481-3764

Circa 1910. Situated on a half-acre hillside this California Craftsman-style bungalow provides panoramic ocean and village views. A versatile structure, it once served as a church and a Roaring Twenties bordello, although not at the same time. The common areas include a large living room with fireplace and a glass-enclosed veranda. Rooms are decorated in antiques and outfitted with down comforters. The famous Del Mar Racetrack is nearby.
*Rates: $75-$135.
Doris Holmes.
10 Rooms. 4 Private Baths. 1 Fireplace. Guest phone available. Beds: KQT. B&B. CCs: MC VISA AX.

Dulzura

Brookside Farm
1373 Marron Valley Rd
Dulzura CA 92017
(619) 468-3043

Circa 1928. Ancient oaks shade terraces leading from the farmhouse to

a murmuring brook. Behind a nearby stone barn there is a grape arbor and beneath it, a spa. Each room in the inn and its two cottages is furnished with vintage pieces and handmade quilts. Adventurous hikers can explore mines nearby, which date from the gold rush of 1908. Innkeeper Edd Guishard is a former award-winning restaurant owner.
Location: Thirty-five minutes southeast of San Diego.

*Rates: $45-$65.
Edd Guishard.
9 Rooms. 6 Private Baths. Guest phone available. Beds: Q. Full breakfast. Jacuzzi. Handicap access. Conference room.
Seen in: *California Magazine, San Diego Home & Garden.*

"Our stay at the farm was the most relaxing weekend we've had in a year."

Elk

Elk Cove Inn
PO Box 367
Elk CA 95432
(707) 877-3321

Circa 1883. This mansard-style Victorian home was built as a guest

house for lumber baron L. E. White. Operated as a full-service country inn for over 21 years, Elk Cove Inn commands a majestic view from atop a scenic bluff. Two cabins and an addition to the house feature large bay windows, skylights, and Victorian fireplaces. Antiques, hand-embroidered linens, and sun-dried sheets add to the amenities. Below the inn is an expansive driftwood-strewn beach. French and German specialities are served in the ocean-view dining rooms.
Location: 6300 S Hwy 1, 15 miles south of Mendocino.
Rates: $98-$138.
Hildrun-Uta Triebess.
6 Rooms. 6 Private Baths. Guest phone available. Beds: Q. AP. Handicap access. Ocean kayaking, beachcombing, tennis, golf, wineries nearby through the redwoods.
Seen in: *AAA & Mobil guidebooks.*

"Quiet, peaceful, romantic, spiritual. This room, the Inn, and the food are all what the doctor ordered."

Harbor House Inn by the Sea
5600 S Hwy 1
Elk CA 95432
(707) 877-3203

Circa 1916. Built by a lumber company for executives visiting from

the East, the inn is constructed entirely of redwood. The parlor's vaulted, carved ceiling and redwood paneling were sealed by hot beeswax and hand rubbed. Edwardian decor adds elegance to the guest rooms. Views of the ocean and arches carved in the massive rocks that jut from the sea may be seen from the blufftop cottages. Benches nestle along a path edged with wild flowers that winds down the bluff to the sea.
Rates: $135-$200.
Dean & Helen Turner.
10 Rooms. 10 Private Baths. 9 Fireplaces. Guest phone available. MAP.
Seen in: *California Visitor's Review.*

Eureka

Carter House
1033 Third St
Eureka CA 95501
(707) 445-1390

Circa 1982. The Carters found a pattern book in an antique shop and

built this inn according to the architectural plans for an 1890 San Francisco Victorian. (The architect, Joseph Newsom, also designed the Carson House across the street.) Three open parlors with bay windows and marble fireplaces, provide an elegant backdrop for relaxing. Guests are free to visit the kitchen in quest of coffee and views of the bay. The inn is famous for its Apple Almond Tart featured in *Gourmet* magazine.
Location: Corner of Third & L streets in Old Town.
Rates: $79-$250.
Mark & Christi Carter.
7 Rooms. 4 Private Baths. 1 Fireplace. Guest phone available. TV available. Beds: Q. B&B. Jacuzzi. Conference room. CCs: MC VISA AX. Carriage rides.
Seen in: *Sunset Magazine, U.S. News & World Report.*

"We've traveled extensively throughout the U.S. and stayed in the finest hotels. You've got them all beat!! The accommodations, the food, the atmosphere and the friendly hosts are the very best of the best."

Old Town B&B Inn
1521 Third St
Eureka CA 95501
(707) 445-3951

Circa 1871. This early Victorian Greek Revival Italianate was the

original family home of Lumber Baron William Carson. It was constructed of virgin redwood and Douglas fir. (Redwood from the Carson's mill was used to build a significant portion of San Francisco.) Try and time your stay on a day when the Timber Beast breakfast menu is served, and be sure to take home a copy of the inn's cookbook.
*Rates: $60-$95.
Leigh & Diane Benson.
5 Rooms. 3 Private Baths. Guest phone available. Beds: KQDT. B&B. CCs: MC VISA AX. Sport fishing, whale watching, hiking, beaches, mountains, museums, redwood forests.

"You set the standard by which other B&B's should be measured. Absolutely top drawer!

Plough & the Stars Country Inn

See: Arcata, CA

Ferndale

Shaw House Inn

PO Box 1125, 703 Main St
Ferndale CA 95536
(707) 786-9958

Circa 1854. The Shaw House is thought to be one of the oldest inns in California. It is an attractive Gothic house with gables, bays and balconies set back on an acre of garden. An old buckeye tree frames the front gate, and in the back a secluded deck overlooks a creek. Nestled under the wallpapered gables are several guest rooms filled with antiques and fresh flowers. New owners have brought new zest to this lovely old inn.

*Rates: $65-$125.
Norma & Ken Bessingpas.
6 Rooms. 2 Private Baths. 2 Fireplaces. Guest phone available. Beds: KQDT. Continental-plus breakfast. Conference room. CCs: MC VISA. Bikes available, hiking, sleeping, reading.

"Lovely place and lovely people." Willard Scott.

Fort Bragg

Avalon House

561 Stewart St
Fort Bragg CA 95437
(707) 964-5555

Circa 1905. This California Craftsman house was built completely of redwood Extensively remodeled in 1988, the Avalon House is furnished with a mixture of antiques and willow furniture. Fireplaces, whirlpool tubs, down comforters and pillows create a romantic ambience. The inn is in a quiet residential area, just three blocks from the Pacific Ocean, and one block from Hwy. 1. The Skunk Train depot is two blocks away.

*Rates: $70-$115.
Anne Sorrells.
6 Rooms. 6 Private Baths. 3 Fireplaces. Guest phone available. TV available. Beds: QDT. B&B. Jacuzzi. CCs: MC VISA AX. Hiking, fishing, biking, horseback riding, whale watching, skunk train. Can arrange and cater small weddings or other events.

"Elegant, private and extremely comfortable. We will never stay in a motel again."

Country Inn

632 N Main St
Fort Bragg CA 95437
(707) 964-3737

Circa 1890. The Union Lumber Company once owned this two-story townhouse built of native red-

wood. It features rooms with slanted and peaked ceilings. Several of the rooms have fireplaces. Camellia trees, flower boxes, and a white picket fence accent the landscaping, while just two blocks away a railroad carries visitors on excursions through the redwoods.

Rates: $65-$105.
Don & Helen Miller.
8 Rooms. 8 Private Baths. Guest phone available. Beds: KQ. Continental-plus breakfast. Handicap access. CCs: MC VISA.

"Each room is so charming, how do you choose one?"

DeHaven Valley Farm

See: Westport, CA

Grey Whale Inn

615 N Main St
Fort Bragg CA 95437
(707) 964-0640 (800) 382-7244 (CA only)

Circa 1915. Built in the Classic style, with weathered, old-growth

redwood, this stately historic building served as the Redwood Coast Hospital until 1971. A skillfully executed renovation has created airy and spacious rooms, most with a special amenity: ocean view, fireplace, whirlpool tub, private deck, or kitchen.

Location: Two blocks from downtown in historic North Fort Bragg.
*Rates: $60-$140.
Colette & John Bailey.
14 Rooms. 14 Private Baths. 2 Fireplaces. Guest phone available. TV available. Beds: KQDT. B&B. Jacuzzi. Handicap access. Game room. Conference room. CCs: MC VISA AX. Fishing, party boats, skunk train, whale watching, beaches.
Seen in: *San Francisco Examiner.*

"Just spent the loveliest week in our traveling history...the inn surpassed any Hyatt Regency in service and attitude. The accommodations were superb."

Noyo River Lodge

500 Casa Del Noyo Dr
Fort Bragg CA 95437
(707) 964-8045

Circa 1868. Located on a two-and-one-half acre pinnacle of wooded

land overlooking Noyo River, the harbor and fishing village, the lodge is a mansion once owned by the local lumber baron. Garden pathways lead to romantic picnic spots under the redwoods. Each guest room is furnished with antiques and is lined with a fine cedar no longer available to builders. The lodge's restaurant provides fireside dining and picturesque views of the river.

Rates: $65-$105.
Joe Patton & Ellie Singel.
7 Rooms. 7 Private Baths. Guest phone available. Beds: KQ. Full breakfast. CCs: MC VISA. Horseback riding on beach, whale watching trips, steam train ride. State and national parks.

"Such beauty and serenity, words cannot describe. We left the city in search of peace and tranquility and discovered it here."

Freestone

Green Apple Inn

520 Bohemian Hwy
Freestone CA 95472
(707) 874-2526

Circa 1862. Located on five acres of redwood trees and meadows, this inn was built by Trowbridge Wells, squire, pundit, grocer and postman for Freestone, the county's first designated historic district. Freestone was once the site of a Russian experimental farm (to grow wheat for Sitka, Alaska in 1814,) a stage coach stop en route to the coast, and a key station on the bootleg Underground Railway. Freestone itself has only one street, and that one is crooked.

Location: Twenty minutes from Bodego Bay.
*Rates: $65-$85.
Rogers & Rosemary Hoffman.
4 Rooms. 2 Private Baths. Guest phone available. Beds: QD. Full breakfast. Handicap access. CCs: MC VISA. Horseback riding nearby, deep-sea fishing, river boats, biking.
Seen in: *Sonoma Monthly, San Francisco Chronicle.*

"The Green Apple is a cosy inn. Not rushed but you can take your time." Emma, age 6.

Garberville

Benbow Inn

445 Lake Benbow Dr
Garberville CA 95440
(707) 923-2124

Circa 1926. The Benbow family commissioned famous architect Al-

bert Far to design this Tudor-style inn. An imposing sight, it is set among Japanese maple trees and an English rose garden. Each summer the park service builds a dam to form a lake, creating a sandy beach and backdrop for Shakespeare plays performed in July and August. The lobby and main rooms of the inn are filled with fine paintings, antiques, old clocks and books. The dining room overlooks green lawns leading down to the banks of the Eel River.

Location: On the Eel River, two miles south of Garberville.
*Rates: $78-$220.
Patsy & Chuck Watts.
55 Rooms. 55 Private Baths. Guest phone available. TV available. Beds: KQDT. EP. Jacuzzi. CCs: MC VISA. Lake swimming, hiking, biking. Afternoon tea & scones, wine.

"An astonishing place with charm by the ton!! This is our fifth visit."

Georgetown

American River Inn

Orleans St, PO Box 43
Georgetown CA 95634
(916) 333-4499

Circa 1853. Just a few miles from where gold was discovered in Coloma stands this completely res-

tored boarding house. Mining cars dating back to the original Woodside Mine Camp are visible. The lode still runs under the inn, although no one knows exactly where. Maybe you can find a nugget as large as the one that weighed in at 126 ounces! Swimmers will enjoy a spring-fed pool on the property.

Rates: $68-$98.
Maria & Will Collin.
27 Rooms. 15 Private Baths. 2 Fireplaces. Guest phone available. Beds: KQ. Full breakfast. Handicap access. Swimming pool. CCs: MC VISA. Fishing, hiking. White water rafting on the American River.

"Our home away from home. We fell in love here in all its beauty and will be back for our 4th visit in April, another honeymoon for six days."

Grass Valley

Annie Horan's

415 W Main St
Grass Valley CA 95945
(916) 272-2418

Circa 1874. Mine owner James Horan built this splendid Victorian

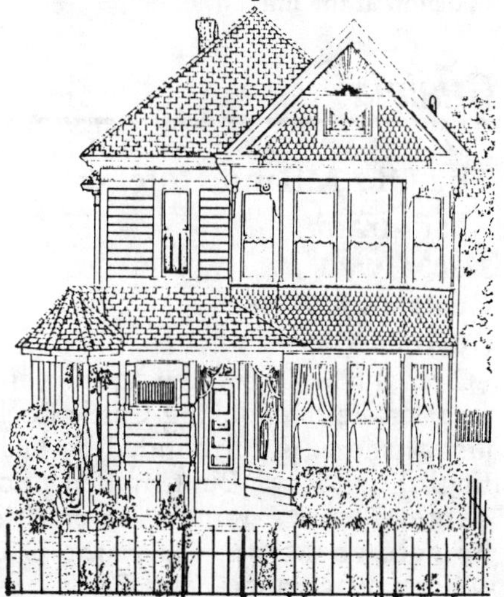

house for his wife Mary. Today the exterior, parlor and guest quarters are as they were at the height of Gold Country opulence. Follow in the footsteps of Mark Twain, Bret Harte and Presidents Grant, Harrison and Cleveland, who visited the shops, pubs, restaurants and other spots located just beyond the inn.

Location: Downtown Grass Valley.
*Rates: $65-$85.
Tom & Pat Kiddy.
4 Rooms. 4 Private Baths. Guest phone available. Beds: Q. Full breakfast. Conference room. CCs: MC VISA AX. Rafting, fishing, boating, gold panning, skiing.

Swan-Levine House

328 S Church St
Grass Valley CA 95945
(916) 272-1873

Circa 1880. Originally built by a local merchant, this Queen Anne Victorian house was converted into a hospital by Dr. John Jones. It served the area as a medical center until 1968. Innkeepers/artists Howard and Margaret Levine renovated the home for their three children, to be used as a printmaking studio and guesthouse. The old surgery is now a guest room, with rose-painted walls and octagonal

white floor tiles, providing a grand view from the wicker-furnished turret.
Rates: $50-$85.
Howard & Peggy Levine.
4 Rooms. 2 Private Baths. Guest phone available. TV available. Beds: KQT. Full breakfast. Swimming pool. CCs: MC VISA. Swimming, badminton and nearby skiing, hiking, fishing. Etching instruction at the inn.

Gualala

The Old Milano Hotel & Restaurant
38300 Hwy 1
Gualala CA 95445
(707) 884-3256

Circa 1905. This three-acre oceanfront estate overlooking Castle Rock just offshore, is surrounded by lush English gardens. Built by Bert Lucchinetti and named after his hometown Milan, Italy, the Old Milano was called "Big Bert's" by local residents. Many rooms offer views of the ocean, and The Caboose, a fanciful cottage, is tucked among the cedars for privacy. Situated atop the bluff is a hot tub overlooking a spectacular view of the Pacific Ocean.
Rates: $75-$160.
Leslie L. Linscheid.
9 Rooms. 3 Private Baths. 2 Fireplaces. Guest phone available. Beds: QD. B&B. Restaurant. Gourmet meals. Jacuzzi. CCs: MC VISA AX. Horseback riding, hiking, whale watching, beach.

Half Moon Bay

Mill Rose Inn
615 Mill St
Half Moon Bay CA 94019
(415) 726-9794

Circa 1903. This Victorian country inn is part of the original Miramon-

tes land grant, and played an important part in local coastal history. English country gardens bloom year-round under the magical hand of innkeeper and landscape designer Terry Baldwin. Canopy beds, claw-foot tubs, hand-painted fireplaces, and an inside garden spa create an opulent setting in which to relax.
*Rates: $145-$225.
Eve & Terry Baldwin.
6 Rooms. 6 Private Baths. 5 Fireplaces. Guest phone in room. TV in room. Beds: KQ. Full breakfast. Jacuzzi. Conference room. CCs: MC VISA. Horseback riding, beach, wineries, whale watching. Musicians and masseuses on call.
Seen in: *New York Times, LA Times, Dallas Morning News.*

"One of the loveliest retreats this side of the Cotswolds." San Diego Union.

Old Thyme Inn
779 Main St
Half Moon Bay CA 94019
(415) 726-1616

Circa 1897. Redwood harvested from nearby forests and dragged by

oxen was used to construct this Queen Anne Victorian home on historic Main Street. Decorated in a distinctly English style by English-born hosts, the inn boasts fireplaces and four-poster and canopy beds. The skylight in the Garden Suite, above a double whirlpool tub, treats bathers to a view of the night sky. Innkeeper Anne Lowings has cultivated 80 varieties of herbs in her garden. Serious herbalists are provided with a cutting kit to take samples back home.
*Rates: $70-$150.
Anne & Simon Lowings.
7 Rooms. 5 Private Baths. 3 Fireplaces. Guest phone available. TV available. Beds: QDT. B&B. Jacuzzi. CCs: MC VISA AX. Golf, tennis, tidepools, horseback riding, fishing, whale watching, beaches.
Seen in: *California Weekends, Los Angeles Magazine.*

San Benito House
356 Main St
Half Moon Bay CA 94019
(415) 726-3425

Circa 1905. The owners at the San Benito House have opened the upper floor as a country inn in the tradition of the auberges of Europe and the wayside inns of New England. An ornate stairway, Victorian and country decor, brass beds, and historic photographs create an Old World atmosphere. Outside, a sun deck, croquet lawn, and flower gardens provide relaxing spots for taking in the ocean air.
Rates: $49-$108.
Carol Mickelsen.
12 Rooms. 9 Private Baths. Guest phone available. Beds: QDT. Full breakfast. Restaurant. Conference room. CCs: MC VISA DC.

Healdsburg

Camellia Inn
211 North St
Healdsburg CA 95448
(707) 433-8182

Circa 1869. An elegant Italianate Victorian town house, the Camellia Inn has twin marble parlor fireplaces and an ornate mahogany dining-room fireplace. Antiques fill the guest rooms, complementing Palladian windows and classic interior moldings. The award-winning grounds feature 30 varieties of camellias and are accentuated with a pool.
Location: Heart of the Sonoma Wine Country.
*Rates: $65-$115.
Ray & Del Lewana.
9 Rooms. 7 Private Baths. Guest phone available. Beds: QT. Full breakfast. Handicap access. Swimming pool. CCs: MC VISA.

Grape Leaf Inn
539 Johnson St
Healdsburg CA 95448
(707) 433-8140

Circa 1900. This magnificently restored Queen Anne home was built in what was considered the "Nob Hill" of Healdsburg. It was typical of a turn-of-the-century middle-class dream house. It is situated near the Russian River and the town center.

Seventeen skylights provide an abundance of sunlight, fresh air, and stained glass. Several of the antique-filled guest rooms have whirlpool tubs.
*Rates: $70-$115.
Karen Sweet.
7 Rooms. 7 Private Baths. Beds: KQ. Full breakfast. Jacuzzi. CCs: MC VISA. Wine tasting, bicycling, canoeing. Lake Sonoma water sports. Complimentary wine and cheese served in the parlor.

"Reminds me of my grandma's house."

Haydon House

321 Haydon St
Healdsburg CA 95448
(707) 433-5228

Circa 1912. Architectural buffs will have fun naming the several ar-

chitectural styles found in the Haydon House. It has the curving porch and general shape of a Queen Anne Victorian home, the expansive areas of siding and unadorned columns of the Bungalow style, and the exposed roof rafters of the Craftsman style.
Location: Western Sonoma County, heart of the wine country.
Rates: $70-$110.
Richard & Joanne Claus.
8 Rooms. 4 Private Baths. Guest phone available. TV available. Beds: QT. Full breakfast. Conference room. CCs: MC VISA.

"Adjectives like class, warmth, beauty, thoughtfulness with the right amount of privacy, attention to details relating to comfort, all come to mind. Thank you for the care and elegance."

Madrona Manor, A Country Inn

PO Box 818 1001 Westside Rd
Healdsburg CA 95448
(707) 433-4231

Circa 1881. The inn is comprised of four historic structures in a National Historic District. Surrounded by eight acres of manicured lawns and terraced flower and vegetable gardens, the stately mansion was built

for John Paxton, a San Francisco businessman. Embellished with turrets, bay windows, porches, and a mansard roof, it provides a breathtaking view of surrounding vineyards. Massive, elegant antique furnishings and a notable restaurant add to the genuine country inn atmosphere. The Gothic-style Carriage House offers more casual lodging.
Location: In the heart of the wine country, Sonoma County.
*Rates: $92.50-$135.
John & Carol Muir.
20 Rooms. 20 Private Baths. 15 Fireplaces. Guest phone in room. Beds: KQDTC. Continental breakfast. Restaurant. Gourmet meals. Handicap access. Swimming pool. Conference room. CCs: MC VISA AX DC DS. Canoeing, wine tasting, picnics, bicycles, antique shopping. Golf and tennis nearby.
Seen in: *Northern California Home & Garden, Gourmet, Country Inns, Woman's Day Home Decorating Ideas.*

"Our fourth visit and better every time."

Hope Valley

Sorensen's Resort

Hwy 88
Hope Valley CA 96120
(916) 694-2203

Circa 1876. Where Danish sheepherders settled in this 7,000-

foot-high mountain valley, the Sorensen family built a cluster of fishing cabins. Thus, began a century-old tradition of valley hospitality. The focal point of Sorensen's is a "stave" cabin - a reproduction of a 13th-century Nordic home. Now developed as a Nordic ski resort, part of the Mormon-Emigrant Trail and Pony Express Route pass near the inn's 165 acres. In the summer, river rafting, fishing, pony express re-rides, and llama treks are popular Sierra pastimes. Lake Tahoe lies twenty miles to the north.
*Rates: $50-$190.
John & Patty Brissenden.
23 Rooms. 22 Private Baths. 11 Fireplaces. Guest phone available. Beds: QDC. B&B. Restaurant. Sauna. Conference room. CCs: MC VISA. Horseback & Llama pack riding, hiking, rafting, fishing, biking, skiing.
Seen in: *Sunset Magazine, San Francisco Chronicle.*

Huntington Beach

Seal Beach Inn & Gardens

See: Seal Beach, CA

Idyllwild

Wilkum Inn

26770 Hwy 243, PO Box 1115
Idyllwild CA 92349
(714) 659-4087

Circa 1939. Much of the knotty pine in the original part of this inn reflects on Idyllwild's history of lumbering and sawmills. Pine-crafted stair rails, unique to the area's construction in the Thirties, were reportedly milled in the area. The inn is noted for its Old World charm.
Location: Three-fourths of a mile South of village center.
*Rates: $55-$75.
Annamae Chambers & Barbara Jones.
5 Rooms. 2 Private Baths. Guest phone available. Beds: QDT. Continental-plus breakfast. Handicap access. Horseback riding. Hiking.

Inverness

Ten Inverness Way

10 Inverness Way
Inverness CA 94937
(415) 669-1648

Circa 1904. Shingled in redwood, this bed and breakfast features a stone fireplace, good books, player

piano and access to a great hiking area. The view from the breakfast room invites you to include a nature walk in your day's plans. According to local folklore a ghost used to call Ten Inverness Way his home. However, since the innkeepers had each room blessed, he seems to have disappeared. The inn is now known for its peace and refreshment.
Location: Near Point Reyes National Seashore.
*Rates: $90-$100.
Mary Davies.
4 Rooms. Guest phone available. Beds: Q. B&B. Jacuzzi. Birdwatching, horsebacking, hiking.
Seen in: *LA Times, New York Times, Travel & Leisure, Sunset.*

Ione

The Heirloom
214 Shakeley Lane
Ione CA 95640
(209) 274-4468

Circa 1863. A two-story Colonial with columns and balconies, and a

private English garden, the antebellum Heirloom is true to its name. It has many family heirlooms and a square grand piano once owned by Lola Montez. The building was dedicated by the Native Sons of the Golden West as a historic site.
Location: California Gold Country.
*Rates: $50-$85.
Melisande Hubbs & Patricia Cross.
6 Rooms. 4 Private Baths. 3 Fireplaces. Guest phone available. Beds: KQDT. Full breakfast. Swings, bicycles, croquet.
Seen in: *San Francisco Chronicle, Country Living.*

"Hospitality was amazing. Truly we've never had such a great time."

Jackson

Court Street Inn
215 Court St
Jackson CA 95642
(209) 223-0416

Circa 1876. This cheery yellow and white Victorian era house is accentuated with green shutters and a front porch stretching across the entire front. Behind the house, a two-story brick structure, that once served as a Wells Fargo office and a museum for Indian artifacts, now houses guests. Hors d'oeuvres and wine are served in the dining room under a pressed, carved tin ceiling. Guests relax in front of a marble fireplace in the parlor topped by a gilded mirror. Guest rooms are decorated in antiques. Downtown is only two blocks away.
*Rates: $75-$85-$125.
Janet & Lee Hammond & Gia & Scott Anderson.
7 Rooms. 3 Private Baths. 3 Fireplaces. Guest phone available. TV in room. Beds: QD. Full breakfast. Jacuzzi. Handicap access. CCs: MC VISA AX.
Seen in: *Amador Dispatch.*

"Warm hospitality, great breakfasts, and genuine family atmosphere. All our friends will only hear wonderful thoughts about the Court Street Inn."

Jamestown

National Hotel
Main Street, PO Box 502
Jamestown CA 95327
(209) 984-3446

Circa 1859. One of the oldest continuously operating hotels in California, the inn maintains its original redwood bar where thousands of dollars in gold dust were spent. The restaurant is considered to be one of the finest in the Mother Lode.
Location: Center of town.
*Rates: $45-$65.
Stephen Willey.

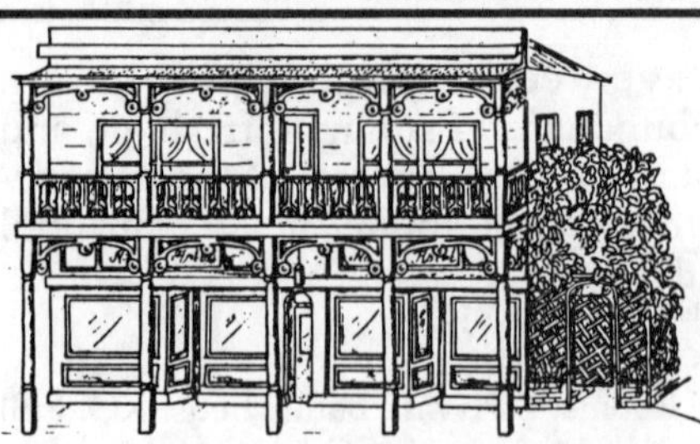

11 Rooms. 5 Private Baths. Guest phone available. TV available. Beds: QT. AP. Restaurant. Gourmet meals. Handicap access. Conference room. CCs: MC VISA. Gold panning, water sports, horseback riding, snow skiing.
Seen in: *Bon Appetit.*

"Excellent, wonderful place!"

Julian

Julian Gold Rush Hotel
2032 Main St, PO Box 1856
Julian CA 92036
(619) 765-0201

Circa 1897. The dream of a former slave and his wife lives on today in

this sole surviving hotel in Southern California's "Mother Lode of Gold Mining." This Victorian charmer is listed in the National Register of Historic Places and is a designated State of California Point of Historic Interest (#SDI-09). Guests enjoy the feeling of a visit to grandma's and a tradition of genteel hospitality.
Location: Center of town.
*Rates: $60-$145.
Steve & Gig Ballinger.
18 Rooms. 5 Private Baths. 1 Fireplace. Guest phone available. Beds: QDT. EP. Conference room. CCs: MC VISA AX. Horseback riding, fishing, hiking, historic gold mining town.
Seen in: *San Diego Union, PSA.*

"Any thoughts you have about the 20th Century will leave you when you walk into the lobby of this grand hotel..." Westways Magazine.

Kyburz

Strawberry Lodge

Hwy 50
Kyburz CA 95720
(916) 659-7030

Circa 1935. Nestled in the Sierra Nevada Mountains high above Lake Tahoe, Strawberry Lodge was named for Ira Fuller Berry. (It was said that he was so tight-fisted that he passed off straw for hay to teamsters driving their wagons up to the lodge. When they arrived, they would yell, "Got any more of that straw, Berry?") The lodge features brass beds and hand-painted furniture. Nearby, golden eagles nest on the high cliffs of Lover's Leap.

Location: 15 miles west of Lake Tahoe.
*Rates: $35-$100.
Richard Mitchell.
39 Rooms. 34 Private Baths. Guest phone available. TV available. Beds: KQT. EP. Swimming pool. Conference room. CCs: MC VISA. German brown and rainbow trout fishing, swimming, tennis. Dancing in the dance room.
Seen in: *San Francisco Examiner, City Sports.*

La Jolla

The B&B Inn at La Jolla

7753 Draper Ave
La Jolla CA 92037
(619) 456-2066

Circa 1913. The architect Irving Gill, father of tilt slab construction, built this home once occupied by John Phillip Souza and his family. All the guest rooms are beautifully designed with garden and ocean views. Honeymooners will be charmed by the room with the white canopy bed, fireplace and white sofa. Each room has one of Innkeeper Betty Albee's fresh floral arrangements.

Location: One block to the ocean.
*❀Rates: $75-$200.
Betty P. Albee.
16 Rooms. 15 Private Baths. Guest phone available. TV available. Beds: QT. Continental breakfast. Handicap access. CCs: MC VISA. Tennis across the street. Swimming, surfing, sunning.
Seen in: *Innsider, Country Inns.*

"Perfection, elegance, style! May I buy this room?"

Laguna Beach

Carriage House

1322 Catalina St
Laguna Beach CA 92651
(714) 494-8945

Circa 1920. A Laguna Beach historical landmark, this inn has a Cape clapboard exterior. It housed

an art gallery and a bakery before it was converted into apartments with large rooms and kitchens. Now as a cozy inn, each room has a private parlor. Outside, a courtyard fountain shaded by a large carrotwood tree with hanging moss provides a welcome respite from 20th Century living.

Location: Two & one-half blocks from the ocean.
*Rates: $85-$125.
Dee & Vernon Taylor.
6 Rooms. 6 Private Baths. Guest phone available. TV available. Beds: KQDT. Continental-plus breakfast. Swimming, shopping.

"A true home away from home with all the extra touches added in."

Casa Laguna

2510 S Coast Hwy
Laguna Beach CA 92651
(714) 494-2996

Circa 1930. A romantic combination of California Mission and Spanish Revival architecture, the

inn's Mission House and cottages were built in the early Thirties. The casitas were added in the Forties. The hillside setting of secluded gardens, winding paths, and flower-splashed patios invites guests to linger and enjoy ocean views. Be sure to arrive at the inn in time to watch the sunset from the Bell Tower high above the inn.

Location: On an ocean view hillside.
*❀Rates: $90-$205.
Jerry & Luanne Siegel.
20 Rooms. 20 Private Baths. 1 Fireplace. Guest phone in room. TV in room. Beds: KQTC. Continental-plus breakfast. Swimming pool. Game room. Conference room. CCs: MC VISA AX DC CB DS.
Seen in: *Los Angeles Magazine, Houston Post.*

"What a fantastic place. Who needs a casa in Spain?"

Eiler's Inn

741 S Coast Hwy
Laguna Beach CA 92651
(714) 494-3004

Circa 1940. This New Orleans-style inn surrounds a lush courtyard and fountain. The rooms are decorated with antiques and wallpapers. Wine and cheese is served during the evening in front of the fireplace. Named after Eiler Larsen, famous town greeter of Laguna, the inn is just a stone's throw from the beach on the ocean-side of Pacific Coast Highway.

Location: In the heart of the village.
*Rates: $100-$170.
Henk & Annette Wirtz.
12 Rooms. 12 Private Baths. 2 Fireplaces. Guest phone available. TV available. Beds: KQDT. B&B. CCs: MC VISA AX. Swimming, sunning.
Seen in: *Home & Garden.*

"Who could find a paradise more relaxing than an old-fashioned bed and breakfast with Mozart and Vivaldi, a charming fountain, wonderful fresh-baked bread, ocean air, and Henk's conversational wit?"

Little River

Glendeven

8221 N Hwy 1
Little River CA 95456
(707) 937-0083

Circa 1867. Lumber merchant Isaiah Stevens built this farmhouse set on a two-acre headland meadow with the bay of Little River in the distance. White clapboard siding and high pitched roof lines reflect the architecture of Stevens' native Maine. The sound of waves rolling onto the beach can often be heard. Ask for the Stevens Suite with its

own fireplace, views of the bay and breakfast in your room.
Location: One and a half miles to Mendocino.
Rates: $80-$140.
Jan & Janet deVries.
10 Rooms. 10 Private Baths. Beds: QDT. Continental-plus breakfast. Jacuzzi. CCs: MC VISA. Tennis, golf, horseback riding nearby. Wonderful hiking.
Seen in: *Arizona Republic, Contra Costa Times.*

The Victorian Farmhouse
7001 N Hwy 1, PO Box 357
Little River CA 95456
(707) 937-0697

Circa 1877. Built as a private residence, this Victorian farmhouse

is located on two-and-a-half acres in Little River. Two miles south of the historic village of Mendocino, the inn offers a relaxed country setting with deer, quail, flower gardens, an apple orchard and a running creek (School House Creek). A short walk will take you to the shoreline.
Rates: $80-$90.
George & Carole Molnar.
10 Rooms. 10 Private Baths. Guest phone available. Beds: KQ. Continental-plus breakfast. Handicap access. Conference room. CCs: MC VISA. Horseback riding, canoeing, fishing, golf and hiking nearby. Garden weddings are popular.
"This morning when we woke up at home we really missed having George deliver breakfast. You have a lovely inn and you do a super job."

Long Beach

Lord Mayor's B&B Inn
435 Cedar Ave
Long Beach CA 90802
(213) 436-0324

Circa 1904. Charles Windham, first mayor of Long Beach, had his Edwardian style home built with granite pillars flanking the veranda. Bay windows and a decorative pediment top the second story. A grand piano occupies the foyer and is often used to play the wedding march for area weddings. Decorated in antiques, such as a carved oak hawaiian bedstead, all the guest rooms have access to a sun deck. The Convention Center is within walking distance.
*Rates: $75-$85.
Laura & Reuben Brasser.
5 Rooms. 5 Private Baths. Guest phone available. TV available. Beds: QDT. Full breakfast. Conference room. CCs: MC VISA AX. Queen Mary, Spruce Goose.
Seen in: *KCET Magazine, Daily News Los Angeles.*
"Your hospitality and beautiful room were respites for the spirit and body after our long trip."

Seal Beach Inn & Gardens
See: Seal Beach, CA

Los Angeles

Channel Road Inn
See: Santa Monica, CA

Eastlake Victorian Inn
1442 Kellam Ave
Los Angeles CA 90026
(213) 250-1620

Circa 1887. Faithfully restored, decorated and furnished, the Eastlake Victorian Inn is situated in

Los Angeles' first historic preservation zone. Private tours of two National Register Victorian homes are available, as well as old-fashioned hot-air ballooning, murder mysteries, and other nearby attractions.
Location: Near downtown and the Music Center.
*Rates: $49-$150.
Murray Burns & Planaria Price.
7 Rooms. 2 Private Baths. Guest phone available. TV available. Beds: Q. B&B. Conference room. CCs: MC VISA.
Seen in: *USA Today, Travel & Leisure, Travel Holiday, Sunset.*
"Incomparably romantic!" Los Angeles Times.

Eye Openers B&B Reservations
See: Altadena, CA

Salisbury House
2273 W 20th St
Los Angeles CA 90018
(213) 737-7817

Circa 1909. Located in Arlington Heights, the inn is part of the old

West Adams area of Los Angeles. It features original stained and leaded glass windows, wood-beamed ceilings, and an abundance of wood paneling. Used as a location for movies and commercials, Salisbury House is known for its gourmet breakfasts and old-fashioned graciousness.
*Rates: $65-$85.
Sue & Jay German.
5 Rooms. 3 Private Baths. 1 Fireplace. Guest phone available. TV available. Beds: KQT. Full breakfast. CCs: MC VISA.
Seen in: *Sunset Magazine, Southern California Magazine.*
"The finest bed and breakfast we've seen. Not only is the house exquisite but the hospitality is unmatched!"

Seal Beach Inn & Gardens
See: Seal Beach, CA

Terrace Manor
1353 Alvarado Terrace
Los Angeles CA 90006
(213) 381-1478

Circa 1902. This three-story Tudor is a National Register Landmark

house. Tastefully decorated, the inn displays extraordinary stained-glass windows installed by the builder who owned a stained glass factory at the turn of the century.
*Rates: $60-$90.
Sandy & Shirley Spillman.
5 Rooms. 5 Private Baths. Guest phone available. TV available. Beds: KQDT. Full breakfast. Conference room. CCs: MC VISA AX DC CB. Entrance to Magic Castle.
Seen in: *Victorian Homes.*

"Lovely! Sandy does magic in the parlor; Shirley in the kitchen!

West Adams B&B Inn
1650 Westmoreland Blvd
Los Angeles CA 90006
(213) 737-5041

Circa 1913. The Rosenblum brothers built this splendid Craftsman home, and added a Ger-

man-lodge style log fireplace. Natural mahogany woodwork and elegant Arts and Crafts light fixtures are among the home's special touches. Built-in furnishings include a rare hideaway bed that has an arched cover which rolls toward the room creating a sleeping porch.
*Rates: $75-$80.
Jon Rake & Jeffrey Stvrtecky.
3 Rooms. 2 Private Baths. 1 Fireplace. Guest phone available. TV available. Beds: KQD. Full breakfast. Conference room. CCs: MC VISA. Convention Center, Los Angeles Music Center, art museums, Exposition Park.
Seen in: *Los Angeles Conservancy Newspaper.*

"You really made us feel at home and treated us as special guests."

Mammoth Lakes

Rainbow Tarns
See: Crowley Lake, CA

Mariposa

Meadow Creek Ranch B&B Inn
2669 Triangle Rd
Mariposa CA 95338
(209) 966-3843

Circa 1858. This Wells Fargo stagecoach stop is now a rambling farmhouse framed by a black walnut tree and old-fashioned climbing roses. A cozy country cottage in back is called the "Chicken Coop", but is decorated with a white carpet, canopy bed and antiques. There are three guestrooms in the main house.
Location: Halfway between two southern entrances into Yosemite.
*Rates: $60-$85.
Bob & Carol Shockley.
4 Rooms. 1 Private Bath. Guest phone available. Beds: QT. Full breakfast. CCs: MC VISA. Yosemite skiing, horseback riding, river rafting.
Seen in: *Gazette, Signature, Los Angeles Times.*

"A wonderful spot to begin a trip through the Gold Country or into Yosemite."

McCloud

McCloud Guest House
PO Box 1510, 606 W Colombero Dr
McCloud CA 96057
(916) 964-3160

Circa 1907. The deep verandas that wrap around this massive Craftsman-style house seem to extend a warm greeting to guests. For 50 years it served as a guest house for the McCloud River Lumber Company, accommodating the company's VIPs and executives. Such luminaries as Herbert Hoover, the Hearst family, and Jean Harlow stayed here. Elegantly restored, the inn includes an acclaimed restaurant enhanced by carved wood-beam ceilings, leaded glass windows and handsome chandeliers. The parlor features a pool table that is part of the Hearst collection.
Rates: $70-$90.
Bill & Patti Leigh & Dennis & Pat Abreu.
5 Rooms. 5 Private Baths. 1 Fireplace. Guest phone available. Beds: D. Continental breakfast. Restaurant. Game room. CCs: MC VISA. Downhill & cross-country skiing, golf, trout fishing.

Mendocino

Agate Cove Inn
PO Box 1150
Mendocino CA 95460
(707) 937-0551

Circa 1860. Perched on a blufftop overlooking the Pacific Ocean, the Agate Cove Inn was constructed by Mathias Brinzwg, owner of the first beer brewery in Mendocino. Cottages are lovingly decorated, and some have stunning white-water views. Views are highlighted by the tall, many-paned windows in the breakfast room where Jake, a former New York City ad agency executive, now reigns supreme. (On his first foray to a country fair, he entered his inn-baked bread and won a blue ribbon.)
Sallie McConnell & Jake Zahavi.
10 Rooms. 10 Private Baths. 9 Fireplaces. Guest phone available. TV in room. Beds: KQ. Full breakfast. CCs: MC VISA AX. River canoeing, hiking, fishing, horseback riding, tennis, golf.
Seen in: *Travel & Leisure, San Francisco Magazine, San Francisco Examiner.*

"Warmest hospitality, charming rooms, best breakfast and view in Menodcino."

DeHaven Valley Farm
See: Westport, CA

Grey Whale Inn
See: Fort Bragg, CA

Harbor House-Inn by the Sea
See: Elk, CA

The Headlands Inn

PO Box 132, Howard & Albion Sts
Mendocino CA 95460
(707) 937-4431

Circa 1868. Originally a small barbershop on Main Street, the building

later became the elegant "Oyster and Coffee Saloon" in 1884. Finally, horses pulled the house over log rollers to its present location. The new setting provides a spectacular view of the ocean, the rugged coastline, and breath-taking sunsets. Antiques, paintings, and fireplaces warm each guest room. There is a romantic honeymoon cottage in the back garden.

Location: Two blocks from the village center.
Rates: $89-$125.
Pat & Rod Stofle.
5 Rooms. 5 Private Baths. 5 Fireplaces. Guest phone available. Beds: KQ. B&B. Gourmet meals. Handicap access. Hiking in state parks, redwood groves, wineries, little theater.

"If a Nobel Prize were given for breakfasts, you would win hands down. A singularly joyous experience!!"

Howard Creek Ranch

See: Westport, CA

Joshua Grindle Inn

44800 Little Lake Rd, PO Box 647
Mendocino CA 95460
(707) 937-4143

Circa 1879. The town banker, Joshua Grindle, built this New England-style home on two acres.

The decor is light and airy, with Early American antiques, clocks and quilts. In addition to lodging in the house, there are rooms in the water tower and in an adjacent cottage. Six of the guest rooms have fireplaces. Some have views over the town to the ocean.

Location: On the Pacific Ocean at the edge of the village.
Rates: $65-$100.
Arlene & Jim Moorehead.
10 Rooms. 10 Private Baths. Guest phone available. Beds: QDT. Full breakfast. Handicap access. CCs: MC VISA DS. Hiking, golf, deep sea fishing, bicycling, art galleries.
Seen in: *Peninsula, Copley News Service.*

"We are basking in the memories of our stay. We loved every moment."

MacCallum House Inn

45020 Albion St
Mendocino CA 95460
(707) 937-0289

Circa 1882. Built by William H. Kelley for his newly wed daughter

Daisy MacCallum, the MacCallum House Inn is a splendid example of New England architecture in the Victorian village of Mendocino. Besides the main house, accommodations include the barn, carriage house, greenhouse, gazebo and water tower rooms.

Location: North Coast.
*Rates: $45-$135.
Melanie & Joe Reding.
20 Rooms. 7 Private Baths. Guest phone available. Beds: KQTC. Continental breakfast. Handicap access. CCs: MC VISA.
Seen in: *California Visitors Review.*

Mendocino Hotel

PO Box 587, 45080 Main St
Mendocino CA 95460
(707) 937-0511

Circa 1878. Rising prominently on the blufftop, the Mendocino Hotel

was originally established as a temperance hotel for lumbermen. Completely renovated, this western-style structure was built with a false front. The historic Heeser House, home of Mendocino's first settler, was annexed by the hotel along with its acre of gardens. Many of the guest rooms and suites boast tall four-poster and canopy beds or fireplaces and coastal views. The hotel offers a choice of several dining rooms.

*Rates: $65-$225.
Paul Cadelago.
50 Rooms. 37 Private Baths. 22 Fireplaces. Guest phone in room. TV in room. Beds: KQD. EP. Restaurant. Handicap access. Conference room. CCs: MC VISA AX. Whale watching, canoeing, river & ocean fishing, golf, tennis, horseback riding.
Seen in: *Los Angeles Times, The Tribune.*

"The hotel itself is magnificent, but more importantly, your staff is truly incredible."

Mendocino Village Inn

44860 Main St, PO Box 626
Mendocino CA 95460
(707) 937-0246

Circa 1882. Originally the home of physician Dr. William McCornack,

this graceful Victorian has been beautifully restored. One of the architectural gems of Mendocino, the inn has a variety of rooms with both Victorian and country decor. Seven of the rooms have fireplaces with neatly stacked wood beside them. The ocean and the pleasures of the North Coast lie just beyond the house's white picket fence.

Location: Walking distance to everything in the village.
Rates: $55-$120.
Sue & Tom Allen.
12 Rooms. 10 Private Baths. 7 Fireplaces. Guest phone available. Beds: Q. Full breakfast. CCs: MC VISA.

"Thanks for making our visit very special! We enjoyed the ambience you provided - Vivaldi, Diamond Lil, homemade breakfast and of course, Mendocino charm!"

Whitegate Inn

PO Box 150, 499 Howard St
Mendocino CA 95460
(707) 937-4892

Circa 1883. When it was first built, the local newspaper called

Whitegate Inn "one of the most elegant and best appointed residences in town." It is resplendent with bay windows, a steep gabled roof, redwood siding and fishscale shingles. The house's original wallpaper adorns one of the double parlors. There, an antique 1827 piano, at one time part of Alexander Graham Bell's collection, and inlaid pocket doors take you back to a simpler time. The silver, Baccarat crystal and Rosenthal china used at breakfast add a crowning touch to the inn's elegant hospitality.
Rates: $65-105.
Patricia Patton.
5 Rooms. 5 Private Baths. 4 Fireplaces. Guest phone available. Beds: KQDT. B&B. Conference room. Horseback riding, canoeing, Pacific Ocean.
Seen in: *Innsider, Country Inns.*

"Made our honeymoon a dream come true."

Mill Valley

Mountain Home Inn

810 Panoramic Hwy
Mill Valley CA 94941
(415) 381-9000

Circa 1912. At one time the only way to get to Mountain Home Inn was by taking the train up Mount Tamalpais. With 22 trestles and 281 curves, it was called "the crookedest railroad in the world". No wonder the round-trip costs only $1.40 from San Francisco. Then as now, the trip was always worth the spectacular view of San Francisco Bay. Each guest room has a view of the mountain, valley or bay.
Location: Mt. Tamalpais.
✻Rates: $112-$178.
Ed & Susan Cunningham.
10 Rooms. 10 Private Baths. 3 Fireplaces. TV available. Beds: KQ. B&B. Jacuzzi. Handicap access. Conference room. CCs: MC VISA. Ocean beach 10 minutes away. Above giant redwoods of Muir Woods.
Seen in: *San Francisco Examiner, California Magazine.*

"A luxurious retreat. Echoes the grand style and rustic feeling of national park lodges." Ben Davidson, *Travel and Leisure.*

Monterey

The Jabberwock

598 Laine St
Monterey CA 93940
(408) 372-4777

Circa 1911. Set in a half-acre of gardens, this Victorian inn provides a

fabulous view of Monterey Bay and its famous barking seals. When you're ready to settle in for the evening, you'll find huge Victorian beds complete with lace-edged sheets and goose-down comforters. Early evening hor d'oeuvres and aperitifs are served in an enclosed veranda.
Location: Four blocks above Cannery Row, the beach and Monterey Aquarium.
Rates: $85-$160.
Jim & Barbara Allen.
7 Rooms. 3 Private Baths. 1 Fireplace. Guest phone available. Beds: KQ. Full breakfast. Conference room. Biking, boating, horseback riding. Fisherman's Wharf, Seventeen-Mile Drive.
Seen in: *Sacramento Bee, San Francisco Examiner, Los Angeles Times.*

"Not only were the accommodations delightful but the people were equally so."

Old Monterey Inn

500 Martin St
Monterey CA 93940
(408) 375-8284

Circa 1929. Built in the Tudor style with half-timbers, the ivy-covered Old Monterey Inn looks and feels like an English country house. Brick pathways and a comfortable hammock beckon guests outside to the garden. Redwood, pine and old oak trees shelter an acre of pansies, roses, peonies and rhododendrons. Most of the guest rooms have wood-burning fireplaces, skylights and stained-glass windows.
Rates: $140-$195.
Ann & Gene Swett.
10 Rooms. 10 Private Baths. 8 Fireplaces. Guest phone available. Beds: KQT. B&B.
Seen in: *Los Angeles Times, PSA Magazine, San Francisco Focus.*

"Bed and Breakfast Inn of the Year." Hideaway Report.

Roserox Country Inn By-The-Sea

See: Pacific Grove, CA

Murphys

Dunbar House, 1880

271 Jones St, PO Box 1375
Murphys CA 95247
(209) 728-2897

Circa 1880. A picket fence frames this Italianate home, built by Willis

Dunbar for his bride. Later, distinguished sons who served in the State Assembly and ran the Dunbar Lumber Company lived here. On the porch, rocking chairs overlook century-old gardens. Inside, are antiques, lace, quilts and claw-foot tubs. Breakfast is delivered to your

room in a picnic basket, or you may join others by the fireplace in the dining room.
Location: Two blocks from the historic gold rush town of Murphys.
*Rates: $80-$85.
Bob & Barbara Costa.
4 Rooms. 4 Private Baths. 4 Fireplaces. Guest phone available. TV available. Beds: QDT. Full breakfast. Jacuzzi. Sauna. Exercise room. Swimming pool. Game room. Conference room. CCs: MC VISA. Tennis, swimming and fishing nearby. Skiing 39 miles. Winery and gold panning tours.
Seen in: *Los Angeles Times, Gourmet Magazine, Victorian Homes.*

"Your beautiful gardens and gracious hospitality combine for a super bed and breakfast."

Napa

Beazley House
1910 First St
Napa CA 94559
(707) 257-1649

Circa 1902. Nestled in green lawns and gardens, this graceful Shingle-

style mansion is frosted with white trim on its bays and balustrades. Stained glass windows and polished wood floors set the atmosphere in the parlor. There are five rooms in the main house and the carriage house features five more, many with fireplaces and whirlpool tubs. The venerable Beazley House was Napa's first bed and breakfast inn.
*Rates: $95-$150.
Jim & Carol Beazley.
10 Rooms. 10 Private Baths. 6 Fireplaces. Guest phone available. Beds: KQT. B&B. Jacuzzi. Handicap access. CCs: MC VISA AX DS. Horseback riding, water sports, wineries.
Seen in: *Los Angeles Times, USA Today.*

"It has everything: history, style, romance."

Calistoga's Wine Way Inn
See: Calistoga, CA

Coombs Residence "Inn on the Park"
720 Seminary St
Napa CA 94559
(707) 257-0789

Circa 1852. Nathan Coombs, who laid out the city of Napa, and who was ambassador to Japan during President Harrison's term, built this two-story Victorian home for his son Frank. The inn is decorated with European and American antiques. Across the street is historic Fuller Park.
Location: One hour from San Francisco.
*Rates: $80-$100.
Dave & Pearl Campbell.
4 Rooms. 1 Private Bath. Guest phone available. TV available. Beds: KQD. Continental breakfast. Jacuzzi. Swimming pool. CCs: MC VISA.

"We feel like we are back in Europe! Your hospitality is unmatched! Simple elegance with warm friendly atmosphere. Our favorite B&B, a house with its own personality."

Country Garden Inn
1815 Silverado Tr
Napa CA 94558
(707) 255-1197

Circa 1860. This historic carriage house is situated on the Napa River and one-and-a-half acres of woodland. A circular rose garden, with a lily pond and fountain add to the natural beauty of the location. Many of the guest rooms have jacuzzis, canopy beds, fireplaces, or private decks looking out over the water. English innkeepers serve hors d'oeuvres in the early evening and desserts later.
Location: South end of Napa Valley.
*Rates: $100-$150.
Usa & George Smith.
13 Rooms. 13 Private Baths. 4 Fireplaces. Guest phone available. Beds: KQ. B&B. Jacuzzi. Handicap access. CCs: MC VISA AX. Wine tasting, hiking, golf, horseback riding.
Seen in: *Los Angeles Times, San Francisco Examiner.*

Napa Inn
1137 Warren St
Napa CA 94559
(707) 257-1444

Circa 1898. This Victorian mansion is nestled in the heart of a serene wine country neighborhood. As

some rooms have kitchens, guests often pack a picnic lunch and start out for an afternoon of wine-touring. Shaded parks, gourmet and family restaurants are a short stroll from the inn.
Location: In the historic district.
Rates: $90-$135.
Doug & Carol Morales.
4 Rooms. 4 Private Baths. 1 Fireplace. Guest phone available. Beds: KQ. Full breakfast. CCs: MC VISA. Horseback riding, wine touring, balloon rides.

Shady Oaks Country Inn
See: St. Helena, CA

Nevada City

Downey House
517 West Broad St
Nevada City CA 95959
(916) 265-2815

Circa 1869. This Eastlake Victorian house is one of Nevada City's noted

Nabob Hill Victorians. There are six sound-proofed guest rooms, a curved veranda, and in the garden, a pond and restored red barn. One can stroll downtown where the evening streets are lit by the warm glow of gas lights.
Location: On Nabob Hill close to the Historic District.
*Rates: $60-$80.
Miriam Wright.
6 Rooms. 6 Private Baths. Guest phone available. TV available. Beds: QD. B&B.

CCs: MC VISA. Tennis, fishing, gold panning, boating, water-sports, wineries, horseback riding, skiing. Horse-drawn carriages, trolley.
Seen in: *San Francisco Examiner, Country Living.*
"The best in Northern California."

Grandmere's Inn

449 Broad St
Nevada City CA 95959
(916) 265-4660

Circa 1856. Arron Sargent, U.S. Congressman, senator, and author

of the women's suffrage bill, was the first owner of this white Colonial Revival house. He and his wife often received Susan B. Anthony here. Shaker pine furnishings and white wooden shutters predominate the interior design. Lavish creature comforts include six pillows to a bed and cut crystal water glasses in the bathrooms. Huge country breakfasts may include Dutch baby pancakes, baked brie in sherry, potatoes with cheddar and the inn's trademark, bread pudding. A half acre of terraced gardens cascade behind the inn to the block below.
Rates: $95-$135.
Annette Meade.
6 Rooms. 6 Private Baths. Guest phone available. TV available. Beds: Q. B&B. CCs: MC VISA. Horseback riding, cross-country & downhill skiing nearby.
Seen in: *Country Living, Gourmet, Sierra Heritage, California Inns.*
"Thanks for making me feel at home - no, better than home!"

The Red Castle Inn

109 Prospect St
Nevada City CA 95959
(916) 265-5135

Circa 1857. The Smithsonian has lauded the restoration of this four-story brick Gothic Revival known as "The Castle" by townsfolk. The roof is laced with wooden icicles and the balconies are festooned with gingerbread. Within, there are intri-

cate moldings, antiques, Victorian wallpapers, canopy beds and woodstoves. Verandas provide views of the historic city through cedar, chestnut and walnut trees, as well as of the terraced gardens with fountain pond.
Location: Within the historic district overlooking the town.
*Rates: $70-$110.
Conley & Mary Louise Weaver.
8 Rooms. 6 Private Baths. Guest phone available. Beds: QD. Full breakfast. CCs: MC VISA. Cross-country skiing, swimming, tennis, golf, white-water rafting. Horse-drawn carriage rides to town.
Seen in: *Sunset, Northern California Home and Garden, Sacramento Bee.*
"The Red Castle Inn would top my list of places to stay. Nothing else quite compares with it." Gourmet.

Nipomo

The Kaleidoscope Inn

Box 1297, 130 E Dana St
Nipomo CA 93444
(805) 929-5444

Circa 1887. Joseph Dana, a sea captain from New England, fell in love

with this area and married a Spanish senorita. Afterwards, he petitioned the Mexican government and was given all the land from the foothills to the sea. Inside this gingerbread Victorian are antique sofas, an old wooden trunk of Patty's great, great grandmother and vintage photographs. Sunlight filtering through the stained glass windows creates a kaleidoscope effect.
Location: Twenty miles south of San Luis Obispo, near Pismo Beach.
**Rates: $65-$70.
Patty & Bill Linane.
3 Rooms. 1 Private Bath. 1 Fireplace. Guest phone available. TV available. Beds: KQ. Continental-plus breakfast. Jacuzzi. CCs: MC VISA. Golfing, horseback riding, mineral springs, wind surfing, water skiing. Dinner & theater reservations.
Seen in: *Santa Maria Times.*
"Beautiful room, chocolates, huge bathroom, fresh flowers, peaceful night's rest, great breakfast."

Nipton

Hotel Nipton

Rt 1, Box 357
Nipton CA 92364
(619) 856-2335

Circa 1904. This southwestern-style adobe hotel with its wide verandas

once housed gold miners and Clara Bow, wife of movie star Rex Bell. It is decorated in period furnishings and historic photos of the area. A 1920s rock and cactus garden is now blooming and an outdoor spa provides the perfect setting for watching a flaming sunset over Ivanpah Valley, the New York Mountains, and Castle Peaks. Later, a magnificent star-studded sky appears undimmed by city lights.
*Rates: $44.94
Jerry & Roxanne Freeman.
4 Rooms. Beds: DT. Continental-plus breakfast. Jacuzzi. CCs: MC VISA. Mining tours, Cottonwood Cove.

Ojai

Bella Maggiore Inn

See: Ventura, CA

Ojai Manor Hotel

210 E Matilija
Ojai CA 93023
(805) 646-0961

Circa 1874. Once a schoolhouse, this is Ojai's oldest building. Turn-of-the-century furnishings are combined with modern prints and sculpture for an original decor. In the parlor are blue velvet couches and a big willow chair next to an old pot-bellied stove where sherry is served in the evening. Several good restaurants are nearby.
Location: One block from Main Street.
Rates: $70-$80.
6 Rooms. Continental-plus breakfast. CCs: MC VISA. Walk to shops & restaurants. Drive to hot springs.
Seen in: *Country Inns.*

"Best hotel we've ever stayed in and best breakfast we've ever had."

Ontario

Christmas House B&B Inn

See: Rancho Cucamonga, CA

Orland

The Inn at Shallow Creek Farm

Rt 3, Box 3176
Orland CA 95963
(916) 865-4093

Circa 1900. This vine-covered farmhouse was once the center of a well-known orchard and sheep ranch. The old barn, adjacent to the farmhouse, was a livery stop. The citrus orchard, now restored, blooms with 165 trees. Apples, pears, peaches, apricots, persimmons, walnuts, figs, and pomegrantes are also grown here. Guests are often found meandering about examining the Polish crested chickens, silver guinea fowl, Muscovy ducks, and African geese. The old caretaker's house is now a four-room guest cottage. Hundreds of narcissus grow along the creek that flows through the property.
Location: Northern California, 3 miles off Interstate 5.
*Rates: $45-$75.
Mary & Kurt Glaeseman.
4 Rooms. 2 Private Baths. 1 Fireplace. Guest phone in room. TV available. Beds: QT. B&B. River boating, fishing, hiking, birding.

Oxnard

Bella Maggiore Inn

See: Ventura, CA

Pacific Grove

Gosby House Inn

643 Lighthouse Ave
Pacific Grove CA 93950
(408) 375-1287

Circa 1887. Built as an upscale Victorian inn for those visiting the old

Methodist retreat, this sunny yellow mansion features an abundance of gables, turrets and bays. During renovation the innkeeper slept in all the rooms to determine just what antiques were needed and how the beds should be situated. Gosby House is in the National Register.
Location: Six blocks from the ocean.
*Rates: $85-$125.
Kelly Short.
22 Rooms. 20 Private Baths. Guest phone in room. Beds: QC. Full breakfast. Conference room. CCs: MC VISA AX. Afternoon tea & hors d'oeuvres.
Seen in: *Los Angeles Times, Travel & Leisure.*

Green Gables Inn

104 5th St
Pacific Grove CA 93950
(408) 375-2095 (800) 841-5252

Circa 1888. This half-timbered Queen Anne Victorian appears as a fantasy of gables overlooking spectacular Monterey Bay. The parlor has stained-glass panels framing the fireplace and bay windows looking out to sea. A favorite focal point is

an antique carousel horse. Most of the guest rooms have panoramic views of the ocean, fireplaces, gleaming woodwork, soft quilts, and flowers.
Location: On Monterey Bay four blocks from Monterey Bay Aquarium.
*Rates: $95-$150.
Roger & Sally Post with Claudia Long.
11 Rooms. 7 Private Baths. Guest phone available. TV available. Beds: QD. Full breakfast. Conference room. CCs: MC VISA DS. Picnicking, scuba diving, swimming, golfing. Honeymoon packages.

Roserox Country Inn By-The-Sea

557 Ocean View Blvd
Pacific Grove CA 93950
(408) 373-7673

Circa 1904. Roserox was designed and built by Dr. Julia Platt, first

woman mayor of Pacific Grove, Doctor of Zoology and world-renowned scientist. This is a warm and intimate four-story inn, enhanced by original patterned-oak floors and ten-foot-high redwood beamed ceilings.
Location: Oceanfront.
Rates: $85-$185.
Dawn Browncroft.
8 Rooms. 4 Private Baths. Guest phone available. Beds: QT. Full breakfast. Conference room.
Seen in: *This Month's Magazine, The Monterey Peninsula Guide.*

"I could never return to Monterey without staying at Roserox."

Seven Gables Inn
555 Ocean View Blvd
Pacific Grove CA 93950
(408) 372-4341

Circa 1886. At the turn of the century, Lucie Chase, a wealthy widow

and civic leader from the East Coast, embellished this Victorian with gables and verandas, taking full advantage of its spectacular setting on Monterey Bay. All guest rooms feature ocean views. There are elegant antiques, intricate Persian carpets, and beveled-glass armoires. Sea otters, harbor seals, and whales may often be seen from the inn.

Rates: $95-$165.
The Flately Family.
14 Rooms. 14 Private Baths. Guest phone available. TV available. Beds: Q. B&B. CCs: MC VISA. Golf, hiking, biking, beaches, whale watching.
Seen in: *Travel & Leisure Magazine.*

"We could not have spent the last two nights at a more charming home."

Palo Alto

The Victorian On Lytton
555 Lytton Ave
Palo Alto CA 94301
(415) 322-8555

Circa 1895. This Queen Anne home was built for Hannah Clapp, a des-

cendant of Massachusetts Bay colonist, Roger Clapp. In 1859, threatened by tuberculosis, she sought health in the West. She crossed the plains on horseback wearing bloomers so she could ride astride. She kept a pistol at her belt to challenge those who thought her costume invited frivolity. Once she arrived in California, she opened a preparatory school. The house has been recently restored with most guest rooms featuring a sitting area and a canopy or four-poster bed.

Rates: $90-135.
Susan Max Hall.
9 Rooms. 9 Private Baths. TV available. Beds: KQT. Continental breakfast. CCs: MC VISA AX.

Pismo Beach

The Kaleidoscope Inn
See: Nipomo, CA

Placerville

Vineyard House
See: Coloma, CA

Quincy

The Feather Bed
542 Jackson St, PO Box 3200
Quincy CA 95971
(916) 283-0102

Circa 1893. Englishman Edward Huskinson built this charming Queen Anne house shortly after he began his mining and real estate ventures. Ask for the secluded cottage with its own deck and clawfoot tub. Other rooms in the main house overlook downtown Quincy, or the mountains. Check out a bicycle to explore the countryside.

Location: In the heart of Plumas National Forest.
*Rates: $55-$80.
Chuck & Dianna Goubert.
7 Rooms. 7 Private Baths. Guest phone in room. TV available. Beds: QD. Full breakfast. Conference room. CCs: MC VISA AX. Horseback riding, water sports, cross country skiing, hiking. Bicycles available.

"After living and traveling in Europe where innkeepers are famous, we have found The Feather Bed to be one of the most charming in the U.S. and Europe!"

Rancho Cucamonga

Christmas House B&B Inn
9240 Archibald Ave
Rancho Cucamonga CA 91730
(714) 980-6450

Circa 1904. This Queen Anne Victorian has been renovated in period

elegance, emphasizing its intricate wood carvings, and red and green stained-glass windows. Once surrounded by 80 acres of citrus groves and vineyards, the home with its wide, sweeping veranda, is still a favorite place for taking in the beautiful lawns and palm trees. The elegant atmosphere attracts the business traveler, romance-seeker and vacationer.

Location: East of downtown Los Angeles, 3 miles from Ontario Airport.
*Rates: $55-$115.
Jay & Janice Ilsley.
5 Rooms. 2 Private Baths. 2 Fireplaces. Guest phone available. TV in room. Beds: QD. B&B. Gourmet meals. Jacuzzi. Conference room. Snow skiing.
Seen in: *Los Angeles Times, Elan Magazine.*

"Coming to Christmas House is like stepping through a magic door into an enchanted land. Many words come to mind...warmth, serenity, peacefulness."

Red Bluff

Faulkner House
1029 Jefferson St
Red Bluff CA 96080
(916) 529-0520

Circa 1890. Built by jeweler Herman Wiendieck, this Queen Anne Victorian was bought by Dr. and Mrs. James L. Faulkner in 1933. The house has original stained-glass windows, ornate molding, and eight-foot pocket doors separating the front and back parlors. Church bells nearby chime the hour as you relax on the porch.

*Rates: $45-$60.

Harvey & Mary Klingler.
4 Rooms. 1 Private Bath. Guest phone available. Beds: QD. Full breakfast. Conference room. Fishing, hiking, skiing, golf.

"A delightful B&B, tastefully decorated with beautiful antiques."

Sacramento

Amber House

1315 22nd St
Sacramento CA 95816
(916) 444-8085

Circa 1905. This Craftsman-style bungalow on the city's Historic

Preservation Register is in a neighborhood of fine old homes eight blocks from the capitol. Each room is named for a famous poet and features stained glass, English antiques, selected volumes of poetry and fresh flowers. Ask for the Lord Byron Room where you can soak by candlelight in the jacuzzi.

Location: Seven blocks to the capitol.
*Rates: $70-$135.
Michael & Jane Richardson.
5 Rooms. 5 Private Baths. Guest phone in room. TV available. Beds: QD. B&B. Jacuzzi. Conference room. CCs: MC VISA AX. Near Old Town, Convention Center. River rafting. Bicycles available.

Briggs House B&B

2209 Capitol Ave
Sacramento CA 95816
(916) 441-3214

Circa 1901. Surrounded by stately elms, this elegantly restored Cube

Colonial house is filled with European and American antiques. The spacious rooms have rich wood paneling, inlaid-hardwood floors, and oriental rugs. Guests are welcome to raid the refrigerator for refreshments any time during the day or night.

Location: Midtown, seven blocks from the capitol.
Rates: $60-$105.
Pam Giordano and Catherine Parker.
7 Rooms. 5 Private Baths. Guest phone in room. Beds: KQT. Full breakfast. Jacuzzi. Sauna. Conference room. CCs: MC VISA.
Seen in: *Motorland, San Francisco Bay Views, California Lodging Update.*

"We have enjoyed country inns around the world and this ranks as one of the top small inns."

Hartley House Inn

700 22nd St
Sacramento CA 95816
(916) 447-7829

Circa 1906. Original hitching posts grace the front of this stunning

Colonial Revival inn. What was formerly known as Mrs. Murphy's boarding house has been restored with elegant antiques and silk wallpapers. There is a large collection of antique wall clocks and chiming grandfather clocks.

Location: Downtown.
*Rates: $75-$105.
Randall Hartley.
5 Rooms. 5 Private Baths. Guest phone in room. TV in room. Beds: Q. Full breakfast. Conference room. Water skiing, horseback riding, bicycling.
Seen in: *Yellow Brick Road, Sacramento Bee, Innviews.*

"Breakfasts are as lavish as the inn."

The Red Castle Inn

See: Nevada City, CA

Sterling Hotel

1300 H St
Sacramento CA 95814
(916) 448-1300

Circa 1894. The gables and bays, turrets and verandas of this 15,000

square-foot Queen Anne Victorian home testify to the affluence of its former owners, the Carter-Hawley Hale family, of Weinstocks department store fame. The foyer and drawing room boast black marble fireplaces and marble floors while guest rooms feature writing desks, designer furnishings, private jacuzzis, and marble baths. A reproduction Victorian glass conservatory houses one of the dining rooms of the inn's four star restaurant, Chanterelle.

*Rates: $95-$225.
Richard Kann.
12 Rooms. 12 Private Baths. Guest phone in room. TV in room. Beds: KQ. Restaurant. Jacuzzi. Conference room. CCs: MC VISA AX DC.
Seen in: *Sacramento Magazine.*

"Fabulous, looking forward to my return."

Vineyard House

See: Coloma, CA

Saint Helena

Cornerstone B&B Inn
1308 Main St
Saint Helena CA 94574
(707) 963-1891

Circa 1891. This renovated European-style hostelry has twelve spacious rooms furnished in the Victorian period. The exterior is stone, the interior has rooms decorated with antiques, hand-made quilts and down comforters. Nearby attractions are the famous hot springs, mud baths and concerts in the vineyards.

*Rates: $65-$115.
Margie Hinton.
12 Rooms. Beds: KQDT. Continental-plus breakfast. Ballooning, gliders, geysers, bicycling, mud baths and hot springs.

Ink House
1575 St Helena Hwy
Saint Helena CA 94574
(707) 963-3890

Circa 1884. Theron H. Ink, owner of thousands of acres in Marin,

Napa and Sonoma counties, invested in livestock, wineries and mining. He built this Italianate Victorian house with a glass-walled observatory on top of the house. From this room, visitors can enjoy 360-degree views of the Napa Valley and surrounding vineyards.

Location: In the heart of Napa Valley wine country.
*Rates: $95-$120.
Lois & George Clark.
4 Rooms. 4 Private Baths. Guest phone available. Beds: QD. Continental breakfast. Nearby wine tours, spas & mud baths, soaring, ballooning.

"Your hospitality of home and heart have made us feel so much at home. This is a place and a time we will long remember."

Shady Oaks Country Inn
399 Zinfandel
Saint Helena CA 94574
(707) 963-1190

Circa 1880. This country home sits on two acres of oak and walnut

trees. Adjacent to the house is a winery built in 1883, possessing original stone walls. It now serves as a luxurious guest suite. Rooms in the main house feature original wallpaper, a claw-foot tub, a private deck, or a view of the gardens and vineyards. Take the afternoon to play croquet, or ask the innkeeper to pack one of her perfect picnic baskets.

Location: Two miles south of town among the finest wineries in the valley.
*Rates: $50-$120.
Lisa Wild-Runnells & Jon Runnells.
4 Rooms. 4 Private Baths. Guest phone available. Beds: KQ. Full breakfast. Handicap access. CCs: MC VISA. Near restaurants, biking, ballooning. Hammock, croquet, bicycles.
Seen in:

"Can't decide which is the most outstanding...the rooms, the breakfast or the sensational hospitality." Rocky Mountain News.

San Diego

Britt House
406 Maple St
San Diego CA 92103
(619) 234-2926

Circa 1887. This lavish Queen Anne Victorian house once belonged to the Scripps family of newspaper publishing fortune. The elder Scripps created a chain of 35 newspapers. One of them, the San Diego Sun, was begun simply to irritate the Spreckels, owners of the

Union-Tribune. The house is noted for an unusual two-story rose and blue stained-glass window depicting morning, noon, and night. Other features of the inn include carved oak fretwork, a golden-oak staircase, turrets, and formal English gardens.

Location: City, parkside.
**Rates: $95-$125.
Elizabeth Lord.
10 Rooms. 1 Private Bath. Guest phone available. TV available. Beds: Q. Full breakfast. Picnics and special dinners by arrangement.
Seen in: *LA Magazine, California Magazine, Toronto Sun, San Diego Home & Gardens.*

"The 'Gold Standard' for California B&B's."

Heritage Park B&B Inn
2470 Heritage Park Row
San Diego CA 92110
(619) 295-7088

Circa 1889. Situated on a seven-acre Victorian park in the heart of

Old Town, this inn is one of seven preserved classic structures. Built for Hartfield and Myrtle Christian it was featured in *The Golden Era* as an "outstandingly beautiful home of Southern California." It has a variety of chimneys, shingles, a two-story corner tower, and a wraparound porch.

Location: In historic Old Town.

✻Rates: $75-$115.
Lori Chandler.
9 Rooms. 5 Private Baths. Guest phone available. Beds: QT. Full breakfast. Handicap access. Conference room. CCs: MC VISA. Walking distance to golf and tennis. Sportsfishing charters located 5 miles away. Candlelight dinners in room.
Seen in: *Los Angeles Herald Examiner, Yellow Brick Road.*

"A beautiful step back in time. Peaceful and gracious."

Julian Gold Rush Hotel

See: Julian, CA

Surf Manor & Cottages

PO Box 7695
San Diego CA 92107
(619) 225-9765

Circa 1930. Surf Manor consists of four original beach cottages in the

popular South Mission Beach area. Each tiny cottage contains a living room, bedroom, kitchen and bath. Guests enter through a picket fence onto a small front porch. Breakfast is self-catered. The ocean and bay are within one block.
Location: South Mission Beach.
✻Rates: $60-$90.
Jerri Grady.
4 Rooms. 4 Private Baths. Beds: D. Continental breakfast. Water sports.

"Enjoyed the many walks along the bay and ocean. Great location."

San Francisco

Art Center/Wamsley Gallery & B&B

1902 Filbert St
San Francisco CA 94123
(415) 567-1526

Circa 1857. The Art Center Bed & Breakfast was built during the Louisiana movement to San Francisco during the Gold Rush. It was the

only permanent structure on the path between the Presido and Yerba Buena village. There are four guest apartments here, convenient to much of San Francisco. Ask for the penthouse apartment. The building is next to what was reputedly Washer Woman's Cove, a freshwater lagoon at the foot of Laguna Street that served as the village laundry. It was the only permanent structure on the path between the Presidio and Yerba Buena village. There are four guest apartments here, convenient to much of San Francisco. Ask for the penthouse apartment.
Location: Two blocks south of Lombard (Rt 101) on the corner of Laguna.
✻Rates: $65-$115.
George & Helvi Wamsley.
4 Rooms. 4 Private Baths. 3 Fireplaces. Guest phone available. TV in room. Beds: QT. Continental-plus breakfast. Jacuzzi. CCs: MC VISA AX DC CB DS. Whale watching, boat cruises.
Seen in: *Richmond News, American Artist Magazine.*

Garratt Mansion

See: Alameda, CA

Golden Gate Hotel

775 Bush St
San Francisco CA 94108
(415) 392-3702

Circa 1913. News travels far when there's a bargain. Half of the guests visiting this four-story Edwardian hotel at the foot of Nob Hill are from abroad. Great bay windows on each floor provide many of the rooms with gracious spaces at humble prices. An original bird cage elevator kept in working order floats between floors. Antiques, fresh flowers, and afternoon tea further add to the atmosphere. Union

Square is two-and-a-half blocks from the hotel.
✻Rates: $50-$79.
John & Renate Kenaston.
23 Rooms. 14 Private Baths. Guest phone available. TV in room. Beds: QDT. B&B. CCs: MC VISA AX DC CB. Cable car, theatre, shopping.
Seen in: *Los Angeles Times, Travel Tips.*

"Stayed here by chance, will return by choice!"

Green Apple Inn

See: Freestone, CA

The Inn San Francisco

943 S Van Ness
San Francisco CA 94110
(415) 641-0188

Circa 1872. Built on Mansion Row, this Italianate Victorian was once the home of city commissioner John English and his family. He was known as "The Potato King" because of his vast holdings in potato commodities. Champion race horses were raised on the grounds. Now, restored to an elegant Victorian inn, Inn San Francisco welcomes guests to enjoy ornate woodwork and marble fireplaces.
✻Rates: $68-$180.
Joel Daily.
20 Rooms. 15 Private Baths. 2 Fireplaces. Guest phone in room. TV in room. Beds: QDT. Continental-plus breakfast. Jacuzzi. Conference room. CCs: MC VISA AX.
Seen in: *Innsider.*

"...in no time at all you begin to feel a kinship with the gentle folk who adorn the walls in their golden frames."

Moffatt House

431 Hugo St
San Francisco CA 94122
(415) 661-6210

Circa 1910. A simple two-story Edwardian home, the Moffatt House has a vivid stained-glass window

that contrasts with its light, neutral interior. Guest rooms are artfully decorated and several face Mt. Sutra's fog-veiled heights. Guests take in the neighborhood shops, bakeries and cafes. The Haight-Ashbury district and Golden Gate Park are nearby.
Location: One block from Golden Gate Park.
Rates: $39-$54.
Ruth Moffatt.
4 Rooms. Guest phone available. Beds: QTC. Continental-plus breakfast. CCs: MC VISA.
"It was neat and clean...excellent breakfast. I would return."

The Nolan House

1071 Page St
San Francisco CA 94117
(415) 863-0384

Circa 1889. This fanciful Victorian features a four-story bay and distinctively painted elements, decorataive moldings, dentil designs and shingles. A double parlor inside boasts two marble fireplaces. The dining room overlooks a sub-tropical garden. French Victorian furnishings, feather beds and marble fireplaces add to a luxurious San Francisco experience. There is a deck and carriage house on the property and Golden Gate Park is two blocks away.

*Rates: $85-$115.
Timothy W. Beaver & Timothy F. Sockett.
4 Rooms. 3 Fireplaces. Guest phone available. TV available. Beds: Q. B&B. Conference room. CCs: MC VISA. Horseback riding, bicycling, tennis.
"...a wonderful home with alot of character and your breakfast was superb. The best we've had at any B&B!"

Old Thyme Inn

See: Half Moon Bay, CA

Petite Auberge

863 Bush St
San Francisco CA 94108
(415) 928-6000

Circa 1919. This five-story hotel features an ornate baroque design with curved bay windows. Now transformed to a French country inn there are antiques, fresh flowers, and country accessories. Most rooms also have working fireplaces. It's a short walk to the Powell Street cable car.

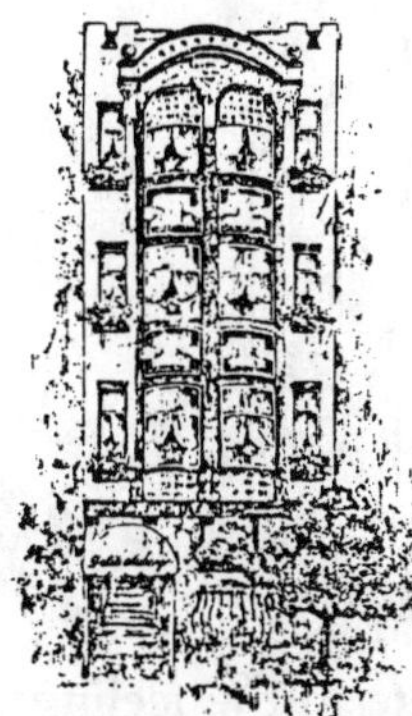

Location: Two-and-a-half blocks from Union Square.
*Rates: $105-$195.
Carolyn Vaughan.
26 Rooms. 26 Private Baths. Full breakfast. CCs: MC VISA. Shopping, theater.
Seen in: *Los Angeles Times, Brides.*
"Breakfast was great, and even better in bed!"

The Red Castle Inn

See: Nevada City, CA

Spencer House

1080 Haight St
San Francisco CA 94117
(415) 626-9205

Circa 1890. This opulent mansion, which sits on three city lots, is one of San Francisco's finest examples of Queen Anne Victorian architecture. Ornate parquet floors, original wallpapers, gaslights, and antique linens are featured. Breakfast is served with crystal and silver in the elegantly paneled dining room.
Location: Ten minutes from the wharf.
*Rates: $95-$155.
Barbara & Jack Chambers.
6 Rooms. 6 Private Baths. Guest phone available. TV available. Beds: KQD. Full breakfast. Conference room.

Spreckels Mansion

737 Buena Vista West
San Francisco CA 94117
(415) 861-3008

Circa 1887. The Spreckels family built this rare Colonial Revival mansion across from Buena Vista Park, on a hill with spectacular views of the city. The stained-glass windows and gaslight fixtures are all original. Request the Sugar Baron Suite and enjoy a canopied bed and free-standing tub in view of the

fireplace. The next morning if you ask, your breakfast will be brought up on a silver tray.
Location: On a wooded hilltop near the Panhandle of Golden Gate Park.
*Rates: $98-$200.
Jonathan Sharron & Kathleen Austin.
10 Rooms. 8 Private Baths. Guest phone in room. Beds: Q. Continental-plus breakfast. CCs: MC VISA. Afternoon social hour before the fireplace.
Seen in: *Travel & Leisure, Bay View Magazine.*
"Well, it's the closest thing to heaven that we've found."

Stanyan Park Hotel

750 Stanyan St
San Francisco CA 94117
(415) 751-1000

Circa 1905. Many of the guest rooms of this restored Victorian inn

overlook Golden Gate Park. The turret suites and bay suites are popular, but all rooms are decorated in a variety of antiques and color schemes. A variety of museums, horseback riding and biking are available in the park, as well as the Japanese Tea Garden.
*Rates: $68-$88.
36 Rooms. 36 Private Baths. Guest phone in room. TV in room. Beds: QTC. Continental breakfast. Handicap access. Conference room. CCs: MC VISA AX DS. Aquarium, planetarium, museums.
Seen in: *San Francisco Chronicle, Metropolitan Home.*

Victorian Inn On The Park

301 Lyon St
San Francisco CA 94117
(415) 931-1830

Circa 1897. This grand three-story Queen Anne inn, built by William

Curlett, has an open belvedere turret with a tea house roof and Victorian railings. Silk-screened wallpapers created especially for the inn, are accentuated by intricate mahogany and redwood paneling. The opulent Belvedere Suite features French doors opening to a Roman tub for two. Overlooking Golden Gate Park, the inn is near the University of San Francisco Medical Center, ten minutes from downtown.

*Rates: $81-$250.
Lisa & William Benau.
12 Rooms. 12 Private Baths. 4 Fireplaces. Guest phone in room. TV in room. Beds: QDT. B&B. CCs: MC VISA AX. Golf, walking trails, Japanese Tea Gardens.
Seen in: *Innsider Magazine, Country Inns, Good Housekeeping.*

"The excitement you have about your building comes from the care you have taken in restoring and maintaining your historic structure."

White Swan Inn

845 Bush St
San Francisco CA 94108
(415) 775-1755

Circa 1908. This four-story Nob Hill hotel with a marble facade was originally the Hotel Louise. Heavy beveled glass doors open to a large reception area with granite floors, an antique carousel horse, and English artworks. Bay windows and

a rear deck contribute to the feeling of an English garden inn. The guest rooms are decorated with softly colored English wallpapers and prints. All rooms have fireplaces and turn-down service is provided.

Location: In the heart of downtown.
*Rates: $145-$250.
Carolyn Vaughan.
27 Rooms. 27 Private Baths. Guest phone in room. Beds: KQC. Continental-plus breakfast. Conference room. CCs: MC VISA. Afternoon tea and hors d'oeuvres.
Seen in: *Victoria Magazine.*

San Jose

Madison Street Inn

See: Santa Clara, CA

San Luis Obispo

The Kaleidoscope Inn

See: Nipomo, CA

Olallieberry Inn

See: Cambria, CA

San Rafael

Casa Soldavini

531 "C" St
San Rafael CA 94901
(415) 454-3140

Circa 1932. The first Italian settlers in San Rafael built this home. Their grandchildren now own it, and proudly hang pictures of their family. Grandfather Joseph, a wine maker, who planned and planted what are now the lush gardens surrounding the home. The many Italian antiques throughout the house complement the Italian-style decor.

Location: Fifteen minutes north of Golden Gate Bridge.
*Rates: $55-$65.
Linda Soldavini-Cassidy & Dan Cassidy.
3 Rooms. 1 Private Bath. Guest phone available. TV available. Beds: QT. Continental-plus breakfast. Within 30-45 minutes of woods, beaches, horses, wineries.

"Scrumptious breakfast, quiet and charming."

Santa Ana

The Craftsman

2900 N Flower St
Santa Ana CA 92706
(714) 543-1168

Circa 1910. This two-story Colonial Revival home with multiple gables was built by the Smiley family. They were orange growers in Orange County and an original orange grove remains across the street. The house is one of the few stately homes still in the area. It has been restored to its original beauty, furnished in American and Danish antiques.

Location: Disneyland area in Orange County.
Rates: $65.
Philip & Irene Chinn.
2 Rooms. Guest phone in room. TV available. Beds: Q. Full breakfast. Swimming pool. Tennis and swimming.

Santa Barbara

Bath Street Inn

1720 Bath St
Santa Barbara CA 93101
(805) 682-9680

Circa 1873. Overlooking the Victorian front veranda, a semi-circular

"eyelid" balcony on the second floor seems to wink, beckoning guests to come in for an old-fashioned taste of hospitality provided by innkeeper Sue Brown. Originally the home of

a merchant tailor, the inn is within a few blocks of the heart of Old Santa Barbara. Guest chambers upstairs have polished hardwood floors, floral wallpapers and antiques. The back garden deck, filled with wicker, or the summer house surrounded by wisteria and blossoming orange trees are among the four locations available for enjoying breakfast.
*Rates: $60-$115.
Susan Brown & Joanne Thorne.
7 Rooms. 7 Private Baths. Guest phone available. TV available. Beds: KQT. Full breakfast. CCs: MC VISA AX. Ocean nearby, all water sports, polo.
Seen in: *Sunset Magazine*.
"Like going to the home of a favorite aunt." Country Inns Magazine.

Bella Maggiore Inn

See: Ventura, CA

Blue Quail Inn

1908 Bath St
Santa Barbara CA 93101
(805) 687-2300

Circa 1915. The main house and adjacent cottages are decorated in a charming country style. The Hummingbird is a cottage guest room featuring a chaise lounge, queen-size, white iron bed, and a private brick patio. Hot apple cider is served each evening and picnic lunches are available.
Location: Quiet residential area near town and the beach.
*Rates: $75-$100.
Jeanise Suding Eaton.
8 Rooms. 6 Private Baths. 1 Fireplace. Guest phone available. TV available. Beds: KQT. Continental-plus breakfast. CCs: MC VISA. Bicycles, sailing, horseback riding, golf tennis. Nearby gliding, wine tasting.
Seen in: *Los Angeles Times, Santa Barbara Magazine.*
"Mahvolous, simply maaahvolous! Loved everything. And just think, I'm here on a business trip - boy, love this job! I'll be back for sure - business of course."

Cheshire Cat Inn

36 W Valerio
Santa Barbara CA 93101
(805) 569-1610

Circa 1892. The Eberle family built two graceful homes side by side, one a Queen Anne, the other a Colonial Revival. President McKinley was entertained here on his visit to Santa Barbara. There is a pagoda-like porch, and a square and a curved bay. There are rose gardens, grassy lawns and a gazebo. Laura Ashley wallpapers are featured here and in the owner's other inn, a 12th century manor in Scotland.
Location: Downtown.
*Rates: $99-$179.
Christine Dunstan.
11 Rooms. 11 Private Baths. Guest phone in room. Beds: KQT. Continental-plus breakfast. Jacuzzi. Conference room. Bicycling.
Seen in: *Two on the Town, KABC, Los Angeles Times, Santa Barbara Magazine.*
"...romantic and quaint."

Glenborough Inn

1327 Bath St
Santa Barbara CA 93101
(805) 966-0589

Circa 1880. This Craftsman-style inn recreates a turn-of-the-century atmosphere in the main house. There is also an 1880's cottage reminiscent of the Victorian era. Inside are antiques, rich wood trim, and elegant fireplace suites with canopy beds. There's always plenty of firewood and an open invitation to the secluded garden hot tub. Breakfast is homemade and has been written up in *Bon Appetit* and *Chocolatier*.
*Rates: $65-$155.
David & Judy Groom & Laurel Ford.
9 Rooms. 5 Private Baths. 3 Fireplaces. Guest phone available. Beds: QD. B&B. Jacuzzi. CCs: MC VISA AX. Nearby sailing, scuba diving, tennis, horseback riding, wineries.
Seen in: *Houston Post, Los Angeles Times.*
"Both Tom & I are terminal romantics and as it is obvious that you must be also, suffice it to say that for grace & style you are hereby awarded the Blue Ribbon."

Harbour Carriage House

420 W Montecito St
Santa Barbara CA 93101
(805) 962-8447

Circa 1900. The Harbour Carriage House, set behind a white picket fence, consists of two historic homes adorned with fish-scale shingles and gabled roofs. Guest rooms, named for wild flowers, are decorated with a combination of French and English country antiques. Try Forget-Me-Not and enjoy a private spa, a fireplace and a view of the mountains from the canopied, king-size bed.
Location: Two blocks to the beach, close to downtown.
*Rates: $85-$155.
JoAnn Adorna.
9 Rooms. 9 Private Baths. 6 Fireplaces. Guest phone in room. TV available. Beds: KQ. Full breakfast. Jacuzzi. Handicap access. CCs: MC VISA. Biking, horseback riding, sailing, wine tasting, gliding.
Seen in: *Los Angeles Times.*
"Thank you for a lovely weekend. If it wouldn't be any trouble could we have your recipes for the delicious breakfast?"

The Old Yacht Club Inn

431 Corona Del Mar
Santa Barbara CA 93103
(805) 962-1277

Circa 1912. This California Craftsman house was the home of the Santa Barbara Yacht Club during the Roaring Twenties. It was opened as Santa Barbara's first B&B and has become renowned for its gourmet food and superb hospitality. Innkeeper Nancy Donaldson is the author of *The Old Yacht Club Inn Cookbook*.
Location: East Beach.
*Rates: $65-$120.
Nancy Donaldson, Sandy Hunt & Lu Carouso.
9 Rooms. 8 Private Baths. Guest phone in room. TV available. Beds: KQDT. Full breakfast. Gourmet meals. Jacuzzi. Conference room. CCs: MC VISA AX. Water sports, bicycling, golf, horseback riding.
Seen in: *Los Angeles Magazine, Valley Magazine.*
"Donaldson is one of Santa Barbara's better-kept culinary secrets."

The Parsonage

1600 Olive St
Santa Barbara CA 93101
(805) 962-9336

Circa 1892. Built for the Trinity Episcopal Church, the Parsonage is one of Santa Barbara's most notable Queen Anne Victorian structures. It is nestled between downtown Santa Barbara and the foothills in a quiet residential, upper eastside neighborhood. The inn has ocean and mountain views and is within walking

distance of the mission, shops, theater, and restaurants.
*Rates: $75-$150.
Hilde Michemore.
6 Rooms. 6 Private Baths. Full breakfast.
Seen in: *Los Angeles Times, Epicurean Review.*

"Things were as close to perfect as newlyweds could want. You and your marvelous house played a major role in making it so."

Simpson House Inn
121 E Arrellaga St
Santa Barbara CA 93101
(805) 963-7067

Circa 1874. If you were one of the Simpson family's first visitors, you

would have arrived in Santa Barbara by stagecoach or sea because the railroad route was not completed for another 14 years after the house was built. A stately Italianate Victorian house, the inn is graciously decorated. It is situated on an acre of lawns and gardens secluded behind a 20-foot-tall eugenia hedge. Mint juleps are often served in the early evening, and are particularly enjoyable under the shade of the Magnolia trees.
Location: Five minute walk to downtown Santa Barbara and the historic district.
**Rates: $75-$150.
Gillean Wilson, Linda & Glyn Davies.
6 Rooms. 5 Private Baths. 1 Fireplace. Beds: KQD. Full breakfast. Handicap access. Conference room. CCs: MC VISA. English croquet, chickens, and ducks. Complementary bicycles.
Seen in: *Country Inns Magazine, Santa Barbara Magazine, Glamour.*

"Perfectly restored and impeccably furnished. Your hospitality is warm and heartfelt and the food is delectable."

Tiffany Inn
1323 De La Vina
Santa Barbara CA 93101
(805) 963-2283

Circa 1898. This Victorian house features a steep front gable and balcony accentuating the entrance.

Colonial diamond-paned bay windows and a front veranda welcome guests to an antique-filled inn. The Honeymoon Suite is a favorite with its secluded garden entrance, canopied bed, jacuzzi tub and fireplace. Other rooms are just as interesting, with antique toy collections, floral chintzes and Victorian beds. Fine restaurants and shops are within walking distance.
*Rates: $90-$195.
Carol & Larry Mac Donald.
7 Rooms. 5 Private Baths. 5 Fireplaces. Guest phone available. Beds: Q. Full breakfast. Jacuzzi. CCs: MC VISA AX. Museums, shops, beaches nearby.

"We have stayed at a number of B&B's, but this is the best. We especially liked the wonderful breakfasts on the porch overlooking the garden."

Santa Clara

Madison Street Inn
1390 Madison St
Santa Clara CA 95050
(408) 249-5541

Circa 1890. This Queen Anne Victorian inn still has its original doors

and locks. "No Peddlers or Agents" is engraved in the cement of the original carriageway, but guests always receive a warm and gracious welcome. High-ceilinged rooms are furnished in antiques, oriental rugs, and Victorian wallpaper.
Location: Ten minutes from San Jose.
Rates: $60-$85.
Ralph & Teresa Wigginton.
5 Rooms. 3 Private Baths. Guest phone in room. TV available. Beds: QT. B&B. Jacuzzi. Sauna. Swimming pool. CCs: MC VISA AX DC.

"The people in our little group travel often and spend many nights in hotels that look and feel exactly alike whether they are in Houston or Boston. Your inn was delightful and best of all, it was wonderful to bask in your warm and gracious hospitality."

Santa Cruz

Babbling Brook B&B Inn
1025 Laurel St
Santa Cruz CA 95060
(408) 427-2437

Circa 1909. This inn was built on the foundations of an 1870 tannery

and a 1790 grist mill. Secluded, yet within the city, the inn features a cascading waterfall and meandering creek on one acre of gardens and redwoods. Country French decor, cozy fireplaces, and deep soaking whirlpool tubs are luxurious amenities of the Babbling Brook.
Location: North end of Monterey Bay.
*Rates: $85-$125.
Tom & Helen King.
12 Rooms. 12 Private Baths. Guest phone available. TV available. Beds: KQ. Full breakfast. Handicap access. CCs: MC VISA DS. Tennis and the ocean are within walking distance. Inn-to-inn tour package.

"We were impressed with the genuine warmth of the inn. The best breakfast we've had outside our own home!"

Bayview Hotel B&B Inn
See: Aptos, CA

Chateau Victorian
118 First St
Santa Cruz CA 95060
(408) 458-9458

Circa 1890. Chateau Victorian was built by a prosperous young sea captain from the east coast who made Santa Cruz his home port. On one of his journeys he met and fell in love with a native girl from the Solomon Islands. After instructing

the crew to tell the story that he had died at sea, he sent his ship on without him. Years later, nearing death, he tried to return home to Santa Cruz but died aboard ship. Now his Victorian house is an elegant inn with a fireplace in each room.
Location: One block from the beach near the boardwalk and wharf.
Rates: $90-$120.
Franz & Alice-June Benjamin.
7 Rooms. 7 Private Baths. 7 Fireplaces. Guest phone available. Beds: Q. Continental-plus breakfast. Conference room. CCs: MC VISA. Golfing, fishing, sailing, ballooning, whale watching.
Seen in: *Times Tribune, Santa Cruz Sentinel, Good Times.*

"Certainly enjoyed our most recent stay and have appreciated all of our visits."

Cliff Crest
407 Cliff St
Santa Cruz CA 95060
(408) 427-2609

Circa 1887. Warmth, friendliness and comfort characterize this elegantly restored Queen Anne Victorian house. An octagonal solarium, tall stained-glass windows, and a belvedere overlook Monterey Bay and the Santa Cruz mountains. The mood is airy and romantic. The spacious gardens were designed by John McLaren, landscape architect for Golden Gate Park. Antiques and fresh flowers fill the rooms, once home to William Jeter, Lieutenant Governor of California.
Location: One-and-a-half blocks from the beach and boardwalk.
*Rates: $80-$125.
Sharon & Bruce Taylor.
5 Rooms. 5 Private Baths. 1 Fireplace. Guest phone available. Beds: KQ. Full breakfast. CCs: MC VISA. Theatre, wineries, train ride. Hammock.
Seen in: *Los Angeles Times.*

"Delightful place, excellent food and comfortable bed."

The Inn at Depot Hill
See: Aptos, CA

Mangels House
See: Aptos, CA

New Davenport B&B
See: Davenport, CA

Santa Maria

The Kaleidoscope Inn
See: Nipomo, CA

Santa Monica

Channel Road Inn
219 West Channel Road
Santa Monica CA 90402
(213) 459-1920

Circa 1910. This shingle-clad building is a rare example of a variation

of the Colonial Revival Period, one of the few remaining in Los Angeles. The abandoned home was saved from the city's wrecking crew by Susan Zolla with the encouragement of the local historical society. Many amenities for business guests and beach visitors are available, and there is a spectacular cliffside spa.
Location: One block from the ocean.
*Rates: $85-$145.
Susan Zolla.
14 Rooms. 14 Private Baths. Guest phone in room. TV in room. Beds: KQDT. B&B. Gourmet meals. Jacuzzi. Handicap access. Conference room. CCs: MC VISA. Horseback riding nearby, bicycles provided for beach bike path. Picnic lunches on request.
Seen in: *Los Angeles-The Daily News, Evening Outlook.*

"The inn is very pretty inside and out, the rooms are handsomely decorated using a variety of furnishings."

Santa Rosa

The Gables
4257 Petaluma Hill Rd
Santa Rosa CA 95404
(707) 585-7777

Circa 1877. Fifteen gables accentuate this striking French-influenced Gothic Revival house situated on three-and-a-half acres in the historic district. It was built by William Roberts for his high-school

sweetheart, after he returned from the goldmines. Inside, there are 12-foot ceilings, a winding staircase with ornately carved ballistrades, and three marble fireplaces. The Brookside Suite overlooks Taylor Creek and is decorated in an Edwardian theme. Other rooms feature views of the Sequoias, meadows and the Gable's barn.
*Rates: $95-$115.
Michael & Judy Ogne.
6 Rooms. 6 Private Baths. 2 Fireplaces. Guest phone in room. TV in room. Beds: KQD. B&B. Gourmet meals. Handicap access. Conference room. CCs: MC VISA AX. Golf, horseback riding, wineries.

"You all have a warmth about you that makes it home here."

Melitta Station Inn
5850 Melita Rd
Santa Rosa CA 95409
(707) 538-7712

Circa 1880. Originally built as a stage-coach stop, this long rambling structure became a freight station for the little town of Melitta's depot. Basalt stone quarried from the near-by hills were sent by rail to San Francisco where they were used to pave the cobblestone streets. Still located down a country lane, the station has been charmingly renovated. Oiled-wood floors, rough-beam cathedral ceiling and French doors opening to a balcony are features of the sitting room. Wineries and vineyards stretch from the station to the town of Sonoma.
*Rates: $80-$90. Season: Nov. - April.
Diane & Vic.
6 Rooms. 4 Private Baths. 2 Fireplaces. Guest phone available. Beds: QD. Full breakfast. Conference room. CCs: MC VISA. Horseback riding, biking, hiking, swimming, fishing, sailing.

Seen in: *Press Democrat.*

"...warm welcome and great food."

Sausalito

Casa Madrona Hotel

801 Bridgeway
Sausalito CA 94965
(415) 332-0502

Circa 1885. This Victorian mansion was first used as a lumber baron's mansion. As time went on, additional buildings were added giving it a European look. A registered Sausalito Historical Landmark, it is the oldest building in town. Each room has a unique name, such as "Lord Ashley's Lookout" or "Kathmandu", and the appointments are as varied as the names. The inn faces San Francisco Bay, enabling guests to enjoy the barking seals, the evening fog and the arousing sunsets.

Location: Downtown Sausalito.
Rates: $90-$185.
John W. Mays.
37 Rooms. 37 Private Baths. Guest phone in room. Jacuzzi. Conference room. Checks not accepted.
Seen in: *Los Angeles Times, The Register.*

"Had to pinch myself several times to be sure it was real! Is this heaven? With this view it sure feels like it."

Sausalito Hotel

16 El Portal
Sausalito CA 94965
(415) 332-4155

Circa 1900. Built in the Mission Revival style, this hotel is nestled

near the ferry landing on the water's edge. There, it has witnessed the transformance of a once sleepy Portugese fishing village into a prohibition headquarters, an artist colony and a European resort. A collection of massive Victorian pieces includes a magnificently carved mahogany bed once belonging to Ulysses S. Grant. Each of the inn's guest chambers displays a view of San Francisco Bay or Vina del Mar Park.

Location: Adjacent to the ferry landing in the heart of Sausalito.
Rates: $75-$160.
Manager Liz MacDonald, owner Gene Hiller.
15 Rooms. 10 Private Baths. 1 Fireplace. Guest phone in room. TV in room. Beds: KQDTC. Continental-plus breakfast. CCs: MC VISA AX DC CB. Windsurfing, sailing, golf, tennis, hiking. All water sports nearby.

"One of our favorite hobbies is to B&B hop. Yours is truly one of our favorites!"

Seal Beach

The Seal Beach Inn & Gardens

212 5th St
Seal Beach CA 90740
(213) 493-2416

Circa 1924. This is an exquisitely restored inn with fine antiques and

historical pieces. Outside, the gardens blaze with color and there are Napoleonic *jardinieres* filled with flowers. A 300-year-old French fountain sits in the pool area and an antique Parisian fence surrounds the property. In the neighboring historic area, you'll find a Red Car on Electric Street. It's a reminder of the time when the Hollywood crowd came to Seal Beach on the trolley to gamble and drink rum.

Location: 300 yards from the ocean, five minutes from Long Beach.
❋❋Rates: $98-$155.
Marjorie Bettenhausen.
22 Rooms. 22 Private Baths. 1 Fireplace. Guest phone in room. TV in room. Beds: KQDTC. B&B. Gourmet meals. Swimming pool. Conference room. CCs: MC VISA AX DC. Swimming, tennis, golf. Gondola & honeymoon packages.
Seen in: *Brides Magazine, Country Inns.*

"The closest thing to Europe since I left there."

Sky Forest

Storybook Inn

PO Box 362
Sky Forest CA 92385
(714) 336-1483

Circa 1939. Formerly known as the Foutch Estate, this 9,000-square-foot

home illustrates Mr. Foutch's romantic flair. Its abundant mahogany paneling was bleached to match the color of his bride's hair! Two massive brick fireplaces dominate the main lobby. The three-story inn has enclosed solariums and porches. A hot tub nestled under ancient oaks provides a view of snow-capped mountains, forests and on clear days, the Pacific Ocean.

Location: 28717 Highway 18.
❋Rates: $95-$155.
Kathleen & John Wooley.
9 Rooms. 9 Private Baths. Guest phone available. TV available. Beds: KQD. Full breakfast. Jacuzzi. Handicap access. Conference room. CCs: MC VISA. Horseback riding, skiing, hiking, water skiing.
Seen in: *Los Angeles Times.*

Sonoma

The Gables

See: Santa Rosa, CA

The Hidden Oak

214 E Napa St
Sonoma CA 95476
(707) 996-9863

Circa 1913. This shingled California craftsman bungalow features a

gabled roof and front porch with stone pillars. Located a block and a

half from the historic Sonoma Plaza, the inn once served as the rectory for the Episcopal Church. Rooms are furnished with antiques and wicker. Nearby wineries may be toured by hopping on one of innkeeper Catherine Cotchett's bicycles.
*Rates: $85-$130.
Catherine S. Cotchett.
3 Rooms. 3 Private Baths. 1 Fireplace. Guest phone available. Beds: Q. B&B. CCs: AX. Bicycles, wineries, festivals.

"The room was delightful and breakfast was excellent."

Overview Farm

15650 Arnold Dr
Sonoma CA 95476
(707) 938-8574

Circa 1880. This Victorian farmhouse was once a part of the famed Spreckels estate. It has been

revitalized to capture the gracious living style of turn-of-the-century Sonoma. Large guest rooms with ten-foot ceilings house a fine collection of early American treasures. Manicured gardens, espaliered fruit trees, and captivating views complement the beauty of the interior.
*Rates: $102.50.
Judy & Robert Weiss.
3 Rooms. 3 Private Baths. 2 Fireplaces. Guest phone available. Beds: QD. Full breakfast.
Seen in: *Los Angeles Times.*

Sonoma Hotel

110 W Spain St Box 1326
Sonoma CA 95476
(707) 996-2996

Circa 1879. Originally built as a two-story adobe house, in the Twenties a third story was added and it became the Plaza Hotel. The first floor now boasts an award-winning restaurant with patio dining under the stars, while the top two floors contain antique-filled guest rooms. The Vallejo Room is furnished with a massive carved rosewood bedroom suite, previously owned by General Vallejo's family. From room 21 Maya Angelou wrote "Gather

Together in My Name." A short walk away from the tree-lined plaza are several wineries.
*Rates: $62-$105.
Dorene Musilli.
17 Rooms. 5 Private Baths. Guest phone available. Beds: DT. B&B. Restaurant. Gourmet meals. CCs: MC VISA AX. Ballooning, horseback riding, wineries, art galleries.
Seen in: *Americana, House Beautiful.*

Victorian Garden Inn

316 E Napa St
Sonoma CA 95476
(707) 996-5339

Circa 1870. Authentic Victorian gardens cover more than an acre of

grounds surrounding this Greek Revival farmhouse. Pathways wind around to secret gardens, and guests can walk to world-famous wineries and historical sites. All rooms are decorated with the romantic flair of the innkeeper, an interior designer. Ask to stay in the renovated water tower.
*Rates: $69-$125.
Donna Lewis.
4 Rooms. 3 Private Baths. 1 Fireplace. Beds: QT. Full breakfast. Swimming pool. Conference room. CCs: MC VISA. Winery tours, swimming, nearby golf, tennis, bicycles. Full concierge services.
Seen in: *Denver Post, Los Angeles Times.*

Sonora

City Hotel

See: Columbia, CA

Lulu Belle's

85 Gold St
Sonora CA 95370
(209) 533-3455

Circa 1886. This sturdy home with its spacious lawns, rambling por-

ches and free form picket fence was built for John Rother, a local builder. "There was always music at the Rother home - early and late you could hear the piano going," wrote Ora Morgan in an early Sonora newspaper. Now the music room is enjoyed by guests for after-dinner entertainment. The house is filled with Victorian antiques. The historic village dotted with 1850's store fronts housing gourmet restaurants and antique shops is two blocks away.
Rates: $55-$85.
Janet & Chris Miller.
5 Rooms. 5 Private Baths. 1 Fireplace. Guest phone available. TV available. Beds: KQDTC. Full breakfast. Jacuzzi. Conference room. CCs: MC VISA AX. Horseback riding, water sports, snow skiing, gold panning, antiquing.
Seen in: *California Magazine, Union Democrat-Gadabout.*

"Hospitality and friendliness matched only by the beautiful accommodations! We'll be back for sure."

The Ryan House B&B

153 S Shepherd St
Sonora CA 95370
(209) 533-3445

Circa 1855. This restored homestead-style house is set well back from the street in a quiet residential

area. Green lawns and gardens with 35 varieties of roses surround the house. Each room is individually decorated with handsome antiques and there is a wood-burning stove in the parlor. An antique-style cookstove sets the mood for a country breakfast served in the dining room.
Location: Two blocks from the heart of historic Sonora.
*Rates: $75-$80.
Nancy & Guy Hoffman.
4 Rooms. 2 Private Baths. Guest phone in room. TV available. Beds: QT. B&B. CCs: MC VISA DC. Golf, gold panning, hiking.
"Everything our friends said it would be: warm, comfortable and great breakfasts. You made us feel like long-lost friends the moment we arrived."

South Lake Tahoe

Sorensen's Resort
See: Hope Valley, CA

Sutter Creek

Nancy & Bob's 9 Eureka Street Inn
55 Eureka St, PO Box 386
Sutter Creek CA 95685
(209) 267-0342

Circa 1916. A California bungalow, this inn mirrors the graciousness and charm of a bygone era. It is filled with rich woods, antiques, and stained-glass windows. All of the guest rooms are decorated in the manner of the past.
Location: Highway 49 in the Gold Country.
Rates: $65-$85. Season: Feb.-Dec.
Nancy & Bob Brahmst.
5 Rooms. 5 Private Baths. Guest phone available. Beds: QT. Full breakfast. Conference room. CCs: MC VISA. Wineries. Close to foundry, where gold was found.

Tahoe City

Mayfield House
256 Grove St, PO Box 5999
Tahoe City CA 95730
(916) 583-1001

Circa 1932. Norman Mayfield, Lake Tahoe's pioneer contractor, built this home of wood and stone.

Julia Morgan, the architect responsible for the Hearst Castle, was a frequent guest. Dark-stained pine-paneling, beamed ceiling, and a large stone fireplace make an inviting living room. Many of the rooms have either mountain, woods, or golf course views.
Location: Downtown on Highway 28.
*Rates: $65-$100.
Cynthia & Bruce Knauss.
6 Rooms. Guest phone available. TV available. Beds: KQT. Continental-plus breakfast. Handicap access. CCs: MC VISA. Horseback riding, skiing, water sports, bicycles, hiking, golf.
Seen in: *Sierra Heritage, Tahoe Today.*
"The place is charming beyond words, complete with down comforters and wine upon checking in. The breakfast is superb."

Templeton

Country House Inn
91 Main St
Templeton CA 93465
(805) 434-1598

Circa 1886. This Victorian home, built by the founder of Templeton, is set off by rose-bordered gardens. It was designated as a historic site in San Luis Obispo County. All of the rooms are decorated with antiques and fresh flowers. Hearst Castle and six wineries are nearby.
Location: Twenty miles north of San Luis Obispo on Hwy 101.
*Rates: $65-$80.
Dianne Garth.

7 Rooms. 3 Private Baths. Guest phone available. Beds: KQ. Full breakfast. CCs: MC VISA. Horseback riding, tennis, waterskiing, wine tasting.
"A feast for all the senses, an esthetic delight."

Ukiah

Toll House Inn
See: Boonville, CA

Ventura

Bella Maggiore Inn
67 S California St
Ventura CA 93001
(805) 652-0277 (800) 523-8479 CA

Circa 1926. Albert C. Martin, the architect of the former Grauman's Chinese Theater, designed and built this Spanish Colonial Revival-style hotel. Located three blocks from the beach, it is noted for its richly-carved caste-stone entrance and frieze. An Italian chandelier and a grand piano dominate the parlor. Rooms surround a courtyard with a fountain. Miles of coastal bike paths are nearby, as well as restaurants and antique shops.
*Rates: $60-$150.
Thomas Wood.
30 Rooms. 30 Private Baths. 6 Fireplaces. Guest phone in room. TV in room. Beds: KQD. Full breakfast. Jacuzzi. Handicap access. Conference room. CCs: MC VISA AX DC DS. Water sports, bicycling, beach.
Seen in: *Ventura County & Coast Reporter, Sunset.*
"Very friendly and attentive without being overly attentive."

La Mer

411 Poli St
Ventura CA 93001
(805) 643-3600

Circa 1890. This three-story Cape Cod Victorian was built for Robert

Brakey, whose house moving company was responsible for moving the Port Huememe Lighthouse. The second floor overlooks the heart of historic San Buenaventura and the spectacular California coastline. Each room is decorated to capture the feeling of a specific European country. French, German, Austrian, Norwegian and English-style accommodations are available. Gisela, your hostess, is a native of Siegerland, Germany.

Location: Second house north of city hall.
*Rates: $98-$135.
Gisela Baida.
5 Rooms. 5 Private Baths. 1 Fireplace. Guest phone available. TV available. Beds: KQDT. Full breakfast. CCs: MC VISA. Swimming, tennis, golf, biking or walking to the beach a few blocks away. Goose down feather beds.
Seen in: *Los Angeles Times, Ventura Star Press.*

"Where to begin? The exquisite surroundings, the scrumptious meals, the warm feeling from your generous hospitality! What an unforgettable weekend in your heavenly home."

Westport

DeHaven Valley Farm

39247 N Highway One
Westport CA 95488
(707) 961-1660

Circa 1875. This farmhouse was built by Alexander Gordon a local businessman who brought prosperity to the Westport area with his saw mill and ranch. A double-tiered porch wraps around the front and side of the house and extends across the wing, offering pleasant

vistas of the inn's 20 acres of meadows, woodland, and coastal hills. A hilltop hot tub provides a panoramic view of the ocean. Guest rooms are in the main house and in cottages. The DeHaven Cottage features cabbage rose prints, a Franklin stove and a king-size bed. Dinner is served each evening in the farm's dining room.

Rates: $85-$125.
Jim & Kathy Tobin.
8 Rooms. 6 Private Baths. 5 Fireplaces. Guest phone available. Beds: KQD. B&B. Restaurant. Jacuzzi. CCs: MC VISA AX. Horseback riding, redwoods, skunk train, ocean fishing, diving (renowned abalone beds).

Howard Creek Ranch

40501 North Hwy, PO Box 121
Westport CA 95488
(707) 964-6725

Circa 1871. First settled as a land grant of thousands of acres, Howard Creek Ranch is now a 20-acre farm with sweeping views of the Pacific Ocean, sandy beaches, and rolling mountains. A 75-foot bridge spans a

creek that flows past barns and outbuildings to the beach 200 yards away. The farmhouse is surrounded by green lawns, an award-winning flower garden, and grazing cows and horses. This rustic rural location is highlighted with antiques and collectibles.

Location: Mendocino Coast on the ocean.
❀Rates: $50-$95.
Charles & Sally Grigg.
7 Rooms. 3 Private Baths. 3 Fireplaces. Guest phone available. Beds: KQD. Jacuzzi. Sauna. Swimming pool. CCs: MC VISA. Horseback riding, whale watching.
Seen in: *California Magazine.*

"Of the dozen or so inns on the West Coast we have visited, this is easily the most enchanting one."

Yosemite

National Hotel

See: Jamestown, CA

Colorado

Boulder

Briar Rose B&B

2151 Arapahoe
Boulder CO 80302
(303) 442-3007

Circa 1897. Known locally as the McConnell House, this English-style

brick house is situated in a neighborhood originally composed of bankers, attorneys, miners and carpenters. The inn recently received the Award of Excellence from the City of Boulder. Fresh flowers, handmade feather comforters and turndown service with chocolates add to the atmosphere.

Rates: $68-$98.
Emily Hunter & Linda McClure.
11 Rooms. 6 Private Baths. Guest phone in room. TV available. Beds: QDTC. Continental-plus breakfast. Conference room.

"It's like being at Grandma's; the cookies, the tea, the welcoming smile."

Goldminer Hotel

See: Eldora, CO

Pearl Street Inn

1820 Pearl St
Boulder CO 80302
(303) 444-5584

Circa 1895. Located in downtown Boulder, the Pearl Street Inn is com-

posed of a restored Victorian brick house and a new addition complete with fish scale siding. The guest rooms, all with private entrances, overlook a courtyard designed to preserve a grandfather apple tree and newly planted with peach and plum trees. Antiques, cathedral ceilings, bleached oak floors and fireplaces are featured and a gourmet continental breakfast is served.

Rates: $65-$95.
Yossi Shem-Avi & Cathy Surratt.
7 Rooms. 7 Private Baths. 7 Fireplaces. Guest phone in room. TV in room. Beds: QDT. Continental-plus breakfast. Gourmet meals. Conference room. CCs: MC VISA AX DC CB. Hiking, bicycling, canoeing, bird watching, golf, tennis, swimming, croquet & lawn bowling.
Seen in: *Bon Appetit, Rocky Mountain News/Travel.*

"Enter the front door and find the sort of place where you catch your breath in awe."

Colorado Springs

Hearthstone Inn

506 N Cascade Ave
Colorado Springs CO 80903
(719) 473-4413

Circa 1885. This elegant Queen Anne is actually two houses joined

by an old carriage house. It has been restored as a period showplace with six working fireplaces, carved oak staircases, and magnificent antiques throughout. A lush, green lawn, suitable for croquet, surrounds the house, and flower beds match the Victorian colors of the exterior.

Location: A resort town at the base of Pikes Peak.
*Rates: $68-$99.
Dot Williams & Ruth Williams.
23 Rooms. 23 Private Baths. 3 Fireplaces. Guest phone available. Beds: KQDTC. Full breakfast. Gourmet meals. Conference room. CCs: MC VISA AX. Jogging, tennis, swimming. Skiing nearby. Working fireplaces.
Seen in: *Rocky Mountain News.*

"We try to get away and come to the Hearthstone at least twice a year because people really care about you!"

Holden House-1902

1102 W Pikes Peak Ave
Colorado Springs CO 80904
(719) 471-3980

Circa 1902. This Victorian home was built by the Holden family who had mining interests in Cripple Creek, Silverton and Leadville. An old iron fence frames the wide

verandas and three-story turret. The inn is filled with Victorian antiques and family heirlooms.
Location: Near the historic district of Old Colorado City.
*Rates: $50-$85.
Sallie & Welling Clark.
3 Rooms. 3 Private Baths. Guest phone available. TV available. Beds: Q. EP. CCs: MC VISA. Horseback riding, skiing, golf, hiking, tennis nearby. Honeymoon package.
Seen in: *Rocky Mountain News, Pikes Peak Journal, Victorian Homes.*
"Your love of this house and nostalgia makes a very delightful experience."

Outlook Lodge
See: Green Mountain Falls, CO

Cripple Creek

Imperial Hotel
123 N Third St
Cripple Creek CO 80813
(719) 689-2922

Circa 1896. Although not a bed and breakfast, this is the only original Cripple Creek hotel still standing. There is a collection of Gay Nineties memorabilia and the inn is known for its excellent cuisine. A cabaret-style melodrama is performed twice daily.
*Rates: $40-$45. Season: Mid May to October.
Stephen & Bonnie Mackin.
26 Rooms. 12 Private Baths. Guest phone available. Beds: QDT. Conference room.
Seen in: *Rocky Mountain News.*
"This was truly an experience of days gone by - we loved our stay!"

Denver

Pearl Street Inn
See: Boulder, CO

Queen Anne Inn
2147 Tremont Place
Denver CO 80205
(303) 296-6666

Circa 1879. This award-winning Queen Anne Victorian was designed

by Colorado's most famous architect, Frank Edbrooke. There are many elegant furnishings, including pillared canopy beds and a wraparound mural of an aspen grove in the turret peak. Music, art, and a grand oak stairway add to the Victorian experience. In an area of meticulously restored homes and flower gardens, the inn is four blocks from the center of the Central Business District.
Location: In the Clement Historic District.
*❀Rates: $54-$111.
Ann & Charles Hillestad.
10 Rooms. 10 Private Baths. Guest phone in room. Beds: KQDT. Continental-plus breakfast. Conference room. CCs: MC VISA AX. Everything legal except bullfighting and surfing.
Seen in: *Elle, New York Times, USA Today, Travel Holiday, New Woman, Bon Appetit.*
Selected by *Bridal Guide Magazine* as one of "America's Top Ten" wedding night locations.

Eldora

Goldminer Hotel
601 Klondyke Ave
Eldora CO 80466
(303) 258-7770

Circa 1897. With its rough-hewn log exterior, this alpine lodge has served continuously as a hotel since 1897. Situated near Indian Peaks wilderness, the scenic old mining town of Eldora is on the banks of Middle Boulder Creek. Except for the rental cabin behind the inn, all guest rooms are on the second floor. The decor is country antiques sup-

plemented with mountain crafts and art work. A stone fireplace set in the log walls of the lobby provide the focal point of the inn. Alpine trout fishing and scenic Rocky Mountain National Park is nearby.
*Rates: $30-$75.
Carol Rinderkrecht & Scott Bruntjen.
5 Rooms. 3 Private Baths. 1 Fireplace. Guest phone in room. TV available. Beds: DTC. B&B. Jacuzzi. Handicap access. Conference room. CCs: MC VISA. Downhill skiing, trout fishing.
Seen in: *Daily Camera.*

Empire

The Peck House
PO Box 428
Empire CO 80438
(303) 569-9870

Circa 1860. Built as a residence for gold mine owner James Peck, this is

the oldest hotel still in operation in Colorado. Many pieces of original furniture brought here by ox cart remain in the inn, including a red antique fainting couch and walnut headboards. Rooms such as Mountain View provide magnificent views of the eastern slope of the Rockies, and a panoramic view of Empire Valley can be seen from the old front porch.
*Rates: $35-$65.
Gary & Sally St. Clair.
11 Rooms. 9 Private Baths. Guest phone available. Beds: DT. EP. Jacuzzi. Cross-

country skiing, fishing, hiking, Rocky Mountain National Park.
Seen in: *American West, Rocky Mountain News, Denver Post, Colorado Homes.*

Estes Park

The Anniversary Inn

1060 Mary's Lake Rd, Moraine Rt
Estes Park CO 80517
(303) 586-6200

Circa 1877. This authentic turn-of-the-century log home is surrounded by spectacular views of the Rockies. There are two acres with a pond and river nearby. The inn features an exposed log living room dominated by a massive mossrock fireplace. Named after Strauss waltzes, the guest rooms boast handmade quilts and stenciling. Refreshments are served at sunset to coincide with the daily stroll of deer through the property. With the addition of the honeymoon cottage the inn specializes in weddings, anniversaries and vow renewals.
Rates: $55+.
Bruce & Janie Hinds.
4 Rooms. 1 Private Bath. Guest phone available. TV available. Beds: KQD. Full breakfast. CCs: MC VISA. Horseback riding, boating, rafting, hiking.

High in the Colorado Rockies at an elevation of 8,946 feet,

Golden

The Dove Inn

711 14th St
Golden CO 80401
(303) 278-2209

Circa 1889. An airy bay window of this charming Victorian overlooks

giant blue spruce and the foothills of the Rockies. Breakfast is served before the 100-year-old fireplace or outdoors on the porch or deck. In the same neighborhood are the beautiful old homes that housed the leaders of the former territorial capital of Colorado and the Colorado School of Mines is two blocks away. The innkeepers prefer married couples.
Rates: $41-$54.
Sue & Guy Beals.
6 Rooms. 6 Private Baths. Guest phone in room. TV in room. Beds: QDC. Continental breakfast. CCs: MC VISA AX DC CB. Cross-country skiing at 8,000 feet.
Seen in: *Rocky Mountain News.*

"Our first experience at a bed and breakfast was delightful, thanks to your hospitality at The Dove Inn."

Green Mountain Falls

Outlook Lodge

Box 5
Green Mountain Falls CO 80819
(719) 684-2303

Circa 1889. Outlook Lodge was originally the parsonage for the historic Little Church in the Wildwood. Hand-carved balustrades surround a veranda that frames the alpine village view, and inside are many original antique furnishings. Marshmallows are roasted by the pine-scented fire in the evening. This secluded mountain village is nestled at the foot of Pikes Peak, 15 minutes from Colorado Springs.
Rates: $37-$65.
Rodney & Sherri Ramsey.
9 Rooms. 6 Private Baths. 1 Fireplace. Guest phone available. TV available. Beds: QDTC. B&B. Handicap access. Swimming pool. Conference room. CCs: MC VISA. Swimming, fishing, volleyball, tennis, riding stables, hiking. Melodramas, concerts.

"Our four days with you were the very best..."

Gunnison

Waunita Hot Springs Ranch

8007 County Rd 877
Gunnison CO 81230
(303) 641-1266

Circa 1915. This dude ranch was built on the site of a summer gathering area for the Ute Indians. In the early 1900s it became a noted health spa. Crystal clear hot springs provide water for the pool, baths and for heating the lodge. Operated by three generations of the Pringle family, accommodations are provided at the main lodge building and feature queen size beds with bunk beds available for children. Ranch animals include lambs, goats, ducks, chickens and pigs. There are stocked lakes for fishing.
*Rates: $96. Season: June-Sept, Dec-April
Rod & Junelle Pringle.
22 Rooms. 22 Private Baths. Guest phone available. TV available. Beds: QDT. AP. Swimming pool. Game room. Horseback riding, 4x4 trips, cookouts, hayrides, float trip, square dancing.
Seen in: *TWA In-flight Magazine.*

"Whether you ride or not, you'll still be struck by the sincerity, simplicity and harmony at Waunita Hot Springs."

Hesperus

Blue Lake Ranch

16919 Hwy 140
Hesperus CO 81326
(303) 385-4537

Circa 1900. Built by Swedish immigrants, this renovated Victorian farmhouse is surrounded by spectacular flower gardens and a white picket fence. The inn is filled with comforts such as down quilts, vases of fresh flowers and family antiques. The property is designated as a wildlife refuge and there are two cabins overlooking trout-filled Blue Lake. In the evening guests enjoy soaking in the jacuzzi under clear, star-studded skies, and in the morning dining on Tia's gourmet breakfasts.
Location: Twenty minutes from Durango.
*Rates: $70-$125. Season: May to October.
David & Tia Alford.
6 Rooms. 5 Private Baths. Guest phone available. TV in room. Beds: Q. Restaurant. Jacuzzi. Sauna. Handicap access. Conference room. Fishing, swimming, hiking.

"What a paradise you have created - we would love to return!!"

Silver Plume

Brewery Inn

246 Main St, PO Box 473
Silver Plume CO 80476
(303) 674-5565

Circa 1890. The Brewery Inn is a restored Victorian with fireplaces, antiques, wallpapers and down comforters. Located within the Silver Plume National Historic District, a walk through the town recaptures the feeling of an 1880's silver mining town. Nearby is the Silver Plume Museum and the Georgetown Loop Narrow Gauge train ride.

Location: Fifty miles west of Denver, I-70 exit 226.
Rates: $40-$65.
Mary P. Joss.
4 Rooms. 1 Private Bath. 2 Fireplaces. Guest phone available. Beds: QT. B&B. Restaurant. Conference room. CCs: MC VISA.

"Charming, cozy, comfortable! It makes one ponder the real need for the 'necessities' of life, (TV, telephone). It was wonderful to go back and be free of everyday stresses."

Connecticut

Bolton

Jared Cone House
25 Hebron Rd
Bolton CT 06043
(203) 643-8538

Circa 1775. Once the town post office and library, this is a lavishly

embellished Georgian post-and-beam house. There are seven fireplaces and a dramatic Palladian window on the second floor. A pond at the rear of the property provides ice skating for both townsfolk and guests, and in spring, sugar maples surrounding the house are tapped for the inn's breakfasts.

Location: Ten miles east of Hartford via I-384 & Exit #5.
Rates: $60-$70.
Jeff & Cinde Smith.
3 Rooms. 1 Private Bath. Guest phone available. TV available. Beds: QTC. Full breakfast. Conference room. Sleigh rides, hay rides, cross-country skiing, canoeing, bicycling, hiking, antiquing. Canoe to lend.
Seen in: *Manchester Herald, Weekend Plus.*

"Beautiful colonial home, delightful breakfasts."

Bristol

Chimney Crest Manor
5 Founders Dr
Bristol CT 06010
(203) 582-4219

Circa 1930. This 32-room Tudor mansion possesses an unusual castle-like arcade and a 45-foot

living room with a stone fireplace at each end. Many of the rooms are embellished with oak paneling and ornate plaster ceilings. The inn is located in the Federal Hill District, an area of large colonial homes.

*Rates: $70-$95.
Dan & Cynthia Cimadamore.
4 Rooms. 4 Private Baths. 2 Fireplaces. Guest phone available. TV in room. Beds: Q. B&B. Swimming pool. Conference room. CCs: MC VISA. Ballooning, cross-country & downhill skiing, sleigh rides, tubing. Honeymoon and anniversary weekends.
Seen in: *Record-Journal.*

"Great get away - unbelievable structure. They are just not made like this mansion anymore."

Chester

Riverwind
See: Deep River, CT

Clinton

Captain Dibbell House
21 Commerce St
Clinton CT 06413
(203) 669-1646

Circa 1865. Built by a sea captain, this graceful Victorian house is only

two blocks from the harbor where innkeeper Ellis Adams sails his own vessel. A ledger of household accounts dating from the mid-1800s is on display, and there are fresh flowers and fruit baskets in each guest room.

Location: Exit 63 & I-95, south on Rt 1, east for 1 block, left on Commerce.
Rates: $50-$70. Season: Closed January.
Ellis & Helen Adams.
3 Rooms. 2 Private Baths. Guest phone available. TV available. Beds: KQDT. Continental-plus breakfast. CCs: MC VISA. Boating, swimming, fishing, hiking, bicycling.
Seen in: *Clinton Recorder.*

"This was our first experience with B&B and frankly, we didn't know what to expect. It was GREAT! The Adams were relaxed and charming and little personal touches added to our delight."

Coventry

Maple Hill Farm B&B

365 Goose Ln
Coventry CT 06423
(203) 742-0635

Circa 1731. This historic farmhouse still possesses its original kitchen

cupboards and a flour bin used for generations. Family heirlooms and the history of the former home owners are shared with guests. There is a three-seat outhouse behind the inn. Visitors, of course, are provided with modern plumbing, as well as a screened porch and greenhouse in which to relax.

*Rates: $50-$60.
Tony & Mary Beth Felice.
4 Rooms. Beds: TDC. Full breakfast. Swimming pool. Swimming, golf, biking, horseback riding, volleyball.

"Comfortable rooms and delightful country ambience."

Deep River

Riverwind

209 Main St
Deep River CT 06417
(203) 526-2014

Circa 1832. Renovated almost single-handedly by the innkeeper herself, this inn has a wraparound gingerbread porch filled with gleaming white wicker furniture. Antiques from Barbara's Virginia home are used throughout and there are fireplaces everywhere including a twelve-foot cooking fireplace in the keeping room.

Rates: $85-$145.

Barbara & Bob.
8 Rooms. 8 Private Baths. Guest phone available. Beds: QD. Full breakfast. CCs: MC VISA AX. Badminton, croquet, theater, swimming, golf.
Seen in: *The Hartford Courant, New Haven Register, Country Living Magazine.*

"If we felt any more welcome we'd have our Time *subscription sent here."*

East Haddam

Riverwind

See: Deep River, CT

East Windsor

The Stephen Potwine House

84 Scantic Rd
East Windsor CT 06088
(203) 623-8722

Circa 1831. Acres of farmland surround this old homestead. In keep-

ing with its rural setting a country decor has been chosen, and rooms look out over a pond shaded by graceful willow trees. Two goats and a barn complete the picture. The hosts' special interests are highlighted in seminars on stress management, music imagery and other renewal experiences. Sturbridge Village is 30 miles away.

Rates: $55-$75. Season: May to Nov.
Bob & Vangy Cathcart.
4 Rooms. 1 Private Bath. Beds: QTD. Full breakfast. Jacuzzi. Swimming, tennis, skiing, ice skating, bicycling, canoeing, jogging.
Seen in: *The Hartford Woman.*

"...a charming mix of antique, Vangies art work & stenciling, fresh flowers, and aura of peace."

Essex

Griswold Inn

48 Main St
Essex CT 06426
(203) 767-1812

Circa 1776. The main building of the colonial Griswold Inn is said to

be the first three-story frame structure built in Connecticut. The Tap Room, just behind the inn, has been called the most handsome barroom in America although it first served as a schoolhouse before it was rolled on logs by a team of oxen to its present location. The inn is famous for its English fox hunt breakfast served at the request of the British after they invaded the harbor at Essex. Fried chicken, scrambled eggs, lamb kidneys with sauteed mushrooms, corn bread and creamed ham are some of the items still available on Sunday mornings. A collection of firearms tracing the development of the hand gun and rifle from the 15th century is among the collections exhibited here. Ask for a quiet room at the back of the inn unless you'd enjoy Fife & Drum corps marching by under your window on Main Street.

Rates: $85-$175.
William & Victoria Winterer.
22 Rooms. 22 Private Baths. 1 Fireplace. Guest phone in room. TV available. Beds: DTC. Continental breakfast. Conference room. CCs: MC VISA AX.
Seen in: *Yankee Magazine, House Beautiful.*

"A man in search of the best Inn in New England has a candidate in the quiet, unchanged town of Essex, Connecticut." Country Journal

Riverwind

See: Deep River, CT

Glastonbury

Butternut Farm

1654 Main St
Glastonbury CT 06033
(203) 633-7197

Circa 1720. This Colonial house sits on two acres of woodlands. Prize-

winning goats, pigeons, and chickens are housed in the old barn on the property. Eighteenth-century Connecticut antiques including a cherry highboy and cherry pencil-post canopy bed, are placed throughout the inn, enhancing the natural beauty of the pumpkin-pine floors and brick fireplaces.

Location: South of Glastonbury Center, 1 1/2 miles, 15 minutes to Hartford.
Rates: $65-$78.
Don Reid.
4 Rooms. 2 Private Baths. 2 Fireplaces. Beds: DT. Full breakfast. CCs: MC VISA.
Seen in: *New York Times, House Beautiful.*

Greenwich

Homestead Inn

420 Field Point Rd
Greenwich CT 06830
(203) 869-7500

Circa 1799. The Homestead began as a typical farmhouse built by a

judge and gentleman farmer, Augustus Mead. Later it was remodeled in a fanciful Carpenter Gothic style. The full veranda is filled with wicker furnishings and offers views of rolling lawns and trees. Renovated by well-known designers John and Virginia Saladino, the inn now has a fine collection of antiques, an intimate library with fireplace, and a classic French restaurant.

Rates: $85-$175.
Nancy & Lessie Davison.
23 Rooms. 23 Private Baths. Guest phone in room. TV in room. Continental breakfast. Nature preserves, antique shops.
Seen in: *Country Inns.*

"Like going to Grandmother's house."

Hartford

Blantyre

See: Lenox, MA

Chimney Crest Manor

See: Bristol, CT

Copper Beech Inn

See: Ivoryton, CT

Fowler House

See: Moodus, CT

The Old Mill Inn

See: Somersville, CT 06072

Ivoryton

Copper Beech Inn

46 Main St
Ivoryton CT 06442
(203) 767-0330

Circa 1890. The Copper Beech Inn was once the home of ivory im-

porter A.W. Comstock, one of the early owners of the Comstock Cheney Company; producer of ivory products and pianos. The village took its name from the ivory trade centered here. An enormous copper beech tree shades the property. Each room in the renovated Carriage House boasts a jacuzzi tub and French doors opening onto a deck. The inn's restaurant has received numerous accolades.

Location: Lower Connecticut river valley.
Rates: $95-$155.
Eldon & Sally Senner.
13 Rooms. 13 Private Baths. 2 Fireplaces. Guest phone available. TV in room. Beds: KQDT. B&B. Restaurant. Gourmet meals. Jacuzzi. Conference room. CCs: MC VISA AX DC CB. Water sports.
Seen in: *Los Angeles Times.*

"The grounds are beautiful...just breathtaking...accommodations are wonderful."

Lakeville

Wake Robin Inn

Rt 41
Lakeville CT 06039
(203) 435-2515

Circa 1898. Once the Taconic School for Girls, this inn is located on 15 acres of landscaped grounds in the Connecticut Berkshires. A library has been added as well as antique furnishings. The recently renovated property also includes a few private cottages.

Rates: $75-$200.
H.J.P. Manassero.
40 Rooms. 40 Private Baths. Beds: KQT. Restaurant. Jacuzzi. Sauna. Conference room. CCs: MC VISA. Swimming, cycling, horseback riding.

Ledyard

Applewood Farms Inn

528 Col Ledyard Hwy
Ledyard CT 06339
(203) 536-2022

Circa 1826. Five generations of the Gallup family worked this farm

near Mystic. The classic center chimney colonial, furnished with antiques and early-American pieces, is situated on 33 acres of fields and

meadows. Stone fences meander through the property and many of the original outbuildings remain. It is in the National Register, cited as one of the best surviving examples of a 19th century farm in Connecticut.
Rates: $75-$105.
Frankie & Tom Betz.
6 Rooms. 3 Private Baths. 4 Fireplaces. Guest phone available. TV available. Beds: KD. Full breakfast. CCs: MC VISA AX. Horseback riding, water sports, hiking, bird watching, surry rides.
Seen in: *Country, New Woman.*

"This bed & breakfast is a real discovery."

Litchfield

The House on the Hill
See: Waterbury, CT

Moodus

Fowler House
PO Box 432
Moodus CT 06469
(203) 873-8906

Circa 1890. Dr. Fowler, manufactured patent medicine and the resulting mail orders forced the

Moodus Post Office to expand to accommodate his 5,000 pieces of mail that arrived each day. With that fortune, Dr. Fowler built this house. It features stained glass windows and a skylight, elegant Lincrusta wallcoverings, (an early interior design material made from horse hair, linseed oil and wood fiber), eight Italian ceramic fireplaces, and extensive displays fo hand carved woodwork. Now refurbished, filled with family heirlooms and painted with more than 75 gallons of paint, the house was voted Connecticut's favorite inn by *Yankee Magazine* readers.
*Rates: $65-$90.
Barbara Ally & Paul Seals.
6 Rooms. 4 Private Baths. 8 Fireplaces. Guest phone available. Beds: QDT. Continental-plus breakfast. Conference room. CCs: MC VISA. Tennis, horseback riding, swimming, boating, sailing, hiking, cross-country skiing, skating.
Seen in: *Daughters of the Painted Ladies, USA Weekend.*

"The proprietors are engaging hosts...the food is delicious and obviously homemade."

Mystic

Applewood Farms Inn
See: Ledyard, CT

The Inn at Mystic
Jct Rt 1 & 27
Mystic CT 06355
(203) 536-9604 (800) 237-2415

Circa 1904. This is a Colonial Revival mansion built by Katherine Haley, widow of one of the owners of the old Fulton Fish Market. A columned Victorian veranda overlooks the harbor and sound. All the rooms are individually decorated and may include a canopy bed, whirlpool tub or a wood-burning fireplace. There is also a motor inn on the property so be sure and request rooms in the original house. Old Mistick Village, Mystic Seaport Museum and the Aquarium are all nearby.
Rates: $100-$175.
Jody Dyer.
68 Rooms. 68 Private Baths. 30 Fireplaces. Guest phone in room. Beds: KQTC. EP. Restaurant. Jacuzzi. Handicap access. Swimming pool. CCs: VISA AX DC DS. Sailing, rowing, canoeing, swimming, walking trails, tennis.
Seen in: *Travel & Leisure.*

Queen Anne Inn & Antique Gallery
See: New London, CT

Red Brook Inn
PO Box 237
Mystic CT 06372
(203) 572-0349

Circa 1740. Situated on a bluff surrounded by seven acres of woodland, the inn and stagecoach stop have been recently restored and each has a traditional center chimney. There are 13 fireplaces in the inn. All rooms are furnished with period antiques such as canopy beds and many rooms have working fireplaces. Breakfast is served in the large keeping room of the Haley Tavern in front of a great hearth.
Rates: $85-$149.
Ruth Keyes.
10 Rooms. 10 Private Baths. 7 Fireplaces. Guest phone available. TV available. Beds: QDT. B&B. Jacuzzi. Game room. CCs: MC VISA. Horseback riding, water skiing, boating, fishing.
Seen in: *Travel & Leisure, Yankee Magazine.*

Mystic - Noank

Palmer Inn
25 Church St
Mystic - Noank CT 06340
(203) 572-9000

Circa 1907. This gracious seaside mansion was built for shipbuilder

Robert Palmer, Jr. by shipyard craftsmen. It features a two-story grand columned entrance, mahogany beams, a mahogany staircase, quarter-sawn oak floors, and 14-foot ceilings. The Lincrusta wallcovering, original light fixtures, and nine stained-glass windows remain.
Location: Two miles from Mystic.
Rates: $105-$175.
Patricia W. Cornish.
6 Rooms. 6 Private Baths. 1 Fireplace. Guest phone available. Beds: KQDT. Continental-plus breakfast. Conference room. CCs: MC VISA. Sailing, tennis, fishing, museums, antiquing.
Seen in: *Boston Globe, Yankee Magazine, The Norwalk Hour.*

"Tops for luxury." Water Escapes, by Whittemann & Webster.

"All the little touches at your place are what make it so special."

New Hartford

Cobble Hill Farm
Steele Rd
New Hartford CT 06057
(203) 379-0057

Circa 1796. This rambling Colonial inn was selected by *Country Living*

Magazine as one of their favorite ten inns in the country. It is located in Litchfield Hills on 40 acres of gardens, meadows, woodlands, and wildlife. Signs of deer and wild turkey can be seen while you are strolling along the dirt road. A spring-fed pond is filled with tadpoles and trout, and the barn houses horses, chickens, and pigs.

Location: Foothills of the Berkshires.
✻Rates: $95. Season: April 1 - Jan 1
Jo & Don McCurdy.
4 Rooms. 3 Private Baths. Guest phone available. TV available. Beds: KQDC. Full breakfast. Hay & sleigh rides, horseback riding, tubing on river, swimming.
Seen in: *New York Post, Country Living.*

"Do you know what it's like to relive one's happy childhood except in technicolor? We loved it. The accommodations and food were excellent, too."

New Haven

The Inn at Chapel West
1201 Chapel St
New Haven CT 06511
(203) 777-1201

Circa 1847. This green-and-white Victorian has recently undergone a two-million-dollar renovation. Its lavish appointments include items such as a Bavarian canopy bed, mahogany and French country furnishings, and a musical doll collection. Maple woodwork, parquet floors and seven fireplaces adorn the inn. There are crystal glasses in the bathrooms and Laura Ashley prints on the walls.

Location: Downtown, one block from the Yale campus.
✻Rates: $150-$175.
Steven Schneider.
10 Rooms. 10 Private Baths. 3 Fireplaces. Guest phone in room. TV in room. Beds: KQTC. Continental-plus breakfast. Handicap access. Conference room. CCs: MC VISA AX DC CB. Tours, theater.
Seen in: *New York Times, Business Digest of Greater New Haven.*

Copper Beech Inn
See: Ivoryton, CT

New London

Queen Anne Inn & Antique Gallery
265 Williams St
New London CT 06320
(203) 447-2600

Circa 1903. Several photographers for historic house books have been

attracted to the classic good looks of the recently renovated and freshly painted Queen Anne Inn. The traditional tower, wrap around verandas, and elaborate frieze invite the traveler to explore the interior with its richly polished oak walls and intricately carved alcoves. Double stained glass windows curve around the circular staircase landing. Period furnishings include brass beds and many rooms have their own fireplace. Afternoon tea is served.

✻❀Rates: $52-$105.
Beth Sievers & Captain Morgan Beatty.
10 Rooms. 8 Private Baths. 2 Fireplaces. Guest phone in room. TV in room. Beds: KQDT. B&B. Jacuzzi. Conference room. CCs: MC VISA. Antiquing, theater, concerts.
Seen in: *New London Day Features, New York Times.*

"Absolutely terrific - relaxing, warm, gracious - beautiful rooms and delectable food."

New Milford

Homestead Inn
5 Elm St
New Milford CT 06776
(203) 354-4080

Circa 1853. Built by the first of three generations of John Prime

Treadwells, the inn was established 80 years later. Victorian architecture includes high ceilings, spacious rooms and large verandas. There is a small motel adjacent to the inn. Marilyn Monroe and Arthur Miller were among the Homestead's famous guests.

Location: North of Danbury, 15 miles.
✻Rates: $60-$78.
Rolf & Peggy Hammer.
14 Rooms. 14 Private Baths. 2 Fireplaces. Guest phone in room. TV in room. Beds: KQDTC. Continental-plus breakfast. CCs: MC VISA AX DS. Golf, hiking, downhill and cross-country skiing.
Seen in: *The Litchfield County Times, ABC Home Show.*

"One of the homiest inns in the U.S.A. with most hospitable hosts. A rare bargain to boot."

Norfolk

Manor House
Maple Ave, Box 447
Norfolk CT 06058
(203) 542-5690

Circa 1898. Charles Spofford, designer of London's underground system, built this home with many

gables, exquisite cherry paneling, and grand staircase. There are Moorish arches and Tiffany windows. Guests can enjoy hot mulled cider after a sleigh ride, hay ride, or horse-and-carriage drive along the country lanes nearby.
❀Rates: $65-$145.
Hank & Diane Tremblay.
9 Rooms. 7 Private Baths. 2 Fireplaces. Guest phone available. TV available. Beds: KQDT. B&B. Conference room. CCs: MC VISA AX. Cross-country skiing, hiking, biking, riding stables, swimming, boating.
Seen in: *Boston Globe, The Journal, Philadelphia Inquirer.*

"Queen Victoria, eat your heart out."

Mountain View Inn
Rt 272
Norfolk CT 06058
(203) 542-5595

Circa 1875. Imagine yourself bundled in blankets in a horse-

drawn sleigh, as it slides silently through virgin snow, back to the warmth and comfort of Victorian Mountain View. There are fine antiques and collectables in all the rooms and gourmet dining on site at Mayfield's restaurant.
*Rates: $60-$100. Season: May - November.
Alan & Michele Sloane.
11 Rooms. 8 Private Baths. Guest phone available. TV available. Beds: TD. Continental-plus breakfast. Restaurant. Conference room. CCs: MC VISA. Swimming, hiking, horseback riding, rafting, cross-country skiing.

"Newly decorated with delightful results." B&B Travelers Review.

Norwalk

Silvermine Tavern
Silvermine & Perry Aves
Norwalk CT 06850
(203) 847-4558

Circa 1786. The Silvermine consists of the Old Mill, the Country Store, the Coach House, and the Tavern itself. Primitive paintings and furnishings, as well as family heirlooms, decorate the inn. Guest rooms and dining rooms overlook the Old Mill, the waterfall, and swans gliding across the millpond.
Rates: $74-$80.
Frank Whitman, Jr.
10 Rooms. 10 Private Baths. B&B. Restaurant.

Old Lyme

Old Lyme Inn
85 Lyme St
Old Lyme CT 06371
(203) 434-2600

Circa 1850. This elegantly restored mansion features original wall

paintings in its front hall, portraying historic Old Lyme buildings and the scenic countryside. Elegance is reflected throughout the inn with marble fireplaces, antique mirrors, and Victorian and Empire furnishings.
*Rates: $95-$125. Season: Jan 15-Dec 31.
Diana Field Atwood.
13 Rooms. 13 Private Baths. 3 Fireplaces. Guest phone in room. TV available. Beds: QT. Continental-plus breakfast. Restaurant. Handicap access. Conference room. CCs: MC VISA AX DC CB DS. Tennis, golf, cross-country skiing, water sports, bicycling.

"Gracious and romantic rooms with exquisite dining, our favorite inn!"

Old Mystic

The Old Mystic Inn
58 Main St, Box 318
Old Mystic CT 06372
(203) 572-9422

Circa 1810. Charles Vincent ran the Old Mystic Bookstore from this house for 35 years. Although it once housed 20,000 old books and maps, it has been renovated to a bed and breakfast inn. The old maps and drawings hung around the stairwell have been preserved. There are stone fireplaces in all the rooms and wide board floors. Furnishings include replica Colonial period pieces.
Rates: $95-$125.
Lois & Kari Taylor.
8 Rooms. 8 Private Baths. 3 Fireplaces. Guest phone available. TV available. Beds: Q. B&B. CCs: MC VISA AX.
Seen in: *The Day.*

"A real delight and the breakfast was sumptuous!"

Salisbury

Under Mountain Inn
Rt 41
Salisbury CT 06068
(203) 435-0242

Circa 1740. Situated on three acres, this was originally the home of iron

magnate Jonathan Scoville. A thorned locust tree, rumored to be the oldest in Connecticut, shades the inn. Paneling that now adorns the pub was discovered hidden between the ceiling and attic floorboards. The boards were probably placed there in violation of a colonial law requiring all wide lumber to be given to the King of England. British-born Peter was happy to reclaim it in the name of the Crown.

*Rates: $75.MAP
Peter & Marged Higginson.
7 Rooms. 7 Private Baths. Guest phone available. Beds: KQDT. MAP. Restaurant. Gourmet meals. CCs: MC VISA AX. Golf, tennis, horseback riding, boating, hiking, swimming, bikes.
Seen in: *Travel & Leisure, Country Inns Magazine.*
"You're terrific!"

Yesterday's Yankee B&B

Rt 44 E
Salisbury CT 06068
(203) 435-9539

Circa 1744. Shaded by ancient towering maples, this Cape home is

unusual because in 1744 the individual Cape Cod design was limited to Cape, 250 miles away. Its original Colonial atmosphere is retained by low ceilings, wide board floors, small paned windows and white-washed walls. Breakfast is served in the keeping room near the fireplace.

*Rates: $65-$80.
Doris & Dick Alexander.
3 Rooms. Guest phone available. TV available. Beds: KQT. B&B. CCs: MC VISA AX. Water sports, hiking, summer theater, music centers, antiquing, winter sports, horseback riding, skiing, sports car racing.
Seen in: *New England Getaways, New England Magazine.*
"Lovely house & hosts, great breakfasts - 5 star!"

Somersville

The Old Mill Inn

63 Maple St
Somersville CT 06072
(203) 763-1473

Circa 1850. Owners of the old woolen mill bought this home at the turn-of-the-century, and it was occupied by the storekeeper of the Somersville general store. The dining room walls are painted with flowering shrubs and trees in keeping with the inn's landscaping. In the old mill there are two furniture factories and a shop producing Shaker reproductions.

Location: Five miles east of Exit 47 on I-91, 1 block south of Rt. 190.
*Rates: $45-$50.
Ralph & Phyllis Lumb.
4 Rooms. 2 Private Baths. 1 Fireplace. Guest phone available. TV available. Beds: TW. Continental-plus breakfast. Golf, horseback riding.
"We loved staying here! You are both delightful. P.S. We slept like a log."

Tolland

Tolland Inn

63 Tolland Green, Box 717
Tolland CT 06084
(203) 872-0800

Circa 1800. This white clapboard house on the village green originally

provided lodging for travelers on the old Post Road between New York and Boston. After extensive renovation, the Tolland Inn has been opened once again and has been refurbished with antiques and many furnishings made by the innkeeper. Nearby is the town hall and the Old Jail Museum.

Location: On the village green, 1/2 mile to exit 68 & I-84.
Rates: $50-$60.
Susan & Stephen Beeching.
5 Rooms. 3 Private Baths. Guest phone available. Beds: DT. B&B. CCs: MC VISA AX. Antiquing, herb farm.
Seen in: *Journal Inquirer.*
"The rooms are very clean, the bed very comfortable, the food consistently excellent and the innkeepers very courteous."

Waterbury

The House On The Hill

92 Woodlawn Terrace
Waterbury CT 06710
(203) 757-9901

Circa 1888. Set on a slope wooded with huge copper beech trees, in the

exclusive hillside neighborhood, is a Queen Anne with a three-story turret and six shades of fresh Victorian color. In the library a lavishly carved mahogany fireplace is flanked by built-in-bookcases with decorative columns and egg-and-dart and dentil designs. The Turret Suite, a favorite guest room, is furnished with an Empire sofa and secretary, and a Victorian love seat. Just beyond the veranda perennial gardens dot the landscape.

Rates: $75-$100.
Marianne Vandenborgh
6 Rooms. 5 Private Baths. 1 Fireplace. Guest phone available. TV available. Beds: QD. B&B. Gourmet meals. Conference room.
Seen in: *Yankee Traveller Guide.*

Westbrook

Captain Stannard House

138 S Main St
Westbrook CT 06498
(203) 399-7565

Circa 1850. Captain Elbert Stannard became a sea man at 14, and

later commanded many famous ships. At 21, he built this gracious Georgian home complete with a

widow's walk. It eventually became the Menunketesuck Inn, and has now been restored to its former beauty. Antiques, a wood-burning stove, and hot mulled cider are available for today's guests.
Rates: $70-$150.
Ray & Elaine Grandmaison.
10 Rooms. 10 Private Baths. Guest phone available. TV available. Beds: DT. Continental-plus breakfast. Conference room. CCs: MC VISA AX DC. Biking, tennis, fishing, evening cruises.
"Excellent accommodations."

Woodbury

Curtis House
Main St
Woodbury CT 06798
(203) 263-2101

Circa 1754. Perhaps the oldest continuously operating inn in the state, the Curtis House began as the Orenaug Inn run by Anthony Stoddard. In 1900, the roof was raised and a third floor of eight rooms laid out in anticipation of a boom from a scheduled trolley service. All the guest rooms in the main house have canopied beds. Regional Yankee fare such as chowders, bisques and crusted pot pies are served at the inn.
Rates: $30-$70.
The Hardisty family.
18 Rooms. 12 Private Baths. Guest phone in room. TV in room. Beds: QDT. EP. Restaurant. Handicap access. Conference room. CCs: MC VISA. Swimming, boating, hiking, bicycling, golf.
Seen in: *New York Times.*
"More charming arrangements could not have been made..."

Woodstock

The Inn at Woodstock Hill
Plaine Hill Rd
Woodstock CT 06267
(203) 928-0528

Circa 1816. This classic Georgian house with its black shutters and

white clapboard exterior reigns over 14 acres of rolling farmland. Inside are several parlors, pegged-wood floors, English country wallpapers, floral chintzes and a fireplace for each room. The inn was recently renovated at a cost of $1.5 million, but the barn with its cupola remains untouched and stalls still display names such as Topsy and Primrose.
*Rates: $55-$140.
Sheila Becks.
19 Rooms. 19 Private Baths. TV available. Beds: QT. Continental-plus breakfast. Conference room. CCs: MC VISA. Horseback riding, skiing.
Seen in: *The Hartford Courant.*

Delaware

Dover

The Inn at Meeting House Square

305 S Governors Ave
Dover DE 19901
(302) 678-1242

Circa 1849. An arched front porch accentuates this two-and-a-half-

story house, located across the street from the Delaware State Museum, formerly the old 1790 Presbyterian Church. A traditional style decor features memorabilia collected on family travels. An old-fashioned swing is a favorite place to relax on the brick-walled sun porch. Walnut bread, French toast and sticky buns are house favorites.

❀Rates: $41-$48.
Sherry & Carolyn DeZwarte.
4 Rooms. 4 Private Baths. Guest phone available. TV in room. Beds: KQDT. B&B. CCs: MC VISA. Water sports, wildlife refuge, museums.

"Thank you for making us so comfortable and keeping us so well-fed."

Laurel

Spring Garden

Rt 1 Box 283-A
Laurel DE 19956
(302) 875-7015

Circa 1780. This gracious white brick and clapboard plantation was

built in a Federal style with Georgian overtones. It features outstandingly preserved 18th-century heart-pine paneling, four fireplaces, and wide-planked floors. Lawns and meadows bloom with lilies and lilacs. A stream meanders through the forest on the property. Spring Garden was awarded first place for "Excellence in Hospitality" by the Delaware Tourism Bureau.

Location: Fourteen miles north of Salisbury, MD.
✻Rates: $55-$75.
Gwen North.
6 Rooms. 2 Private Baths. Guest phone available. TV available. Beds: DT. Full breakfast. Handicap access. Conference room. Bicycling, horseback riding, badminton, tennis, swimming, fishing.
Seen in: *The Sun, Newsday*.

"The warmest, most gracious hostess on the Eastern Shore. We rated all the inns we stayed in on a scale of one to ten. You got the ten."

New Castle

The Jefferson House B&B

The Strand at the Wharf
New Castle DE 19720
(302) 323-0999

Circa 1800. Overlooking the Strand and the Delaware River, the Jeffer-

son House served as a hotel, a rooming house, and a shipping company office during colonial times. On the side lawn is a "William Penn landed here" sign. The inn features heavy paneled doors, black marble mantels over the fireplaces and a fanlight on the third floor. There is private access to the river. Cobblestone streets add to the quaintness of the first capital city of the colonies.

Location: Mid-Atlantic region.
✻Rates: $55-$75.
Chris Bechstein.
3 Rooms. 3 Private Baths. 1 Fireplace. Guest phone available. TV in room. Beds: D. B&B. Restaurant. CCs: MC VISA. Kyacking, walking, bicycling.

William Penn Guest House

206 Delaware St
New Castle DE 19720
(302) 328-7736

Circa 1680. William Penn slept here. In fact, his host Arnoldus de LaGrange witnessed the ceremony in which Penn gained possession of the Three Lower Colonies. Mrs. Burwell who lived next door to the historic house 'gained possession' of it one day about 20 years ago while her husband was away. After recovering from his wife's surprise purchase, Mr. Burwell rolled up his sleeves and began restoring the house. Guests may stay in the very room slept in by Penn.
Rates: $40.
Irma & Richard Burwell.
4 Rooms. Guest phone available. TV in room. Beds: DT. Continental breakfast. CCs: MC VISA.

Rehoboth Beach

Pleasant Inn Lodge

31 Olive Ave
Rehoboth Beach DE 19971
(302) 227-7311

Circa 1928. Originally on the ocean front, this Victorian four-square house was moved a block away after Rehoboth's Great Storm of 1918. The inn is comfortably furnished with antiques. Broad verandas and several common rooms

invite guests to lounge, whether they choose a bedroom or apartment. No meals are served, but coffee is available. Many restaurants are within walking distance.
Rates: $45-$65.
Peck Pleasanton.
10 Rooms. 10 Private Baths. Guest phone available. TV available. Beds: KQDT. Continental-plus breakfast. CCs: MC VISA. Water skiing, fishing, charter boats, ocean.

Florida

Amelia Island

The 1735 House

584 S Fletcher Ave
Amelia Island FL 32034
(904) 261-5878

Circa 1928. Perched right at the edge of the Atlantic, the inn is just

15 steps across the sand to the ocean (any closer and it would be below the tide line). All rooms in this New England clapboard-style inn are actually suites. Antiques, wicker and rattan add to the decor and comfort of the rooms. A lighthouse-type building is popular with families. Breakfast is delivered to your door in a picnic hamper.

Location: Oceanfront.
*Rates: $65-$105.
Gary & Emily Grable.
6 Rooms. 6 Private Baths. Guest phone available. TV in room. Beds: KQDT. B&B. CCs: MC VISA AX. Tennis, golf, horseback riding.

"It was a delightful surprise to find a typical old New England inn in Florida. The charm of Cape Cod with warm ocean breezes and waves lapping at the door."

Apalachicola

Gibson Inn

PO Box 221
Apalachicola FL 32320
(904) 653-2191

Circa 1907. James Buck of South Carolina handpicked the cypress and heart pine lumber that was used in the construction of this Victorian hotel. Purchased by the Gibson sisters in the Twenties, the inn was known for its elegant parties. Recently renovated, two stories of verandas and a roof-top cupola adorn the inn. Rich woodwork, a flaired staircase and globe lamps prepare guests for antique-filled rooms and a pleasing dining room.

Location: Highway U.S. 98.
*Rates: $50-$125.
Michael J. Koun & JoAnn Dearing.
31 Rooms. 31 Private Baths. Guest phone in room. TV in room. Beds: KQTC. B&B. Restaurant. Handicap access. Conference room. CCs: MC VISA AX. Tennis, golf, fishing.
Seen in: *Travel & Leisure, Tallahassee Democrat.*

Bradenton

Harrington House B&B

See: Holmes Beach, FL

Cedar Key

Historic Island Hotel

Box 460
Cedar Key FL 32625
(904) 543-5111

Circa 1849. This old hotel was never elegant but it has tremendous character and a rich history. At one time, it housed both Union and Confederate armies, although not at

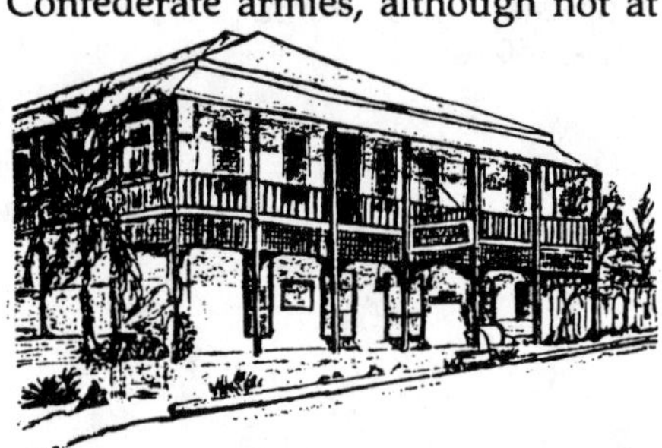

the same time. A leisurely veranda, a pot-bellied stove, paddle-fans, and canopies of mosquito netting are reminiscent of days gone by. Pearl Buck used the hotel as a writing retreat. Two red-headed parrots maintain a vigil in the lobby.

Location: Gulf of Mexico Islands - 55 miles west of Gainesville.
Rates: $70-$80.
Marcia Rogers.
10 Rooms. 6 Private Baths. Guest phone available. TV available. Beds: KD. Full breakfast. Restaurant. Handicap access. Conference room. Swimming, boating.
Seen in: *NBC TV, New York Times.*

"When you step through the double screen doors, you enter a different world, a world of the Caribbean Islands, or even the South Pacific."

Coral Gables

Hotel Place St. Michel

162 Alcazar Ave
Coral Gables FL 33134
(305) 444-1666

Circa 1926. Although the architecture is Spanish in character, the inn's carefully selected paintings and antiques help to establish a French country inn feeling in many of the rooms. Fresh flowers, and

turn down service with Italian chocolates add to the ambience. The hotel's restaurant is locally favored for its French deli takeout and French-Continental cuisine.
*Rates: $105-$125.
Stuart N. Bornstein & Alan H. Potamkin.
28 Rooms. 28 Private Baths. Guest phone in room. TV in room. Beds: KQ. Continental breakfast. Handicap access. Conference room. CCs: MC VISA DC. Golf, water skiing, tennis.
Seen in: *Esquire, Miami Herald, South Florida.*

"It was positively divine, all of it. I look forward to returning."

Fernandina Beach

Bailey House
PO Box 805
Fernandina Beach FL 32034
(904) 261-5390

Circa 1895. This elegant Queen Anne Victorian was a wedding present steamship agent Effingham

W. Bailey gave to his bride. He shocked the locals by spending the enormous sum of $10,000 to build the house with all its towers, turrets, gables, and verandas. The parlor and dining room open to a fireplace in a reception hall with the inscription "Hearth Hall - Welcome All". A spirit of hospitality has reigned in this home from its beginning.
Location: On Amelia Island.
*Rates: $65-$95.
Tom & Diane Hay.
4 Rooms. 4 Private Baths. 2 Fireplaces. Guest phone available. TV in room. Beds: QDT. B&B. CCs: MC AX. Beach, horseback riding, tennis & golf in the vicinity. Bicycles for guests.
Seen in: *Innsider Magazine, Southern Living, Victorian Homes, St. Petersburg Times.*

"Well, here we are back at Mickey Mouse land. I think we prefer the lovely Bailey House!"

Holmes Beach

Harrington House B&B
5626 Gulf Dr
Holmes Beach FL 34217
(813) 778-5444

Circa 1925. A mere 40 feet from the water, this gracious home is set

among oak trees and palms. Constructed of 14-inch-thick coquina blocks the house features a living room with a 20-foot-high beamed ceiling, fireplace, Twenties wallpaper and French doors. All the guest rooms have four-poster beds, antique wicker furnishings, and French doors opening onto a deck overlooking the swimming pool and water.
*Rates: $85-$100.
Walt & Betty Spangler.
5 Rooms. 5 Private Baths. Guest phone available. TV in room. Beds: KDT. Full breakfast. Handicap access. Swimming pool. CCs: MC VISA. Moonlight beach walks, theater, water skiing, boating.
Seen in: *Sarasota Herald Tribune, Island Sun, Islander Press.*

"Elegant house and hospitality..."

Jacksonville

1735 House
See: Amelia Island, FL

Casa de la Paz
See: Saint Augustine, FL

Key West

Colours Key West
The Guest Mansion
410 Fleming St
Key West FL 33040
(305) 294-6977

Circa 1889. Completely renovated, this Victorian mansion has main-

tained all the original architectural detail, including 14-foot ceilings, chandeliers, polished wood floors and graceful verandas. The house is said to be haunted by Hetty, a ghost who has been seen by many folks over the years. The innkeeper says that the inn is for the liberal-minded adult only.
Location: Historic Old Town District.
*Rates: $50-$140.
James Remes.
12 Rooms. 10 Private Baths. Guest phone in room. Beds: KD. Continental-plus breakfast. Swimming pool. CCs: MC VISA. Water skiing, snorkeling, scuba diving, boating. Turn-down service, cocktails.
Seen in: *Sunshine News, Sun Sentinel.*

"I have stayed at several guest houses in Key West - none compare. Constant clean towels and the freshness of everything is impressive."

"Colours is going into my book as THE place to stay in Key West!"

Eden House
1015 Fleming
Key West FL 33040
(305) 296-6868 (800) 533-5397

Circa 1924. This simply furnished hotel is located in the historic dis-

trict. French doors open from the

lobby onto the pool area, where a handsome new gazebo has been constructed around the base of a palm tree. Painted iron bedsteads, ceiling fans and verandas add to the tropical ambiance.
*Rates: $45-$155.
41 Rooms. 19 Private Baths. Guest phone in room. TV available. Beds: QDT. Swimming pool. CCs: MC VISA AX. Sailing, snorkeling, scuba diving, para-sailing.
Seen in: *Glamour, Cosmopolitan, Woman's Day.*
"We feel lucky to have found such a relaxing place, and we look forward to returning."

Heron House

512 Simonton St
Key West FL 33040
(305) 294-9227

Circa 1856. One of the oldest homes remaining in Key West, this

house is an early pre-1860 example of Conch architecture. Bougainvillea, jasmine and orchids bloom in the tropical gardens. Light and airy rooms with wicker furnishings have a tropical feeling.
Location: One block from Duval St. in center of Historic District.
*Rates: $45-$155.
Fred Gribelt.
18 Rooms. 18 Private Baths. Guest phone available. Beds: D. Continental-plus breakfast. Swimming pool. CCs: MC VISA. Complete free-weight gym.
Seen in: *Sun Sentinel.*

Key West B&B Popular House

415 William St
Key West FL 33040
(305) 296-7274

Circa 1890. This pink and white Victorian sits elegantly behind a white picket fence. It was constructed by shipbuilders with sturdy heart-pine walls and 13-foot ceilings. With two stories of porches, the inn is located in the center of the Historic District.
Location: Two blocks from the Gulf.
*Rates: $55-$110.
Jody Carlson.
7 Rooms. 2 Private Baths. Guest phone available. Beds: KQDT. Continental-plus breakfast. Jacuzzi. Sauna. Conference room. CCs: MC VISA AX DS. Fishing, shopping, Hemmingway House Tours, all water sports.
Seen in: *Palm Beach Life.*
"The essence of charming."

The Watson House

525 Simonton
Key West FL 33040
(305) 294-6712

Circa 1860. Purchased by an Ohio couple during the Civil War this

home was remodeled as a Bahama-style home, ideal for its sub-tropical climate. In 1986, after two years of restoration, the house became the recipient of the Excellence in Rehabilitation award granted by the Historic Florida Keys Preservation Board.
*Rates: $75-$215.
Joe Beres, Ed Czaplicki.
3 Rooms. 3 Private Baths. Guest phone in room. TV in room. Beds: Q. AP. Jacuzzi. Swimming pool. CCs: MC VISA. All suites with kitchens.
Seen in: *Florida Wayfarer.*
"Your home is absolutely beautiful. It was truly a delightful treat."

Whispers B&B Inn at Gideon Lowe House

409 William St
Key West FL 33040
(305) 294-5969

Circa 1846. This columned Greek Revival-style house shows the architectural influence of the Victorian period with ornamental fretwork on the porch railings. Bahamian tropical additions include shuttered windows, ceiling scuttles and double-decked porches. Air-conditioned rooms are furnished in antiques. Ceiling fans and lush gardens add to the atmosphere. In the center of the historic district, the house is in view of the Gulf harbor.
Location: Heart of Old Town Key West.
*Rates: $65-$85.
Marilyn & Les Tipton.
6 Rooms. Guest phone available. TV in room. Beds: KDT. Full breakfast. CCs: MC VISA. Reef diving, fishing, tennis, bicycles, biplane rides, sunset cruises, beaches.

Lake Wales

Chalet Suzanne

319 W Starr Ave, Drawer AC
Lake Wales FL 33859-9003
(813) 676-6011 (800)288-6011

Circa 1921. Carl & Vita Hinshaw are carrying on the traditions begun

by Carl's mother, Bertha, who was known as a world traveler, gourmet cook and antique collector. Following the stock market crash and the double disaster of her husband's death, she turned her home into an inn and dining room. The whimsical architecture includes gabled roofs, balconies, spires and steeples. The restaurant received the Craig Claiborne award, as one of the 121 best restaurants in the world.
Location: Four miles north of Lake Wales.
*Rates: $95-$165.
Carl & Vita Hinshaw.
30 Rooms. 30 Private Baths. Guest phone in room. TV in room. Beds: KDTC. EP. Restaurant. Handicap access. Swimming pool. Conference room. CCs: MC VISA AX DC CB DS. Lawn games, golf and tennis nearby. Private airstrip and lake. Murder mystery weekends.
Seen in: *USA Today, Dallas Morning News, Woman's Day.*
"I now know why everyone always says 'Wow!' when they come up from dinner. Please don't change a thing."

Orlando

Chalet Suzanne

See: Lake Wales, FL

Saint Augustine

Carriage Way B&B

70 Cuna St
Saint Augustine FL 32084
(904) 829-2467

Circa 1883. A two-story veranda dominates the facade of this square Victorian. Painted creamy white with blue trim, the house is located in the heart of the historic district. It's within a four-block walk to restaurants and shops, and only one block to the Intracoastal Waterway. Guest rooms reflect the charm of a light Victorian touch, with brass and wicker beds incorporating many furnishings that have been in the house for sixty years. On weekend evenings the dining room table is laden with scrumptious desserts and coffee. A buffet breakfast is provided in the morning.
*Rates: $49-$85.
Karen Burkley.
7 Rooms. 7 Private Baths. Guest phone available. TV available. Beds: QDC. B&B. Gourmet meals. CCs: MC VISA. Beach, tennis.
Seen in: *Miami Herald, Florida Times Union.*

"Charming in every detail."

Casa de la Paz

22 Avenida Menendez
Saint Augustine FL 32084
(904) 829-2915

Circa 1915. Overlooking Matanzas Bay, Casa de la Paz was built after

the devastating 1914 fire leveled much of the old city. An ornate stucco Mediterranean Revival house, it features clay barrel tile roofing, ornate iron work, bracketed eaves, verandas, and a walled courtyard. Bookcases in the dining room and living room attest to the scholarly background of your philosophy professor innkeeper Harvy Stafford. Guest rooms offer ceiling fans, central air, hardwood floors, antiques and chocolates. The favored top suite has views of the bay and Anastasia Island beyond.
*Rates: $75-$135.
Brenda Sugg & Harry Stafford.
5 Rooms. 5 Private Baths. Guest phone available. TV in room. Beds: KQDT. Continental-plus breakfast. CCs: MC VISA AX. Boat rides, beach, golf, tennis, biking.
Seen in: *Innsider.*

"...your elegant home, beautifully restored, which we will always recommend."

Casa de Solana

21 Aviles St
Saint Augustine FL 32084
(904) 824-3555

Circa 1763. Spanish military leader, Don Manuel Solana built this home

in the early European settlement and Spanish records show that a Solana child was the first child born in America. The thick coquina-shell walls (limestone formed of broken shells and corals cemented together), high ceilings with dark, hand-hewn beams and polished hand-pegged floors are part of the distinctive flavor of this period. Two working Majorcan fireplaces are in the carriage house. A southern breakfast is served at an elegant ten-foot-long mahogany table.
Location: In the Historic District.
*Rates: $100-$125.
Faye L. McMurray.
4 Rooms. 4 Private Baths. 2 Fireplaces. Guest phone available. TV in room. Beds: KQD. EP. Handicap access. Conference room. CCs: MC VISA AX. Bicycles.
Seen in: *House Beautiful.*

Kenwood Inn

38 Marine St
Saint Augustine FL 32084
(904) 824-2116

Circa 1865. Originally built as a summer home the Kenwood Inn has

taken in guests for over a hundred years. Early records show that it was advertised as a private boarding house as early as 1886. Rooms are decorated in periods ranging from the simple Shaker decor to more formal colonial and Victorian styles.
Location: One block from the bay front.
Rates: $55-$100.
Mark, Kerrianne & Caitlin Constant.
12 Rooms. 12 Private Baths. 1 Fireplace. Guest phone available. TV available. Beds: KQD. B&B. Swimming pool. Game room. CCs: MC VISA. Boating, beaches, golf.

St. Francis Inn

279 St George St
Saint Augustine FL 32084
(904) 824-6068

Circa 1791. Long noted for its hospitality, the St. Francis Inn is

near the oldest house in town. A classic example of Old World architecture, it was built by Senor Garcia who received a Spanish grant to the plot of land. Coquina, was the main building material. St. Augustine was founded in 1565.
Location: In the St. Augustine Historic District, the nation's oldest city.
*Rates: $45-$95.
Marie Register.
14 Rooms. 14 Private Baths. 7 Fireplaces. TV in room. Beds: KQTC. Continental

breakfast. Swimming pool. CCs: MC VISA. Bicycles.

"We have stayed at many nice hotels but nothing like this. We are really enjoying it."

Saint Petersburg

Bayboro House on Old Tampa Bay

1719 Beach Dr, SE
Saint Petersburg FL 33701
(813) 823-4955

Circa 1904. The Bayboro has a Victorian flavor and was built by one

of the founding fathers of the city, C. A. Harvey. He was the first real estate developer and the first to have the vision to construct the port. Across from Lassing Park, the house has an unobstructed view of Old Tampa Bay.

Location: Off exit 9 (I-275), downtown St. Petersburg.

*Rates: $55-$70.

Gordon & Antonia Powers.

4 Rooms. 4 Private Baths. 1 Fireplace. Guest phone available. TV in room. Beds: QT. Continental-plus breakfast. CCs: MC VISA.

Seen in: *Miami Herald, Mobil Travel Guide.*

"A lovely room and the house itself a handsome structure. Special touches from the fine linen, pretty quilts, plants, shells and lovely antique furniture made my brief stay enjoyable."

Sarasota

Harrington House B&B

See: Holmes Beach, FL

St. Augustine Beach

Casa de Solana

See: Saint Augustine, FL

Tallahassee

Susina Plantation Inn

See: Thomasville, GA

Wakulla Springs Lodge & Conference Ctr

See: Wakulla Springs, FL

Tampa

Harrington House B&B

See: Holmes Beach, FL

Tarpon Springs

Spring Bayou Inn

32 W Tarpon Ave
Tarpon Springs FL 34689
(813) 938-9333

Circa 1905. The massive two story rotunda of this Victorian house is surrounded by an encircling veranda and a balcony. Inside, glowing curly pine paneling adorns the staircase and fireplace. In addition to Victorian furnishings, a variety of miniature collections are gathered in polished cabinets throughout the inn. The butler's pantry, not to be left undecorated, features a dressmaker's form attired in an 1800s black lace frock. A scenic bayou surrounded by high green banks and huge oak trees is only a block from the inn. The sponge docks, made famous by Greek sponge divers are within walking distance.

Rates: $50-$65. Season: Oct. 1 - August 15.

Ron & Cher Morrick

5 Rooms. 4 Private Baths. 1 Fireplace. Guest phone available. TV available. Beds: QDT. B&B. Golf, tennis, parks, beaches, fishing.

Wakulla Springs

Wakulla Springs Lodge & Conference Ctr

1 Spring Dr
Wakulla Springs FL 32305
(904) 224-5950

Circa 1937. Financier Ed Ball built this Spanish-Moorish style lodge with its multitude of arches and fan

windows. Now situated on 2,900 acres, the lodge's marbled terrace overlooks grounds lush with azaleas, camellias, dogwood and magnolias. The dining room overlooks Wakulla Springs, one of the world's largest natural springs, forming a four-and-a-half-acre lagoon. Glass-bottomed boats glide along the river inhabited with alligators, turtles, deer, nine species of herons and egrets, osprey and bald eagles. Films made here include early *Tarzan* movies with Johnny Weissmuller, and *Creature from the Black Lagoon*. Rooms are furnished in the Thirties style.

*Rates: $53-$75.

John Puskar/John Harvey.

27 Rooms. 27 Private Baths. Guest phone in room. TV available. Beds: KQDTC. EP. Restaurant. Handicap access. Conference room. Capital Building, museums, vineyard.

Seen in: *Southern Living Magazine, Family Circle.*

"...the lodge and surroundings cannot be matched anywhere!"

Georgia

Atlanta

Glen-Ella Springs Hotel

See: Clarkesville, GA

Shellmont B&B Lodge

821 Piedmont NE
Atlanta GA 30308
(404) 872-9290

Circa 1891. This grand Victorian showplace derives its name from

two distinctions: the shell motif embossed on the exterior bay and portico, and its prominent location on Piedmont Avenue. Architect W.T. Downing further carried out the shell theme with carved wooden shells, bows, and garlands. Five panels of stained glass, two stories high accentuate the foyer and are thought to have been designed by Tiffany & Co. Victorian wallpapers and appropriate antiques add to the inn's romantic ambiance.

*Rates: $75-$90.
Ed & Debbie McCord.
4 Rooms. 4 Private Baths. 3 Fireplaces. Guest phone available. TV available. Beds: D. B&B. CCs: MC VISA AX. Tennis, jogging, theater, Botanical Gardens.
Seen in: *Southern Homes.*

"Thanks for the warm welcome and good cheer."

The Veranda - Hollberg Hotel

See: Senoia, GA

Augusta

Oglethorpe Inn

836 Greene St
Augusta GA 30901
(404) 724-9774

Circa 1888. The Oglethorpe, named after General James Oglethorpe, Augusta's founder, is actually two Victorian era houses and a carriage house. Shaded by 100 year-old magnolias, the inn is located in the heart of the central business district near Riverwalk, Civic Center and the Federal Courts. There are whirlpool tubs and fireplaces in many of the rooms, as well as original antique furnishings. An outdoor hot tub is available as well.

*Rates: $60-$130.
Margaret Black & Molly Maloney.
20 Rooms. 20 Private Baths. 12 Fireplaces. Guest phone in room. TV in room. Beds: KQDTC. B&B. Gourmet meals. Jacuzzi. Conference room. CCs: MC VISA AX DC. Water sports, horse events, river events.
Seen in: *Southern Homes, Augusta Magazine.*

"Thanks for giving us a break from the world."

Chickamauga

Gordon-Lee Mansion B&B

217 Cove Rd
Chickamauga GA 30707
(404) 375-4728

Circa 1847. Serving as a museum house for over 15 years, the Gordon-

Lee Mansion is now also open for lodging. In the grand Greek Revival style, the house features giant Doric columns overlooking stands of oak and maple trees that line the driveway to the mansion. During the Civil War, the home served as headquarters for General William Rosecrans. It was the only building that survived the Battle of Chickamauga.

Rates: $65.
Richard Barclift.
4 Rooms. 3 Private Baths. 3 Fireplaces. Guest phone available. TV available. Beds: QDT. B&B. CCs: MC VISA.
Seen in: *Chattanooga News Free-press, Atlanta Journal and Constitution.*

"Margaret Mitchell never saw the Gordon-Lee house, but if she had, she certainly would have used it as her model for Tara in 'Gone With the Wind.'"

Clarkesville

Glen-Ella Springs Hotel

Rt 3, Bear Gap Rd
Clarkesville GA 30523
(404) 754-7295 (800) 552-3479

Circa 1875. This renovated hotel adjacent to the Chattahoochee National Forest is an outstanding example of early 19th and 20th century inns that dotted the Georgia countryside. The luxury of private baths and a plethora of porches have been added. A great stone fireplace is the focal point of the parlor, decorated in bright chintzes. Local handcrafted pieces and antiques furnish the guest rooms. Two suites feature whirlpool baths. Bordered by Panther Creek, the property includes 17 acres of meadows, flower and herb gardens, fruit trees and an original mineral springs.

*Rates: $65-$130.
Barrie & Bobby Aycock.
16 Rooms. 16 Private Baths. 2 Fireplaces. Guest phone in room. TV in room. Beds: KQDTC. EP. Restaurant. Gourmet meals. Jacuzzi. Handicap access. Swimming pool. Conference room. CCs: MC VISA AX. Horseback riding, hiking, white-water rafting, golf, boating, tennis.
Seen in: *Atlanta Magazine, Southern Homes.*

Macon

1842 Inn

353 College St
Macon GA 31201
(912) 741-1842

Circa 1842. Judge John J. Gresham, cotton merchant and founder of the Bibb Manufacturing Company, built this antebellum Greek Revival house. It features graceful columns, elaborate mantels, crystal chandeliers and oak parquet floors inlaid with mahogany. Guest rooms boast cable television discreetly tucked into antique armoires. There are whirlpool baths available in the main house, and in an adjoining Victorian cottage.

*Rates: $60-$90.
Aileen P. Hatcher
22 Rooms. 22 Private Baths. 8 Fireplaces. Beds: KQTC. Full breakfast. Jacuzzi. Handicap access. Conference room. CCs: MC VISA.
Seen in: *The Christian Science Monitor, Southern Living, Daily News.*
"The best B&B we've seen! Deserves all four stars!."

The Carriage Stop Inn

1129 Georgia Ave
Macon GA 31201
(912) 743-9740

Circa 1840. Pictured in the Library of Congress as an excellent example of Greek Revival architecture, this three-story house was built for Judge Thaddeus Holt. Eleven fluted Doric columns rise from the portico across the front and side of the inn. At one time, the wrought iron handrails flanking the double horseshoe stairs had newels topped with solid silver balls. High ceilings, chandeliers, panelled doors and heart of pine floors echo a gracious life style. Original gold-framed mantel mirrors are hung over the dining and drawing room fireplaces. Guest rooms are furnished with a collection of English and European antiques.

Rates: $95-$105.
Vic & Judy Wilkinson.
4 Rooms. 4 Private Baths. 3 Fireplaces. Guest phone in room. TV in room. Beds: QT. B&B. Swimming pool. Conference room. CCs: MC VISA. Tours of historic downtown.
Seen in: *Daily News, Macon Telegraph and News.*
"We loved every minute and look forward with eagerness to a return visit."

Mountain City

The York House

Box 126
Mountain City GA 30562
(404) 746-2068

Circa 1896. Bill and Mollie York opened the York House as an inn in 1896, and it has operated continuously ever since. Two stories of shaded verandas overlook tall hemlocks, Norwegian spruce, lawns and mountains. Adjacent to the Old Spring House is a stand of pines that provide a romantic setting for weddings. Breakfast is carried to the room each morning on a silver tray and each room is plumbed with natural spring water.

*Rates: $50-$75.
Phyllis & Jimmy Smith.
13 Rooms. 13 Private Baths. Guest phone available. Beds: DC. Full breakfast. Handicap access. Conference room. CCs: MC VISA. Skiing, horseback riding, hiking, swimming.

Saint Mary's

Riverview Hotel

105 Osborne St
Saint Mary's GA 31558
(912) 882-3242

Circa 1916. This hotel is located on the banks of the St. Mary's River

near the ferry to Cumberland Island National Seashore. It was renovated in 1976, and there is a veranda filled with rocking chairs. Guests can tour pre-Civil-War Oak Grove Cemetery. The Okefenokee Swamp is an hour away.
Location: St. Mary's river, 30 miles north of Jacksonville, Florida.
*Rates: $32-$49.
Jerry Brandon.
18 Rooms. 18 Private Baths. Guest phone available. Beds: KD. Restaurant. CCs: MC VISA DC.

Sautee

Stovall House
Rt 1 Box 1476
Sautee GA 30571
(404) 878-3355

Circa 1837. This house was built by Moses Harshaw who was infamous

in the area for being "the meanest man who ever lived." The handsome farm house has an extensive wraparound porch providing vistas of 28 acres of cow pasture, meadows and creek. High ceilings, polished walnut woodwork and decorative stenciling provide a pleasant backdrop for the inns collection of antiques. Victorian bathroom fixtures include pull-chain toilets and pedestal sinks. The inn has its own restaurant.
Rates: $68.75.
Ham Schwartz.
5 Rooms. 5 Private Baths. 1 Fireplace. Guest phone available. Beds: KDC. Continental breakfast. Restaurant. CCs: MC VISA. Horseback riding, rafting, hiking.
Seen in: *The Atlanta Journal.*

"Great to be home again."

Savannah

417 The Haslam-Fort House
417 East Charlton St
Savannah GA 31401
(912) 233-6380

Circa 1872. This is a free-standing, three-story brick town house built in

an Italianate style with a colorful side garden. Located on a quiet square, the two-bedroom suite has a living room with fireplace, full bath and country kitchen. The inn's attractive decor has been featured in many national magazines and newspapers.
Location: In the heart of Savannah's Historic District.
Rates: $65-$150.
Alan Fort & Richard McClellan.
2 Rooms. 1 Private Bath. Beds: KQC. Continental-plus breakfast. Handicap access.

"Alan is by far the most qualified host I've met. He gives 'home away from home' a brand new meaning."

Ballastone Inn
14 E Oglethorpe Ave
Savannah GA 31401
(912) 236-1484

Circa 1853. The inn is located in the heart of the largest historic dis-

trict in the nation (two-and-a-half square miles). Four stories of luxurious furnishings are accentuated with authentic Savannah colors and Scalamandre fabrics. Theme rooms include Greek Revival, English, and Egyptian. Turn-down service features pralines and brandy, a southern touch.
*Rates: $90-$125.
Richard Carlson & Tim Hargus.
18 Rooms. 18 Private Baths. Guest phone in room. TV in room. Beds: KQD. B&B. Jacuzzi. Handicap access. CCs: MC VISA AX. Carriage rides. Ocean is 17 miles away for boating, swimming. Elevator, jacuzzis, breakfast in bed.
Seen in: *New York Times, Bride's Magazine.*

"To a fabulous inn - magnificent!" Patricia Neal.

Foley House Inn
14 W Hull St
Savannah GA 31401
(912) 232-6622

Circa 1896. Fine craftsmen have faithfully restored the inn, and there

is a fireplace in each room. Antiques, silver, china, oriental rugs and hand-colored engravings come from around the world. Churches, museums, galleries and the waterfront are within walking distance.
*Rates: $100-$190.
Susan Steinhauser.
20 Rooms. 20 Private Baths. Beds: KDTC. Continental-plus breakfast. Jacuzzi. CCs: MC VISA.

"I'll send all my romantic friends here."

The Forsyth Park Inn
102 W Hall St
Savannah GA 31401
(912) 233-6800

Circa 1893. This graceful yellow and white three-story Victorian fea-

tures bay windows and a large veranda overlooking Forsyth Park. Sixteen-foot ceilings, polished parquet floors of oak and maple, and a handsome oak stairway provide an elegant background for the guest rooms. There are several whirlpool tubs, marble baths and four-poster beds.
Location: Savannah's historic district, opposite Forsyth Park.
Rates: $75-$145.
Hal & Virginia Sullivan.
10 Rooms. 10 Private Baths. 9 Fireplaces. Guest phone available. TV in room. Beds: KQT. Continental breakfast. Jacuzzi. CCs: MC VISA. Tennis, jogging. Honeymoon package.
Seen in: *Savannah Morning News.*

"Breathtaking, exceeded my wildest dreams."

Jesse Mount House

209 W Jones St
Savannah GA 31401
(912) 236-1774

Circa 1854. A Greek Revival town house, Jesse Mount has two spacious, luxurious three-bedroom suites complete with gas-burning fireplaces. There is a Savannah-style walled garden. Exceptional antiques include a coach used by Tom Thumb to meet Queen Victoria, gilded harps and a grand piano. The hostess is an internationally-known concert harpist. A pre-Revolutionary London clock chimes gently to urge you to step from your historic lodgings into the compelling charm of Old Savannah.
Location: In historic district of Savannah.
*Rates: $75.
Howard Crawford & Lois Bannerman.
2 Rooms. 2 Private Baths. Beds: QC. Full breakfast.
Seen in: *Savannah Morning News.*

"Marvelous. We enjoyed your gracious hospitality, delicious breakfast, and elegant surroundings."

Liberty Inn 1834

128 W Liberty St
Savannah GA 31401
(912) 233-1007

Circa 1834. In 1949, the innkeepers met for their first date at the Liberty Cafe. Many years later, they purchased it and converted it to an inn. A National Register Landmark, it was constructed of clapboard over

brick and has survived many Savannah fires. The builder, Colonel Williams, was a publisher, bookseller, and six-time mayor of the city. Period pieces, original fireplaces, and exposed interior brick walls are featured.
Location: Northeast corner of Liberty & Barnard Streets.
Rates: $95-$165.
Frank & Janie Harris.
5 Rooms. 7 Private Baths. Beds: Q. Continental breakfast. Jacuzzi. CCs: MC VISA. River harbor cruises.
Seen in: *The Orlando Sentinel, Savannah Morning News.*

"Incredibly beautiful. Perfectly charming."

Magnolia Place Inn

503 Whitaker St
Savannah GA 31401
(912) 236-7674 (800) 238-7674

Circa 1878. This southern Victorian features a two-story, ornately styled veranda that stretches across the entire facade providing views of Forsyth Park Square. It was built for a descendant of the Declaration of Independence signer Thomas W. Hyward. Romantic four-poster or canopy beds are complimented by antiques, fireplaces and an occasional whirlpool tub. Turn down service is provided.
*Rates: $85-$165. Season: Mid Feb. - Mid Jan.
Ron J. Strahan, Andrea Harrelson.
13 Rooms. 13 Private Baths. 12 Fireplaces. Guest phone in room. TV in room. Beds: KQ. Continental-plus breakfast. Jacuzzi. CCs: MC VISA AX. Tennis nearby, golf in area.
Seen in: *Esquire, New York Magazine.*

"Absolutely quintessential southern excess."

Olde Harbour Inn

508 E Factors Walk
Savannah GA 31401
(912) 234-4100

Circa 1892. This building once housed Tidewater Oil Company and in 1930 the Alexander Blue Jean Manufactory. Now converted to condos, the units are decorated in a traditional style and each suite overlooks the Savannah River.
*Rates: $95-$135.
Pamela Barnes.
24 Rooms. 24 Private Baths. Guest phone available. TV available. Beds: QDTC. Continental-plus breakfast. CCs: MC VISA AX. Riverfront vacation package.

"Wonderful time. Loved the river view."

Presidents' Quarters

225 E President St
Savannah GA 31401
(912) 233-1600 (800) 233-1776

Circa 1855. Situated in the heart of the largest urban historic landmark district in America is the President's Quarters. The facade of this inn was used in Alex Haley's television version of *Roots*. Each of the nine rooms and seven suites is named for a United States president who visited Savannah. The decor varies from mahogany period reproductions to white pine rustic, but each room carries out the presidential theme by displaying memorabilia (such as authentic campaign posters) of the life of a president. Room service, a pool, in-room jacuzzis and stocked refrigerators are among this inn's luxury amenities.
*Rates: $97-$147.
Muril L. Broy.
16 Rooms. 16 Private Baths. 16 Fireplaces. Guest phone in room. TV in room. Beds: KQDC. Continental-plus breakfast. Jacuzzi. Handicap access. Conference room. CCs: MC VISA AX DC. Beach nearby.
Seen in: *Country Inn Magazine, Southern Homes.*

"Presidents' Quarters was truly a home away from home." Karl Malden.

"Will never forget our delicious and warm stay. Southern hospitality at its best."

Remshart-Brooks House

106 W Jones St
Savannah GA 31401
(912) 234-6928

Circa 1853. Remshart-Brooks House is in the center of the historic

district. Guests enjoy a terrace-garden suite with bedroom, living room, bath and kitchen. Home-baked delicacies enhance the continental breakfast.

Location: Center of historic district.
Rates: $65.
Anne Barnett.
1 Room. 1 Private Bath. 2 Fireplaces. Guest phone in room. Beds: Q. Continental-plus breakfast.

RSVP Savannah B&B Reservation Service

417 E Charlton St
Savannah GA 31401
(912) 232-7787 (800) 673-9350

This service specializes in the traveler seeking history and beauty,

from South Carolina's Low Country to Georgia's Sea Islands. Accommodations are available in elegantly restored inns, guest houses, private homes or villas on the water. Areas include Savannah, Tybee and St. Simons Islands, in Georgia, and Beaufort and Charleston in South Carolina.

Rates: $60-$175.
Alan Fort.
250 Rooms. 250 Private Baths. Beds: KQTC. Continental breakfast. Restaurant. Jacuzzi. Handicap access. Swimming pool. CCs: MC VISA. Golf, tennis, sailing, deep sea fishing, water sports.
Seen in: *National Geographic Traveler, Innsider.*

Senoia

Culpepper House

Corner of Broad & Morgan
PO 462
Senoia GA 30276
(404) 599-8182

Circa 1871. This Queen Anne Victorian was built by a Confederate veteran and later occupied for 50 years by Dr. Culpepper. With original moldings, stained-glass windows and mantelpieces the house is decorated in cozy Victorian clutter and comfortable whimsy. The inn offers guests Southern hospitality at its finest.

Rates: $50-$60.
Mary Brown.
3 Rooms. 1 Private Bath. Guest phone available. TV available. Beds: QDT. B&B.

The Veranda - Hollberg Hotel

252 Seavy St
Senoia GA 30276-0177
(404) 599-3905

Circa 1907. Doric columns adorn the verandas of this 9,000 square-

foot neo-classical hotel. William Jennings Bryan stayed here and it is said that Margaret Mitchell (Gone With the Wind) came here to interview Georgia veterans of the Civil War who held their annual reunion at the hotel. Furnishings include walnut bookcases owned by President William McKinley and a rare Wurlitzer player piano — pipe organ. There are Victorian collections of hair combs, walking canes, books and one of the largest assortments of kaleidoscopes in the Southeast.

Location: Thirty miles south of Altanta airport.
*Rates: $75-$95.
Jan & Bobby Boal.
9 Rooms. 9 Private Baths. Guest phone available. Beds: QT. B&B. Gourmet meals. Jacuzzi. Handicap access. Conference room. CCs: MC VISA AX. Golf, tennis, fishing.
Seen in: *The Newnan Times Herald, Good Times, After Hours.*

"The mystique and reality of The Veranda are that you're being elaborately entertained by friends in their private home."

Thomasville

Susina Plantation Inn

Rt 3 Box 1010
Thomasville GA 31792
(912) 377-9644

Circa 1841. Four towering columns support the enormous portico of

this Greek Revival plantation home designed by John Wind. Its commanding position provides a view of 115 acres of lawns, woodlands and ancient oak and magnolia trees. The gracious interiors, including a dining room, drawing rooms and verandas, are furnished with fine antiques. A deep well on the property is noted for its superb drinking water. Horseback riding and fishing the stocked pond are popular plantation activities.

Rates: $150.
Anne-Marie Walker.
8 Rooms. 8 Private Baths. Guest phone available. Beds: KQDT. MAP. Restaurant. Gourmet meals. Swimming pool. Conference room. Golf.

"We saved the best for last!"

Hawaii

Haiku, Maui

Haikuleana B&B Inn

69 Haiku Rd
Haiku, Maui HI 96708
(808) 575-2890

Circa 1850. A true plantation house, the Haikuleana sits in the midst of pineapple fields and Norfolk pine trees. With high ceilings and a tropical decor the inn has all of the flavor of Hawaiian country life. The porch looks out over exotic gardens. Beaches and waterfalls are nearby.

Location: Twelve miles east of Kahului.
*Rates: $65.
Denise & Clark Champion.
2 Rooms. Guest phone available. TV available. Beds: KQTC. B&B. Windsurfing, golf, tennis.
Seen in: *Neighbor Island Feature.*

"Great, great, extra great! Maui is paradise thanks to your daily guidance, directions and helpful hints."

Honolulu

The Manoa Valley Inn

2001 Vancouver Dr
Honolulu HI 96822
(808) 947-6019 (800) 634-5115

Circa 1915. An Iowa lumber executive built this mansion situated on a half-acre of lush greenery. Gables supported by fanciful buttresses add unique detail to the inn, now in the National Register. Lanais furnished with white wicker overlook Diamond Head. The guest rooms are filled with carefully chosen antiques, reproduction wallpaper and cozy comforters.

Location: On the island of Oahu.

Rates: $85-$145.
Marianne Schultz.
8 Rooms. 5 Private Baths. Beds: KQD. Continental-plus breakfast. Parlour piano, pool table, croquet.
Seen in: *Travel & Leisure, LA Style.*

"A wonderful place!! Stepping back to a time of luxury!"

Lahaina, Maui

The Lahaina Hotel

127 Lahainaluna Rd
Lahaina, Maui HI 96761
(808) 661-0577

Circa 1963. Originally built in the 1860s as a hotel for whalers, the bar was famous for brawls. A 16-foot killer whale stuffed and hanging overhead was the target for harpoons, a version of barroom darts. After a fire in 1963, the hotel was rebuilt in a frontier storefront style. Recently renovated by Rick Ralston, founder of Crazy Shirts, Inc., a chain of T-shirt stores, the inn has been appointed in furnishings chosen from Ralston's warehouse of 12,000 antiques. All rooms have balconies and some have ocean views.

*Rates: $110-$170.
Ken Eisley.
12 Rooms. 12 Private Baths. Beds: D. Restaurant. CCs: MC VISA.
Seen in: *Tour & Travel News.*

Poipu Beach, Kauai

Poipu B&B Inn

2720 Hoonani Rd
Poipu Beach, Kauai HI 96756
(808) 742-1146 (800) 552-0095

Circa 1933. This restored plantation house is located one block from the beach. Handcrafted wood interiors,

traditional lanais, carousel horses, and pine antiques decorate the inn. Each room has a private bath, and some have whirlpool tubs. One can hear the sound of the ocean and a nearby stream.

Location: Poipu Beach.
*Rates: $75-$125.
Dotti Cichon.
6 Rooms. 6 Private Baths. Guest phone available. TV in room. Beds: KQTC. Continental-plus breakfast. Jacuzzi. Handicap access. Swimming pool. Conference room. CCs: MC VISA AX. Surfing, boating, horseback riding, golf, tennis. Afternoon tea, popcorn with movies.
Seen in: *Travel & Leisure, Travel-Holiday.*

"Thank you for sharing your home as well as yourself with us. I'll never forget this place, it's the best B&B we've stayed at."

Idaho

Coeur d'Alene

Greenbriar B&B

315 Wallace
Coeur d'Alene ID 83814
(208) 667-9660

Circa 1908. Winding mahogany staircases, woodwork and window seats are features of Greenbriar, now in the National Register. Antiques, imported Irish down comforters with linen covers, sheer curtains, and gabled ceilings decorate the guest rooms. It is four blocks from Lake Coeur d'Alene, one of the most beautiful lakes in the country.

❀Rates: $35-$65.
Kris McIlvenna.
7 Rooms. 4 Private Baths. Guest phone available. Beds: KQTC. Full breakfast. Restaurant. CCs: MC VISA. Canoeing, bicycling, skiing, snowmobiling.
Seen in: *Spokesman Review Chronicle, Downwind.*

"It made our wedding celebration so special. You're a real professional."

Illinois

Chicago

Burton House B&B Inn

1454 N Dearborn Pkwy
Chicago IL 60610
(312) 787-9015

Circa 1877. The Bullock-Folsom Mansion, as it is known locally, was the Chicago White House during Grover Cleveland's term. It has been owned by the same family since it was built, and much of early California was built by members of the Bullock and Folsom families. A grand lobby on the first floor displays the magnificent Eastlake interiors seen throughout the inn. Each bedroom has a marble fireplace and gilded ceiling.

*Rates: $90-$120.
Ralph d'Neville-Raby.
3 Rooms. 3 Private Baths. Guest phone available. Beds: QTD. EP. CCs: MC. Shopping.

Chateau des Fleurs

See: Winnetka, IL

The Manor House

See: Kenosha, WI

Collinsville

Maggie's B&B

2102 N Keebler Rd
Collinsville IL 62234
(618) 344-8283

Circa 1890. A rustic, two-acre wooded area surrounds this friendly Victorian inn, once a boarding house. Rooms with 14-foot ceilings are furnished with exquisite antiques and art objects collected on world wide travels. Downtown St.

Louis, the Gateway Arch and the Mississippi riverfront are just 10 minutes away.

Location: Ten minutes from St. Louis.
Rates: $35-$50.
Maggie Leyda.
5 Rooms. 1 Private Bath. Guest phone available. TV available. Beds: QDTC. B&B. Jacuzzi. Handicap access. Game room. Conference room.

"We enjoyed a delightful stay. You've thought of everything. What fun!"

Galena

Avery Guest House

606 S Prospect St
Galena IL 61036
(815) 777-3883

Circa 1848. Avery Guest House is named for Major George Avery who served in the Civil War and later led parades through Galena each year. The house was originally owned by a steamboat captain and later by a wagon-maker. There is a porch swing for leisurely evenings. Breakfast is served in the sunny dining

room with bay windows overlooking the Galena River Valley.

Rates: $45-$60.
Flo & Roger Jensen.
4 Rooms. 2 Private Baths. Guest phone available. TV available. Beds: QTC. Continental-plus breakfast. Handicap access. CCs: MC VISA AX. Horseback riding, swimming, skiing, hiking, bicycling.
Seen in: *The Galena Gazette.*

"We've stayed in several B&Bs and this one is the most pleasant and friendly."

Belle Aire Mansion

11410 Rt 20 W
Galena IL 61036
(815) 777-0893

Circa 1834. Situated on 16 acres including a barn and windmill, the

Belle Aire Mansion was originally a log cabin. Remodeled in 1879, the charming white Federal-style house features a two-story columned porch looking out over lawns and a

circular drive. Original logs and flooring, as well as a fieldstone basement remain. Decor is early American and country. With two small children of their own, the hosts welcome children of all ages.
Location: Thirteen miles east of Dubuque, Iowa.
Rates: $55-$75.
Jan & Lorraine Svec.
4 Rooms. 2 Private Baths. Guest phone available. TV available. Beds: KDC. B&B. Downhill and cross-country skiing, golf, horseback riding, hiking.
"Loved the house and the hospitality!"

DeSoto House Hotel
230 S Main St
Galena IL 61036
(815) 777-0090 (800) 343-6562

Circa 1855. Abraham Lincoln, Theodore Roosevelt, and Mark Twain are among the DeSoto's famous guests. An original winding staircase still graces the lobby and a ballroom with floor-to-ceiling windows is now used for banquets. The hotel is appointed in antiques and other comfortable furnishings. A restaurant is on the premises.
Rates: $65-$115.
George Bush.
55 Rooms. 55 Private Baths. Guest phone in room. TV in room. Beds: KD. Continental-plus breakfast. CCs: MC VISA AX.

Hellman Guest House
318 Hill St
Galena IL 61036
(815) 777-3638

Circa 1895. A corner tower and an observatory turret rise above the gabled roofline of this Queen Anne house built of Galena brick. The house was constructed from designs drawn by Schoppel of New York. An antique telescope in the parlor is a favorite of guests who wish to view the town. Stained glass, pocket doors and antique furnishings add to the inn's pleasure. The tower room with its brass bed and village views is recommended.
Rates: $65-$95.
Merilyn Tommaro.
4 Rooms. 4 Private Baths. Guest phone available. Beds: QD. B&B. CCs: MC VISA AX. Horseback riding, golf, swimming, cycling, cross-country & downhill skiing.
Seen in: *Innsider, Midwest Living, Chicago Tribune.*

Standish House
See: Lanark, IL

Stillman's Country Inn
513 Bouthillier
Galena IL 61036
(815) 777-0557

Circa 1858. This grand Victorian mansion, built by merchant Nelson

Stillman, is just up the hill from Ulysses S. Grant's house. In fact, Grant and his wife dined here often. The tower of the house was a hideout for slaves escaping through the Underground Railroad. Original working fireplaces and handsome antiques grace the guest rooms.
Location: Across from General Grant's house.
Rates: $65-$95.
Pam & Bill Lozeau.
5 Rooms. 5 Private Baths. Guest phone available. TV in room. Beds: QD. Continental breakfast. Conference room. CCs: MC VISA DS.
Seen in: *National Geographic Traveler, Midwest Living.*

Lanark

Standish House
540 W Carroll St
Lanark IL 61046
(815) 493-2307

Circa 1892. Four generations of Standishes are associated with this

Queen Anne Victorian house. The current owner is Norman Standish, descendant of Captain Myles Standish. Furnishings include English antiques from the 17th and 18th centuries. During Thanksgiving, the innkeepers sponsor a series of lectures on pilgrim history.
Location: One-hundred-twenty miles west of Chicago on route 64.
Rates: $50-$65.
Maggie Aschenbrenner.
5 Rooms. 1 Private Bath. Guest phone available. TV available. Beds: Q. B&B. CCs: MC VISA. Skiing, fishing, hunting, hiking. Pilgrim history lectures.
Seen in: *Prairie Advocate, Northwestern Illinois Dispatch.*

Oregon

Pinehill B&B
400 Mix St
Oregon IL 61061
(815) 732-2061

Circa 1874. This Italianate country house is noted for its unusual T-shape. It was constructed by local artisans from a sketch found in a Chicago home sketch shop. A three-story cupola, 10-foot windows, arched doorways and seven marble fireplaces are special features. Mural wallpaper along the stairway was silk-screened in Paris in 1919 especially for the house. Somerset Maugham was a frequent visitor in the Thirties.
*Rates: $75-$85.
Lois & George Fischer
3 Rooms. 3 Private Baths. 3 Fireplaces. Guest phone available. TV available. Beds: D. Continental-plus breakfast. Jacuzzi. Conference room. CCs: MC VISA. Golf, nature trails, fishing, boating, water skiing.
Seen in: *Oregon Republican Reporter, Freeport Journal.*

Rockford

Pinehill B&B
See: Oregon, IL

Springfield

Corinne's B&B Inn

1001 S Sixth St
Springfield IL 62703
(217) 527-1400

Circa 1883. This gabled Queen Anne house was built for the niece of wholesale grocer William Bunn, whose business still flourishes. The house was part of the "Aristocracy Hill" neighborhood. The foyer features built-in window seats, oriental carpets and oak wainscotting leading to the open staircase lit by leaded glass windows. Abraham Lincoln's home is five blocks away. The Capitol Complex, Governor's Mansion and Lincoln Depot are within walking distance.

*Rates: $55-$70.
Corinne Gramlich.
5 Rooms. 3 Private Baths. Guest phone in room. TV available. Beds: K. Continental-plus breakfast. CCs: MC VISA. Horseback riding, carriage rides.
Seen in: *USA Today, Weekend Journal.*

"We had the best of times at your inn. It couldn't have been more perfect."

Winnetka

Chateau des Fleurs

552 Ridge Rd
Winnetka IL 60093
(312) 256-7272

Circa 1936. This is an authentic French-style country home near Lake Michigan. The lawn and terraced English gardens are shaded by cottonwood, willow and apple trees. A Steinway baby grand piano is in the living room and there is a library available to guests. The Northwestern Train to the Chicago Loop is four blocks away.

Location: Thirty minutes to the Chicago Loop.
Rates: $80.
Sally Ward.
3 Rooms. 3 Private Baths. Guest phone in room. TV available. Beds: KDT. Continental-plus breakfast. Jacuzzi. Swimming pool. Conference room. Jogging, golf, croquet.
Seen in: *Pioneer Press.*

"We will always remember your wonderful hospitality and your delightful gardens."

Indiana

Batesville

Sherman House Restaurant & Inn

35 S Main St
Batesville IN 47006
(812) 934-2407

Circa 1852. This hotel has been in business for more than 100 years. During this century it acquired a Tudor facade. The inn's restaurant is the focal point of town, with business meetings and frequent banquets in the Chalet Room. There are several covered bridges nearby.

*Rates: $32-$55.
Bertha Vogt.
25 Rooms. 25 Private Baths. Guest phone available. TV in room. Beds: KDTC. Full breakfast. Conference room. CCs: MC VISA. Weekend and tour packages.

Bloomington

The Rock House

See: Morgantown, IN

Story Inn

See: Nashville, IN

Columbus

The Columbus Inn

445 Fifth St
Columbus IN 47501
(812) 378-4289

Circa 1895. Dances, basketball games and poultry shows once convened in the auditorium of the old Columbus City Hall during its years as the focal point of town. Now, renovated and in the National

Register, the building is luxurious. The original terra-cotta floors, enormous brass chandeliers, and handcarved oak woodwork now welcome overnight guests. Lavishly decorated rooms feature reproduction antiques such as cherry sleigh beds. Twelve-foot high windows and 21-foot ceilings grace the Charles Sparrell Suite, where a separate level for sleeping beacons the weary traveler. A horse and buggy stops at the inn's front door.

Rates: $80-$245.
Paul A. Staublin.
34 Rooms. 34 Private Baths. Guest phone in room. TV in room. Beds: QDC. B&B. Restaurant. Gourmet meals. Handicap access. Game room. Conference room. CCs: MC VISA AX DC CB DS. Horse and buggy rides, fishing, canoeing.
Seen in: *Chicago-Sun Times, Country Inns, Home & Away, The Cincinnati Enquirer, Glamour.*

"The Inn gives one a real feeling of escape from the everyday hustle and bustle with the ambience of yesteryear and of course the delicious and beautifully served breakfast was the crowning glory of our stay."

Story Inn

See: Nashville, IN

Crawfordsville

Davis House

1010 W Wabash Ave
Crawfordsville IN 47933
(317) 364-0461

Circa 1870. Sampson Houston built this Italianate-style house from brick manufactured on site. He was a

colonel in the home guards, a farmer, minister, and a land speculator who was partially responsible for the town's development. Stately bedrooms have private baths and comfortable beds.

Location: South on I-74.
*Rates: $35-$60.
Jan Stearns.
4 Rooms. 4 Private Baths. TV available. Beds: QTDC. Full breakfast. Conference room. CCs: MC VISA. Canoeing, fishing, hiking.

"This is just wonderful."

Decatur

Cragwood Inn

303 N Second St
Decatur IN 46733
(219) 728-2000

Circa 1900. This Queen Anne Victorian with four porches, gingerbread frosting, a turret and a

graceful bay facade was built by a local Decatur banker. Finely carved oak is magnificently displayed in the paneled ceilings, staircase and pillars of the parlor. An Ornate tin ceiling, leaded glass windows, and a crystal chandelier are among other highlights. The four-poster bed in the Garden Room looks out through a Palladian window. The turret suite and the Blue Room have their own fireplace.
*Rates: $45-$55.
George & Nancy Craig.
5 Rooms. 3 Private Baths. 2 Fireplaces. Guest phone available. TV available. Beds: QD. B&B. Gourmet meals. Conference room. CCs: MC VISA. Tennis, biking, swimming, golf, bowling.
Seen in: *Inside Chicago, Nipsco Folks.*

"Your wonderful hospitality, beautiful home and company made my trip that much more enjoyable."

Evansville

Brigadoon B&B Inn
1201 SE Second St
Evansville IN 47713
(812) 422-9635

Circa 1892. Situated in a historic residential area, this Victorian inn is approached through a white picket fence. Built for a railroad executive, it is near downtown and the river. The house has been completely restored and insulation has been added to the interior bedroom walls. The parlor and library are open to guests.
Location: Old Ohio River city.
Rates: $45.
Katelin Forbes.
4 Rooms. 2 Private Baths. TV available. Beds: QC. Full breakfast. Handicap access. Conference room. CCs: MC VISA. Museums, horse racing, zoo.

"These 14 hours of pure enjoyment have been a delight. Throughout the 26 countries I've traveled not one B&B has matched your hospitality."

Hagerstown

Teetor House
300 W Main St
Hagerstown IN 47346
(317) 489-4422

Circa 1936. Inventor Ralph Teetor (cruise control) built this luxurious

mansion on acres of rolling lawns. The house's gracious stairway is a replica of the Waldorf Astoria's stairways and also boasts cherry paneling and a two-story leaded and stained-glass window. A Steinway grand piano has been converted as an electric player piano in the inn's parlor and there are hundreds of old piano rolls. Among Mr. Teetor's early guests were Lowell Thomas, Wendell Wilkie, and probably his friend Henry Ford.

Location: Five miles N of I70 in east-central Indiana, 1 hour from Dayton, Ohio and Indianapolis, Indiana.
Rates: $75-$85.
Jack & Joanne Warmoth.
4 Rooms. 4 Private Baths. Guest phone available. TV in room. Beds: KT. B&B. Conference room. CCs: MC VISA. Golf, swimming, health recreation center.
Seen in: *Palladium-Item, Midwest Living.*

Indianapolis

The Columbus Inn
See: Columbus, IN

Knightstown

Old Hoosier House
Rt 2 Box 299-I
Knightstown IN 46148
(317) 345-2969

Circa 1836. The Old Hoosier House was owned by the Elisha Scovell family, friends of President Martin Van Buren. They named their child after him. Features of this early Vic-

torian house include tall, arched windows and a gabled entrance. Rooms are air-conditioned and decorated with antiques and lace curtains. Only Hoosier breakfasts are served here.
Location: Greensboro Pike & Rd. 750 S.
*Rates: $55. Season: May to Nov.
Jean & Tom Lewis.
4 Rooms. 3 Private Baths. 1 Fireplace. Guest phone in room. TV available. Beds: KQT. B&B. Golf, fishing, hiking, bicycling, tennis.
Seen in: *Indianapolis Star News.*

"We had such a wonderful time at your house. Very many thanks."

Mishawaka

The Beiger Mansion Inn
317 Lincoln Way E
Mishawaka IN 46544
(219) 256-0365

Circa 1907. This neo-classical limestone mansion was built to satisfy

Susie Beiger's wish to copy a friend's Newport, Rhode Island estate. Palatial rooms that were once a gathering place for local society now welcome guests who seek gracious accommodations. Notre Dame, St. Mary's and Indiana University in South Bend are nearby.
Location: Northern Indian.
*Rates: $65-$125.
Ron Montandon & Phil Robinson.
10 Rooms. 3 Private Baths. 2 Fireplaces. Guest phone available. TV available. Beds: DTC. B&B. Conference room. CCs: MC VISA AX DS. Afternoon hors d'oeuvres.
Seen in: *Tribune.*

"Can't wait until we return to Mishawaka to stay with you again!"

Morgantown

The Rock House

380 W Washington St
Morgantown IN 46160
(812) 597-5100

Circa 1894. James Smith Knight built this stone house with tower

rooms, a three-room basement, and an attic and delivery room. Knight made concrete blocks years before they were popular, and embedded stones and rocks in them before they were dry. He also used seashells, jewelry, china dolls and even an animal skull to decorate the blocks. There is still a dumbwaiter used to lower food to the basement for cooling during the summer.

Location: Ten miles north of Brown County and Nashville.
Rates: $60-$75.
Doug & Marcia Norton.
6 Rooms. 3 Private Baths. Guest phone available. TV available. Beds: QDT. Full breakfast. Horseback riding, skiing, water sports.
Seen in: *Bloomington Herald-Times, Outdoor Indiana Magazine.*

"I was so impressed with your hospitality and the little extra touches that added so much. I've already started spreading the word and I'll be back myself."

Nashville

Story Inn

PO Box 64
Nashville IN 47448
(812) 988-2273

Circa 1916. Marking the center of town, this rustic "Dodge-City" style general store with its weathered tin facade, is flanked by two illuminated Red and Gold Crown gas pumps set on the front porch. There's a first floor restaurant that draws guests from hours away for its fancy desserts and farm-fresh produce. Upstairs, where Studebaker buggies were previously assembled, attractive guest rooms now feature antique four-poster beds, down comforters and flannel sheets.

Rates: $65-$85.
Benjamin & Cynthia Schultz.
13 Rooms. 12 Private Baths. TV available. Beds: QDTC. Full breakfast. Restaurant. Gourmet meals. CCs: MC VISA AX DC. Pool, tennis, horseback riding, hiking.
Seen in: *New York Times, Chicago Tribune, Los Angeles Times, Midwest Living.*

"I never wanted to leave."

Paoli

Braxtan House Inn B&B

210 N Gospel St
Paoli IN 47454
(812) 723-4677

Circa 1893. Thomas Braxtan, son of original Quaker settlers, was a business owner and stock trader who built this Victorian house. With 21 rooms, the inn became a hotel when

nearby mineral springs lured guests to Paoli. Oak, cherry, chestnut, and maple woodwork are featured. The inn is furnished in antiques and highlighted with stained and leaded glass.

Location: Downtown Paoli on state road 37N.
❄❀Rates: $40-$70.
Terry & Brenda Cornwell.
5 Rooms. 3 Private Baths. Guest phone available. TV available. Beds: QDT. Full breakfast. Conference room. CCs: MC VISA. Skiing, swimming, fishing, golf, tennis, hiking. Ski packages.
Seen in: *Paoli News-Republican, Bloomington Herald Times.*

Wonderful. Lovely hospitality."

Richmond

Teetor House

See: Hagerstown, IN

South Bend

Beiger Mansion Inn

See: Mishawaka, IN

Iowa

Amana Colonies

Die Heimat Country Inn

Main St
Amana Colonies IA 52236
(319) 622-3937

Circa 1854. The Amana Colonies is a German settlement listed in the National Register. This two-story clapboard inn houses a collection of handcrafted Amana furnishings of walnut and cherry. Country-style quilts and curtains add personality to each guest room. Nearby, you'll find museums, a winery, and a woolen mill that imports wool from around the world.

Location: South of Cedar Rapids, west of Iowa City.
Rates: $35-$49.
Don & Sheila Janda.
19 Rooms. 19 Private Baths. Guest phone available. TV in room. Beds: QD. Continental-plus breakfast. CCs: MC VISA DS. Nature trail, golf course. Hayrack tour package.

"Staying at Die Heimat has been one of our life's highlights. We loved the clean rooms, comfortable beds and history."

Avoca

Victorian B&B Inn

425 Walnut St
Avoca IA 51521
(712) 343-6336 (800) 397-3914

Circa 1904. This Victorian home was built by Fred Thielsen, a local contractor and builder. The house is noted for its fishscale shingling and golden pine woodwork. Detailed columns enhance the parlor and dining rooms. Midwestern antiques and locally made quilts decorate the guest rooms. Guests may arrange to have dinner at the inn, either down-home Iowa cooking or gourmet selections, all served on fine china, crystal, and sterling.

*Rates: $48-$50.
Jan & Gene Kuehn.
4 Rooms. 1 Private Bath. Guest phone available. TV available. Beds: QD. B&B. Gourmet meals. CCs: MC VISA.
Seen in: *Kansas City Star, Des Moines Register.*

"Your hospitality was exceptional. We'll be back...with our friends!"

Bellvue

Mont Rest

300 Spring St
Bellvue IA 52031
(319) 872-4220 (800) 369-REST

Circa 1893. Mont Rest was built by Seth Lewellyn Baker, developer of the Chicago suburb of Glen Ellyn. A compulsive gambler, he played high-stakes poker from the turret. Within three years he lost his home. Because the architecture is an unusual mix of styles, the owners and the Iowa Historical Society labeled it Gothic Steamboat Revival. A clearly Victorian atmosphere prevails inside.

Location: On a nine-acre wooded bluff overlooking the Mississippi River.
Rates: $50-$75.
Bob & Christine Gelms.
5 Rooms. Guest phone available. TV available. Beds: Q. Full breakfast. Jacuzzi. Conference room. CCs: MC VISA. Potter's Mill, fishing, doll museum, mystery weekends, ski packages. Lunch and dinner on request.
Seen in: *Quad City Times, The Register.*

Decorah

Old World Inn

See: Spillville, IA

Dubuque

Redstone Inn

504 Bluff St
Dubuque IA 52001
(800) 331-5454 (319) 582-1894

Circa 1894. The Redstone Inn, a 23 room duplex, was built by pioneer industrialist A. A. Cooper as a wedding gift for his daughter Nell. The side occupied by Nell's family is of grand Victorian decor, generously embellished with turrets and porches. Maple and oak woodwork, beveled, leaded and stained-glass windows and marble and tile fireplaces are elegant features. Dubuque conservationists and business people converted the mansion into a luxurious antique-filled inn.

*Rates: $65-$100.
Debbie Griesinger, Manager.
15 Rooms. 15 Private Baths. Guest phone available. TV in room. Beds: QD. Full breakfast. Conference room. CCs:

MC VISA AX DC. Dickens Christmas and ski packages.
Seen in: *Country Inns, Journal Star.*
"Very nice!"

The Richards House

1492 Locust St
Dubuque IA 52001
(319) 557-1492

Circa 1883. Innkeeper David Stuart estimates that it will take several

years to remove the concrete-based brown paint applied by a bridge painter in the Sixties to cover the 7,000 square-foot Queen Anne Victorian house. The interior, however, only needed a tad of polish. The varnished cherry and bird's eye maple woodwork is set aglow under electrified gas lights. Ninety stained-glass windows, eight pocket doors with stained glass, and a magnificent entry way reward those who pass through.
*Rates: $35-$75.
Michelle, Delaney, David Stuart.
5 Rooms. 3 Private Baths. 5 Fireplaces. Guest phone in room. TV in room. Beds: QC. Full breakfast. CCs: MC VISA.

Stout House

1105 Locust
Dubuque IA 52001
(800) 331-5454 (319) 582-1894

Circa 1894. This Richardsonian-Romanesque mansion was built by Frank D. Stout for $300,000. The intricate wood carvings were a showcase for the finest skilled craftsmen of the day, working in rosewood, maple, oak and sycamore. One of the 10 wealthiest men in Chicago, Stout entertained Dubuque's upper crust elegantly in his rough-hewn sandstone house.
*Rates: $62-$160.
Deborah Griesinger.
15 Rooms. 15 Private Baths. 2 Fireplaces. Guest phone in room. TV in room. Beds: QDT. Restaurant. Jacuzzi. Conference room. CCs: MC VISA AX DC.
Seen in: *Telegraph Herald, Country Inns Magazine.*
"The surroundings were exquisite."

Newton

La Corsette Maison Inn

629 First Ave East
Newton IA 50208
(515) 792-6833

Circa 1909. This unusual Mission-style building has an Arts and Crafts interior. All the woodwork is of quarter-sawn oak and the dining room furniture was designed by Limbert. Stained and beveled glass is found throughout. French bed-chambers feature reproduction and antique furnishings. The inn's restaurant has received four-and-one-half stars from the *Des Moines Register's* Grumpy Gourmet.
Rates: $55-$175.
Kay Owen.
4 Rooms. 4 Private Baths. 1 Fireplace. Beds: KQD. Full breakfast. CCs: MC VISA.

Spencer

The Hannah Marie Country Inn

Rt 1, Hwy 71 S
Spencer IA 51301
(712) 262-1286

Circa 1910. This beautifully restored farmhouse is Northwest Iowa's first country inn. Guest

rooms are decorated with Iowa-made quilts, antiques and lace curtains. The Sweetheart room has an in-room claw-foot tub with pillows. Amenities include dessert, evening wine, fruit baskets and flowers. Afternoon teas include Queen Victoria's Chocolate Tea, or Tea with the Mad Hatter, all served in costume. Green lawns, the scent of freshly mowed hay, and golden fields of corn surround the inn. Guests are given walking sticks and parasols for strolling to the old creek for a country picnic.
Location: Six miles south of Spencer.
*Rates: $50-$60. Season: May - Mid-Dec.
Mary & Dave Nichols.
3 Rooms. 3 Private Baths. Guest phone in room. Beds: QD. Full breakfast. Gourmet meals. Jacuzzi. CCs: MC VISA. Museums, antique shops. Afternoon tea included in price of room.
Seen in: *Innsider, Midwest Living, Country Woman.*
"Loved everything. The food was elegant, thank you, thank you again."

Spillville

Old World Inn

331 S Main St
Spillville IA 52168
(319) 562-3739 (319)562-3186

Circa 1871. This brick general store has been a brewery, livery stable,

hardware store and residence. Most recently it was a Czech restaurant. It is located in the Czech village that inspired Antonin Dvorak to compose the "American Quartet." He worked on the New World Symphony here in 1893 and played organ for daily mass at nearby St. Wenceslaus Church. Lodging is upstairs.
Location: Walking distance to Dvorak exhibit.
Rates: $40.
Juanita Loven.
4 Rooms. 4 Private Baths. Guest phone available. Beds: DTC. EP. Restaurant. Gourmet meals. Conference room. CCs: MC VISA. Skiing, canoeing, bicycling, golf, tennis.
Seen in: *Des Moines Register, Cedar Rapids Gazette, USA Today.*
"Rooms are delightful! Very charming atmosphere."

Kansas

Council Grove

The Cottage House Hotel

25 N Neosho
Council Grove KS 66846
(316) 767-6828 (800) 888-8162

Circa 1872. The inn is located in Council Grove, the birthplace of the

Santa Fe Trail. The Cottage House is located on the old Santa Fe Trail which originated in Council Grove. The building grew from a boarding house to an elegant home before it became the hotel of a local banker. Listed in the National Register of Historic Places, the inn has been completely renovated and is a beautiful example of Victorian architecture in a prairie town.

Location: Northeast Kansas, intersection of 56 & 177.
*Rates: $30-$55.
Connie Essington.
26 Rooms. 26 Private Baths. Guest phone in room. TV in room. Beds: KQDWC. Continental breakfast. Jacuzzi. Sauna. Handicap access. Conference room. CCs: MC VISA AX DS. Historic sites, golf in town, lake nearby, fishing, skiing. Dinner package, group tours.
Seen in: *Manhattan Mercury, The Gazette, Globe and Mail.*

"A walk back into Kansas history; preserved charm and friendliness."

Topeka

Heritage House

3535 SW 6th St
Topeka KS 66606
(913) 233-3800

Circa 1900. This was the original mid-western farm home of the Menninger Clinic. A wide porch that wraps around the front is filled with wicker furnishings. Each room was decorated by a different design firm when the inn appeared as a designer showcase home. Dr. Karl's Study is popular with its luminous paneling and desk. The bridal suite boasts a four-poster bed and whirlpool.

Rates: $45-$105.
Sarah Rich.
15 Rooms. 13 Private Baths. Guest phone available. Beds: KQDT. Full breakfast. Conference room. CCs: MC VISA AX DC DS.

Valley Falls

The Barn B&B

RR 2 Box 87
Valley Falls KS 66088
(913) 945-3303

Circa 1892. This century old barn tucked in the rolling countryside of northeast Kansas has been modernized and converted to a bed and breakfast inn. King size beds, down comforters and an exercise room are among the Barn's special amenities. A hearty farm-style breakfast is served in the glassed-in sundeck. By special arrangement, dinner taken with the family, is available. Swimmers will appreciate the indoor, heated pool available all year. The inn also has its own fishing ponds.

*Rates: $49-$54.
Tom & Marcella Ryan.
18 Rooms. 18 Private Baths. Guest phone in room. TV available. Beds: KC. AP. Conference room. CCs: MC VISA AX.

Wichita

Inn at the Park

3751 E Douglas
Wichita KS 67208
(316) 652-0500

Circa 1910. Cyrus Beachy, of Steffen Ice & Ice Cream Company built this massive three-story brick house with a two-level wraparound porch in the best part of town. A Symphony Showcase house, 27 designers converged to decorate the rooms. French Country, Oriental, Neo Classic and Art Nouveau are among the themes carried out in the 12 guest rooms. The carriage house suites feature extra amenities such as a hot tub and a private courtyard. Breakfast is offered in bed, the garden or breakfast room.

*Rates: $85-$135.
12 Rooms. 12 Private Baths. 8 Fireplaces. Guest phone in room. TV in room. Beds: KQ. Continental breakfast. Jacuzzi. Conference room. CCs: MC VISA AX. Carriage rides.
Seen in: *Wichita Business Journal.*

"This is truly a distinctive hotel. Your attention to detail is surpassed only by your devotion to excellent service."

Kentucky

Bardstown

Jailer's Inn

111 W Stephen Foster Ave
Bardstown KY 40004
(502) 348-5551

Circa 1819. This old jail was constructed of native limestone. There were two cells and an upstairs dungeon to house prisoners. The back building, sometimes referred to as the new jail, is completely surrounded by a stone wall. Jailer's Inn was a residence for many years before becoming a bed and breakfast.

Location: South of Louisville 35 miles.
Rates: $55-$75. Season: March to Dec.
Challen & Fran McCoy.
4 Rooms. Guest phone available. TV available. Continental breakfast. CCs: VISA. Dinner train and drama package.

"One of the oldest and most picturesque houses in Bardstown, a city noted for its fine homes." Joe Creason of the Courier Journal.

Berea

Boone Tavern Hotel

Main St CPO 2345
Berea KY 40403
(606) 986-9358

Circa 1909. This white, three-story Georgian hotel is run by a non-

profit organization for the benefit of Berea College. The school is famous for a work-study program that makes a college education available to motivated students from the Kentucky mountains. To enjoy an example of Kentucky's finest dining, make reservations and be sure to arrive on time, since there is only one seating.

Location: Center of Berea College campus.
Rates: $52-72.
J.B. Morgan.
59 Rooms. 59 Private Baths. Guest phone in room. TV in room. Beds: QD. Full breakfast. Handicap access. Conference room. CCs: MC VISA DS. Tennis, gym. Alumni packages.

Covington

Amos Shinkle Townhouse

215 Garrard St
Covington KY 41011
(606) 431-2118

Circa 1854. The facade of this restored mansion is Greco-Italianate.

The cast iron fence and gate in front are echoed in the cast iron filigree on the porch. Inside there are impressive crown moldings highlighted by stenciling in a surrounding border. Massive carved bedsteads, 16-foot ceilings, and rococo Revival chandeliers add to the formal elegance. Here, Southern hospitality is at its finest.

Location: Fifteen-minute walk to downtown Cincinnati.
*Rates: $68-$105.
Bernie Moorman.
7 Rooms. 7 Private Baths. 3 Fireplaces. Guest phone available. TV available. Beds: D. Full breakfast. Jacuzzi. Conference room. CCs: MC VISA AX DC DS. Stroll to an authentic paddlewheel boat, or carriage ride.
Seen in: *Bluegrass Magazine, Cincinnati Magazine, Cincinnati Post.*

"It's like coming home to family and friends."

Georgetown

Log Cabin B&B

350 N Broadway
Georgetown KY 40324
(502) 863-3514

Circa 1809. This rustic Kentucky log cabin, with its shake-shingle roof and chinked logs was restored by the McKnight family. The huge fieldstone fireplace often holds a roaring fire and there is a kitchen and upstairs loft bedroom. Country decor and collections fill the house. Art Linkletter and Alex Haley enjoyed visits here.

Location: Two miles off I-75, 10 miles from Lexington.
Rates: $64.
Clay & Sanis McKnight.
1 Fireplace.
Seen in: *Lexington Herald Leader.*

Harrodsburg

Canaan Land Farm B&B

4355 Lexington Rd
Harrodsburg KY
(606) 734-3984

Circa 1795. This National Register farm house was built of Flemish

bond brick set over a fieldstone foundation. The innkeepers' collies and Italian Anatolian and Shar Planinetz sheep dogs herd white Polypay and black Border Leicester sheep on 168 acres of woodland and rolling pastureland. New lambs are born in November and in the spring. Nuebian dairy goats are raised. A clapboard addition houses two of the guest rooms and the Wool Room where the innkeeper spins and weaves. Antiques, quilts, and featherbeds add to the ambiance.

Rates: $45-$60. Season: Nov - March.
Fred & Theo Bee.
3 Rooms. Guest phone available. Beds: DT. Full breakfast. Swimming pool. Swimming, golf, crafts, river boat rides, village tours.

Shakertown At Pleasant Hill

Rt 4
Harrodsburg KY 40330
(606) 734-5411

Circa 1805. A non-profit organization preserves this 19th-century Shaker village set atop a pleasant meadow. Guest rooms are in 15 restored buildings. The old road running through the village is a National Landmark and is restricted to foot traffic. Reproductions of authentic Shaker furnishings fill the guest rooms. Air conditioning is hidden and there are no closets. Instead, clothes (and sometimes chairs and lamps) are hung on Shaker Pegs spaced one foot apart on all four walls. Costumed interpreters in the craft buildings describe Shaker culture and craft.

Location: Twenty-five miles southwest of Lexington off Harrodsburg Road.
Rates: $40 - $70
Anne Voris.
78 Rooms. 78 Private Baths. Guest phone in room. TV in room. Beds: TD. EP.

"We can't wait to return! We treasure our memories here of peaceful, pleasant days."

Lexington

Log Cabin B&B

See: Georgetown, KY

Murray

The Diuguid House

603 Main St
Murray KY 42071
(502) 753-5470

Circa 1895. When this Victorian house was built there was a tax on the number of rooms each house contained. Because each closet was counted as a room, the family did without closets, using freestanding wardrobes. Thick brick walls make

it soundproof. There are stained glass windows and intricate oak woodwork.

Location: Downtown Murray.
*Rates: $30-$40.
Helena & Lorene Celano.
3 Rooms. Guest phone available. TV available. Beds: QTC. Full breakfast. Conference room. CCs: MC VISA. Horseback riding, tennis, boating within 15 miles.
Seen in: *The Murray State News.*

"We enjoyed our visit in your beautiful home and your hospitality was outstanding."

Louisiana

Napoleonville

Madewood Plantation

Rt 2 Box 478
Napoleonville LA 70390
(504) 369-7151

Circa 1848. Six massive Ionic columns support the central portico

of this striking Greek Revival mansion. Framed by live oaks and ancient magnolias, Madewood, on 20 impeccably groomed acres, overlooks Bayou Lafourche. It was designed by Henry Howard, a noted architect from Cork, Ireland. Elegant double parlors, a ballroom, library, music room and dining room are open to guests. Breakfast and dinner are included.

Location: Seventy-five miles from New Orleans.
*Rates: $85-$150.
Keith & Millie Marshall.
9 Rooms. 9 Private Baths. 2 Fireplaces. Guest phone available. TV available. Beds: QDT. MAP. Conference room. CCs: MC VISA AX DC. Swamp and plantation tours.
Seen in: *Travel & Leisure, New York Times, Southern Living, Los Angeles Magazine.*

"We have stayed in many hotels, other plantations and English manor houses and Madewood has surpassed them all in charm, hospitality and food."

New Orleans

A Hotel, the Frenchman

417 Frenchman St
New Orleans LA 70116
(504) 948-2166

Circa 1860. Two town houses built by Creole craftsmen have been totally renovated, including the slave quarters. The original site was chosen to provide convenient access to shops and Jackson Square. The location today is still prime. Historic homes, quaint shops, and fine restaurants are immediately at hand. The Old Mint and French Market are across the way. All rooms are furnished with period antiques.

Location: The French Quarter.
*Rates: $68-$108.
Mark Soubie, Jr.
25 Rooms. 25 Private Baths. Guest phone in room. TV in room. Beds: QC. Full breakfast. Restaurant. Jacuzzi. Handicap access. Swimming pool. Conference room. CCs: MC VISA. Swimming.

"Still enjoying wonderful memories of my stay at your charming hotel...such a delightful respite from the frantic pace of the Quarter."

Columns Hotel

3811 St Clarles Ave
New Orleans LA 70115
(504) 899-9308

Circa 1883. The Columns was built by Simon Hernsheim, a tobacco merchant, who was the wealthiest philanthropist in New Orleans. The floors are three layers deep made of oak, mahogany and pine. The two-story columned gallery and portico provide a grand entrance into this restored mansion. The estate was selected by Paramount Studios for the site of the movie *Pretty Baby* with Brook Shields. The hotel has been nominated to be included in the National Register of Historic Places.

*Rates: $50-$125.
Claire & Jacques Creppel.
19 Rooms. 9 Private Baths. Guest phone in room. Beds: KDTW. Continental breakfast. Restaurant. Gourmet meals. Conference room. CCs: MC VISA AX. Audubon Zoo, shopping.
Seen in: *Good Housekeeping, New York Times, Vogue, Good Morning America.*

"...like experiencing life of the Old South, maybe more like living in a museum."

The Cornstalk Hotel

915 Royal St
New Orleans LA 70116
(504) 523-1515

Circa 1805. This home belonged to Judge Francois Xavier-Martin, the author of the first history of Louisiana and one of Louisiana's first State Supreme Court Chief Justices. Andrew Jackson stayed here and another guest, Harriet Beecher Stowe wrote *Uncle Tom's Cabin* after viewing the nearby slave markets. The Civil War followed the widely-

read publication. Surrounding the inn is a 150-year-old wrought-iron cornstalk fence. Stained-glass windows, oriental rugs, fireplaces and antiques grace the inn.
Location: In the heart of the French Quarter.
Rates: $85-$115.
Debbie & David Spencer.
14 Rooms. 14 Private Baths. 8 Fireplaces. Guest phone in room. TV in room. Beds: KQDT. B&B. CCs: MC VISA AX DC.
Seen in: *London Sunday Times.*

Dauzat House

337 Burgandy St
New Orleans LA 70130
(504) 524-2075

Circa 1788. Located three blocks from Canal Street and two blocks from Bourbon Street, Dauzat House conveniently located to both the French Quarter and downtown New Orleans. A lobby was once the cottage of Marie Lareau, voodoo queen. There are two slave quarters converted to full suites complete with living rooms and kitchens. The house includes a 200-year-old courtyard with a swimming pool. Because of its location in the heart of the French Quarter the innkeepers require adherence to a list of policies and regulations. Write to the inn for information.
Rates: $75-$500.
Richard Nicolais & Donald Dauzat.
8 Rooms. 5 Private Baths. Beds: T. Full breakfast. Swimming pool. Conference room. Swimming.
Seen in: *Esquire Magazine, Playboy Magazine.*

Grenoble House

329 Dauphine
New Orleans LA 70112
(504) 522-1331

Circa 1854. Grenoble House is really several renovated historic buildings in the French Quarter. There are several suites. A spa and pool are available.
Location: In the heart of the French Quarter.
*Rates: $95-$195.
Peggy Martin.
EP. Jacuzzi. Swimming pool. CCs: MC VISA.

Hotel Ste. Helene

508 Rue Chartres St
New Orleans LA 70130
(504) 522-5014

Circa 1835. This elegantly refurbished hotel once housed Hart's Pharmaceuticals. The company was known throughout the country for Harts Elixirs. With its 20% alcohol content, it was guaranteed to "cure what ails you." The inn is decorated in a European style. Guests gravitate to the hotel's courtyard for breakfast, or for a dip in the pool. Within a one-block radius are Jackson Square and St. Louis Cathedral, Bourbon Street, as well as world-famous Brennan's and Antoines restaurants.
*Rates: $65-$115.
Ian Hardcastle, Barbara Coffey.
16 Rooms. 16 Private Baths. Guest phone in room. TV in room. Beds: KDT. B&B. Swimming pool. CCs: MC VISA AX. Horseback riding, water sports, riverboat cruises, zoo.
Seen in: *Los Angeles Times.*

"Our memories of our stay is promoting a desire to return in the near future."

Lafitte Guest House

1003 Bourbon St
New Orleans LA 70116
(504) 581-2678

Circa 1849. This elegant French manor house has been meticulously restored. The house is filled with fine antiques and paintings collected from around the world. Located in the heart of the French Quarter, the inn is near world-famous restaurants, museums, antique shops and rows of Creole and Spanish cottages.
Location: Heart of the French Quarter.

**Rates: $65-$115.
Pat Twohey.
14 Rooms. 14 Private Baths. TV available. Beds: KQ. Continental breakfast. CCs: MC VISA.
Seen in: *Glamour Magazine, Antique Monthly.*

"This old building offers the finest lodgings we have found in the city." McCall's Magazine.

Lamothe House

621 Esplanade Ave
New Orleans LA 70116
(504) 947-1161

Circa 1840. A carriageway that formerly cut through the center of

many French Quarter buildings was enclosed at the Lamothe House in 1866, and is now the foyer. Splendid Victorian furnishings enhance moldings, high ceilings, and hand-turned mahogany stairway railings. Gilded opulence goes unchecked in the Mallard and Layfayette suites. Registration takes place in the second-story salon above the courtyard.
*Rates: $75-$205.
Carol Chauppette.
20 Rooms. 20 Private Baths. Beds: TD. Continental breakfast. Conference room. CCs: MC VISA.

Seen in: *Houston Post, Travel & Leisure.*

Nine-O-Five Royal Hotel

905 Rue Royal St
New Orleans LA 70116
(504) 523-4068

Circa 1890. A quaint European-style hotel, the Nine-O-Five is a

colonial with balconies overlooking the southern charm of Royal Street. It has been owned and operated by the same family since it was built. There are 18-foot ceilings, antique furnishings and kitchenettes.

Location: French quarter.
Rates: $45-$95.
J.J. Morell.
14 Rooms. 14 Private Baths. Guest phone available. TV in room. Beds: KQD. EP.

Prytania Inn

1415 Prytania St
New Orleans LA 70130
(504) 566-1515

Circa 1852. The Prytania received the Historic District Landmark Commission's 1984 award for its restoration. Eleven-foot ceilings, old plaster moldings and hand-carved cornices set a pleasant background for the inn's collection of white wicker. A double parlor boasts two black marble mantels over the fireplaces. Eggs Benedict is a popular choice for breakfast and is served with china and fresh flowers. Petunias and hibiscus bloom in the inn's courtyard.

❊Rates: $35-$55.
Sally & Peter Schreiber.
18 Rooms. 18 Private Baths. Guest phone available. TV available. Beds: KQDTW. B&B. CCs: MC VISA AX. Sightseeing.
Seen in: *Times Picayune.*

St. Charles Guest House

1748 Prytania St
New Orleans LA 70130
(504) 523-6556

Circa 1850. Reminiscent of a European *pensione*, the St. Charles

Guest House has served visitors for more than 30 years. The inn is located in the residential Lower Garden District near the St. Charles Streetcar. This is a good choice for seasoned travelers who want an economical, clean and basic accommodation with friendly and helpful hosts.

Rates: $35-$60.
Joanne & Dennis Hilton.
36 Rooms. 23 Private Baths. Guest phone available. Beds: TD. Continental breakfast. Swimming pool. CCs: MC VISA.
Seen in: *Chicago-Sun Times.*

"You had an intuitive understanding of how a group like ours should experience New Orleans."

Terrell House Mansion

1441 Magazine St
New Orleans LA 70130
(504) 524-9859

Circa 1858. Cotton broker Richard Terrell built his Classical Revival

mansion with floor to ceiling windows, balconies and galleries. It's located in the Lower Garden District, the oldest purely residential neighborhood outside the French Quarter. A collection of Prudent Mallard furnishings made by the famous New Orleans craftsman in the 1840s, is featured in rooms one and three. Other heirlooms and antiques are accentuated with a collection of gas lighting fixtures, oriental rugs, paintings and gold leaf mirrors.

❊Rates: $60-$90.
Frederick H. Nicaud.
9 Rooms. 9 Private Baths. 12 Fireplaces. Guest phone in room. TV in room. Beds: KQDT. Continental breakfast. CCs: MC VISA AX.
Seen in: *San Francisco Examiner.*

New Roads

Pointe Coupee B&B

605 E Main St
New Roads LA 70760
(504) 638-6254

Circa 1898. The inn is actually three houses, two embellished with gingerbread. One of the houses was constructed at Waterloo, but because of frequent floods was moved here around 1900. The False River is four blocks away.

❊Rates: $40.
Rev. and Mrs. Miller Armstrong.
13 Rooms. 9 Private Baths. Guest phone available. TV available. Beds: DT. Full breakfast. Handicap access. Conference room. Water sports.

Saint Francisville

Barrow House

524 Royal St
Saint Francisville LA 70775
(504) 635-4791

Circa 1809. This saltbox with a Greek Revival addition was built during Spanish Colonial times. Antiques dating from 1840-1860, include a Mississippi plantation bed with full canopy and a massive rosewood armoire crafted by the famous New Orleans cabinetmaker Mallard. One room has a Spanish moss mattress, traditional Louisiana bedding material used for more than 200 years. Six nearby plantations are open for tours.

Rates: $65-$75.
Shirley Dittloff
4 Rooms. 4 Private Baths. 3 Fireplaces. Beds: KQD. Continental breakfast. Gourmet meals. Golf.
Seen in: *Louisiana Life.*

Shreveport

Fairfield Place

2221 Fairfield Ave
Shreveport LA 71104
(318) 222-0048

Circa 1890. This blue Victorian structure is located in the Highland Restoration District, a neighborhood of gracious mansions framed by stately oaks. French hand-printed Victorian reproduction wallpaper adorns the foyer. Bradbury papers provide the background for the French, English, German and Scandinavian antiques in the guest rooms. Two rooms feature upholstered walls of English floral chintz. Guests enjoy the secluded New Orleans-type courtyard, porches and gardens that bloom year round.

Rates: $85-$95.
Janie Lipscomb.
6 Rooms. 6 Private Baths. Guest phone in room. TV in room. Beds: KQ. B&B. CCs: MC VISA AX. Horse races, lakes. Smoking in courtyard and gardens only. Seen in: *Dallas Herald, Veranda Magazine.*

White Castle

Nottoway

PO Box 160, Mississippi River Rd
White Castle LA 70788
(504) 545-2409

Circa 1859. Virginian John Hampden Randolph built the South's largest plantation home. Twenty-two columns support the exterior structure, a combination of Greek Revival and Italianate architecture. Listed in the National Register, the mansion is over 53,000 square feet. The White Ballroom is

the most famous of Nottoway's 64 rooms.

*Rates: $95-$250.
Faye Russell, Manager.
13 Rooms. 13 Private Baths. Guest phone available. Beds: QDT. Full breakfast. Swimming pool. CCs: MC VISA AX. Tennis nearby.

"Southern hospitality at its finest. Your restaurant has got to be Louisiana's best kept secret."

Maine

Bangor

Ledgelawn Inn
See: Bar Harbor, ME

The Old Parsonage Inn
See: Bucksport, ME

Surry Inn
See: Surry, ME

Bar Harbor

The Inn at Canoe Point
Rt 3 Box 216A - Hull's Cove
Bar Harbor ME 04644
(207) 288-9511

Circa 1889. This oceanfront inn has served as a summer residence for several generations of families escaping city heat. Guests are treated to the gracious hospitality of the past, surrounded by the ocean and pine forests. They can relax on the deck overlooking Frenchman's Bay, or pursue outdoor activities in the National Park.

Rates: $55-$175.
Don Johnson.
5 Rooms. 5 Private Baths. 1 Fireplace. Guest phone available. TV available. Beds: KQT. B&B. Conference room. Ocean.
Seen in: *The New York Times, Portland Monthly Magazine.*

Canterbury Cottage
12 Roberts Ave
Bar Harbor ME 04609
(207) 288-2112

Circa 1901. This house is one of three year-round cottages designed by architect Fred Savage. It was built for station master Frank Whitmore of the Maine Central Railroad Ferry service, which operated from the Bar Harbor Pier and brought all the visitors to the island. The inn is furnished with antiques and accessories of the Victorian period.
Rates: $65-$85. Season: June - Oct.
Michele & Richard Suydam.
4 Rooms. 2 Private Baths. Beds: QD. Continental breakfast. Horseback riding, hiking, bicycling, swimming, boating, wind surfing, fishing, tennis, golf.

Cottage Inns of Bar Harbor
16 Roberta Ave
Bar Harbor ME 04609
(207) 288-3443

Circa 1900. Two gabled Victorian cottages, the Ridgeway and the Maples were built on quiet residential streets to house summer visitors to Bar Harbor. Recently refurbished, guest chambers include comfortable rooms and suites. The Wingwood Suite, for instance, features a queen-size four-poster bed and a working fireplace tucked in the corner. Shops, restaurants and the scenic harbor are within walking distance.

Rates: $45-$110.
Esther Cavagnaro & Katie Wood.
12 Rooms. 10 Private Baths. 2 Fireplaces. Guest phone available. Beds: KQDT. B&B. Conference room. CCs: MC VISA. Acadia National Park.
Seen in: *New England Guide.*

Graycote Inn
40 Holland Ave
Bar Harbor ME 04609
(207) 288-3044

Circa 1881. On an acre of land in town, this summer house was built for Christopher Leffingwell, the Episcopal Bishop of Maine. It has served as a guest house since 1929 and was recently restored. King-size canopy beds, antiques, and fireplaces provide luxury. The ocean, harbor and shops are a four-block stroll from the inn.

Rates: $75-$98. Season: May - Nov.
William & Darlene DeMao.

10 Rooms. 4 Private Baths. Guest phone available. Beds: KQ. Full breakfast. CCs: MC VISA. Hiking, bicycling, horseback riding, canoe and kayak rentals.

"We appreciated your hospitality. Your inn is by far our favorite."

Hearthside Inn B&B

7 High St
Bar Harbor ME 04609
(207) 288-4533

Circa 1907. Originally built for a doctor, this three-story shingled

house sits on a quiet street in town. Guests enjoy four working fireplaces and a porch. The parlor includes a library and fireplace, and the music room holds a studio grand piano. Acadia National Park is five minutes away.

Rates: $65-$110.
Susan & Barry Schwartz.
9 Rooms. 7 Private Baths. 3 Fireplaces. Guest phone available. Beds: QD. B&B. CCs: MC VISA. Near skiing, hiking, whale watching, boating, swimming.

"I have only one word to describe this place, Wow! My wife and I are astonished at the splendor, the warmth of your care and the beauty of the surroundings."

Holbrook House

74 Mount Desert St
Bar Harbor ME 04609
(207) 288-4970

Circa 1876. A local merchant built this Victorian inn in the Bar Harbor

double-bracket style, for vacationers who came to enjoy the beauty of Mt. Desert Island. The inn is located in the town's historic corridor. There is a library, sunroom, and parlor.

Location: Mt. Desert Island.
Rates: $85-$110. Season: June 15-Oct 15.
Dorothy & Mike Chester.
10 Rooms. 10 Private Baths. Guest phone available. TV available. Beds: QDT. B&B. CCs: MC VISA AX. Tennis, golf, swimming, hiking, bike riding, canoeing, horseback riding, sailing. Acadia National Park entrance one mile.

"When I selected Holbrook House all my dreams of finding the perfect little country inn came true."

Ledgelawn Inn

66 Mount Desert
Bar Harbor ME 04609
(207) 288-4596

Circa 1904. Gables, bays, columns and verandas are features of this

rambling three-story summer house located on an acre of wooded land within walking distance to the waterfront. The red clapboard structure sports black shutters and a mansard roof. Filled with antiques and fireplaces the inn features a sitting room and library.

*Rates: $85-$185. Season: April-Nov.
Nancy & Mike Cloud.
35 Rooms. 35 Private Baths. 10 Fireplaces. Guest phone in room. TV in room. Beds: KQD. EP. Jacuzzi. Sauna. Swimming pool. Conference room. CCs: MC VISA AX. Bike riding, canoeing, water sports, sailing.
Seen in: *New York Times*.

"A lovely place to relax and enjoy oneself. The area is unsurpassed in beauty and the people friendly."

Manor House Inn

W St Historic District
Bar Harbor ME 04609
(207) 288-3759

Circa 1887. Colonel James Foster built this 22-room Victorian mansion

now in the National Register. It is an example of the tradition of gracious summer living for which Bar Harbor was and is famous. In addition to the main house, there are several charming cottages situated in the extensive gardens on the property. The innkeeper has written a history of the inn and Bar Harbor.

Location: 106 West Street.
Rates: $79-$149. Season: April 15 - Nov.
Mac Noyes, Jim Dennison.
14 Rooms. 14 Private Baths. Guest phone available. TV available. Beds: KQDT. Continental-plus breakfast. Swimming pool. CCs: MC VISA AX. Horseback riding, bicycling, hiking, canoeing, tennis, swimming, boating.

"Wonderful honeymoon spot!"

Mira Monte Inn

69 Mt Desert St
Bar Harbor ME 04609
(207) 288-4263

Circa 1864. A gracious 18-room Victorian mansion, the Mira Monte has been newly renovated in the style of early Bar Harbor. It features period furnishings, pleasant common rooms, a library and wraparound porches. Situated on estate grounds, there are sweeping lawns, paved terraces, and many gardens. The inn was one of the earliest of Bar Harbor's famous summer cottages.

Location: Five minute walk from the waterfront, shops and restaurants.
*Rates: $75-$125. Season: May - Oct.
Marian Burns.
11 Rooms. 11 Private Baths. Beds: KQT. Full breakfast. CCs: MC VISA. Swimming, outdoor games, tennis.

"On our third year at your wonderful inn in beautiful Bar Harbor. I think I enjoy it more each year. A perfect place to stay in a perfect environment."

Surry Inn

See: Surry, ME

Bar Mills

Royal Brewster B&B

Box 307, Corner Rt 202 & 112
Bar Mills ME 04004
(207) 929-3012

Circa 1805. Master builder Joseph Woodman constructed this impressive Federal house for Dr. Royal Brewster. There is an Adams-style carved mantle over the library

fireplace, and a semi-flying staircase. Original sliding Indian shutters remain in many window casings. The hostess is from Manchester, England and the atmosphere is reminiscent of an English bed and breakfast where guests are treated as one of the family.
Location: 20 minutes from Kennebunkport and Portland.
*Rates: $65.
Marian & Bill Parker.
4 Rooms. Guest phone available. TV available. Beds: DT. Full breakfast. Conference room. CCs: VISA. Golf, beaches, amusement parks, mountains.
Seen in: *Portland, Maine, Evening Express.*
"Thank you for your warm hospitality, the lovely breakfasts, the coziness of your inn and its elegance."

Bath

Elizabeth's B&B
360 Front St
Bath ME 04530
(207) 443-1146

Circa 1820. This early Federal house was built by a family of shipbuilders. From its location on the Kennebec River, Elizabeth's provides a relaxing atmosphere with country antiques and "Mr. T." the resident cat. The dining room features stenciled walls and flagstone and brick floors. Choose the Captain's Quarters for a king-size bed, wide pine flooring, window seat and river view.
Rates: $40-$60. Season: May 15 - Dec. 31.
Elizabeth A. Lindsay.
5 Rooms. 2 Fireplaces. Guest phone available. TV available. Beds: KDT. Continental-plus breakfast. Tennis, beaches, boating, hiking.
Seen in: *The Times Record.*
"It was truly a warming experience to feel so at home, away from home."

Fairhaven Inn
RR 2 Box 85, N Bath Rd
Bath ME 04530
(207) 443-4391

Circa 1790. With its view of the Kennebec River, this site was so attractive that Pimbleton Edgecomb built his Colonial house where a log cabin had previously stood. His descendants occupied it for the next 125 years. Antiques and country furniture fill the inn. Meadows and lawns, and woods of hemlock, birch and pine cover the inn's 27 acres.
Rates: $50-$70.
George & Sallie Pollard.
9 Rooms. 1 Private Bath. Guest phone available. TV available. Beds: QT. Full breakfast. Conference room. Cross-country skiing, snowshoeing, beaches nearby.
"The Fairhaven is now marked in our book with a red star, definitely a place to remember and visit again."

Belfast

The Jeweled Turret Inn
16 Pearl St
Belfast ME 04915
(207) 338-2304

Circa 1898. This grand Victorian is named for the staircase that winds

up the turret, lighted by stained and leaded-glass panels and jewel-like embellishments. It was built for attorney James Harriman. Dark pine beams adorn the ceiling of the den, and the fireplace is constructed of bark and rocks from every state in the Union. Elegant antiques furnish the guest rooms of this National Register home.
Rates: $50-$75.
Carl & Cathy Heffentrager.
7 Rooms. 7 Private Baths. Guest phone available. TV available. Beds: QDT. Full breakfast. Swimming, horseback riding, golf, tennis, deep sea fishing. Afternoon tea.
Seen in: *The Republican Journal.*
"This was the most fun we had in all of the places we've seen all week."

Northport House B&B
City One, Mounted Rt, US Rt. 1
Belfast ME 04915
(207) 338-1422

Circa 1873. A graceful mansard roof tops this three-story early Vic-

torian house. At one time it was an overnight stop on the Portland/Bar Harbor road. Guest rooms feature New England period furnishings. A few rooms have their own kitchens.
Rates: $43-$53.
Peter Mankevetch & Mary Lou Wood.
8 Rooms. 5 Private Baths. Beds: DT. B&B. CCs: MC VISA. Beach, tennis, golf, fishing, hunting, skiing, snowmobiling, hiking, foliage.
Seen in: *Country Inn & Bed & Breakfast Cookbook.*
"Rating: on a scale of 1 to 10, 15+ - couldn't be better."

The Old Parsonage Inn
See: Bucksport, ME

Bethel

Hammons House
Broad St
Bethel ME 04217
(207) 824-3170

Circa 1859. Built by Congressman David Hammons, this is an elegant Greek Revival with a side-hall plan. William Upson converted the adjacent barn to a small summer theater in the early 1920s. Every day a full country breakfast is served. The inn is surrounded by porches, a patio, and beautiful perennial gardens.
Location: Centrally located on the village common.
Rates: $65-$75.

Sally Rollinson.
4 Rooms. Guest phone available. TV available. Beds: DT. Full breakfast. Conference room. CCs: MC VISA. Downhill & cross-country ski areas nearby.
Seen in: *Lewiston Sunday newspaper.*

"The charm of your home was a highlight of our New England tour."

Blue Hill

Blue Hill Farm Country Inn

Rt 15 Box 437
Blue Hill ME 04614
(207) 374-5126

Circa 1900. This farm, situated at the foot of Blue Hill Mountain, spans 48 acres of woods and fields. There is a trout pond and brook on the property, and the restored barn holds a comfortable living room and dining area. Dinner may be arranged while making room reservations. The farm has been in continuous operation since 1840.
Rates: $58 & up.
Jim & Marcia Schatz.
14 Rooms. 7 Private Baths. Guest phone available. Beds: QD. Full breakfast.

"One of the most relaxing experiences ever - perfect beds, ultimate quiet."

Boothbay

Kenniston Hill Inn

Rt 27
Boothbay ME 04537
(207) 633-2159

Circa 1786. Six fireplaces warm this white clapboard, center-chimney Colonial set amidst four acres of gardens and woodlands. It was built by David Kenniston, a prominent shipbuilder and landowner, and was occupied by the Kennistons for

more than 100 years. The parlor has a huge, open hearth fireplace. For several years the inn was used as a country club and later as a restaurant.
*Rates: $60-$80. Season: April - Nov.
Paul & Ellen Morissette.
8 Rooms. 8 Private Baths. Guest phone available. Beds: KQD. Full breakfast. CCs: MC VISA. Golf, deep sea fishing, horseback riding, bicycling, sailing, antiquing.

"England may be the home of the original bed and breakfast, but Kenniston Hill Inn is where it has been perfected!"

Bridgton

The 1859 Guest House

60 S High St
Bridgton ME 04009
(207) 647-2508

Circa 1789. Built on the site of an old tavern, this Federal house features Italianate arched windows and shutters and a large side porch. More than 100 clocks tick away in corners and on mantels throughout the inn. Hailing from Pennsylvania Dutch country, the hosts provide a lavish Pennsylvania farm breakfast served with china and silver in the kitchen or sun room. Highland Lake is 500 yards away, for canoeing or swimming.
Rates: $50-$65.
Mary S. & William W. Zeller, M.D.
4 Rooms. 1 Private Bath. 1 Fireplace. Guest phone available. TV in room. Beds: DTC. Full breakfast. Handicap access. Horseback riding, skiing, cross-country skiing, water skiing, miniature golf, swimming, fishing. Antique shops, craft sales, bazaars.
Seen in: *The Bridgton News, Down East Magazine.*

"The accommodations and our hosts were wonderful and very hospitable. The friendly atmosphere is charming and reminds us of the villages of England."

Noble House

PO Box 180
Bridgton ME 04009
(207) 647-3733

Circa 1903. This inn is tucked among three acres of old oaks and a

grove of pine trees, providing an estate-like view from all guest rooms. The elegant parlor contains a library, grand piano and hearth. Bed chambers are furnished with antiques, wicker and quilts. A hammock placed at the water's edge provides a view of the lake and Mt. Washington. The inn's lake frontage also allows for canoeing at sunset and swimming.
Location: Forty miles northwest of Portland.
Rates: $75-$130. Season: June to Oct. 15.
The Starets Family.
10 Rooms. 7 Private Baths. Guest phone available. TV available. Beds: QDT. Full breakfast. Jacuzzi. CCs: MC VISA AX. Golf, tennis, horseback riding, fishing, hiking, boating.

Brunswick

The Bagley House

See: Freeport, ME

Brunswick B&B

165 Park Row
Brunswick ME 04011
(207) 729-4914

Circa 1860. This completely restored Greek Revival home overlooks the park in the Brunswick Historic District. The inn features twin front parlors with park views. A tasteful collection of antiques fill the rooms. In 1987 the inn was a Christmas show house for American University Women. A separate guest house apartment featuring brick floors and skylights is available. Bowdoin College is two blocks

away. L.L. Bean and Freeport are within a ten minute drive.
Rates: $60-$70.
Travis B. & Nancy Keltner.
5 Rooms. 3 Private Baths. 3 Fireplaces. Guest phone available. TV available. Beds: DT. Full breakfast. Water sports, golf, cross-country skiing.

Harriet Beecher Stowe House

63 Federal St
Brunswick ME 04011
(207) 725-5543

Circa 1807. Built during the Federal Period, Henry Wadsworth Longfellow boarded here while he

attended nearby Bowdoin College. Frequent visitors were Nathaniel Hawthorne and Franklin Pierce. Later Calvin Stowe and his wife Harriet Beecher Stowe lived here while Mrs. Stowe wrote Uncle Tom's Cabin - said to be the book that started the Civil War. During the house's Victorian era, marble fireplaces and Victorian ornamentation were added. It is a designated National Historical Landmark. There is a modern motel on the property, so be sure and request rooms in the main house.
Bob & Peggy Mathews.
48 Rooms. 48 Private Baths. Guest phone in room. TV in room. Beds: DC. EP. Restaurant. Handicap access. Conference room. CCs: MC VISA AX DC CB. Water sports, golf, tennis.

Bucksport

The Old Parsonage Inn

PO Box 1577, 190 Franklin St
Bucksport ME 04416
(207) 469-6477

Circa 1800. The inn was built as a federal style, double house with front entrances on the gable ends. The rooms and winding staircases on either side are mirror images. The third floor was originally a meeting hall. The bowed ceiling and

built-in benches remain. The local Masonic lodge held their first meeting here in 1809. Eight fireplaces, two with beehive ovens, remain, along with wide board wainscotting, pine floors and cornices.
Rates: $35-$50.
Brian & Judith Clough.
3 Rooms. 1 Private Bath. Guest phone available. TV available. Beds: DT. Full breakfast. CCs: MC VISA. Boating, fishing, Acadia National Park, Penobscot Bay.
Seen in: *Maine Times, Bucksport Free Press.*

"Your kindness, great food, and beautiful location gave us a favorable opinion of bed and breakfasts in general."

Camden

Blackberry Inn

82 Elm St
Camden ME 04843
(207) 236-6060

Circa 1860. The exterior of this elaborate Italianate Victorian-style home is highlighted by contrasting shades of Blackberry Purple outlining its bays and friezes. The interiors are lavished with elaborate plaster ceiling designs, polished parquet floors, finely crafted fireplace mantels, and original tin ceilings. A collection of antique Bar Harbor wicker fills the Morning Parlor, once enjoyed by Bette Davis when she visited the inn when it was known as Broadlawn. Most guest rooms have views of Mt. Battie.
Rates: $50-$100.
Vicki & Ed Doudera.
8 Rooms. 3 Private Baths. 1 Fireplace. Guest phone available. Beds: QDT. B&B. CCs: MC VISA. Horseback riding, golf, cross-country & downhill skiing, sailing, swimming, shopping.
Seen in: *The Miami Herald, Daughters of Painted Ladies.*

"Charming. An authentic reflection of a grander time."

Blue Harbor House

67 Elm St, Rt 1
Camden ME 04843
(207) 236-3196

Circa 1835. James Richards, Camden's first settler, built this Cape house on a 1768 homesite.

(The King granted him the land as the first person to fulfill all the conditions of a settler.) An 1806 carriage house has been refurbished to offer private suites. The bustling harbor is a five-minute walk away.
Location: Camden Village.
Rates: $50-$110.
Jody Schmoll & Dennis Hayed.
6 Rooms. 4 Private Baths. Beds: QD. Full breakfast. CCs: MC. Sailing, fishing, swimming, hiking, horseback riding, golf, bikes.

Camden Harbour Inn

83 Bayview St
Camden ME 04843
(207) 236-4200

Circa 1874. This inn was first visited by steamship passengers as a

stop from Boston to Bangor. Guests were picked up by the inn's horse-drawn carriages and driven along the harbor's edge, through the village and up the hill to the inn. There they were delighted by the spectacular panoramic views of both harbor and mountains.

Location: Mid-coast of Maine, Penobscot Bay.
Rates: $145-$185.
Sal Vella & Patti Babij.
22 Rooms. 22 Private Baths. 8 Fireplaces. Guest phone available. TV available. Beds: QDT. Full breakfast. Restaurant. Handicap access. Conference room. CCs: MC VISA AX.
Seen in: *Chicago Tribune, Travel & Leisure, Glamour Magazine.*

"One of the six best seafood restaurants on the Maine Coast." Yankee Magazine.

Edgecombe-Coles House

64 High St, HCR 60 Box 3010
Camden ME 04843
(207) 236-2336

Circa 1830. Admiring the view of Penobscot Bay, Chicago lawyer Chauncey Keep built this house on

the foundation of a sea captain's house. By 1900, his 22-room cottage was too small and he built a 50-room mansion up the hill, retaining this as a guest house. Country antiques set the tone and many rooms command a spectacular ocean view.
Location: North of Camden Harbor on Highway 1.
Rates: $75-$145.
Terry & Louise Price.
6 Rooms. 6 Private Baths. 1 Fireplace. Guest phone available. Beds: KQDT. Full breakfast. CCs: MC VISA DC. Skiing, mountain climbing, fishing, sailing, hiking, tennis, golf.
Seen in: *Uncommon Lodgings.*

"A beautiful view, beautiful decor and a lovely hostess make this a very special place." Shelby Hodge, *Houston Post.*

The Elms

84 Elm St, Rt 1
Camden ME 04843
(207) 236-6250

Circa 1806. Captain Calvin Curtis built this Colonial a few minutes stroll from the picturesque harbor. Candlelight shimmers year round from the inn's windows. A sitting room, library, and parlor are open for guests and tastefully appointed bed chambers scattered with antiques are available in both the main house and the carriage house.
Rates: $65-$85.
Joan A. James.
6 Rooms. 3 Private Baths. 2 Fireplaces. Guest phone available. Beds: D. Full breakfast. Sailing, skiing, hiking, tennis, golf.

"The warmth of your home is only exceeded by the warmth of yourself."

Hawthorn Inn

9 High St
Camden ME 04843
(207) 236-8842

Circa 1894. This yellow and white, towered Victorian sits on a green lawn set against a backdrop of woods near the harbor. The spacious grounds offer many water views. A carriage house boasts private decks, jacuzzis and apartments. There are additional rooms in the main house. The English hostess serves afternoon tea and biscuits in the drawing room.
*Rates: $55-$125.
Pauline & Brad Staub.
11 Rooms. 5 Private Baths. 3 Fireplaces. Guest phone available. TV in room. Beds: DTWC. B&B. Jacuzzi. Conference room. CCs: MC VISA. Sailing, boating, skiing, cycling, outdoor theater, photo workshop, boat building. Wedding packages during the off season.

Maine Stay B&B

22 High St
Camden ME 04843
(207) 236-9636

Circa 1802. Listed in the National Register of Historic Places, this

treasured Colonial is one of the oldest of the 66 houses which comprise High Street Historic District. The inn's antiques include interesting pieces from the 17th, 18th, and 19th century. It is a short five-minute walk down High Street to the center of the village and the Camden Harbor. The innkeeper is known for his down-east stories told in a heavy down-east accent.
Rates: $74-$86.
Peter & Donny Smith and Diana Robson.
8 Rooms. 2 Private Baths. Guest phone available. TV available. Beds: QDT. B&B. Conference room. CCs: MC VISA. Sailing, windsurfing, skiing, tennis, golf, hiking, swimming, biking, whale watching.
Seen in: *The Miami Herald, Lewiston Sun-Journal, Waterville Sentinel.*

"Everything was delicious, beautifully served with a smile, a story and a bit of wit!"

Northport House B&B

See: Belfast, ME

Center Lovell

Center Lovell Inn

Rt 5
Center Lovell ME 04016
(207) 925-1575

Circa 1805. A wraparound porch connects the original farmhouse with a Cape-style annex added in

1830. Governor of Florida, Eckley Stearns, transformed this house into its present Mississippi steamboat style with the addition of a mansard roof and third floor. Acclaimed by *Architectural Digest*, the inn overlooks Kezar Lake Valley with a panoramic view of the White Mountains.
Location: Western Maine mountains along the New Hampshire border.
*Rates: $42-$145. Season: May - Oct.
Bil & Susie Mosca.
11 Rooms. 7 Private Baths. Guest phone available. TV available. Beds: DT. EP. Jacuzzi. Swimming pool. Conference room. CCs: MC VISA. Horseback riding, golf, hiking, canoeing, kayaking.
Seen in: *New York Magazine, Architectural Digest.*

"Finest food I have ever eaten in 40 states and 30 countries, located in one of the most beautiful areas anywhere."

Clark Island

Craignair Inn
Clark Island Rd
Clark Island ME 04859
(207) 594-7644

Circa 1930. Craignair originally was built to house stonecutters

working in nearby granite quarries. Overlooking the docks of the Clark Island Quarry, where granite schooners once were loaded, this roomy, three-story inn is tastefully decorated with local antiques.

Rates: $63-$80. Season: March - Dec.
Norman & Terry Smith.
16 Rooms. 5 Private Baths. Guest phone available. Beds: DTC. Full breakfast. Restaurant. Handicap access. CCs: MC VISA DS. Tennis, horseback riding, sailing, skiing, water sports, boating, fishing.
Seen in: *Boston Globe, Free Press.*

"We thoroughly enjoyed our stay with you. Your location is lovely and private. Your dining room and service and food were all 5 star!"

Damariscotta

The Brannon Bunker
PO Box 045, HCR 64
Damariscotta ME 04543
(207) 563-5941

Circa 1820. This Cape-style house has been a home to many genera-

tions of Maine residents, one of whom was captain of a ship that sailed to the Arctic. During the Twenties, the barn served as a dance hall. Later, it was converted into comfortable guest rooms.

*Rates: $45-$55.
Joe & Jeanne Hovance.
8 Rooms. 5 Private Baths. Guest phone available. TV available. Beds: QDTC. B&B. Handicap access. CCs: MC VISA. Bicycling, fishing, golf, hiking, hay rides, hunting, fishing, sailing, cross-country skiing, sleigh rides, tennis.
Seen in: *The Times-Beacon Newspaper.*

"Wonderful beds, your gracious hospitality and the very best muffins anywhere made our stay a memorable one."

Deer Isle Village

Laphroaig B&B
Rte 15, PO Box 67
Deer Isle Village ME 04627
(207) 348-6088

Circa 1854. Laphroaig (la froyg) is Scottish for the beautiful hollow by

the broad bay, which describes the inn's location overlooking Penobscot Bay. The inn is known locally as "Doc's house" for Dr. Kopfmann who lived here for 40 years while serving as the island's medical officer, often making house calls by boat. Collections of glass slippers, miniature pitchers and dolls are displayed throughout. Rooms with Virginia antiques can also be found. A Cheney chair lift is available for handicapped guests.

Rates: $68.
John & Andrea Maberry.
2 Rooms. 2 Private Baths. Guest phone available. TV in room. Beds: QD. B&B. Gourmet meals. Cross-country skiing, golf, tennis, swimming, hiking, sailing.
Seen in: *The American Staff.*

"An unexpected delight, good rest, delicious food and genuine hospitality - to a Southern boy, that means a lot."

Dennysville

Lincoln House Country Inn
Rts 1 & 86
Dennysville ME 04628
(207) 726-3953

Circa 1787. Theodore Lincoln, ancestor of Abraham Lincoln and son

of Benjamin Lincoln, who accepted the sword of surrender from Cornwallis after the American Revolution, built this house. The four-square colonial looks out to the Dennys River and its salmon pools. John James Audubon stayed here on his way to Labrador. He loved the house and family so much that he named the Lincoln Sparrow in their honor.

Rates: $58-$140. Season: May - October.
Mary & Jerry Haggerty.
6 Rooms. 2 Fireplaces. Guest phone available. Beds: QDT. MAP. Restaurant. Conference room. CCs: MC VISA. Bird watching, hiking, fishing, boating, cross-country skiing.
Seen in: *Good Housekeeping, Washington Post.*

"The food was delicious, the ambiance special.

Eastport

Todd House
Todd's Head
Eastport ME 04631
(207) 853-2328

Circa 1775. Todd House is a typical full Cape with a huge center chimney. In 1801, Eastern Lodge No. 7 of the Masonic Order was chartered here. It became a temporary barracks when Todd's Head was fortified. Guests may use barbecue facilities overlooking Passamaquoddy Bay.

Rates: $35-$75.
Ruth McInnis.
6 Rooms. 2 Private Baths. 3 Fireplaces. Guest phone available. TV in room. Beds: QDT. Continental-plus breakfast. Handicap access. Boat rides, whale watching.
Seen in: *Portland Press Herald.*

"Your house and hospitality were real memory makers of our vacation."

Weston House

26 Boynton St
Eastport ME 04631
(207) 853-2907

Circa 1810. Jonathan Weston, an 1802 Harvard graduate, built this

Federal-style house on a hill overlooking Passamaquoddy Bay. John Audubon stayed here as a guest of the Westons while awaiting passage to Labrador in 1833.
Rates: $40-$60.
John & Jett Peterson.
5 Rooms. Guest phone available. Beds: KQT. Full breakfast. Conference room. Fishing, golf, hiking, bicycling, boating.
Seen in: *Downeast Magazine, Los Angeles Times.*

"The most memorable bed and breakfast experience we have ever had."

Eliot

High Meadows B&B

Rt 101
Eliot ME 03903
(207) 439-0590

Circa 1736. A ship's captain built this house, now filled with remembrances of colonial days. At

one point, it was raised and a floor added underneath, so the upstairs is older than the downstairs. It is conveniently located to factory outlets in Kittery, Maine, and great dining and historic museums in Portsmouth, NH.
Rates: $50-$60. Season: April - Dec. 31.
Elaine Raymond.
5 Rooms. 3 Private Baths. Guest phone available. TV available. Beds: QDTW. Continental-plus breakfast. Conference room. Golf, tennis, whale watching.

"High Meadows was the highlight of our trip."

Ellsworth

The Old Parsonage Inn

See: Bucksport, ME

Freeport

The Bagley House

RR 3 Box 269C
Freeport ME 04032
(207) 865-6566

Circa 1772. Six acres of fields and woods surround the Bagley House,

once an inn, a store, and a schoolhouse. Guest rooms are decorated with colonial furnishings and handsewn Maine quilts. Many boast working fireplaces. For breakfast, guests gather in the country kitchen in front of a huge brick fireplace and beehive oven.
Location: Route 136, Durham.
*Rates: $55-$85.
Sigurd A. Knudsen, Jr.
5 Rooms. 3 Private Baths. 1 Fireplace. Guest phone available. Beds: QDF. B&B. Conference room. CCs: MC VISA AX. Cross-country skiing, hiking, croquet.
Seen in: *Los Angeles Times, New England Getaways.*

"I had the good fortune to stumble on the Bagley House. The rooms are well appointed and the new innkeeper is as charming a host as you'll find."

Captain Josiah Mitchell House

188 Main St
Freeport ME 04032
(207) 865-3289

Circa 1779. Captain Josiah Mitchell was commander of the clipper ship Hornet, which sailed in the 1800s. In 1865, en route from New York to San Francisco it caught fire, burned and was lost. The passengers and crew survived in three longboats, drifting for 45 days. It is the longest recorded survival at sea in an open boat. When the boats finally drifted into one of the South Pacific Islands, Mark Twain was there. He befriended the Captain and both sailed back to the Mainland together. The diary of Captain Mitchell parallels episodes of *Mutiny on the Bounty.* Flower gardens and a porch swing on the veranda now welcome guests to Freeport and the Captain's House.
*Rates: $68 & up.
Alan & Loretta Bradley.
7 Rooms. 7 Private Baths. Guest phone available. TV in room. Beds: DT. Full breakfast. Jacuzzi. CCs: MC VISA.

Fairhaven Inn

See: Bath, ME

Harraseeket Inn

162 Main St
Freeport ME 04032
(207) 865-9377

Circa 1850. The tavern and drawing room of this inn are decorated

in the Federal style. Guest rooms are furnished with antiques and half-canopied beds. Some have whirlpools and fireplaces. The L.L. Bean store is just two blocks away, with other outlet stores nearby, such as Ralph Lauren, Laura Ashley and Anne Klein.
*Rates: $85-$165.
Paul & Nancy Gray.
54 Rooms. 54 Private Baths. 16 Fireplaces. Guest phone in room. TV in room. Beds: KQD. EP. Restaurant. Gourmet meals. Jacuzzi. Handicap access. Conference room. CCs: MC VISA AX DC DS. Boating, fishing, golf, tennis, hiking, skiing.
Seen in: *Village Bed & Breakfast.*

Isaac Randall House

Independence Drive
Freeport ME 04032
(207) 865-9295

Circa 1823. Isaac Randall's Federal-style farmhouse was once a dairy farm and a stop on the Underground Railway for slaves escaping into Canada. Randall was a descendant of John Alden and Priscilla Mullins of the *Mayflower*. Longfellow immortalized their romance in *The Courtship of Miles Standish*.
Rates: $50-$85. Season: May - Oct. 31.
Jim & Glyn Friedlander.
8 Rooms. 6 Private Baths. Guest phone available. Beds: KQC. Full breakfast. Jacuzzi. Handicap access. Conference room. Cross-country skiing, hiking.

"Enchanted to find ourselves surrounded by all your charming antiques and beautiful furnishings."

Greenville

Greenville Inn

Norris St, PO Box 1194
Greenville ME 04441
(207) 695-2206

Circa 1895. The Greenville Inn sits on a hill, one block from town. It's

also one block from the shore line of Moosehead Lake, the largest lake completely contained in any one state. A wealthy lumbering family built the house. Ten years were needed to complete the cherry and mahogany paneling. There are six fireplaces with carved mantels and mosaics. From the dining room, guests have an excellent water view.

Location: Moosehead Lake.
Rates: $55-$75.
The Schnetzer's.
10 Rooms. 6 Private Baths. 2 Fireplaces. Guest phone available. TV available. Beds: KQDT. EP. Restaurant. Gourmet meals. Handicap access. Game room. Conference room. CCs: MC VISA DS. Cross-country & downhill skiing, boating, hunting, fishing, white-water rafting.
Seen in: *Maine Times, Portland Monthly Magazine.*

"The fanciest place in town."

Harpswell

Lookout Point House

141 Lookout Point Rd
Harpswell ME 04079
(207) 833-5509

Circa 1761. Once a cookhouse for the Lookout Point shipyards that flourished during the Civil War, this three-story inn is situated on the ocean overlooking Casca Bay. An old bell atop the house rings to inform guests when breakfast is ready. The same bell was used in the 1860s to call local shipbuilders to their meals. Bowdoin College is nearby.
Location: Eight miles from Brunswick.
*Rates: $55-$90.
Marilyn & Alden Sewall.
13 Rooms. 2 Private Baths. 3 Fireplaces. Guest phone available. TV available. Beds: KQDT. Full breakfast. Conference room. CCs: MC VISA. Walking trails, seal watching, antiquing, lobstering.

"A gracious, luxurious home in a most wonderful setting."

Isle Au Haut

The Keeper's House

PO Box 26
Isle Au Haut ME 04645
(207) 367-2261

Circa 1907. Designed and built by the U.S. Lighthouse Service, the

handsome 48-foot high Robinson Point Light guided vessels into this once bustling island fishing village. Guests arrive on the 11 a.m. mailboat. Innkeeper Judi Burke, whose father was a keeper at the Highland lighthouse on Cape Cod, provides picnic lunches so guests may explore the scenic island trails. Dinner is served in the keeper's dining room. The lighthouse is adjacent to the most remote section of Acadia National Park. It's not uncommon to hear the cry of an osprey, see deer approach the inn, or seals and porpoises cavorting off the point. Guest rooms are comfortable and serene, with stunning views of the island's ragged shore line, forests and Duck Harbor.
Rates: $205. Season: May - Oct. 31.
Jeff & Judi Burke.
5 Rooms. 3 Fireplaces. Beds: D. AP. Hiking.

"Simply one of the unique places on Earth."

Kennebunk Beach

Sundial Inn

PO Box 1147
Kennebunk Beach ME 04043
(207) 967-3850

Circa 1891. This yellow and white clapboard house faces the ocean and

Kennebunk Beach. The inn is decorated with country Victorian antiques, and some rooms have a whirlpool bath. An elevator makes for easy access. Beachcombing for sand dollars, sea shells and sea urchins is a popular pastime, along with enjoying splendid views from the porch rockers and guest rooms.
Location: Beach Avenue #48.
Rates: $60-$170.
Pat & Larry Kenny.
34 Rooms. 34 Private Baths. Guest phone in room. TV in room. Beds: KQT. B&B. Jacuzzi. Handicap access. Conference room. CCs: MC VISA AX DC CB.
Seen in: *New England Travel.*

" My time on your porch watching the sea was the best part of my vacation. Whenever I am stressed I wander back in my mind to a day at the Sundial where I found such inner peace."

Kennebunkport

1802 House

Box 646A Locke St
Kennebunkport ME 04046
(207) 967-5632

Circa 1802. Many of the guest rooms in the 1802 House possess private fireplaces. All are decorated with colonial wallpaper and antiques, such as four-poster beds. The ringing of a ship's bell announces breakfast. Guests dine overlooking a golf course next to the inn. Water sports, fall foliage, cross-country skiing and the Seashore Trolley Museum are all popular attractions.

*Rates: $80-$115.
Pat Ledda.
6 Rooms. 6 Private Baths. 2 Fireplaces. TV available. Beds: QTD. EP. CCs: MC VISA AX. Golf, tennis, cross-country skiing, hiking, boating.

Captain Lord Mansion

Pleasant & Green, PO Box 800
Kennebunkport ME 04046
(207) 967-3141

Circa 1812. In the National Register, the Captain Lord Mansion was built during the War of 1812,

and is one of the finest examples of Federal architecture on the coast of Maine. A four-story spiral staircase winds up to the cupola where one can view the town and the Kennebunk River and Yacht Club. At one time, there was a street entrance so villagers could climb the stairs to view inbound ships without bothering the family. Thirteen rooms have fireplaces and there's a cottage with a fireplace in the bathroom.

Rates: $59-$79.
Bev Davis & Rick Litchfield.
18 Rooms. 18 Private Baths. Beds: K Full breakfast. Jacuzzi. Conference room. CCs: MC VISA DS. Cross Country Skiing, Cruises, Sailing, Beaches
Seen in: *AAA, Colonial Homes, Yankee, New England Get Aways.*

"A showcase of elegant architecture, with lovely remembrances of the past. Meticulously clean and splendidly appointed. It's a shame to have to leave."

The Inn at Harbor Head

Pier Rd, RFD #2 Box 1180
Kennebunkport ME 04046
(207) 967-5564

Circa 1890. This rambling, shingled saltwater farmhouse is right on the

water in historic Cape Porpoise - the quiet side of Kennebunkport. Elegantly restored, the inn offers outstanding views of the harbor, ocean and islands. Ancient apple trees shield the inn from the road affording visitors tranquil privacy. A back terrace leads guests down to the seashore.

Location: On the rocky shore of Cape Porpoise Harbor.
Rates: $95-$160.
Joan & David Sutter.
4 Rooms. 4 Private Baths. Guest phone available. Beds: KQT. Full breakfast. Gourmet meals. Jacuzzi. CCs: MC VISA DS. Swimming, beach, horseback riding, golf, boat cruises all nearby.
Seen in: *The Boston Globe, Country Inns.*

"Your lovely home is our image of what a New England B&B should be. Unbelievably perfect!"

Harbor Inn

PO Box 538A
Kennebunkport ME 04046
(207) 967-2074

Circa 1903. Tucked behind a white iron Victorian fence is the Harbor

Inn. A yellow canopy covers the stairs leading to the veranda. There, you can hear the quiet purring of fishing boats or smell the fresh, sea air. Guest rooms are furnished with canopied or four-poster beds, period lighting, oriental rugs, and antique coverlets. The inn's kitchen has blue iris stained-glass windows and an old wood stove set on a brick hearth. Just past the inn, where the Kennebunk River runs to the sea, are Spouting Rock and Blowing Cave.

Rates: $75-$120. Season: May 15-Nov. 1.
Charlotte & Bill Massmann.
8 Rooms. 8 Private Baths. Guest phone available. TV available. Beds: QDT. Full breakfast. Horseback riding, golf, tennis, biking, boating, fishing, water sports.
Seen in: *Country Inns, Yankee Travel Guide.*

"Everything is beautifully done. It's the best we've ever been to."

Kylemere House 1818

South Street, PO Box 1333
Kennebunkport ME 04046
(207) 967-2780

Circa 1818. Located in Maine's largest historic district, Kylemere

House was built by Daniel Walker, descendant of an original Kennebunkport family. In 1895, Maine artist and architect Abbot Graves purchased the property, using the barn as his studio. He named the house Crosstrees for the husband and wife maple trees planted on either side of the front door. Today, only one maple remains.

Rates: $60-$85. Season: May - Dec.
Mary & Bill Kyle.
5 Rooms. 3 Private Baths. 1 Fireplace. Guest phone available. Beds: KQT. Full breakfast. CCs: AX. Water sports, bicycling, hiking, tennis, golf.
Seen in: *Boston Globe.*

"Beautiful inn. Outstanding hospitality. Thanks for drying our sneakers, fixing our bikes. You are all a lot of fun!"

Maine Stay Inn and Cottages

Maine St, PO Box 500A
Kennebunkport ME 04046
(207) 967-2117

Circa 1860. In the National Register, this is a square-block Italianate contoured in a low hip-

roof design. Later additions of the Queen Anne period include a suspended spiral staircase, crystal windows, ornately carved mantels and moldings, bay windows and porches. A sea captain built the handsome cupola that became a favorite spot for making taffy. In the Twenties, the cupola was a place from which to spot offshore rum-runners. Guests enjoy afternoon tea with stories of the Maine Stay's heritage.

Location: In the Kennebunkport National Historic District.
*Rates: $85-$150.
Lindsay & Carol Copeland.
17 Rooms. 17 Private Baths. 1 Fireplace. Guest phone available. TV in room. Beds: QDTC. B&B. Handicap access. Conference room. CCs: MC VISA AX. Beaches, golf.

"Beautifully decorated home. Clean, clean accommodations, cute cottages."

Morning Dove B&B

See: Ogunquit, ME

Old Fort Inn

Old Fort Ave, PO Box M 24
Kennebunkport ME 04046
(207) 967-5353

Circa 1880. The Old Fort Inn is a luxurious mini-resort nestled in a secluded setting with an English garden. It has a tennis court, fresh-water swimming pool and shuffleboard. Bikes are also available. Country furniture, primitives, and china are featured in an antique shop on the property. The ocean is just a block away.

Rates: $90-$195. Season: April-Oct.
Sheila & David Aldrich.

16 Rooms. 16 Private Baths. Guest phone available. Beds: KQT. Full breakfast. Jacuzzi. CCs: MC VISA DS. Bicycling, swimming, golf.
Seen in: *Country Inns.*

"My husband and I have been spending the last two weeks in August at the Old Fort Inn for years. It combines for us a rich variety of what we feel a relaxing vacation should be."

Port Gallery Inn

PO Box 1367
Kennebunkport ME 04046
(207) 967-3728

Circa 1891. This Victorian mansion was given to Captain Titcomb,

builder of the largest ships on the Kennebunk River. Kennebunkport, summer home of the rich and famous, is in the National Register of Historical Places featuring 26 different architectural styles. The inn's Marine Art Gallery specializes in paintings of old seafaring days.

Location: Corner of Spring & Main Streets.
*Rates: $98-$149.
Francis & Lucy Morphy.
7 Rooms. 7 Private Baths. Beds: QD. Continental breakfast. CCs: MC VISA DC. Golf, tennis, hiking, canoeing, bicycling.
Seen in: *The Globe Pequot Press, Colonial Homes.*

The Inn on South Street

PO Box 478A, South St
Kennebunkport ME 04046
(207) 967-5151

Circa 1807. Built in the Greek Revival style, the inn now stands on a quiet side street. It was towed here by oxen from its original location on the village green, after a wealthy citizen complained that it was cutting off her river view. The inn boasts a handsome 'good-morning' staircase, original pine-plank floors, hand-planed wainscoting and an old-fashioned herb garden.

*Rates: $75-$110.
Jacques & Eva Downs.
4 Rooms. 4 Private Baths. 3 Fireplaces. Guest phone available. Beds: DT. B&B. Jacuzzi. Conference room. CCs: AX. Water sports, hiking, bicycling, walking.
Seen in: *Summertime.*

"Superb hospitality. We were delighted by the atmosphere and your thoughtfulness."

The Welby Inn

Ocean Ave, PO Box 774
Kennebunkport ME 04046
(207) 967-4655

Circa 1900. The Welby Inn possesses a gambrel-style roof and a large common room with a country motif. The innkeeper's watercolors of flowers and her floral arrangements decorate the interiors. Breakfast is served in the dining room or on the adjoining sun porch. It is a five-minute walk to the ocean, galleries and fine restaurants.

Rates: $75-$90.
The Knox family, Betsy, David & Jessica.
7 Rooms. 7 Private Baths. Guest phone available. Beds: QTF. Full breakfast. Conference room. Golf, tennis, bicycling, fishing, whale watching.

"I'm glad we found this place before Gourmet Magazine *discovers it and the rates increase!"*

The White Barn Inn

Beach St, RR 3 Box 387
Kennebunkport ME 04046
(207) 967-2321

Circa 1810. Over the past 150 years, various owners have added onto this farmhouse and its signa-

ture white barn. Each addition to

the rambling grey structure has been distinctive. Stately Queen Anne furnishings, soft down sofas, bright floral prints, and country tweeds decorate the suites. There are four-posters and whirlpool tubs in some rooms. Candlelight dining is popular in the three-story barn.
Location: South of Portland 1/2 hour, I-95 1-1/2 hour North of Boston.
*Rates: $85-$220.
Laurie Bongiorno & Carole Hackett.
24 Rooms. 24 Private Baths. 7 Fireplaces. Guest phone in room. TV in room. Beds: KQDT. MAP. Restaurant. Gourmet meals. Jacuzzi. Conference room. CCs: MC VISA AX. Golf, tennis, cross-country & downhill skiing, beach, sailing, fishing.
Seen in: *Colonial Homes, U.S.A. Today.*

"It is clear you are in the business of very fine hospitality and we appreciated the warm welcome we received from you and your staff."

Kingfield

Herbert Inn
PO Box 67
Kingfield ME 04947
(800) 533-INNS (207)265-2000

Circa 1915. This three-story Beaux-Arts style hotel with terrazzo marble floors was built by Maine legislator Herbert Wing. A sink remaining on the dining room wall once provided stagecoach patrons a place to wash up before dining. Finely crafted oak paneling adorns the lobby. A moosehead is the focal point above the fireplace. Simply furnished rooms are equipped with jacuzzis or steam baths.
*Rates: $77-$90.
Bud Dick, Sue & Faye
31 Rooms. 31 Private Baths. Guest phone available. TV available. Beds: QDTC. MAP. Restaurant. Gourmet meals. Jacuzzi. Sauna. Conference room. CCs: MC VISA AX DC CB DS. Hiking, golf, white water rafting, canoeing, fishing. Sugarloaf/USA skiing 20 minutes away.
Seen in: *New England Monthly.*

The Inn on Winter's Inn
Box 587
Kingfield ME 04947
(207) 265-5421

Circa 1898. The twin Stanley brothers (Stanley Steamer) designed this house on a lazy summer after-

noon. Their creative genius resulted in an exciting example of Georgian Revival architecture, now restored to its original beauty. Today, it houses Julia's Restaurant which specializes in New England cuisine and 15 guest rooms. There is a lighted skating rink and shuttle service to and from Sugarloaf USA.
Rates: $120+.
Diane Winnick.
15 Rooms. 15 Private Baths. Guest phone in room. TV in room. Beds: QDC. EP. Restaurant. Jacuzzi. Handicap access. Swimming pool. Conference room. CCs: MC VISA AX DS. Golf, white water rafting, canoeing, downhill & cross-country skiing, ice skating.
Seen in: *The Franklin Journal.*

Lewiston/Auburn

The Bagley House
See: Freeport, ME

Naples

The Augustus Bove House
RR 1 Box 501
Naples ME 04055
(207) 693-6365

Circa 1856. A long front lawn nestles up against the stone founda-

tion and veranda of this house, once known as the Hotel Naples, one of the area's summer hotels in the 1800s. The guest rooms are decorated in a colonial style with antiques and wallpapers. Many rooms provide a view of Long Lake. A fancy country breakfast is provided.
Rates: $49-$75.
David & Arlene Stetson.
12 Rooms. 5 Private Baths. 1 Fireplace. Guest phone available. TV available. Beds: KQDTC. EP. CCs: MC VISA AX. Hiking, canoeing, fishing, cycling, swimming, golf, horseback riding, theaters, boating, cross-country & downhill skiing, ice fishing, skating, sliding.
Seen in: *Brighton Times.*

"Beautiful place, rooms, and people."

The Inn at Long Lake
Lake House Rd, PO Box 806
Naples ME 04055
(207) 693-6226

Circa 1906. This recently reopened inn housed the overflow guests

from the Lake House Resort 80 years ago. Guests traveled to the resort via the Oxford-Cumberland Canal. Each room is named for a historic canal boat and is decorated to match.
Rates: $70-$75. Season: Closed March.
Terry & Bob Denner.
16 Rooms. 16 Private Baths. 1 Fireplace. Guest phone available. TV in room. Beds: QDT. Continental-plus breakfast. CCs: MC VISA AX. Golf, water skiing, boating, bicycling, cross-country skiing.
Seen in: *The Bridgton News.*

"Convenient location, tastefully done and the prettiest inn I've ever stayed in."

New Harbor

Gosnold Arms
Northside Rd, Rt 32
New Harbor ME 04554
(207) 677-3727

Circa 1870. This remodeled, sparkling-white saltwater farmhouse has

a steamboat wharf and a glassed-in dining porch overlooking the water. A Smith College dorm mother assembled several cottages in addition

to the rooms in the house, creating a congenial family atmosphere. One cottage is a rustic pilot house picked up, helm and all, from the top of a steamboat, and relocated bayside.
Rates: $110-$140. Season: May - Nov.
The Phinney family.
24 Rooms. 24 Private Baths. Guest phone available. Beds: QDTC. MAP. Conference room. CCs: MC VISA.
Seen in: *New York Magazine.*

Newcastle

The Newcastle Inn

River Rd
Newcastle ME 04553
(207) 563-5685

Circa 1860. The Newcastle Inn is a Federal-style colonial that has been

in operation since the early 1920s. Located on the Damariscotta River, the neighbors just behind the inn are 97 sailboats. Honeymooners like the room with the old-fashioned canopy bed, and many rooms look out over the water and the town. Breakfast consists of four courses, and there is a five-course dinner.
Location: Tidal Damariscotta River.
Rates: $80-$90.
Ted & Chris Sprague.
15 Rooms. 15 Private Baths. Guest phone available. Beds: KQT. MAP. Gourmet meals. CCs: MC VISA. Cross-country skiing, golf, bicycling, swimming, fishing.
Seen in: *Yankee Magazine, Coastal Journal, The Weekly Courier.*

"Standing ovation for the food, atmosphere and innkeepers!"

North Waterford

Olde Rowley Inn

Rt 35 N
North Waterford ME 04267
(207) 583-4143

Circa 1790. Two hundred years ago, settlers from Rowley, Massachusetts who had served together

in the French Revolution moved here. This farm belonged to one of those families. It later became a stagecoach stop and inn, and for over 100 years the Rice family served here as innkeepers. Recently restored, the inn offers pleasant and spacious guest rooms. The dining rooms are in the carriage house and barn.
Rates: $50-$65.
Brian & Meredith Thomas.
6 Rooms. 3 Private Baths. Guest phone available. Beds: D. Full breakfast. Restaurant. CCs: MC VISA AX. Skiing, horse-drawn sleigh and hay rides.

"Our accommodations were clean and neat. With your hospitality we felt very welcomed and at home."

Ogunquit

Morning Dove B&B

5 Bourne Ln, PO Box 1940
Ogunquit ME 03907
(207) 646-3891

Circa 1860. The Moses Littlefields lived in this three-story farmhouse for over 100 years and the family still retains the adjacent property. Renovated by Pete and Eeta Sachon, it is filled with carefully collected antiques and paintings by local artists. A Palladian window spreads sunlight around Grandma's Attic, a favorite room. Surrounded by bright and blooming gardens, the inn is a short stroll to beaches, restaurants and galleries.
*Rates: $55-$100.
Peter & Eeta Sachon.
8 Rooms. 4 Private Baths. Guest phone available. Beds: KQDT. B&B. Conference room. CCs: MC VISA AX. Bird watching, outlet malls.

Portland

The Bagley House

See: Freeport, ME

Harraseeket Inn

See: Freeport, ME

The Inn at Long Lake

See: Naples, ME

Pomegranate Inn

49 Neal St
Portland ME 04102
(207) 772-1006 (800)356-0408

Circa 1884. Known locally as the Barbour-Miliken house, this three-

story inn is furnished with a mix of contemporary and antiques. *Faux*-finished woodwork painted by the innkeeper's daughter includes mouldings, fireplace mantels and columns. Another local artist hand-painted the guest room walls. Two bathrooms contain Grecian marble.
Alan & Isabel Smiles
6 Rooms. 6 Private Baths. Guest phone in room. TV in room. Beds: QDT Continental-plus breakfast. Conference room. CCs: MC VISA AX.

Royal Brewster B&B

See: Bar Mills, ME

The White Barn Inn

See: Kennebunkport, ME

Portsmouth

The White Barn Inn

See: Kennebunkport, ME

Searsport

Homeport Inn

Rt 1 E Main St
Searsport ME 04974
(207) 548-2259

Circa 1863. Captain Joshua Nickels built this home on Penobscot Bay. On top of the two-story house is a

widow's walk. A scalloped picket fence frames the property. Fine antiques, black marble fireplaces, a collection of grandfather clocks and elaborate ceiling medallions add to the atmosphere.
*Rates: $60-$75.
Dr. & Mrs. F. George Johnson.
10 Rooms. 6 Private Baths. Guest phone available. TV available. Beds: QT. Full breakfast. Handicap access. CCs: MC VISA. Golf, sailing, cruises, bicycle rentals.
"Your breakfast is something we will never forget."

McGilvery House
PO Box 588
Searsport ME 04974
(207) 548-6289
Circa 1860. A prominent sea captain, William McGilvery, built this

handsome estate in the mansard domestic style, with a soaring center-gambrel gable. Guest rooms provide an excellent view of Penobscot Bay, and some feature ornate marble fireplaces.
*Rates: $55.
Sue Omness.
3 Rooms. 3 Private Baths. Guest phone available. Beds: Q. Continental breakfast. Boating, museums.
Seen in: *The Courier-Gazette.*
"It was a thrill being in your lovely home. Your personal touches are evident everywhere. The breakfasts are tops. We'll be back."

Southwest Harbor

The Island House
Box 1006
Southwest Harbor ME 04679
(207) 244-5180
Circa 1830. The first guests arrived at Deacon Clark's door as early as

1832. when steamboat service from Boston began in the 1850s. The Island House became a popular summer hotel. Among the guests was Ralph Waldo Emerson. In 1912, the hotel was taken down and rebuilt as two separate homes using much of the woodwork from the original building.
Location: Mount Desert Island (Acadia National Park).
Rates: $50-$60. Season: May - Oct. 31.
Ann R. Gill.
4 Rooms. 1 Private Bath. Guest phone available. TV available. Beds: QW. Continental-plus breakfast. Horseback riding, swimming, canoeing, sailing, cycling. Piano.
"Island House is a delight from the moment one enters the door! We loved the thoughtful extras. You've made our vacation very special!"

Kingsleigh Inn
PO Box 1426, 100 Main St
Southwest Harbor ME 04679
(207) 244-5302
Circa 1904. This seaside village has been home to fishermen and boatbuilders for generations. After stopping by the inn's country kitchen for lemonade, guests gravitate to the flower-filled veranda to watch the harbor waters. Waverly wall coverings and fabrics decorate the rooms. Book the Turret Suite with its spectacular harbor views and four-poster bed.
Rates: $55-$145. Season: May to Nov. 1.
Jim & Kathy King.
8 Rooms. 8 Private Baths. Beds: Q. Full breakfast. Horseback riding, canoeing, hiking, swimming, sailing.
Seen in: *McCall's.*
"Very romantic and wonderfully decorated. We'll always treasure our stay with you."

Lindenwood Inn
PO Box 1328
Southwest Harbor ME 04679
(207) 244-5335
Circa 1906. Sea Captain Mills named his home "The Lindens" after stately linden trees that line the front lawn. The cypress paneling retains its original finish and adorns the entrance and dining room. Gull's Nest and Casablanca are among the rooms overlooking the harbor.
Location: Mt. Desert Island.
Rates: $35-$75.
T. Gardiner, Marilyn & Matthew Brower.
7 Rooms. 3 Private Baths. Guest phone available. TV available. Beds: QDT. Full breakfast. Hiking, lake across the street.
"We had a lovely stay at your inn. Breakfast, room and hospitality were all first rate. You made us feel like a special friend instead of a paying guest."

Surry

Surry Inn
PO Box 25, Rte 172
Surry ME 04684
(207) 667-5091
Circa 1834. Surry inn was originally built for passengers traveling by steamship. The driveway is called Stagecoach Lane because the steamboat met the stage at the inn's private beach in Contention Cove. The inn features stenciled walls and New England decor. You won't need to leave the property for dinner. The inn is noted for its excellent cooking.
Rates: $62.
Peter Krinsky.
13 Rooms. 11 Private Baths. 3 Fireplaces. Guest phone available. TV available. Beds: DT. Full breakfast. Restaurant. Gourmet meals. Handicap access. Conference room. CCs: MC VISA. Boating, swimming, croquet.
Seen in: *Bar Harbor Times, Ellsworth American.*
"Wonderful food! Peaceful, quiet and comfortable."

Waldoboro

Broad Bay Inn & Gallery

Main St, PO Box 607
Waldoboro ME 04572
(207) 832-6668

Circa 1830. This colonial inn lies in the heart of an unspoiled coastal village. You'll find Victorian furnishings throughout and some guest rooms have canopy beds. Afternoon tea is served on the deck. An established art gallery displays works by renowned artists, as well as limited edition prints. Television, games and an art library are available in the common room.

✼❀Rates: $45-$70.
Jim & Libby Hopkins.
5 Rooms. 3 Private Baths. Guest phone available. TV available. Beds: FT. Full breakfast. Restaurant. CCs: MC VISA. Swimming, fishing, cross-country skiing, sleigh rides.

"Breakfast was so special - I ran to get my camera. Why, there were even flowers on my plate."

Waterford

Lake House

Rts 35 & 37
Waterford ME 04088
(207) 583-4182

Circa 1797. Situated on the common, the Lake House was first a hotel and stagecoach stop. In 1817, granite baths were constructed below the first floor. The inn opened as "Dr. Shattuck's Maine Hygienic Institute for Ladies." It continued as a popular health spa until the 1890s. Now noted for excellent country cuisine, there are two dining rooms, one for non-smokers. Four guest rooms are upstairs. The spacious Grand Ballroom Suite features curved ceilings, a sitting room and a canopy bed. Views of Lake Keoka are enjoyed from the inn's veranda.

Rates: $65-$89.
Suzanne & Michael Uhl-Myers
4 Rooms. 4 Private Baths. Guest phone available. Beds: DT. Full breakfast. Restaurant. CCs: MC VISA. Hiking, lake across the street.
Seen in: *Country Inns.*

Wiscasset

The Squire Tarbox Inn

RR 2 Box 620
Wiscasset ME 04578
(207) 882-7693

Circa 1765. North of Bath, deep into the country and woods, Squire Tarbox built his rambling farmhouse around a building originally constructed in 1763. Today, the rooms are warm and comfortable in the inn and in the remodeled hayloft. The innkeepers raise Nubian goats, all photogenic, that have become part of the entertainment (milking and goat cheese). A house-party atmosphere pervades the inn.

Location: Route 144, 8½ miles on Westport Island.
✼Rates: $110-$175. Season: May - Oct.
Bill & Karen Mitman.
11 Rooms. 11 Private Baths. 4 Fireplaces. Guest phone available. Beds: KQTD. AP. CCs: MC VISA. Sailing, fishing, sand dunes, ocean.
Seen in: *Washington Post, Hartford Courant.*

"Your hospitality was warm, friendly, well-managed and quite genuine. That's a rarity, and it's just the kind we feel best with."

York

Dockside Guest Quarters

PO Box 205, Harris Island
York ME 03909
(207) 363-2868

Circa 1885. Harris Island, the site of Dockside and its companion marina, was York's smallpox quarantine area in 1632. This Maine house is typical of the large, cottage-style New England summer homes. It sits on a peninsula overlooking York Harbor and the ocean. Antiques of museum quality are found throughout the inn. Guest accommodations occupy the main house and several newer cottages.

Location: Harris Island, Maine Rt. 103
✼Rates: $44-$105. Season: May - October.
The David Lusty family.
21 Rooms. 19 Private Baths. 1 Fireplace. Guest phone available. TV available. Beds: KQDTC. EP. Restaurant. Handicap access. Conference room. CCs: VISA DS. Deep sea fishing, tennis, golf.
Seen in: *Boston Globe.*

"We've been back many years – it's a paradise for us, the scenery, location, maintenance, living quarters,."

York Harbor

York Harbor Inn

Rt 1A Box 573
York Harbor ME 03911
(207) 363-5119

Circa 1637. The core building of the York Harbor Inn is a small log cabin constructed on the Isles of Shoals. Moved and reassembled at this dramatic location overlooking the entrance to York Harbor, the cabin is now a gathering room with a handsome stone fireplace. There is an English-style pub in the cellar with booths made from horse stalls.

✼Rates: $55-$89.
Joe, Jean, Garry & Nancy Dominguez.
32 Rooms. 27 Private Baths. 2 Fireplaces. Guest phone in room. TV available. Beds: DC. Restaurant. Gourmet meals. Jacuzzi. Handicap access. Conference room. CCs: MC VISA AX. Golf, tennis, boating, fishing, theater.
Seen in: *New York Times, Down East.*

"It's hard to decide where to stay when you're paging through a book of country inns. This time we chose well."

Maryland

Annapolis

Gibson's Lodgings

110-114 Prince George
Annapolis MD 21401
(301) 268-5555

Circa 1786. This Georgian house in the heart of the Annapolis Historic

District was built on the site of the Old Courthouse, circa 1680. Two historic houses make up the inn and there is an annex built in 1988. All the rooms, old and new, are furnished with antiques. Only a few yards away is the City Dock Harbor and within two blocks is the Naval Academy visitor's gate.

*Rates: $55-$120.
Holly Perdue.
20 Rooms. 7 Private Baths. Beds: QT. Continental breakfast. Conference room. CCs: MC VISA.

Historic Inns of Annapolis

16 Chruch Circle
Annapolis MD 21401
(301) 263-2641

Circa 1700. Five beautifully restored historic inns comprise Paul Pearson's Historic Inns of Annapolis: Robert Johnson House, State House, Maryland Inn, Reynolds Tavern and the Governor Calvert House. The Tavern, for instance, took seven years to restore. During that time, workers confirmed local legends that the tavern was once a center for smuggling and included a network of tunnels

extending to the Annapolis waterfront. Architectural styles include Victorian, Georgian and Colonial with furnishings of the same period. (The Maryland Inn has been in continuous operation for over 200 years.) There is also a new hotel attached to the State House.

*Rates: $85-$175.
William Burrurs, Jr.
141 Rooms. 141 Private Baths. Guest phone in room. TV in room. Beds: KQDTC. EP. Restaurant. Jacuzzi. Handicap access. Conference room. CCs: MC VISA AX DC. Swimming, sailing, power boat, all water sports.
Seen in: *Washingtonian, Historic Preservation, Boating.*

Prince George Inn

232 Prince George St
Annapolis MD 21401
(301) 263-6418

Circa 1884. The Prince George Inn is a three-story brick town house comfortably furnished with an emphasis on Victorian decor. The guest parlor, breakfast room, porch and courtyard offer areas for relaxing. In the heart of the colonial city, the inn is near restaurants, museums, shops, and the City Dock. The Naval Academy is two blocks away. Your

hostess operates a walking-tour service.

Location: Historic District of Annapolis.
*Rates: $75.
Bill & Norma Grovermann.
4 Rooms. Guest phone available. TV available. Beds: QDT. Continental-plus breakfast. CCs: MC VISA. Sailing, walking tours, golf, tennis.

William Page Inn B&B

8 Martin St
Annapolis MD 21401
(301) 626-1506

Circa 1908. This turn-of-the-century four-square house served the First Ward Democratic Club as the center of social politics in Annapolis. For 30 years a "crap" game was held every Friday night. Now renovated, its distinctively decorated rooms include a suite with a sitting area and a whirlpool bathtub. Antiques and period reproductions are found throughout.

*Rates: $70-$120.
Robert L. Zuchelli & Greg Page.
5 Rooms. 3 Private Baths. Guest phone available. TV available. Beds: Q. Continental-plus breakfast. Jacuzzi. Sailing, water sports, tennis, swimming, baseball & softball fields.
Seen in: *The Evening Capital Newspaper, Country Inns.*

"It was such a pleasure to see such a very elegantly appointed Victorian inn."

Baltimore

Admiral Fell Inn
888 S Broadway
Baltimore MD 21231
(301) 522-7377 (800) 292-INNS

Circa 1720. This inn is three buildings, the oldest of which is a red

brick, three-story columned structure with a Victorian facade. At one time the complex served as a boarding house for sailors and a vinegar bottling plant. Each room is tastefully furnished with period pieces.
✻❀Rates: $90-$115.
Jim Widman.
38 Rooms. 38 Private Baths. Guest phone in room. TV in room. Beds: KD. Continental breakfast. Restaurant. Gourmet meals. Jacuzzi. Handicap access. Conference room. CCs: MC VISA AX. Boating, sailing, shopping.
Seen in: *New York Times, Cover of Mid-Atlantic Country.*

"Beautiful rooms, excellent services."

Betsy's B&B
1428 Park Ave
Baltimore MD 21217
(301) 383-1274

Circa 1895. This four-story town house with 13-foot ceilings features

many elegant architectural touches. The hallway floor is laid in alternating strips of oak and walnut and there are six carved marble fireplaces. The most elaborate, carved in fruit designs, is in the dining room. The inn is decorated with handsome brass rubbings made by the owner during a stay in England.
Location: Downtown, about 1.5 miles north of Inner Harbor.
✻Rates: $65-$70.
Betsy Grater.
3 Rooms. 1 Private Bath. Guest phone available. TV in room. Beds: KQT. Continental-plus breakfast. Jacuzzi. Swimming pool. CCs: VISA AX DS. Tennis.
Seen in: *Peabody Reflector, Baltimore/Washington Business Journal.*

"What hotel room could ever compare to a large room in a 115-year old house with 10-foot ceilings and a marble fireplace with hosts that could become dear long-time friends?"

The Shirley-Madison Inn
205 W Madison St
Baltimore MD 21201
(301) 728-6550

Circa 1880. An elegant Victorian mansion located in a downtown historic neighborhood, the Shirley-Madison Inn has an English stairway of polished ash that winds up four stories. The original 100-year-old lift still carries no more than three guests. The inn is decorated with Victorian and Edwardian antiques and turn-of-the-century artwork. The Inner Harbor, business district, and cultural centers are a short walk away.
Location: Ten blocks from the Inner Harbor.
✻❀Rates: $65-$95.
Herman Lantz.
25 Rooms. 25 Private Baths. Guest phone in room. TV in room. Beds: KQDTC. Continental breakfast. Conference room. CCs: MC VISA AX DC. Boating, museums.
Seen in: *Mid Atlantic Country, New York Magazine.*

"Charming, comfortable rooms, reasonable rates and friendly staff."

"One of the most enjoyable experiences I have been priviledged to have has been to stay at the Shirley House."

Society Hill Government House
1125 N Calvert St
Baltimore MD 21202
(301) 752-7722

Circa 1897. This is the official guest house for Baltimore's visiting dignitaries, as well as the general public. Three town houses comprise the inn, located in the Mt. Vernon historic district. Features include chandeliers, ornate wallpapers, and Victorian antiques. Each bedchamber has its own view.
Rates: $95-$115.
Peggy Bannister.
18 Rooms. 18 Private Baths. Beds: KQDC. Continental breakfast. Handicap access. Conference room. CCs: MC VISA.

Society Hill Hopkins
3404 St Paul St
Baltimore MD 21218
(301) 235-8600

Circa 1920. The embassy-like atmosphere of this inn makes it popular for small meetings as well

as romantic getaways. Antiques and original art fill the rooms, decorated in a variety of period styles. Breakfast may be taken in the guest room or dining room.
Rates: $65-$135.
Joanne Fritz & Toni Pietrowitz.
26 Rooms. 26 Private Baths. Guest phone in room. TV in room. Beds: QC. Continental-plus breakfast. Conference room. CCs: MC VISA AX DC CB. Museum of Art.
Seen in: *Baltimore Business Journal, New York Times, Weekend Getaways.*

"...most friendly and comfortable and very efficiently run."

Society Hill Hotel
58 W Biddle St
Baltimore MD 21201
(301) 837-3630

Circa 1890. This town house has been converted for lodging and includes a distinctive bar and restaurant with romantic dining rooms. The country-inn decor includes brass beds, fresh flowers and elaborate Victorian furnishings. Breakfast is brought to the room. Within walking distance is Meyerhoff Symphony Hall, and the Lyric Opera House.
Rates: $80-$120.

Kate Hopkins.
15 Rooms. 15 Private Baths. Beds: KQDT. Full breakfast. Restaurant.

Twin Gates

308 Morris Ave
Baltimore MD 21093
(301) 252-3131

Circa 1857. While renovating Twin Gates, the innkeepers discovered

two secret rooms used to hide runaway slaves heading north by means of the Underground Railroad. One of them is a small, half-height room that, prior to renovation, was accessed through a trap-door in the room above. All the public rooms have 12-foot ceilings and are decorated with antiques.
Location: Lutherville, a Victorian village north of Baltimore.
*Rates: $70.
Gwen & Bob Vaughan.
6 Rooms. 2 Private Baths. Guest phone available. TV available. Beds: Q. Full breakfast. Winery tours. National Aquarium.
Seen in: *The Towson Flier, Baltimore Magazine.*

Chestertown

Brampton

RR2, Box 107
Chestertown MD 21620
(301) 778-1860

Circa 1860. Situated on 35 acres of Maryland's Eastern Shore between the Chester River and Chesapeake Bay, Brampton is a three-story brick, Greek Italianate Revival house. A massive walnut staircase winds to the second and third floor. Swiss Innkeeper Danielle Hanscom selected family antiques to furnish the parlor and dining room. Upstairs the spacious rooms feature canopied beds, antiques and reproductions. A full country breakfast is served.
Rates: $75-$85.
Michael & Danielle Hanscom.
5 Rooms. 5 Private Baths. 4 Fireplaces. Guest phone available. TV available. Beds: QDT. EP. CCs: MC VISA. Hunting, crabbing, fishing, cycling, antiquing.

Seen in: *The Washington Post.*

"A stately beauty that exudes peace and tranquility."

White Swan Tavern

231 High St
Chestertown MD 21620
(301) 778-2300

Circa 1730. During the 1978 restoration of this inn, an archaeological dig made an interesting discovery. Before 1733, the site was a tannery operated by the Shoemaker of Chestertown. His one-room dwelling is now a converted guest room. After additions to the building, it became a tavern in 1793, and was described as *situated in the center of business...with every attention given to render comfort and pleasure to such as favor it with their patronage."*
Location: Eastern shore of Maryland. Downtown historic district.
Rates: $75-$100.
Mary Susan Maisel.
6 Rooms. 6 Private Baths. Guest phone available. TV available. Beds: QDTC. Full breakfast. Conference room.

Denton

Sophie Kerr House

Rt 3 Box 7-B, Kerr & 5th Aves
Denton MD 21629
(301) 479-3421

Circa 1861. This two-story white Colonial sits on a spacious lawn away from the road. It was the birthplace of Sophie Kerr, an Eastern Shore writer. A four-star French country restaurant is within walking distance. Two state parks are nearby.

Location: Downtown Denton, Route 404 to Fifth Avenue.
Rates: $40.
John & Thelma Lyons.
5 Rooms. TV available. Beds: KQTC. Full breakfast. Swimming pool. Antique and craft shops.
Seen in: *Pittsburg Press.*

"John and Thelma make a stay there fun. We met them in the garden with two guests from Manhattan. We joined the party and had a terrific time."

Frederick

Spring Bank Inn

7945 Worman's Mill Rd
Frederick MD 21701
(301) 694-0440

Circa 1880. Both Gothic Revival and Italianate architectural details

are featured in this brick Victorian in the National Register. High ceilings accommodate 10-foot arched windows. The original interior shutters remain. The parlor has a marbleized slate fireplace, and there is original hand-stenciling in the billiards room. Victorian and Chippendale furnishings have been collected from the family's antique shop. Black birch, pine, maple, and poplar trees dot the inn's 10 acres.
Location: Two and a half miles north of Frederick Historic District.
Rates: $70-$85.
Beverly & Ray Compton.
6 Rooms. 1 Private Bath. Guest phone available. Beds: DT. Continental-plus breakfast. CCs: MC VISA AX. Fishing, bicycling, canoeing, cross-country skiing.
Seen in: *The Washington Post, Los Angeles Times.*

"From two B&B frequenters - this one wins the blue ribbon."

Tran Crossing

121 E Patrick St
Frederick MD 21701
(301) 663-8449

Circa 1877. This elegant three-story town house in the heart of the Frederick Historic District is noted for its attractive mansard roof and stately entrance. A spiral staircase leads to gas-lit rooms with period furnishings. Historical sites within

walking distance include the location of the first official rebellion against the Stamp Act.
*Rates: $80-$100.
Fred & Becky Tran.
2 Rooms. 1 Private Bath. 1 Fireplace. Guest phone in room. Beds: QD. Continental-plus breakfast. Conference room. Hiking, tennis, swimming, bicycling, carriage rides. Golf nearby.

"The room was perfect, as fine a B&B as we have stayed at anywhere. You'll see us again."

Hagerstown

The Mercerburg Inn
See: Mercerburg, PA

Harwood

Oakwood
4566 Solomons Island Rd
Harwood MD 20776
(301) 261-5338

Circa 1840. A private lane winds through towering poplar, hickory and maple trees to Oakwood, a gracious two-and-a-half story Federal-style manor. Extensive terraced gardens include old-fashioned flowers. There are deep woods surrounding the inn. Interiors feature 11-foot ceilings and six fireplaces. An imposing dining room is appointed with a large dining table, a period sideboard, and chandeliers. Guest rooms are filled with antiques. Outbuildings include a spring house, butler's house and pond.
Location: Thirty miles southeast of Washington, D.C.
*Rates: $60-$65. Season: March - Nov 15.
Dr. Joan and Dennis Brezina.
2 Rooms. Guest phone available. TV available. Beds: DT. Continental-plus breakfast. Water sports.
Seen in: *The Washington Post.*

"A special glimpse at nature's beauty. Such a tranquil spot. Delightful!"

New Market

National Pike Inn
9-11 W Main St, PO Box 299
New Market MD 21774
(301) 865-5055

Circa 1796. This red shuttered brick Federal house has a unique

widow's watch added in 1900. The National Pike was the East-West connection between Baltimore and points west. Towns along the road were located eight miles apart, which was as far as herds could be driven in one day. Of the eight inns in New Market, only two remain. The inn's colonial decor includes wingback chairs, oriental rugs and four-poster beds.
Rates: $60-$100.
Tom & Terry Rimel.
5 Rooms. 2 Private Baths. 2 Fireplaces. Guest phone available. TV available. Beds: QDT. Full breakfast. CCs: MC VISA. Tennis, golf, cross-country skiing, hiking.
Seen in: *Mid-Atlantic Country.*

"A total joy! A relaxed, charming, and romantic setting."

Oxford

1876 House
110 N Morris St
Oxford MD 21654
(301) 226-5496

Circa 1876. This early Victorian house has a welcoming front porch, ten-foot ceilings and wide-planked pine floors. A queen-size four-poster bed is in the master suite, which looks out over North Morris Street. A continental breakfast is served in the formal dining room.
Rates: $75-$86. Season: Closed Dec.24-Jan.1
Eleanor & Jerry Clark.
3 Rooms. 1 Private Bath. Guest phone available. Beds: QDT. Continental-plus breakfast.

The Robert Morris Inn
Box 70, On The Tred Avon
Oxford MD 21654
(301) 226-5111

Circa 1710. Once the home of Robert Morris, Sr., a representative of an English trading company, the house was constructed by ship carpenters with wooden pegged paneling, ships nails and hand-hewn beams. Bricks brought to Oxford as ballast in trading ships were used to build the fireplaces. Robert Morris, Jr., a partner in a Philadelphia law firm, used his entire savings to help finance the Continental Army. He signed The Declaration of Independence, The Articles of Confederation and The United States Constitution.
Rates: $60-$150. Season: March to January.
Jay Gibson, Wendy & Ken Gibson.
33 Rooms. 30 Private Baths. Guest phone available. TV available. Beds: KQDT. EP. CCs: MC VISA AX. Golf, tennis, antiquing, sailing, goose hunting (seasonal), private beach.
Seen in: *Southern Accents, The Evening Sun.*

Saint Michaels

Kemp House Inn
412 S Talbot St
Saint Michaels MD 21663
(301) 745-2243

Circa 1805. This two-story Georgian house was built by Col. Joseph Kemp, a shipwright and one of the town forefathers. The inn is appointed in period furnishings accentuated by candlelight. Guest rooms include patchwork quilts, a collection of four-poster rope beds, and old-fashioned nightshirts. There are several working fireplaces. Robert E. Lee is said to have been a guest.
Rates: $55-$95.

Stephen & Diane Cooper.
8 Rooms. 3 Private Baths. Beds: Q. Full breakfast. CCs: MC VISA. Waterskiing, hunting, boating, fishing, bicycling, crabbing.

Parsonage Inn
210 N Talbot St
Saint Michaels MD 21663
(301) 745-5519

Circa 1883. A striking Victorian steeple rises next to the wide bay of

this brick residence, once the home of Henry Clay Dodson, state senator, pharmacist and brickyard owner. The house features brick detail in a variety of patterns and inlays - perhaps a design statement for brick customers. Porches are decorated with filagree and spindled columns. Laura Ashley linens, late Victorian era furnishings, fireplaces and decks add to the creature comforts. Four 12-speed bikes await guests who wish to ride to Tilghman Island or over the ferry to Oxford.
✻Rates: $72-$94.
Betty & Chuck Oler.
7 Rooms. 7 Private Baths. 4 Fireplaces. Guest phone available. TV available. Beds: KQDC. Continental-plus breakfast. Handicap access. Conference room. CCs: MC VISA. Chesapeake Bay Maritime Museum.
Seen in: *Wilmington, Delaware News Journal.*

"Striking. Extensively renovated."

Scotland

St Michael's Manor B&B
St Michael's Manor
Scotland MD 20687
(301) 872-4025

Circa 1805. Twice featured on the Maryland House and Garden Tour, St. Michael's is located on Long Neck Creek, a half mile from Chesapeake Bay. The original handcrafted woodwork provides a hand-

some backdrop for the inn's antique collection. A three-acre vineyard is on the property.
Joe & Nancy Dick.
3 Rooms. 1 Private Bath. Guest phone available. TV available. Beds: DT. Full breakfast. Swimming pool. Bicycles and canoe to use.

"You made our stay the most unforgettable B&B experience we've had to date."

Sharpsburg

The Inn at Antietam
PO Box 119
Sharpsburg MD 21782
(301) 432-6601

Circa 1908. Eight acres of meadows surround this gracious white Victorian framed by English walnut trees. A columned veranda provides a view of the countryside, the town with its old stone churches, and the Blue Mountains. Gleaming floors accentuate romantically designed Victorian guest rooms. An inviting smokehouse features beamed ceilings, a wide brick fireplace, and handsome upholstered chairs.
Rates: $65-$95.
Betty N. Fairbourn.
5 Rooms. 5 Private Baths. Guest phone available. Beds: QDT. EP. Conference room. CCs: AX. Hiking, bicycling, cross-country skiing, golf, tennis. Civil War battlefield tours.

"A romantic setting and a most enjoyable experience."

Westminster

The Winchester Country Inn
430 S Bishop St
Westminster MD 21157
(301) 876-7373

Circa 1760. William Winchester the founder of Westminster, built this unusual English-style house. It has a steeply slanted roof, similar to those found in the Tidewater area. A central fireplace opens to both the parlor and the central hall. Colonial period furnishings prevail, with some items loaned by the local historic society. Community volunteers, historians, craftsmen, and designers helped restore the inn. A non-profit agency provides some of the housekeeping and gardening staff from its developmentally disabled program.
Rates: $60-$65.
Estella Williams.
5 Rooms. 3 Private Baths. Guest phone available. TV available. Beds: QDT. B&B. CCs: MC VISA. Horseback riding, museums.
Seen in: *Country Living, Evening Sun, The Towson Flier.*

"We give your inn an A+. Our stay was perfect."

Massachusetts

Amherst

The Wildwood Inn
See: Ware, MA

Andover

Sherman-Berry House
See: Lowell, MA

Ashfield

Ashfield Inn
Main St, PO Box 129
Ashfield MA 01330
(413) 628-4571

Circa 1919. This handsome Georgian mansion was built as a summer

home for Milo Belding. Enormous porches overlook spectacular perennials and herb gardens, and there are views of the lake, hills and countryside. Nestled in the gardens are several tree swings. The romantic interior includes a reception hall and a grand stairway.

*Rates: $75-$90.
Scott & Stacy Alessi.
8 Rooms. 3 Fireplaces. Guest phone available. TV available. Beds: QDTC. Full breakfast. Conference room. CCs: MC VISA AX. Golf, skiing, hiking, swimming, tennis.

"Privacy, elegance, fabulous food, amenities (like terry robes, flowers and fruit) that made me feel pampered. Wonderful hospitality in a spectacular romantic setting."

Auburn

Captain Samuel Eddy House Inn
609 Oxford St S
Auburn MA 01501
(508) 832-5282

Circa 1765. This beautiful 18th-century farmhouse has been painstak-

ingly restored by the innkeepers. The south parlor is decorated with colonial furniture, while the north parlor has modern furnishings and a TV. Innkeeper Carilyn O'Toole often cooks over the hearth and sometimes dresses in a colonial frock to present breakfast. An herb garden and flock of geese are behind the inn.

*Rates: $60-$85.
Jack & Carilyn O'Toole.
5 Rooms. 5 Private Baths. Guest phone available. TV available. Beds: KQDTC. MAP. Restaurant. Gourmet meals. Swimming pool. Game room. Conference room. CCs: MC VISA. Hiking, skating, fishing.
Seen in: *The Boston Herald, Auburn News, New York Times.*

"Like stepping back in time."

Barnstable

Ashley Manor
3660 Olde Kings Hwy PO Box 856
Barnstable MA 02630
(508) 362-8044

Circa 1699. The first addition to this house was built in 1750. A suc-

cession of expansions occurred over the years. Besides the wide-board flooring (usually reserved for the king) and huge, open-hearth fireplaces with beehive ovens, there is a secret passageway connecting the upstairs and downstairs suites. It was thought to be a hiding place for Tories during the Revolutionary War. The inn now rests gracefully on two acres of manicured lawns sprinkled with cherry and apple trees.

Location: In the heart of Cape Cod's historic district.
*Rates: $100-$165.
Donald & Fay Bain.
6 Rooms. 6 Private Baths. 5 Fireplaces. Guest phone available. Beds: KQD. B&B. CCs: MC VISA AX. Sportfishing, boating, tennis, horses, bicycles, croquet, museums, antiques.
Seen in: *Boston Globe.*

"This is absolutely perfect! So many very special, lovely touches."

Thomas Huckins House

2701 Main St, Rt 6A
Barnstable MA 02630
(508) 362-6379

Circa 1705. Merchants and shippers, the Huckins family settled in

Barnstable in 1639. Thomas built this Cape half-house across from Calves Pasture Lane, common grazing land used by the colonists. There is a ten-foot fireplace and original paneling, windows, hinges and latches. American antique furnishings with canopy beds add to the gracious feeling of the inn. Just down the road is a graveyard where slate headstones bear the names of early residents.
Location: Cape Cod
Rates: $60-$95.
Burt & Eleanor Eddy.
4 Rooms. 4 Private Baths. 2 Fireplaces. Guest phone available. TV available. Beds: QD. Full breakfast. CCs: MC VISA.

"Your home is even warmer and more charming in person than the lovely pictures in Early American Life.*"*

Barnstable Village

Beechwood

2839 Main St
Barnstable Village MA 02630
(508) 362-6618

Circa 1853. Beechwood is a carefully restored Queen Anne house offer-

ing period furnishings, fireplaces and ocean views. Its warmth and elegance make it a favorite hideaway for couples looking for a peaceful return to the Victorian era. The inn is named for rare old beech trees that shade the veranda.
Location: Cape Cod's historic North Shore.
Rates: $95-$135.
Anne & Bob Livermore.
6 Rooms. 6 Private Baths. 2 Fireplaces. Guest phone available. Beds: KQD. Full breakfast. CCs: MC VISA AX. Golf, beaches, whale watching, bicycles.
Seen in: *National Trust Calendar.*

"Your inn is pristine in every detail. We concluded that the innkeepers, who are most hospitable, are the best part of Beechwood."

Charles Hinckley House

Olde Kings Hwy, PO Box 723
Barnstable Village MA 02630
(508) 362-9924

Circa 1809. Built by shipwright Charles Hinckley, direct descendant

of the last governor of Plymouth Colony, the inn is a fine example of Federal colonial architecture. A twin chimney, hip-roofed, post-and-beam structure, the house is an award-winning restoration. Standing watch over one of Cape Cod's most photographed wild flower gardens, the inn is a short walk down a quiet lane to the bay.
❄Rates: $108-$138.
Les & Miya Patrick.
4 Rooms. 4 Private Baths. 4 Fireplaces. Guest phone available. Beds: QD. Full breakfast. Gourmet meals. Beach, golf, antiquing.
Seen in: *Country Living Magazine, Boston Globe, Historic Preservation.*

"A wonderful, sophisticated and intimate hideaway. This inn experience was truly fantastic, punctuated by Miya's incredible gourmet breakfasts."

Bernardston

Bernardston Inn

Church St
Bernardston MA 01337
(413) 648-9282

Circa 1905. The present building was erected on the site of an old

coach inn. Recently renovated, the Bernardston Inn has ceiling fans, claw-foot bathtubs, and guest rooms with antique furnishings.
Location: Junction Routes 5 & 10.
Rates: $39-$72.
Lanelle & Michael Mikolaitis.
7 Rooms. 7 Private Baths. Guest phone available. TV available. Beds: QT. Full breakfast. Restaurant. CCs: MC VISA AX.

"Delighted with the charming atmosphere, excellent accommodations and outstanding service."

Boston

Amelia Payson Guest House

See: Salem, MA

Beacon Street Guest House

See: Brookline, MA

Caron House

See: Lynn, MA

Host Homes of Boston

PO Box 117, Waban Branch
Boston MA 02168
(617) 244-1308

Circa 1864. This stately town house on Commonwealth Avenue in Boston's chic Back Bay area is less than one block away from the Boston Common, and a short walk to Copley Square. The house was built for the Robbins family, prominent clockmakers of the period. Since 1890, it has served as a private professional club providing cultural and intellectual programs. Overnight lodging is now offered for B&B guests as well as for members.
Location: Homes in Beacon Hill, Back Bay, Cambridge, Greater Boston.

Rates: $60-$90.
Marcia Whittington.
7 Rooms. 4 Private Baths. Beds: DT. Continental breakfast. Handicap access. CCs: MC VISA AX.
Seen in: *Changing Times, Boston/Newton.*
"Very special."

Land's End Inn
See: Provincetown, MA

Seafarer Inn
See: Rockport, MA

Sears-Withington House
See: West Newton, MA

Brewster

Bramble Inn
Rt 6a 2019 Main St
Brewster MA 02631
(508) 896-7644

Circa 1861. The venerable Bramble Inn is composed of three buildings. The main house containing a restaurant and lodging, and the house next door with five guest rooms, are of Greek Revival architecture. The Captain Bangs Pepper House on the other side of the main house of the Federal style, built in 1793. Williamsburg and Laura Ashley fabrics and wall coverings decorate the inn.

Location: Walking distance to the ocean.
*Rates: $75-$105. Season: April - Dec.
Ruth & Cliff Manchester.
11 Rooms. 11 Private Baths. Guest phone available. Beds: QD. Full breakfast. Restaurant. CCs: MC VISA DC. Tennis, swimming, cycling.
Seen in: *The Boston Globe, The Boston Herald, Bon Appetit.*
"Adventurous cuisine in a romantic setting." Providence Journal.

Old Manse Inn
1861 Main St, PO 839
Brewster MA 02631
(508) 896-3149

Circa 1800. This old sea captain's house is tucked behind tall trees and has a gracious mansard roof. It was built by Captain Knowles, and served as a link in the Underground Railroad during the Civil War. The rooms are decorated with old-fashioned print wallpapers, original paintings and antiques.
Location: Cape Cod.
Rates: $60-$85. Season: March - Jan.
Sugar & Doug Manchester.
9 Rooms. 9 Private Baths. Guest phone available. Beds: KQTD. Full breakfast. Restaurant. Handicap access. CCs: MC VISA. Tennis, golf, swimming, bicycling, fishing.
"Our stays at the Old Manse Inn have always been delightful. The innkeepers are gracious, the decor charming and the dining room has a character all its own."

Old Sea Pines Inn
2553 Main St
Brewster MA 02631
(508) 896-6114

Circa 1900. This turn-of-the-century mansion on three-and-one-half

acres of lawns and trees was formerly the Sea Pines School of Charm and Personality for Young Women, established in 1907. Recently renovated, the inn displays elegant wallpapers and a grand sweeping stairway. It is located near beaches and bike paths, as well as village shops and restaurants.
Location: Cape Cod.
*Rates: $40-$90.
Stephen & Michele Rowan.
21 Rooms. 16 Private Baths. 3 Fireplaces. Guest phone available. TV in room. Beds: QDT. Full breakfast. Restaurant. Handicap access. Conference room. CCs: MC VISA AX DC CB. Beaches, tennis, golf.
Seen in: *Boston, For Women First.*
"The loving care applied by Steve, Michele and staff is deeply appreciated."

Brookline

Beacon Street Guest House
1047 Beacon St
Brookline MA 02146
(800) 872-7211 (617) 232-0292

Circa 1900. This four-story brick and sandstone building was originally a private home built by Silas and Luther Merril and designed by G. Wilton Lewis. Providing good basic lodging, the house is an example of Queen Anne and Romanesque Revival and is five minutes from Harvard and five blocks from Fenway. Restaurants, theaters, and shops are nearby.
Location: West of Boston, 10 minutes to downtown by subway.
*Rates: $35-$65. Season: April - Nov.
Jessica McGovern & Morris Fuller.
14 Rooms. 9 Private Baths. Guest phone available. TV available. Beds: TDC. Continental breakfast. CCs: MC VISA DC.
"Quiet, charming. Real Boston flavor."

Buckland

1797 House
Charlemont Rd
Buckland MA 01338
(413) 625-2975

Circa 1797. This house was built by Zenas Graham who married the

same year and went on to have 12 children. The Graham family retained the house well into the 1940s. At one time, it served as the Winter School for Young Ladies, run by Mary Lyon, founder of Mount Holyoke College. Features include 12-over-12 windows, four fireplaces, and a peaceful screened porch. Comfort is everywhere and very enticing after a day of sightseeing.
Location: Three miles south of Mohawk Trail.
Rates: $65. Season: Jan. 15-Oct.
Janet Turley.
3 Rooms. 3 Private Baths. Guest phone available. TV available. Beds: DT. B&B. Conference room. Hiking, downhill & cross-country skiing, tennis, swimming.
"The most restful nights ever spent away from home. When I become stressed I send my mind to your porch."

Cambridge

A Cambridge House B&B Inn

2218 Massachusetts Ave
Cambridge MA 02140
(617) 491-6300

Circa 1892. Listed in the National Register, A Cambridge House has

been restored to its turn-of-the-century elegance. A remarkable carved cherry fireplace dominates the den, and some rooms have four-poster canopy beds and fireplaces. The library is often the setting for mulled cider, wine or tea served fireside on brisk afternoons. Parking is available and the subway is four blocks away.

Location: Minutes from downtown Boston.
*Rates: $59-$139.
Ellen Riley & Tony Femmino.
12 Rooms. 1 Private Bath. Beds: QT. Full breakfast. CCs: MC VISA.
Seen in: *Evening Magazine, Glamour Magazine.*

"I'm afraid you spoiled us quite badly! Your home is elegant, charming and comfortable. Breakfasts were delicious and beautifully served."

Cape Cod

Old Sea Pines Inn

See: Brewster, MA

For Cape Cod see also:

Barnstable, Brewster, Centerville, Chatham,,Dennis, Dennis Port, East Sandwich, Eastham, Harwich Port, Hyannis, Falmouth, Monument Beach, North Falmouth, Orleans, Osterville, Provincetown, Sandwich, South Yarmouth, Wellfleet, West Hyannisport, West Yarmouth, Woods Hole, Yarmouth Port

Cape Cod-Eastham

Over Look Inn

PO Box 771
Cape Cod-Eastham MA 02642
(508) 255-1886 (800) 649-5782 (MA)

Circa 1869. Schooner Captain Barnabus Chipman built this three-story home for his wife. In 1920 it opened as an inn and was frequented by author and naturalist Henry Beston as he wrote "The Outermost House." Located on one-and-a-half acres of grounds, the inn is furnished with Victorian antiques and reproductions. A collection of Winston Churchill books fills the inn's library. The Aitchisons, from Edinboro, are known for their warm Scottish charm and occasional bagpipe serenades.

*Rates: $70-$90.
Ian & Nan Aitchison.
10 Rooms. 10 Private Baths. Guest phone available. Beds: QDT. Full breakfast. CCs: MC VISA AX. Afternoon tea, billiard room, library.
Seen in: *Conde Nast Traveler, Victorian Homes.*

"A delightful experience." Max Nichols, *Oklahoma City Journal Record.*

Centerville

Copper Beech Inn

497 Main St
Centerville MA 02632
(508) 771-5488

Circa 1830. At the site of the largest European copper beech tree

on Cape Cod you'll find this white clapboard house, built by Captain Hillman Crosby. The Crosby name has long been associated with boat builders and fast sailing ships. Preserved and restored, this Cape-style inn is a walk away to Craigville Beach, considered one of the ten best beaches in the United States. Summer theater and fine restaurants are also nearby.

Rates: $65-$75.
Joyce & Clark Diehl.
3 Rooms. 3 Private Baths. Guest phone available. TV available. Beds: KD. Full breakfast. CCs: MC VISA AX. Bicycling, ocean beach.
Seen in: *Innsider, Cape Cod Life.*

"Everything we were looking for, clean and private, but best of all were our wonderful hosts. They made us feel very much at home and made delicious breakfast."

Chatham

The Cranberry Inn at Chatham

359 Main St, Cape Cod
Chatham MA 02633
(508) 945-9232

Circa 1830. Continuously operating for over 150 years, this inn was originally called the Traveler's Lodge, then the Monomayie after a local Indian tribe. A cranberry bog adjacent to the property inspired the current name. Recently restored, the inn is located in the heart of the historic district. It's within walking distance of the lighthouse, beaches, shops and restaurants. Guest rooms feature four-poster beds, wide planked floors and coordinated fabrics. An award-winning restaurant and a tap room are on the premises.

*Rates: $85-$135. Season: March - Mid Dec.
Richard Morris & Peggy DeHan.
14 Rooms. 14 Private Baths. Guest phone in room. TV in room. Beds: QDT. Continental-plus breakfast. CCs: MC VISA AX. Swimming, water sports, golf, tennis (all nearby).
Seen in: *Cape Cod Chronicle.*

Chatham, Cape Cod

Chatham Town House Inn

11 Library Ln
Chatham, Cape Cod MA 02633
(508) 945-2180 (508) 945-3990 (FAX)

Circa 1881. This three-story sea captain's house was built by Daniel Webster Nickerson, a descendant of William Nickerson who came over on the *Mayflower*. Resting on two acres in the village, the inn is sur-

rounded with charming gardens. Victorian wallpapers, hand stenciling and canopy beds are features of most guest rooms and there are two cottages with fireplaces. Hospitality is provided by an international staff and Scandinavian hosts.
*Rates: $115-$175. Season: Closed Jan.
Russell & Svea Marita Peterson.
22 Rooms. 22 Private Baths. 2 Fireplaces. Guest phone in room. TV in room. Beds: KQDC. EP. Jacuzzi. Handicap access. Swimming pool. Conference room. CCs: MC VISA AX DC CB DS. Horseback riding, water skiing, sport fishing, swimming, surf sailing. Full-service restaurant with Swedish chef.
Seen in: *Cape Cod Times, New York Times, Yankee Magazine.*

Concord

Anderson-Wheeler Homestead

154 Fitchburg Turnpike
Concord MA 01742
(508) 369-3756

Circa 1890. When Route 117 was the main road between Boston and Fitchburg the Lee family operated a stagecoach stop here. They provided room and board, a change of horses, and a leather and blacksmith shop. The building burned in 1890, and a Victorian house was built by Frank Wheeler, developer of rust-free asparagus. The property has remained in the family, and the veranda overlooks an extensive lawn and Sudbury River.
*Rates: $70-$85.
David & Charlotte Anderson.
5 Rooms. 2 Private Baths. 2 Fireplaces. Guest phone available. TV in room. Beds: KDTC. Continental-plus breakfast. Conference room. CCs: MC VISA AX DC CB. Bird-watching, horseback riding, cross-country skiing.
Seen in: *New England Getaways, Concord Journal.*

"The five nights spent with you were the most comfortable and most congenial of the whole cross-country trip."

Colonel Roger Brown House

1694 Main St
Concord MA 01742
(508) 369-9119

Circa 1775. The oldest house in West Concord was the home of Minuteman Roger Brown who fought at the Old North Bridge. The frame for this center-chimney colonial was raised April 19th, the day the battle took place. Other parts of the house were built in 1708. Next door is the Damon Mill, now developed as an office complex with a fitness club available to guests.
Rates: $65-$75.
Kate Williams.
5 Rooms. 5 Private Baths. 1 Fireplace. Guest phone in room. TV in room. Beds: QDT. Continental-plus breakfast. Jacuzzi. Sauna. Swimming pool. CCs: MC VISA DC. Golf, canoeing, skiing, tennis.
Seen in: *Middlesex News.*

"My boss won't stay anywhere else!" Secretary.

Hawthorne Inn

462 Lexington Rd
Concord MA 01742
(508) 369-5610

Circa 1870. The Hawthorne Inn is situated on land that once belonged

to Ralph Waldo Emerson, the Alcotts and Nathaniel Hawthorne. It was here that Bronson Alcott planted his fruit trees, made pathways to the Mill Brook, and erected his Bath House. Hawthorne purchased the land and repaired a path leading to his home with trees planted on either side. Two of these trees still stand. Across the road is Hawthorne's House, The Wayside. Next to it is the Alcott's Orchard House, and Grapevine Cottage where the Concord grape was developed. Nearby is Sleepy Hollow Cemetery where Emerson, the Alcotts, the Thoreaus, and Hawthorne were laid to rest.
*Rates: $110-$150.
G. Burch & M. Mudry.
7 Rooms. 7 Private Baths. Guest phone available. Beds: TCD. Continental-plus breakfast. Cross-country skiing, swimming.
Seen in: *New York Times, Boston Globe, Yankee Magazine.*

"Surely there couldn't be a better or more valuable location for a comfortable, old-fashioned country inn."

Sherman-Berry House

See: Lowell, MA

Deerfield

Deerfield Inn

The Street
Deerfield MA 01342
(413) 774-5587

Circa 1885. Deerfield was settled in 1670 and a few years later survived

an Indian massacre. Farmers still unearth bones and axe heads when they plow. Now, 50 beautifully restored Colonial and Federal homes line mile-long The Street, considered by many to be the loveliest street in New England. Twelve of these houses are museums open to the public. The inn is situated at the center of this peaceful village and is filled with antiques from historic Deerfield's remarkable collection. The village has been designated a national historic landmark.
Location: Middle of historic village.
Rates: $115-$125.
Karl & Jane Sabo.
23 Rooms. 23 Private Baths. TV available. Beds: KQT. Full breakfast. Restaurant. Handicap access. Conference room. CCs: MC VISA DC. Golf, downhill & cross-country skiing, buggy rides.
Seen in: *The Recorder-Greenfield, Travel Today, Daily Hampshire Gazette.*

"We've stayed at many New England inns, but the Deerfield Inn ranks among the best."

Dennis

Four Chimneys Inn

946 Main St, Rt 6A
Dennis MA 02638
(508) 385-6317

Circa 1881. This spacious Victorian stands across from Lake Scargo. Legend says the lake was created at the command of an Indian chief whose daughter needed a larger fishbowl for her goldfish. The village maidens dug the lake with clam shells and all the fish happily multiplied. The inn has eight-foot windows, high ceilings, a cozy library and parlor, and a gracious summer porch from which to view the "fishbowl."

Location: Cape Cod.
Rates: $50-$95.
Christina Jervant & Diane Robinson.
9 Rooms. 7 Private Baths. Guest phone available. Beds: QDT. Continental breakfast. Conference room. CCs: MC VISA AX. Bicycling, tennis, golf, fishing, swimming, theater.
Seen in: *The Littleton Independent.*

Isaiah Hall B&B Inn

152 Whig St
Dennis MA 02638
(508) 385-9928

Circa 1857. Adjacent to the Cape's oldest cranberry bog is this Greek

Revival farmhouse built by Isaiah Hall, a cooper. His brother was the first cultivator of cranberries in America and Isaiah designed and patented the original barrel for shipping cranberries. In 1948, Dorothy Ripp, an artist, established the inn. Many examples of her art work remain.

Location: Cape Cod.
*Rates: $48-$85. Season: Mid March-Mid Nov.
Marie & Dick Brophy.
11 Rooms. 10 Private Baths. 1 Fireplace. Guest phone available. TV available. Beds: QDT. B&B. Conference room. CCs: MC VISA AX. Swimming, golf, tennis, bike trails.
Seen in: *Cape Cod Life.*

Duxbury

Black Friar Brook Farm

636 Union St
Duxbury MA 02332
(617) 834-8528

Circa 1708. Josiah Soule, grandson of pilgrim George Soule, built this saltbox house on 11 acres of farmland. Part of an original land grant of 150 acres, the house has gun-stock beams and colonial antiques. The private guest suite includes a bedroom, sitting room and dining area. The hostess runs a reservation service for other New England homestays.

Location: Close to Historic Plymouth with easy access to both Boston and Cape Cod.
Rates: $45-$50. Season: March - Nov.
Ann & Walter Kopke.
2 Rooms. 2 Private Baths. Guest phone available. Beds: DT. Full breakfast. Beach.
Seen in:

East Orleans

The Parsonage

202 Main St, PO Box 1016
East Orleans MA 02643
(508) 255-8217

Circa 1770. This 18-century parsonage is a Cape house, complete

with ancient wavy glass in the windows and antique furnishings throughout. There are dormer windows and a sitting area in the spacious loft room. Breakfast is served in the courtyard or in guest rooms. Main Street, the road to Nauset Beach, is lined with the old homes of sea captains and other early settlers.

Rates: $60-$90.
Chris & Lloyd Shand.
5 Rooms. 5 Private Baths. Guest phone available. Beds: QD. Continental-plus breakfast. CCs: MC VISA. Beaches, tennis, bicycling.
Seen in: *Miami Herald.*

"Your hospitality was as wonderful as your home. Your home was as beautiful as Cape Cod. Thank you!!"

Ships Knees Inn

Beach Rd
East Orleans MA 02643
(508) 255-1312

Circa 1817. This restored sea captain's house is located just a

short walk from the ocean and Nauset Beach. Guest rooms feature beamed ceilings, four-poster beds piled with quilts, and a special colonial color scheme. Several cottages and efficiencies overlook Orleans Cove.

Location: One-and-a-half hours from Boston.
*Rates: $38-$98.
Carol & Dick Hurlburt.
22 Rooms. 9 Private Baths. Guest phone available. Beds: KQDTC. Continental breakfast. Swimming pool. Golf. Tennis on the premises.

"Warm, homey and very friendly atmosphere. Very impressed with the beamed ceilings."

East Sandwich

Wingscorton Farm Inn

11 Wing Blvd
East Sandwich MA 02537
(508) 888-0534

Circa 1757. Wingscorton is a working farm on seven acres of lawns, gardens and orchards. It adjoins a short walk to a private ocean beach. This Cape Cod manse, built by a

Quaker family, is a historical landmark on what was once known as the King's Highway, the oldest historical district in the United States. All the rooms are furnished with working fireplaces (one with a secret compartment where runaway slaves hid), as well as fully restored antiques. Breakfast features fresh produce with eggs, meats and vegetables from the farm's livestock and gardens.
Location: North Side of Cape Cod, off Route 6A.
Rates: $115-$150.
Dick Loring & Sheila Weyers.
7 Rooms. 7 Private Baths. 7 Fireplaces. Guest phone available. TV available. Beds: QTC. EP. Gourmet meals. Jacuzzi. CCs: MC VISA AX. Boating, fishing, whale watching.
Seen in: *The Boston Globe, The New York Times.*
"Absolutely wonderful. We will always remember the wonderful time."

Edgartown

The Arbor
222 Upper Main St
Edgartown MA 02539
(508) 627-8137
Circa 1890. Originally built on the adjoining island of Chappaquidick,

this house was moved over to Edgartown on a barge at the turn of the century. Located on the bicycle path, it is within walking distance from downtown and the harbor. Guests may relax in the hammock, have tea on the porch, or walk the unspoiled island beaches of Martha's Vineyard.
Location: Martha's Vineyard.
*Rates: $50-$110. Season: May - Oct.
Peggy Hall.
10 Rooms. 8 Private Baths. Guest phone available. Beds: QDWT. Continental breakfast. CCs: MC. Beaches, bike trails, sailing, fishing, nature.
"Thank you so much for your wonderful hospitality! You are a superb hostess. If I ever decide to do my own B&B your example would be my guide."

Captain Dexter House of Edgartown
35 Pease's Point Way
Edgartown MA 02539
(508) 627-7289
Circa 1840. Located a little over a block from the ferry landing, this green- shuttered sea captain's house has a graceful lawn and terraced flower gardens. A gentle colonial atmosphere is enhanced by original wooden beams, exposed floor boards, working fireplaces, old-fashioned dormers, and a collection of period antiques. Luxurious canopy beds are featured.
Location: On a tree-lined residential street in downtown Edgartown.
**Rates: $65-$175.
Michael Maultz.
11 Rooms. 11 Private Baths. 4 Fireplaces. Guest phone available. TV available. Beds: QD. Continental breakfast. CCs: MC VISA AX. Horseback riding, boating, tennis, golf, bird watching, bicycling, fishing, hiking.
Seen in: *Island Getaways, Vineyard Gazette.*
"It was a perfect stay!"

Chadwick Inn
67 Winter St
Edgartown MA 02539
(508) 627-4435
Circa 1840. The winding staircase in this Greek Revival house was

crafted by the carpenter who built the Edgartown Old Whaling Church tower. You may wish to stay in the original house with its high ceilings, fireplaces, antiques, and canopy beds, or in the newer Garden Wing. Guests enjoy the veranda, with views of the spacious lawn and blooming flower beds. Numerous shops and galleries are just down the block.
Location: Center of Edgartown.
Rates: $75-$260.
Peter & Jurate Antioco.
15 Rooms. 15 Private Baths. Guest phone available. TV available. Beds: KQT. Full breakfast. Handicap access. CCs: MC VISA. Swimming, horseback riding, bicycling.
Seen in: *Cape Cod Life.*
"Wonderful hospitality. I hated to leave, it's such a comfortable, caring inn."

Edgartown Inn
56 N Water
Edgartown MA 02539
(508) 627-4794
Circa 1798. The Edgartown Inn was originally built as a home for whaling Captain Worth. (Fort Worth, Texas, was later named for his son.) The house was converted to an inn around 1820, when Daniel Webster was a guest. The innkeeper admonished his children not to "sop the platter" in Webster's presence, that is, not to dip their bread into the gravy. To the delight of the children, Webster himself "sopped the platter." Later, Nathaniel Hawthorne stayed here and proposed to the innkeeper's daughter Eliza Gibbs (who turned him down).
Location: Martha's Vineyard.
Rates: $50-$135. Season: April - Nov. 1.
Liliane & Earle Radford.
21 Rooms. 13 Private Baths. Guest phone available. TV available. Beds: KDT. Full breakfast. Tennis, golf, sailing.

Kelly House
PO Box 37
Edgartown MA 02539
(508) 627-4394
Circa 1742. Located in the heart of both downtown Edgartown and the historic district, this is one of the island's oldest inns. Over the years four additional buildings have been added, all maintaining the inn's colonial style. It has recently been extensively restored and refurbished. The Island Ferry is across the street.
*Rates: $95-$300.
Jonathan Louis.
60 Rooms. 60 Private Baths. Guest phone in room. TV in room. Beds: KQD. EP. Restaurant. Swimming pool. Conference room. CCs: MC VISA AX.
Seen in: *Boston Globe, Boston Magazine.*

Point Way Inn
104 Main St, Box 128
Edgartown MA 02539
(508) 627-8633

Circa 1840. The reception area of Point Way Inn is papered with

navigational charts from a 4,000-mile cruise the innkeepers made with their two daughters. After the voyage, they discovered this old sea captain's house. They completely renovated it, filling it with New England antiques, period wallpapers, and canopied beds. There are working fireplaces and French doors opening onto private balconies.
Location: Martha's Vineyard.
✻Rates: $75-$210.
Ben & Linda Smith.
15 Rooms. 15 Private Baths. Guest phone available. TV available. Beds: KQDTC. Continental-plus breakfast. Conference room. CCs: MC VISA. Croquet, golf, horseback riding, bicycling.
Seen in: *Boston Herald American.*

"One of the most pleasant old New England inns around." The Boston Monthly.

Fairhaven

Edgewater B&B
2 Oxford St
Fairhaven MA 02719
(508) 997-5512

Circa 1760. On the historic Moby Dick Trail, Edgewater overlooks the harbor from the grassy slopes of Poverty Point. The inn is a recently restored home in the charming, rambling, eclectic-style of the area. Across the harbor in New Bedford, is Herman Melville's "dearest place in all New England". There, visitors immerse themselves in the history and lore of whaling. Near the inn is the Gothic Revival-style Unitarian Church with stained glass by Tiffany.
Kathy Reed.
5 Rooms. 5 Private Baths. 2 Fireplaces. Guest phone available. TV in room. Beds: KQDT. Continental breakfast. CCs: MC VISA AX. Beach, tennis, golf, factory outlet shopping.

Falmouth

Captain Tom Lawrence House
75 Locust St
Falmouth MA 02540
(508) 540-1445

Circa 1861. After completing five whaling trips around the world,

each four years in length, Captain Lawrence retired at 40 and built this house. There is a Steinway piano here now, and elegantly furnished guest rooms, some with canopied beds. The house is near the beach, bikeway, ferries and train station. Freshly ground organic grain is used to make Belgian waffles with warm strawberry sauce, crepes Gisela and pancakes.
Location: Cape Cod.
Rates: $65-$95.
Barbara Sabo-Feller.
6 Rooms. 6 Private Baths. Guest phone available. Beds: KQT. B&B. CCs: MC VISA. Golf, tennis, bicycling.
Seen in: *Country Inns, Honda Acura magazine.*

"This is our first B&B experience. Better than some of the so-called 4-star hotels!! We loved it here."

Mostly Hall B&B Inn
27 Main St
Falmouth MA 02540
(508) 548-3786

Circa 1849. Albert Nye built this southern plantation house with wide verandas and a cupola to observe shipping in Vineyard Sound. It was a wedding gift for his New Orleans bride. Because of the seem-

ingly endless halls on every floor (some 30 feet long) it was whimsically called Mostly Hall.
Location: In the historic district across from the village green.
Rates: $75-$95. Season: Feb. 15-Dec. 31.
Caroline & Jim Lloyd.
6 Rooms. 6 Private Baths. Guest phone available. TV available. Beds: Q. B&B. Bicycling, tennis, golf, swimming, boating, theater.
Seen in: *Bon Appetit.*

"Of all the inns we stayed at during our trip, we enjoyed Mostly Hall the most. Imagine, southern hospitality on Cape Cod!!"

Palmer House Inn
81 Palmer Ave
Falmouth MA 02540
(508) 548-1230

Circa 1901. It's just a short walk to the village common from this turn-

of-the-century Victorian. The original stained-glass windows and rich woodwork are typical of the gracious homes in the historic district of Falmouth.
Rates: $85-$95.
Phyllis & Bud Peacock.
8 Rooms. 8 Private Baths. 1 Fireplace. Guest phone available. TV available. Beds: DWT. B&B. Gourmet meals. CCs: MC VISA. Beach, tennis, golf, bicycling.

"Exactly what a New England inn should be!"

Village Green Inn

40 W Main St
Falmouth MA 02540
(508) 548-5621

Circa 1804. The inn was originally built in the Federal style for Brad-

dock Dimmick, son of Revolutionary War General Joseph Dimmick. Later, cranberry king John Crocker, moved the house onto a granite slab foundation, remodeling it in the Victorian style. There are inlaid floors, large porches and gingerbread trim.

Location: Falmouth's historic village green.
Rates: $65-$95.
Linda & Don Long.
5 Rooms. 5 Private Baths. 5 Fireplaces. Guest phone available. TV available. Beds: QDT. Full breakfast. Boating, sailing, fishing, water skiing, tennis, horses, golf, swimming.
Seen in: *Country Inns.*

"Like we've always said, it's the innkeepers that make the inn!"

Woods Hole Passage

186 Woods Hole Rd
Falmouth MA 02540
(508) 540-7469

Circa 1889. This magnificent barn was moved from an estate to its present location overlooking one-and-a-half acres of rolling lawns adjacent to a conservation area. An enormous sitting area (30' x 30') is painted in a raspberry sorbet color with accents of hunter green and white. Furnishings include large wing-back chairs and couches, antiques and a piano. Four-poster beds and views of the fish pond and the woodlands are special attractions to guests. An ivy-covered stone wall encloses a patio. Beaches and ferries are nearby.

Rates: $70-$85.
3 Rooms. 3 Private Baths. Guest phone available. Beds: QT Full breakfast. CCs: MC VISA. Summer theaters, bike paths, fine restaurants.

"The art of hospitality in a delightful atmosphere, well worth travelling 3,000 miles for."

Great Barrington

Round Hill Farm

17 Round Hill Rd
Great Barrington MA 01230
(413) 528-3366

Circa 1907. The hayloft of the farm's 1820 dairy barn has been transformed into a handsome apart-

ment and studio with cathedral ceilings, visible posts and beams, and skylights. Seven of the guest rooms are in the farm house next door. Two-hundred and sixty-six acres of rolling, open meadows surround the inn, adjacent to Great Pine Farm. Dr. Tom Whitfield is a pediatrician turned therapist with his office in a wing of the house. This bed and breakfast inn caters exclusively to non-smokers.

*Rates: $65-$140.
Dr. & Mrs. Thomas J. Whitfield.
8 Rooms. 3 Private Baths. Guest phone in room. Beds: QDT. B&B. CCs: MC VISA AX.
Seen in: *Berkshire Eagle.*

Seekonk Pines Inn

142 Seekonk Cross Rd
Great Barrington MA 01230
(413) 528-4192

Circa 1832. Known as the Crippen Farm from 1835-1879, Seekonk Pines

Inn now includes both the original farmhouse and a Dutch Colonial wing. Throughout the years, major alterations were made to this New England frame house. Green lawns, gardens and meadows surround the inn. The name *Seekonk* was the local Indian name for the Canadian geese which migrate through this part of the Berkshires.

Rates: $60-$87.
Linda & Chris Best.
7 Rooms. 3 Private Baths. 1 Fireplace. Guest phone available. TV available. Beds: QTDC. Full breakfast. Swimming pool. Cross-country & downhill skiing, theater.
Seen in: *Los Angeles Times, The Boston Sunday Globe.*

"Of all the B&Bs we trekked through, yours was our first and most memorable!

Harwich Port

Captain's Quarters

85 Bank St
Harwich Port MA 02646
(508) 432-0337 (800) 992-6550

Circa 1850. This Victorian house features a classic wraparound porch,

gingerbread trim, an authentic turret room and a graceful, curving front stairway. It is situated on an acre of sunny lawns, broad shade trees and colorful gardens. The inn is a five-minute walk to sandy Bank Street Beach and is close to town.

Location: One-and-a-half hours from Boston.
*Rates: $50-$95.
David & Kathleen Van Gelder.
6 Rooms. 6 Private Baths. Guest phone available. TV available. Beds: QT. Continental-plus breakfast. Swimming pool. CCs: MC VISA. Golf, bicycling, fishing, boating, tennis, pool nearby. A housekeeping cottage with two beds is set in the gardens.

"Accommodations are very comfortable and attractive. This is our favorite inn!"

Country Inn Acres

86 Sisson Rd
Harwich Port MA 02646
(508) 432-2769

Circa 1700. Roses cascading over a picket fence frame this rambling Cape Cod house located on six-and-a-half acres. Comfortable furnish-

ings and an unhurried pace set a relaxing tone. Hearty New England cookery is featured in the public dining room. An in-ground pool and three hard-surfaced tennis courts on the grounds are for guests' use.
Rates: $50-$75.
Jim & Lois Crapo.
8 Rooms. 8 Private Baths. Guest phone available. TV available. Beds: KQDT. Continental breakfast. Restaurant. Swimming pool. CCs: MC VISA AX. Horseback riding, bike trail, tennis.

Holyoke

Yankee Pedler Inn
1866 Northampton St
Holyoke MA 01040
(413) 532-9494

Circa 1875. Five buildings comprise this Connecticut River Valley

inn. There is a tavern and dining room decorated with brass lamps, Blue Onion china, copper pieces and Currier & Ives prints. The kitchen has no doors, an invitation to guests to visit and watch their dinner being prepared. All the rooms are decorated in an Early American style and some include canopy beds.
*Rates: $58-$80.
The Banks family.
47 Rooms. 47 Private Baths. Guest phone in room. TV in room. Beds: KQDTC. EP. Conference room. CCs: MC VISA DC. Ten minutes to skiing Mt. Tom.

Hyannis

Chatham Town House Inn
See: Chatham, MA

Martin's Guest House
See: Nantucket Island, MA

Hyannisport

Copper Beech Inn
See: Centerville, MA

Lawrence

Sherman-Berry House
See: Lowell, MA

Lenox

Birchwood Inn
7 Hubbard St, Box 2020
Lenox MA 01240
(413) 637-2600

Circa 1764. This house was enlarged to become Hubbard Tavern in 1798. Lenox was considered the

nation's literary center in the 1800s with Edith Wharton, Henry Ward Beecher, Nathaniel Hawthorne, Henry Wadsworth Longfellow and Herman Melville living in the area. The inn's gracious parlor, dining room with an elegant fireplace, and showcase gardens add to the atmosphere.
Location: Near Berkshire.
*Rates: $75-$175.
Arnold, Sandra & Laura Hittleman.
11 Rooms. 9 Private Baths. Guest phone available. TV available. Beds: QT. Full breakfast. Handicap access. Conference room. CCs: MC VISA. Cross country & downhill skiing, hiking, biking, golf, tennis.

"Inn-credible! Inn-viting! Inn-spiring! Inn-comparable! Our ultimate getaway. Wonderful ambiance, great food and the finest hosts we ever met."

Blantyre
Rt 20
Lenox MA 01240
(413) 637-3556 (413)298-3806

Circa 1900. The facade of this Tudor manor is dominatd by a large

portico. Grandly sized rooms include the Great Hall and an elegantly paneled dining room. The formal grounds feature a tennis court, authentic croquet court, pool and carriage house. Season: May - Nov.
Roderick Anderson.
23 Rooms. 23 Private Baths. 7 Fireplaces. Guest phone in room. TV in room. Beds: KQDT. Continental-plus breakfast. Restaurant. Gourmet meals. Jacuzzi. Sauna. Swimming pool. Conference room. CCs: MC VISA AX DC CB DS. Riding, croquet, tennis.
Seen in: *The Hideaway Report.*

"There was not a single aspect of our stay with you that was not worked out to total perfection."

Brook Farm Inn
15 Hawthorne St
Lenox MA 01240
(413) 637-3013

Circa 1890. Brook Farm Inn is named after the original Brook Farm, a literary commune that sought to combine thinker and worker through a society of intelligent, cultivated members. In keeping with that theme, this gracious Victorian inn offers poetry and writing seminars and has a 650-volume poetry library. Canopy beds and Mozart tend to the spirit.
Rates: $55-$135.
Bob & Betty Jacob.
12 Rooms. 12 Private Baths. 5 Fireplaces. Guest phone available. Beds: QTF. Full breakfast. Swimming pool. CCs: MC VISA. Hiking, swimming.
Seen in: *Berkshire Eagle.*

"We loved everything about your inn, especially the friendliness and warmth of both of you. The only bad thing about your inn is leaving it!"

Cornell House
197 Main St
Lenox MA 01240
(413) 637-0562

Circa 1880. This graceful Queen Anne Victorian first welcomed paying guests back in the Thirties. Back then, it was a guest house with a speakeasy in the adjacent carriage house. All the rooms in the main house are decorated in antiques. Many have working fireplaces. The carriage house was developed into four contemporary condominium-style suites, complete with jacuzzi bathtubs, fireplaces, and kitchens.

Rates: $50-$150.
David A. Rolland.
17 Rooms. 17 Private Baths. 7 Fireplaces. Guest phone available. TV available. Beds: KQDTC. B&B. Jacuzzi. Sauna. CCs: MC VISA. Horseback riding, skiing.

East Country Berry Farm

830 East St
Lenox MA 01240
(413) 442-2057

Circa 1798. At the time of the French and Indian War, this land

was given to the widow and children of Captain Stevens. Later, the farm was owned by the Sears family for approximately 150 years. Now, two historic, restored farmhouses combine to create the inn which is located on 23 acres of lawn, fields, trees and flowers.
Location: Three-and-a-half hours from Boston.
*Rates: $55-$145.
Rita F. Miller.
7 Rooms. 3 Private Baths. Guest phone in room. Beds: KQTC. Continental-plus breakfast. Downhill & cross-country skiing, horseback riding, golf & tennis nearby.
Seen in: *Boston Globe.*

"You have all the cultural advantages and all the country setting."

The Gables Inn

103 Walker St, Rt 183
Lenox MA 01240
(413) 637-3416

Circa 1885. At one time, this was the home of Pulitzer Prize-winning novelist Edith Wharton. The Queen Anne-style Berkshire cottage features a handsome eight-sided library and Mrs. Wharton's own four-poster bed. An unusual indoor swimming pool with jacuzzi is available in warm weather. The inn also features tennis courts and a popular gourmet restaurant.
Location: Within walking distance to Tanglewood summer home of the Boston Symphony Orchestra.
Rates: $60-$175.
Mary & Frank Newton.
14 Rooms. 14 Private Baths. 5 Fireplaces. Guest phone available. TV available. Beds: QDT. Continental-plus breakfast. Jacuzzi. CCs: MC VISA. Skiing, hiking, golf.
Seen in: *P.M. Magazine, New York Times.*

"You made us feel like old friends and that good feeling enhanced our pleasure. In essence it was the best part of our trip."

Garden Gables Inn

141 Main St
Lenox MA 01240
(413) 637-0193

Circa 1770. Several distinctive gables adorn this home set on five

wooded acres. Deer occasionally wander into the garden to help themselves to fallen apples. Breakfast is served in the dining room which overlooks tall maples, flower gardens and fruit trees. The swimming pool was the first built in the county, and is still the longest.
*Rates: $60-$140.
Mario & Lynn Mekinda.
11 Rooms. 11 Private Baths. Guest phone available. Beds: KQDT. Full breakfast. Jacuzzi. Skiing, hiking, tennis, golf, horseback riding.
Seen in: *Berkshire Eagle.*

"Charming and thoughtful hospitality. You restored a portion of my sanity and I'm very grateful."

Underledge Inn

76 Cliffwood St
Lenox MA 01240
(413) 637-0236

Circa 1876. Drive along Cliffwood Street under an archway of greenery, then up Underledge's winding drive to a peaceful setting overlooking the Berkshire Hills. The

inn sits resplendently atop four acres, providing rooms with sunset views. In the foyer you'll find an exquisite oak staircase and floor-to-ceiling oak fireplace. A solarium is the setting for breakfast. Just down the street are quaint shops and fine restaurants.
Rates: $75-$160.
Marcie & Cheryl Lanoue.
9 Rooms. 9 Private Baths. Guest phone available. TV available. Beds: KQT. Continental breakfast. CCs: VISA. Golf, tennis, swimming.

"We were received like a guest in a luxurious private house. We now think of Underledge as our summer home."

Village Inn

16 Church St
Lenox MA 01240
(413) 637-0020

Circa 1771. Four years after the Whitlocks built this Federal-style

house they converted it and two adjoining barns for lodging. Since 1775, it has operated as an inn, and a six-year renovation has just been completed. Stenciled wallpapers, maple floors, and four-poster canopied beds decorate the rooms. Best of all, traditional afternoon tea includes scones and clotted cream.
Location: In the heart of the Berkshires.
*Rates: $40-$135.
Clifford Rudisill & Ray Wilson.
29 Rooms. 27 Private Baths. 5 Fireplaces. Guest phone available. TV available. Beds: KQDT. AP. Restaurant. Gourmet meals. Jacuzzi. Handicap access. Game room. Conference room. CCs: MC VISA AX DC CB. Hiking, cross-country & downhill skiing, tennis, golf, horseback riding, fishing, boating.
Seen in: *The London Independent.*

"Kathy and I stayed at your beautiful inn in early October. It was the highlight of our trip to New England."

Walker House

74 Walker St
Lenox MA 01240
(413) 637-1271

Circa 1804. This beautiful Federal-style house sits in the center of the

village on three acres of graceful woods and restored gardens. Guest rooms have fireplaces and private baths. Each is named for a favorite composer such as Beethoven, Mozart, or Handel. The innkeepers' musical backgrounds include associations with the San Francisco Opera, the New York City Opera, and the Los Angeles Philharmonic. Walker House concerts are scheduled from time to time.

Location: Route 183 & 7A.
Rates: $50-$140.
Richard & Peggy Houdek.
8 Rooms. 8 Private Baths. Guest phone available. TV available. Beds: KQT. Continental-plus breakfast. Handicap access. Conference room. Bicycles, croquet, badminton, skiing, hiking.
Seen in: *Boston Globe, PBS, Los Angeles Times.*

"We had a grand time staying with fellow music and opera lovers! Breakfasts were lovely."

Whistler's Inn

5 Greenwood St
Lenox MA 01240
(413) 637-0975

Circa 1820. Whistler's Inn is an English Tudor home surrounded by eight acres of woodland and gardens. Inside, elegance is abundant. In the impressive Louis XVI music room you'll find a Steinway piano, chandeliers, and gilt palace furniture. There is an English library with chintz-covered sofas, hundreds of volumes of books, and a fireplace of black marble. Here, guests have sherry or tea and perhaps engage in conversation with their well-traveled hosts, both authors. A baronial dining room features a Baroque candelabrum.

Rates: $65-$180.
11 Rooms. 11 Private Baths. Guest phone available. Beds: KQDT. B&B. Conference room. CCs: MC VISA AX. Skiing, hiking, horseback riding 100 yards away.
Seen in: *The Berkshire Book.*

Lowell

Sherman-Berry House

163 Dartmouth St
Lowell MA 01851
(508) 459-4760

Circa 1893. This Queen Anne Victorian is shaded by a spreading sugar maple that drops leaves onto

the wraparound porch when fall begins. You'll have a choice to relax in either the front or back parlors. Both have fireplaces and are filled with antiques. Beside the staircase is a dramatic stained-glass window. Well-behaved children of all ages are invited to pump the player piano, turn the kaleidoscope, and peer through the stereoscope.

*Rates: $50-$55.
Susan Scott & David Strohmeyer.
2 Rooms. TV available. Full breakfast. Conference room.
Seen in: *The Sun.*

"A fantastic two night stay! Loved all the lovely things surrounding us, the table settings and food fantastic."

Lynn

Caron House

142 Ocean St
Lynn MA 01902
(617) 599-4470

Circa 1911. This 22-room Georgian house was built for shoe manufacturer P.J. Harney-Lynn. The Charles Pinkham family (son of Lydia Pinkham - health tonic producer) later purchased it. Many of the original fixtures and wall coverings remain. There are several views of the ocean from the house, but the porch is the most popular spot for sea gazing. Breakfast is brought to your room, the dining room or porch.

*Rates: $75.
Sandra & Jerry Caron.
5 Rooms. 5 Private Baths. Guest phone in room. TV in room. Beds: QDT. Continental-plus breakfast. Conference room. CCs: MC VISA AX. Swimming, jogging, biking.

"The room was spectacular and breakfast was served beautifully."

Marblehead

Harbor Light Inn

58 Washington St
Marblehead MA 01945
(617) 631-2186

Circa 1712. This handsomely restored Federal home has been filled with antique mahogany furnishings, oriental carpets and expertly framed etchings to enhance its 18th-century architecture. Chandeliers and brasswork add to the decor. There are two suites with their own spas. A roof top walk provides a view of the Marblehead light and the harbor. Sam, an enormous marmalade colored cat is the inn's mascot.

Rates: $75-$175.
12 Rooms. 12 Private Baths. 6 Fireplaces. Guest phone in room. TV in room. Continental breakfast. Jacuzzi.
Seen in: *Los Angeles Times, New England Get Aways.*

"This is fabulous. Beautifully decorated and delightful in every way. One of the finest places I have visited."

Spray Cliff on the Ocean

25 Spray Ave
Marblehead MA 01945
(508) 741-0680 (508)631-6789

Circa 1910. Panoramic views stretch out in grand proportions from this English Tudor mansion set high above the Atlantic. The inn provides a spacious and elegant atmosphere inside. The grounds of the inn include a brick terrace surrounded by lush flower gardens where eider ducks, black cormorants and seagulls abound.

Location: Fifteen miles north of Boston.
*Rates: $90-$125.

Richard & Diane Pabich.
6 Rooms. 6 Private Baths. 2 Fireplaces. Guest phone available. Beds: KQD. Full breakfast. CCs: MC VISA DC.

"I prefer this atmosphere to a modern motel. It's more relaxed and love is everywhere!"

Martha's Vineyard

Captain Dexter House of Vineyard Haven

100 Main St, PO Box 2457
Martha's Vineyard MA 02568
(508) 693-6564

Circa 1843. Captain Dexter House was the home of sea captain Rodolphus Dexter. Authentic 18th-century antiques, early-American oil paintings and oriental rugs are among the inn's appointments. There are Count Rumford fireplaces and hand-stenciled walls in several rooms. Located on a street of fine historic homes, the inn is a short stroll to the beach.

Location: Martha's Vineyard.
✻✻Rates: $65-$160.
Alisa Lengel.
8 Rooms. 8 Private Baths. 2 Fireplaces. Guest phone available. TV available. Beds: QD. Continental breakfast. Conference room. CCs: MC VISA AX. Horseback riding, wind surfing, bicycling, tennis, boating, golf.
Seen in: *Martha's Vineyard Times.*

"The house is sensational. Your hospitality was all one could expect. You've made us permanent bed and breakfast fans."

Durant Sail Loft Inn

See: New Bedford, MA

Thorncroft Inn

See: Vineyard Haven, MA

For Martha's Vineyard see also: Edgartown, Oak Bluffs, Vineyard Haven

Nantucket Island

The Carlisle House Inn

26 N Water St
Nantucket MA 02554
(508) 228-0720

Circa 1765. For over 100 years, the Carlisle House has served as a

notable Nantucket lodging establishment. Three floors of picture-perfect rooms provide accommodations from the simple to the deluxe. Hand stenciling, polished wide-board floors, handsome color schemes and carpets fill each room. Special candelight dinners are occasionally served at a harvest table in the kitchen. The ferry is a five-minute walk.

Rates: $65-$135.
Peter & Suzanne Conway.
14 Rooms. 10 Private Baths. 4 Fireplaces. Guest phone available. TV available. Beds: QDT. B&B. CCs: AX. Swimming, tennis, golf, fishing.
Seen in: *Cape Cod Life, Boston Globe, Los Angeles Times.*

Century House

10 Cliff Rd Box 603
Nantucket MA 02554
(508) 228-0530

Circa 1833. Captain Calder built this Federal-style house and supple-

mented his income by taking in guests when the whaling industry slowed down. This is the oldest continually operating inn on the island. It is surrounded by other large homes on a knoll in the historic district. Museums, beaches and restaurants are a short walk away. The inn's motto for the last 100 years has been, "An inn of distinction on an island of charm." Ask about the inn's secluded rose-covered cottage.

✻Rates: $75-$140.
Gerry & Jean Heron-Connick.
14 Rooms. 10 Private Baths. Guest phone available. Beds: KQDTW. Continental-plus breakfast. Surfing, wind surfing, sandcastle building, biking.
Seen in: *Palm Beach Daily News.*

"We loved the inn and the staff. Our stay here really was enjoyed."

Corner House

49 Centre St, PO Box 1828
Nantucket Island MA 02554
(508) 228-1530

Circa 1723. The Corner House is a charming 18th-century inn. Ar-

chitectural details such as the original pine floors, paneling and fireplaces have been preserved. A screened porch overlooks the English perennial garden, where guests often take afternoon tea. Many of the romantically appointed bed chambers feature canopy beds.

✻Rates: $55-$130. Season: Feb. 15-Jan. 3.
Sandy & John Knox-Johnston.
16 Rooms. 16 Private Baths. 3 Fireplaces. Guest phone available. TV available. Beds: KQDT. Continental-plus breakfast. Gourmet meals. Conference room. CCs: MC VISA.
Seen in: *Detroit Free Press, The Atlanta Journal, Newsday.*

"The most beautiful place we've ever been to and the most comfortable!!"

The Folger Hotel & Cottages

Easton St
Nantucket MA 02554
(508) 228-0313

Circa 1891. This large Victorian hotel was built for turn-of-the-century vacationers who usually stayed a month at a time and brought the whole family. Its weathered, brown-

shingled exterior is brightened with white trim, balustraded porches, white lawn furniture and a rose-covered picket fence. Several cottages are available and a restaurant adjoins the hotel.
*Rates: $103. Season: June - Oct. 12.
Bob & Barb Bowman.
60 Rooms. 40 Private Baths. Guest phone in room. TV available. Beds: KQDTC. Full breakfast. Restaurant. CCs: MC VISA AX DC DS. Horseback riding, sailing, water sports, tennis, bicycling.
Seen in: *Boston Globe.*
"A busy and fun hotel."

Four Chimneys
38 Orange St
Nantucket Island MA 02554
(508) 228-1912

Circa 1835. The Four Chimneys is located on famous Orange Street where 126 sea captains built mansions. Captain Frederick Gardner built this Greek Revival, one of the largest houses on Nantucket Island. The Publick Room is a double parlor with twin fireplaces. Porches stretch across three levels of the house providing views of the harbor and beyond.
Rates: $90-$145. Season: April - Dec.
Betty York.
10 Rooms. 10 Private Baths. Guest phone available. TV available. Beds: QD. Continental breakfast. Conference room. CCs: MC VISA AX. Golf, boating, fishing, swimming, tennis.
Seen in: *Country Home.*

Jared Coffin House
29 Broad St
Nantucket MA 02554
(508) 228-2400

Circa 1845. Jared Coffin was one of the island's wealthiest shipowners

and the first to build a three-story mansion. The house's brick walls and slate roof resisted the Great Fire of 1846 and, in 1847, it was purchased by the Nantucket Steamship Company for use as a hotel. Additions were made and a century later, the Nantucket Historical Trust purchased and restored the house. Today, the inn consists of five historic houses and a 1964 building. The oldest is the Swain House.
*Rates: $100-$175.
Phil and Peg Read.
60 Rooms. 60 Private Baths. Guest phone in room. TV in room. Beds: QDT. EP. Restaurant. Gourmet meals. Conference room. CCs: MC VISA AX DC CB. Swimming, boating, sailing, tennis, golf, charter fishing.

Martin's Guest House
61 Centre St
Nantucket Island MA 02554
(508) 228-0678

Circa 1803. Known as Wonoma Inn in the Twenties, this shingled mariner's house in the historic dis-

trict is tucked behind a picket fence. In summer, roses climb to the six-over-six windows and the hammock gently sways on the side veranda. Authentic period pieces include Chippendale chests, Windsor rockers and Victorian settlers, all set against white woodwork and floral wallpapers. There are four-poster and canopy beds in the guest rooms. The cobblestone streets of Nantucket's Main Street are a stroll away.
*Rates: $65-$125.
Anne Foye.
13 Rooms. 9 Private Baths. 2 Fireplaces. Guest phone available. TV available. Beds: QDT. B&B. CCs: MC VISA AX. Beach, wind surfing, tennis, sailing, bird watching.
Seen in: *Cape Cod Life.*

Quaker House
5 Chestnut St
Nantucket MA 02554
(508) 228-0400

Circa 1847. The recently renovated Quaker House is situated in the Natucket Historic District on a quiet side street once known as Petticoat Lane because during the whaling era women operated most of the businesses here. Guest rooms are furnished with oriental rugs and period antiques that include brass, iron and carved wood. Its restaurant is recommended for reasonable rates and outstanding breakfasts.
Rates: $75-$110. Season: May - Sept.
Caroline & Bob Taylor.
9 Rooms. 9 Private Baths. Guest phone available. Beds: Q. Restaurant. CCs: MC VISA. Beaches, sailing, surfing, fishing, tennis, golf, whale watching.
Seen in: *Boston Magazine.*
"From two Quakers, it was enlightening and grand."

Ships Inn
13 Fair St
Nantucket MA 02554
(508) 228-0040

Circa 1812. Located near the waterfront, this four-story house

was built by Captain Obed Starbuck and is the birthplace of abolitionist Lucretia Mott. Many of the guest rooms are named for ships that the Captain commanded. Authentic furnishings have been selected. The Captain's Table is the inn's restaurant.
Location: Nantucket Island.
Rates: $55-$100.
Joyce Berruet & John Krebs.
12 Rooms. 10 Private Baths. Beds: DT. Continental breakfast. Restaurant. CCs: MC VISA. Fishing, swimming, boating.

West Moor Inn
Off Cliff Rd
Nantucket MA 02554
(508) 228-0877

Circa 1917. Only 300 yards from the beach, this house was built as a wedding gift for a member of the

Vanderbilt family. Situated on two acres at the crest of a hill, West Moor provides a splendid view of meadows, moors and the village. The yellow shingled house has a library furnished with antique wicker. The wallpapered guest rooms have fine percale sheets and antique pillow covers.
Location: One mile from Nantucket center.
Rates: $150-$225.
Nancy & John Drahzale.
14 Rooms. 14 Private Baths. Guest phone available. TV available. Beds: KQ. Full breakfast. CCs: MC VISA. Beach, tennis, bicycles. Complimentary wine and cheese is served in the evenings.
Seen in: *Inquirer, Mirror.*

"Thank you for a wonderful week. Super place, super innkeeper."

The Woodbox
29 Fair St
Nantucket MA 02554
(508) 228-0587

Circa 1709. Nantucket's oldest inn was built by Captain Bunker. In 1711, the Captain constructed an adjoining house. Eventually the two houses were made into one by cutting into the sides of both. Guest rooms are furnished with period antiques. The inn's gourmet dining room features an Early American atmosphere with low-beamed ceilings and pine-paneled walls.
Rates: $105-$170. Season: June - Mid Oct.
Dexter Tutein.
9 Rooms. 9 Private Baths. 6 Fireplaces. Guest phone available. Beds: KQDT. EP. Restaurant. Handicap access. Conference room. Swimming, tennis, bicycling.
Seen in: *Wharton Alumni Magazine.*

"Best breakfast on the island." Yesterday's Island.

New Bedford

Durant Sail Loft Inn
1 Merrill's Wharf
New Bedford MA 02740
(508) 999-2700

Circa 1848. This massive granite block structure, once the Bourne

Counting House, was owned by whaling merchant Jonathan Bourne. Located on the waterfront at Merrills Wharf it offers an authentic Portugese/Spanish cafe, an elegant penthouse restaurant overlooking the scenic working waterfront, and lodging rooms.
*Rates: $58-$68.
Michael DeLacey.
18 Rooms. 18 Private Baths. Guest phone in room. TV in room. Beds: KQTC. Restaurant. Conference room. CCs: MC VISA AX. Beach, museums.
Seen in: *The Standard-Times, Money.*

"We had always assumed B&Bs lacked privacy and were too expensive. What a wonderful surprise!"

Salt Marsh Farm
See: South Dartmouth, MA

Newburyport

Garrison Inn
On Brown Square
Newburyport MA 01950
(617) 465-0910

Circa 1809. This recently renovated four-story townhouse is located near Newburyport's restored downtown and waterfront areas. Originally built as a residence, the house served as a doctor's office, boarding house, and embroidery business. At the turn of the century it became an inn. Exposed brick walls, hewn beams and furnishings that reflect the colonial era add character to the guest rooms. There is elevator service to all levels. The Moses Brown Pub boasts vaulted brick arches, a wood burning stove and granite walls.
Location: Downtown.
*Rates: $70-$140.
Roy Hamond.
24 Rooms. 24 Private Baths. Guest phone in room. TV in room. Beds: KQD. Restaurant. Handicap access. Conference room. CCs: MC VISA AX DC CB. Beaches, golf, skiing, boating, fishing. Restaurant on the premises.
Seen in: *Yankee Travel Guide, New England Getaways.*

Newton

Host Homes of Boston
See: Boston, MA

North Eastham

The Penny House
Rt 6 Box 238
North Eastham MA 02651
(508) 255-6632

Circa 1751. Captain Isaiah Horton built this house with a shipbuilder's bow roof. Traditional wide-planked floors and 200-year-old beams buttress the ceiling of the public room. The Captain's Quarters, the largest guest room with its own fireplace bears the motto: *Coil up your ropes and anchor here, Til better weather doth appear.*
Location: One mile from National seashore. Route 6, Cape Cod.
*Rates: $65-$100.
Bill & Margaret Keith.
12 Rooms. 7 Private Baths. Guest phone available. Beds: KQT. Full breakfast. CCs: MC VISA AX. Bicycling, fishing.

"Enjoyed my stay tremendously. My mouth waters thinking of your delicious breakfast."

Oak Bluffs

Nashua House
30 Kennebec Ave, PO Box 803
Oak Bluffs MA 02557
(508) 693-0043

Circa 1873. Methodist campgrounds first occupied Oak Bluffs as a religious retreat. Later, the area was designed by William

Copeland, a landscape architect. His idea was to provide "curving ways around open spaces that lent themselves to a meandering stroll, casual encounters between neighbors, a sense of grace, ease, leisure and appreciation of natural beauty." The Victorian guest house is part of Copeland's design.
Location: Martha's Vineyard.
Rates: $29-$60. Season: April - Oct.
15 Rooms. TV available. Beds: DT. Continental breakfast. Exercise room. CCs: MC VISA AX. Bicycling, beach activities, water sports, golf.
Seen in: *The Boston Sunday Globe.*

Oak House
Box 299
Oak Bluffs MA 02557
(508) 693-4187

Circa 1872. Massachusettes Governor William Claflin purchased this gingerbread cottage because of its fine location and splendid view of the ocean. He imported oak timbers and employed ship's carpenters to carve oak ceilings, wall panels and interior pillars. A servants' wing, an additional floor, and a wide veranda were added, all for the purpose of entertaining important Massachusettes leaders. As a bed and breakfast, the Oak House maintains the grand style with authentic Victorian furnishings and refined hospitality.
*Rates: $75-$200. Season: May - Oct. 15.
Betsi Convery-Luce.
10 Rooms. 10 Private Baths. Guest phone available. TV available. Beds: KQ. B&B. CCs: MC VISA. Fishing, golf, biking, riding, tennis.

Petersham

Winterwood at Petersham
North Main St
Petersham MA 01366
(508) 724-8885

Circa 1842. The town of Petersham is often referred to as a museum of

Greek Revival architecture. One of the grand houses facing the common is Winterwood. It boasts fireplaces in almost every room and the two-room suite has twin fireplaces. Private dining is available for small groups.
*Rates: $80-$100.
Jean & Robert Day.
5 Rooms. 5 Private Baths. 4 Fireplaces. Guest phone available. Beds: TF. Continental-plus breakfast. Conference room. CCs: MC VISA AX. Hiking, cross-country skiing, museums.
Seen in: *Boston Globe.*

"Between your physical facilities and Jean's cooking, our return to normal has been made even more difficult. Your hospitality was just a fantastic extra to our total experience."

Provincetown

Bradford Gardens Inn
178 Bradford St
Provincetown MA 02657
(508) 487-1616

Circa 1820. Framed by a split-rail fence, this Cape Cod house is con-

veniently located within a mile of all of Provincetown. Behind the inn is the Loft Lodge with cathedral ceilings, a kitchen, and its own fireplace. An informal New England decor with period furnishings is enhanced by a collection of original paintings. If your visit is in the spring, request the Cherry Tree Room and enjoy the delicate blossoms from your window.
*Rates: $69-$118. Season: Apr. - Dec.
Susan Culligan.
12 Rooms. 12 Private Baths. 10 Fireplaces. Guest phone available. TV in room. Beds: QD. EP. CCs: MC VISA AX.
Seen in: *Country Inns.*

"We return year after year for the gourmet breakfasts, incredibly beautiful gardens and the warm atmosphere."

Chatham Town House Inn
See: Chatham, MA

Land's End Inn
22 Commercial St
Provincetown MA 02657
(508) 487-0706

Circa 1907. Built as a shingle-style summer cottage for Boston merchant Charles Higgins, Land's End stands high on a hill overlooking Provincetown and all of Cape Cod Bay. Part of the Higgins' collection of oriental wood carvings and stained glass is housed at the inn. Furnished lavishly in a Victorian style, the inn offers a comforting atmosphere for relaxation and beauty.
Rates: $66-$106.
David Schoolman.
14 Rooms. 10 Private Baths. Guest phone available. Beds: DT. B&B. Swimming, bicycling.

Rose And Crown
158 Commercial St
Provincetown MA 02657
(508) 487-3332

Circa 1787. Located in what will soon be Massachusett's second largest historic district, this Geor-

gian "shingled square rigger" is framed by an ornate iron fence. Above the paneled entrance, a ship's figurehead of Jane Elizabeth is posed. Victorian antiques and art work fill the inn. A cottage and an apartment are available in addition to the two rooms in the main house, named The Crown and The Rose.
*Rates: $65-$120.
Preston Babbitt, Jr.
8 Rooms. 5 Private Baths. Guest phone available. TV in room. Beds: KQDT. Continental breakfast. CCs: AX. Water sports, golf, bicycling, horseback riding.
Seen in: *Hotels.*

"We had a great time due to your hospitality."

Watership Inn

7 Winthrop St
Provincetown MA 02657
(508) 487-0094

Circa 1820. George Miller built this home, used as a private residence until 1948. Over the past 10 years it has been renovated, with careful attention given to providing an 1880s Victorian style. Guests enjoy the inn's sun decks. Season: April to Nov.

James F. Foss.

16 Rooms. 11 Private Baths. Guest phone available. Beds: D. B&B. CCs: MC VISA AX. Horseback riding, beaches, pool access.

"We found your hospitality and charming inn perfect for our brief yet wonderful escape from Boston."

Rehoboth

Perryville Inn

157 Perryville Rd
Rehoboth MA 02769
(508) 252-9239

Circa 1824. The Perryville Inn was a dairy farm for more than 140 years. During that time, in 1897, the original two-story colonial was remodeled into a handsome three-story Victorian. (The house was raised and an additional floor added underneath.) The pasture is now a public golf course, but the icehouse remains. There are old stone walls, a mill pond, trout stream and wooded paths. Inside the inn, cozy rooms are decorated with comfortable antiques.

*Rates: $40-$75.

Tom & Betsy Charnecki.

5 Rooms. 3 Private Baths. Guest phone available. Beds: QTD. Continental-plus breakfast. Conference room. CCs: MC VISA. Hay & sleigh rides, cross-country skiing, golf, tennis, bicycles, hot air balloon rides.

Seen in: *The Providence Journal-Bulletin, Evening Magazine.*

"The family voted the Perryville the best place we stayed on our entire trip, without hesitation!"

Rockport

Addison Choate Inn

49 Broadway
Rockport MA 01966
(508) 546-7543

Circa 1851. Addison Choate built his home on the site of a blueberry

bog. He became the talk of the town when he installed the first bathtub of the area in his kitchen. A long petunia-filled porch wraps around the inn. Inside are pumpkin pine floors, polished woodwork and a delightful assortment of guest rooms. If Addison returned to the house today, surely he would choose the ocean-view suite with a bathtub under a stained glass ceiling and skylight. Other guest rooms feature canopied, or brass beds and are decorated with a personal collection of antiques.

Rates: $77-$85.

Peter & Chris Kelleher.

10 Rooms. 10 Private Baths. Guest phone available. Beds: KQDT. B&B. Swimming pool. Golf, tennis, boating, horseback riding, cross-country skiing, whale watching.

Seen in: *Los Angeles Times, Detroit Free Press, Gloucester Daily Times.*

"Lovely! Charming and quaint."

The Inn on Cove Hill

37 Mt Pleasant St
Rockport MA 01966
(508) 546-2701

Circa 1791. Pirate gold found at Gully Point paid for this Federal-style house. An exquisitely-crafted spiral staircase, random-width, pumpkin-pine floors, and hand-forged hinges display the artisan's handiwork. A picket fence and granite walkway welcome guests.

Rates: $46-$86. Season: April - Oct.

John & Margorie Pratt.

11 Rooms. 9 Private Baths. Guest phone available. TV in room. Beds: QDT. B&B. Ocean swimming, whale watching, bicycling.

Seen in: *The Boston Globe, Yankee Magazine.*

"Everything was superb. Love your restorations, your muffins and your china."

Rocky Shores Inn

Eden Rd
Rockport MA 01966
(508) 546-2823

Circa 1905. This grand country mansion was built on wooded land

selected to provide maximum views of Thacher Island and the open sea. There are seven unique fireplaces, handsome woodwork, and a graceful stairway. Guest rooms are in the main house, or in several cottages nestled among the trees. Lawns flow from the mansion down to the picturesque shoreline.

Location: On a knoll overlooking the ocean.

*Rates: $76-$93. Season: March 30 - Oct. 27.

Gunter & Renate Kostka.

10 Rooms. 10 Private Baths. 7 Fireplaces. Guest phone available. TV in room. Beds: QDT. Continental-plus breakfast. Conference room. CCs: MC VISA. Nearby whale watching, sailing, fishing, diving, tennis, golf.

"Fabulous! You and your inn are a five-star rating as far as we are concerned."

Seafarer Inn

86 Marmion Way
Rockport MA 01966
(508) 546-6248

Circa 1890. Built in the early 1890s, the Seafarer Inn has been in continuous operation since the turn-of-

the-century. Originally part of a large seaside inn and cottage complex that was known as Straitsmouth, the gambrel-roofed Seafarer stands at the edge of Gap Cove, overlooking Straitsmouth Island. An old-fashioned porch wraps around the inn to take full advantage of the ocean view and breezes. Lloyds of London brass certification plates identify each of the eight ocean-view guest rooms.
*Rates: $60-$90.
Leigh Reynolds.
8 Rooms. 8 Private Baths. Guest phone available. TV in room. Beds: DT. Continental-plus breakfast. CCs: MC VISA. Beaches, sailing, hiking, whale watching, bird-watching.

Salem

Amelia Payson Guest House

16 Winter St
Salem MA 01970
(508) 744-8304

Circa 1845. This elegantly restored two-story wooden house is a prime example of Greek Revival architecture. Located in the heart of the Salem Historic District, it is a short walk to shops, museums and the wharf. Ask for the room with the canopy bed.

Location: Thirteen miles north of Boston.
❀Rates: $55-$85.
Ada & Donald Roberts.
4 Rooms. 2 Private Baths. Guest phone available. TV available. Beds: DT. Continental-plus breakfast. CCs: MC VISA AX. Whale watching.

"Your hospitality has been a part of my wonderful experience."

Coach House Inn

284 Lafayette St
Salem MA 01970
(508) 744-4092

Circa 1879. Captain Augustus Emmerton was one of the last Salem

natives to earn his living from maritime commerce. He was master of the barkentine *Sophronia* and the ship *Neptune's Daughter* that sailed to Zanzibar and the Orient. Emmerton's house is an imposing example of Second Empire architecture situated two blocks from the harbor. The House of Seven Gables and the Salem Witch Museum are nearby.
Rates: $69-$85.
11 Rooms. 9 Private Baths. 7 Fireplaces. Guest phone available. TV in room. Beds: DT. B&B. CCs: MC VISA. Museums.
Seen in: *The North Shore.*

The Salem Inn

7 Summer St
Salem MA 01970
(508) 741-0680

Circa 1834. Captain Nathaniel West, first owner of this historic building, believed that at all times his home should be maintained in readiness for his return from sea. Today that same philosophy is practiced for guests of the Salem Inn. The guest rooms are uniquely decorated with homey touches and there are two-room suites with kitchens for families.
Location: Historic downtown.
*Rates: $80-$100.
Richard & Diane Pabich.
23 Rooms. 23 Private Baths. 10 Fireplaces. Beds: KQT. Full breakfast.

"Delightful, charming. Our cup of tea."

Stephen Daniels House

1 Daniels St
Salem MA 01970
(508) 744-5709

Circa 1667. This lovely 300-year-old captain's house is one of the few three-story homes of this vintage still intact. Two large walk-in fireplaces grace the common room and each guest room includes antique furnishings, a canopy bed, and a fireplace. A pleasant English garden is filled with colorful blooms. Well behaved pets are welcome.
*Rates: $60-$77.
Catherine Gill.
5 Rooms. 3 Private Baths. 2 Fireplaces. TV available. Beds: DT. Continental breakfast. Conference room. Bicycles available.

"Like going back to earlier times."

Sandwich

Captain Ezra Nye House

152 Main St
Sandwich MA 02563
(800) 388-2278 (508) 888-6142

Circa 1829. Captain Ezra Nye built this house after a record-shattering

Halifax to Boston run, and the stately Federal-style house reflects the opulence and romance of the clipper ship era. Hand-stenciled walls and museum-quality antiques decorate the interior. Within walking distance are the Doll Museum, the Glass Museum, restaurants, shops, the famous Heritage Plantation, and the beach and marina.
*Rates: $55-$80.
Elaine & Harry Dickson.
6 Rooms. 4 Private Baths. 1 Fireplace. Guest phone available. TV available. Beds: KQT. Continental-plus breakfast. Conference room. CCs: MC VISA AX. Beaches, tennis, bike trails, piano.
Seen in: *Sandwich, A Cape Cod Town.*

"The prettiest room and most beautiful home we have been to. Thank you

for everything. We had a wonderful time."

The Dan'l Webster Inn

149 Main St
Sandwich MA 02563
(508) 888-3622

Circa 1692. Originally built as a parsonage, this property became

Patriot headquarters when it later served as the Fessenden Tavern. Daniel Webster came here to hunt and fish in the 1850s and to complain when the new glass factory workers began to discover his favorite hunting spots. The inn was destroyed by a devastating fire in 1970 and was rebuilt. The 1826 Ezra Nye House next door was added to the property a few years later. The inn holds a Travel-Holiday Distinctive Dining Award.

Steve Catania, Paul Rumul.
46 Rooms. 46 Private Baths. 6 Fireplaces. Guest phone in room. TV in room. Beds: KQDT. MAP. Restaurant. Gourmet meals. Jacuzzi. Handicap access. Swimming pool. Conference room. CCs: MC VISA AX DC CB. Golf, tennis, horse & carriage tours, charter fishing, whale-watching, beaches.
Seen in: *Bon Appetit, New York Times, Great Weekends.*

"Excellent accommodations and great food."

Isaiah Jones Homestead

165 Main St
Sandwich MA 02563
(508) 888-9115

Circa 1849. This fully restored Victorian homestead is situated on

Main Street in the village. Eleven-foot ceilings and two bay windows are features of the Gathering Room. Guest rooms contain antique Victorian bedsteads such as the half-canopy bed of burled birch in the Deming Jarves room. This room also features an over-sized whirlpool tub. Candlelight breakfasts are highlighted with the house speciality, freshly baked cornbread, inspired by nearby Sandwich Grist Mill.

*Rates: $65-$110.
Steve & Kathy Catania.
4 Rooms. 4 Private Baths. Guest phone available. Beds: Q. B&B. CCs: MC VISA AX. Bike paths, tennis, beach, museums.
Seen in: *Cape Cod Life.*

"Excellent! The room was a delight, the food wonderful, the hospitality warm & friendly. One of the few times the reality exceeded the expectation."

The Summer House

158 Main St
Sandwich MA 02563
(508) 888-4991

Circa 1835. The Summer House is a handsome Greek Revival in a set-

ting of historic homes and public buildings. (Hiram Dillaway, one of the owners, was a famous mold maker for the Boston & Sandwich Glass Company.) The house is fully restored and decorated with antiques and hand-stitched quilts. Four of the guest rooms have black marble fireplaces. The porch overlooks old-fashioned perennial gardens, antique rose bushes, and a 70-year-old rhododendron hedge.

Location: Center of village, Cape Cod.
*Rates: $50-$70.
David & Kay Merrell.
5 Rooms. 1 Private Bath. 4 Fireplaces. Guest phone available. Beds: KQDT. Continental-plus breakfast. CCs: MC VISA AX. Beach, museums.
Seen in: *Country Living Magazine.*

"This is just full of charm. As beautiful as a fairy world."

Sheffield

Staveleigh House

PO 608, S Main St
Sheffield MA 01257
(413) 229-2129

Circa 1821. The Reverend Bradford, minister of Old Parish Congregational Church, the oldest church in the Berkshires, built this home for his family. Mysteriously, the name Staveleigh is carved into the mantel of the living room fireplace. Afternoon tea is served here. The house is located next to the town green, in the shade of century-old trees.

❀Rates: $70-$85.
Dorothy Marosy & Marion Whitman.
5 Rooms. 2 Private Baths. Guest phone available. Beds: KQTD. B&B. Skiing, horseback riding, hiking, bicycling, canoeing, golf.
Seen in: *Los Angeles Times.*

"Exceptionally good."

South Dartmouth

Salt Marsh Farm

322 Smith Neck Rd
South Dartmouth MA 02748
(508) 992-0980

Circa 1775. In 1665, John Smith traded his house in Plymouth for this land in Dartmouth so he could escape the overcrowding in Plymouth. The land was called Smith's Neck. Later, Isaac Howland built this two-story Federal house. The farm has 90 acres of salt meadows, tidal marshes, hay fields, and woodlands. The innkeeper is a descendant of John Smith and enjoys sharing local history.

Location: Southeastern Massachusetts.
Rates: $55-$65.
Larry & Sally Brownell.
2 Rooms. 2 Private Baths. Guest phone available. Beds: DT. Full breakfast. CCs: MC VISA. Tandem bicycle, nature trails.

"A peaceful setting for the refreshment of both body & spirit."

South Egremont

Egremont Inn

Old Sheffield Rd
South Egremont MA 01258
(413) 528-2111

Circa 1780. This three-story inn is adjacent to a quiet, tree-lined stream

where guests have spent many a summer day. There are private tennis courts on the premises. A wraparound porch is decorated with white wicker and guest rooms are furnished with antiques. There is a tavern and a dining room.

Rates: $90-$155.
John Black.
22 Rooms. 22 Private Baths. Guest phone available. TV available. Beds: DTC. MAP. Restaurant. Swimming pool. Conference room. CCs: MC VISA AX. Tennis, golf, hiking, riding, skiing.

"To say our stay at the Egremont Inn was unforgettable would be understating the case."

Weathervane Inn

PO Box 388
South Egremont MA 01258
(413) 528-9580

Circa 1785. Nine years were spent restoring this rambling old house

that was formerly a kennel, store, and dance studio. Long ago, it was also an inn. Today high ceilings, handsome moldings, and a beehive oven are featured attractions.

Location: Main Street, Route 23.
Vincent & Anne Murphy and Robert & Olena Murphy.
10 Rooms. 10 Private Baths. Guest phone available. TV available. Beds: KQT. Full breakfast. Restaurant. Handicap access. Conference room. CCs: MC VISA. Downhill & cross-country skiing, fishing, tennis, golf.
Seen in: *New York Times, Berkshire Eagle, Berkshire Business Journal, Boston Herald.*

"...the Murphy family exemplifies the best tradition of New England hospitality." Berkshire Business Journal.

South Lee

Merrell Tavern Inn

Rt 102 Main St
South Lee MA 01260
(413) 243-1794

Circa 1794. This elegant stagecoach inn was carefully preserved under

supervision of the Society for the Preservation of New England Antiquities. Architectural drawings of Merrell Tavern have been preserved by the Library of Congress. Eight fireplaces in the inn include two with original beehive and warming ovens. An antique circular birdcage bar serves as a check-in desk. Comfortable rooms feature canopy and four-poster beds with Hepplewhite and Sheraton-style antiques.

Rates: $65-$130.
Charles & Faith Reynolds.
9 Rooms. 9 Private Baths. Guest phone available. Beds: TD. Full breakfast. CCs: MC VISA. Downhill & cross-country skiing.

"One of the most authentic period inns on the East Coast." The Discerning Traveler.

Springfield

Blantyre

See: Lenox, MA

The Old Mill Inn

See: Somersville, CT 06072

Sterling

Sterling Orchards B&B

60 Kendall Hill Rd
Sterling MA 01564
(508) 422-6595

Circa 1740. The orchards planted in 1920 by Shirley Smiley's father-in-law provide a suitable setting to frame the 250-year old farmhouse that has been thoroughly renovated. Original Indian shutters are still in place. A hiding place in the 12-square-foot center chimney, originally built by settlers can still be found. The largest guest room (20x30) served as the town ballroom at the 1881 centennial. Afternoon tea is available in the Appleseed Tea Room, the inns dining room.

Rates: $65. Season: April - Dec.
Robert & Shirley Smiley.
2 Rooms. 2 Private Baths. Guest phone in room. TV in room. Beds: QT. Full breakfast. Swimming pool. Conference room. Wineries.
Seen in: *Boston Globe, Worcester Telegram.*

"It's like stepping back in time with every modern convenience."

Stockbridge

Historic Merrell Tavern Inn

See: South Lee, MA

Sturbridge

Captain Samuel Eddy House Inn

See: Auburn, MA

Commonwealth Inn

11 Summit Ave
Sturbridge MA 01566
(508) 347-7603

Circa 1890. This 16-room Victorian house overlooks the Quinebaug

River just a few minutes from Old Sturbridge Village. Two parlors,

each with a marble fireplace, are available to guests. The inn is decorated in a country style. The veranda has two gazebos, one on each end.
Rates: $40-$55.
Kevin MacConnell.
8 Rooms. 5 Private Baths. Guest phone available. Full breakfast. Jacuzzi. Fishing, boating, tennis, golf, cross-country skiing, hiking.

Sturbridge Country Inn

530 Main St
Sturbridge MA 01566
(508) 347-5503

Circa 1840. Shaded by an old silver maple, this classic Greek Revival house boasts a two-story columned entrance. The attached carriage house now serves as the lobby and displays the original post-and-beam construction and exposed rafters. All guestrooms have individual fireplaces and whirlpool tubs. They are gracefully appointed in reproduction colonial furnishings, including queen-size four posters and cherry sleigh beds. A patio and gazebo are favorite summertime retreats.
Rates: $69-$110.
Kevin MacConnell.
9 Rooms. 9 Private Baths. 9 Fireplaces. Guest phone in room. TV in room. Beds: KQDT. Continental breakfast. Jacuzzi. CCs: MC VISA AX. Fishing, boating, tennis, golf, cross-country skiing, hiking.
Seen in: *Southbridge Evening News, Worcester Telegram & Gazette.*

"Best lodging I've ever seen."

Tolland Inn

See: Tolland, CT

The Wildwood Inn

See: Ware, MA

Vineyard Haven

Lothrop Merry House

Owen Park Box 1939
Vineyard Haven MA 02568
(508) 693-1646

Circa 1790. Eight yoke of oxen moved this house to its present beach-front location. A wedding gift from father to daughter, the house has a classic center chimney and six fireplaces. Breakfast is served in season on the flower bedecked patio overlooking stunning harbor views.

A private beach beckons at the end of a sloping lawn.
Location: Martha's Vineyard.
Rates: $68-$145.
John & Mary Clarke.
7 Rooms. 4 Private Baths. Guest phone available. Beds: QTC. Continental breakfast. CCs: MC VISA. Golf, tennis, bicycling, sailing, canoeing.
Seen in: *Cape Cod Life.*

"It is the nicest place we've ever stayed."

Thorncroft Inn

278 Main St, PO Box 1022
Vineyard Haven MA 02568
(508) 693-3333

Circa 1918. The Thorncroft Estate is a classic craftsman bungalow with

a dominant roof and neo-colonial details. It was built by Chicago grain merchant John Herbert Ware as the guest house of a large ocean front estate. Guests experience an authentic turn-of-the-century ambience with canopied beds, walnut Victorian suites, and balconies, situated on three and one-half acres of lawns and woodlands.
*Rates: $105-$225.
Karl & Lynn Buder.
19 Rooms. 19 Private Baths. 7 Fireplaces. Guest phone available. TV available. Beds: QDT. B&B. Jacuzzi. CCs: MC VISA AX. Beaches, bicycles.

"It's the type of place where we find ourselves falling in love all over again."

Ware

The Wildwood Inn

121 Church St
Ware MA 01082
(413) 967-7798

Circa 1880. This yellow Victorian has a wraparound porch and a beveled glass front door. American primitive antiques include a collection of New England cradles, and there is a cobbler's bench, a sled, and a spinning wheel. The inn's two acres are dotted with maple, chestnut and apple trees. Through the woods you'll find a river.
Rates: $37-$64.
Margaret Lobenstine.
5 Rooms. Guest phone available. Beds: QTD. Full breakfast. CCs: MC VISA. Tennis, canoeing, swimming, hiking, cross-country skiing.
Seen in: *The Boston Globe.*

West Barnstable

Honeysuckle Hill

591 Main St
West Barnstable MA 02668
(508) 362-8418

Circa 1810. This Queen Anne Victorian built by Josiah Goodspeed is

in the National Register. Guest rooms are decorated with Victorian sofas, Peter Rabbit memorabilia, and St. Louis antiques. Feather beds, Laura Ashley linens and fluffy pillows are among the other amenities.
Location: Cape Cod.
*Rates: $90-$105.
Barbara & Bob Rosenthal.
3 Rooms. 3 Private Baths. 1 Fireplace. Guest phone available. TV available. Beds: KQ. Full breakfast. Game room. Conference room. CCs: MC VISA DS. Bicycling, beach.

"The charm, beauty, service and warmth shown to guests are impressive, but the food overwhelms. Breakfasts

were divine!" Judy Kaplan, *St. Louis Journal.*

West Harwich

Lion's Head Inn

186 Belmont Rd PO 444
West Harwich MA 02671
(508) 432-7766

Circa 1804. This Cape half-house was built by sea captain Thomas Snow. Original pine floors and a ship's ladder staircase are features of the inn. It is decorated in antiques and traditional furnishings. Several old maps hang in the Map Room, once used as a study for Captain Snow.

*Rates: $57-$125.
Kathleen & William Lockyer.
6 Rooms. 6 Private Baths. Guest phone available. TV available. Beds: KT. Full breakfast. Swimming pool. CCs: MC VISA. Badminton, beach, fishing, boating, golf.

"The best innkeepers we have met on the Cape!"

Sunny Pines B&B Inn

77 Main St, PO Box 667
West Harwich MA 02671
(508) 432-9628

Circa 1900. Caleb Chase of Chase and Sanbourne coffee fame built this

house as a parsonage for the local Baptist Church. It later became the town library and in the Forties, a guest house. An Irish candlelight breakfast is served. The innkeeper was an oceanographer for 20 years.

*Rates: $80.
Jack & Eileen Connell.
6 Rooms. 6 Private Baths. 1 Fireplace. Guest phone in room. TV in room. Beds: KQT. B&B. Gourmet meals. Swimming pool. CCs: MC VISA AX. Hiking, bicycling, water sports, tennis, golf, croquet, horseshoes, darts, barbecue.

West Hyannisport

B&B Cape Cod

Box 341
West Hyannisport MA 02672
(508) 775-2772

Circa 1709. This reservation service represents many exquisitely restored historic houses in almost every nook and cranny on the Cape. One of the oldest, an Early American home, was built two blocks from Cape Cod Bay by the founder of Barnstable. Furnished in an early 1700s decor, the home has four-poster beds and period antiques. A hearty country breakfast is served.

Rates: $45-$177.
4 Rooms. 2 Private Baths. 2 Fireplaces. Guest phone available. Full breakfast. CCs: MC VISA AX.

West Newton

Sears-Withington House

274 Otis St
West Newton MA 02165
(617) 332-8422

Circa 1840. Situated on West Newton Hill, this 16-room Italianate

mansion is in the National Register of Historic Places. There are seven fireplaces and an antique decor that includes collections of cribs and birdcages gathered by the innkeeper on world travels. Dedicated preservationists, the innkeepers sometimes entertain guests at their private club. A stately poodle, Baron Brian de Breffny, is in residence. Boston, Cambridge and the airport are 20 minutes away.

Rates: $75.
Marise Tracey Zellmann.
3 Rooms. 3 Private Baths. 3 Fireplaces. Guest phone available. TV available. Beds: DT. Full breakfast.

Woods Hole

Marlborough

320 Woods Hole
Woods Hole MA 02543
(508) 548-6218

Circa 1939. Although not centuries old, this is a faithful reproduction of

a Cape cottage complete with picket fence and rambling roses, set on spacious grounds. Although the inn is beautifully decorated with antiques, designer sheets and wall coverings, children are welcome. In winter, a proper high tea with finger sandwiches, pate, and scones with clotted cream is served. An English paddle-tennis court, a swimming pool, and a gazebo are popular spots in summer.

Rates: $85.
Patricia Morris.
6 Rooms. 6 Private Baths. 1 Fireplace. Guest phone available. TV available. Beds: QDTC. B&B. Swimming pool. Private beach.
Seen in: *Cape Cod Life.*

"Our stay at the Marlborough was a little bit of heaven."

Worcester

Captain Samuel Eddy House Inn

See: Auburn, MA

Worcester-Rutland

The General Rufus Putnam House

344 Main St
Worcester-Rutland MA 01543
(508) 886-4256

Circa 1750. This restored Federal house, listed in the National

Register, was the home of General Rufus Putnam, founder of Marietta, Ohio. A memorial tablet on the house states that "to him it is owing...that the United States is not now a great slaveholding empire." Surrounded by tall maples and a rambling stone fence, the inn rests on seven acres of woodlands and meadows. There are eight fireplaces, blue Delft tiles, and a beehive oven. Afternoon tea and breakfast is served fireside in the keeping room where the hostess may often be found in period dress.

Location: Rural/Central Massachusetts.
Rates: $75-$90.
Gordon & Marcia Hickory.
3 Rooms. 1 Private Bath. Guest phone available. TV available. Beds: DTC. Full breakfast. Swimming pool. Golf, fishing, concerts.
Seen in: *Sunday Telegram, The Land Mark, Washusett People.*

"We were thrilled not only with the beauty of the place but the luxury and the best hospitality."

Yarmouth Port

Crook' Jaw Inn

186 Main St, Rt 6A
Yarmouth Port MA 02675
(508) 362-6111

Circa 1790. This Georgian full-cape was named Crook Jaw after the notorious whale hunted in the 1700s by Yarmouth sea captains. The inn is situated on two-and-a-half acres (much of it English country gardens), in the center of Yarmouth Valley. The area is called Captains' Row, named for the sea captains who lived there. The innkeeper, a former Catholic Priest, provides both breakfast and dinner in the price of the room.

Rates: $85-$99.
7 Rooms. 7 Private Baths. 8 Fireplaces. Guest phone available. TV available. Beds: KD. AP. CCs: MC VISA AX. Golf, tennis, swimming, cross-country skiing.
Seen in: *Cape Cod Times, Cape Cod Life Magazine.*

"Hospitality is fantastic, food superb, atmosphere delightful."

Liberty Hill Inn

77 Main St, Rt 6A
Yarmouth Port MA 02675
(508) 362-3976

Circa 1825. This Greek Revival mansion is located on the site of the

original Liberty Pole dating from Revolutionary times. To benefit the Cape Cod Conservatory of Music several local decorators restored the rooms. There are outstanding English gardens and the inn's setting on the hill affords views of Cape Cod Bay. On historic Old King's Highway, it's a brief walk to antique shops, auctions, and restaurants.

*Rates: $75-$100.
Beth & Jack Flanagan.
5 Rooms. 5 Private Baths. Guest phone available. TV available. Beds: KQT. B&B. Gourmet meals. Conference room. Beaches, nature trails, golf.
Seen in: *Cape Cod Life.*

"Your homey hospitality makes us want to return."

Old Yarmouth Inn

223 Main St
Yarmouth Port MA 02675
(508) 362-3191

Circa 1696. The Old Yarmouth was originally built as an inn and is one of America's oldest. There is a guest register from the 1860s when it was called the Sears Hotel. Traveling salesmen often stayed here and according to the register they sold such items as Henry's Vermont Linament, lightning rods, sewing machines and drilled-eye needles. Today this venerable inn has rooms with antiques, but also cable television and air-conditioning.

Location: King's Highway, Route 6A.
Rates: $55-$80.
Shane Peros.
5 Rooms. 5 Private Baths. 2 Fireplaces. Guest phone available. TV in room. Beds: KQ. B&B. Restaurant. Handicap access. CCs: MC VISA AX DC DS. Beaches.
Seen in: *The Register, Travel News.*

Wedgewood Inn

83 Main St
Yarmouth Port MA 02675
(617) 362-5157

Circa 1812. This three-story Greek Revival home was built for a

maritime attorney and was the first architecturally designed home in town. A built-in hallway clock is written up in the town's local history. Wide-board floors, pencil-post beds, antiques and fireplaces create a romantic ambiance. Afternoon tea is served.

*Rates: $85-$145.
Milt & Gerrie Graham.
6 Rooms. 6 Private Baths. 4 Fireplaces. Guest phone available. TV available. Beds: Q. Full breakfast. CCs: MC VISA AX DC. Water sports, bike & hiking trails, golf, tennis, horseback riding, whale watching.

Michigan

Allegan

Winchester Inn

524 Marshall St
Allegan MI 49010
(616) 673-3621

Circa 1863. This neo-Italian Renaissance mansion was built of double-

layer brick and has been restored to its original beauty. Surrounded by a unique hand-poured iron fence, the inn is decorated with period antiques and romantically furnished bed chambers. Depending on your wishes, you can have breakfast in the elegant dining room, or in bed.
*Rates: $45-$95.
Dave & Denise Ferber.
5 Rooms. 5 Private Baths. Guest phone available. TV available. Beds: QT. Full breakfast. Handicap access. Conference room. CCs: MC VISA. Skiing, boating, horseback riding, fishing. Murder mystery weekends.
Seen in: *Architectural Digest.*

"This is one of Michigan's loveliest country inns."

Big Bay

The Big Bay Point Lighthouse B&B

3 Lighthouse Rd
Big Bay MI 49808
(906) 345-9957

Circa 1896. With 4,500 feet of frontage on Lake Superior, this landmark lighthouse commands 534 acres of forests and a five-acre lawn. The interior of the lighthouse features a brick fireplace. Several guest rooms look out to the water. The tower room on the top floor boasts truly unforgettable views.
Location: Four miles northeast of Big Bay.
*Rates: $90-$115.
Buck & Marilyn Gotschall.
6 Rooms. 4 Private Baths. 1 Fireplace. Guest phone available. Beds: DT. B&B. Sauna. Exercise room. Conference room. Hiking, bicycling, skiing.
Seen in: *Los Angeles Times, USA Today.*

"The fact that anyone who has ever met Buck Gotschall or stayed at the Lighthouse will tell everyone they know that they have to go there, in my opinion, makes Buck Gotschall the Ambassador of the year." Vic Krause, State Representative.

Detroit

The Blanche House Inn

506 Parkview Dr
Detroit MI 48214
(313) 822-7090

Circa 1905. This massive "White House" style Victorian mansion has two-story columns supporting a rotunda entrance. Located on the Stanton Canal a block from the Detroit River, the inn provides an expansive view of Detroit's waterways. Polished wood floors, etched glass, Pewabic tile, gleaming woodwork and antiques fill the inn's 10,000 square feet. The home was built by Marvin Stanton, former overall manufacturer and Detroit lighting commissioner. In the Twenties this house and adjoining "Castle" served as a private boys' school where Henry Ford II attended.
Location: Three miles east of downtown on the canal.
Rates: $60-$70.
Mary Jean & Sean Shannon.
8 Rooms. 8 Private Baths. Guest phone in room. TV in room. Beds: QT Continental-plus breakfast. Conference room. CCs: MC VISA AX. Near the theater district.
Seen in: *Detroit Monthly, Crain's Detroit Business.*

Victorian Inn

See: Port Huron, MI

Escanaba

The House of Ludington

223 Ludington St
Escanaba MI 49829
(906) 786-4000

Circa 1865. Located on the shore of Little Bay de Noc, this large four-story historic hotel with its green awnings and medieval tower dominates the waterfront scene. There are two dining rooms accommodating parties up to 200. Guest rooms are individually decorated.
Rates: $55 & up.
Gerald & Vernice Lancour.
21 Rooms. 21 Private Baths. Guest phone in room. TV in room. Beds: Q.

Continental breakfast. Restaurant. Gourmet meals. Conference room. CCs: MC VISA AX DC CB DS.
Seen in: *Country Inns, Michigan Living.*

Fennville

The Kingsley House
626 W Main St
Fennville MI 49408
(616) 561-6425

Circa 1886. Complete with a three-story turret, construction of this

Queen Anne Victorian was paid for in silver bricks by the Kingsley family. Mr. Kingsley is noted for having introduced the apple tree to the area. In recognition of him, guest rooms are named Dutchess, Golden Delicious and Granny Smith. A winding oak staircase leads to the antique-filled guest chambers. Family heirlooms and other period pieces add to the inn's elegance.
*Rates: $50-$65.
David & Shirley Witt.
5 Rooms. 5 Private Baths. Guest phone available. TV available. Beds: QDT. Full breakfast. Conference room. CCs: MC VISA. Walking trails, bicycling, cross-country skiing, Lake Michigan nearby.
Seen in: *The Fennville Herald, The Commercial Record.*

"It was truly enjoyable. You have a lovely home and a gracious way of entertaining."

Grand Rapids

Kemah Guest House
See: Saugatuck, MI

Holland

The Kingsley House
See: Fennville, MI

The Old Holland Inn
133 W 11th St
Holland MI 49423
(616) 396-6601

Circa 1895. Innkeeper Dave Plaggemars is a descendant of one of

Holland's ten original founding families. The entrance hall to his National Register Victorian home opens to an oak staircase. Grecian columns support an elaborate fireplace with brass inlays and an 1895 heat-reflecting insert. The oak pocket doors were crafted by first-generation Dutch woodworkers. Now, family collections and period antiques are scattered throughout the spacious guest rooms. A pear hedge on the property provided the inspiration for Innkeeper Dave Plaggemar's Poached Pears in Cranberry Sauce.
Rates: $45-$75.
Dave & Fran Plaggemars.
5 Rooms. 2 Private Baths. TV available. Beds: DT. Continental-plus breakfast. Conference room. CCs: VISA DS. Tennis, trout fishing, Lake Michigan.
Seen in: *The Ann Arbor News, Holland Evening Sentinel, Country Inn Cookbook.*

"We enjoyed the touches of live flowers, a selection of books and the wonderful deck."

The Parsonage
6 E 24th St
Holland MI 49423
(616) 396-1316

Circa 1908. Members of Prospect Park Christian Reformed Church built this Queen Anne structure as their parsonage. Over the years, it housed nine different pastors and their families. Rich oak woodwork, antique furnishings, and leaded glass are found throughout the inn. There are two sitting rooms, a formal dining room, garden patio and summer porch. The inn flies a B&B flag designed by the hosts and available to guests.
Location: Close to Hope College.
Rates: $65-$70.
Bonnie Verwys.
4 Rooms. 1 Private Bath. 1 Fireplace. Guest phone available. TV available. Beds: DT. Continental-plus breakfast. Conference room. CCs: MC. Cross-country skiing, golf, tennis, boating.

"Charming. We slept so well!"

Hudson

The Sutton-Weed Farm
18736 Quaker Rd
Hudson MI 49247
(517) 547-6302 (517) 339-1492

Circa 1874. This farm with its 170 acres has been in the same family

ever since it was purchased by Albert Clinton-Weed in 1873. The seven-gabled Victorian house features furnishings collected from five generations of family. There is a secretary made without nails, with poured glass windows. A rope bed, a spinning wheel, and antique chests are featured. Corn, soy beans or wheat are planted. In the woods where maple syrup is still collected are ancient sugar maples once 'tapped' by the Potowatami Indians.

*Rates: $55.
Jack & Barb Sutton.
13 Rooms. Guest phone available. TV available. Beds: QDTC. Continental-plus breakfast. CCs: MC VISA. Golf, cross-country skiing, lakes all nearby.
Seen in: *Hudson Post Gazette.*

"Just like going home to Grandma's—complete with homemade maple syrup at the breakfast table."

Kalamazoo

Hall House

106 Thompson St
Kalamazoo MI 49007
(616) 343-2500

Circa 1923. This Georgian Colonial Revival-style house was constructed

by builder H.L. Vander Horst as his private residence. During the depression when the construction slowed, Mr. Vander Horst busied himself painting the vaulted ceiling with a Dutch landscape now much admired. Other special features of the house include a ten- head shower, an early intercom system and secret drawers. The hillside campus of Kalamazoo College and the city center are nearby.

Rates: $70.
Pam & Terry O'Connor.
4 Rooms. 4 Private Baths. 1 Fireplace. Guest phone available. TV in room. Beds: Q. Continental-plus breakfast. CCs: MC VISA AX DS. Fishing, winery tours, museums.
Seen in: *Canton Observer, Encore Magazine.*

"A step into the grace, charm and elegance of the 19th century, but with all the amenities of the 20th century right at hand."

Lakeside

The Pebble House

15093 Lakeshore Rd
Lakeside MI 49116
(616) 469-1416

Circa 1912. Across the street from a private beach on Lake Michigan, this was the main house of a summer cottage colony for Orthodox Jews. It is named for the local stones collected to construct the fireplace, some of the exterior walls and fence posts. There are three

guest buildings connected by wooden walks and pergolas. Rooms feature antique and wicker furnishings. The hosts give seminars on the Arts & Crafts Movement.

Rates: $90-$130.
Jean & Ed Lawrence.
7 Rooms. 7 Private Baths. Guest phone available. Beds: KQ. Full breakfast. Handicap access. CCs: MC VISA. Tennis, cross-country skiing, beach, nature centers.
Seen in: *Chicago Sun-Times.*

"Beautiful place, wonderful hospitality, cute cats."

Mackinac Island

Haan's 1830 Inn

Box 123
Mackinac Island MI 49757
(906) 847-3403 (312) 234-5682

Circa 1830. The clip-clopping of horses is still heard from the front porch of this inn as carriages and wagons transport visitors around the island. Said to be the oldest Greek Revival-style house in the Northwest Territory, Haan's 1830 Inn is behind a picket fence and just across the street from the bay. Victorian antiques include a writing desk used by Colonel Preston, an officer at Fort Mackinac at the turn-of-the-century. A cannonball bed built in 1790 still sports a horsehair mattress.

Rates: $60-$98. Season: May 25 - Oct. 15.
Joyce & Vernon and Nicholas & Nancy Haan.
7 Rooms. 5 Private Baths. Guest phone available. Beds: QDTC. B&B. Golf, horseback riding, carriage trips & tours.
Seen in: *Detroit Free Press, Chicago Tribune.*

The ambiance, service and everything else was just what we needed."

Mendon

The Mendon Country Inn

440 W Main St
Mendon MI 49072
(616) 496-8132

Circa 1873. This two-story inn was constructed with St. Joseph River clay bricks fired on the property. There are eight-foot windows, high ceilings and a walnut staircase. Country antiques are accentuated with rag rugs, collectables, and bright quilts. The Indian Room has a fireplace. A creek runs by the property and a romantic courting canoe is available to guests. Depending on the season, guests may also borrow a tandem bike or arrange for an Amish sleigh ride.

Location: Halfway between Chicago and Detroit.
*Rates: $45-$115.
Dick & Dolly Buerkle.
11 Rooms. 11 Private Baths. Guest phone available. TV available. Beds: QD. Continental breakfast. Jacuzzi. Handicap access. Conference room. CCs: MC VISA DS. Fishing, tennis, golf, bicycles, swimming, cross-country skiing.
Seen in: *Innsider.*

"A great experience. Good food and great hosts. Thank you."

Niles

Yesterday's Inn

518 N 4th
Niles MI 49120
(616) 683-6079

Circa 1875. Nearly every style of architecture can be found on Fourth Street in the historical district. This distinctive Italianate house has a graceful porch and tall shuttered windows. The walls are 12 inches thick, with the interior plaster applied directly onto the brick.

Location: Eight miles north of South Bend.
Rates: $55.
Elizabeth Baker.
4 Rooms. 4 Private Baths. Jacuzzi.

Northport

Old Mill Pond Inn
202 W Third St
Northport MI 49670
(616) 386-7341

Circa 1895. This three-story summer cottage nestled among tall trees

is surrounded by extensive gardens including a Roman garden with fountain and statues. Inside the house is an unusual collection of memorabilia from around the world. Breakfast is served by the fireside or on the screened porch with its white wicker furnishings. Shops and restaurants are within two blocks and the beach is a quarter of a mile.
Rates: $65.
David Chrobak.
6 Rooms. Guest phone available. TV available. Beds: QT. Full breakfast. CCs: MC VISA. Sailing, fishing, swimming.

Port Huron

Victorian Inn
1229 Seventh St
Port Huron MI 48060
(313) 984-1437

Circa 1896. This finely renovated Queen Anne Victorian house has both an inn and restaurant. Gleaming carved-oak woodwork, leaded-glass windows, and fireplaces in almost every room reflect the home's gracious air. Authentic wallpapers and draperies provide a background for carefully selected antiques. Victorian inspired menus include such entrees as Partridge with Pears and Filet of Beef Africane, all served on antique china.
Rates: $45-$60.
Sheila Marinez.
4 Rooms. 2 Private Baths. Guest phone available. TV available. Beds: QDT. Continental breakfast. Restaurant. CCs: MC VISA AX DS. Water sports, golf, tennis, museums of art & history.
Seen in: *Detroit Free Press.*

"In all of my trips, business or pleasure, I have never experienced such a warm and courteous staff."

Port Sanilac

Raymond House Inn
M-25, 111 S Ridge St
Port Sanilac MI 48469
(313) 622-8800

Circa 1871. Uri Raymond, owner of Michigan's first hardware store,

built this Gothic house with its gingerbread facade and white icicle trim dripping from the eaves. The inn is filled with antiques and features classic moldings, high ceilings and a winding staircase. The innkeeper is a sculptor who works as a restoration artist at the U. S. Capitol. Be sure to visit the historic lighthouse nearby.
Location: I-94 to Port Huron, then 30 miles on M-25.
*Rates: $50-$60. Season: May to Nov.
Shirley Denison.
7 Rooms. 7 Private Baths. Guest phone available. TV available. Beds: Q. Continental-plus breakfast. CCs: MC VISA. Sport fishing, swimming, sailing, golf, bicycling, scuba diving.
Seen in: *Adventure Magazine.*

"A warm, friendly, relaxed, homey atmosphere like visiting friends and family."

Saugatuck

Kemah Guest House
633 Pleasant St
Saugatuck MI 49453
(616) 857-2919

Circa 1906. Stained-glass windows, beamed ceilings, and stone and tile

fireplaces are trademarks of this house. There is a billiard room, and a Bavarian rathskeller has German inscriptions on the wall and original wine kegs. Deco Dormer, a guest room with a mahogany bedroom suite, was featured in a 1926 *Architectural Digest.* That same year, a Frank Lloyd Wright-style solarium with its own waterfall was added to the house. Kemah is situated on two hilltop acres with a view of the water. Spelunkers will want to explore the cave found on the property.
*❀Rates: $50-$95.
Cindi & Terry Tatsch.
7 Rooms. 3 Fireplaces. Guest phone available. TV available. Beds: DT. Continental-plus breakfast. Game room. Conference room. CCs: MC VISA. Golf, sailing, cross-country skiing.
Seen in: *Innsider.*

"What a wonderful time we had at Kemah. Thank you for a delightful stay. Your home is very special."

The Kingsley House
See: Fennville, MI

The Kirby House
294 W Center St, PO Box 1174
Saugatuck MI 49453
(616) 857-2904

Circa 1890. This impressive Victorian home sits behind a picket fence. It's framed by tall trees and a veranda that wraps around three

sides. The inn has four fireplaces and a grand staircase.
Location: Near Lake Michigan.
Rates: $85-$100.
Marsha & Loren Kontio.
10 Rooms. 4 Private Baths. Guest phone available. Beds: QDT. Full breakfast. Jacuzzi. Swimming pool. CCs: MC VISA. Beachcombing, hiking, swimming.
Seen in: *Michigan Today Magazine, Lansing State Journal.*

Maplewood Hotel
428 Butler St Box 1059
Saugatuck MI 49453
(616) 857-1771

Circa 1860. Maplewood Hotel stands on the quiet village green in the center of Saugatuck. Built during Michigan's lumber era, the elegant three-story Greek Revival hotel boasts four massive wooden pillars, each 25-feet high. The interiors include crystal chandeliers, period furniture, and well-appointed lounge areas.
Rates: $45-$134.
Donald & Harriet Mitchell.
13 Rooms. 13 Private Baths. Guest phone in room. TV in room. Beds: KQC. Continental breakfast. Swimming pool. Conference room. CCs: MC VISA. Swimming.

"Staying at the Maplewood provided the pleasure of listening to classical music on the player grand piano. It was so easy vacationing...steps from boutiques, art galleries and antique shops."

The Park House
888 Holland St
Saugatuck MI 49453
(616) 857-4535

Circa 1857. This Greek Revival-style home is the oldest residence in Saugatuck and was constructed for

the first mayor. Susan B. Anthony was a guest here for two weeks in the 1870s, and the local Women's Christian Temperance League was established in the parlor. A country theme pervades the inn, with antiques, old woodwork, and pine floors.
*Rates: $65-$85.
Lynda & Joe Petty.
8 Rooms. 8 Private Baths. Guest phone available. TV available. Beds: Q. Continental-plus breakfast. Handicap access. Conference room. CCs: MC VISA DS. Cross-country skiing, swimming, hiking.
Seen in: *Detroit News, Innsider, Gazette, South Bend Tribune.*

Traverse City

The Victoriana
622 Washington St
Traverse City MI 49684
(616) 929-1009

Circa 1898. Egbert Ferris, a partner in the European Horse Hotel, built this Italianate Victorian manor and a two-story carriage house. Later, the bell tower from the old Central School was moved onto the property, and now serves as a handsome Greek Revival gazebo. The house

has three parlors, all framed in fretwork. Etched and stained glass is found throughout. Guest rooms are furnished with family heirlooms. The house speciality is Belgian waffles topped with homemade cherry sauce.
*Rates: $45-$65.
Flo & Bob Schermerhorn.
4 Rooms. 2 Private Baths. 1 Fireplace. Guest phone available. TV available. Beds: KQDT. Full breakfast. CCs: MC VISA. Bicycling, water sports, downhill & cross-country skiing, wineries, theater.
Seen in: *Midwest Living.*

"We will long remember your beautiful home, those delectable breakfast creations and our pleasant chats."

Warwickshire Inn
5037 Barney Rd
Traverse City MI 49684
(616) 946-7176

Circa 1902. The Warwickshire is a farm home located in a country setting, yet with a panoramic view of Traverse City. Spacious rooms feature turn-of-the century Victorian furnishings. Afternoon tea and breakfast are served elegantly on fine china.
Location: Two miles west of City Center.
Rates: $68.
Dan & Pat Warwick.
3 Rooms. 3 Private Baths. Full breakfast.

Minnesota

Cannon Falls

Quill & Quilt

615 W Hoffman St
Cannon Falls MN 55009
(507) 263-5507

Circa 1897. This three-story, gabled colonial Revival house has six bay

windows and several porches and decks. The inn features a well-stocked library, a front parlor with a fireplace, and handsomely decorated guest rooms. A favorite is the room with a double whirlpool tub, two bay windows, king-size, oak canopy bed and Victorian chairs.

Location: Forty-five miles from Minneapolis/St. Paul, and Rochester.
*Rates: $45-$95.
Denise Anderson & David Karpinski.
4 Rooms. 4 Private Baths. TV available. Beds: KQD. AP. Jacuzzi. CCs: MC VISA. Bicycling, hiking, canoeing, cross-country skiing, tubing.
Seen in: *Minneapolis Tribune, Country Quilts.*

"What a pleasure to find the charm and hospitality of an English country home while on holiday in the United States."

Chaska

Bluff Creek Inn

1161 Bluff Creek Dr
Chaska MN 55318
(612) 445-2735

Circa 1864. This two-story brick Victorian folk home was built on land granted by Abe Lincoln to one of the earliest settlers in the area. It boasts a wide veranda and three summer porches. Family antiques are accentuated by Laura Ashley and Merrimekko quilts and linens. A three-course breakfast is served in the country dining room with Bavarian Crystal and old English China.

Rates: $65-$85.
Anne Karels.
4 Rooms. 1 Private Bath. Guest phone available. Beds: QD. Full breakfast. CCs: MC VISA. Bike trails, cross-country skiing, walking paths.

Grand Marais

Cascade Lodge

PO Box 693
Grand Marais MN 55604
(218) 387-1112

Circa 1938. A main lodge and several vintage cabins (1920s) comprise Cascade Lodge set in the midst of Cascade River State Park overlooking Lake Superior. Cascade Creek meanders between the cabins towards the lake. The lodge has a natural-stone fireplace and lounge areas decorated with the skins of moose, coyote, wolves and bear. Canoeing, hiking to Lookout Mountain, walking along Wild Flower Trail and watching the sunset from the lawn swing are favorite summer activities. Skiing, snowshoeing, photography and fireside conversations are popular in winter.

Location: Highway 61.
*Rates: $50-$90.
Gene & Laurene Glader.
26 Rooms. 26 Private Baths. 6 Fireplaces. Guest phone in room. TV available. Beds: QDT. MAP. Restaurant. Game room. Conference room. CCs: MC VISA AX.
Seen in: *Country Inns.*

"We needed to get away and recharge ourselves. This was the perfect place."

Naniboujou Lodge

HC 1 Box 505
Grand Marais MN 55604
(218) 387-2688

Circa 1928. Built originally as an exclusive private club, this cedar

and cypress lodge was constructed on land that includes a mile of Lake Superior shoreline. Babe Ruth and Jack Dempsey were charter members, but after the stock market crash of 1929 the club fell into financial straits. Now rejuvenated, the

lodge possesses Minnesota's largest native rock fireplace. It also features a dining room painted in brilliant colors, with Cree Indian designs on the vaulted ceilings and walls.
Location: On the shores of Lake Superior, 15 miles east of Grand Marais.
Rates: $37-$64.
Tim & Nancy Ramey.
29 Rooms. 15 Private Baths. Guest phone available. TV available. Beds: QDT. EP. CCs: MC VISA DC. Hiking, cross-country skiing.
Seen in: *Twin Cities Reader, City Pages, House & Gardens.*

Lanesboro

Scanlan House
708 Park Ave S
Lanesboro MN 55949
(507) 467-2158

Circa 1889. This gracious Victorian, a National Register house, was built

by the Scanlans, successful merchants and bankers. Since then, more recent owners have added window boxes and garden areas. There are stained-glass windows throughout, and carved oak woodwork adorns the dining room and staircase.
*Rates: $45-$90.
Mary, Gene & Kirsten Mensing.
5 Rooms. 1 Private Bath. Guest phone available. Beds: QD. Full breakfast. CCs: MC VISA. Skiing, bicycles, golf, tennis, tubing, canoeing.
Seen in: *Post-Bulletin, Lacrosse Tribune.*

"We were refreshed and inspired and when the sun was out, wanted not to budge from the balcony."

Minneapolis

Quill & Quilt
See: Cannon Falls, MN

Red Wing

Pratt-Taber Inn
706 W Fourth
Red Wing MN 55066
(612) 388-5945 (612) 388-0166

Circa 1876. City treasurer A. W. Pratt built this Italianate house

during the town's centennial. He added star-studded porch detailing to the gingerbread trim to celebrate the event. Feather-painted slate fireplaces and gleaming butternut woodwork provide a backdrop for early Renaissance Revival and country Victorian furnishings. There is a Murphy bed hidden in the library buffet. Other library items include 1,000 stereoptican slides and a Victrola. Secret bureau drawers, authentic Victorian wallpapers, dress-up clothes and hand-stenciling add to the atmosphere.
Location: Fifty-five miles south of the Twin Cities.
*Rates: $69-$89.
Jane Walker, Darrell Molander.
6 Rooms. 2 Private Baths. 4 Fireplaces. Guest phone available. TV available. Beds: KQDT. B&B. Jacuzzi. Handicap access. Conference room. CCs: MC VISA. Golf, hiking, bicycling, boating, dinner cruises.
Seen in: *Better Homes & Gardens, Midwest Living.*

"When I need a peaceful moment I dream of the Pratt-Taber and the big screened-in porch with church bells chiming a favorite tune."

Rochester

Canterbury Inn B&B
723 2nd St SW
Rochester MN 55902
(507) 289-5553

Circa 1890. Scrollwork adorns the many gables of this three-story, red Victorian. Carved oak spindles grace the stairway. Polished hardwood floors, stained glass windows, Oriental rugs and a fireplace add to the graciousness of the inn. Afternoon tea is served. The Mayo Clinic is a three-block walk from the inn.
*Rates: $60-$75.
Mary Martin & Jeffrey Van Sant.
4 Rooms. 4 Private Baths. TV available. Beds: KQT. Full breakfast. CCs: MC VISA. Canoeing, golf, tennis, cross-country skiing. Pick up service from airport.
Seen in:

"Rochester's B&B treasure." Bill Farmer, *St. Paul Pioneer Press.*

Quill & Quilt
See: Cannon Falls, MN

Saint Paul

Chatsworth B&B
984 Ashland
Saint Paul MN 55104
(612) 227-4288

Circa 1902. This three-story red Victorian is framed by maple and

basswood trees. Guest rooms are decorated in an international theme except for the Four Poster Room. It features a canopy bed, whirlpool bath, mirrored armoire, and a wallpaper of roses that covers both the ceiling and the walls. Vegetarian breakfasts are available. Don't forget to ask the innkeeper for her famous cranberry bread.
Rates: $55-$90.
Donna & Earl Gustafson.
5 Rooms. 2 Private Baths. Guest phone available. TV available. Beds: KQDT. B&B. Conference room. Jogging, biking, museums.
Seen in: *St. Paul Pioneer Press and Dispatch.*

"Wonderful and romantic surroundings everywhere. So beautifully kept, fresh and clean. Tremendous service."

Quill & Quilt

See: Cannon Falls, MN

University Club of St. Paul

420 Summit Ave
Saint Paul MN 55102
(612) 222-1751

Circa 1912. Established to enhance literary, cultural and social activities

for the well-educated, this Tudor Revival club is modeled after the Cambridge and Oxford Clubs in London. Fine English antiques and oil paintings of English landscapes decorate the interiors. In the Grill Bar, F. Scott Fitzgerald's initials can be found carved beside those of other club members. There is a library, dining room, Fireside Room and a fitness center.

Rates: $45-$85.
John Rupp.
5 Rooms. 5 Private Baths. TV available. Beds: QT. Restaurant. Sauna. Swimming pool. Conference room. CCs: MC VISA DC. Tennis, exercise room, playground.
Seen in: *Minnesota USA Magazine, Corporate Report.*

Spring Valley

Chase's

508 N Huron Ave
Spring Valley MN 55975
(507) 346-2850

Circa 1879. This brick, Second Empire house is listed in the National Register. It features a mansard roof, arched windows, and a long porch. Several parlors and the guest rooms display antiques for sale. Beds include a walnut Renaissance Revival hooded bed, a pine canopy bed, and a golden oak, six-foot-tall double bed.

*Rates: $50-$60. Season: March - Dec.
Bob & Jeannine Chase.

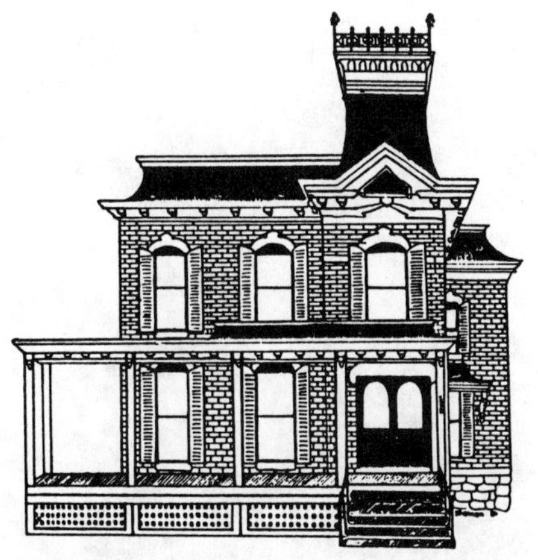

5 Rooms. 2 Private Baths. Guest phone available. TV available. Beds: KQD. Full breakfast. CCs: MC VISA. Trout fishing, cross-country skiing, hiking, canoeing.

"It's so beautiful!"

Stillwater

Lowell Inn

102 N Second St
Stillwater MN 55082
(612) 439-1100

Circa 1930. The Palmer family has operated this Williamsburg-style

hotel since Christmas Day 1930, collecting antiques and fine tableware all this time. The George Washington Room is a parlor containing collections of Dresden china, a Charles III Sheffield silver service, Williamsburg ladder-back chairs, and colonial draperies. A natural spring bubbles in the Garden Room. Guest rooms include four suites with jacuzzi baths.

Rates: $89-$239.
Arthur & Maureen Palmer.
21 Rooms. 21 Private Baths. Beds: KQC. AP. Restaurant. Jacuzzi. Conference room. CCs: MC VISA. Downhill & cross-country skiing, hiking, canoeing, biking, swimming.
Seen in: *New York Times.*

Rivertown Inn

306 W Olive St
Stillwater MN 55082
(612) 430-2955

Circa 1882. This three-story Victorian was built by lumber mill

owner John O'Brien. Framed by an iron fence, the home is enveloped by a wraparound veranda. Each guest room has been decorated with care, but we suggest the honeymoon suite, or Patricia's Room with its giant whirlpool and tall oak bedstead. A burl wood buffet in the dining room is laden each morning with home-baked breads and cakes. The St. Croix River is a short walk away.

Rates: $45-$115.
Chuck & Judy Dougherty.
9 Rooms. 9 Private Baths. 2 Fireplaces. Guest phone available. Beds: D. B&B. Jacuzzi. Conference room. CCs: MC VISA. Golf, biking, skiing, canoeing, swimming, river excursions.

Twin Cities

Rivertown Inn

See: Stillwater, MN

Walker

Chase On The Lake Lodge & Motor Inn

PO Box 206
Walker MN 56484
(218) 547-1531 (800) 533-2083

Circa 1921. Located on the shoreline of Leech Lake, this Tudor-style hotel, in the National Register, was renovated in 1987. A Twenties-style predominates. The hotel has a private sandy swimming beach. The city docks are a block away and Main Street is two blocks.

❀Rates: $52-$68.
Jim & Barb Aletto.
20 Rooms. 20 Private Baths. Guest phone in room. TV in room. Beds: QDTC. B&B. Restaurant. Conference room. CCs: MC VISA AX DS. Golf, water slide, movie theater, shopping, tennis, boating, launch fishing.
Seen in: *Minneapolis Star Tribune, Fargo Forum.*

"We thoroughly enjoyed ourselves with the wonderful view, excellent menu and friendly service."

Mississippi

Aberdeen

Rosemont
407 S Meridian
Aberdeen MS 39730
(601) 369-9434

Circa 1909. This Mississippi Landmark is a 22-room, neo-classical Victorian house. It includes a pillared second-story balcony and first-floor veranda. The builder, Addison Brannin, was a local artisan who showcased his talents in the art of interior graining. Leaded glass and hand-screened wallpapers provide an elegant background for Queen Anne walnut furnishings in the inn's main rooms. Guest rooms are furnished with Victorian oak pieces.

*Rates: $60.
Melany & Shane Fortenberry.
2 Rooms. 2 Private Baths. 1 Fireplace. Guest phone in room. TV available. Beds: D. Full breakfast. Gourmet meals. CCs: MC VISA. Fishing, skiing, boating, walking & exercise track.
Seen in: *Aberdeen Examiner.*

"We are going to tell all our friends about your delightful inn."

Columbus

Rosemont
See: Aberdeen, MS

Jackson

Millsaps-Buie House
628 N State St
Jackson MS 39202
(601) 352-0221

Circa 1888. Major Millsaps, founder of Millsaps College, built this stately mansion 100 years ago. Today the house still remains in the family. A handsome, columned entrance, bays and gables are features of the house, decorated by Berle Smith, designer for Mississippi's governor's mansion. The parlor features a French dating bench and a grand piano. The guestrooms are appointed in antiques and canopied beds.

*Rates: $75-$130.
Judy Fenter, Nancy Fleming, Rivers Carroll.
11 Rooms. 11 Private Baths. Guest phone in room. TV in room. Beds: KQDT. Full breakfast. Handicap access. Conference room. CCs: MC VISA AX DC.
Seen in: *New York Times, Jackson Daily News, Mississippi.*

Lorman

Rosswood Plantation
Hwy 552
Lorman MS 39096
(601) 437-4215

Circa 1857. Rosswood is a stately, columned mansion in an original plantation setting. Here, guests may find antiques, buried treasure, ghosts, history of a slave revolt, a Civil War battleground, the first owner's diary and genuine southern hospitality. Voted the "prettiest

place in the country" by *Farm & Ranch Living*, the manor is a Mississippi Landmark and is in the National Register.

*Rates: $75-$90.
Jean & Walt Hylander.
4 Rooms. 4 Private Baths. Beds: QDTC. Full breakfast. Conference room. CCs: MC VISA.
Seen in: *Southern Living, New York Times.*

"The plantation to see if you can only see one."

Meridian

Lincoln, Ltd. B&B
PO Box 3479
Meridian MS 39303
(601) 482-5483

Circa 1830. Lincoln, Ltd. Bed and Breakfast is a Mississippi reservation service representing over 50 properties throughout the state and Western Alabama, Eastern Louisiana, and Tennessee. Over 225 rooms are available, many in private historic homes, such as an antebellum mansion and a historic log cabin.

Rates: $70-$100.
May White, Kathy Tanner.
9 Rooms. 9 Private Baths. Guest phone in room. TV in room. Beds: QDTC. Continental breakfast. Jacuzzi. Swimming pool. CCs: MC VISA.

Natchez

The Burn

712 N Union St
Natchez MS 39120
(601) 442-1344 (800) 654-8859

Circa 1834. White Doric columns support the front portico of this

Greek Revival gem set in four blossoming acres of dogwoods, magnolias and camellias. An extensive antique collection graces the inn with gas light chandeliers, Belgian draperies and finely carved woodwork adding to the genteel setting. The lavish Pink Room features an exquisite antique four-poster bed built by master craftsman Prudent Mallard, and canopied with swaged damask draperies. Further pampering is provided with a plantation breakfast served at a polished mahogany dining table, set with crystal and silver. The innkeeper has served for twenty years as mayor of Natchez.
*Rates: $75-$125.
Loveta & Tony Byrne.
6 Rooms. 6 Private Baths. Guest phone available. TV in room. Beds: QDT. B&B. Gourmet meals. Swimming pool. Conference room. CCs: MC VISA AX DC CB DS. Swimming.
Seen in: *Country Inns, Bon Appetit.*

"We are still basking in the pleasures we found at The Burn."

Port Gibson

Oak Square Plantation

1207 Church St
Port Gibson MS 39150
(601) 437-4350

Circa 1850. Six, 22-foot tall fluted Corinthian columns support the front gallery of this 30-room Greek Revival plantation. The owners furnished the mansion with Mississippi

heirloom antiques, some as old as 200 years. The parlor holds a carved rosewood Victorian suite, original family documents, and a collection of Civil War memorabilia. Enormous oaks and magnolia trees grace the grounds.
Location: US 61 between Natchez & Vicksburg.
*Rates: $65-$75.
Mr. & Mrs. William D. Lum.
10 Rooms. 10 Private Baths. Beds: QT. Full breakfast. CCs: MC VISA.
Seen in: *Quad-City Times, The Dallas Morning News.*

"We just cannot say enough about the wonderful ambiance of Oak Square...except it is even better than four stars."

Starkville

Rosemont

See: Aberdeen, MS

Tupelo

Rosemont

See: Aberdeen, MS

Vicksburg

Cedar Grove Mansion Inn

2300 Washington St
Vicksburg MS 39180
(800) 862-1300 (800)448-2820 MS

Circa 1840. It's easy to relive *Gone With the Wind* at this grand antebel-

lum estate built by John Klein as a wedding present for his bride. Visitors sip mint juleps and watch gas chandeliers flicker in the finely appointed parlors. The children's rooms and master bedroom contain their original furnishings. Although Cedar Grove survived the Civil War, a Union cannonball is still lodged in the parlor wall. There is a magnificant view of the Mississippi from the terraces and front galleries. Four acres of gardens include fountains and gazebos.
*Rates: $85-$130.
Estelle Mackey.
18 Rooms. 7 Private Baths. 5 Fireplaces. Guest phone in room. TV in room. Beds: KQD. Full breakfast. Jacuzzi. Handicap access. Swimming pool. Conference room. CCs: MC VISA AX.
Seen in: *Vicksburg Post.*

The Corners

601 Klein St
Vicksburg MS 39180
(800) 444-7421 (601) 636-7421

Circa 1872. Listed in the National Register, the Corners was built as a

wedding present. It is an interesting combination of architectural styles, including Steamboat Gothic, Louisiana Raised Cottage, Italianate, Greek Revival, and Vicksburg Pierced Columns. Lovely antiques and canopy beds fill the mansion. It's the only inn in Vicksburg with original parterre gardens and a view of the Mississippi River from the front gallery.
*Rates: $65-$95.
Cliff & Bettye Whitney.
7 Rooms. 7 Private Baths. 3 Fireplaces. Guest phone in room. TV in room. Beds: QDT. B&B. Gourmet meals. Handicap access. Conference room. CCs: MC VISA AX. Golf, boating, museums.
Seen in: *Vicksburg Post.*

"The highlight of our trip was the night we spent in Vicksburg with you. It was just great!"

The Duff Green Mansion

1114 First East St
Vicksburg MS 39180
(601) 636-6968

Circa 1856. The 12,000 square-foot Duff Green Mansion is considered

one of the finest examples of Palladian architecture in Mississippi. It was a wedding gift to Mary Lake Green from her parents, Judge and Mrs. William Lake, who built the adjacent house, Lakemont. During the siege of Vicksburg, Mary Green gave birth in one of the caves next to the mansion and named her son Siege Green. Handsome furnishings highlight the spacious and elegantly renovated rooms.

Location: Vicksburg Historic District.
*Rates: $75-$150. Season: March to Dec.
Sally Bullard & Tom DeRossette.
7 Rooms. 7 Private Baths. 12 Fireplaces. Guest phone available. Beds: KQC. Full breakfast. Jacuzzi. Sauna. Conference room. CCs: MC VISA. Swimming.
Seen in: *The Washington Post, Chicago Sun Times.*

"The service could not have been better. We've stayed in a number of B&B inns in different parts of the country over the years and we rate you #1."

Missouri

Branson

Branson House

120 4th St
Branson MO 65616
(417) 334-0959

Circa 1923. A landscape architect for the Missouri State Park system,

A. L. Drumeller built this bungalow house, surrounding it with rock walls, gardens and orchards. Exposed beam ceilings, built-in glass cabinets, and pine woodwork add to the house's charm. From its hillside location, the veranda overlooks the town and Lake Taneycomo. Sherry is served in the late afternoon. In the evening, cookies and milk are set out for the guests.

Location: Downtown.
Rates: $50-$65. Season: March - Dec.
Opal Kelly.
7 Rooms. 7 Private Baths. Guest phone available. TV available. Beds: TW. Full breakfast. Fishing, boating, water sports.

"Thank you so much for your warm hospitality. It really made our trip special."

Hannibal

The Fifth Street Mansion B&B

213 S Fifth St
Hannibal MO 63401
(314) 221-0445

Circa 1868. This 20-room Italianate house displays the typical extended

eaves and heavy brackets, tall windows, and decorated lintels. A cupola affords a view of the town. Mark Twain was invited to dinner here by the Garth family and joined Laura Frazer (his Becky Thatcher) for the evening. An enormous stained-glass window lights the stairwell. The library stained-glass window holds the family crest. The library also features hand-grained walnut paneling.

Location: North of St. Louis 100 miles.
⁂Rates: $50-$70.
Donalene & Mike Andreotti.
7 Rooms. 4 Private Baths. Guest phone available. TV available. Beds: QDTC. B&B. Conference room. CCs: MC VISA. Water sports, fishing, Mississippi River cruises.
Seen in: *Innsider.*

"We thoroughly enjoyed our visit. Terrific food and hospitality!"

Garth Woodside Mansion

RR 1
Hannibal MO 63401
(314) 221-2789

Circa 1871. This Italian Renaissance mansion is set on 39 acres of

meadow and woodland. Authentic Victorian antiques fill the house. An unusual flying staircase with no visible means of support vaults three stories. Best of all, is the Samuel Clemens room where Mark Twain slept in a "button bed." It has been said that Buffalo Bill Cody and Mr. Clemens met here.

Location: Just off highway 61.
⁂Rates: $51-$68.
Irv & Diane Feinberg.
8 Rooms. 4 Private Baths. 8 Fireplaces. Guest phone available. TV available. Beds: D. Full breakfast. Conference room. CCs: MC VISA. Riverboat rides.
Seen in: *Country Inns, Chicago-Sun Times.*

"So beautiful and romantic and relaxing, we forgot we were here to work." Jeannie and Bob Ransom, *Innsider.*

Jamesport

Richardson House B&B

PO 227
Jamesport MO 64648
(816) 684-6664

Circa 1900. This intimate, five-room house is situated on a farm at

the edge of Jamesport. It was built by the Richardson family, who delivered rural mail by horse and buggy. Careful restoration makes an attractive background for the country antiques that furnish the house, now owned by the Richardsons' granddaughter. The entire house is rented to one party at a time. Home-cooked meals fresh from the farm are available.

*Rates: $60.
Jayla Smith, Rebecca Richardson, owner.
5 Rooms. Guest phone available. TV available. Beds: QDT. Full breakfast. Gourmet meals. Conference room. CCs: MC VISA. Fishing, hunting, hiking, bicycling, canoeing, horseback riding. Farm tours for children.
Seen in: *St. Joseph News-Press/Gazette.*

Kansas City

Richardson House B&B

See: Jamesport, MO

Saint Charles

Boone's Lick Trail Inn

1000 South Main St
Saint Charles MO 63301
(314) 947-7000

Circa 1840. This Greek Revival brick and limestone house overlooks the Missouri River State Trail and the Lewis and Clark Trail. From the galerie porch guests may watch the Missouri River flow by Frontier Park. The inn is furnished with antiques, lace curtains and old quilts.

Location: 10 minutes from St. Louis airport.
Rates: $40-$75.
V'Anne Mydler
6 Rooms. 4 Private Baths. Guest phone available. TV available. Beds: QD. Continental-plus breakfast. CCs: MC VISA DS. Art museums, the ferry, historic district. Missouri River, Louis & Clark launching site.
Seen in: *St. Louis Post Dispatch, Midwest Motorist, Midwest Living.*

"Makes your trip back in time complete."

Saint Joseph

Harding House

219 N 20th St
Saint Joseph MO 64501
(816) 232-7020

Circa 1903. This turn-of-the-century, four-square home was built for George Johnson. At the time, Johnson was vice-president and general manager of Wyeth Hardware, the world's largest hardware supply company. Fourteen beveled leaded-glass windows, beautiful oak woodwork and gracious pocket doors are among its features. Furnishings are antique. Lemon bread and tea, or other beverages are served in the late afternoon.

Rates: $40-$50.
Glen & Mary Harding.
4 Rooms. 1 Private Bath. 1 Fireplace. Guest phone available. TV available. Beds: D. Full breakfast. Conference room. CCs: MC VISA AX. Horseback riding, museums, river boat rides, surrey rides.
Seen in: *Country, The News Press Gazette.*

"Our stay in your home has been an experience of pure delight."

"Can't say enough about your breakfasts...they are the best we have had in the dozens of bed and breakfasts we have stayed in."

Saint Louis

The Coachlight B&B

1 Grandview Heights
Saint Louis MO 63131
(314) 965-4328

Circa 1904. This three-story, brick house is in an exclusive district of

elegant homes. These homes were once considered "private places" where home owners even owned the streets. The neighborhood has been beautifully maintained and is near St. Louis and Washington Universities. The parlor features Queen Anne furnishings with Laura Ashley prints. Please request Coachlight when you call the reservation center.

Location: Central West End.
Rates: $60 & up.
Reservations are made by River Country B&B.
3 Rooms. 3 Private Baths. Beds: QDT. Continental-plus breakfast. Conference room. CCs: MC VISA AX. Golf, handball, zoo, art museums.

Lafayette House

2156 Lafayette Ave
Saint Louis MO 63104
(314) 772-4429

Circa 1876. Captain James Eads, designer and builder of the first

trussed bridge across the Mississippi River, built this Queen Anne mansion as a wedding present for his daughter Margaret. The rooms are furnished in antiques and there is a suite with a kitchen on the third floor. The house overlooks Lafayette Park.

Location: In the center of St. Louis.
*Rates: $40-$70.
Sarah & Jack Milligan.
6 Rooms. 2 Private Baths. Guest phone available. TV available. Beds: DTC. Full breakfast.

"We had a wonderful stay at your house and enjoyed the furnishings, delicious breakfasts, and friendly pets."

Maggie's B&B

See: Collinsville, IL

Springfield

Walnut Street B&B

900 E Walnut St
Springfield MO 65806
(417) 864-6346

Circa 1894. This three-story Queen Anne gabled house has cast iron

Corinthian columns and a veranda. Polished wood floors and antiques are featured throughout. Upstairs you'll find the gathering room with a fireplace. Ask for the McCann guest room with two bay windows. A full breakfast is served, including items such as Peach Stuffed French Toast.

Rates: $60-$95.
Nancy & Karol Brown.
6 Rooms. 6 Private Baths. Guest phone available. TV available. Beds: QDT. Full breakfast. Handicap access. Conference room. CCs: MC VISA. Boating, fishing, sports center.

Washington

Schwegmann House

438 West Front Street
Washington MO 63090
(314) 239-5025

Circa 1853. John F. Schwegmann, a native of Germany, built a flour mill on the Missouri riverfront. His

stately three story home was constructed to provide extra lodging for over-night customers who traveled long hours to town. Today, guests enjoy the formal gardens and patios overlooking the river, as well as gracious rooms decorated with antiques and air-conditioning. A country store is on the property.

Location: One hour west of St. Louis.
✻Rates: $60.
George Bocklage.
9 Rooms. 7 Private Baths. 2 Fireplaces. Guest phone available. Beds: DT. Continental-plus breakfast. Handicap access. CCs: MC VISA. Wineries, antique shopping.
Seen in: *St. Louis Post-Dispatch, West County Journal.*

"Like grandma's house many years ago."

Zachariah Foss Guest House

4 Lafayette
Washington MO 63090
(314) 239-6499

Circa 1846. Zachariah and Amelia Foss arrived here from Maine with their five children. They selected this spot on the Missouri River, across from the steamboat landing, for their new home. Amelia was a schoolteacher who opened the first private English-speaking schoolhouse in this German settlement. Constructed in a Federal style, the house is three stories of clapboard and stone. This private historic retreat is rented to one party at a time, and can accommodate from one to six guests. Antique-filled rooms, a his-and-hers claw-foot bathtub, a tandem bike and Missouri wine are among the luxuries provided.

Location: West of St. Louis, 45 minutes.
Rates: $110-$130.
Sunny & Joy Drewel, Janet Berlener.
7 Rooms. 1 Private Bath. Beds: DT. B&B. CCs: MC VISA. Linen & Lace shop on the premises.
Seen in: *Country Home.*

Montana

Big Sky

Lone Mountain Ranch

PO Box 145
Big Sky MT 59716
(406) 995-4644

Circa 1920. A cross-country ski center and guest ranch, this was one of the first ranches in Gallatin Canyon. Situated in a meadow, posh log cabins with fireplaces border a tumbling trout stream. An extensive Indian artifact collection is housed in several ranch buildings. There are 45 miles of groomed trails for skiers and in summer, guests fish world-famous trout streams or take part in dozens of other activities.

Location: Fifty miles south of Bozeman Mountain.
*Rates: From $725pp/wk Season: June 1-Oct/Dec 1-Apr
Mike Amkeny, Bob & Viv Schaap.
22 Rooms. 22 Private Baths. Guest phone available. Beds: QT. AP. Jacuzzi. Handicap access. Conference room. CCs: MC VISA. Horseback riding, cross-country skiing, fly fishing. Horse-drawn sleigh ride dinners.
Seen in: *The New York Times, Town & Country Magazine.*

"Meals couldn't be better! From the sack lunches to the gourmet dinner, it was all delicious. We'll be back with friends."

Bozeman

Voss Inn

319 S Willson
Bozeman MT 59715
(406) 587-0982

Circa 1883. The Voss Inn is a restored two-story house with a large front porch and a Victorian parlor. Old-fashioned furnishings include an upright piano and chandelier. A full breakfast is served, with fresh baked rolls kept in a unique warmer that's built into an ornate 1880s radiator.

Location: Four blocks south of downtown.
*Rates: $50-$70.
Bruce & Frankee Muller.
6 Rooms. 6 Private Baths. Guest phone available. TV available. Beds: KQ. Full breakfast. CCs: MC VISA DC. Skiing, hiking, fishing, hunting, biking, horseback riding.
Seen in: *Sunset Magazine, Cosmopolitan.*

"...first class all the way."

Essex

Izaak Walton Inn

PO Box 653
Essex MT 59916
(406) 888-5700

Circa 1939. The Izaak Walton Inn was built as an overnight lodging for Great Northern Railway workers. It is located now on the Burlington-Northern Mainline and is served twice daily by Amtrak. The inn is in a strategic location for enjoying Glacier National Park. You can take trails and rivers into the Rocky Mountain forests and meadows.
*Rates: $55-$74.
Larry & Lynda Vielleux.
30 Rooms. 10 Private Baths. Guest phone available. Beds: DT. Restaurant. Sauna. Game room. Conference room. CCs: MC VISA. Hiking, fishing, rafting, horseback riding, cross-country skiing, white-water rafting.
Seen in: *Outdoor America-Summer, Seattle Times.*

"The coziest cross-country ski resort in the Rockies."

Great Falls

Three Pheasant Inn

626 5th Ave N
Great Falls MT 59401
(406) 453-0519

Circa 1910. This Victorian house, newly opened as an inn, features glassed-in sun porches. The common rooms include a parlor and library. Guest rooms are filled with English Victorian-style antiques and Oriental rugs. A 100-year-old fountain and a gazebo grace the garden.

The inn is popular for weddings and parties.
Rates: $35-$55.
David & Amy Sloan
5 Rooms. 2 Private Baths. Guest phone available. Full breakfast. Walk to museums, shops and businesses. Golf, walking trails, fishing, hunting and skiing nearby.
"Have stayed at many B&Bs in England, Scotland and Ireland, but yours has been the nicest."

Red Lodge

Willows Inn

224 S. Platt Ave, PO Box 886
Red Lodge MT 59068
(406) 446-3913

Circa 1903. This shuttered three-story farmhouse, framed by spruce trees and a white picket fence, was once a boarding house for Finnish mine workers. Rooms feature Victorian and comfortable country furnishings. Some have mountain views. Charles Kuralt called the Beartooth Highway that runs through Red Lodge, "the most beautiful drive in America." Rock Creek, noted for its trout fishing is a block from the inn.
*Rates: $45-$60.
Elven Boggio.
5 Rooms. 3 Private Baths. Guest phone available. TV available. Beds: KQT. Continental-plus breakfast. CCs: MC VISA. Cross-country and downhill skiing, hiking, fishing, hunting, golf, biking, Yellowstone Park.
Seen in: *The Billings Gazette.*
"It was heavenly, the bed was comfortable and we loved the decor."

Nebraska

Lincoln

Rogers House
2145 B St
Lincoln NE 68502
(402) 476-6961

Circa 1914. Ivy covers one wing of the three-story Jacobean Revival Rogers House. In the Hillsdale National Historic District, the house is a few blocks from the University of Nebraska and the Capitol building. A ballroom on the third floor has been converted to three guest rooms but the original built-in ballroom benches remain. Mahogany paneling, cross-beamed ceilings, fireplaces and antique bedsteads are featured.

Rates: $45-$55.
Nora Houstma.
Beds: QDT.
Seen in: *Innsider.*

"Here I am in Egypt enjoying travel on the Nile in luxury almost up to the Rogers House standards." Guest's postcard.

Omaha

Offutt House
140 N 39th St
Omaha NE 68131
(402) 553-0951

Circa 1894. This two-and-a-half story, 14-room house is built like a chateau with a steep roof and tall

windows. During the 1913 tornado, although almost every house in the neighborhood was leveled, the Offutt house stood firm. It is said that a decanter of sherry was blown from the dining room to the living room without anything spilling. The large parlor features a handsome fireplace, a wall of books and an inviting sofas. A bridal suite is tucked under the gables of the third floor.

Location: One block from downtown.
*Rates: $40-$60.
Jeannie K. Swoboda.
7 Rooms. 2 Private Baths. Beds: KDT. Continental breakfast. Conference room. CCs: MC VISA. Sightseeing, walking.
Seen in: *Midwest Living, Innsider.*

"Hospitable, comfortable, lovely."

Nevada

Virginia City

Edith Palmer's Country Inn

South B Street, PO Box 756
Virginia City NV 89440
(702) 847-0707

Circa 1862. This white clapboard two-story country house has a wine cellar with walls two feet thick. The addition of a skylight makes this a romantic setting for dining and for weddings. Furnishings are country antiques, and the inn is within easy walking distance of the historic district of Virginia City.

Rates: $65-$75.
Earlene Brown.
5 Rooms. 3 Private Baths. Full breakfast. Conference room.
Seen in: *San Francisco Chronicle, Great Getaways.*

New Hampshire

Ashland

Glynn House Victorian Inn

43 Highland St, PO Box 819
Ashland NH 03217
(603) 968-3775

Circa 1895. A three-story turret, gables and verandas frosted with

Queen Anne gingerbread come together in an appealing mass of Victoriana in the Glynn House. Carved oak woodwork and pocket doors accentuate the foyer. Period furnishings and ornate oriental wall coverings decorate the parlor. The village of Ashland is a few minutes from "On Golden Pond," (Squam Lake) and the White Mountains.

Rates: $65-$80.
Karol & Betsy Paterman.
4 Rooms. 2 Private Baths. 2 Fireplaces. Guest phone available. TV available. Beds: QDT. Full breakfast. Gourmet meals. Jacuzzi. Conference room. Skiing, boating, hiking.

Bartlett

The Country Inn at Bartlett

Rt 302, PO Box 327
Bartlett NH 03812
(603) 374-2353

Circa 1885. This New England farmhouse, built as a summer home by a Portland sea captain, rests in a stand of tall pines adjacent to national forest land. For the last 50

years it has provided a homey atmosphere for families and friends coming to the White Mountains. Accommodations are in the house or in private cottages. An outdoor hot tub takes advantage of the crisp pinescented air. A hearty family-style dinner is served.

*Rates: $64-$72.
Mark Dindorf.
17 Rooms. 11 Private Baths. 2 Fireplaces. Guest phone available. TV available. Beds: DT. B&B. Jacuzzi. CCs: MC VISA AX. Hiking, downhill & cross-country skiing.

"Walking through your door felt like stepping back in time."

Bedford

Bedford Village Inn

2 Old Bedford Rd
Bedford NH 03102
(603) 472-2001

Circa 1810. Built by Josiah Gordon, the Bedford Inn stands as a landmark restoration of a farm estate. There are Indian shutters, exposed chestnut beams, and working fireplaces. Situated in the converted barn, the inn's guest rooms feature king-size beds and canopied four-posters. Public spaces include the

Milk Room Lounge and viewing porches perched in the original barn silos. A herd of French *Charolais* cows graze with their calves in adjacent pastures.

*Rates: $125-$225 MAP.
Michael Downing.
14 Rooms. 14 Private Baths. Guest phone in room. TV in room. Beds: K. Continental breakfast. Restaurant. Jacuzzi. Handicap access. Conference room. Cross-country skiing on property. Corporate packages.
Seen in: *Travelhost Magazine.*

"Thank you for the gracious hospitality. I was extremely happy with the accommodations and the food and wine were exquisite."

Bethlehem

The Bells

Strawberry Hill, PO Box 276
Bethlehem NH 03574
(603) 869-2647

Circa 1892. This unique Queen Anne house is a wonderful example

of Victorian ingenuity. Basically square with wraparound porches, the roof line has an oriental influence which makes the house look like a pagoda. Eighty hand-carved wooden bells hang under the second floor eaves and eight large tin bells hang from the upper corners of the roofs. According to local folklore the builder constructed the house for his son, a missionary to the Far East.

Location: In the heart of the White mountains.
Rates: $50-$70.
Bill & Louise Sims.
3 Rooms. 3 Private Baths. Guest phone available. TV available. Beds: TD. Full breakfast. Golf, fishing, tennis, swimming, hiking, cross-country skiing.
Seen in: *Charlotte Observer, New England Get Aways.*

"It was so nice to be fussed over, not to mention being treated like old friends. Everything was superb and we went bananas over the decor!"

The Mulburn Inn

Main St
Bethlehem NH 03574
(603) 869-3389

Circa 1913. This summer cottage was known as The Ivie Estate. Mrs. Ivie and Mrs. Frank Woolworth of 'Five and Dime' fame were sisters. Many of the Ivie and Woolworth family members vacationed here in summer. Cary Grant and Barbara

Hutton spent their honeymoon at the mansion. Polished oak staircases and stained glass windows add to the atmosphere.

*Rates: $50-$65.
Linda & Moe Mulkigian, Bob & Cheryl Burns.
7 Rooms. 7 Private Baths. 3 Fireplaces. Guest phone available. TV available. Beds: KQTD. Full breakfast. CCs: MC VISA. Hiking, bicycling, swimming, fishing, tennis, skiing.

"You have put a lot of thought, charm, beauty and warmth into the inn. Your breakfasts were oh so delicious!!"

Bradford

The Bradford Inn

Main St
Bradford NH 03221
(603) 938-5309

Circa 1898. The Bradford Hotel was the most elaborate lodging in

town when it first boasted of electricity, a coal furnace and a large dining room. Now restored and polished to its original turn-of-the-century charm, guests can once again enjoy the grand staircase, the wide halls, parlors, high ceilings and sunny rooms.

Location: Rural country village.
*Rates: $59-$99.
Connie & Tom Mazol.
12 Rooms. 12 Private Baths. Guest phone available. TV available. Beds: DTC. MAP. Restaurant. Handicap access. Conference room. CCs: MC VISA AX DC CB DS. Lake cruises, hiking, skiing, antiques, auctions.

"We enjoyed excellent breakfasts and dinners as well as a clean and spacious suite and a most pleasant host and hostess."

Mountain Lake Inn

Rt 114
Bradford NH 03221
(603) 938-2136 (800) 662-6005

Circa 1760. This white colonial house is situated on 167 acres, 17 of

which are lakefront. A sandy beach on Lake Massasecum is inviting for sunning, but guests often prefer to take out the canoe and the rowboat. The Pine Room has floor-to-ceiling windows that look out to the garden. A 75-year-old Brunswick pool table is in the lounge, along with a wood-burning fireplace.

*Rates: $80.
Carol & Phil Fullerton.
9 Rooms. 9 Private Baths. Guest phone available. TV available. Beds: KQDT. Full breakfast. Gourmet meals. Conference room. CCs: MC VISA DS. Swimming, skiing, snowshoeing packages, boating, fishing, country cooking weekend.
Seen in: *Country Inns, Boston Globe.*

"We loved your place! From the moment I entered the door that afternoon and caught the aroma of a country dinner I was hooked. You give the inn such personal warmth."

Bridgewater

Pasquaney Inn On Newfound Lake

Star Rt 1 Box 1066
Bridgewater NH 03222
(603) 744-9111

Circa 1840. The Pasquaney Inn was a stopover point on the Old Star

Route from Boston to Montreal. It

was built originally for lodging and is in the classic style of a New England resort with white clapboard siding, tall windows and a broad veranda stretching the length of the inn. It faces the sandy beaches of what is purported to be one of the cleanest, clearest lakes in the world. The mountains are just beyond.
Rates: $36-$104.
Barbara & Bud Edrick - Pamela & Sean Smith.
14 Rooms. 14 Private Baths. Beds: QT. AP. CCs: MC VISA. Swimming, fishing, boating, cross-country & downhill skiing.

Campton

Mountain Fare Inn

Mad River Rd
Campton NH 03223
(603) 726-4283

Circa 1850. This white farm house is surrounded by flower gardens in

the summer and unparalleled foliage in the fall. Often, ski teams, family reunions and other groups are found enjoying the outdoors here with Mountain Fare as a base. In the winter everyone seems to be a skier and in the summer there are boaters and hikers. The inn is decorated in a casual New Hampshire-style country decor.
Location: Two hours from Boston in the White Mountains.
Rates: $48-$70.
Susan & Nick Preston.
8 Rooms. 5 Private Baths. 1 Fireplace. Guest phone available. TV available. Beds: DTC. AP. Golf, hiking, canoeing, biking, cross-country skiing, tennis, fishing.
"Charming and casual. Truly country."

Canaan

Inn On Canaan Street

The Kremzners
Canaan NH 03741
(603) 523-7310

Circa 1800. This white colonial situated on 14 acres of woodland,

lawn, meadows of wild flowers, and lake shore is located in a National Historic District. With its white-steepled churches, venerable old maple and oak trees, an 18th-century meeting house and handsome colonial homes, it is called one of New Hampshire's prettiest streets. The inn is furnished with period pieces such as an English bachelor's chest, Victorian drawing easels and Hitchcock chairs. Canoes are lined up at the lake for guests to use.
Rates: $65-$85.
Louise & Lee Kremzner.
5 Rooms. 3 Private Baths. 3 Fireplaces. Guest phone available. TV available. Beds: KQDT. B&B. Gourmet meals. CCs: VISA. Skiing, canoeing.
Seen in: *The Granite State Vacationer.*
"Every room filled with sunlight. A special country inn overflowing with welcome."

Centre Harbor

Red Hill Inn

RD 1 Box 99M
Centre Harbor NH 03226
(603) 279-7001

Circa 1904. The mansion was once the centerpiece of a 1000-acre estate.

It was called "keewaydin" for the strong north wind that blows across Sunset Hill. When the Depression was over, the inn was sold. New owners included European royalty escaping from Nazi Germany. Now the mansion is a lovely restored country inn with spectacular views of the area's lakes and mountains. From your room you can see the site of the filming of *On Golden Pond.*
Location: Central New Hampshire in the Lakes Region.
*Rates: $75-$135.
Don Leavitt & Rick Miller.
21 Rooms. 21 Private Baths. 19 Fireplaces. Guest phone in room. TV available. Beds: DTC. EP. Restaurant. Jacuzzi. Conference room. CCs: MC VISA AX DC CB. Cross-country skiing on groomed trails. Rental equipment available.
Seen in: *New England Getaways.*
"Our stay was very enjoyable."

Chichester

Hitching Post B&B

Dover Rd #2, Box 790
Chichester NH 03263
(603) 798-4951

Circa 1787. This New England Colonial with its attached carriage

house and barn was built by a Revolutionary War General, Jonathan Blake. From 1939 to 1965 it served as a tourist house recommended by the Duncan Hynes tourist home book. There are wide-planked floors with an eclectic decor reminiscent of a visit to Grandma's. Lis, born in Denmark, loves to cook. The couple honed their hospitality skills while living in Philadelphia and serving as international hosts and tour guides.
*Rates: $45-$55. Season: Feb. to Nov.
Lis & Gil Lazich.
4 Rooms. Guest phone available. TV available. Beds: KQDT. B&B. Gourmet meals. Exercise room. Canoeing, antiquing.
Seen in: *Concord Monitor.*
"Terrific place!! Food excellent-hospitality generous, company great!"

Concord

The Bradford Inn
See: Bradford, NH

Hitching Post B&B
See: Chichester, NH

Maria Atwood Inn
See: West Franklin, NH

Conway

The Darby Field Inn
Bald Hill, PO Box D
Conway NH 03818
(603) 447-2181

Circa 1826. This rambling, blue clapboard farmhouse has a huge fieldstone fireplace, stone patio and

outstanding views of the Mt. Washington Valley and the Presidential Mountains. For many years it was called the Bald Hill Grand View lodge but was renamed to honor the first man to climb Mt. Washington, Darby Field.
Location: Half a mile south of Conway.
Rates: $65-$90pp. Season: Jan-March 15,May-Oct
Marc & Maria Donaldson.
16 Rooms. 14 Private Baths. TV available. Beds: DT. AP. Swimming pool. CCs: MC VISA. Swimming, skiing.

"If an inn is a place for a weary traveler to relax, recover and feel the hospitality and warmth of the innkeeper, then the Darby Field Inn is one of the finest."

Mountain Valley Manner
148 Washington St
Conway NH 03818
(603) 447-3988

Circa 1885. Built on the Revolutionary era mustering grounds of the Conway volunteer militia, this Victorian farm house is located within 200 yards of the historic Swift River covered bridge and Saco River covered bridge. Three of the guest rooms overlook the Swift River covered bridge and Mt. Washington. On weekends your hosts serve a hearty mountain climber's breakfast. A continental breakfast is provided mid-week.
*Rates: $50-$70.
Bob, Lynn & Amy Lein.
4 Rooms. 2 Private Baths. Guest phone available. TV available. Beds: KQDW. B&B. Swimming pool. CCs: MC VISA AX. Golf, hiking, skiing, tubing, fishing. Tennis, pool & skating rink nearby.

"Accommodations excellent, hospitality better than the Ritz, surroundings very nice, meals way above expectation, highest recommendation."

Cornish

Chase House B&B
Rt 12 A, RR 2 Box 909
Cornish NH 03745
(603) 675-5391

Circa 1775. Cornish's first English settler, Dudley Chase, built this Federal house noted for its fine architecture. In 1845 it was moved to accommodate the Sullivan County Railroad. Designated a National Landmark, it was the birthplace of Salmon Chase, Governor of Ohio, Secretary of the Treasury for President Lincoln and Chief Justice of the Supreme Court. The Chase Manhattan Bank was named after him.
Location: Two-and-a-half hours from Boston.
Rates: $75-$95.
Hal & Marilyn Wallace.
5 Rooms. 5 Private Baths. Guest phone available. TV available. Beds: QDT. Full breakfast. CCs: MC VISA. Hiking, canoeing, cross-country skiing, swimming, tennis, golf.
Seen in: *New Hampshire Sunday News, Newsday.*

Dover

Pinky's Place
38 Rutland St
Dover NH 03820
(603) 742-8789

Circa 1890. A front veranda shaded by towering trees encases the first floor bay of the three-story rounded turret rising from this Queen Anne Victorian home. A turned oak stair-

case and fretwork welcome guests to a turn-of-the-century era. Bob Kram, an engineer, enjoys sailing and making wine, while German-born Pinky, a gerontologist, provides a gourmet breakfast for guests.
Rates: $50.
Pinky & Bill Kram.
2 Rooms. Guest phone in room. TV available. Beds: D Full breakfast. Beaches, shopping.
Seen in: *Foster's Daily Democrat.*

"Just like being with family."

Durham

Maple Lodge B&B
See: Stratham, NH

Pinky's Place
See: Dover, NH

East Hebron

Six Chimneys
Star Rt Box 114
East Hebron NH 03232
(603) 744-2029

Circa 1791. This was once a stagecoach stop where 20 fresh hor-

ses were kept for changes. Beds and a drink of rum were 10 cents. Located on five acres, at the head of Newfound Lake, the home retains wide pine boards, pine paneling, and old beams.

Location: Newfound Lake.
*Rates: $45-$55.
Peter & Lee Fortescue.
6 Rooms. 3 Private Baths. Guest phone available. TV available. Beds: KQDT. B&B. CCs: MC VISA. Skiing, hiking. Tennis & golf nearby.
Seen in: *Bristol Enterprise.*

Etna

Moose Mountain Lodge
Moose Mountain Rd
Etna NH 03750
(603) 643-3529

Circa 1938. This old log lodge is perched high on the western side of

Moose Mountain providing views of the Connecticut River Valley and the Green Mountains. The inn's land connects with the Appalachian Trail for extended hikes and ski tours. In the summer the lodge participates in "Canoeing Inn to Inn" on the Connecticut River. Bountiful gardens provide fresh vegetables for lunch and dinner.
Location: Part of town of Hanover.
Rates: $100-$140. Season: Jan-March,June-Oct
Peter & Kay Shumway.
12 Rooms. Guest phone available. Beds: QTD. AP. Restaurant. Gourmet meals. Game room. Conference room. CCs: MC VISA. Cross-country skiing, bicycling, hiking, swimming.

"Moose Mountain is just like some of the old European ski lodges, relaxed, warm, friendly, and very comfortable."

Fitzwilliam

Amos Parker House
119 West
Fitzwilliam NH 03447
(603) 585-6540

Circa 1780. An antique liberty pole is attached to the original part of

this appealing Federal house (Liberty poles were used to identify meeting places for Revolutionaries). Situated on three acres, with mountain views, the house is bordered by green lawns and perfect flower beds. Antiques, Spode china, beautiful stenciling, carpet and needlepoint collections add grace and style to the rooms. Freda, a former travel agent from Chicago, exudes enthusiasm for all New Hampshire's sights and is an expert on the area. Hopefully, your arrival will coincide with a breakfast menu of spinach souffle' with mushroom Newburg sauce or "Praline French Toast."
Rates: $55-$80.
Freda B. Houpt.
5 Rooms. 3 Private Baths. 6 Fireplaces. Guest phone available. TV available. Beds: KQDT. B&B. CCs: MC VISA. Cross-country skiing, biking, water sports, mountain climbing.
Seen in: *New York Times, Washington Post, The Tampa Tribune-Times.*

Care and solicitation is what makes staying here more the experience of visiting a wealthy and hospitable relative in the country than simply staying at an inn or hotel."

Fitzwilliam Inn
Fitzwilliam NH 03447
(603) 585-9000

Circa 1796. For almost 200 years this old New England inn has of-

fered food, lodging and grog. Over the parlor presides a portrait of the Earl of Fitzwilliam, the 18th century nobleman for whom the town is named. In the rustic pub the innkeeper still provides his own special grog.
Rates: $40-$55.
John Wallace.
28 Rooms. 14 Private Baths. Guest phone available. TV available. Beds: QDTC. EP. Restaurant. Handicap access. Swimming pool. Conference room. CCs: MC VISA AX DC. Cross-country skiing, hiking, fishing.
Seen in: *Boston Globe.*

"Like a dream, no, it was a dream come true!"

Franconia

Bungay Jar B&B
PO Box 15
Franconia NH 03580
(603) 823-7775

Circa 1967. A century old barn was taken down and moved piece by piece to Easton Valley six miles from Franconia. A post and beam barn-style home was constructed, nestled onto eight wooded acres with a stream nearby and the White Mountains in view. The two-story living room, reminiscent of a hay loft, is decorated with antique country furnishings, as are all the guest rooms. Your host, a landscape architect, has planted herb and perennial gardens.
*Rates: $55-$85.
Kate Kerivam, Lee Strimbeck.
6 Rooms. 4 Private Baths. 1 Fireplace. Guest phone available. Beds: KQDT. B&B. Gourmet meals. Sauna. CCs: MC VISA AX DS. Skiing, hiking, bird-watching.

"Such a perfect spot with such a great view."

Franconia Inn
Easton Rd
Franconia NH 03580
(603) 823-5542

Circa 1936. This inn was originally built in 1868 when most of the

area's farmers took in summer boarders. Each farmer had a wagon marked with his farm's name and would pick up guests at the train

station in Littleton. In the 30s, fire destroyed the old house and it was rebuilt as an inn. A basement rathskeller is well known by the ski-touring circuit. There is also an oak-paneled library upstairs.
Location: Exit 38 off I-93, two-and-a-half miles south on Route 116.
*Rates: $60-$90. Season: May 20-April.
Alec & Richard Morris.
35 Rooms. 35 Private Baths. 3 Fireplaces. Guest phone available. TV available. Beds: KQDTC. MAP. Restaurant. Gourmet meals. Jacuzzi. Swimming pool. Game room. Conference room. CCs: MC VISA AX. Croquet, bicycles, pool, soaring, swimming, cross-country skiing, tennis, horseback riding, bicycles, hiking, horse drawn sleigh rides, ice skating - All on premises.
Seen in: *The Philadelphia Inquirer, Boston Globe.*
"The piece de resistance of the Franconia Notch is the Franconia Inn." Philadelphia Inquirer.

Lovett's Inn
Rt 18, Profile Rd
Franconia NH 03580
(603) 823-7761

Circa 1784. In the National Register, the main building consists

of two connected Cape-style houses. The lower floor functioned as the kitchen, woodshed and milk room, and the old wash oven remains today next to the original fireplace. Other rooms are in cottages and new additions. Trout streams, Lafayette Brook and a pond dot the inn's 90 acres.
Rates: $85-$130, MAP.
Lan Finlay, General Manager.
30 Rooms. 19 Private Baths. Guest phone available. TV available. Beds: QDTC. AP. Handicap access. Swimming pool. Conference room. Gliding, horseback riding, golf nearby. Ski trails on premises.
"Room very pleasant, comfortable and clean. Delicious dinner. We appreciated being made to feel welcome and at home."

Gilford

Cartway House Inn
83 Old Lake Shore Rd
Gilford NH 03246
(603) 528-1172

Circa 1771. Overlooking mountains and meadows, this clapboard colonial was built by shipbuilders and is one of ten historic homes in Gilford. This is a popular area for bike tours, cross-country skiing, horseback riding and golf. The innkeepers speak several languages.
*Rates: $52-$58.
Gretchen & Tony Shortway.
9 Rooms. 1 Private Bath. Guest phone available. TV available. Beds: TD. Full breakfast. Jacuzzi. CCs: MC VISA. Skiing, swimming, golf, horseback riding, bicycling.
"Gretchen really knows how to make you feel welcome."

Greenfield

The Greenfield Inn
Box 156
Greenfield NH 03047
(603) 547-6327

Circa 1817. In the 1850s this inn was purchased by Henry Dunklee, innkeeper of the old Mayfield Inn across the street. When there was an overflow of guests at his tavern, Mr. Dunklee accommodated them here. Three acres of lawn and a veranda provide views of Crotched, Temple and Monadnock Mountains. Inside are polished wide-board floors and cozy comfortable furnishings.
Location: Southern New Hampshire, 90 minutes from Boston.
*Rates: $45-$60.
Barbara & Vic.
9 Rooms. 5 Private Baths. Guest phone available. TV in room. Beds: KDT. B&B. Jacuzzi. Conference room. CCs: MC VISA. Mountain climbing, skiing, bicycling, swimming, hunting, golf.
Seen in: *New England Getaways, Manchester Union Leader.*

Hampstead

Stillmeadow B&B at Hampstead
545 Main St, PO Box 565
Hampstead NH 03841
(603) 329-8381

Circa 1850. The old Ordway home rests on several acres on the Main

Street of Hampstead, just across a meadow from the Hampstead Croquet Associations' grass courts. The Dawn Suite features a working fireplace, sitting area and an extra single bed for children, while the Tulip Suite has two queen beds and a double bathroom. Private stairs lead from this room to a playroom. The cookie jar at Stillmeadow is said to be always full.
Rates: $55-$80.
Lori & Randy Offord.
4 Rooms. 4 Private Baths. 1 Fireplace. Guest phone available. TV in room. Beds: QDTWC. Continental-plus breakfast. Conference room. CCs: AX. Skiing, tennis, croquet, fenced in children's playground.
Seen in: *Lawrence Eagle Tribune, New Hampshire Profiles.*
"No less than monumental."

Hanover

Inn On Canaan Street
See: Canaan, NH

Moose Mountain Lodge
See: Etna, NH

The Trumbull House
Box C29
Hanover NH 03755
(603) 643-1400

Circa 1919. This handsome two-story farmhouse was concocted and built by Harvey Trumbull from materials he gathered from old Dartmouth College buildings and fraternity houses. Presiding over 16 acres with stands of maple and pine, and a meandering brook, the inn of-

fers a cozy refuge for all, including cross-country skiers and Dartmouth College alumni and parents. The parlor features Country English chairs, sofas and lace curtains.
Rates: $110-$130.
Ann C. Fuller.
5 Rooms. 5 Private Baths. Guest phone available. TV available. Beds: QT. B&B. Alpine & cross-country skiing, golf, swimming, riding, sailing, canoeing, biking, hiking.
Seen in: *Boston Globe, Upper Valley News.*
"From the beautiful setting outdoors through every elegant and thoughtful detail indoors, including your exquisite sunlit breakfast, we were in Heaven!"

Haverhill

Haverhill Inn
Box 95
Haverhill NH 03765
(603) 989-5961

Circa 1810. This handsome Federal house commands sweeping views of

the Upper Connecticut River Valley and the Vermont hills. Indian shutters, a fireplace in every room, and an old kitchen hearth and bake oven add to the charm. Cross-country trails start at the back door and in summer, guests often canoe inn-to-inn.
Location: On Route 10.
Rates: $75.
Stephen Campbell.
4 Rooms. 4 Private Baths. 4 Fireplaces. Guest phone available. Beds: QT. Full breakfast. Hiking, cross-country skiing, canoeing.
Seen in: *Sunday Boston Globe.*

Henniker

The Meeting House Inn & Restaurant
35 Flanders Rd
Henniker NH 03242
(603) 428-3228

Circa 1850. Just up the road from this rural country farmstead is the site of the first meeting house in Henniker. Hearty New England cooking is served in the 200-year-old barn/restaurant. Wide pine floors, brass beds and antique accessories decorate guest rooms in the main house.
Location: Off 114S, 2 miles from Henniker Center.
Rates: $63-$88.
June & Bill Davis, Peter & Cheryl Bakke.
6 Rooms. 6 Private Baths. Guest phone available. TV available. Beds: QTDC. Full breakfast. Restaurant. Jacuzzi. Sauna. Conference room. CCs: MC VISA. Downhill & cross-country skiing, golf, swimming, hiking, bicycling
"Thank you for giving us a honeymoon worth waiting eleven years for."

Holderness

The Inn on Golden Pond
Rt 3 Box 680
Holderness NH 03245
(603) 968-7269

Circa 1879. Framed by meandering stone walls and split-rail fences more than 100 years old, this inn is situated on 55 acres of woodlands. Most rooms overlook picturesque countryside and nearby is Squam Lake, setting for the film *On Golden Pond*. An inviting, 60-foot screened porch provides a place to relax during the summer.
Location: Four miles from Exit 24, I-93.
*Rates: $75-$85.
Bill & Bonnie Webb.
9 Rooms. 7 Private Baths. Guest phone available. TV available. Beds: QT. Full breakfast. CCs: MC VISA. Skiing, boating, fishing, swimming.

Manor On Golden Pond
Rt 3 Box T
Holderness NH 03245
(603) 968-3348

Circa 1903. An Englishman and land developer had a boyhood dream of living in a beautiful man-

sion high on a hill overlooking lakes and mountains. After he discovered these beautiful 13 acres he brought craftsmen from around the world to build an English-style country mansion. Old world charm is accentuated by marble fireplaces and the hand-carved mahogany lobby.
Location: On Squam Lake, 40 minutes north of Concord.
*Rates: $96-$170.
Andre' R. Lamoureux.
27 Rooms. 27 Private Baths. 10 Fireplaces. Guest phone available. TV in room. Beds: KQDT. AP. Swimming pool. Conference room. CCs: MC VISA AX DC CB DS. Boating, canoeing, clay tennis court, swimming, cross-country skiing, fishing, golf, hiking, horseback riding, private beach.
Seen in: *Summer Week.*
"The setting, the inn itself, the dining, the staff, the fascinating boat tour. Everything was outstanding!".

Jackson

Ellis River House
Rt 16 Box 656
Jackson NH 03846
(603) 383-9339

Circa 1890. Andrew Harriman built this colonial farmhouse, as well as

the village town hall and three-room schoolhouse where the innkeepers' child attends school. Classic antiques fill the guest rooms and each window reveals views of magnificent mountains, the vineyard, or

spectacular Ellis River. As a working farm, the Ellis River House includes a population of chickens, geese, ducks, a pony and pigs.
Location: White Mountain area.
Rates: $25-$50pp.
Barry & Barbara Lubao.
6 Rooms. 1 Private Bath. Guest phone available. TV available. Beds: QT. AP. Jacuzzi. CCs: MC VISA. Cross-country skiing, horseback riding, tennis, golf, biking.
Seen in: *The Mountain Ear.*

"We have stayed at many B&Bs all over the world and are in agreement that the beauty and hospitality of Ellis River House is that of a world class bed & breakfast."

The Inn at Jackson
PO Box H
Jackson NH 03846
(603) 383-4321

Circa 1890. Architect Stanford White built this inn overlooking the

village and White Mountains. The atmosphere is comfortable and inviting, and breakfast is served in a glassed-in porch which provides a panoramic view. In winter, sleigh rides can be arranged and in summer, hay rides and horseback riding.

*Rates: $70-$80.
Lori & Steve Tradewell.
6 Rooms. 6 Private Baths. 3 Fireplaces. Guest phone available. TV available. Beds: DT. B&B. CCs: MC VISA AX. Golf, skiing, tennis, hiking.
Seen in: *Country Inns.*

"We had a terrific time and found the inn warm and cozy and most of all relaxing."

The Inn at Thorn Hill
PO Box A, Thorn Hill Rd
Jackson NH 03846
(603) 383-4242

Circa 1895. Follow a romantic drive through the Honeymoon Covered Bridge to Thorn Hill Road where this country Victorian stands, built by architect Stanford White. Its 11 acres are adjacent to the Jackson Ski Touring trails. Inside, the decor

is Victorian and a collection of antique light fixtures accentuates the guest rooms, pub, drawing room, and parlor.
*Rates: $65-$96. Season: May to March.
Peter & Linda LaRose.
20 Rooms. 18 Private Baths. Guest phone available. TV available. Beds: KQDT. MAP. Restaurant. Gourmet meals. Swimming pool. Conference room. CCs: MC VISA AX DS. Cross-country skiing, golf, tennis, horseback riding.
Seen in: *Mature Outlook, The Reporter, New England GetAways.*

"Magnificent, start to finish! The food was excellent but the mountain air must have shrunk my clothes!"

Village House
Rt 16A Box 359
Jackson NH 03846
(603) 383-6666

Circa 1860. Village House was built as an annex to the larger Hawthorne

Inn which eventually burned. It is a colonial building, with a porch winding around three sides. The Wildcat River flows by the inn's seven acres, and there is a clay tennis court and shuffleboard set in view of the White Mountains.
Rates: $50-$90.
Robin Crocker, Lori Allen.
10 Rooms. 8 Private Baths. Guest phone available. TV available. Beds: TW. EP. Swimming pool. CCs: MC VISA. Clay tennis courts, hiking, downhill & cross-country skiing, golf, ice skating, horses, hay & sleigh rides.
Seen in: *The Foxboro Reporter.*

"Your hospitality and warmth made us feel right at home. The little extras, such as turn-down service, flowers and baked goods are all greatly appreciated."

Jaffrey

The Benjamin Prescott Inn
Rt 124 East
Jaffrey NH 03452
(603) 532-6637

Circa 1853. Colonel Prescott arrived on foot in Jaffrey in 1775, with

an ax in his hand and a bag of beans on his back. The family built this classic Greek Revival many years later. Now candles light the windows, seen from the stonewall-lined lane adjacent to the inn. Each room bears the name of a Prescott family member.
*Rates: $60-$130.
Barry & Jan Miller.
10 Rooms. 10 Private Baths. Guest phone available. TV in room. Beds: KQDT. B&B. CCs: MC VISA. Hiking, climbing, cross-country skiing, sleigh rides.

Jefferson

The Jefferson Inn
Rt 2
Jefferson NH 03583
(603) 586-7998

Circa 1896. This rambling Victorian house features a turret, gables, and

verandas. English antiques fill the inn and there are complimentary desserts in the evening.
*Rates: $40-$65. Season: Dec-March,May-Oct.
Greg Brown & Bertie Koelewijn.
10 Rooms. 5 Private Baths. Guest phone available. TV available. Beds: QDT. B&B. Handicap access. Conference

room. CCs: MC VISA AX. Skiing, hiking, swimming, golf, tennis, cycling, horseback riding.

"Marvelous breakfast and a warm, comfortable atmosphere."

Littleton

Beal House Inn

247 West Main St
Littleton NH 03561
(603) 444-2661

Circa 1833. This Federal Renaissance farmhouse has been an inn for 54 years. The original barn still stands, now covered with white clapboard and converted to an antique shop. The inn is furnished with antiques, that are for sale. Beal House is a Main Street landmark as well as the area's first bed and breakfast inn.

*Rates: $45-$85.
Jim & Ann Carver & son John.
14 Rooms. 12 Private Baths. Guest phone available. Beds: KQDT. B&B. CCs: MC VISA AX DC. Downhill & cross-country skiing, hiking, golf, canoeing.
Seen in: *Country Inn, Glamour Magazine.*

"These innkeepers know and understand people, their needs and wants. Attention to cleanliness and amenities, from check-in to check-out is a treasure."

Thayers Inn

136 Main St
Littleton NH 03561
(603) 444-6469

Circa 1843. Ulysses Grant is said to have spoken from the inn's balcony during a federal court hearing. In those days, fresh firewood and candles were delivered to guest rooms each day as well as a personal thunderjug. The handsome facade features four 30-foot, hand-carved pillars and a cupola with views of the surrounding mountains.

Rates: $30-$40.
Don & Carolyn Lambert.
40 Rooms. 36 Private Baths. Guest phone in room. TV in room. Beds: KDTC. AP. Restaurant. CCs: MC VISA AX DS. Skiing, hiking, natural wonders.
Seen in: *Business Life, Vacationer, Upcountry.*

"This Thanksgiving Russ and I spent a lot of time thinking about the things that are most important to us. It seemed appropriate that we should write to thank you for your warm hospitality as innkeepers."

Manchester

Stillmeadow B&B at Hampstead

See: Hampstead, NH

Nashua

Sherman-Berry House

See: Lowell, MA

New London

The Bradford Inn

See: Bradford, NH

Follansbee Inn

See: North Sutton, NH

New London Inn

Box 8 Main St
New London NH 03257
(603) 526-2791 (800) 526-2791

Circa 1792. This classic New England inn is situated right on Main Street and features a two-story

veranda. Inside are bed chambers decorated in colonial furnishings. Guests may dine beside the fire at the inn's restaurant. Colby-Sawyer College is nearby.

*Rates: $75-$90.
Maureen & John Follansbee.
30 Rooms. 30 Private Baths. Guest phone in room. TV available. Beds: KQDT. MAP. Restaurant. Gourmet meals. Conference room. CCs: MC VISA AX. Skiing, water sports, golf, tennis, theater, museums, antiquing.
Seen in: *Boston Globe, New Hampshire Profiles.*

Newport

The Inn at Coit Mountain

HCR 63, PO 3 Rt 10
Newport NH 03773
(603) 863-3583 (800)367-2364

Circa 1790. This gracious Georgian was once the home of Rene Cheronette-Champollion a descendant of the famous Egyptologist who deciphered the Rosetta stone. A 35-foot, two-story library adds elegance with its oak paneling and massive granite fireplace. Lake Sunapee is nearby.

Location: Lake Sunapee Region, 8 miles south from Exit 13 on Route 10.
Rates: $85-$150.
Dick & Judi Tatem.
5 Rooms. 1 Private Bath. 2 Fireplaces. Guest phone available. Beds: KQDTC. B&B. Gourmet meals. Handicap access. Conference room. CCs: MC VISA. Skiing, swimming, boating, fishing, snowmobiling, sleigh rides.
Seen in: *The Advisor.*

"We stopped at many B&Bs on our trip. Yours is the loveliest by far!"

North Conway

The 1785 Inn

Rt 16 at The Scenic Vista
North Conway NH 03860
(603) 356-9025

Circa 1785. The main section of this center-chimney house was built by Captain Elijah Dinsmore of the New Hampshire Rangers. He was granted the land for service in the American Revolution. Original hand-hewn beams, corner posts, fireplaces, and a brick oven are still visible and operating.

*Rates: $60-$115.
Charlie & Becky Mallar.
17 Rooms. 12 Private Baths. Guest phone available. TV available. Beds: KC. AP. Swimming pool. Conference room. Downhill & cross-country skiing, swimming, fishing, bicycling.
Seen in: *The Valley Visitor, Bon Appetite*

"Occasionally in our lifetimes is a moment so unexpectedly perfect that we use it as our measure for our unforgettable moments. We just had such an experience at The 1785 Inn."

The Buttonwood Inn

Mt Surprise Rd, PO Box 1817A
North Conway NH 03860
(603) 356-2625

Circa 1820. This center-chimney, New England-style inn was once a

working farm of more than 100 acres on the mountain. Of the original outbuildings only the granite barn foundation remains. Through the years the house has been extended to twenty rooms.

✻Rates: $24-$41.
Ann & Hugh Begley & Family.
9 Rooms. 2 Private Baths. Guest phone available. TV available. Beds: DTC. AP. Swimming pool. CCs: MC VISA AX. Swimming, downhill & cross-country skiing, golfing, hunting.

"The very moment we spotted your lovely inn nestled midway on the mountainside in the moonlight, we knew we had found a winner."

Cranmore Mt Lodge

Kearsarge Rd, PO Box 1194
North Conway NH 03860
(603) 356-2044

Circa 1850. Babe Ruth was a frequent guest at this old New England farmhouse when his daughter was the owner. There are many rare Babe Ruth photos displayed in the inn and one guest room is still decorated with his furnishings. The barn on the property is held together with wooden pegs and contains dorm rooms.

Location: Village of Kearsarge.
Rates: $56-$140.
Dennis & Judy Helfand.
20 Rooms. 5 Private Baths. 2 Fireplaces. Guest phone available. TV in room. Beds: DTC. MAP. Jacuzzi. Handicap access. Swimming pool. Game room. CCs: MC VISA AX DS. Tennis, fishing, hiking, bicycling, basketball, cross-country skiing, tobogganing.

"Your accommodations are lovely, your breakfasts delicious."

The Darby Field Inn

See: Conway, NH

Mountain Valley Manner

See: Conway, NH

Peacock Inn

PO Box 1012
North Conway NH 03860
(603) 356-9041

Circa 1773. The guest book at this inn dates from 1875. Since that time

the inn has been renovated and placed on the federal map as a national landmark. Some of the rooms have skylights as well as brass beds or canopy beds and antique rockers. Breakfast is served fireside. Across the street flows a babbling brook.

Location: Kearsarge Road, 1 mile from Mt. Cranmore.
✻Rates: $39-$56.50.
Claire & Larry Jackson.
18 Rooms. 16 Private Baths. 1 Fireplace. Guest phone available. TV available. Beds: KQTC. Full breakfast. Sauna. Swimming pool. Conference room. CCs: MC VISA AX DS. Swimming, hiking.
Seen in: *The Irregular.*

"Although I expected this to be a nice, cozy place, I was not prepared for the royal treatment my family and I received. We cast our vote for Larry and Claire as innkeepers of the year."

Stonehurst Manor

Rt 16
North Conway NH 03860
(603) 356-3271

Circa 1876. This English-style manor stands on lush, landscaped

lawns and 30 acres of pine trees. It was built as the summer home for the Bigelow family, founder of the Bigelow Carpet Company. Inside the tremendous front door is an elegant display of leaded and stained-glass windows, rich oak woodwork, a winding staircase and a massive, hand-carved oak fireplace.

Rates: $50-$135.
Peter Rattay.
24 Rooms. 22 Private Baths. Guest phone available. Beds: QTD. AP. Restaurant. Jacuzzi. Handicap access. Swimming pool. Conference room. CCs: MC VISA. Swimming, canoeing, hiking.
Seen in: *The Boston Globe, New York Daily News.*

"An architecturally preserved replica of an English country house, a perfect retreat for the nostalgic-at-heart." Phil Berthiaume, *Country Almanac.*

Sunny Side Inn

Seavey St
North Conway NH 03860
(603) 356-6239

Circa 1850. This vintage farmhouse became the Sunny Side Inn back in the 1930s when steam trains brought thousands of skiers to North Conway every winter weekend. It has been open continuously since that time. In the summer guests gather on the front porch, festooned with flowers, while in winter guests are drawn to the fireplace and wood stove. The North Conway Village is a short walk away.

Location: Walking distance to North Conway Village.
Rates: $38-$60.
Chris & Marylee.
10 Rooms. 2 Private Baths. Guest phone available. TV available. Beds: DT. B&B. CCs: MC VISA. Golf, tennis, swimming, fishing, hiking, biking, rock climbing, downhill & cross-country skiing.

"I would just like to thank you both again for your tremendous hospitality. The accommodations were extremely cozy and comfortable."

North Sutton

Follansbee Inn

PO Box 92, Keyser St
North Sutton NH 03260
(603) 927-4221

Circa 1840. This New England farmhouse was enlarged in 1929, becoming an inn, no doubt because of its attractive location on the edge of Kezar Lake. It has a comfortable porch, sitting rooms with fireplaces, and antique-furnished bedrooms. Cross-country skiing starts at the doorstep.

Rates: $65-$85.
Sandy & Dick Reilein.
23 Rooms. 11 Private Baths. Guest phone available. Beds: KDT. Full break-

fast. Conference room. CCs: MC VISA. Skiing, golf, tennis, boating, fishing, swimming, row boat, sail board, canoe & paddle boat. Wind surfer, paddleboat.
Seen in: *Country Inns.*
"Bravo! A great inn experience. Super food."

North Woodstock

Mt. Adams Inn
Rt 3, South Main St
North Woodstock NH 03262
(603) 745-2711

Circa 1875. Situated at a choice spot on the banks of the Moosalauki

River, this is the only hotel remaining in the area from the 1800s. Original tin ceilings and cobblestone fireplaces were first enjoyed when visitors came for the summer, taking carriage rides through the mountains. Unique rock formations along the river behind the inn are called the "mummies" and tourists have explored them for more than a century. Authentic Polish cuisine is served in the restaurant.
Rates: $36-$56.
Gloria & Joe Town.
20 Rooms. 2 Fireplaces. Guest phone available. Beds: DT. Full breakfast. Restaurant. CCs: MC VISA. Horseback riding, skiing, golf, tennis, swimming, mountain climbing.
Seen in: *Outlook.*
"Last of the grand inns when guests were dropped off by train right across the road."

Plymouth

Crab Apple Inn
RR 4 Box 1955
Plymouth NH 03264
(603) 536-4476

Circa 1835. Behind an immaculate, white picket fence is a brick Federal

house beside a small brook at the foot of Tenney Mountain. There are fireplaces on the second floor and panoramic vistas from the third floor, and rooms are furnished with canopy beds and claw-foot tubs. The grounds include an English garden and meandering wooded paths.

Location: The Baker River Valley.
Rates: $65-$85.
Bill & Carolyn Crenson.
5 Rooms. 2 Private Baths. Guest phone available. Beds: QDT. B&B. CCs: MC VISA. Skiing, hiking, horseback riding, golf.
"We are still excited about our trip. The Crab Apple Inn was the unanimous choice for our favorite place to stay."

Six Chimneys
See: East Hebron, NH

Portsmouth

Leighton Inn
69 Richards Ave
Portsmouth NH 03801
(603) 433-2188

Circa 1809. Immediately after cabinetmaker Samuel Wyatt built this fashionable clapboard Federal house, the *Portsmouth Oracle* advertised it for auction in their December 23, 1809 edition. Through an impressive entranceway, Empire antiques accentuate the gracious atmosphere of this handsome home.
Location: North of Boston 55 miles.
Rates: $55-$75.
Catherine Stone.
5 Rooms. 3 Private Baths. Guest phone available. TV available. Beds: QDT. Full breakfast. CCs: MC VISA. Tennis, swimming, sailing.
Seen in: *Country Inns, Portsmouth Herald.*

"Your hospitality, charm and friendliness was greatly appreciated. You're a terrific cook."

Maple Lodge B&B
See: Stratham, NH

Martin Hill Inn
404 Islington St
Portsmouth NH 03801
(603) 436-2287

Circa 1820. Lieutenant-Governor George Vaughan sold this land in 1710 for 50 British pounds. The Main House, a colonial, contains three guest rooms and the Guest House has four. All bedrooms are decorated in elegant antiques including canopy and four-poster beds, writing tables and sofas or sitting areas. Amenities include air-conditioning.
Rates: $75-$90.
Jane & Paul Harnden.
7 Rooms. 7 Private Baths. Guest phone available. Beds: QDT. Full breakfast. CCs: MC VISA.
Seen in: *New Hampshire Profiles, Country Inn Magazine.*
"Beautifully furnished with antiques. Delicious gourmet breakfasts served on exquisite china."

York Harbor Inn
See: York Harbor, ME

Snowville

Snowvillage Inn
Box 83, Foss Mt. Rd
Snowville NH 03849
(603) 447-2818

Circa 1850. Frank Simonds, noted World War I historian and govern-

ment consultant, called his retreat

here "Blighty." The beams in the main house are hand-hewn and were taken from the original 1850 farmhouse. The inn has a spectacular sweeping view of Mt. Washington, and resembles a European mountain home with an Austrian flavor. (The hostess was born in Austria.)
Location: In White Mountains.
Rates: $40-$80.
Peter, Trudy & Frank Cutrone.
19 Rooms. 19 Private Baths. 4 Fireplaces. Guest phone available. Beds: KQDT. AP. Restaurant. Sauna. Conference room. CCs: MC VISA. Cross-country skiing, hiking, tennis, volleyball, swimming, majestic view.
Seen in: *New England GetAways, Los Angeles Times, The Boston Globe.*

"A jewel of a country inn and gourmet food."

Stratham

Maple Lodge B&B
68 Depot Rd
Stratham NH 03885
(603) 778-9833

Circa 1900. Built by an old sea captain, the living room of Maple Lodge overlooks Great Bay. An enormous stone fireplace is a favored place for guests in winter, while the screened veranda is popular in summer. Guest rooms are spacious with comfy beds and floral wallpapers. A hearty breakfast is served in keeping with the country setting.
Rates: $55.
John & Natalie Fortin.
3 Rooms. 1 Fireplace. Guest phone available. Beds: DT. B&B. CCs: MC VISA. Beaches, whale watches.

"The personal, caring touch given to every small detail captured our satisfaction to the fullest."

Sugar Hill

The Homestead
Sugar Hill NH 03585
(603) 823-5564

Circa 1802. The current innkeepers are seventh generation descendants of Sugar Hill's first settler. In 1880, the Teffits began taking in "city boarders". Early settlers carted many of the inn's antiques here

with their ox-drawn wagons. In 1917, the Chalet was built with stones from nearby meadows.
Rates: $70-$80.
Essie Serafini & Paul Hayward.
19 Rooms. 9 Private Baths. Guest phone available. TV available. Beds: KQDT. Full breakfast. CCs: MC VISA. Cross-country skiing, swimming, tennis, golf, hiking.
Seen in: *Yankee Magazine, Boston Globe, Playboy, Reader's Digest, Bon Appetit.*

Ledgeland Inn & Cottages
Sugar Hill NH 03585
(603) 823-5341

Circa 1926. The main house of this inn is open from June to October

but the private cottages surrounding the inn are available all year. Furnishings are contemporary and there are fireplaces in many of the cottages.
Rates: $60-$110.
23 Rooms. 23 Private Baths. 12 Fireplaces. Guest phone available. TV available. Beds: KDTC. Continental-plus breakfast. Cross-country skiing, hiking, fishing, tennis, swimming.

"We loved it at Ledgeland. Your place offered the kind of peace and beauty we desperately needed."

Tamworth

Tamworth Inn
Main St
Tamworth NH 03886
(603) 323-7721

Circa 1833. This rambling village inn was originally a stagecoach stop. A sparkling trout stream borders its two acres. Across the street

is the Barnstormer's Theater, one of the country's oldest summer stock theaters, now in its 57th year under the direction of Francis Cleveland, son of President Grover Cleveland. A New England-style decor features a variety of antiques. The Tamworth Pub is in the inn.
❀Rates: $50-$75.
Phil & Kathy Bender.
18 Rooms. 18 Private Baths. 4 Fireplaces. Guest phone available. TV available. Beds: KQDT. EP. Restaurant. Gourmet meals. Swimming pool. Conference room. CCs: MC VISA. Swimming, fishing, cross-country & downhill skiing, hiking.
Seen in: *Boston Globe.*

"It was great spending the day touring and returning to the quiet village of Tamworth and your wonderful inn."

Wakefield

Wakefield Inn
Mountain Laurel Rd, Rt 1 Box 2185
Wakefield NH 03872
(603) 522-8272

Circa 1803. Early travelers pulled up to the front door of the Wakefield Inn by stagecoach and

while they disembarked, their luggage was handed up to the second floor. It was brought in through the door which is still visible over the porch roof. A spiral staircase, ruffled curtains, wallpapers and a wraparound porch all create the romantic ambience of days gone by. In the dining room an original three-sided fireplace casts a warm

glow on dining guests as it did 186 years ago.
Location: Historic district.
Rates: $65.
Harry & Lou Sisson.
6 Rooms. 6 Private Baths. Guest phone available. TV available. Beds: DT. Full breakfast. Restaurant. CCs: MC VISA DC. Cross-country & downhill skiing, horseback riding, snowmobiling, hiking, biking, golf.
Seen in: *New England GetAways.*

"Comfortable accommodations, excellent food and exquisite decor highlighted by your quilts."

West Franklin

Maria Atwood Inn

RFD 2, Rt 3a
West Franklin NH 03235
(603) 934-3666

Circa 1830. This brick colonial was constructed with double-course brick made on the property by builder, Henry Greenleaf. Original Indian shutters, Count Rumford fireplaces, wide-plank wood floors

and original paneling remain. The innkeepers have filled the rooms with their antique collection and maintain a small antique shop nearby.
*Rates: $65.
Phil & Irene Fournier.
7 Rooms. 7 Private Baths. 4 Fireplaces. Guest phone available. TV available. Beds: QDT. Full breakfast. CCs: MC VISA AX DC. Horseback riding, canoeing, fishing, boating, downhill & cross-country skiing, biking, historic sightseeing.
Seen in: *Concord Newspaper, Alumni Magazine.*

"Wouldn't stay anywhere else."

Wolfeboro

Tuc'Me Inn

PO 657
Wolfeboro NH 03894
(603) 569-5702

Circa 1880. Wolfeboro, on the shores of New Hampshire's largest lake, Lake Winnipesaukee, is said to be the oldest summer resort in the United States. This colonial inn is two blocks from the lakefront. A library and two screened porches offer inviting areas for relaxation.
Rates: $50-$90.
Irma Limberger.
7 Rooms. 3 Private Baths. Guest phone available. TV available. Beds: QT. Full breakfast. CCs: MC VISA. Skiing, swimming.
Seen in: *Granite State News.*

"This is the most delightful place I have ever stayed."

Wakefield Inn

See: Wakefield, NH

New Jersey

Bay Head

Conover's Bay Head Inn

646 Main Ave
Bay Head NJ 08742
(201) 892-4664

Circa 1905. This shingle-style house is one of many similar summer cottages in Bay Head. Most of these are still owned by the original families who came from Princeton. Downstairs rooms feature tones of lavender and mauve surrounding antique photographs and furnishings. Guest rooms are decorated with antiques and Laura Ashley and Ralph Lauren fabrics. Views of the ocean, bay and marina may be seen.

Rates: $70-$140.
Carl & Beverly Conover and son Timothy.
12 Rooms. 12 Private Baths. 1 Fireplace. Guest phone available. Beds: QDT. Continental-plus breakfast. Gourmet meals. Jacuzzi. CCs: MC VISA AX. Horseback riding, water sports, sailing, windsurfing, tennis.
Seen in: *New Jersey Monthly, Good Housekeeping.*

"If you want action look elsewhere; this is a place to go to relax." Great Getaways.

Cape May

Abigail Adams B&B

12 Jackson St
Cape May NJ 08204
(609) 884-1371

Circa 1888. The front porch of this Victorian, one of the Seven Sisters, is only 100 feet from the ocean. There is a free-standing circular staircase, and original fireplaces and woodwork throughout. The decor is highlighted with flowered chintz and antiques, and the dining room is hand-stenciled.

Rates: $65-$105. Season: April to Oct.
Ed & Donna Misner.
5 Rooms. 5 Private Baths. 2 Fireplaces. Guest phone available. Beds: QD. B&B. CCs: MC VISA. Biking, beaches.

"Warm and friendly innkeepers added to the specialness."

Barnard-Good House

238 Perry St
Cape May NJ 08204
(609) 884-5381

Circa 1865. The Barnard-Good House is a Second Empire Victorian

with a mansard roof and original shingles. A wraparound veranda adds to the charm of this lavender, blue and tan cottage along with the original picket fence and a concrete-formed flower garden. The inn was selected by *New Jersey Magazine* as the #1 spot for breakfast in New Jersey.

Rates: $85-$110. Season: March 15 - Nov. 15.
Nan & Tom Hawkins.
5 Rooms. 5 Private Baths. Guest phone available. Beds: KD. Full breakfast. CCs: MC VISA. Water sports, tennis, historic tours.
Seen in: *The New York Times.*

"Even the cozy bed can't hold you down when the smell of Nan's breakfast makes its way upstairs."

Captain Mey's Inn

202 Ocean St
Cape May NJ 08204
(609) 884-7793

Circa 1881. Named after a Dutch West India captain who named the

area, the inn displays its Dutch heritage with table-top Persian rugs, Delft china and imported Dutch lace curtains. The dining room features chestnut and oak Eastlake paneling. Breakfast is served by candlelight.

❀Rates: $65-$125.
Milly LaCanfora & Carin Feddermann.
9 Rooms. 2 Private Baths. Guest phone available. Beds: QT. Full breakfast. Conference room. CCs: MC VISA. Swimming, tennis, horse & buggy rides.
Seen in: *Americana Magazine, Country Living.*

"The innkeepers pamper you so much you wish you could stay forever."

The Chalfonte

301 Howard St
Cape May NJ 08204
(609) 884-8409

Circa 1876. This 103-room hotel has a rambling veranda, rooms are

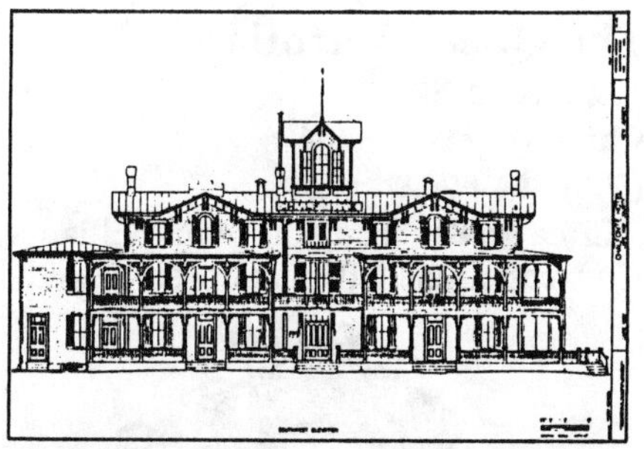

simple, and the cooking is southern. The cook Helen Dickerson, now in her seventies, has been with the hotel since her mother brought her here at the age of four.
Location: Centrally located in the historic district, 2 blocks from beaches.
*Rates: $80-$130. Season: May to Oct.
Anne LeDuc & Judy Bartella.
103 Rooms. 11 Private Baths. Guest phone available. TV available. Beds: KQDTC. MAP. Restaurant. Game room. Conference room. CCs: MC VISA. Swimming, sailing, tennis, golf, bicycling, bird watching, nature trails. Special workshops.
Seen in: *Travel & Leisure, Philadelphia Inquirer.*
"The well-loved building, enthusiastic innkeepers, great food and friendly atmosphere made the weekend a success."

COLVMNS by the Sea
1513 Beach Dr
Cape May NJ 08204
(609) 884-2228

Circa 1905. Dr. Davis, the Philadelphia physician who created calamine lotion, built this house in

the days when a summer cottage might have 20 rooms, 12-foot ceilings, three-story staircases and hand-carved ceilings. Large, airy rooms provide magnificent views of the ocean. The innkeepers supply beach tags and towels as well as bikes. Afternoon tea is served.
Rates: $95-$135. Season: 4/27-10/31.
Barry & Cathy Rein.
11 Rooms. 11 Private Baths. 2 Fireplaces. Guest phone available. TV available. Beds: KQDT. B&B. Conference room. CCs: MC VISA.

Dormer House, International
800 Columbia Ave
Cape May NJ 08204
(609) 884-7446

Circa 1899. This Colonial Revival estate is three blocks from the ocean

and the historic walking mall. It was built by marble-dealer John Jacoby and retains much of the original marble and furniture. Several years ago the inn was converted into guest suites with kitchens.
Location: Corner of Franklin & Columbia in the historic district.
Rates: $Call.
Ruth & Stephen Fellin.
8 Rooms. 8 Private Baths. 1 Fireplace. Guest phone available. TV available. Beds: DT. EP. CCs: MC VISA. Beach, water sports, tennis, golf.
Seen in: *Cape May Star & Wave.*
"Our 7th year here. We love it."

Duke of Windsor Inn
817 Washington St
Cape May NJ 08204
(609) 884-1355

Circa 1896. This Queen Anne Victorian was built by Delaware River

boat pilot Harry Hazelhurst and his wife Florence. They were both six feet tall, so the house was built with large open rooms and doorways, and extra wide stairs. The inn has a carved, natural oak open staircase with stained-glass windows at top and bottom. Five antique chandeliers grace the dining room.
Rates: $60-$105. Season: Feb. to Dec.
Bruce, Fran & Barbara Prichard.
9 Rooms. 7 Private Baths. Guest phone available. Beds: DT. B&B. Conference room. CCs: MC VISA. Tennis, beach.
Seen in: *Philadelphia Inquirer.*
"Tom and I loved staying in your home! We certainly appreciate all the hard work you put into renovating the house."

Gingerbread House
28 Gurney St
Cape May NJ 08204
(609) 884-0211

Circa 1869. The Gingerbread is one of eight original Stockton Row Cottages, summer retreats built for families from Philadelphia and Virginia. It is a half-block from the ocean and breezes waft over the wicker-filled porch. The inn is decorated with period antiques and a fine collection of paintings.
Location: One-half block from the beach.
Rates: $72-$125.
Fred & Joan Echevarria.
6 Rooms. 3 Private Baths. 1 Fireplace. Guest phone available. Beds: D. Continental-plus breakfast.

Henry Ludlam Inn
See: Woodbine, NJ

Humphrey Hughes House
29 Ocean St
Cape May NJ 08204
(609) 884-4428

Circa 1903. Stained-glass windows mark each landing of the staircase,

and intricately carved American chestnut columns add to the atmosphere in this 30-room summer cottage. The land was purchased by the Captain Humphrey Hughes family in the early 1700s and remained in the family till 1980. Dr. Harold Hughes' majestic grandfather clock

remains as one of many late Victorian antiques.
Rates: $85-$120.
Lorraine & Terry Schmidt.
10 Rooms. 10 Private Baths. Guest phone available. Beds: KQ. Full breakfast. Handicap access. Biking, golf, beach.

"Thoroughly enjoyed our stay. You should be proud of your home and operation."

Mainstay Inn & Cottage

635 Columbia Ave
Cape May NJ 08204
(609) 884-8690

Circa 1872. This was once the elegant and exclusive Jackson's Clubhouse popular with gamblers.

Many of the guest rooms and the grand parlor look much as they did in the 1840s. Fourteen-foot ceilings, elaborate chandeliers, a sweeping veranda and a cupola add to the atmosphere. Tom and Sue Carroll received the annual American Historic Inns award in 1988 for their preservation efforts.
Rates: $80-$135. Season: March 15-Dec 15
Tom & Sue Carroll.
12 Rooms. 12 Private Baths. Guest phone available. Beds: KQDT. Full breakfast. Conference room. Beach, tennis, bicycling, croquet, bird watching.
Seen in: *The Washington Post, Good Housekeeping, The New York Times.*

"By far the most lavishly and faithfully restored guesthouse...run by two arch-preservationists." Travel and Leisure.

The Mason Cottage

625 Columbia Ave
Cape May NJ 08204
(609) 884-3358

Circa 1871. Since 1940, this house has been open to guests. The curved mansard wood-shingle roof was built by local shipyard carpenters. Much of the original furniture remains in the house, and it has endured both hurricanes and the 1878 Cape May fire.
*Rates: $70-$120. Season: May to Nov.

Dave & Joan Mason.
5 Rooms. 4 Private Baths. Guest phone available. Beds: D. Continental-plus breakfast. CCs: MC VISA. Trolley tours, carriage rides, walking tours. Honeymoon packages.

"We look forward so much to coming back each summer and enjoying your hospitality and very special inn."

Poor Richard's Inn

17 Jackson St
Cape May NJ 08204
(609) 884-3536

Circa 1882. The unusual design of this Second Empire house has been

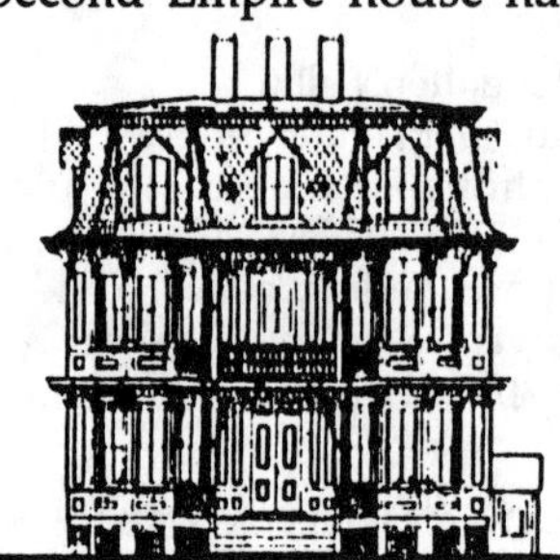

accentuated with five colors of paint. Arched gingerbread porches tie together the distinctive bays of the house's facade. The combination of exterior friezes, ballustrades and fretwork has earned the inn an individual listing in the National Register. Some rooms sport an eclectic country Victorian decor with patchwork quilts and pine furniture, while others tend toward a more traditional turn-of-the-century ambiance. Many rooms are air-conditioned. A few apartment suites are available.
Rates: $30-$89. Season: Feb. 14 - Dec. 31.
Harriett & Richard Samuelson.
9 Rooms. 4 Private Baths. Guest phone available. TV available. Beds: DC. Continental breakfast. CCs: MC VISA. Riding, golf, fishing, bird watching, historic tours, ocean.
Seen in: *Washington Post, New York Times, National Geographic.*

"Hold our spot on the porch, we'll be back before you know it."

The Queen Victoria

102 Ocean St
Cape May NJ 08204
(609) 884-8702

Circa 1881. The Sherwin-Williams Company used this restored seaside

villa to illustrate its line of Victorian paints, and *Victorian Homes* featured 23 color photographs of it. Amenities include afternoon tea and mixers, a fleet of bicycles, and evening turn-down service. Suites feature a jacuzzi, fireplace or private porch.
Location: In the heart of the historic district, one block from the beach.
Rates: $55-$180.
\ane & Joan Wells.
24 Rooms. 20 Private Baths. 2 Fireplaces. Guest phone available. TV in room. Beds: KQTDC. B&B. Jacuzzi. Handicap access. Conference room. CCs: MC VISA. Bicycling, beach, nature trails, bird watching.

"Everything was perfect in a beautiful surrounding."

Sand Castle Guest House

829 Stockton Ave
Cape May NJ 08204
(609) 884-5451

Circa 1873. This Carpenter Gothic was built by John Bullitt, a wealthy

Philadelphia lawyer and a key figure in the development of Cape May in the mid-19th century. The inn is one block from the ocean and

the two-mile-long promenade. The decor is a light blend of country and Victorian with lace, oak, quilts and chintz.
Rates: $65-$125.
Peg Barradale.
7 Rooms. 6 Private Baths. Beds: DT. Continental-plus breakfast. CCs: MC VISA. Beach.

"Your friendly atmosphere and decor can't be beat. Thanks for making a needed vacation such a pleasant one."

Seventh Sister Guesthouse

10 Jackson St
Cape May NJ 08204
(609) 884-2280

Circa 1888. Most of the Seventh Sister's guest rooms have ocean views. The inn is in the National Register. Extensive wicker and original art collections are featured and three floors are joined by a spectacular central circular staircase. The center of town is one block away.
Rates: $50-$75.
Bob & Jo-Anne Myers.
6 Rooms. Guest phone available. Beds: D. Bicycling, beach.
Seen in: *New York Times, 1001 Decorating Ideas.*

Springside

18 Jackson St
Cape May NJ 08204
(609) 884-2654

Circa 1891. This Renaissance Revival Cottage with three bright and airy stories is one of the Seven

Sister houses built by architect Stephen Decatur Button. Most rooms have a partial ocean view and the front porch provides rocking chair views of the water, half a block away. The inn is furnished with mahogany pieces built in the thirties. A large doll house and collections of art and sculpture are featured.
Rates: $50-$65.
Meryl & Bill Nelson.
4 Rooms. 2 Private Baths. Guest phone available. Beds: K. EP. CCs: MC VISA. Beach.

"A unique combination of historic atmosphere and creature comforts."

Windward House

24 Jackson St
Cape May NJ 08204
(609) 884-3368

Circa 1905. The three stories of the blue Edwardian-style cottage con-

tain antique-filled guest rooms in the heart of the historic district. Three porches include a wraparound front veranda furnished with wicker. Outstanding beveled and stained-glass casts rainbows of flickering light from the windows and French doors, while gleaming chestnut and oak paneling set off a collection of museum-quality antiques and Innkeeper Sandy Miller's mannequins adorned in Victorian dress. The Eastlake and Empire rooms feature ocean views.
Rates: $85-$115.
Owen & Sandy Miller.
8 Rooms. 8 Private Baths. Guest phone available. Beds: QD. B&B. CCs: MC VISA. Bicycles, beach, shopping.
Seen in: *New Jersey Monthly, Delaware Today, Mid Atlantic Country.*

"The loveliest and most authentically decorated of all the houses we visited."

The Wooden Rabbit

609 Hughes St
Cape May NJ 08204
(609) 884-7293

Circa 1838. Robert E. Lee brought his wife to stay at this sea captain's house to ease her arthritis. The house was also part of the Underground Railroad. Throughout the inn are whimsical touches such as the "rabbit hutch" in the living room which holds a collection of Beatrix Potter figures. The decor is country, with folk art and collec-

tables that can accommodate hands-on exploration. Children are welcome.
Rates: $65-$130.
Greg & Debby Burow.
3 Rooms. 3 Private Baths. Guest phone available. Beds: KQT. Full breakfast. CCs: MC VISA. Swimming, bicycling, tennis, golf.
Seen in: *The Sandpaper.*

"The room was perfect, our breakfast delicious. We will be back."

Woodleigh House

808 Washington St
Cape May NJ 08204
(609) 884-7123

Circa 1866. Woodleigh House actually consists of two country Vic-

torians side-by-side, both built by sea captain Isaac Smith. Collections of glass and Royal Copenhagen are found throughout along with Victorian era furnishings. The two front porches sport rocking chairs and wicker furniture. The Woods, both educators, attend to guests needs. Beach bikes are available.
*Rates: $75-$100.
Buddy & Jan Wood.
8 Rooms. 8 Private Baths. Guest phone available. TV available. Beds: DT. B&B. CCs: MC VISA. Beach, biking.

"What a warm and friendly home..."

Frenchtown

Old Hunterdon House
12 Bridge St
Frenchtown NJ 08825
(201) 996-3632

Circa 1865. Framed by an antique wrought iron fence, this Italianate

Victorian is crowned with a handsome cupola that provides views of the Delaware River, a block away, and rolling green hills beyond. Empire and Victorian antiques include massive burled four-poster beds. Frenchtown is noted for a number of fine restaurants.
Rates: $68-$100.
Rick Carson.
7 Rooms. 7 Private Baths. 1 Fireplace. Guest phone available. Beds: QDT. B&B. CCs: MC VISA. Horseback riding, cycling, hiking, ballooning & gliding, river activities.
Seen in: *Innsider, New York Times.*

"We are so fortunate to have the luxury of a retreat like this, and it definitely re-charges the batteries."

Lambertville

Colligan's Stockton Inn
See: Stockton, NJ

Lyndhurst

The Jeremiah J. Yereance House
410 Riverside
Lyndhurst NJ 07071
(201) 438-9457

Circa 1841. In the National Register, this tiny house was built by a ship joiner who worked at the shipyards on the Passaic River. The inn is adjacent to a one-room schoolhouse built in 1804 which is now a museum of local history. There are cobblestone walks and a wisteria arbor. It is across from a riverside park.
*Rates: $55-$75.
Evelyn & Frank Pezzolla.
4 Rooms. 1 Private Bath. 2 Fireplaces. Guest phone available. TV available. Beds: DT. Continental breakfast. CCs: AX. Tennis, bicycling, walking trails.
Seen in: *The Record.*

"A perfect setting to start our honeymoon!"

Ocean Grove

Cordova
26 Webb Ave
Ocean Grove NJ 07756
(201) 774-3084 (212)751-9577 (winter)

Circa 1886. Founded as a Methodist retreat, ocean-bathing and cars were not allowed here until

a few years ago, so there are no souvenir shops along the white sandy beach and wooden boardwalk. The inn has hosted Presidents Wilson, Cleveland and Roosevelt who were also speakers at the Great Auditorium with its 7,000 seats. Guests here feel like family and have the use of kitchen, lounge and barbecue.
*Rates: $30-$66. Season: May to Sept.
Doris & Vlad Chernik.
17 Rooms. 3 Private Baths. Guest phone available. TV available. Beds: TDC. B&B. Swimming, tennis, volleyball, bicycling, jogging, fishing.
Seen in: *New Jersey Magazine, Asbury Park Press.*

"Warm, helpful and inviting, homey and lived-in atmosphere."

Pine Tree Inn
10 Main Ave
Ocean Grove NJ 07756
(201) 775-3264

Circa 1880. This small Victorian hotel is operated by long-standing residents of the area. Guestrooms are decorated in antiques and all the rooms are equipped with sinks. Bicycles are available as well as beach towels.
Rates: $30-$85.
Karen Mason & Francis Goger.
13 Rooms. 3 Private Baths. Guest phone available. Beds: KQT. Full breakfast. CCs: MC VISA. Swimming, bicycling, jogging.
Seen in: *Country Living.*

Princeton

Logan Inn
See: New Hope, PA

Spring Lake

Chateau
500 Warren Ave
Spring Lake NJ 07762
(201) 974-2000

Circa 1888. In addition to the lake, this village has a two-mile

boardwalk along the ocean. The Chateau is a Victorian era inn with many rooms providing scenic vistas of the park, lake and gazebo. Borders of flowers surround the white pillared verandas and there are brick patios, sun-filled balconies and private porches. The Spring Lake Trolley departs every half hour from the front door.
*Rates: $49-$132. Season: April to Nov.
Scott Smith.
40 Rooms. 40 Private Baths. 4 Fireplaces. Guest phone in room. TV in room. Beds: KQDTC. B&B. Handicap access. Conference room. CCs: MC VISA AX. Swimming, surfing, boating, fishing, tennis, golf, bicycling.
Seen in: *Great Water Escapes.*

"One of the top five inns in New Jersey." Mobil Travel Guide.

Kenilworth
1505 Ocean Ave
Spring Lake NJ 07762
(201) 449-5327

Circa 1883. This Victorian inn provides an unobstructed view of

the Atlantic from the front porch, and is located across the street from the boardwalk. The parlor is filled with books, and a Victorian bridal chamber has recently been added. Guests are welcome to barbecue on the side lawn or use the fully equipped kitchen.
*Rates: $60-$135. Season: June 15-Oct.15.
Pam Meehan.
23 Rooms. 14 Private Baths. Guest phone available. TV available. Beds: KDTC. Full breakfast. Conference room. Swimming, fishing, tennis, golf.
Seen in: *The Christian Science Monitor, Holiday Shore Magazine.*
"Entered as strangers and left as friends."

The Normandy Inn
21 Tuttle Ave
Spring Lake NJ 07762
(201) 449-7172

Circa 1888. An Italianate villa with Queen Anne influences, the Nor-

mandy Inn features sunburst designs and neoclassical interiors. Victorian antiques are accentuated by Victorian colors documented and researched by Roger Moss. The house was moved onto the present site around 1910.
Rates: $90-$125.
Michael & Susan Ingino.
19 Rooms. 19 Private Baths. Guest phone available. TV available. Beds: DTC. Full breakfast. Conference room. Bicycling.
"The cozy and delicious accommodations of your inn were beyond expectations; memories of the lingering scent of hazelnut coffee will keep me going until we can visit again."

Sandpiper Hotel
7 Atlantic Ave
Spring Lake NJ 07762
(201) 449-6060

Circa 1888. This historic Victorian inn is just one-quarter of a block from the ocean. It offers romantically appointed rooms, a large wraparound porch, and old-fashioned hospitality. Spring Lake is a lovely Victorian-era community with an uncluttered two-mile-long oceanfront boardwalk.
Rates: $59-$155.
15 Rooms. 15 Private Baths. Guest phone in room. TV in room. Beds: KQDTC. B&B. Restaurant. Jacuzzi. Swimming pool. CCs: MC VISA AX DC CB.

Stone Post Inn
115 Washington Ave
Spring Lake NJ 07762
(201) 449-1212

Circa 1882. Originally built as a lodging establishment, the inn was known as the Rest-A-While and then The Washington House. It is located in a quiet residential area surrounded by tree-shaded lawns and gardens, giving it the atmosphere of a private home. European antiques are complemented by a varied collection of family antiques and art.
Location: One block from the ocean and the village.
*Rates: $50-$100.
Julia Paris & daughters Janine & Connie.
20 Rooms. 9 Private Baths. Guest phone available. TV available. Beds: QT. Full breakfast. Conference room. CCs: MC VISA. Tennis, horseback riding, golf, fishing.
"Your charming inn and warm hospitality were the perfect ingredients for a lovely holiday weekend."

Stanhope

Whistling Swan Inn
Box 791, 110 Main Street
Stanhope NJ 07874
(201) 347-6369

Circa 1900. This Queen Anne Victorian has a limestone wraparound veranda and a tall steep-roofed turret. Family antiques fill the rooms and highlight the polished ornate woodwork, pocket doors and winding staircase. It is a little over a mile from Waterloo Village and the International Trade Zone.
Rates: $60-$80.
Paula Williams & Joe Mulay.
10 Rooms. 10 Private Baths. Beds: Q. Full breakfast. Conference room. CCs: MC VISA AX. Skiing, boating, golf, horseback riding, hunting, fishing.
Seen in: *Sunday Herald.*

Stockton

Colligan's Stockton Inn
Rt 29
Stockton NJ 08559
(609) 397-1250

Circa 1710. Colligan's has operated as an inn since 1796. It received na-

tional prominence when Richard Rogers & Lorenz Hart included reference to it in a song from musical comedy — "There is a small hotel with a wishing well". (The Broadway show was "On Your Toes".) Later, band leader Paul Whiteman signed off his radio and television shows announcing he was going to dinner at "Ma Colligan's". Guest rooms are scattered throughout the inn's four buildings and feature fireplaces, balconies or canopy beds. There are two restaurants on the premises.
Rates: $60-$130.
Andrew McDermott.
11 Rooms. 11 Private Baths. 8 Fireplaces. Guest phone available. TV in room. Beds: QDT. B&B. Restaurant. Conference room. CCs: MC VISA AX DC CB. Horseback riding, skiing, ballooning, canoeing, hiking, antiquing.
Seen in: *New York Times, Philadelphia Magazine, New York Magazine.*
"My well-traveled parents say this is their favorite restaurant."

Woolverton Inn

6 Woolverton Rd
Stockton NJ 08559
(609) 397-0802

Circa 1793. This charming mansard-roofed inn was built by John Prall, a merchant who owned the

Prallsville Mills nearby. The stone manor house is set among formal gardens. Each room is decorated in a different era and named after one of the previous owners or noted people of the area.
Rates: $60-$95.
Louise Warsaw.
12 Rooms. 2 Private Baths. Guest phone available. Beds: KTD. Handicap access. CCs: MC VISA. Horse back riding, tennis, swimming, cross-country skiing.
Seen in: *New York Magazine, Colonial Homes.*

"Thank you for providing a perfect setting and relaxed atmosphere for our group. You're terrific."

Woodbine

Henry Ludlam Inn

124 S Delsea Dr, RD 3 Box 298
Woodbine NJ 08270
(609) 861-5847

Circa 1760. Each of the guest rooms has a fireplace and view of Ludlam Lake. Canoeing and fishing are popular activities and the innkeepers make sure you enjoy these

at your peak by providing you with a full country breakfast.
Location: Cape May County.
✻❀Rates: $65-$90.
Ann & Marty Thurlow.
5 Rooms. 3 Private Baths. 3 Fireplaces. Guest phone available. TV available. Beds: DT. Full breakfast. Gourmet meals. Conference room. CCs: MC VISA. Cross-country skiing, hiking, biking, fishing, canoeing, ice skating.
Seen in: *Atlantic City Press, Herald Dispatch.*

"By the time we left we felt like old friends!...I'm afraid that staying with you spoiled us!"

New Mexico

Alamagordo

The Lodge

See: Cloudcroft, NM

Albuquerque

Casita Chamisa

850 Chamisal Rd NW
Albuquerque NM 87107
(505) 897-4644

Circa 1850. Beneath her old adobe, Kit an archaeologist, discovered a deeply stratified Indian village attributed to the Pueblo IV Period, 1300-1650 A.D. After a two-year excavation a viewing site was created. There is an indoor swimming pool and bicycles are available. An aerial tram and hot air ballooning is nearby.

Location: Fifteen minutes from town.
Rates: $60. Season: Closed Jan. & Feb.
Kit & Arnold Sargeant.
3 Rooms. 2 Private Baths. Beds: KQT. Continental-plus breakfast. Swimming pool. CCs: MC VISA.

W.E. Mauger Estate

701 Roma Ave NW
Albuquerque NM 87102
(505) 242-8755

Circa 1897. This former boarding house is now an elegantly restored Victorian in the National Register. Third floor rooms are done in Art Deco with views of downtown Albuquerque and the Sandia Mountains beyond. The second floor is decorated with antiques and lace. The inn is located in an area undergoing renovation, six blocks from the Convention Center.

Location: Central Albuquerque.

*Rates: $60-$95
Richard & Uta Carleno.
6 Rooms. 6 Private Baths. Guest phone available. Beds: QD. Continental-plus breakfast. Conference room. CCs: MC VISA AX DC CB DS. Water skiing, horseback riding, fishing. Daily Indian dances. Organized tours of Indian Pueblos & petroglyphs.
Seen in: *Albuquerque Journal.*

"All because of your hospitality, kindness and warmth, we will always be comparing the quality of our experience to what we experienced during our stay in W.E. Mauger."

Cloudcroft

The Lodge

PO Box 497
Cloudcroft NM 88317
(505) 682-2566 (800) 842-4216

Circa 1899. This Bavarian style lodge building, topped with an enormous cupola, is situated at 9,200 feet in the Southern Rockies. Eleven of the rooms are located in The Pavillion - the lodge's bed and breakfast inn. These rooms have stone fireplaces, knotty pine walls and down comforters. The four-story high copper-domed observatory contains a sitting room and has views that stretch 150 miles towards White Sands, the San Andres Mountains and the Black Range. Past guests were Pancho

Villa, Judy Garland and Clark Gable. The country's highest golf course is here.

*Rates: $59-$150.
Mike Coy.
59 Rooms. 47 Private Baths. 3 Fireplaces. Guest phone in room. TV in room. Beds: KQDTC. B&B. Restaurant. Gourmet meals. Jacuzzi. Sauna. Handicap access. Swimming pool. Conference room. CCs: MC VISA AX DC DS. Biking, golf, tennis, cross-country skiing, fishing, snowmobiling, hunting, hiking, ice skating.
Seen in: *New Mexico Architecture, The Golf Traveler.*

Galisteo

Galisteo Inn

Box 4
Galisteo NM 87540
(505) 982-1506

Circa 1750. In the historic Spanish village of Galisteo, this adobe hacienda is surrounded by giant cottonwoods. The inn features a comfortable southwestern decor, a library, and eight fireplaces. Located on eight acres, there is a duck pond and a creek (the Galisteo River) forms the boundary of the property. Sophisticated cuisine includes dishes such as Brie Quesadilla with

Pineapple Salsa. Blue corn waffles are favorites for breakfast.
Location: Twenty-three miles southeast of Santa Fe, 1 block east of Hwy 41.
Rates: $60-$150.
Joanna Kaufman & Wayne Aarniokoski.
11 Rooms. 7 Private Baths. Guest phone available. Beds: KQDT. Continental-plus breakfast. Swimming pool. CCs: MC VISA. Horseback riding, hiking, massage, ghost towns, 8 miles to petroglyphs. At the beginning of Turquoise Trail.
Seen in: *Physicians Lifestyle Magazine, Insider.*

Kingston

Black Range Lodge
Star Rt 2, Box 119
Kingston NM 88042
(505) 895-5652

Circa 1884. Ivy covers the three-story viga (log-beamed ceilings) and

stone walls of this old hotel, a remnant of the bustling days when silver was discovered nearby and the town mushroomed to 7,000 people. Now only 30 citizens populate the village. Calvary soldiers are said to have headquartered here while protecting miners from the Indians. Hosts, Catherine & Mike pursue movie-script editing and writing careers. Furnishings from the Forties fill the guest rooms on the second floor. There is a room with pool table and video games. Pets and children are welcome.
Rates: $40-$50.
Catherine Wanek & Mike Sherlock.
7 Rooms. 7 Private Baths. Guest phone available. TV available. Beds: QDT. B&B. Game room. Conference room. Swimming, hiking, water sports.
Seen in: *El Paso Times, El Paso Herald Post.*

"Experience serenity and solitude."

Las Cruses

The Lodge
See: Cloudcroft, NM

Las Vegas

Plaza Hotel
230 Old Town Plaza
Las Vegas NM 87701
(505) 425-3591

Circa 1882. This brick Italianate Victorian hotel, once frequented by the likes of Doc Holliday, Big Nose Katy and Billy the Kid, was renovated in 1982. A stencil pattern found in the dining room inspired the selection of Victorian wallpaper borders in the guest rooms, decorated with a combination of contemporary and period furnishings. Guests are still drawn to the warm, dry air and the hot springs north of town.
David Fenzi.
37 Rooms. 37 Private Baths. Guest phone in room. TV in room. Beds: QDC. EP. Restaurant. Gourmet meals. Handicap access. Conference room. CCs: MC VISA AX DC CB DS. Horseback riding, water skiing, wind surfing, hiking, fishing.

Ruidosa

The Lodge
See: Cloudcroft, NM

Santa Fe

El Paradero
220 W Manhattan
Santa Fe NM 87501
(505) 988-1177

Circa 1912. This was originally a two-bedroom Spanish farmhouse that doubled in size to a Territorial style in 1860, was remodeled as a Victorian in 1912, and became a Pueblo Revival in 1920. All styles are present and provide a walk through many years of history.
Location: Downtown.
*Rates: $45-$95.
Ouida MacGregor & Thom Allen.
14 Rooms. 10 Private Baths. TV available. Beds: QT. EP. Handicap access. Conference room. Hiking, horseback riding, white water rafting, indian ruins.
Seen in: *Insider Magazine, Country Inns.*

"I'd like to LIVE here."

Grant Corner Inn
122 Grant Ave
Santa Fe NM 87501
(505) 983-6678

Circa 1905. Judge Robinson and his family lived in this colonial manor

for 30 years and many couples were married in the parlor. Still a romantic setting, the inn is secluded by a garden with willow trees, and there is a white picket fence. Rooms are appointed with antique furnishings and the personal art collections of the Walter family.
*Rates: $50-$110. Season: Feb. to Dec.
Louise Stewart & Martin Walter.
13 Rooms. 7 Private Baths. 1 Fireplace. Guest phone in room. TV in room. Beds: KQDTC. B&B. Gourmet meals. Handicap access. Conference room. CCs: MC VISA. Downhill & cross-country skiing, hiking, fishing, horseback riding.

"The very best of everything - comfort, hospitality, food and T.L.C."

Inn of the Animal Tracks
707 Paseo de Peralta
Santa Fe NM 87501
(505) 988-1546

Circa 1902. Los Andadas is the Spanish phrase that may be trans-

lated "animal tracks" or "end of the trail." Each guest room of this turn-of-the-century house carries an animal theme. The Soaring Eagle room has an inviting fireplace and six large windows with views of apple, pear and honey locust trees in the garden. The vibrant Santa Fe colors selected for Loyal Wolf reflect

the impressive sunsets visible from the windows. Lilac trees and fragrant junipers are just outside. Breakfast and afternoon tea are all made from scratch and reflect the ten years Daun spent as proprietor of one of California's first bed & breakfast inns.
*Rates: $85-$95.
Daun Martin.
4 Rooms. 4 Private Baths. 1 Fireplace. Guest phone in room. TV available. Beds: Q. B&B. Handicap access. CCs: MC VISA AX.

Pueblo Bonito
138 W Manhattan
Santa Fe NM 87501
(505) 984-8001

Circa 1883. A large adobe wall surrounds the grounds of this estate,

once the home of a circuit judge. An original Indian oven is attached to the house. Flagstone pathways, old oak trees and a rose garden add to the atmosphere.
Location: Downtown.
*Rates: $55-$150.
Amy & Herb Behm.
15 Rooms. 15 Private Baths. 15 Fireplaces. Guest phone available. Beds: QD. Continental-plus breakfast. Jacuzzi. Sauna. Handicap access. Swimming pool. Conference room. CCs: MC VISA. Hiking, skiing, tennis, golf, horseback riding, bicycles, exercise equipment.
Seen in: *Innsider Magazine.*

"You captured that quaint, authentic Santa Fe atmosphere, yet I didn't feel as if I had to sacrifice any modern conveniences."

Taos

Hacienda del Sol
109 Mabel Dodge Ln, Box 177
Taos NM 87571
(505) 758-0287

Circa 1800. Mabel Dodge, patron of the arts, purchased this old hacienda as a hideaway for her Indian husband Tony Luhan. The spacious adobe sits among huge cottonwoods, blue spruce, and ponderosa pines, with an uninterrupted view of the mountains across 95,000 acres of Indian lands. Among Dodge's famous guests were Georgia O'Keefe, who painted here, and D. H. Lawrence. The mood is tranquil and on moonlit nights guests can hear Indian drums and the howl of coyotes.
Location: North of Santa Fe at the base of Sangre de Cristo Mountains.
*Rates: $45-$100.
Mari & Jim Ulmer.
7 Rooms. 5 Private Baths. 5 Fireplaces. Guest phone available. TV available. Beds: KQDTC. Continental-plus breakfast. Jacuzzi. CCs: MC VISA. Downhill & cross-country skiing, hiking, fishing, hunting, white water rafting.
Seen in: *Phoenix Gazette, Rocky Mountain News.*

"Your warm friendliness and gracious hospitality have made this week an experience we will never forget!"

La Posada De Taos
309 Juanita Ln, PO Box 1118
Taos NM 87571
(505) 758-8164

Circa 1900. Located within the historic district in a secluded residential area, La Posada is built in the adobe vernacular of the southwest. Log-beamed ceilings (viga), polished floors, Mexican headboards, handwoven spreads, and whitewashed walls hung with local serigraphs contribute to the southwestern decor. French doors open onto a garden with views of Taos Mountain. There are four guest rooms and a honeymoon cottage.
Rates: $46-$85.
Sue Smoot.
5 Rooms. 5 Private Baths. TV available. Beds: QT. B&B. Handicap access. Horseback riding, skiing, biking, fishing.
Seen in: *New York Times, Bon Appetit, Country.*

"Since we left your inn we have talked of our time there often. We look forward to coming again."

The Taos Inn
125 Paseo del Pueblo Norte
Taos NM 87571
(505) 758-2233 (800) 826-7466

Circa 1660. The Taos Inn is a historic landmark with sections dating

back to the 1600s. It is a rustic wood and adobe setting with wood-burning fireplaces, vigas, and wrought iron. The exotic tri-cultural heritage of Spanish, English, and Indian is displayed in hand-loomed Indian bedspreads, antique armoires, Taos furniture, and Pueblo Indian fireplaces.
Location: A quarter block north of historic Taos Plaza.
*Rates: $50-$95.
The Sangers, Carolyn Haddock, Douglas Smith.
40 Rooms. 40 Private Baths. 32 Fireplaces. Guest phone in room. TV in room. Beds: KQDTC. EP. Restaurant. Jacuzzi. Handicap access. Swimming pool. CCs: MC VISA AX DC CB. Horseback riding, skiing, water sports, golf, museums.
Seen in: *Bon Appetit, The Toronto Sun, The Naples Daily News.*

"It is charming, warm, friendly and authentic in decor with a real sense of history."

New York

Albany

Blantyre
See: Lenox, MA

Greenville Arms
See: Greenville, NY

The Gregory House
See: Averill Park, NY

Mansion Hill Inn & Restaurant
115 Philip St
Albany NY 12202
(518) 465-2038 (518) 434-2313

Circa 1865. This old Victorian store houses guest rooms and apartment

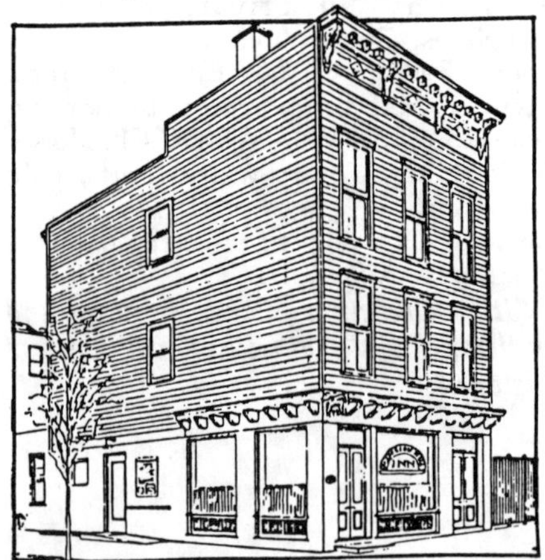

suites on the top two floors and a restaurant on the street level. Originally the home of brush maker, Daniel Brown, it later served as a bulk grocery store. It is located in the historic district just around the corner from the Governor's Executive Mansion in the Mansion Neighborhood. It is a few minutes walk to the State Capitol and the downtown Albany business district.

Rates: $95-$135.
Maryellen & Steve Stofelano, Jr.
7 Rooms. 7 Private Baths. Guest phone in room. TV in room. Beds: QDC. Restaurant. Handicap access. Conference room. CCs: MC VISA AX DC. Swimming pool, private health club.
Seen in: *The Albany Review.*

"Rooms were beautiful and comfortable down to the shower curtain."

The Westchester House
See: Saratoga Springs, NY

Altamont

Appel Inn
Rte 146
Altamont NY 12009
(518) 861-6557

Circa 1765. Originally built as a tavern by Hendrick Appel, this was

the site of the first town meeting of Guilderland. A century later, pillars, porches and a Victorian solarium were added. Guests often breakfast here and enjoy views through the trees to winding Black Creek. The innkeeper was a chef in Europe.

Location: 15 miles to Albany & 8 miles to Schenectady.
Rates: $45-$60.
Laurie & Gerd Beckmann.
4 Rooms. 2 Fireplaces. Guest phone available. TV available. Beds: QDTC. B&B. Gourmet meals. Swimming pool. Conference room. CCs: MC VISA. Nearby lakes, golf. Fireplaces in bedrooms.
Seen in: *Capital Region.*

"Accommodations were superb, hosts were gracious and food was delicious. We were delighted."

Amenia

Troutbeck
Box 26, Leedsville Rd
Amenia NY 12501
(914) 373-9681

Circa 1918. This English country estate on 422 wooded acres enjoyed

its heyday in the Twenties. The NAACP was conceived here and the literati and liberals of the period, including Teddy Roosevelt, were overnight guests. Weekend room rates include all meals and spirits as well as luxurious accommodations for a couple. During the week the inn is a corporate retreat and has been awarded Executive Retreat of the Year.

Location: Foothills of the Berkshires.
*Rates: $550-$790.
James Flaherty & Bob Skibsted.
34 Rooms. 29 Private Baths. 6 Fireplaces. Guest phone available. TV available. Beds: QTDC. MAP. Restaurant. Gourmet meals. Jacuzzi. Sauna. Exercise room. Swimming pool. Game room. Conference room. CCs: AX. Horseback riding, downhill & cross-country skiing, fishing. Tennis courts.

Seen in: *Good Housekeeping, New York Magazine.*

"Connoisseurs of country inns rummage fruitlessly through their memories to summon up an establishment that satisfies their expectations as completely as Troutbeck." Travel & Leisure.

Averill Park

The Gregory House
PO Box 401
Averill Park NY 12018
(518) 674-3774

Circa 1837. This colonial house was built in the center of the village by stockbroker Elias Gregory. It became a restaurant in 1984. The historic section of the building now holds the restaurant while a new portion accommodates overnight guests. It is decorated with Early American braided rugs and four-poster beds.

Location: Minutes from Albany.
*Rates: $55-$75.
Bette & Bob Jewell.
12 Rooms. 12 Private Baths. Guest phone available. TV available. Beds: QT. EP. Restaurant. Swimming pool. CCs: MC VISA DC CB.
Seen in: *The Courier, The Sunday Record.*

Binghamton

Sarah's Dream
See: Dryden, NY

Buffalo

Asa Ransom House
See: Clarence, NY

Burdett

The Red House Country Inn
Picnic Area Rd
Burdett NY 14818
(607) 546-8566

Circa 1844. Nestled within the 13,000-acre Finger Lakes National Forest, this old farmstead has a large veranda overlooking groomed lawns, flower gardens and picnic areas. Pet Samoyeds, goats, and horses share the seven acres. Next to the property are acres of wild

blueberry patches and stocked fishing ponds. The Red House is near Seneca Lake, world-famous Glen Gorge, and Cornell University.

Location: Near Watkins Glen.
*Rates: $55-$75.
Sandy Schmanke & Joan Martin.
6 Rooms. 1 Fireplace. Guest phone available. TV available. Beds: QDT. Full breakfast. Handicap access. Swimming pool. CCs: MC VISA AX. Cross-country skiing, hiking, 36 wineries.
Seen in: *New York Alive.*

"Delightful. Beautifully located for hiking, cross-country skiing. Guest rooms are charming."

Cazenovia

Brae Loch Inn
5 Albany St, US Rt 20
Cazenovia NY 13035
(315) 655-3431

Circa 1805. The innkeeper here wears a kilt to highlight the Scottish

theme. Four of the oldest rooms have fireplaces. There are Stickley furnishings, and the Princess Diana Room has a canopy of white eyelet. Guest rooms are on the second floor above the restaurant.

Location: U.S. Route 20.
*Rates: $59-$125.
H. Grey Barr & Doris L. Barr.
12 Rooms. 12 Private Baths. Guest phone available. Beds: KQDC. Continental-plus breakfast. Restaurant. Conference room. CCs: MC VISA DC. Horseback riding, cross-country skiing, golf, hiking.
Seen in: *The Globe and Mail, Traveler Magazine.*

Clarence

Asa Ransom House
10529 Main St
Clarence NY 14031
(716) 759-2315

Circa 1853. Set on spacious lawns, behind a white picket fence, the Asa

Ransom House rests on the site of the first grist mill built in Erie County. Silversmith Asa Ransom, constructed an inn and grist mill here in response to the Holland Land Company's offering of free land to anyone who would start and operate a tavern. A specialty of the dining room is "Chicken & Leek Pie" and "Pistachio Banana Muffins."

**Rates: $85-$105. Season: Feb. to Dec. 31.
Bob & Judy Lenz.
4 Rooms. 4 Private Baths. 2 Fireplaces. Guest phone in room. TV available. Beds: KQDT. EP. Restaurant. Gourmet meals. CCs: MC VISA DS. Antiquing.
Seen in: *Country Living Magazine.*

"Popular spot keeps getting better."

Cooperstown

The Inn at Cooperstown
16 Chestnut St
Cooperstown NY 13326
(607) 547-5756

Circa 1874. In 1986, New York State awarded the Certificate of Achievement in Historic Preserva-

tion for the restoration of this three-story, Second Empire house. A block from Otsego Lake, the inn is within

walking distance of most of Cooperstown's attractions.
*Rates: $75-$90.
Michael Jerome.
17 Rooms. 17 Private Baths. Guest phone available. TV available. Beds: QT. B&B. Handicap access. Conference room. CCs: MC VISA AX DC DS. Swimming, cross-country skiing, horseback riding, snow tubing, golf, tennis, hang gliding, boating.
Seen in: *The Plain Dealer.*
Nicest place to stay on Earth."

The Davenport Inn
See: Davenport, NY

The Inn at Mill Pond
PO Box 167
Cooperstown NY 13326
(315) 858-1654

Circa 1890. This quaint bed and breakfast is located on a mill pond in a historic area. The house has been restored and is furnished with local antiques. Late afternoon tea is served.
Location: Route 80, 10 minutes north of Cooperstown.
Rates: $45. Season: May to October.
Ed & Gail Newton-Condon.
3 Rooms. 1 Private Bath. Guest phone available. Beds: D. Full breakfast. Golf, fishing, swimming.
"Great stay, we loved it!"

Corning

Rosewood Inn
134 E First St
Corning NY 14830
(607) 962-3253

Circa 1855. Rosewood Inn was originally built as a Greek Revival house. In 1917, the interior and exterior were remodeled in an English Tudor style. The facade includes four square columns two stories high and arched windows and doors. Original black walnut and oak woodwork grace the interior, decorated with authentic wallpapers, period draperies and fine antiques.
Location: Off U.S. Route 17.
Rates: $70-$110.
Winnie & Dick Peer.
6 Rooms. 4 Private Baths. 1 Fireplace. TV available. Beds: QTDC. Full breakfast. CCs: MC VISA DC.
Seen in: *Syracuse Herald-Journal.*
"Rosewood Inn is food for the soul! You both made us feel like friends instead of guests. We'll be back!"

Cortland

Sarah's Dream
See: Dryden, NY

Davenport

The Davenport Inn
Main St
Davenport NY 13750
(607) 278-5068

Circa 1819. In 1799, a tavern was built on this lot, part of an original

land grant of John Jacob Astor. The inn has always catered to working folk and was a gathering place for townsfolk. Grazing cattle and meadows studded with farmhouses may be seen from guest rooms. Fine and hearty family-style meals are served on weekends.
Rates: $34-$46.
Stewart Wohlrab, Bill Hodge.
5 Rooms. 4 Private Baths. Guest phone available. TV in room. Beds: QDT. Continental-plus breakfast. Restaurant. Gourmet meals. Conference room. CCs: MC VISA. Horseback riding, swimming, golf, tennis.
Seen in: *Oneonta Daily Star.*
"The operators of the Davenport Inn with their innate hospitality, graciousness, comfort and gourmet meals make it a place worth stopping and staying."

Dryden

Sarah's Dream
49 W Main St, PO Box 970
Dryden NY 13053
(607) 844-4321

Circa 1828. This graceful Greek Revival was built for physician Daniel Page who originated the Bunker Hill apple, working with a small orchard on the property. Antique filled guest chambers include one with a fringed canopy bed and

an old trunk. Upon arrival, guests are greeted with refreshments. In the morning a lavish breakfast is presented with a table set with antique dinnerware and silver.
*Rates: $50-$120.
Judi Williams & Ken Morusty.
7 Rooms. 7 Private Baths. 1 Fireplace. Guest phone available. TV available. Beds: KQDT. B&B. Conference room. CCs: MC VISA. Downhill skiing, golf, sailing, wind surfing, antiquing.
Seen in: *Ithaca Times, The Grapevine.*
"Gracious hosts. Tastefully decorated. Blockbuster breakfast. A real 'find'."

Forestburgh

The Inn at Lake Joseph
PO Box 81
Forestburgh NY 12777
(914) 791-9506

Circa 1879. This Queen Anne Victorian, with a massive screened veranda is set on 20 acres and was once the vacation home of Cardinal Hayes and Cardinal Spellman. The inn is surrounded by rolling lawns and woodlands and a small swimming beach is located within a short walk. It is in the National Register.
Rates: $118-$218.
Ivan Weinger & Meri Kramer.
9 Rooms. 4 Private Baths. 2 Fireplaces. Guest phone available. TV available. Beds: KQD. MAP. Gourmet meals. Game room. Conference room. CCs: MC VISA AX. Golf, horseback riding, skiing, snowmobiling, rafting, ballooning, hunting, tennis, boating, fishing.
Seen in: *New York Times, Kaatskill Life Magazine.*
"This is a secluded spot where every detail is attended to, making it one of the country's best inns."

Fulton

Battle Island Inn

RD 1 Box 176
Fulton NY 13069
(315) 598-3985

Circa 1840. Topped with a gothic cupola, this family farmhouse over-

looks the Oswego River and a golf course. There are three antique-filled parlors. Guest accommodations are furnished in a variety of styles including Victorian and Renaissance Revival. There are four wooded acres with lawns and gardens. Guests are often found relaxing on one of the inn's four porches, enjoying the views.

Location: Seven miles South of Oswego on Lake Ontario.
Rates: $55-$75.
Richard & Joyce Rice.
6 Rooms. 6 Private Baths. Guest phone in room. TV in room. Beds: QDT. Full breakfast. Conference room. CCs: MC VISA. Golf, cross-country skiing, fishing, museums.
Seen in: *Lake Effect.*

"We will certainly never forget our wonderful weeks at Battle Island Inn."

Garrison

Bird & Bottle Inn

Rt 9
Garrison NY 10524
(914) 424-3000

Circa 1761. Built as Warren's Tavern this three-story yellow farmhouse served as a lodging and

dining spot on the old New York-to-Albany Post Road, now a national historic landmark. George Washington, Hamilton, Lafayette and many other historic figures frequently passed by. The inn's four acres include secluded lawns, a bubbling stream and Hudson Valley woodlands. Timbered ceilings, old paneling and fireplace mantels maintain a Revolutionary War era ambiance for the inn's notable restaurant. Second floor guest rooms have canopied or four-poster beds and each is warmed by its own fireplace.

*Rates: $195-$215.
Ira Boyar.
4 Rooms. 4 Private Baths. 4 Fireplaces. Guest phone available. Beds: QD. MAP. Restaurant. Gourmet meals. CCs: MC VISA AX DC. Cross-country skiing, golf, horseback riding, hiking, swimming, boating.
Seen in: *Colonial Homes, Westchester Spotlight, Hudson Valley Living.*

Geneseo

American House

39 Main St
Geneseo NY 14454
(716) 243-5483

Circa 1897. The American House was a tavern and stagecoach stop in the early 1800s. When it burned, a private home was built and it is now in the National Register. Centrally located in the village, it's a short walk to the campus of the State University of New York. The second oldest active fox hunt in the country is the Genesee Valley Hunt.

Location: Thirty miles south of Rochester, 60 miles east of Buffalo.
*Rates: $50-$65.
Harry & Helen Wadsworth.
6 Rooms. 2 Private Baths. 2 Fireplaces. Guest phone available. TV available. Beds: QTD. B&B. Cross-country skiing, horseback riding, swimming, boating.

"You certainly set the tone for Jodi's wedding day. Many thanks from a grandmother who enjoyed every moment of that memorable stay."

Geneva

The Inn at Belhurst Castle

PO 609
Geneva NY 14456
(315) 781-0201

Circa 1889. Red Medina stone was chosen to construct this Richardson Romanesque mansion. The inn's sweeping lawns and views of Seneca Lake may be enjoyed from anywhere on the property, but the most stunning experience is from the balcony of the Tower suite, a special room with a hot tub and a private staircase that winds up the turret. Exquisitely carved woodwork throughout the inn serves as a backdrop to surprising decorative touches such as a stuffed partridge or a suit of armor.

Rates: $80-$115.
Robert & Nancy Golden.
12 Rooms. 12 Private Baths. 4 Fireplaces. Guest phone in room. TV in room. Beds: QT. Restaurant. Handicap access. CCs: MC VISA AX DC CB. Swimming, sailing, fishing, cross-country skiing.

Glens Falls

The Crislip's B&B

RD 1 Box 57, Ridge Rd
Glens Falls NY 12801
(518) 793-6869

Circa 1820. This Federal-style house was built by Quakers. It was

owned by the area's first doctor who used it as a training center for young interns. There are historic stone walls on the property.

Location: Lake George, Saratoga area.
Rates: $55-$75.
Ned & Joyce Crislip.
3 Rooms. 3 Private Baths. Guest phone available. Beds: KD. CCs: MC VISA.

Greenville

Greenville Arms
South St
Greenville NY 12083
(518) 966-5219

Circa 1889. William Vanderbilt had this graceful Victorian built with

Queen Anne gables and cupolas. Seven acres of lush lawns are dotted with gardens of daffodils, tulips and lilacs. There are floor-to-ceiling fireplaces, chestnut woodwork and wainscoting, and Victorian bead work over the doorways. Painting workshops are held in summer and fall.
*Rates: $80-$110.
Laura & Barbara Stevens.
20 Rooms. 14 Private Baths. Guest phone available. TV available. Beds: DT. Full breakfast. Swimming pool. Conference room. CCs: MC VISA. Golf, tennis, horseback riding, hiking, bicycling, skiing, airplane rides.
Seen in: *Victorian Homes, New York Magazine, Yankee.*

"Just a note of appreciation for all your generous hospitality, and wonderful display of attention and affection!"

Groton

Benn Conger Inn
206 W Cortland
Groton NY 13073
(607) 898-5817

Circa 1921. Once home to Benn Conger, founder of Smith-Corona typewriters, this Greek Revival

mansion overlooks the village and presides over 18 acres of rolling fields. The inn is owned and operated by Chef Mark Bloom and wife Patricia who specialize in French and Italian cuisine. Guest rooms are furnished in antiques and feature flannel sheets and warm comforters for frosty evenings.
Location: Finger Lakes area between Ithaca and Cortland.
Rates: $60-$100. Season: April - Feb.
Mark & Patricia Bloom.
4 Rooms. 4 Private Baths. 1 Fireplace. Guest phone available. TV available. Beds: KQD. B&B. Restaurant. Conference room. CCs: MC VISA AX DC. Hiking, cross country skiing on premises. Nearby wineries. Award-winning wine cellar.
Seen in: *Andrew Harper's Hideaway Report.*

Ithaca

Benn Conger Inn
See: Groton, NY

Falconer Inn
140 College Ave
Ithaca NY 14850
(607) 272-0919

Circa 1874. This eight-bedroom brick Victorian was built by an Englishman who came to town to work on Ezra Cornell's house. It is three blocks from the edge of Cornell campus and a block away from several ethnic restaurants.
*Rates: $79-$99.
Nancy Falconer & Susan Vance.
8 Rooms. 5 Private Baths. Beds: QTD. Full breakfast. CCs: MC VISA. Boating, swimming, ice skating, cross-country skiing.
Seen in: *Ithaca Daily Journal, Cornell Daily Sun.*

"Elegant, warm, first rate. One is made to feel comfortable and relaxed."

Rose Inn
Rt 34 N, Box 6576
Ithaca NY 14851-6576
(607) 533-7905

Circa 1851. This classic Italianate mansion has long been famous for its circular staircase made of Honduran mahogany by a mysterious craftsman. Charles Rosemann is a German hotelier with a degree from the Hotel School in Heidelberg. Sherry is a noted interior designer

specializing in pre-Victorian architecture and furniture. The inn is on 20 landscaped acres 15 minutes from Ithaca and Cornell University.
*❀Rates: $95-$165.
Sherry & Charles Rosemann.
15 Rooms. 15 Private Baths. 1 Fireplace. Guest phone available. TV available. Beds: KQT. Full breakfast. Jacuzzi. Handicap access. Conference room. CCs: CB. Downhill & cross-country skiing, sailing, windsurfing.
Seen in: *Ithaca Times, New Woman Magazine.*

"The blending of two outstanding talents, which when combined with your warmth, produce the ultimate experience in being away from home. Like staying with friends in their beautiful home."

Sarah's Dream
See: Dryden, NY

Keene

The Bark Eater
Alstead Mill Rd
Keene NY 12942
(518) 576-2221

Circa 1830. Originally a stagecoach stop on the old road to Lake Placid,

The Bark Eater (English for the Indian word Adirondacks) has been in almost continuous operation since the 1800s. Then it was a full day's journey over rugged, mountainous terrain with two teams of horses. The inn features wide-board floors, fireplaces and rooms filled with antiques.
Location: One mile from town.
*Rates: $75 to $110.
Joe Pete Wilson.
12 Rooms. 6 Private Baths. Guest phone available. TV available. Beds: KQTC. AP. Handicap access. Conference room.

CCs: AX. All summer & winter sports, horseback riding, cross country skiing. Adironacks high peaks climbing.

"Staying at a country inn is an old tradition in Europe, and is rapidly catching on in the United States... A stay here is a pleasant surprise for anyone who travels." William Lederer, *Ugly American.*

Kingston

The Jacob Kip River House B&B

See: Rhinebeck, NY

Village Victorian Inn

See: Rhinebeck, NY

Lake George

The Lamplight Inn

See: Lake Luzerne, NY

The Westchester House

See: Saratoga Springs, NY

Lake Luzerne

Lamplight Inn

PO Box 70, 2129 Lake Ave (9N)
Lake Luzerne NY 12846
(518) 696-5294

Circa 1890. Howard Conkling, a wealthy lumberman, built this Vic-

torian Gothic estate on land that had been the site of the Warren County Fair. The home was designed for entertaining since Conkling was a very eligible bachelor. It has 12-foot beamed ceilings, chestnut wainscoting and moldings and a chestnut keyhole staircase all crafted in England.

*Rates: $60-$125.
Gene & Linda Merlino
10 Rooms. 10 Private Baths. 5 Fireplaces. Guest phone available. TV available. Beds: QD. Full breakfast. Conference room. CCs: AX. Horseback riding, swimming, cross-country & downhill skiing, boating, white water rafting.
Seen in: *Getaways for Gourmets.*

"Rooms are immaculately kept and clean. The owners are the nicest, warmest, funniest and most hospitable innkeepers I have ever met."

Lake Placid

Highland House Inn

3 Highland Pl
Lake Placid NY 12946
(518) 523-2377

Circa 1910. This inn is situated on the hill in the village, a five-minute

walk to Main Street and the Olympic Center. The rooms are decorated in a charming country style. A separate cottage on the property accommodates groups of up to six people.

Location: Above Main Street in the Lake Placid Village.
*Rates: $45-$85.
Teddy & Cathy Blazer.
9 Rooms. 5 Private Baths. Guest phone available. TV available. Beds: DT. Full breakfast. Conference room. CCs: MC VISA. Lakes, beaches, skiing.
Seen in: *Weekender.*

"You have the perfect place to rest and relax."

Livingston Manor

Lanza's Country Inn

RD 2 Box 446, Shandelee Rd
Livingston Manor NY 12758
(914) 439-5070

Circa 1901. Located on seven acres, the inn has a country taproom with a fireplace. It is furnished with antiques and there is a separate cottage on the property for groups of four.

Rates: $69-$79.

Dick, Pat & Mickey Lanza.
8 Rooms. 8 Private Baths. Guest phone available. TV available. Beds: KQDT. B&B. Restaurant. CCs: MC VISA AX. Horseback riding, water sports, golf, tennis.
Seen in: *Hudson Valley Magazine.*

"We were treated like family. Excellent food."

Mayville

Plumbush B&B at Chautauqua

Chautauqua - Stedman Rd, Box 332
Mayville NY 14757
(716) 789-5309

Circa 1865. Situated on 125 acres of meadows and woodlands, Plum-

bush is a mauve and pale pink, Italianate Victorian shaded by towering maples. Eleven-foot ceilings accommodate the nine-foot tall arched windows. There is a music room and a staircase winds up to the three-story turret.

*Rates: $55-$75.
George & Sandy Green.
4 Rooms. 4 Private Baths. Guest phone available. TV available. Beds: QDT. Continental-plus breakfast. CCs: MC VISA. Hiking, cross-country ski trails, bicycles. One mile to Chautauqua Institute.
Seen in: *Buffalo News, Mayville Sentinel.*

"A wonderful piece of Heaven."

Mount Tremper

Mt. Tremper Inn
Rt 212 & Wittenberg Rd
Mount Tremper NY 12457
(914) 688-5329

Circa 1850. Nettie & Charles Lamson built this Victorian inn to ac-

commodate families who would stay all summer with fathers commuting by rail from New York City on the weekends. Now with Hunter Mountain skiing 20 miles away, the inn is popular all year. Romantic classical music wafts through the Victorian parlor decorated with velvet Empire sofas, burgundy velvet walls, oriental carpets, and museum quality antiques. A large blue stone fireplace warms guests who gather for evening chats. Each bedchamber has Victorian wallpapers, French lace curtains, luxury linens, and antique bedsteads.

Location: Corner of Route 212 and Wittenberg Road.
Rates: $60-$90.
Lou Caselli & Peter Lascala.
12 Rooms. 2 Private Baths. Guest phone available. Beds: DT. B&B. CCs: MC VISA. Horseback riding, hiking, swimming, fishing, cross-country skiing.
Seen in: *The New York Times, Mature Outlook, Staten Island Advance, Ski Magazine.*

Mumford

Genesee Country Inn
948 George St
Mumford NY 14511
(716) 538-2500

Circa 1833. This stone house with two-and-a-half-foot-thick limestone walls served as a plaster mill and later as a hub and wheel factory. Now it is an inn set on six acres with views of streams, woodlands and ponds. There is a deck adjacent to a 16-foot waterfall. Ask for a garden room and enjoy a fireplace and your own balcony overlooking the mill ponds.
*Rates: $80-$95.
Gregory & Glenda Barcklow.
9 Rooms. 9 Private Baths. 2 Fireplaces. Guest phone in room. TV in room. Beds: QD. B&B. Conference room. CCs: MC VISA AX DC DS. Trout fishing, museum.

"You may never want to leave..."

New York

Incentra Village House
32 8th Ave
New York NY 10014
(212) 206-0007

Circa 1841. Located in the Greenwich Village area, this guest house is decorated in period furnishings. Most rooms have kitchens and some have fireplaces and air conditioning.
Location: Greenwich Village area.
*Rates: $85-$110.
Gaylord Hofteizer.
10 Rooms. 10 Private Baths. 7 Fireplaces. Guest phone in room. TV in room. Beds: QDT. EP. CCs: MC VISA AX.

The Jeremiah J. Yereance House
See: Lyndhurst, NJ

Shadowbrook
See: Irvington-on-Hudson, NY

Oneida

The Pollyanna
302 Main St
Oneida NY 13421
(315) 363-0524

Circa 1862. Roses and iris grace the gardens of this Italian villa. Inside are special collections, antiques and three Italian-marble fireplaces. Of the two crystal chandeliers, one is still piped for original gas. A handcrafted white wool and mohair rug runs up the staircase to the rooms where guests are pampered with bed warmers and down quilts. The innkeeper teaches spinning, felting, bobbin lace and other crafts.
Location: Route 46, 5 miles from Thruway 90, exit off route 5.
*Rates: $48-$68.

Doloria & Ken Chapin.
6 Rooms. Guest phone available. TV available. Beds: QDT. Full breakfast. Gourmet meals. Conference room. CCs: MC VISA AX. Water skiing, hiking.
Seen in: *Oneida Daily Dispatch.*

"Great hospitality and super breakfast. We really enjoyed all the interesting things."

Oneonta

The Davenport Inn
See: Davenport, NY

Oswego

Battle Island Inn
See: Fulton, NY

Penfield

Strawberry Castle B&B
See: Rochester, NY

Poughkeepsie

Village Victorian Inn
See: Rhinebeck, NY

Rhinebeck

Beekman Arms
Rt 9, 4 Mill St
Rhinebeck NY 12572
(914) 876-7077

Circa 1766. Said to be the oldest landmark inn in America, some walls of the Beekman Arms are two and three-feet-thick. It has seen a variety of guests - including pioneers, trappers, Indians and Dutch farmers. Among the famous were Aaron Burr, William Jennings

Bryan, Horace Greeley and Franklin Roosevelt. Like most old taverns and inns it provided a meeting place for leaders of the day. Victorian furnishings are found throughout. Mr. LaForge is the 28th innkeeper at Beekman Arms.
Location: Center of Village of Rhinebeck.
*Rates: $55-$95.
Charles LaForge.
54 Rooms. 54 Private Baths. 21 Fireplaces. Guest phone in room. TV in room. Beds: QDT. Continental breakfast. Restaurant. Handicap access. Conference room. CCs: MC VISA AX DC. Cross-country skiing, golf, tennis.
Seen in: *New York Times.*

The Jacob Kip River House B&B
Long Dock Rd
Rhinebeck NY 12572
(914) 876-8330

Circa 1708. Nestled into a hillside overlooking the Hudson River 100 yards away is this stone house built by Hendrick Kip for his brother Jacob. They purchased the land from Sapasco Indians in 1686. The house served as a tavern for the travelers taking the ferry service to Kingston. During a recent restoration a hidden chamber, thought to have been used on the Underground Railroad, was found beneath the dining room. George Washington slept here in 1783 during his triumphal tour following the Revolutionary War.
*Rates: $60-$85.
Katherine Mansfield & Norman Shatkin.
3 Rooms. 1 Private Bath. Guest phone available. TV available. Beds: KDT. B&B. CCs: MC VISA. Tennis, swimming, cross-country skiing, bird-watching.

Village Victorian Inn
31 Center St
Rhinebeck NY 12572
(914) 876-8345

Circa 1860. A white picket fence surrounds this appealing yellow-and-white Victorian. It is furnished in French Victorian fabrics, floral wallpapers, local antiques and canopy or brass beds. Cheese blintzes or eggs Benedict are often the choices for breakfast which is served in the dining room.
*Rates: $95-$130.
Judy & Rich Kohler.

5 Rooms. 5 Private Baths. 2 Fireplaces. Guest phone available. TV available. Beds: KQ. B&B. Conference room. CCs: MC VISA AX. Sailing, cross-country skiing, antiquing.
Seen in: *Travel & Leisure Magazine, Weekend Trader.*

"Thank you for all your hospitality and for making our stay so wonderful. Breakfast was delicious."

Rochester

Strawberry Castle B&B
1883 Penfield Rd, Rt 441
Rochester NY 14526
(716) 385-3266

Circa 1875. A rosy brick Italianate villa, Strawberry Castle was once

known for the grapes and strawberries grown on the property. Ornate plaster ceilings and original inside shutters are special features. There are six roof levels, carved ornamental brackets, and columned porches topped by a white cupola.
Location: East of Rochester on Route 441.
Rates: $60-$75.
Charles & Cynthia Whited.
3 Rooms. Guest phone available. TV available. Continental-plus breakfast. Swimming pool. Conference room. CCs: MC VISA. Swimming.
Seen in: *Upstate Magazine.*

"You have a most unusual place. We applaud your restoration efforts and are thankful you've made it available to travelers."

Saranac Lake

The Point
Star Route
Saranac Lake NY 12983
(518) 891-5674

Circa 1930. Designed by renowned architect William Distin and built

for William Rockefeller, this Adirondack Great Camp has hosted fashionable house parties for the Vanderbilts, Whitneys and Morgans. No expense was spared to create the elegant, rustic lakefront estate with its walk-in-granite fireplaces, rare Adirondack antiques and massive hand-hewn beams. Each day a cord of wood is needed to fuel all the fireplaces. This lavish camp welcomes those who prefer to rough it with style.
*Rates: $475-$650.
Bill & Claudia McNamee.
11 Rooms. 11 Private Baths. 9 Fireplaces. Guest phone available. TV available. Beds: K. AP. Game room. Conference room. CCs: AX. Swimming, canoeing, water-skiing, horseback riding. Snow picnics, snow skiing. Old mahogany runabouts.
Seen in: *New York Magazine, House & Garden.*

"Simply the most attractive private home in America." Irene Miki Rawlings, *New York Times.*

Saratoga

Appel Inn
See: Altamont, NY

Saratoga Springs

Adelphi Hotel
365 Broadway
Saratoga Springs NY 12866
(518) 587-4688

Circa 1877. This Victorian hotel is one of two hotels still remaining

from Saratoga's opulent spa era. A piazza overlooking Broadway features three-story columns topped with Victorian fretwork. Recently refurbished with lavish turn-of-the-century decor, rooms are filled with antique furnishings and opulent draperies and wall coverings, highlighting the inn's high ceilings and ornate woodwork. Breakfast is delivered to each room in the morning.
Rates: $65-$190. Season: May - October.
Gregg Siefher & Sheila Parkert.
34 Rooms. 34 Private Baths. Guest phone in room. TV in room. Beds: QTDC. B&B. Restaurant. CCs: MC VISA AX. Horseback riding, skiing, racetracks, boating, water skiing, sailing.
Seen in: *New York Times.*

Inn on Bacon Hill
See: Schuylerville, NY

The Lamplight Inn
See: Lake Luzerne, NY

The Westchester House
102 Lincoln Ave, PO Box 944
Saratoga Springs NY 12866
(518) 587-7613

Circa 1880. This gracious Queen Anne Victorian has been welcoming

vacationers for more than 100 years. Antiques from four generations of the Melvin's family grace the rooms. Saratoga was a favorite Victorian resort for vacationers who packed their Saratoga trunks and headed off for summers in the Adirondacks. The tradition of high living, culture, romance and health ran strong. Strains of Victor Herbert's music filled the air and Mark Twain, Diamond Jim Brady, and Lil Langtree all participated in the Saratoga summer.
Location: Thirty miles north of Albany in the Adirondack foothills.
Rates: $60-$175.
Bob & Stephanie Melvin.
7 Rooms. 5 Private Baths. Guest phone available. Beds: KD. Continental-plus breakfast. Conference room. CCs: VISA DC DS. Golf, tennis, swimming, cross-country skiing, ice skating, mineral spas, Philadelphia Orchestra. NYC Ballet & Opera at the Arts Center.
Seen in: *Getaways for Gourmets, The Albany Times Union.*

"I adored your B&B and have raved about it to all. One of the most beautiful and welcoming places we've ever been to."

Schuylerville

Inn on Bacon Hill
200 Wall Street
Schuylerville NY 12871
(518) 695-3693

Circa 1865. State legislator Alexander Baucus built his mid-Vic-

torian mansion in the country a few miles from Saratoga Springs. Two parlors, marble fireplaces, a carved staircase and original moldings add to the gracious country gentleman lifestyle. Four-poster beds are piled with flowered quilts in the guest rooms.
Rates: $50-$85.
Andrea Collins-Breslin.
4 Rooms. 2 Private Baths. Guest phone available. Beds: DT. Full breakfast. CCs: MC VISA. Tennis, golf, swimming, cross-country skiing, ballet & opera.
Seen in: *Boston Globe, The Saratogian.*

"We'll long remember the warmth and pleasures of sharing a little piece of summer with you."

Skaneateles

Sherwood Inn
26 W Genesee St
Skaneateles NY 13152
(315) 685-3405

Circa 1807. During the Knickerbocker Tours of the 1820s stagecoaches making the rounds between New York and Niagara Falls

chose Isaac Sherwood's tavern as their favorite stopping place. Many of the rooms face scenic Skaneateles Lake. The inn is noted for its continental and American menu.
*Rates: $70-$100.
Ellen Seymour.
17 Rooms. 17 Private Baths. Guest phone in room. TV available. Beds: DT. Continental breakfast. Restaurant. Conference room. CCs: MC VISA AX DC. Boating, swimming, tennis, skiing, horseback riding, golf, polo.
Seen in: *Glamour, Travel & Leisure.*

Southold

Goose Creek Guesthouse
1475 Waterview Dr
Southold NY 11971
(516) 765-3356

Circa 1780. Grover Pease left for the Civil War from this house, and

after his death his widow Harriet ran a summer boarding house here. The basement actually dates from the 1780s and is constructed of large rocks. The present house was moved here and put on the older foundation. Southold has many old historic homes and a guidebook is provided for visitors.
Rates: $65.
Mary J. Mooney-Getoff.
4 Rooms. Guest phone available. TV available. Beds: KQT. Full breakfast. Tennis, golf, horseback riding, beaches, museums, antique shops.
Seen in: *New York Times, Newsday.*

"We will be repeat guests. Count on it!!"

Stony Brook

Three Village Inn

150 Main St
Stony Brook NY 11790
(516) 751-0555

Circa 1751. Since 1751, generations of innkeepers, including Captain

Jonas Smith, the Melvilles, and the Roberts have managed this Long Island colonial inn. The original part of the inn is a tavern room, the Sandbar. Good food, twilight walks by the marina and Laura Ashley decorated guest rooms make for a refreshing getaway.

Rates: $85-$110.
Jimmy & Lou Miaritis.
32 Rooms. B&B. Restaurant. Handicap access. CCs: MC VISA AX. Horse-drawn carriage rides, nature walks, fishing, swimming, golf, tennis, biking, antiquing, apple picking.

Syracuse

Brae Loch Inn

See: Cazenovia, NY

The Pollyanna

See: Oneida, NY

Sarah's Dream

See: Dryden, NY

Sherwood Inn

See: Skaneateles, NY

Troy

The Gregory House

See: Averill Park, NY

Utica

Brae Loch Inn

See: Cazenovia, NY

Waterloo

The Historic James R. Webster Mansion

115 E Main St - Rts 5 & 20
Waterloo NY 13165
(315) 539-3032

Circa 1845. James Russell Webster, relative of Noah and Daniel Webster

and friend of Abraham Lincoln, built this Greek Revival mansion with a classical pillared Greek temple front. In addition to its fine furnishings, there are many collections including rare European clocks of the 17th and 18th centuries. Richly crafted woodwork is found throughout. The inn's fine cuisine was recently acknowledged by membership in the Master Chefs Institute of America.

Location: Routes 5 & 20 between Geneva and Seneca Falls, Exit 41 off I-90.
*Rates: $250.
Leonard & Barbara N. Cohen.
2 Rooms. 2 Private Baths. 2 Fireplaces. Guest phone available. Beds: D. Continental-plus breakfast. Restaurant. Gourmet meals. Conference room. CCs: MC VISA. Horseback riding, skiing, fishing, water skiing.
Seen in: *New York Times.*

"Thank you for making our honeymoon a fabulous fairy tale. Wonderful antiques. Absolutely gourmet meals. We think you have reached perfection."

Watkins Glen

The Red House Country Inn

See: Burdett, NY

Westfield

Westfield House

E Main Rd, PO Box 505
Westfield NY 14787
(716) 326-6262

Circa 1840. Westfield was part of the Granger Homestead. Benjamin

Hopson, a local ice merchant, built a magnificent Gothic Revival addition in 1860. His daughter Lucy used the living room with its large crystal windows as a tea room. The Gothic detailed interiors include a winding staircase to the six upstairs bed chambers.

Location: Southwestern New York state. Historic Chautauqua County.
Rates: $45 to $65.
Betty & Jud Wilson
6 Rooms. 6 Private Baths. Guest phone available. Beds: KQ. B&B. Handicap access. Conference room. CCs: MC VISA. Horseback riding, skiing, water sports. Complimentary boat rides on Chautauqua Lake.

"Your accommodations and hospitality are wonderful! Simply outstanding. The living room changes its character by the hour."

The William Seward Inn

RD 2, S Portage Rd, Rt 394
Westfield NY 14787
(716) 326-4151

Circa 1821. This two-story Greek Revival estate stands on a knoll

overlooking the forest and Lake Erie. Seward was a Holland Land Company agent before becoming governor of New York. He later served as Lincoln's Secretary of State and is known for the Alaska

Purchase. George Patterson bought Seward's home and also became governor of New York. Most of the mansion's furnishings are dated 1790 to 1870 from the Sheraton-Victorian period.
Location: Three hours from Cleveland, Pittsburgh and Toronto.
Rates: $58-$88.
Peter & Joyce Wood.
10 Rooms. 10 Private Baths. 1 Fireplace. Guest phone available. TV available. Beds: KQT. Full breakfast. Gourmet meals. Conference room. CCs: MC VISA. Downhill & cross-country skiing, lakes, Chautauqua Institution.
Seen in: *New York Times, Pittsburgh Post-Gazette.*

"The breakfasts are delicious. The solitude and your hospitality are what the doctor ordered."

Westhampton Beach

1880 Seafield House

2 Seafield Lane
Westhampton Beach NY 11978
(516) 288-1559 (800)346-3290

Circa 1880. On Westhampton Beach's exclusive Seafield Lane, this country estate includes a pool and tennis court, and it is just a short walk to the ocean beach. The inn is decorated with Victorian antiques, Shaker benches, and Chinese porcelain creating a casual, country inn atmosphere.
Location: Ninety minutes from Manhattan.
❊Rates: $75.
Elsie Collins.
2 Rooms. 2 Private Baths. Guest phone available. TV in room. Beds: D. B&B. Swimming pool. Tennis.

"From the moment we stepped inside your charming home we felt all the warmth you sent our way which made our stay so comfortable and memorable."

Woodstock

The Jacob Kip River House B&B

See: Rhinebeck, NY

Mt. Tremper Inn

See: Mount Tremper, NY

North Carolina

Asheville

Albemarle Inn

86 Edgemont Rd
Asheville NC 28801
(704) 255-0027

Circa 1907. Tall Grecian columns mark the majestic entrance to Albemarle. A wide veranda, shaded by mountain pines, provides a welcoming invitation to guests. Inside, a carved oak staircase and massive oak panelled doors are polished to a high gleam. Guest rooms feature 11-foot ceilings and claw foot tubs. The Hungarian composer Bela Bartok is said to have written his third concerto for piano while in residence at the inn.

*Rates: $58-$74.
John & Rosina Mellin.
12 Rooms. 12 Private Baths. 2 Fireplaces. Guest phone in room. TV in room. Beds: KQD. Full breakfast. Swimming pool. CCs: MC VISA. Tennis, white-water rafting, hiking.

Cedar Crest Victorian Inn

674 Biltmore Ave
Asheville NC 28803
(704) 252-1389

Circa 1891. This Queen Anne mansion is one of the largest and most opulent residences surviving Asheville's 1890's boom. A captain's walk, projecting turrets, and expansive verandas welcome guests to lavish interior woodwork and stained glass. All rooms are furnished in antiques with satin and lace trappings.

Rates: $70-$100.
Barbara & Jack McEwan.
13 Rooms. 10 Private Baths. 1 Fireplace. Guest phone in room. TV available. Beds: QDT. B&B. CCs: MC VISA AX DS. Tennis, skiing, rafting all nearby. Afternoon beverage, evening hot chocolate & tea.
Seen in: *New Woman, Southern Living, Good Housekeeping, House Beautiful.*

Cornerstone Inn

230 Pearson Dr
Asheville NC 28801
(704) 253-5644

Circa 1924. This Dutch Tudor house was built by Dr. Charles Cocke. Standing in the heart of the Montford Historic District, it is surrounded by other homes of distinctive architecture, in an active restoration area. The inn is filled with antiques the Wyatts gleaned from their southern families and collected from ten years of living and traveling in Europe. Local wildflowers grown within a rock walled garden provide the summertime breakfast setting.

*Rates: $60-$65.
Lonnie & Evelyn Wyatt.
4 Rooms. 4 Private Baths. Guest phone available. TV in room. Beds: D. B&B. CCs: MC VISA. Hiking, horseback riding, festivals, botanical gardens.
Seen in: *Asheville Citizen-Times.*

"A wonderful place to stay with very friendly innkeepers."

Dry Ridge Inn

See: Weaverville, NC

Flint Street Inn

100 & 116 Flint St
Asheville NC 28801
(704) 253-6723

Circa 1915. Side by side, these two lovely old family homes are located in Asheville's oldest neighborhood and are within comfortable walking distance of downtown. A lovely breakfast room invites guests to linger and 200-year-old oaks, old-fashioned gardens and a fish pond add to the atmosphere.

Location: Montford Historic District.
*Rates: $75.
Rick, Lynne & Marion Vogel.
8 Rooms. 8 Private Baths. 3 Fireplaces. Guest phone available. TV available. Beds: D. CCs: MC VISA AX DS.

"Our home away from home."

Heritage Hill

64 Linden Ave
Asheville NC 28801
(704) 254-9336

Circa 1909. Twelve white pillars and a large veranda filled with rocking chairs greet visitors to this colonial house. There are three fireplaces and on cool evenings guests often enjoy wine in front of a cozy fire. The house sits on an acre of park-like grounds with giant maple, oak, pine and dogwood trees. It's a three-block walk to town.

*Rates: $40-$60.
Linda & Ross Willard.
9 Rooms. 9 Private Baths. 5 Fireplaces. Guest phone available. TV in room. Beds: KDT. B&B. CCs: MC VISA. Swimming, skiing, hiking, tennis. Champagne for honeymooners.

"It was the highlight of our trip!"

Marshall House

See: Marshall, NC

The Old Reynolds Mansion

100 Reynolds Hgts
Asheville NC 28804
(704) 254-0496

Circa 1855. This handsome three-story brick, antebellum mansion

listed in the National Register is furnished with antiques. Guests enjoy mountain views from all rooms, wood-burning fireplaces, a two-story wraparound veranda, and a swimming pool. It is situated on a four-acre knoll of Reynolds Mountain.

Location: Ten minutes north of downtown Asheville.
Rates: $40-$75.
Fred & Helen Faber.
10 Rooms. 8 Private Baths. 4 Fireplaces. Guest phone available. Beds: QDT. B&B.
Seen in: *Greensboro News & Record, Blue Ridge Country.*

"This was one of the nicest places we have ever stayed. We spent every sundown on the porch waiting for the fox's daily visit."

Reed House B&B

119 Dodge St
Asheville NC 28803
(704) 274-1604

Circa 1892. This yellow and white Queen Anne Victorian, in the National Register, sports a handsome, three-story tower. During renovation, the owners discovered a secret passageway from the top of the tower down between the walls to an exit in the crawl space under the house. Inside the house, rose-colored cherubs decorate the fireplace tile. Rockers and a porch swing occupy the veranda.

Location: South of Asheville.
Rates: $40-$50. Season: May to Nov.
Marge Turcot.
5 Rooms. 1 Private Bath. 5 Fireplaces. Guest phone available. TV available. Beds: DTC. B&B. CCs: MC VISA. Golfing, fishing, hiking, rafting.
Seen in: *Old House Journal, CBS Morning Show.*

Richmond Hill Inn & Conference Center

87 Richmond Hill Dr
Asheville NC 28806
(704) 252-7313

Circa 1889. This newly renovated 30-room Victorian mansion was designed for the Pearson family by

James Hill, architect of the U. S. Treasury Building. Richmond Pearson was a renowned statesman, Congressman, and friend of Theodore Roosevelt. This elegant estate featured innovations such as running water, a communication system, and a pulley-operated elevator for moving furniture.

Rates: $80-$160.
12 Rooms. 12 Private Baths. Beds: KQTC. Full breakfast. Jacuzzi. Conference room. CCs: MC VISA. Fishing, rafting, downhill skiing.
Seen in: *Winston-Salem Journal, The Atlanta Journal and Constitution.*

"A great adventure into history."

The Waverly Inn

See: Hendersonville, NC

Beaufort

Captains' Quarters Bed & Biscuit

315 Ann St
Beaufort NC 28516
(919) 728-7711

Circa 1902. This two-story, balloon-frame house has a wraparound front porch. Politician and railroad owner W. S. Chadwick, built the heart-pine home for his daughter Corinne. It is furnished with Victorian antiques and family heirlooms that date to the American Revolution.

Location: Corner of Ann & Turner Streets in the heart of historical district.
*Rates: $50-$90.
Ruby & Captain Dick Collins.
3 Rooms. 3 Private Baths. Guest phone available. TV available. Beds: DT. Continental-plus breakfast. Conference room. CCs: MC VISA AX. Fishing, golf, tennis, beaches.
Seen in: *The News-Times.*

"Your family is simply delightful and your hospitality was more than a pleasure."

Langdon House

135 Craven St
Beaufort NC 28516
(919) 728-5499

Circa 1733. This three-story colonial house witnessed Beaufort pillaged by pirates in 1747, plundered by the British in 1782, occupied by the Union army in 1862, and pounded by the great hurricane of 1879. The atmosphere of the inn is enhanced by a 19th-century pump organ, an Empire secretary, and other antiques. A colonial garden features daisies, cabbage roses and a collection of herbs.

*Rates: $59-$115.
Jimm Prest.
4 Rooms. 4 Private Baths. Guest phone available. Beds: Q. Full breakfast. Conference room. Sailing, fishing, swimming, boating, tennis, golf, water skiing. Gourmet Belgian waffles.
Seen in: *McCalls, Lookout Magazine, Mid-Atlantic Country Magazine, Atlanta Journal, Florida Home Journal.*

"Prest is a historian, a guide, a maitre'd', a confidant. Your friend."

Belhaven

River Forest Manor

600 E Main St
Belhaven NC 28710
(919) 943-2151

Circa 1898. Both Twiggy and Walter Cronkite have passed through the two-story, pillared rotunda entrance of this white mansion lo-

cated on the Atlantic Intercoastal Waterway. Ornate, carved ceilings, cut and leaded-glass windows, and crystal chandeliers grace the inn. Antiques are found throughout. Each evening a Smorgasbord buffet features over 65 items from the inn's kitchen.
Rates: $60-$75.
Melba G. Smith.
12 Rooms. 12 Private Baths. 5 Fireplaces. Guest phone in room. TV in room. Beds: KQDW. Full breakfast. Restaurant. Jacuzzi. Swimming pool. CCs: MC VISA. Tennis, fishing, water sports.
Seen in: *Southern Living, National Geographic.*

Brevard

Red House Inn
412 W Probart St
Brevard NC 28712
(704) 884-9349

Circa 1851. Originally built as a trading post, this inn was also the county's first post office and railroad station. It survived the Civil War and years of neglect. Recently renovated, it is furnished with Victorian antiques. The center of town is four blocks away.
*❀Rates: $43-$49. Season: May to Dec.
Alynne MacGillycuddy Ong.
6 Rooms. 1 Private Bath. TV available. Beds: D. Full breakfast. Handicap access. Hiking.
Seen in: *The Transylvania Times.*

"Lovely place to stay - clean and bright."

Bryson City

Folkestone Inn
767 W Deep Creek Rd
Bryson City NC 28713
(704) 488-2730

Circa 1926. This farmhouse is constructed of local stone and rock. Pressed tin ceilings, stained-glass windows and claw-foot tubs remain. The dining room, where breakfast is

served, features floor-to-ceiling windows on all sides with views of the mountains. There is a stream with a rock bridge on the property and you can walk ten minutes to waterfall views in the Smoky Mountain National Park.
*Rates: $62-$79. Season: March to Dec.
Norma & Peter Joyce.
9 Rooms. 9 Private Baths. Guest phone available. Beds: D. Full breakfast. Hiking, horseback riding, fishing, tubing, rafting.
Seen in: *Asheville Citizen Times.*

"Thanks to you we were able to stop and smell the flowers last weekend! You have a lovely place."

Fryemont Inn
PO Box 459
Bryson City NC 28713
(704) 488-2159

Circa 1923. Captain Amos Frye, a lumber baron, built this rough-sawn hilltop lodge with the choicest chestnut, walnut, oak and cherry woods found in the region. His architect was Richard Hunt, architect of the Biltmore Estate in Ashville. A wide cedar porch overlooks the Tuckaseigee Valley and the Great Smoky Mountains National Park. Massive fireplaces were crafted of stone — one large enough to burn eight-foot logs. All bedrooms are paneled in chestnut and are furnished with antiques, including hand-hewn furniture original to the lodge. Meals in the dining room feature fresh mountain trout and southern fried chicken.
Rates: $75-$160.
Sue & George Brown.
39 Rooms. 39 Private Baths. 3 Fireplaces. Guest phone available. TV in room. Beds: KDTC. MAP. Restaurant. Gourmet meals. Swimming pool. Conference room. CCs: MC VISA. Horseback riding, train ride, white water rafting, tennis.

Chapel Hill

Arrowhead Inn
See: Durham, NC

Colonial Inn
See: Hillsborough, NC

Fearrington House
See: Pittsboro, NC

Charlotte

The Homeplace B&B
5901 Sardis Rd
Charlotte NC 28226
(704) 365-1936

Circa 1902. This country Victorian house sits on two-and-one-half wooded acres and has a wraparound porch with a gabled entrance. The foyer features a handcrafted staircase, 10-foot beaded ceilings, and heart-of-pine floors. Peggy's father, John Gentry, has been painting for several years (since age 79) and his art joins collections of antiques and other family treasures found in the inn.
*Rates: $68-$75.
Frank & Peggy Dearien.
3 Rooms. 3 Private Baths. 3 Fireplaces. Guest phone available. TV available. Beds: Q. Full breakfast. CCs: MC VISA AX. Antiques.
Seen in: *Birmingham News.*

"Everything was perfect. The room was superb, the food excellent!"

Clinton

The Shield House
216 Sampson St
Clinton NC 28328
(919) 592-2634 (800) 462-9817

Circa 1916. Built for timberjack, Robert Herring, this Greek Revival house is dominated by four colossal

fluted columns rising 30 feet to support a portico. The veranda, with 12 Ionic columns, wraps around three sides. Intricately designed leaded glass highlights the entrance and inside are walnut and mahogany antiques. A 22-foot long mural of Orton Plantation can be seen in the dining room. The innkeepers are twin sisters who are also nurses.
*Rates: $45-$50.
Anita Green & Juanita G. McLamb.
5 Rooms. 5 Private Baths. 5 Fireplaces. Guest phone in room. TV in room. Beds: QDTC. Full breakfast. Conference room. CCs: MC VISA. Horseback riding, tennis, volleyball, basketball, golf.
Seen in: *The Sampson Independent.*

"I have never been pampered so much. A beautiful home and a beautiful spirit."

Durham

Arrowhead Inn

106 Mason Rd
Durham NC 27712
(919) 477-8430

Circa 1775. The Lipscombe family and later owners made additions to

the original white colonial manor house, but none destroyed the handsome fanlight, moldings, wainscoting, mantelpieces, and heart-of-pine floors. Past its doors, Catawba and Waxhaw Indians traveled the Great Path to Virginia. A stone arrowhead and marker at the inn's front door designate the path. Current visitors enjoy a long tradition of hospitality. From time to time, the hosts conduct classes for prospective innkeepers.
*Rates: $50-$85.
Jerry & Barbara Ryan.
8 Rooms. 4 Private Baths. 4 Fireplaces. Guest phone in room. TV available. Beds: QDT. Full breakfast. Conference room. CCs: MC VISA AX. Golf, tennis, horseback riding, croquet, horseshoes, fishing nearby.
Seen in: *The Daily Courier, Los Angeles Times.*

"Thanks a million for your hospitality."

Colonial Inn

See: Hillsborough, NC

Edenton

The Lords Proprietors' Inn

300 N Broad St
Edenton NC 27932
(919) 482-3641

Circa 1787. On Albemarle Sound, Edenton was one of the colonial

capitals of North Carolina. The inn consists of three houses providing elegant accommodations within walking distance of town. A guided walking tour from the Visitor's Center provides an opportunity to see museum homes.
Location: Main street of town.
Rates: $48-$70.
Arch & Jane Edwards.
20 Rooms. 20 Private Baths. Guest phone in room. TV in room. Beds: KQTC. Continental-plus breakfast. Gourmet meals. Handicap access. Swimming pool. Conference room. Guided walking tours.
Seen in: *Southern Living, Mid Atlantic Country, House Beautiful, Washington Post.*

"One of the friendliest and best-managed inns I have ever visited."

Flat Rock

Woodfield Inn

PO Box 98
Flat Rock NC 28731
(704) 693-6016

Circa 1852. Henry Farmer constructed this inn and later, when it was ready to be furnished, started a furniture factory. He created the famous southern "Flat Rock Rocker," a fine walnut rocker noted for its absence of creaking. Squire Farmer planted lemon trees that flourished and provided him the inspiration for the Lemon Juleps still served at the inn. Poet and neighbor Carl Sandburg proclaimed upon entering, "These walls speak to me". In 1981 the National Register awarded the Woodfield Inn first place as "Inn of the South" for its meticulous restoration.
Rates: $40-$75.
Jeane Smith
19 Rooms. 9 Private Baths. 14 Fireplaces. TV available. Beds: KQDTC. B&B. Restaurant. Gourmet meals. Conference room. CCs: MC VISA. Horseback riding, swimming, hiking, rafting.
Seen in: *Americana.*

"One didn't have to be a newlywed to sense a romantic atmosphere here."

Greensboro

Colonel Ludlow Inn

See: Winston-Salem, NC

Colonial Inn

See: Hillsborough, NC

Greenwood B&B

205 N Park Dr
Greensboro NC 27401
(919) 274-6350

Circa 1905. Greenwood is a fully renovated, stick-style chalet on the

park in the historic district. President Hayes was once a guest here. The inn is decorated with wood carvings and art from around the world. There are two living rooms, each with a fireplace. Air-conditioning and a swimming pool in the backyard are among the amenities.
Location: Central Greensboro in the historic district.
*Rates: $40-$70.
JoAnne Green.
5 Rooms. 3 Private Baths. Guest phone in room. TV available. Beds: KQT. B&B.

Game room. CCs: MC VISA AX. Tennis, hiking, golf.
Seen in: *Triad Style.*

"Marvelous renovation. Courteous, helpful, knowledgeable hostess and perfectly appointed room and bath. Interesting fine art interior decorating."

Hendersonville

Claddagh Inn at Hendersonville

755 N Main St
Hendersonville NC 28739
(800) 225-4700 (704)697-7778

Circa 1898. Claddagh has been host for 85 years to visitors staying

in Hendersonville. The wide, wraparound porch is filled with inviting rocking chairs. Many of North Carolina's finest craft and antique shops are just two blocks from the inn. Carl Sandburg's house and the Biltmore Estate are nearby, and within a short drive are spectacular sights in the Great Smoky Mountains and the Blue Ridge Parkway.

Location: One-half block north from 7th Avenue (US 64 W) & Main St.
*Rates: $49-$69.
Marie & Fred Carberry.
14 Rooms. 14 Private Baths. 4 Fireplaces. Guest phone in room. TV available. Beds: KQDTC. Full breakfast. Conference room. CCs: MC VISA AX DS. Horseback riding, swimming, tennis, golf, fishing, racquetball, boating.
Seen in: *New York Times, New Yorker Magazine.*

"Excellent food, clean, home atmosphere."

Pine Crest Inn

See: Tryon, NC

The Waverly Inn

783 N Main St
Hendersonville NC 28739
(800) 537-8195 (704)692-1090

Circa 1898. In the National Register, this three-story Queen Anne and Eastlake blend Victorian

house has a two-tiered sawn work trimmed porch, and widow's walk. In the last 90 years there have been only two cooks - Annie May Smith has been serving breakfast here for 47 years. A beautifully carved Eastlake staircase and an original registration desk grace the inn. The Waverly is the only surviving operational inn remaining from the turn-of-the-century tourism boom in Hendersonville.

Location: Corner of 8th Avenue & Main Street (Rt. 25 North)
*Rates: $45-$85.
John & Diane Sheiry.
20 Rooms. 15 Private Baths. Guest phone available. TV available. Beds: KQTDC. B&B. CCs: MC VISA AX DS. Tennis, golf, murder mystery weekends, fishing, hiking. Biltmore Estates, Flatrock Playhouse.
Seen in: *The New York Times, Country Magazine.*

"Our main topic of conversation while driving back was what a great time we had at your place."

Hertford

Gingerbread Inn

103 S Church St
Hertford NC 27944
(919) 426-5809

Circa 1904. In a Colonial Revival style this yellow and white house has a wraparound porch with

paired columns and turned balusters. There are gables and leaded glass windows, and the spacious rooms are furnished comfortably. The hallmark of the inn is freshly baked gingerbread.

Rates: $40.
Jenny Harnisch
3 Rooms. 3 Private Baths. Guest phone available. TV in room. Beds: KQT. Full breakfast. CCs: MC VISA. On the historical walking tour. Fishing nearby.
Seen in: *The Daily Advance, The Raleigh Times.*

Hillsborough

Arrowhead Inn

See: Durham, NC

Colonial Inn

153 W King St
Hillsborough NC 27278
(919) 732-2461

Circa 1759. This historic inn is said to be one of the oldest continuously

operating inns in the United States. The original section was built on the site of a tavern constructed in 1752 but destroyed by fire in 1758. Cornwallis stayed at the inn and used it as his headquarters. Aaron Burr, who fought a duel with Alexander Hamilton and was Vice President of the United States, was also a guest.

*Rates: $48-$65.
Carolyn B. Welsh & Evelyn B. Atkins.
10 Rooms. 6 Private Baths. Guest phone available. TV available. Beds: QTC. Full breakfast. Restaurant. Conference room. CCs: MC VISA.

Kill Devil Hills

Ye Olde Cherokee Inn

500 N Virginia Dare Trail
Kill Devil Hills NC 27948
(919) 441-6127

Circa 1940. Originally a hunting and fishing lodge, this large pink beach house is just across the road

from the ocean. Guest rooms are paneled in knotty cypress creating a rustic cabin atmosphere. Behind the inn is the Wright Brothers Memorial, and nearby, the spot where they made their first flight.
Location: Outer Banks.
*Rates: $55-$75. Season: April to Oct.
Phyllis & Robert Combs.
6 Rooms. 6 Private Baths. Guest phone available. TV in room. Beds: D. MAP. CCs: MC VISA AX. Swimming, fishing, sailing, golf, tennis, hang gliding.
Seen in: *The North Carolina Independent, This Week.*

"Thanks for another wonderful visit! It gets harder to leave each time we come."

Kitty Hawk

First Colony Inn

See: Nags Head, NC

Lake Junaluska

Providence Lodge

1 Atkins Loop
Lake Junaluska NC 28745
(704) 456-6486

Circa 1915. This is a simple and very rustic lodge in the Blue Ridge Mountains 26 miles from Asheville. Dinner is available and the inn is noted for its dining.
Rates: $30-$40. Season: June - Sept. 15.
Ben & Wilma Cato.
16 Rooms. 10 Private Baths. Guest phone available. MAP. Handicap access. Swimming pool.

Marshall

Marshall House

Box 865
Marshall NC 28753
(704) 649-9205

Circa 1903. Richard Sharp Smith, a resident architect for the Biltmore Estates, designed this house with a large veranda to maximize the view of the French Broad River and Appalacian Mountains. Pebble-dash, a type of masonry brought to the area by George Vanderbilt, was applied to the exterior. Currently under renovation, the 5,200-square-foot house is filled with a bountiful supply of antiques to compliment the original pocket doors, wavy glass and wood floors.
*Rates: $35-$50.
James & Ruth Boylan, Linda McWhorter.
8 Rooms. 2 Private Baths. 1 Fireplace. Guest phone available. TV available. Beds: DT. B&B. Handicap access. Conference room. CCs: MC VISA AX DC CB DS. Horseback riding, skiing, whitewater rafting, fishing, golf, hiking.
Seen in: *Blue Ridge Business.*

Mount Airy

Pine Ridge Inn

2893 W Pine St
Mount Airy NC 27030
(919) 789-5034

Circa 1949. Pine Ridge is a grand English-style mansion set on eight

acres at the foot of the Blue Ridge Mountains. This 10,000 square-foot country inn prides itself on providing many of the amenities found in large hotels such as its wood-paneled library, Nautilus-equipped exercise room and hot tub. An old barn remains on the property.
Rates: $50-$85.
Ellen & Manford Haxton.
6 Rooms. 5 Private Baths. Guest phone in room. TV in room. Beds: QDTC. Continental breakfast. Restaurant. Handicap access. Swimming pool. Game room. Conference room. CCs: MC VISA AX. Golf.

"The Haxtons have updated all the facilities without destroying its grandeur. Their attitude is one of warmth and charm, openness and pleasantness."

Nags Head

First Colony Inn

Route 1, Box 748
Nags Head NC 27959
(919) 441-2343 (704) 249-1114

Circa 1932. First Colony Inn is a large beach hotel built with veran-

das on all four sides. It is said to be the last of the original hotels built on the Outer Banks. To save it from the eroding beach front of its original location, it was moved in three sections to a new waterfront location three miles away. During the midnight move, townsfolk lined the streets cheering and clapping to see the preservation of this historic building. With its own private, sandy beach, it reopens in the summer of 1990, with ocean views from the second and third floors rooms. Antiques and reproduction pieces will be used throughout.
*Rates: $115-$200.
The Lawrences.
26 Rooms. 26 Private Baths. Guest phone in room. TV in room. Beds: KQC. B&B. Jacuzzi. Handicap access. Conference room. CCs: MC VISA DS. Sailing, swimming, surf fishing, hiking.
Seen in: *Virginia News Leader.*

"I want to book the room with the ghost. I've experienced the ghost! Fun!"

Ye Olde Cherokee Inn

See: Kill Devil Hills, NC

New Bern

The Aerie

509 Pollock St
New Bern NC 28560
(919) 636-5553

Circa 1882. This late Victorian home was built by Samuel Street,

proprietor of the Old Gaston House Hotel, as his private residence. An appealing three-sided bay houses

the downstairs parlor and an upstairs guest chamber. Fine antiques add to the gracious atmosphere of the inn and include an old mahogany player piano tuned and waiting for guests. Tryon Palace is a one block walk from the inn.
*Rates: $80.
Rick & Lois Cleveland.
7 Rooms. 7 Private Baths. 5 Fireplaces. Guest phone in room. TV in room. Beds: QTC. B&B. CCs: MC VISA AX. Swimming, camping, hiking.

Harmony House Inn

215 Pollock St
New Bern NC 28560
(919) 636-3810

Circa 1850. Long ago, this two-story Greek Revival was sawed in half and the west side moved nine feet to accommodate new hallways, additional rooms and a staircase. A wall was then built to divide the house into two sections. The rooms are decorated with antiques, family heirlooms, and collectables. Offshore breezes sway blossoms in the lush garden. Cross the street to an excellent restaurant or take a picnic to the water.
Location: Walk to Tryon Palace.
Rates: $70.
Diane & A.E. Hansen.
9 Rooms. 9 Private Baths. 9 Fireplaces. Beds: QTC. Full breakfast. Conference room. CCs: MC VISA. Complimentary juices and sodas.
Seen in: *Americana.*

We feel nourished even now, six months after our visit to Harmony House."

King's Arms Inn

212 Pollock St
New Bern NC 28560
(919) 638-4409

Circa 1848. Four blocks from the Tyron Palace, in the heart of the

New Bern Historic District, this colonial-style inn features a mansard roof and touches of Victorian architecture. Two doors down from the inn is the federal-style Henderson House, the town's most notable restaurant. Guest rooms are decorated with antiques, canopy and four-poster beds and fireplaces. An old tavern in town was the inspiration for the name of the inn.
*Rates: $69.
David & Diana Parks.
9 Rooms. 9 Private Baths. 8 Fireplaces. Guest phone available. TV in room. Beds: QDTC. Continental-plus breakfast. CCs: MC VISA AX. Tennis, golf, windsurfing, sailing, biking, hiking, canoeing.
Seen in: *Washington Post, Southern Living.*

"Delightful."

New Berne House

709 Broad St
New Bern NC 28560
(800) 842-7688 (919)636-2250

Circa 1921. Using bricks salvaged from Tryon Palace, this stately red

brick Colonial Revival replica was built by the Taylor family, known for their historic preservation work in North Carolina. Located in the historic district, it is one block to the governor's mansion, Tryon Palace, now a Williamsburg-style living museum. The splendidly refurbished formal parlor is the setting for afternoon tea, and a graceful sweeping staircase leads to guest rooms with canopy beds and antique furnishings.
*Rates: $55-$75.
Joel & Shan Wilkins.
6 Rooms. 6 Private Baths. 2 Fireplaces. Guest phone in room. TV in room. Beds: KQDT. B&B. Gourmet meals. Conference room. CCs: MC VISA AX DC CB DS. Sailing, golf, swimming, tennis, boating.
Seen in: *Charlotte Observer, Raleigh News & Observer, Pinehurst Outlook.*

"In six months of traveling around the country New Berne House was our favorite stop!"

Ocracoke

The Berkley Center Country Inn

Box 220
Ocracoke NC 27960
(919) 928-5911

Circa 1860. Once a harbor for the pirate Blackbeard, Ocracoke is a

fishing village on a small island in the middle of Hattaras National Seashore, accessible only by ferry or private boat. Located on three acres in the village, the inn is framed by red and white myrtles. The weathered shingled main house boasts an enormous square tower rising from a second-story gable. The walls of the tower room are lined with windows looking out to Pamlico Sound and the Atlantic. With cedar paneling and wooden ceilings, the inn has a lodge-like atmosphere is filled with comfortable furnishings.
*Rates: $60-$80. Season: March 15-Nov. 15.
Ruth & Wes Egan.
14 Rooms. 12 Private Baths. Guest phone available. TV available. Beds: D. B&B. Handicap access. Conference room. Swimming, fishing, hiking, biking.
Seen in: *Mid Atlantic Country.*

Old Fort

Inn at Old Fort

W Main St, Box 1116
Old Fort NC 28762
(704) 668-9384

Circa 1890. Mr. Westerman, a ship builder from Wilmington, North Carolina, had this Gothic Revival house built with steep double gables as a summer retreat. In spring, dogwood graces the three-and-a-half

acres of terraced lawns that surround the house. Antiques and the works of local artisans are featured. Breakfast is served in the inn's parlor or on the enclosed porch.
Rates: $34-$40.
Chuck & Debbie Aldridge.
5 Rooms. 3 Private Baths. Guest phone available. TV available. Beds: DTC. Continental-plus breakfast. Hiking, golf, swimming, snow skiing, horseshoes, croquet.
Seen in: *The McDowell News.*

"What a wonderful place. A nice surprise!"

Pittsboro

The Fearrington House
Fearrington Village Ctr
Pittsboro NC 27312
(919) 542-2121 (919)542-4000

Circa 1927. The Fearrington is an old dairy farm. Several of the

original outbuildings, including the silo and barn, have been converted into a village with a potter's shop, bookstore, jewelry shop, and a southern garden shop. The original homestead houses an award-winning restaurant. The inn itself was built three years ago.
Rates: $95-$175.
Richard & Debbie Delany.
14 Rooms. 14 Private Baths. TV available. Beds: Q. Continental breakfast. Handicap access. Swimming pool. Conference room. CCs: MC VISA. Swimming, bicycling, golf and tennis nearby.

"There is an aura of warmth and caring that makes your guests feel like royalty in a regal setting!"

Raleigh

Arrowhead Inn
See: Durham, NC

Colonial Inn
See: Hillsborough, NC

Fearrington House
See: Pittsboro, NC

The Oakwood Inn
411 N Bloodworth St
Raleigh NC 27604
(919) 832-9712

Circa 1871. Presiding over Raleigh's Oakwood Historic District, this lavender and gray Victorian beauty is in the National Register. A formal parlor is graced by rosewood and red velvet, while guest rooms exude an atmosphere of vintage Victoriana.
*Rates: $75-$90.
Diana Newton.
6 Rooms. 6 Private Baths. 6 Fireplaces. Guest phone available. TV available. Beds: KQD. Full breakfast. CCs: MC VISA AX.
Seen in: *Connoisseur.*

"Resplendent and filled with museum-quality antique furnishings." Kim Devins, *Spectator.*

Tarboro

Little Warren
304 E Park Ave
Tarboro NC 27886
(919) 823-1314

Circa 1913. The wide, wraparound front porch of this gracious family home overlooks the Town Common, said to be one of two originally chartered commons remaining in the United States. The house is in the historic district and is designated with a National Register plaque.
Rates: $65.
Patsy & Tom Miller.
3 Rooms. 3 Private Baths. Guest phone available. TV available. Beds: DT. EP. CCs: MC VISA AX. Tennis. English & American Southern breakfast.

"It is indeed a unique ambience."

Tryon

Pine Crest Inn
PO Box 1030, 200 Pine Crest Ln
Tryon NC 28982
(704) 859-9135 (800) 633-3001

Circa 1906. Carter Brown purchased this former sanitarium on a wooded knoll close to the center of town and in 1917 opened a small

resort. Each of the cabins he added to the complex were given a secluded porch, a terrace, a fireplace and a private bath. The inn's dining room has rough-hewn decor reminiscent of a colonial tavern. Mr. Brown initiated the fox hunts, steeplechase racing and horse shows that have made Tryon a popular equine center.
*Rates: $77-$107.
Bob & Diane Johnson.
29 Rooms. 29 Private Baths. 24 Fireplaces. Guest phone in room. TV in room. Beds: KQDTC. Full breakfast. Restaurant. Gourmet meals. Handicap access. Conference room. CCs: MC VISA. Golf, tennis, hiking, fox hunting.
Seen in: *Southern Living.*

Washington

Pamlico House
400 E Main St
Washington NC 27889
(919) 946-7184

Circa 1906. This gracious Colonial Revival home once served as the

rectory for St. Peter's Episcopal Church. A veranda wraps around the house in a graceful curve. Furnished in Victorian antiques, the inn has the modern convenience of air conditioning. Nearby is the city's quaint waterfront. Washington is on the Historic Albemarle Tour Route and within easy driving distance to the Outer Banks.

Location: Eastern North Carolina.
Rates: $45-$65.
Jeanne & Lawrence Hervey.
4 Rooms. 4 Private Baths. Guest phone in room. Beds: KQDT. Full breakfast. CCs: MC VISA. Air conditioning. Tennis, fishing, sailing.

Waynesville

Grandview Lodge

809 Valley View Cir Rd
Waynesville NC 28786
(704) 456-5212

Circa 1800. Grandview Lodge is located on two-and-a-half acres in the Smokey Mountains. The land surrounding the lodge has an apple orchard, rhubarb patch, grape arbor and vegetable garden for the inn's kitchen. Rooms are available in the main lodge and in a newer addition. The inn's dining room is known throughout the region and Linda, a home economist, has written "Recipes from Grandview Lodge".
*Rates: $75-$85.
Stan & Linda Arnold.
15 Rooms. 15 Private Baths. 3 Fireplaces. Guest phone available. TV in room. Beds: QDT. MAP. Restaurant. Gourmet meals. Handicap access. Game room. Horseback riding, golf, hiking, tennis, swimming.
Seen in: *Asheville Citizen, Winston-Salem Journal, Raleigh News and Observer.*

Hallcrest Inn

299 Halltop Cir
Waynesville NC 28786
(704) 456-6457

Circa 1880. This simple white frame farmhouse was the home of the owner of the first commercial

apple orchard in western North Carolina. Atop Hall Mountain, it commands a breathtaking view of Waynesville and Balsam Mountain Range. A gathering room, a dining room, and eight guest rooms are furnished with family antiques. The side porch features four rooms with balconies. Family-style dining is offered around lazy-susan tables.
Location: US 276N from Waynesville, left on Mauney Cove Road.
*Rates: $50-$70. Season: May 15 to Oct.
Russell & Margaret Burson.
12 Rooms. 12 Private Baths. 5 Fireplaces. Guest phone available. TV available. Beds: D. MAP. Restaurant. Golf, hiking, horseback riding, white-water rafting.
Seen in: *Asheville Citizen.*

"Country charm with a touch of class."

The Palmer House B&B

108 Pigeon St
Waynesville NC 28786
(704) 456-7521

Circa 1885. This rambling old inn reflects the small-town charm so

often found in the mountains. A full breakfast is served and suppers are available. The hosts are book lovers as is evidenced by the stocked library and the bookstore at the rear of the inn. Nearby activities include hiking, golfing and skiing.
Rates: $45.
Kris Gillet & Jeff Minick.
7 Rooms. 7 Private Baths. Guest phone available. Continental-plus breakfast.

"Each guest room has its own particular charm."

The Swag

Rt 2 Box 280-a
Waynesville NC 28786
(704) 926-0430

Circa 1970. The Swag is composed of six hand-hewn log buildings, one dating to 1795. They were moved

here and restored. An old church was reassembled and became the cathedral-ceilinged common room. The fireplace in this room was constructed of river stones with no mortar in order to maintain authenticity. The inn's 250 acres feature a nature trail, a spring-fed pond with gazebo and hammock, and thick forests. A two-and-a-half mile gravel road winds through a heavily wooded hillside to the inn. In the evening, dinner is served on pewter ware at long walnut tables. Listening to folk music and mountain storytelling is popular afterwards.
Location: On edge of Great Smoky Mountain National Park.
Rates: $128-$198. Season: May to Oct. 31.
Deener Matthews.
12 Rooms. 12 Private Baths. 7 Fireplaces. Guest phone available. TV available. Beds: KQDTC. AP. Restaurant. Jacuzzi. Sauna. Handicap access. Conference room. CCs: MC VISA. Riding, rafting, hiking, racquet ball, croquet, badminton.

Seen in: *The Atlanta Journal, Mid-Atlantic Country.*

"The Swag gives us both a chance to relax our bodies and re-vitalize our brains."

Weaverville

Dry Ridge Inn

26 Brown St
Weaverville NC 28787
(704) 658-3899

Circa 1849. This three-story house was built as the parsonage for the

Salem Campground, an old religious revival camping area. Because of the high altitude and pleasant weather, it was used as a camp hospital for Confederate soldiers suffering from pneumonia during the Civil War. The area was called Dry Ridge by the Cherokee

Indians before the campground was established.
Location: Ten minutes North of Asheville.
Rates: $50-$55.
John & Karen VanderElzen.
6 Rooms. 6 Private Baths. Guest phone available. Beds: DC. B&B. CCs: MC VISA. Bicycling, hiking, golf, skiing, rafting, fishing.
Seen in: *Asheville Citizen Times, Marshall News Record.*

"Best family vacation ever spent."

Wilmington

Anderson Guest House

520 Orange St
Wilmington NC 28401
(919) 343-8128

Circa 1851. The main house, a brick Italianate, features cherry woodwork, stained glass, and gas lights that still work. The guest house, built from the remnants of an old children's playhouse and shed, has its own fireplace and overlooks the lawn and garden. Breakfast is served in the main house.
Location: Wilmington's Historic District.
Rates: $65.
Landon & Connie Anderson.
2 Rooms. 2 Private Baths. 2 Fireplaces. Guest phone available. TV available. Beds: Q. EP. Golfing, water skiing.
Seen in: *Star-News.*

"The most gracious hostess in the state."

James Place B&B

9 S Fourth St
Wilmington NC 28401
(919) 251-0999

Circa 1909. On a tree-lined street of two-story, turn-of-the-century houses, this neatly painted grey home has gleaming white trim highlighting the porch and shutters. Each room features air conditioning and ceiling fans. Fresh coffee is brought to guest rooms in the morning and later, a full breakfast is served downstairs. The downtown waterfront is a short stroll away.
Rates: $55.
J.W. Smith.
3 Rooms. 2 Private Baths. Guest phone available. TV available. Beds: KQDW. B&B. CCs: MC VISA. Boating, fishing, golf, tennis, ocean beaches.
Seen in: *Encore Magazine.*

Worth House
A Victorian Inn

412 S Third St
Wilmington NC 28401
(919) 762-8562

Circa 1893. This handsome Queen Anne Victorian boasts two turrets

and a wide double veranda, all framed by a white iron fence. The paneled front hall, crystal chandelier, and spindled staircase welcome guests to a retreat of quiet elegance. There is a player piano and a Victrola, and all rooms feature wood-burning fireplaces, fine linens and antiques. A gourmet breakfast is served in the dining room, in bed or on the veranda.
Location: Historic District.
Rates: $70.
Kate Walsh & Terry Meyer.
4 Rooms. 4 Private Baths. 4 Fireplaces. Guest phone available. Beds: KQD. B&B. Golf, paddle boats, horse drawn carriages, dinner cruises, ocean.

Wilson

Pilgrims Rest

600 W Nash St
Wilson NC 27893
(919) 243-4447

Circa 1858. This Italianate house is on Nash Street which was once described as one of the ten most beautiful streets in the world. It was built by the grandson of the state's

first printer. Twelve-foot ceilings in the parlor are accentuated with borders. Victorian wallpapers and antiques are featured in the guest rooms.
Location: Central North Carolina, near I-95 highway.
*Rates: $45-$65.
June & Doug Stewart.
4 Rooms. 2 Private Baths. Guest phone available. Beds: DT. Full breakfast. CCs: MC VISA. Bicycling.

Winston-Salem

Colonel Ludlow Inn

Summit & W 5th
Winston-Salem NC 27101
(919) 777-1887

Circa 1887. This Queen Anne house features graceful wraparound porches and a hipped gable roof. There is an ornate entrance

and several stained-glass windows bordering the stairway. The dining room has a gold-plated chandelier and reproduction wallpaper. The guest rooms feature antique beds and more stained glass windows, and some have two-person whirlpool tubs.
Location: Off highway I-40.
*Rates: $55-$108.
Terri Jones, Manager.
9 Rooms. 9 Private Baths. 3 Fireplaces. Guest phone in room. TV in room. Beds: KQD. B&B. Jacuzzi. CCs: MC VISA AX DS. Parks, swimming, tennis, fine arts.
Seen in: *Charlotte Observer, Mid-Atlantic Country.*

"I have never seen anything like the meticulous and thorough attention to detail in Col. Ludlow's, a splendiferous Victorian spa." Dannye Romine, *The Charlotte Observer.*

North Dakota

Medora

The Rough Riders

Medora ND 58645
(701) 623-4444

Circa 1865. This old hotel has the branding marks of Teddy Roosevelt's cattle ranch as well as other brands stamped into the rough-board facade out front. A wooden sidewalk helps to maintain the turn-of-the-century cow-town feeling. Rustic guest rooms are above the restaurant and are furnished with homesteader antiques original to the area. In the summer an outdoor pageant is held complete with stagecoach and horses. In October deer hunters are accommodated. The hotel along with two motels is managed by the non-profit Theodore Roosevelt Medora Foundation.

Rates: $55. Season: May to September.
9 Rooms. 9 Private Baths. Continental breakfast. CCs: MC VISA.

Ohio

Akron

Inn At Brandywine Falls

See: Sagamore Hills, OH

Canton

Pleasant Journey Inn

See: Dellroy, OH

Cincinnati

Amos Shinkle Townhouse

See: Covington, KY

Wind's Way B&B

See: Newtown, OH

Cleveland

Inn At Brandywine Falls

See: Sagamore Hills, OH

Clinton

Old Stone House on the Lake

See: Marblehead, OH

Columbus

Central House

See: Pickerington, OH

Danville

The White Oak Inn

29683 Walhonding Rd
Danville OH 43014
(614) 599-6107

Circa 1915. Begonias hang from the wide front porch of this three-story

farmhouse situated on 13 green acres. It is adjacent to the Indian trail and pioneer road that runs along the Kokosing River, and an Indian mound has been discovered on the property. The inn's woodwork is all original white oak and guest rooms are furnished in antiques. Visitors often shop for maple syrup, cheese and handicrafts at nearby Amish farms.

Location: North central Ohio.
❀Rates: $60-$90.
Joyce & Jim Acton.
7 Rooms. 7 Private Baths. 2 Fireplaces. Guest phone available. TV available. Beds: QDC. Full breakfast. Restaurant. Conference room. CCs: MC VISA. Fishing, hunting, hiking, canoeing, cross-country skiing, bicycles
Seen in: *Ladies Home Journal, Columbus Monthly, News Journal-Mansfield.*

"We are moving, but we would go well out of our way to stay with the Acton's. It was lovely."

Dayton

H.W. Allen Villa B&B

See: Troy, OH

Willowtree Inn

See: Tipp City, OH

Dellroy

Pleasant Journey Inn

4247 Roswell Rd SW
Dellroy OH 44460
(216) 735-2987

Circa 1868. This 14-room Victorian mansion is situated on 12 acres of woodland, stream and garden near the Atwood Lake area. Four years were spent building the house, but the depression which followed the Civil War prevented the original family from moving in. Seven marble fireplaces, a curved staircase of gleaming walnut, an oil chandelier, and antiques and crafts collected locally add to the inn's gracious atmosphere. A favored fishing spot is a short walk out the back door.

Rates: $46-$60.
Jim & Mary Etterman.
4 Rooms. 1 Private Bath. Guest phone available. TV available. Beds: DT. Continental-plus breakfast. CCs: MC VISA. Horseback riding, boating, golf, tennis, hiking, swimming, skiing.
Seen in: *Western Reserve, Free Press Standard.*

"The atmosphere at the inn is so serene and relaxing."

Kelleys Island

The Beatty House

South Shore Dr, PO Box 402
Kelleys Island OH 43438
(419) 746-2379

Circa 1861. In the National Register, this 14-room limestone house was built by Ludwig Bette, a Russian immigrant who became a grape-grower and winemaker. Large, cave-like wine cellars beneath the house stored more than 75,000 gallons of wine. Antiques include those of the original owner and the innkeepers. Guest rooms and parlors have both the views and breezes of Lake Erie. Vineyards, a winery, and a state park are also on this three-by-five-mile island.

Location: Twenty-minute ferry ride from Marblehead.
Rates: $50-$60. Season: May to Nov.
Martha & Jim Seaman.
3 Rooms. 1 Private Bath. 1 Fireplace. Guest phone available. TV available. Beds: DC. B&B. Hiking, biking, fishing, cruise boats.
Seen in: *Sandusky Register, Toledo Metropolitan Magazine.*

"Your warmth and hospitality made our first stay at a B&B a memorable one."

Marblehead

Old Stone House Inn

133 Clemons St
Marblehead OH 43440
(419) 798-5922

Circa 1861. Built by Alexander Clemons, owner of the first stone

quarry in the area, the Stone House overlooks Lake Erie. Now a guest room, the enclosed Captain's Tower features a 15-foot ceiling, spindled railings around the staircase, and the best view of the lake and shoreline. The inn's green lawns and gardens slope to the shore where guests may fish from the rocks or swim.

Location: Marblehead Peninsula.
Rates: $60-$85.
Dorothy Bright and Pat Whiteford Parks.
14 Rooms. 1 Private Bath. Guest phone available. TV available. Beds: DT. Continental-plus breakfast. Conference room. CCs: MC VISA. Island tours, winter ice fishing, cross-country skiing, lake swimming.
Seen in: *Marion Star, Cleveland Plain Dealer.*

"Thank you so much!! Everything was wonderful!"

Mount Vernon

The Russell-Cooper House

115 E Gambier St
Mount Vernon OH 43050
(614) 397-8638

Circa 1829. Dr. John Russell and his son-in-law Colonel Cooper modeled a simple brick Federal

house into a unique Victorian. Its sister structure is the Wedding Cake House of Kennebunk, Maine. There is a hand-painted plaster ceiling in the ballroom, and a collection of Civil War items and antique medical devices. Woodwork is of cherry, maple and walnut, and there are etched and stained-glass windows. Hal Holbrook called the town America's Hometown.

❀Rates: $45-$68.
Tim & Maureen Tyler.
6 Rooms. 6 Private Baths. Guest phone available. Beds: QDT. Full breakfast. Conference room. CCs: MC VISA. Downhill & cross-country skiing, fishing, canoeing, golf. Mystery weekends.

"A salute to the preservation of American history and culture. Most hospitable owners!"

Newtown

Wind's Way B&B

3851 Edwards Rd
Newtown OH 45244
(513) 561-1933

Circa 1840. This handsome Federal mansion was built for William Ed-

wards on property obtained through a Revolutionary War land grant. It was owned by Ray's grandfather and named by him. The 29 rooms include a first floor antique shop that features 18th and 19th-century American furniture. Some of the choicest pieces are in the guest rooms and include four-poster and canopied beds, antique sewing rockers and panelled dressers. "Peach Melba Muffins", "Stuffed French Toast", and "Wild Spinach Swiss Quiche" are Brenda's specialties.

*Rates: $55-$120.
Ray & Brenda Raffurty.
4 Rooms. 4 Private Baths. 1 Fireplace. Guest phone available. TV in room. Beds: QC. B&B. Jacuzzi. CCs: MC VISA. Horseback riding, golf, canoeing, river boat rides, live theater, antiquing.
Seen in: *The Cincinnati Enquirer, Cincinnati Post Neighbors.*

"Thank you for the wonderful time you have given us."

Pickerington

Central House

27 W Columbus St, Old Village
Pickerington OH 43147
(614) 837-0932

Circa 1860. The restoration of the old Central Hotel began after the possums, honeybees and other wildlife were evicted. It required extensive reconstruction because the log foundations had rotted away. The house had to be jacked up, straightened, and a new foundation poured underneath. The Victorian

atmosphere makes guests feel as though they had been to Grandma's. The inn is famous for its giant cinnamon rolls.
Rates: $55.
Jim & Sue Maxwell, Mary Lou Boyd.
4 Rooms. 4 Private Baths. Guest phone available. TV available. Beds: D. B&B. Restaurant. Tennis. Golf nearby.
Seen in: *Lancaster Eagle Gazette, Fairfield North, NeighborNews East.*

"Pleasant, charming, comfortable, relaxing and wonderful hostesses."

Poland

The Inn at the Green

500 S Main St
Poland OH 44514
(216) 758-4688

Circa 1876. Main Street in Poland has a parade of historic houses including Connecticut Western Reserve Colonials, Federal and Greek Revival houses. The Inn at the Green is a Victorian Baltimore townhouse. All the common rooms including a greeting room, parlor, sitting room and library have working marble fireplaces. Interiors evoke an authentic turn-of-the century atmosphere with antiques that enhance the moldings, twelve-foot ceilings and poplar floors.
Location: Seven miles southeast of Youngstown, Ohio.
Rates: $40-$50.
Ginny & Steve Meloy.
4 Rooms. 2 Private Baths. 2 Fireplaces. TV available. Beds: DT. Continental breakfast. Conference room. CCs: MC VISA. Cross-country skiing, golf, tennis, fly fishing, canoeing, sailing

Sagamore Hills

The Inn at Brandywine Falls

8230 Brandywine Rd
Sagamore Hills OH 44067
(216) 467-1812 (419) 650-4965

Circa 1848. Overlooking Brandywine Falls, and situated snuggly on national parkland, this National Register Greek Revival house has recently been restored. Antiques made in Ohio are featured in the colonial-style rooms and include sleigh and four-poster beds. The kitchen has been designed to allow

guests to chat with the innkeepers while sipping coffee in front of a crackling fireplace, watching breakfast preparations. Choose the Simon Perkins Room (he was the founder of Akron) for views of the waterfall. George and Kate give Sunday tours of the falls and park, sometimes on Lolly the trolly.
Location: The Cuyahoga Valley National Park.
Rates: $75-$95.
Katie & Geore Hoy.
6 Rooms. 6 Private Baths. 1 Fireplace. Guest phone in room. TV in room. Beds: QDT. B&B. Gourmet meals. Jacuzzi. Handicap access. Exercise room. Conference room. CCs: MC VISA. Hiking, bicycling, cross-country and downhill skiing, golf, sledding.
Seen in: *The Plain Dealer, The Vindicator, Western Reserve Magazine.*

"A beauty amidst beauty."

Sandusky

Old Stone House on the Lake

See: Marblehead, OH

Wagner's 1844 Inn

230 E Washington St
Sandusky OH 44870
(419) 626-1726

Circa 1844. Originally constructed as a log cabin, additions and renovations were made and the house evolved into an Italianate-style accented with brackets under the eaves and black shutters on the second story windows. A wrought-iron fence frames the house and there are ornate wrought-iron porch rails. A billiard room and screened-in porch are available to guests. The ferry to Cedar Point and Kellys Island is within walking distance.
Rates: $65.
Walt & Barbara Wagner.
3 Rooms. 3 Private Baths. 1 Fireplace. Guest phone available. TV available. Beds: D. B&B. CCs: MC VISA. Cedar Point Amusement Park, lakes, history.
Seen in: *Lorain Journal.*

Tipp City

Willowtree Inn

1900 W State, Rt 571
Tipp City OH 45371
(513) 667-2957

Circa 1830. This Federal-style mansion is a copy of a similar house in North Carolina, former home of the builders. Antique period furnishings and polished wood floors add to the atmosphere of this rambling homestead.
❀Rates: $65.
Tom & Peggy Nordquist.
4 Rooms. 1 Private Bath. Guest phone available. TV in room. Beds: D. Full breakfast. Conference room. CCs: MC VISA. Golf, museums, antiquing.
Seen in: *Troy Daily News, Dayton News.*

"Very quiet place to stay. The grounds are beautiful, service excellent!"

Toledo

Mansion View

2035 Collingwood Blvd
Toledo OH 43620
(419) 244-5676

Circa 1887. This corbeled brick Queen Anne house, in the National Register, was built for Fred Reynolds, a wealthy grain merchant. A Vermont slate roof tops the gabled roof. The Italian marble entry leads to an ornately carved grand hall. A few antiques original to the house remain and others have been collected to fill the guest rooms. The owners plan to add six more guest rooms and a restaurant.

❀Rates: $75.
Tam Gagen, Matt Jasin, Tim Oller.
4 Rooms. 4 Private Baths. 2 Fireplaces. Guest phone in room. TV in room. Beds: D. Continental breakfast. Conference room. CCs: MC VISA.

"Thank you for a beautiful alternative to the pre-fab, broken neon hotels we had on our honeymoon. We'll remember it always and be back for our anniversaries."

Troy

H.W. Allen Villa B&B

434 S Market St
Troy OH 45373
(513) 335-1181

Circa 1874. Originally constructed for the president of the local First National Bank, this Italianate Victorian is three stories high and has 14 rooms in its 7,000 square feet.

Restored and refurbished with Victorian era antiques, the inn features butternut walnut woodwork and a gleaming walnut staircase. Handsomely restored crown ceiling molding and repainted stenciling are the finishing touches.

*Rates: $60.
Robert W. & F. June Smith.
4 Rooms. 4 Fireplaces. Guest phone in room. TV in room. Beds: DT. Full breakfast. Conference room. CCs: MC VISA AX. Tennis, golf, swimming, ice skating, bicycling, nature walks, wineries.
Seen in: *Miami Valley Sunday News.*

"Such a beautiful place to stay and such a congenial greeting."

Youngstown

Inn at the Green

See: Poland, OH

Oklahoma

Aline

Heritage Manor

RR1, Box 33
Aline OK 73716
(405) 463-2563

Circa 1903. A wonderful way to experience Oklahoma history is to stay at the Heritage Manor, two turn-of-the century restored homes. One is an American Four Square house and the other, a glorified Arts-and-Crafts style home. Antiques were gathered from area pioneer homes and include an Edison Victrola Morning Glory Horn and a cathedral pump organ. Antique sofas and English leather chairs fill the sitting room. Mannequins dressed in pioneer clothing add to the decor. There are several fireplaces and a widow's walk tops the main house.

Rates: $50.
A.J. & Carolyn Rexroat.
4 Rooms. Beds: D. Full breakfast. Caverns, the Great Salt Plains Lake, Glass Mountain State Park.
Seen in: *Country Magazine, Enid Morning News, the Daily Oklahoman.*

Guthrie

Harrison House

124 W Harrison
Guthrie OK 73044
(405) 282-1000

Circa 1902. This is the old Guthrie Savings Bank. Totally restored, Harrison House is Oklahoma's first bed and breakfast inn. The rooms are named after famous citizens such as Tom Mix, a Guthrie bartender who became a Hollywood cowboy star. The original vault is still in the inn,

now completely furnished with Victorian antiques. Patchwork quilts, lace curtains and antique washstands are featured in each room. Guthrie, the original capital of Oklahoma, has a turn-of-the-century downtown.

Location: 30 minutes N. of Oklahoma City
*Rates: $60-$80.
Phyllis Murray.
23 Rooms. 23 Private Baths. Guest phone in room. TV available. Beds: KDT. B&B. CCs: MC VISA AX DC CB DS. Horseback riding, fishing. Pollar Theater, Lazy E Ranch nearby.
Seen in: *Country Inns, Glamour, Historic Preservation, Country, Tulsa Tribune, Houston Cronicle.*

"I'd been in 10 different hotels in 10 days and couldn't remember a thing about the other nine or where they were. Harrison House, I'll remember forever."

Oklahoma City

The Grandison

1841 NW 15th
Oklahoma City OK 73106
(405) 521-0011

Circa 1896. This brick and shingled three-story house is situated on lawns and gardens shaded by pecan, apple and fig trees. You'll also find a pond and gazebo. Original Belgian stained glass remains and the decor is an airy country Victorian. The bridal suite includes a working fireplace, white lace curtains and a claw-foot tub.

Rates: $40-$90.
Bob & Claudia Wright.
5 Rooms. 5 Private Baths. 3 Fireplaces. Guest phone in room. TV available. Beds: QD. B&B. Gourmet meals.
Seen in: *The Daily Oklahoman, Oklahoma Pride.*

"Like going home to Grandma's!"

Tulsa

Holloway House

PO Box 52423
Tulsa OK 74152-0423
(918) 582-8607 (800) 657-6040

Circa 1924. This New England clapboard house was built by businesswoman, Nelle Shields Jack-

son. Rooms are decorated in a variety of styles, including Victorian and Art Deco. The Williamsburg room boasts a canopy bed and private Jacuzzi bath, as well as a handsome fireplace. The dining room or terrace may be chosen for breakfast.

Location: Riverparks Historic District.
Rates: $45-$55.
Mary Claire Holloway.
3 Rooms. 2 Private Baths. Beds: QD. Full breakfast. Jacuzzi. CCs: MC VISA AX.
Seen in: *Oklahoma Life Style, ABC.*

"What a wonderful experience walking into your paradise today."

Oregon

Ashland

Cowslip's Belle

159 N Main St
Ashland OR 97520
(503) 488-2901

Circa 1913. Cowslip's Belle is a Craftsman bungalow, the simple

design a rebellion against the ornate and often over-decorated Victorian. The inn is named for a flower mentioned in *A Midsummer Night's Dream,* and each of the guest rooms is named for one of Shakespeare's favorite flowers.
Rates: $60-$82.
Jon & Carmen Reinhardt.
4 Rooms. 4 Private Baths. Guest phone available. Beds: QT. Full breakfast. CCs: VISA DS. Snow skiing, water sports, water skiing, wind surfing, wineries.
Seen in: *The Daily Tidings.*

"The atmosphere was delightful, the decor charming, the food delicious and the company grand. Tony says he's spoiled forever."

Edinburgh Lodge B&B

586 E Main St
Ashland OR 97520
(503) 488-1050

Circa 1908. The Edinburgh, built by a miner, became the J. T. Currie Boarding House for teachers and railroad workers. Handmade quilts and period furnishings adorn each guest room and afternoon tea is served at 5:00 p.m. The country gar-

den features hollyhocks and delphiniums.
Rates: $49-$65.
Ann Rivera.
6 Rooms. 6 Private Baths. Guest phone available. Beds: QT. Full breakfast. CCs: MC VISA.

"The rooms are so warm and quaint... like visiting family. Breakfast was delicious. I'm sure there's an Edinburgh Cookbook on its way. I want a copy!"

Hersey House

451 N Main St
Ashland OR 97520
(503) 482-4563

Circa 1904. A saltbox Victorian built with leaded-glass windows,

the inn also features an L-shaped staircase. James Hersey, Ashland city councilman, was the first of five generations of Herseys to occupy the house.
*Rates: $70-$85. Season: May - Nov.
Gail E. Orell & K. Lynn Savage.
4 Rooms. 4 Private Baths. Guest phone available. Beds: QT. Full breakfast. Bicycling, tennis, horseback riding, fishing, swimming.
Seen in: *San Francisco Examiner, Pacific Northwest Magazine, Mature Outlook.*

"Delicious breakfasts and thoughtful social hour. We couldn't have asked for anything more. Your house and gardens are beautiful."

Royal Carter House

514 Siskiyou Blvd
Ashland OR 97520
(503) 482-5623

Circa 1909. Listed in the National Register, the Royal Carter House is surrounded by tall trees and lovely gardens. The inn has a secluded deck and four guest rooms.
Location: Four blocks from the Shakespeare theater.
Rates: $50-$70.
Roy & Alyce Levy.
Beds: KQDT.

"Thank you! I really feel special here!"

Astoria

Rosebriar Inn

636 14th St
Astoria OR 97103
(503) 325-7427

Circa 1902. Commanding a spectacular view of the harbor, the Rosebriar is a neoclassical clapboard house on a hill overlooking the village. Built by banker Frank Patton, it grew to 7,000 square feet when it housed the Holy Name Convent.

The house features hand stenciling, carved ceilings, leaded glass and polished woodwork. Astoria is the oldest American settlement west of the Rockies, dating from a fur trading post established in 1811.
Location: Near the mouth of the Columbia River, 100 miles from Portland.
*Rates: $40-$88.
Ann Leenstra & Judith Papendick.
10 Rooms. 3 Private Baths. Guest phone available. Beds: QT. Full breakfast. Conference room. CCs: MC VISA DS. Fishing, parks, beaches.
"A perfect getaway for historic Astoria."

Cloverdale

Sandlake Country Inn
8505 Galloway Rd
Cloverdale OR 97112
(503) 965-6745

Circa 1894. This two-story farmhouse was built of 3 x 12 bridge

timbers from a Norwegian sailing vessel. It shipwrecked on the beach south of Cape Lookout on Christmas Day 1890. On two acres adjacent to the Suislaw National Forest, the inn's garden is occasionally host to deer and other wildlife. Both the guest rooms feature canopied beds, down comforters and fresh flowers.
Location: On the Oregon Coast.
*Rates: $45-$75.
Margo Underwood.
2 Rooms. 2 Private Baths. Guest phone available. TV in room. Beds: Q. B&B. Jacuzzi. Hiking, fishing, hang gliding, clamming, crabbing, creek-side hammock, croquet, horseback riding on beach nearby.
Seen in: *Headlight Herald, The Bridal Connection of Oregon.*
"A wonderful pampered retreat, revitalizing!"

Eugene

Campus Cottage
1136 E 19th Ave
Eugene OR 97403
(503) 342-5346

Circa 1922. The three guest rooms of Campus Cottage are appointed in a country French decor with antiques, cozy comforters and fresh flowers. The Cottage Room, for instance, has a queen-size oak bed and a day bed, with a vaulted ceiling, bay window and private entrance. Bicycles are available for traveling about the University of Oregon, located two blocks from the inn.
Rates: $68-$80.
Ursula Bates.
3 Rooms. 3 Private Baths. Beds: QT. Full breakfast.
Seen in: *New York Times, PM Magazine.*

House in the Woods
814 Lorane Hwy
Eugene OR 97405
(503) 343-3234

Circa 1910. This handsome Craftsman house on two landscaped acres was built by a Minnesota lawyer. It was originally accessible by streetcar. Antiques include a rosewood, square grand piano and a collection of antique wedding photos. This house is attractively furnished and surrounded by flower gardens.
*Rates: $55-$60.
Eunice & George Kjaer.

2 Rooms. 1 Private Bath. Guest phone available. TV available. Beds: QTDC. Full breakfast. Conference room. Golf, tennis, hiking, bicycling, swimming, fishing.
Seen in: *The Register-Guard, The Oregonian.*
"Lovely ambiance and greatest sleep ever. Delicious and beautiful food presentation."

Grants Pass

Lawnridge House
1304 NW Lawnridge
Grants Pass OR 97526
(503) 479-5186

Circa 1909. This graceful, gabled clapboard house is shaded by a tall

old oak tree. There is a bridal suite with a hand-crafted king-size bed. The house features air conditioning. Breakfast often includes quiche or baked salmon and croissants. Nearby, the Rogue River provides kayaking, river rafting and salmon and steelhead fishing.
*Rates: $45-$67.
Barbara Head.
2 Rooms. 2 Private Baths. Beds: KQ. Full breakfast. Tennis, golf, horseback riding, hiking, skiing.
"Thank you for your incredible friendliness, warmth, and energy expended on our behalf! I've never felt so nestled in the lap of luxury - what a pleasure!"

Hood River

State Street Inn

1005 State St
Hood River OR 97031
(503) 386-1899

Circa 1932. This traditionally styled English house with gabled roof and leaded-glass windows overlooks the Columbia River and Mt. Adams. Each of the four guest rooms is decorated in a different style Colorado Old West, Massachusetts Colonial, California Sunshine and Southern Maryland. Guests may sample Oregon wines at nearby wineries, or take a scenic train ride through local orchards.
Location: Close to Columbia River.
Rates: $50-$70.
Mac Lee & Amy Goodbar.
4 Rooms. Guest phone available. Beds: QD. Full breakfast. Conference room. CCs: MC VISA. Fishing, windsurfing, white-water rafting, wineries, antiquing.
Seen in: *Northwest Best Places.*

Portland

John Palmer House

4314 N Mississippi Ave, Ste AA
Portland OR 97217
(503) 284-5893 Ext. 400

Circa 1890. Located in a redevelopment area, this Queen Anne house features five gables, elaborate spool and spindle work, and roof cresting. It was once the Multnomah Conservatory of Music. The former owners, Oskar and Lotta Hoch, were founders of the Portland Symphony. Inside, a total of 37 splendid silk-screened and gold-leafed Victorian wallpapers adorn the walls and ceil-

ings, often with five papers to a room. Polished woodwork and lavish antiques add to an opulence not easily forgotten.
Location: City Center.
✻❀Rates: $30-$95.
Mary & Richard Sauter.
7 Rooms. 2 Private Baths. Guest phone available. TV available. Beds: DT. Full breakfast. Restaurant. Gourmet meals. Jacuzzi. Handicap access. Conference room. CCs: MC VISA. Horse drawn carriage tours. One hour to skiing, wine country, wind surfing, Pacific Ocean.
Seen in: *The Oregonian.*

"We stayed a whole week, a wonderful week! Can't believe breakfast could be so fantastic each day."

Salem

State House B&B

2146 State St
Salem OR 97301
(503) 588-1340

Circa 1920. This three-story house sits on the banks of Mill Creek where ducks and geese meander past a huge old oak down to the water. (A baby was abandoned here because the house looked "just right" and "surely had nice people there." The baby grew up to become a circuit judge and legal counsel to Governor Mark Hatfield.) The inn is close to everything in Salem.
Location: One mile from the I-5 Santiam turn-off.
Rates: $45-$65.
Mike Winsett & Judy Uselman.
7 Rooms. 5 Private Baths. 1 Fireplace. Guest phone in room. TV available. Beds: QDWC. B&B. Jacuzzi. CCs: MC VISA DS.
Seen in: *Statesman-Journal.*

"You do a wonderful job making people feel welcome and relaxed."

The Dalles

Williams House Inn

608 W 6th St
The Dalles OR 97058
(503) 296-2889

Circa 1899. This handsome, green-and-white gingerbread Victorian possesses a veranda, gazebo and belvedere. Lush green lawns, trees and shrubs slope down to Mill Creek. The popular Harriet's Room overlooks Klickitat Hills and the Columbia River, and has a canopied four-poster bed, chaise lounge and period writing desk. Each spring the hosts harvest their 25-acre cherry orchard. They are active in the historic preservation of the area.
✻Rates: $55-$75.
Don & Barbara Williams.
3 Rooms. 1 Private Bath. Guest phone in room. TV in room. Beds: DC. Full breakfast. CCs: MC VISA AX. Hiking, surfing, skiing, rafting.
Seen in: *Country Inns, New York Times, Glamour Magazine.*

"A fantasy come true, including the most gracious, delightful company in conversation, Barb and Don Williams!"

Pennsylvania

Airville

Spring House
Muddy Creek Forks
Airville PA 17302
(717) 927-6906

Circa 1798. Spring House, always the prominent home in this pre-

Revolutionary War village, was constructed of massive stones over a spring that supplies water to most of the village. The walls are either whitewashed or retain their original stenciling. Furnished with country antiques, quilts, Oriental rugs, and paintings, the guest rooms are cozy with featherbeds in winter. There is a library and grand piano.

*Rates: $60-$85.
Ray Constance Hearne.
5 Rooms. 3 Private Baths. 3 Fireplaces. Guest phone available. Beds: Q. Full breakfast. Fishing, hiking, bicycling, horseback riding, scenic railroads, wineries, antiquing, exploring Amish country.
Seen in: *Woman's Day, Country Decorating.*

"What a slice of history! Thank you for your hospitality. We couldn't have imagined a more picturesque setting."

Allentown

Salisbury House
See: Bethlehem, PA

Bear Creek

Bischwind
Box 7, One Coach Rd
Bear Creek PA 18602
(717) 472-3820

Circa 1881. This spacious Tudor estate was built on prime acreage above the waterfall in Bear Creek Village by lumber and ice baron Albert Lewis. Dr. & Mrs. Von Dran have spent many years restoring the mansion. Filled with antiques, some rooms boast furnishings original to the house. An elegant breakfast with silver, crystal and fine linens is served by a maid in French uniform. Horses are raised on the property.

Location: In a village in the Pocono mountains.
Rates: $150-$200.
3 Rooms. 3 Private Baths. 3 Fireplaces. Guest phone in room. TV in room. Beds: QD. Full breakfast. Swimming pool. Cross-country & downhill skiing, horse races, golf, white-water rafting, walking trails.

"The breakfast was the ultimate."

Bedford

Newry Manor B&B
See: Everett, PA

Bethlehem

Salisbury House
910 East Emmaus Ave
Bethlehem PA 18103
(215) 791-4225

Circa 1810. Built in the plantation style, this enchanting stone house

was operated as an inn for more than a century and then became a private home. A formal boxwood garden and lotus pond are framed by pleasant woodlands. Spacious rooms include an elegant dining room and a well-stocked, paneled library warmed with a fireplace. Family heirlooms, plank floors, wallpapers and more fireplaces fill the guest rooms.

Location: Three miles from Route 309.
Rates: $125-$145.
Judith & Ollie Orth.
5 Rooms. 2 Private Baths. Guest phone available. TV available. Beds: T. B&B. Conference room. CCs: MC VISA AX. Nature trails.
Seen in: *The Morning Call.*

Bloomsburg

The Inn at Turkey Hill

991 Central Rd
Bloomsburg PA 17815
(717) 387-1500

Circa 1839. Turkey Hill is an elegant, white brick farmhouse. All the guest rooms are furnished with handcrafted reproductions from Habersham Plantation in Georgia, and all have views of the duck pond and the gazebo. In the dining room are hand-painted scenes of the rolling Pennsylvania countryside.

Location: Two miles north of Bloomsburg at Exit 35 on Interstate 80.
*Rates: $80-$130.
Babs & Andrew B. Pruden.
18 Rooms. 18 Private Baths. 2 Fireplaces. Guest phone in room. TV in room. Beds: KQC. B&B. Restaurant. Jacuzzi. Handicap access. Conference room. CCs: MC VISA AX DC CB DS. Golf, tennis, fishing, hunting.
Seen in: *The Baltimore Sun, Tempo Magazine.*

"How nice to find an enclave of good taste and class, a special place that seems to care about such old-fashioned virtues as quality and the little details that mean so much." Art Carey, *Philadelphia Inquirer.*

Brookville

Clarion River Lodge

See: Cooksburg, PA

Canadensis

Brookview Manor B&B Inn

Rt 1 Box 365
Canadensis PA 18325
(717) 595-2451

Circa 1911. By the side of the road, hanging from a tall evergreen is the

welcoming sign to this forest retreat. There are brightly decorated common rooms and four fireplaces. The carriage house has three bedrooms and is suitable for small groups. The innkeepers like to share a "secret waterfall" within a 20-minute walk from the inn.

Location: On scenic route 447, Pocono Mountains.
Rates: $50-$85.
John Ward.
8 Rooms. 7 Private Baths. Guest phone available. TV available. Beds: QTD. Full breakfast. CCs: MC VISA. Cross-country skiing, fishing, hiking.
Seen in: *Mid-Atlantic Country.*

"Thanks for a great wedding weekend. Everything was perfect."

Churchtown

Churchtown Inn

Rt 23
Churchtown PA 17555
(215) 445-7794

Circa 1735. This handsome, stone Federal house with its panoramic

views was once known as the Edward Davies Mansion, but was also once a tinsmith shop and rectory. It has heard the marching feet of Revolutionary troops and seen the Union Army during the Civil War. Tastefully furnished with antiques and collectables, the inn features canopy, pencil-post and sleigh beds. There is music everywhere, as the innkeeper directed choruses appearing at Carnegie Hall and the Lincoln Center. By prior arrangement, guests may dine in an Amish home.

Location: Five miles from Pennsylvania Turnpike.
Rates: $49-$75.
Hermine & Stuart Smith, Jim Kent.
8 Rooms. 6 Private Baths. Guest phone available. Beds: QT. Full breakfast. Conference room. CCs: MC VISA. Swimming, hiking, bicycling.
Seen in:

"Magnificent atmosphere. Outstanding breakfasts. Our favorite B&B."

The Foreman House B&B

2129 Main St, Rt 23
Churchtown PA 17555
(215) 445-6713

Circa 1919. A prominent local farmer, Peter Foreman, built this

house and then forbade all seven of his children to marry or they would lose their inheritance. Six obeyed. Surrounded by Amish farmlands, the inn provides views of horse-drawn carriages. A selection of the most sought after quilts in the country may be purchased in the parlors of farm ladies nearby.

Location: Lancaster County on Route 23.
Rates: $50.
Jacqueline & Stephen Mitrani.
2 Rooms. Guest phone available. Beds: DT. Full breakfast. Golf, boating & swimming nearby.
Seen in: *Lancaster Daily Newspaper.*

"We couldn't have been happier staying anywhere else! You have a lovely home."

Clarion

Clarion River Lodge

See: Cooksburg, PA

Danville

The Pine Barn Inn

1 Pine Barn Place
Danville PA 17821
(717) 275-2071

Circa 1860. The inn is a restored Pennsylvania German barn. Original

stone walls and beams accent the restaurant and a large stone

fireplace warms the tavern. It was the first all-electric residence in the state.
*Rates: $40-$60.
Susan Dressler.
75 Rooms. 69 Private Baths. Guest phone in room. TV in room. Beds: KQDTC. B&B. Restaurant. Conference room. CCs: MC VISA AX DC CB DS. Swimming, golf, tennis, racquetball, horseback riding, fishing.

"For four years we have stayed at the Pine Barn Inn. I thought then, and still think, it is truly the nicest inn I have been in and I've been in many."

Doylestown

Logan Inn
See: New Hope, PA

Doylestown, Bucks Co

The Inn at Fordhook Farm
105 New Britain Rd
Doylestown, Bucks Co PA 18901
(215) 345-1766

Circa 1760. Three generations of Burpees (Burpee Seed Company) have dispensed hospitality on this

60-acre farm. Guest rooms are in the family's 18th-century fieldstone house and Victorian carriage house. The inn is filled with family heirlooms and guests can sit at the famous horticulturist's desk in the secluded study where Mr. Burpee wrote his first seed catalogs.
Location: Two miles west of Doylestown on route 202, Bucks County.
Rates: $94-$175.
Elizabeth Romanella & Blanche Burpee Dohan.
7 Rooms. 4 Private Baths. 2 Fireplaces. Guest phone available. TV available. Beds: KQD. B&B. Conference room. CCs: MC VISA AX. Cross-country skiing, hiking.
Seen in: *Bon Appetit, Mid-Atlantic Country.*

"The inn is absolutely exquisite. If I had only one night to spend in Bucks County, I'd do it all over again at Fordhook Farms!"

East Berlin

The Bechtel Mansion Inn
400 West King St
East Berlin PA 17316
(717) 259-7760

Circa 1897. The town of East Berlin, near Lancaster and Gettysburg,

was settled by Pennsylvania Germans prior to the American Revolution. William Leas, a wealthy banker, built this many-gabled Queen Anne mansion, now listed in the National Register. The inn is furnished with an abundance of Victorian antiques and collections.
*Rates: $72-$125.
Ruth Spangler & Mary Doyle.
7 Rooms. 7 Private Baths. Guest phone available. TV available. Beds: QTD. Continental-plus breakfast. Conference room. CCs: MC VISA. Skiing.
Seen in: *The Washington Post.*

"Ruth was a most gracious hostess and took time to describe the history of your handsome museum-quality antiques and the special architectural details."

Ephrata

Gerhart House B&B
287 Duke St
Ephrata PA 17522
(717) 733-0263

Circa 1926. Originally built as a combination home, office and detached butcher shop, the house is unique in its use of hardwoods for inlaid floor designs and its chestnut trim work. Sunny, stenciled guest rooms include one with a queen-size canopy bed covered with a Mennonite quilt. Ephrata Cloister is seven blocks away.
Rates: $50-$75.
Richard & Judith Lawson.
5 Rooms. 3 Private Baths. Guest phone available. Beds: QDTC. Full breakfast. CCs: MC VISA. Fishing, community pool.

"Thank you for making our weekend very special."

Guesthouse and 1777 House at Doneckers
318-324 N State St
Ephrata PA 17522
(717) 733-8696

Circa 1770. Jacob Gorgas, devout member of the Ephrata Cloister and

a clock maker (noted for crafting 150 Eight-Day Gorgas Grandfather Clocks), built this stately home. It was restored and filled with European antiques collected by Bill Donecker, owner of the Community of Doneckers, a village with shops, a restaurant and the 19-room Guesthouse of Doneckers. Original thick stone walls add atmosphere to the breakfast room. Guest chambers may include features such as jacuzzi tubs, fireplaces, inlaid floors or stained-glass windows. One room sports a hand-painted bed purchased from the Liberace estate.
Location: Junction of Routes 222 & 322 in Lancaster County.
Rates: $59-$130.
Jan Grobengeiser.
29 Rooms. 22 Private Baths. 4 Fireplaces. Guest phone in room. TV available. Beds: QDTC. B&B. Restaurant. Gourmet meals. Jacuzzi. Conference room. CCs: MC VISA AX DC CB DS.
Seen in: *Daily News.*

"A peaceful refuge."

Smithton Inn

900 W Main St
Ephrata PA 17522
(717) 733-6094

Circa 1763. Henry Miller opened this inn and tavern on a hill over-

looking the Ephrata Cloister, a religious society he belonged to known as Seventh Day Baptists. Several of their medieval-style German buildings are now a museum. The bedchambers have working fireplaces, canopy beds, candlelight and nightshirts for each guest.

Location: Lancaster County.
Rates: $55-$105.
Dorothy Graybill.
7 Rooms. 7 Private Baths. 7 Fireplaces. Guest phone available. Beds: KQDTC. AP. Jacuzzi. Handicap access. CCs: VISA AX DS. Touring Amish farms, historic sites, crafts, antiques.
Seen in: *New York Magazine, Country Living.*

"After visiting over 50 inns in four countries Smithton has to be one of the most romantic picturesque inns in America. I have never seen its equal!"

Erie

Brown's Village Inn

See: North East, PA

Erwinna

Evermay-on-the-Delaware

River Rd
Erwinna PA 18920
(215) 294-9100

Circa 1740. Twenty-five acres of Bucks County at its best — rolling green meadows, lawns, stately maples and the silvery Delaware River, surround this three-story brick manor. Serving as an inn since 1871, it has hosted such guests as the Barrymore family. Rich walnut wain-scotting, a grandfather clock and twin fireplaces warm the parlor, scented by vases of roses or gladiolus. Antique-filled guest rooms overlook the river or gardens.

Rates: $70-$120.
Ronald Strouse & Frederick Cresson.
16 Rooms. 16 Private Baths. Guest phone in room. Beds: KQD. Continental-plus breakfast. Gourmet meals. Handicap access. Conference room. CCs: MC VISA. Rafting, canoeing, sailing, horseback riding, ballooning, hiking, cross-country skiing.
Seen in: *New York Times, Philadelphia Magazine, Travel and Leisure.*

"The experience was old-fashioned in the best sense of the word." Nao Hauser, *Food & Wine.*

Golden Pheasant Inn

River Rd
Erwinna PA 18920
(215) 294-9595

Circa 1857. Originally built to serve the mule barge workers and

travelers, the Golden Pheasant is located between the Pennsylvania Canal and the Delaware River. Features of the inn include fieldstone walls, exposed beams, and hardwood floors. There is a greenhouse dining room with views of the historic canal, lit in the evenings with spotlights. The cuisine here is highly rated.

Location: Bucks County.
Rates: $95-$125.
Barbara & Michel Faure.
6 Rooms. 1 Private Bath. Guest phone available. Beds: QT. Restaurant. Conference room. CCs: MC VISA. Horseback riding, hiking, swimming, bicycling, cross-country skiing, canoeing.
Seen in: *The Philadelphia Inquirer.*

"A more stunningly romantic spot is hard to imagine. A taste of France on the banks of the Delaware."

Everett

Newry Manor

Rt 1 Box 475
Everett PA 15537
(814) 623-1250

Circa 1805. Newry Manor and the adjacent stone woolen mill are both listed in the National Register. Four generations of the Lutz family lived in and expanded the house into its current blend of stone, brick and log. The inn is filled with family heirlooms and antiques. A beautiful Prussian blue fireplace mantel is in the keeping room. On quiet days, guests can hear the trickle of the Raystown Branch of the Juniata River flowing past the old mill.

Location: Lutzville Road, 1 mile south of U.S. Route 30, near Everett.
Rates: $30-$60. Season: April - Nov.
Rosie & Carl Mulert.
3 Rooms. 3 Private Baths. 2 Fireplaces. Guest phone available. TV available. Beds: QT. Continental-plus breakfast. Canoeing.
Seen in: *Bedford Gazette, Bedford County Shoppers Guide.*

"You are wonderful people. We will always remember this as our honeymoon home!"

Gardners

Goose Chase

200 Blueberry Rd
Gardners PA 17324
(717) 528-8877

Circa 1762. Originally a settler's log cabin, Goose Chase was en-

larged in 1820 and 1988, with stone additions. Comfortable interiors include polished wide floorboards, stenciled walls, rag rugs and antiques. Troops en route to the Gettysburg Battlefield once passed by. Located on 25 acres, this home is one of the oldest in the Gettysburg area.

Location: Fourteen miles north of Gettysburg.
Rates: $55-$65.
Marsha & Rich Lucidi.
3 Rooms. 1 Private Bath. TV available. Beds: KDT. Full breakfast. Gourmet meals. Swimming pool. CCs: MC VISA. Cross-country & downhill skiing, fishing, golf, horseback riding. Afternoon wine and tea.
Seen in: *Gettysburg Times.*

"Everything was just perfect. We were amazed at your fine decor."

Gettysburg

Bechtel Mansion Inn

See: East Berlin, PA

Beechmont Inn

See: Hanover, PA

The Brafferton Inn

44 York St
Gettysburg PA 17325
(717) 337-3423

Circa 1786. The earliest deeded house in Gettysburg, the inn was

designed by James Gettys, and is listed in the National Register of Historic Places. The walls of this huge brownstone range from 18 inches to two-and-one-half-feet thick. There are skylights in all the guestrooms and a primitive mural of famous scenes in the area painted on the four dining room walls.
Location: Ninety miles north of Washington, D.C.
*Rates: $60-$80.
Mimi & Jim Agard.
10 Rooms. 6 Private Baths. Guest phone available. Beds: DT. EP. Handicap access. CCs: MC VISA. Horseback riding, skiing, hiking, biking, swimming, golf.
Seen in: *Early American Life, Country Living.*

"Your house is so beautiful - every corner of it - and your friendliness is icing on the cake. It was fabulous!"

The Doubleday Inn

104 Doubleday Ave
Gettysburg PA 17325
(717) 334-9119

Circa 1929. Located directly on the Gettysburg Battlefield and bordered

by original stone breastworks, this restored Colonial home is furnished with Victorian sofas and period antiques. Available to guests is one of the largest known Civil War libraries with over 500 volumes devoted exclusively to the Battle of Gettysburg. On selected evenings, guests can participate in discussions with a Civil War historian who brings the battle alive with accurate accounts and authentic memorabilia and weaponry.
Location: On the Gettysburg Battlefield.
*Rates: $65-$100.
Joan & Sal Chandon with Olga Krossick.
9 Rooms. 5 Private Baths. Guest phone available. Beds: DT. B&B. CCs: MC VISA. Horseback riding, skiing, golfing, battlefield touring. Afternoon tea, hor d'oeuvres.
Seen in: *Innsider Magazine, New York Magazine.*

"What you're doing for students of Gettysburg & the Civil War in general is tremendous! Our stay was wonderful!!"

Goose Chase

See: Gardners, PA

Hickory Bridge Farm

See: Orrtanna, PA

Keystone Inn B&B

231 Hanover St
Gettysburg PA 17325
(717) 337-3888

Circa 1913. Furniture-maker Clayton Reaser constructed this three-story brick Victorian with a wide-columned porch hugging the north and west sides. Cut stone graces every door and windowsill,

each with a keystone. A chestnut staircase ascends the full three stories, and the interior is decorated with comfortable furnishings, ruffles and lace.
Location: Route 116 East of Gettysburg.
Rates: $55-$65.
Wilmer & Doris Martin.
4 Rooms. 2 Private Baths. Beds: QT. Full breakfast. CCs: MC VISA. Tennis, bicycling.
Seen in: *Gettysburg Times, Hanover Sun.*

"We slept like lambs. This home has a warmth that is soothing."

Gordonville

The Osceola Mill House

313 Osceola Mill Rd
Gordonville PA 17529
(717) 768-3758

Circa 1766. This limestone mill house rests on the banks of Pequea Creek, surrounded by Amish farms in a quaint historic setting. Fireplaces in the keeping room and in the bedrooms provide warmth and charm.
Location: Lancaster County, 15 miles east of Lancaster near Intercourse.
Rates: $50-$70. Season: Closed Xmas & Easter
Barry & Joy Sawyer.
3 Rooms. 2 Fireplaces. Guest phone available. Beds: QD. Full breakfast.
Seen in: *The Journal, Country Living, Washington Times.*

"This is the first time we've stayed in a bed and breakfast- it was a wonderful experience."

Hanover

Beechmont Inn

315 Broadway
Hanover PA 17331
(717) 632-3013

Circa 1834. This gracious Georgian inn was a witness to the Civil War's

first major battle on free soil, the Battle of Hanover. Decorated in pre-Victorian antiques, several guest rooms are named for the battle's commanders. The romantic Diller Suite contains a marble fireplace and queen canopy bed. The inn is noted for elegant breakfasts, often served by candlelight.
Rates: $70-$90.
Terry & Monna, Glenn & Maggie Hormel.
7 Rooms. 7 Private Baths. 1 Fireplace. Guest phone available. TV available. Beds: QD. Full breakfast. Handicap access. CCs: MC VISA. Boating, horseback riding, wineries, swimming. Dutch Days, Gettysburg National Park, outdoor breakfast area.

Harrisburg

Cameron Estate Inn
See: Mount Joy, PA

Herr Farmhouse Inn
See: Manheim, PA

Hawley

Settlers Inn
4 Main Ave
Hawley PA 18428
(717) 226-2993

Circa 1927. When the Wallenpaupack Creek was dammed up to form the lake, the community hired

architect Louis Welch and built this Grand Tudor Revival-style hotel featuring chestnut beams, leaded-glass windows and an enormous stone fireplace. The dining room, the main focus of the inn, is decorated with hand-made quilts, hanging plants and chairs that once graced a Philadelphia cathedral. If you're looking for trout you can try your luck fishing the Lackawaxen River, which runs behind the inn.
Rates: $60.
Jeanne & Grant Genzlinger.
18 Rooms. 18 Private Baths. Guest phone available. TV available. Beds: D. B&B. Restaurant. Gourmet meals. Conference room. CCs: MC VISA AX. Swimming, boating, hiking, tennis, museums, fishing.
Seen in: *Travel Holiday Magazine, New Jersey Monthly.*

Holicong

Ash Mill Farm
PO Box 202
Holicong PA 18928
(215) 794-5373

Circa 1790. This estate includes a Federal addition completed in 1830.

The finish on the house is 18th-century plaster over stone. The original section has a five-foot walk-in fireplace with a beehive oven and original cooking crane. Breakfast is served here, and afternoon tea is also available. Grazing sheep dot the farm pastures.
Location: Route 202 located midway between Lahaska and Buckingham.
*Rates: $70-$110.
Patricia & Jim Auslander.
6 Rooms. 4 Private Baths. 2 Fireplaces. Guest phone available. Beds: Q. EP. CCs: MC VISA. Horseback riding, canoeing, biking, hiking, golf, tennis.

"The home's appointments are lovely and the quaint characteristics of the house itself a pleasure to look at."

Barley Sheaf Farm
Rt 202 Box 10
Holicong PA 18928
(215) 794-5104

Circa 1740. Situated on part of the original William Penn land grant,

this beautiful stone house with white shuttered windows and mansard roof is set on 30 acres of farmland. Once owned by noted playwright George Kaufman, it was the gathering place for the Marx Brothers, Lillian Hellman, and S. J. Perlman. The bank barn, pond, and majestic old trees round out a beautiful setting.
Location: Fifty miles north of Philadelphia in Bucks County.
Rates: $100-$150.
Ann & Don Mills, Amy Donohoe.
10 Rooms. 10 Private Baths. 1 Fireplace. Guest phone available. Beds: KQD. Full breakfast. Handicap access. Swimming pool. Conference room. CCs: AX.
Seen in: *Country Living.*

Jim Thorpe

Harry Packer Mansion
Packer Hill
Jim Thorpe PA 18229
(717) 325-8566

Circa 1874. This extravagant Second Empire mansion was con-

structed of New England sandstone, and local brick and stone trimmed in cast iron. Past ornately carved columns on the front veranda,

guests enter 400-pound, solid walnut doors. The opulent interior includes marble mantels, hand-painted ceilings, and elegant antiques.
Location: Six miles south of Exit 34.
*Rates: $75-$110.
Bob & Pat Handwerr.
13 Rooms. 8 Private Baths. Guest phone available. Beds: QD. Full breakfast. Conference room. CCs: MC VISA. Downhill & cross-country skiing, swimming, rafting, fishing. Mystery weekends.
"The best B&B we have ever stayed at! We'll be back."

Kane

Kane Manor Country Inn
230 Clay St
Kane PA 16735
(814) 837-6522

Circa 1896. This Georgian Revival inn, on 250 acres of woods and trails, was built for Dr. Elizabeth Kane, the first female doctor to practice in the area. Many of the family's possessions dating back to the American Revolution and the Civil War remain. (Ask to see the attic.) Decor is a mixture of contemporary and old family items in an unpretentious homey style. Locals frequent the inn's pub.
Rates: $59-$85.
Laurie Anne.
10 Rooms. 6 Private Baths. Guest phone available. Beds: DT. Full breakfast. CCs: MC VISA AX. Cross-country skiing, fishing, hunting, swimming, bicycling, golf, tennis. Afternoon tea.
Seen in: *The Pittsburg Press, News Herald.*
"It's a place I want to return to often for rest and relaxation."

Kennett Square

Meadow Spring Farm
201 E St Rd
Kennett Square PA 19348
(215) 444-3903

Circa 1836. This working, 245-acre dairy farm has more than 300 holsteins grazing in pastures beside the old red barn. The two-story, white-brick house is decorated with old family pieces and collections of whimsical animals and antique wedding gowns. A Victorian doll collection fills one room. Breakfast is

hearty country style. Afterwards, guests may see the milking operation, gather eggs or pick vegetables from the garden.
Location: Forty-five minutes from Philadelphia, 2 hours from New York.
*Rates: $40-$65.
Anne Hicks.
6 Rooms. 3 Private Baths. 1 Fireplace. Guest phone available. TV in room. Beds: QT. Full breakfast. Gourmet meals. Jacuzzi. Swimming pool. Game room. Hiking and fishing on premises.
Seen in: *Weekend GetAways.*

Lahaska

Golden Plough Inn
Rt 263-Rt 202, Box 218
Lahaska PA 18931
(215) 794-7438

Circa 1750. This Early American house features French Colonial in-

fluences including a mansard roof. It is located in Peddler's Village, a reproduction 18th-century colonial village. There are high-quality specialty shops here, and the Pearl Buck house, Bucks County Playhouse and Dinner Theater are nearby. The inn is five miles from New Hope and the Delaware River.
Location: Peddler's Village, Route 263-Route 202.
*Rates: $80-$200.
Earl Jamison.
45 Rooms. 45 Private Baths. 7 Fireplaces. Guest phone in room. TV in room. Beds: KQT. MAP. Restaurant. Gourmet meals. Jacuzzi. Handicap access. Conference room. CCs: MC VISA AX DC CB. Horseback riding, hot air balloon, boating, tubing.
Seen in: *The Washington Post, New York Times, Bon Appetit.*
"We were very pleased with everything. It was great being here in the village, within walking distance of the shops and restaurants."

Lancaster

The Alden House
See: Lititz, PA

Bechtel Mansion Inn
See: East Berlin, PA

Cameron Estate Inn
See: Mount Joy, PA

Foreman House B&B
See: Churchtown, PA

Gerhart House B&B
See: Ephrata, PA

Herr Farmhouse Inn
See: Manheim, PA

Smithton Inn
See: Ephrata, PA

Spring House
See: Airville, PA

Witmer's Tavern - Historic 1725 Inn
2014 Old Philadelphia Pike
Lancaster PA 17602
(717) 299-5305

Circa 1725. This pre-Revolutionary War inn opened 265 years ago, and

is the sole survivor of 62 inns that once lined the old Lancaster-to-Philadelphia turnpike. Conestoga wagon trains were loaded and prepared here for western and southern journeys. Designated as a National Landmark property, a painstaking restoration is in progress. Highlights are hand-carved stone, original woodwork,

and a brick-floored, beamed-ceiling tavern. Guest rooms feature antiques, original fireplaces in all rooms, old quilts, and freshly-cut flowers.
Location: One mile east of Lancaster on Route 340.
*Rates: $55-$75.
Brant Hartung & his sister Pamela Hartung.
5 Rooms. Beds: D. Continental breakfast. Canoeing, hiking, biking, flying, antiquing.

"Your personal attention and enthusiastic knowledge of the area and Witmer's history made it come alive and gave us the good feelings we came looking for."

Lititz

The Alden House
62 E Main St
Lititz PA 17543
(717) 627-3363

Circa 1850. For over 200 years, breezes have carried the sound of church bells to the stately brick homes lining Main Street. The Alden House is a town house in the center of this historic district, and within walking distance of the Pretzel House (first in the country) and the chocolate factory. A favorite room choice is the suite with a sleeping loft, appealing to families traveling with youngsters. A breakfast buffet is served, often carried to one of the inn's three porches.
Rates: $65-$95.
Gloria Adams.
7 Rooms. 5 Private Baths. Guest phone available. TV available. Beds: QDT. Continental-plus breakfast. CCs: MC VISA.
Seen in: *Early American Life, Travel.*

"Truly represents what bed & breakfast hospitality is all about."

Lumberville

Black Bass Hotel
River Rd
Lumberville PA 18933
(215) 297-5770

Circa 1745. Located on the River Road north of New Hope, the Black Bass Hotel originally opened as a canal stop. In those days, the innkeepers were of Tory persuasion and attracted a Loyalist clientele. Today, the hotel is noted for its excellent cuisine. Electrified oil and tin lamps and railroader's lanterns are displayed, along with a collection of British Royal Family memorabilia. Guest rooms are furnished with 18th and 19th-century antiques. Some rooms have private balconies overlooking the Delaware River.
Rates: $55-$175.
Herbert E. Ward.
10 Rooms. 3 Private Baths. Guest phone available. Beds: DT. Continental breakfast. Restaurant. Conference room. CCs: MC VISA AX DC CB. Horseback riding, water sports.
Seen in: *New York Times, Country Living Magazine.*

"...like the European country hotel."

Manheim

Herr Farmhouse Inn
2256 Huber Dr
Manheim PA 17545
(717) 653-9852

Circa 1738. One of the earliest in Lancaster County, this fully restored

stone farmhouse sits on 26 acres of scenic farmland. All woodwork including moldings, doors, cabinets and pine flooring is original. Lancaster quilts enhance the inn's colonial decor. Six working fireplaces add warmth in the winter while air conditioning cools in summer.
Location: Nine miles west of Lancaster off Route 283 (Mt. Joy 230 exit).
Rates: $65-$85.
Barry & Ruth Herr.
4 Rooms. 2 Private Baths. 2 Fireplaces. Guest phone available. TV available. Beds: DT. Continental-plus breakfast. CCs: MC VISA.

"Your home is lovely. You've done a beautiful job of restoring and remodeling."

Mercer

Magoffin Guest House B&B
129 S Pitt St
Mercer PA 16137
(412) 662-4611

Circa 1884. Dr. Magoffin built this house for his Pittsburgh bride, Hen-

rietta Bouvard. The Queen Anne style is characterized by patterned brick masonry, gable detailing, bay windows and a wraparound porch. The technique of marbelizing was used on six of the nine fireplaces. Magoffin Muffins are featured each morning. Lunch is available Monday through Saturday, and dinner, Tuesday through Saturday.
Location: Near I-79 and I-80.
Rates: $45-$85.
Jacque McClelland, Gene Slagle.
10 Rooms. 8 Private Baths. Beds: QDC. Full breakfast. Conference room. CCs: MC VISA. Swimming, golf, tennis, fishing.
Seen in: *Western Reserve Magazine, Youngstown Vindicator.*

"While in Arizona we met a family from Africa who had stopped at the Magoffin House. After crossing the United States they said the Magoffin House was quite the nicest place they had stayed."

Mercerburg

The Mercerburg Inn
405 S Main St
Mercerburg PA 17236
(717) 328-5231

Circa 1909. Situated on a hill overlooking the Blue Ridge Mountains, the valley and village, this 20,000 square-foot Georgian Colonial mansion was built for industrialist Harry Byron. Six massive columns mark the entrance, which opens to a majestic marble hall with an elegant

double stairway. All the rooms are furnished with antiques and reproductions. A local craftsman built the inn's four-poster, canopied, king-size beds. Many of the rooms have their own balconies and a few have fireplaces. A bowling alley once occupied the entire basement and originally determined the dimensions of the house. An antique billiard table now occupies that site. The inn's chef is noted for his six-course New England dinners.
Rates: $85-$120.
Fran Wolfe.
15 Rooms. 15 Private Baths. 2 Fireplaces. Guest phone in room. TV available. Beds: KQDT. MAP. Restaurant. Gourmet meals. Game room. Conference room. CCs: MC VISA AX. Horseback riding nearby, rafting, boating, tennis.
Seen in: *Mid-Atlantic Country, Washington Post.*
"Elegance personified! Outstanding ambience and warm hospitality."

Mertztown

Longswamp B&B
RD 2 PO Box 26
Mertztown PA 19539
(215) 682-6197

Circa 1789. Country gentleman Colonel Trexler added a mansard roof to this stately Federal mansion in 1860. Inside, is a magnificent walnut staircase and pegged wood floors. As the story goes, the colonel discovered his unmarried daughter having an affair and shot her lover. He escaped hanging, but it was said that after his death his ghost could be seen in the upstairs bedroom watching the road. In 1905, an exorcism was reported to have sent his spirit to a nearby mountaintop.
Rates: $60-$65.
Elsa Dimick.
9 Rooms. 5 Private Baths. 2 Fireplaces. Guest phone available. TV available. Beds: QC. B&B. Gourmet meals. CCs: MC VISA. Horseback riding, biking, bocci, horseshoes.
Seen in: *Washingtonian, Weekend Travel, The Sun.*
"The warm country atmosphere turns strangers into friends."

Montoursville

The Carriage House at Stonegate
RD 1 Box 11A
Montoursville PA 17754
(717) 433-4340

Circa 1830. President Herbert Hoover was a descendant of the original settlers of this old homestead in the Loyalsock Creek Valley. Indians burned the original house, but the present farmhouse and numerous outbuildings date from the early 1800s. The Carriage House is set next to a lovely brook.
Location: Six miles off I-180, north of Montoursville.
Rates: $45-$70.
Harold & Dena Mesaris.
4 Rooms. 2 Private Baths. TV available. Beds: QTC. Continental-plus breakfast. Conference room. Hiking, golf, cross-country skiing, canoeing.
"A very fine B&B - the best that can be found. Gracious hosts."

Mount Joy

Cameron Estate Inn
RD 1 Box 305
Mount Joy PA 17552
(717) 653-1773

Circa 1805. Simon Cameron, Abraham Lincoln's first Secretary of

War, entertained his guests in this Federal-period estate situated on 15 acres of towering oaks with an old stone bridge and trout stream. There are oriental rugs, antiques, and working fireplaces. Groff's Farm Restaurant is at the inn. The pen and ink drawing is by Tom Hermansader.
*Rates: $55-$105.
Carol, Eugene, Stephanie & Betty Groff, owner.
18 Rooms. 16 Private Baths. 7 Fireplaces. Guest phone available. TV available. Beds: KQDT. Continental breakfast. Restaurant. Conference room. CCs: MC VISA AX DC. Tennis, swimming, cross-country skiing, golf, hiking, biking, sky diving, ballooning, yard games.
Seen in: *Chicago Sun-Times, San Francisco Examiner, Mid-Atlantic Country.*
"Betty runs from pillar to post, filled with joy!" Stephanie Edwards, Los Angeles talk show host.

New Hope

Backstreet Inn
144 Old York Rd
New Hope PA 18939
(215) 862-9571

Circa 1750. Tucked away on a quiet street, this inn sits on three

acres of park-like lawns that include a stream, an old wishing well, and a gurgling brook. Several rooms reveal the stone walls of the house and are decorated with antiques. A favorite is the Anne Frank Room down a small hallway hidden by a sliding bookcase.
❀Rates: $89-$125.
Bob Puccio.
7 Rooms. 5 Private Baths. Guest phone available. TV available. Beds: D. Full breakfast. Gourmet meals. Swimming pool. CCs: MC VISA. Horse and carriage rides.
Seen in: *Treutonian Press, Newark Star Ledger.*
"Just felt like taking my shoes off and being right at home, most relaxing."

Colligan's Stockton Inn
See: Stockton, NJ

Hotel Du Village

N River Rd
New Hope PA 18938
(215) 862-9911

Circa 1907. Secluded on 10 acres of lawns, creek and trees, once part of a land grant to the Ely family by William Penn, Hotel du Village is a hotel and restaurant. The Tudor-style hotel served as a boarding school for girls, while the restaurant is part of the old White Oaks estate. Chestnut panelling, Persian carpets and three working fireplaces provide a backdrop to chef Omar Arbanis' French cuisine.

Rates: $80-$95.
Barbara & Omar Arbani.
20 Rooms. 20 Private Baths. Guest phone available. Beds: KQDT. B&B. Restaurant. Handicap access. Swimming pool. Conference room. CCs: AX. Horseback riding nearby, tennis.
Seen in: *Trenton Times, The Burlington County Times.*

"The food is wonderful - fireplaces burning makes everything so romantic!"

Joseph Ambler Inn

See: North Wales, PA

Logan Inn

Main & Ferry Sts
New Hope PA 18938
(215) 862-2300

Circa 1722. Said to be one of the five oldest inns in America, the

Logan was originally known as the Ferry Tavern, established by John Wells, founder of New Hope. The oldest section of the inn contains the tavern (open until 2 a.m.), with a Colonial fireplace, murals and antique woodwork. Original art, antiques, and four-poster canopy beds are featured in each guest room. A private stone-walled cottage has its own fireplace. Under new ownership, the inn's dining rooms are becoming known for their excellent cuisine and gracious service.

Rates: $95-$125.
Gwen Davis.
16 Rooms. 16 Private Baths. Guest phone in room. TV in room. Beds: KQDTC. B&B. Restaurant. Conference room. CCs: MC VISA AX DC CB. Horse-drawn carriage tours, ghost tours, boats, bicycles, canoeing, balloon rides, children's amusement park, museums.
Seen in: *The Philadelphia Inquirer, The Home News.*

"...the food was PERFECTION and served in a gracious and extremely courteous manner...our intentions had been to explore different restaurants, but there was no reason to explore, we had found what we wanted."

Old Hunterdon House

See: Frenchtown, NJ

The Wedgwood Inn

111 W Bridge
New Hope PA 18938
(215) 862-2570

Circa 1870. A Victorian and a Classic Revival house sit side by side and compose the Wedgewood Inn. Twenty-six-inch walls are in the stone house. Lofty windows, hardwood floors and antique furnishings add to the warmth and style. Pennsylvania Dutch surreys arrive and depart from the inn for nostalgic carriage rides.

Rates: $80-$160.
Nadine Silnutzer & Carl Glassman.
10 Rooms. 8 Private Baths. 2 Fireplaces. Guest phone available. Continental-plus breakfast. Pool, antiques, arts & craft shops.
Seen in: *National Geographic, Traveller, Women's Day, Inc.*

"The Wedgewood has all the comforts of a highly professional accommodation yet with all the warmth a personal friend would extend."

New Oxford

Beechmont Inn

See: Hanover, PA

North East

Brown's Village Inn

51 E Main St
North East PA 16428
(814) 725-5522

Circa 1832. Nestled in the heart of Pennsylvania wine country, along

the eastern shore of Lake Erie, this red brick Federal house once served as a stagecoach stop. Slave quarters, in the secret cellar beneath the kitchen, later provided shelter for families escaping slavery on the underground railroad. A restaurant and parlor occupy the first floor. A circular oak staircase winds to the upstairs guest chambers. Lake Erie, several wineries, a cider mill and the world-famous Chautauqua Institution are nearby.

*Rates: $55-$65.
Rebecca Brown.
3 Rooms. 3 Private Baths. Guest phone available. TV available. Beds: KDTC. Full breakfast. Restaurant. Gourmet meals. Conference room. CCs: MC VISA. Horseback riding, skiing, boating, swimming, tennis, wineries.
Seen in: *Pennsylvania Traveller, Erie Times.*

"Your inn is lovely and the meal was superb, but it is your warmth that is so keenly felt."

North Wales

Joseph Ambler Inn

1005 Horsham Rd
North Wales PA 19454
(215) 362-7500

Circa 1734. This beautiful fieldstone-and-wood house was built over a period of three centuries. Originally, it was part of a grant that Joseph Ambler, a Quaker wheelwright, obtained from William Penn in 1688. A large stone bank barn and tenant cottage on 12 acres constitute the remainder of the property. Guests enjoy the cherry wainscoting and walk-in fireplace in the schoolroom.

Rates: $87-$140.
Steve & Terry Kratz.
28 Rooms. 28 Private Baths. Beds: QD. Full breakfast. Restaurant. Conference room. CCs: MC VISA AX DC CB DS. Golf, tennis.
Seen in: *Colonial Homes, Country Living.*

"What a wonderful night my husband and I spent. It was special because of the great pains taken to make the inn quaint and unique. We are already planning to come back to your wonderful get-away."

Orrtanna

Hickory Bridge Farm

96 Hickory Bridge Rd
Orrtanna PA 17353
(717) 642-5261

Circa 1750. The oldest part of this farmhouse was constructed of mud

bricks and straw, on land that once belonged to Charles Carroll, father of a signer of the Declaration of Independence. Inside, there is an attractive stone fireplace for cooking. There are several country cottages in addition to the rooms in the farmhouse. The host family have been innkeepers for nearly 20 years.
Location: Eight miles west of Gettysburg.
Rates: $65-$80.
The Hammetts, Robert & Mary Lynn Martin.
7 Rooms. 6 Private Baths. 4 Fireplaces. TV available. Beds: Q. B&B. Conference room. CCs: MC VISA. Fishing, golfing, swimming, skiing.
Seen in: *Hanover Times, The Northern Virginia Gazzette.*

"Beautifully decorated and great food!"

Philadelphia

B&B of Valley Forge

See: Valley Forge, PA

Golden Plough Inn

See: Lahaska, PA

Society Hill Hotel

301 Chestnut St
Philadelphia PA 19106
(215) 925-1919

Circa 1830. The small cozy rooms of this urban inn are decorated with

brass beds, fresh flowers and other amenities expected by guests of the Society Hill group in Maryland. Breakfast is brought to the room. For other meals, there is an outdoor cafe and a restaurant with nightly jazz piano.
*Rates: $92-$127.
Jacky Hagner.
12 Rooms. 12 Private Baths. Guest phone in room. TV in room. Beds: D. B&B. CCs: MC VISA DC. Close to all historic sites.

Pittsburgh

The Priory

614 Pressley St
Pittsburgh PA 15212
(412) 231-3338

Circa 1888. The Priory, now a European-style hotel, was built to

provide lodging for Benedictine priests traveling through Pittsburgh. It is adjacent to St. Mary's German Catholic Church in historic East Allegheny. The inn's design and maze of rooms and corridors give it a distinctly Old World flavor. All rooms are decorated with Victorian furnishings.
*Rates: $65-$130.
Mary Ann Graf.
27 Rooms. 27 Private Baths. Beds: QDTC. Continental-plus breakfast. Handicap access. Conference room. Complimentary wine in sitting room.
Seen in: *The Pittsburg Press.*

"Although we had been told that the place was elegant, we were hardly prepared for the richness of detail. We felt as though we were guests in a manor."

Pottstown

Fairway Farm B&B

Vaughn Rd
Pottstown PA 19464
(215) 326-1315

Circa 1734. This beautiful old fieldstone house is in a parklike set-

ting that includes a spring-fed outdoor pool, a tennis court, a pond, gazebo and flower gardens. The barn contains an internationally-known trumpet museum. The hosts' European tastes are reflected in a collection of hand-painted Bavarian furnishings and feather beds. Breakfast is served in the gazebo, or on the terrace.
Location: Twenty six miles southwest of Philadelphia.
Rates: $60-$65.
Franz & Katherine Streitwieser.
4 Rooms. 4 Private Baths. Guest phone available. TV available. Beds: KQ. Full breakfast. Jacuzzi. Sauna. Swimming pool. Conference room.

Seen in: *Today Show, Philadelphia Magazine.*

"Looks and feels like a touch of Bavaria."

Starlight

The Inn at Starlight Lake

Starlight PA 18461
(717) 798-2519

Circa 1909. Acres of woodland and meadow surround the last surviving

railroad inn on the New York, Ontario and Western lines. Originally a boarding house, the inn had its own store, church, school, blacksmith shop and creamery. Platforms first erected to accommodate tents for the summer season, were later replaced by individual cottages. The inn is situated on the 45-acre spring-fed Starlight Lake, providing summertime canoeing, swimming, fishing and sailing. (No motor boats are allowed on the lake.)

*Rates: $110-$140.
Jack & Judy McMahon.
26 Rooms. 18 Private Baths. 1 Fireplace. Guest phone available. TV available. Beds: KQDTC. MAP. Restaurant. Gourmet meals. Jacuzzi. Game room. CCs: MC VISA. Hiking, biking, cross-country skiing. Golf nearby.

Seen in: *The Philadelphia Inquirer, Newsday.*

"Delicious food and very relaxing."

Strasburg

Limestone Inn B&B

33 E Main St
Strasburg PA 17579
(717) 687-8392

Circa 1786. The Limestone Inn was built for Jacob Fouts and it later became the Headmaster's House for Strasburg Academy. Its five-bay formal Georgian plan is tempered with the medieval influence of stone work. Mrs. Kennell is often attired in period costume at breakfast. Located in the Strasburg Historic District, the house is in the National Register. The surrounding scenic Amish farmlands offer sightseeing and antique & craft shopping.

Location: Three miles from route 30.
Rates: $49-$69.
Jan & Dick Kennell.
5 Rooms. 1 Private Bath. Guest phone available. Beds: QDT. Continental-plus breakfast. CCs: AX. Horseback riding, golf, cycling.
Seen in: *Lancaster New Era, Intelligencer Journal, Strasburg Weekly.*

Valley Forge

B&B of Valley Forge

PO Box 562
Valley Forge PA 19481-0562
(215) 783-7838

Circa 1692. Venerable boxwood hedges border this 15-room Pennsylvania stone farmhouse near Valley Forge. A flagstone path leads to a long, white-pillared facade overlooking acres of fields. Breakfast is served in the summer kitchen, the oldest part of the house. A tunnel that leads from the keep, a cold storage shed, allowed the owners to escape from the British during the Revolutionary War. Later, it was part of the Underground Railroad for slaves escaping to the North. Carolyn Williams represents over 100 bed and breakfasts and country inns, all rich in history, in the Valley Forge area.

Location: One half mile on Route 202, Exit 24.
Rates: $55-$70.
Carolyn J. Williams, Director.
3 Rooms. 3 Private Baths. Guest phone in room. TV in room. Beds: KQDTC. B&B. Restaurant. Gourmet meals. Jacuzzi. Handicap access. Swimming pool. Game room. Conference room. CCs: MC VISA AX. Skiing, hunting, horses.
Seen in: *Suburban Business Review, Entertainment Magazine.*

"I'll never go back to a hotel. This is the way to get a real feel for the people and a chance to really discover the area. You often get the bonus of making lasting friends."

York

Bechtel Mansion Inn

See: East Berlin, PA

Beechmont Inn

See: Hanover, PA

Cameron Estate Inn

See: Mount Joy, PA

Spring House

See: Airville, PA

Rhode Island

Block Island

New Shoreham House
PO Box 356, Water St
Block Island RI 02807
(401) 466-2651

Circa 1890. Complete with resident ghost and crooked stairs, the New

Shoreham House maintains a fresh, newly papered and painted Victorian seaside charm. A deck faces out to sea and there's a mystical herb garden in the backyard called the Sea Star. Afternoon tea and hors d'oeuvres are served.
Rates: $35-$120.
Robert & Kathleen Schleimer.
15 Rooms. Guest phone available. TV available. Beds: DC. Continental-plus breakfast. CCs: MC VISA AX. Bicycling, white sand beaches.

The Inn at Old Harbour
Water St, Box 994
Block Island RI 02807
(401) 466-2212

Circa 1882. This three-story Victorian with its gingerbread trim and double porch attracts many photographers. Recently renovated, all the rooms are appointed with period furnishings and most have views of the Atlantic. Block Island's beaches and seaside cliffs are enjoyed by wind surfers, sailers, cyclists and those just sunning on the sand. A noted wildlife sanctuary at Sandy

Point is popular for bird-watchers.
Location: Overlooking the harbor and the Atlantic Ocean.
*Rates: $85-$140. Season: May-Oct.
Kevin & Barbara Butler.
10 Rooms. 5 Private Baths. Guest phone available. TV available. Beds: KDTC. B&B. CCs: MC VISA AX. Horseback riding, wind surfing, fishing & sailing charters, parasailing, jet skiing.

"The most romantic enchanting inn we have stayed at and what gracious innkeepers!"

Bristol

The Joseph Reynolds House
956 Hope St, PO Box 5
Bristol RI 02809
(401) 254-0230

Circa 1693. The Joseph Reynolds house is a National Historic Landmark and the oldest known

17th-century, three-story wooden structure in New England. It was the military headquarters of General Lafayette in 1778. Gradually being restored to its original elegance, guest rooms are on the second and third floors. Most of the common rooms have high ceilings and were painted to look like marble. There is a Jacobean staircase, a keeping room and a great room.
Location: Twenty-five minutes from Newport.
Rates: $55-$65.
Richard & Wendy Anderson.
7 Rooms. Guest phone available. Beds: KDT. B&B.
Seen in: *American Design, The New England Colonial.*

"Wonderful, restful week after chaos."

Jamestown

Bay Voyage Inn
Jamestown RI 02835
(401) 423-2100

Circa 1889. To reach its present waterfront location, this hotel was

floated across Narragansett Bay from Newport back in 1889. That was the easy part - the real challenge was moving the hotel across fields, stone walls, marshes and high railroad banks. In celebration of success, 30 rooms were added. Recently renovated, it sits proudly with its giant bay windows providing stunning views of Narragansett Bay and its sailboats.
*Rates: $55-$210.
Mary Beth LaMotte.
32 Rooms. 32 Private Baths. Guest phone in room. TV in room. Beds: Q. Continental breakfast. Restaurant. Gour-

met meals. Jacuzzi. Handicap access. Exercise room. Swimming pool. Conference room. CCs: MC VISA AX DC CB DS. Sailing, beaches, tennis, theaters, historical interests.
Seen in: *Newport Daily News, Rhode Island Monthly.*

Calico Cat Guest House

14 Union St
Jamestown RI 02835
(401) 423-2641

Circa 1860. This Victorian house is only 250 feet from East Harbour in Jamestown. The inn features high ceilings and spacious rooms. Children are welcome and the innkeeper stocks toys and games and will arrange for babysitting. Guests can walk to shops and restaurants and it's 10 minutes to Newport's shops and historic mansions across the bay.

*Rates: $70-$100.
Lori Lacaille.
10 Rooms. 5 Private Baths. Guest phone available. TV available. Beds: KQDTC. Continental-plus breakfast. Handicap access. Conference room. CCs: MC VISA. Water sports. Babysitting available.

"Jamestown is very quiet and the Calico Cat is like being home!"

Narragansett

Ilverthorpe Cottage

41 Robinson St
Narragansett RI 02882
(401) 789-2392

Circa 1896. Edgar & Jessie Watts built their home while Jessie was reading a Victorian novel entitled Ilverthorpe, thus the name. During the following summers they moved out of their home and provided it as a summer rental — one family returned for 30 summers. A new wraparound porch is furnished with wicker rockers. Guest rooms are filled with flowers and family antiques. The beach, restaurant and shops are a short walk away.

Rates: $50-$70. Season: May - Nov.
Chris & Jill Raggio.
4 Rooms. 2 Private Baths. Guest phone available. Beds: KDT. Full breakfast. Tennis, golf, fishing charter boats, sailboat charters.
Seen in: *Narragansett Times.*

"Informal elegance is the best way to describe Ilverthorpe Cottage. A real first class operation!"

Stone Lea

40 Newton Ave
Narragansett RI 02882
(401) 783-9546

Circa 1884. This rambling Victorian estate is situated on two magnificent

ocean front acres at the mouth of Narragansett Bay. One of a handful of summer homes built during the peak period of high society in Narragansett, it was designed by McKim, Mead & White of New York. Waves crashing along the rocky shore may be seen and heard from most guest rooms. English antiques and collections of Victorian china clocks, miniature cars, and ship models are incorporated into the decor. An antique billiard table dominates a large sitting room.

*Rates: $60-$125.
Carol & Ernie Cormier.
4 Rooms. 4 Private Baths. 1 Fireplace. Guest phone available. TV available. Beds: QDT. Full breakfast. Swimming, sailing, boating, fishing, golf, tennis.

"Very beautiful; well prepared food and helpful and concerned hosts."

Newport

Admiral Benbow Inn

93 Pelham St
Newport RI 02840
(401) 846-4256

Circa 1855. Augustus Littlfield built this home two blocks up the hill from the harbor as a boarding house. Gingerbread trim covers the porch, and an enormous bay addition displays tall arched windows. A roof deck, now available at the top of the three-story building, provides a panoramic view of Narragasett Bay. Antiques and brass or four-poster beds are featured. Some rooms have harbor views. The inn maintains a private collection of 18th and 19th century barometers.

*Rates: $55-$110.
Joan Fleming.
15 Rooms. 15 Private Baths. 1 Fireplace. Guest phone in room. TV available. Beds: QDT. Continental-plus breakfast. CCs: MC VISA AX. Sailing, swimming, cliff walk.
Seen in: *New York Magazine, Country Inns.*

"It is refreshing to find a place away from home in which one can feel at ease among familiar faces of those who are eager to make your visit as pleasant as they possibly can."

Admiral Farragut Inn

31 Clarke St
Newport RI 02840
(401) 846-4256

Circa 1702. General Rochambeau, commander of the French forces, quartered his personal staff at the Admiral Farragut house in 1776. It was enlarged to two stories in 1755. Now framed by roses and a white picket fence, this yellow clapboard house showcases colonial cove moldings and 12-over-12 paned windows. In addition to the handcrafted reproduction Shaker four-poster beds, the inn features handpainted armoires and a handpainted fireplace mantel.

*Rates: $55-$110.
Lillian Barnes.
10 Rooms. 10 Private Baths. 1 Fireplace. Guest phone in room. TV available. Beds: Q. Continental-plus breakfast. CCs: MC VISA AX. Sailing, swimming, tennis (grass courts).
Seen in: *Country Living, Country Inns.*

The Admiral Fitzroy

398 Thames St
Newport RI 02840
(401) 846-4256

Circa 1902. This four-story shingled inn, designed by architect Dudley Newton, was originally built as a nunnery. In the heart of Newport's waterfront district, it is tucked back from the street. Spirited guest rooms feature hand-painted stenciling and antique beds, such as a sleigh bed or brass bed. Fine linens include down comforters. You can reach the top-floor harbor-view rooms without hassle, because the inn has its own elevator. A gift shop is located on the lowest level.

*Rates: $65-$150.
Anita Gillia.
18 Rooms. 18 Private Baths. Guest phone in room. TV in room. Beds: QT. Full breakfast. Handicap access. Conference room. CCs: MC VISA AX. Sail-

ing, swimming, hiking, shopping.
Seen in: *Country Inns.*

Bay Voyage Inn
See: Jamestown, RI

The Brinley Victorian Inn
23 Brinley St
Newport RI 02840
(401) 849-7645

Circa 1850. This is a three-story Victorian with a mansard roof and

long porch. A cottage on the property dates from 1850. There are two parlors and a library providing a quiet haven from the bustle of the Newport wharfs. Each room is decorated with period wallpapers and furnishings. There are fresh flowers and mints on the pillows. The brick courtyard is planted with bleeding heart, peonies and miniature roses, perennials of the Victorian era.

Location: Newport Historic District.
*Rates: $85-$115. Season: May - October.
Peter Carlisle & Claire Boslem.
17 Rooms. 13 Private Baths. 6 Fireplaces. Guest phone available. TV available. Beds: D. Full breakfast. Conference room. CCs: MC VISA. Sailing, swimming.
Seen in: *New Hampshire Times, Boston Woman.*

"Ed and I had a wonderful anniversary. The Brinley is as lovely and cozy as ever! The weekend brought back lots of happy memories."

Cliff View Guest House
4 Cliff Terrace
Newport RI 02840
(401) 846-0885

Circa 1871. This charming Victorian is cited in *Architectural History of Newport, Rhode Island* as one of the "Seaview Cottages" formerly located on the Cliff Walk. It was moved half a mile to its present location on one of Newport's most

beautiful tree-lined streets. Guests can walk a short distance to the beach, along the Cliff Walk, or to the wharfs and shopping areas.

Rates: $55-$65. Season: April to Oct.
Pauline & John Shea.
4 Rooms. 2 Private Baths. Guest phone available. TV available. Beds: DTC. Continental-plus breakfast. CCs: MC VISA. Beach, shopping.

"I give it a 10! A happy house and great location."

Cliffside Inn
2 Seaview Ave
Newport RI 02840
(401) 847-1811

Circa 1870. The governor of Maryland, Thomas Swann, built this Newport summer house in the style of a Second Empire Victorian. It features a mansard roof and many bay windows. The rooms are decorated in a Victorian motif set off by ceiling moldings painted in pastel colors. The entrance to Cliff Walk is located one block from the inn.

Rates: $95-$195.
Annette King.
11 Rooms. 11 Private Baths. Guest phone in room. TV available. Beds: KQDT. Full breakfast. Jacuzzi. Conference room. CCs: MC VISA AX.

Durant Sail Loft Inn
See: New Bedford, MA

Ilverthorpe Cottage
See: Narragansett, RI

Jail House Inn
13 Marlborough St
Newport RI 02840
(401) 847-4638

Circa 1772. The owner of another B&B, the Yankee Peddler, has had a good bit of fun restoring and

renovating the old Newport Jail. Prison-striped bed coverings, and tin cups and plates for breakfast express the jail house motif. Guests can stay in the Cell Block, Maximum Security or Solitary Confinement, each on a separate level of the inn. Nevertheless, because guests pay for their time here, there are luxuries in abundance.

Rates: $55-$125.
Beth Hoban & Carol Panaccione.
22 Rooms. 22 Private Baths. Beds: Q. Continental-plus breakfast. Handicap access. CCs: MC VISA. Beaches, centrally located with plenty of parking for shopping, etc.
Seen in: *The Providence Journal.*

"I found this very relaxing and a great pleasure. Our hosts were excellent."

The Melville House
39 Clarke St
Newport RI 02840
(401) 847-0640

Circa 1750. This attractive two-story colonial once housed aides to

General Rochambeau during the American Revolution. Early American furnishings decorate the interior. There is also an unusual collection of old appliances including a cherry-pitter, mincer, and dough maker collected by Innkeeper Sam Rogers, a former household appliance designer. The inn is a pleasant walk to the waterfront and historic sites.

Location: In the heart of Newport's Historic Hill.
Rates: $40-$90. Season: March - Jan.
Rita & Sam Rogers.
7 Rooms. 5 Private Baths. 1 Fireplace. Guest phone available. Beds: DT. B&B. CCs: MC VISA AX. Swimming, boating,

fishing, tennis, golf.

"Comfortable with a quiet elegance."

The Old Dennis House

59 Washington St
Newport RI 02840
(401) 846-1324

Circa 1740. The Dennis House is situated on the oldest residential

street in Newport. Its elaborate pineapple-carved doorway is among the most attractive in Newport. It was built by a sea captain and boasts the city's only flat widow's walk. This marvelous house now provides several inviting rooms for those who want to experience historic Newport at its best.

Rates: $50-$150.
Rev. Henry G. Turnbull.
5 Rooms. 3 Private Baths. 3 Fireplaces. Guest phone available. TV in room. Continental breakfast.
Seen in: *The New York Times.*

"It was like home away from home."

The Pilgrim House

123 Spring St
Newport RI 02846
(401) 846-0040

Circa 1809. Next door to historic Trinity Church, this mansard-roofed

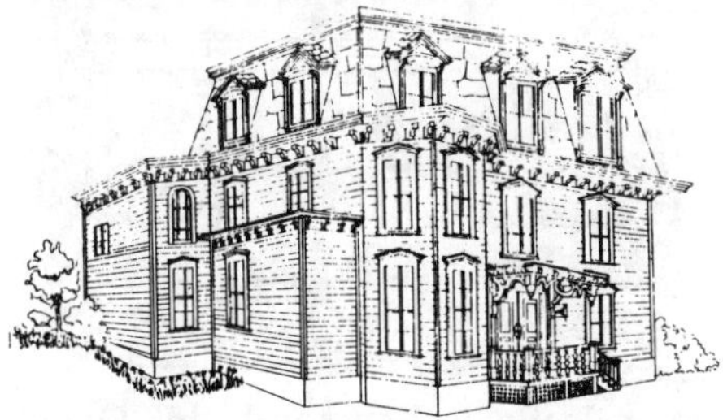

Victorian features a third-floor deck to savor expansive views of Newport Harbor, three streets away. The inn is decorated with Victorian period furnishings. A working fireplace in the living room invites a guest to browse through restaurant menus and the inn's library. Eucalyptus wreaths pleasantly scent the air when it's not filled with the fragrance of freshly baked breads and muffins.

Rates: $45-$125.
Pam & Bruce Bayuk.
10 Rooms. 8 Private Baths. Guest phone available. TV available. Beds: D. B&B. CCs: MC VISA. Sailing, tennis, golf.
Seen in: *The Times.*

Stone Lea

See: Narragansette, RI

Yankee Peddler Inn

113 Touro St
Newport RI 02840
(401) 846-1323

Circa 1830. This handsome Greek Revival inn is a five-minute walk

from the harbor. Features include a deck on the third floor where guests enjoy a view of the water. The inn is furnished in both contemporary and antique pieces. A garden and lounge are popular spots.

Rates: $60-$105.
Kitty Saleknik.
19 Rooms. 17 Private Baths. Guest phone available. TV available. Beds: QDT. Continental breakfast. Conference room. CCs: MC VISA. Sailing, hunting, sightseeing, antiquing. Afternoon tea.

"So comfortable! We return four times each year, once per season. The Yankee Peddler is our home in Newport."

Providence

Old Court B&B

144 Benefit St
Providence RI 02903
(401) 751-2002

Circa 1863. Adjacent to the historic Rhode Island Courthouse, this Italianate building originally served as an Episcopal rectory. Indoor shutters, chandeliers hanging from 12-foot ceilings and elaborate Italian marble mantelpieces provide the gracious setting for antique Victorian beds. Some rooms overlook the Capitol. Brown University, Rhode Island School of Design and downtown Providence are a short walk away.

*Rates: $105-$115.
Jon Rosenblatt.
10 Rooms. 10 Private Baths. 9 Fireplaces. Guest phone in room. TV in room. Beds: KQDT. B&B. CCs: MC VISA AX.
Seen in: *New England Monthly.*

"My only suggestion is that you do everything in your power not to change it."

Perryville Inn

See: Rehoboth, MA

Westerly

Shelter Harbor Inn

Rt 1
Westerly RI 02891
(401) 322-8883

Circa 1800. This farmhouse at the entrance to the community of Shel-

ter Harbor has been renovated and transformed to create a handsome country inn. Rooms, many with fireplaces, are in the main house, the barn and a carriage house. A third floor deck provides panoramic vistas of Block Island Sound. The dining room features local seafood and other traditional New England dishes. Nearby are secluded barrier beaches, stone fences and salt ponds.

*Rates: $72-$96.
Jim & Debbye Dey.
24 Rooms. 24 Private Baths. Full breakfast. Restaurant. Jacuzzi. Conference room. CCs: MC VISA DC. Paddle tennis, golf, tennis.

South Carolina

Aiken

Willcox Inn

100 Colleton Ave at Whiskey Rd
Aiken SC 29801
(803) 649-1377

Circa 1898. The Willcox was established by English valet Frederick Willcox and features a handsome, white columned facade. It is surrounded by horse farms and golf courses. Guest rooms often feature fireplaces, four-poster beds and reproduction furnishings in keeping with the inn's National Register status. Fine dining is presented in the Pheasant Room.

*Rates: $74-$200.
Stig Jorgensen.
30 Rooms. 30 Private Baths. 27 Fireplaces. Beds: QTC. Restaurant. Handicap access. Conference room. CCs: MC VISA. Tennis, golf, horseback riding.

"The beauty and elegance of the inn, the warmth and helpfulness of all the employees and a truly memorable dinner!"

Anderson

Evergreen Inn

1109 S Main
Anderson SC 29621
(803) 225-1109

Circa 1830. This gracious Greek Revival house features tall columns rising to the third-story pediment and a wraparound veranda. It is located on two-and-a-half acres, next to another fine National Register mansion, which houses the inn's restaurant. Scarlet's Room features a tall four-poster bed and burgundy velvet drapes. Another guest room boasts an exotic navy satin canopy bed. Antique shops and the downtown area is within walking distance.

Myrna & Peter Ryter.
7 Rooms. 6 Private Baths. 8 Fireplaces. Guest phone available. TV available. Beds: KDT. Continental-plus breakfast. Handicap access. Conference room. CCs: MC VISA AX DC. Lake nearby.
Seen in: *Travel Host Magazine, Greenville News.*

"Fantastic! Very imaginative & fun."
"Such class is rare."

Beaufort

Bay Street Inn

601 Bay St
Beaufort SC 29902
(803) 524-7720

Circa 1850. Built by one of Beaufort's major cotton planters, the

inn is a fine example of Greek Revival architecture. Cracks remain on the front steps where trunks were thrown from the upper gallery when the Union fleet approached during the Civil War. There are 14-foot ceilings, marble fireplaces, and a two-story veranda. All the rooms have unobstructed water views and fireplaces. Joel Pointsett planted the original poinsettia plants while visiting the builder.

Location: On the water in the historic district.
*Rates: $70-$80.
Gene & Kathleen Roc.
6 Rooms. 6 Private Baths. 6 Fireplaces. Guest phone available. TV available. Beds: QDW. EP. Conference room. CCs: MC VISA. Golf, tennis, ocean bathing, bikes, fishing, full library.
Seen in: *New York Times, Southern Living.*

"From the huge piano in the music room to the lush panelling of the library, the old house is an elegant reminder of bygone days of gracious Southern living."

Old Point Inn

212 New St
Beaufort SC 29902
(803) 524-3177

Circa 1898. Built by William Waterhouse as a wedding present to his

wife, Isabelle Richmond, this Queen Anne Victorian has wraparound verandas in the "Beaufort Style." Guests often rock, swing, or recline in the hammock while watching boats ply the Intercoastal Waterway. Four pillared fireplaces, pocket doors and eyelash windows are fea-

tures of the house. Located in the historic district, there is a waterfront park, a marina, restaurants, and downtown shopping nearby.
Rates: $60-$75.
Joe & Joan Carpentiere.
3 Rooms. 3 Private Baths. Guest phone available. Beds: KQDTC. Continental-plus breakfast. CCs: MC VISA. Beaches.
Seen in: *A Guide to Historic Beaufort.*
"We are still cruising on our memories of a wonderful honeymoon. It certainly had a great start staying at the Old Point Inn. We couldn't have done better."

The Rhett House Inn
1009 Craven St
Beaufort SC 29902
(803) 524-9030

Circa 1820. Most people cannot pass this stunning two-story clap-

board house without wanting to step up to the long veranda and try the hammock. Guest rooms are furnished in antiques, with quilts and fresh flowers. Many have fireplaces. Handsome gardens feature a fountain and are often the site for romantic weddings. Bicycles are available.
Location: In historic downtown.
✻✻Rates: $70-$100.
Marianne & Steve Harrison.
8 Rooms. 8 Private Baths. 3 Fireplaces. Guest phone available. Beds: QDT. Full breakfast. Handicap access. Game room. CCs: MC VISA. Bicycles, tennis, golf, sailing, swimming, horseback riding, hunting, fishing.

Bluffton

Fripp House Inn
Bridge & Boundary, Box 857
Bluffton SC 29910
(803) 757-2139

Circa 1835. Shaded by old oaks and magnolias, this antebellum low-country house was built on eight-foot high, brick pillars. The Fripp House was constructed when families of cotton and rice planters would come to the high bluff of the May River to escape the summer heat. Brick pathways meander through gardens of azaleas and camelias, providing a lush setting for the inn. There are ten fireplaces, and the house is furnished with period antiques and canopy beds. The innkeeper serves breakfast on heirloom china inherited from her great-great grandfather.
✻Rates: $48.
Grant & Dana Tuttle.
3 Rooms. 3 Private Baths. 2 Fireplaces. Guest phone in room. TV in room. Beds: QDTC. B&B. Swimming pool. CCs: MC VISA. Golf, beaches, sailing, fishing, tennis.
Seen in: *The Island Packet, Bluffton Eccentric.*
"We really enjoyed your savory breakfasts. The care that goes into your hospitality will reward you."

Charleston

1837 B&B & Tea Room
126 Wentworth St
Charleston SC 29401
(803) 723-7166

Circa 1800. Originally owned by a cotton planter, this three-story town house is situated in the historic district. Red cypress wainscoting, cornice molding and heart-of-pine floors adorn the formal parlor, while pine-beamed ceilings and red-brick walls are features of the carriage house.
Location: In the historic district.
Rates: $39-$85.
Sherri Weaver Dunn & Richard Dunn.
7 Rooms. 7 Private Baths. Guest phone available. Beds: QD. Full breakfast. CCs: MC VISA. Beach, water sports, tennis, golf.
"The room where tea is served has an open kitchen and is a perfect place to unwind." New York Times.

Barksdale House Inn
27 George St
Charleston SC 29401
(803) 577-4800

Circa 1778. George Barksdale was a wealthy Charleston planter and a member of the South Carolina House of Representatives. The Barksdale family stayed in this gracious town house when they were not at their country residence, Younghall Plantation. Lavish interiors of the three stories include Scalamandre borders and 18th-and 19th-century fabrics. Gas-log fireplaces framed by marbelized or stenciled slate mantels are beside almost every bed.
✻Rates: $75-$150.
Suzanne W. Chesnut.
10 Rooms. 10 Private Baths. 6 Fireplaces. Guest phone in room. TV in room. Beds: KQD. Continental breakfast. Jacuzzi. CCs: MC VISA. Beaches & water sports within 20 miles. Bicycles available to rent.

Cannonboro Inn
184 Ashley Ave
Charleston SC 29403
(803) 723-8572

Circa 1840. The city of Charleston considered the Cannonboro ir-

replaceable because of its semi-circular two-story, columned piazzas. Shaded by crepe myrtles and palmettos, the inn is also air-conditioned. Rooms are appointed with reproduction antiques such as four-poster and rice beds.
✻Rates: $69-$89.
Robert Warley & James Hare.
6 Rooms. 4 Private Baths. Guest phone available. TV in room. Beds: QDC. Full breakfast. CCs: VISA DS. Water sports, tennis, golf.
Seen in: *Chicago Sun-Times.*
"Thanks for your warm hospitality."

Charleston Society B&B
84 Murray Blvd
Charleston SC 29401
(803) 723-4948

Circa 1800. All the homes represented by this reservation service are located in the Charleston Historic District and include pre-

Revolutionary, post-Revolutionary and antebellum homes. Handsome interiors include period furniture and all homes have air-conditioning and private baths.
Location: Historic district.
Rates: $50-$150.
Eleanor Rogers.
15 Rooms. 15 Private Baths. Guest phone available. TV available. Beds: QTC. Continental breakfast.

Elliott House Inn
78 Queen St
Charleston SC 29401
(803) 723-1855

Circa 1886. Located in the center of the Charleston Historic District, the

Elliott House was once a private single home. A renovation has added a carriage house with shutters and flower boxes. Canopy beds are numerous as are balconies overlooking the garden.
*Rates: $95-$125.
26 Rooms. 26 Private Baths. Guest phone in room. TV in room. Beds: KQDT. Continental breakfast. Jacuzzi. CCs: MC VISA. Complimentary bicycles.
Seen in: *Innsider, Southern Living, Gourmet, Charlotte Observer.*

Guilds Inn
See: Mt. Pleasant, SC

Hayne House
30 King St
Charleston SC 29401
(803) 577-2633

Circa 1755. Located one block from the Battery, this handsome clap-

board house has an 1840 addition and is surrounded by a wrought iron garden fence. It was built three stories tall to capture the harbor breese. The inn is furnished in antiques.
Rates: $55-$75.
Ben Chapman.
4 Rooms. 4 Private Baths. Guest phone available. TV available. Beds: DT. B&B. Tennis, golf, beach.

"A fantasy realized. What a wonderful gift of hospitality."

Historic Charleston B&B
43 Legare St
Charleston SC 29401
(803) 722-6606

Circa 1713. Listings in this reservation service include flamboyant Victorian mansions, narrow "single houses", pre-Revolutionary carriage houses and rooms overlooking the Battery. The oldest home open to guests was built in 1713. Some hosts are from old Charleston families that go back several generations. Family heirlooms, period antiques and silver tea service are often featured.
Location: Historic district.
Rates: $65-$125.
Charlotte Fairey.
65 Rooms. 65 Private Baths. Beds: KQTC. Continental-plus breakfast. Jacuzzi. Swimming pool. CCs: MC VISA. Swimming, bicycling.
Seen in: *The New York Times, Southern Living.*

John Rutledge House Inn
116 Broad St
Charleston SC 29401
(803) 723-7999 (800) 845-6119

Circa 1763. John Rutledge, first governor of South Carolina, Supreme Court Justice, and author and signer of the Constitution of the United States wrote first drafts of the document in the stately ballroom of his Charleston home. In 1791 George Washington dined in this same room. Both men would be amazed by the house's recent restoration which includes two lavish suites with elaborately carved Italian marble fireplaces, personal refrigerators, jacuzzi baths, air conditioning, and televisions along with fine antiques and reproductions. Exterior ironwork on the house was designed in the 19th century and features Palmetto trees and American eagles to honor Mr. Rutledge's service to the state and country.
*Rates: $125-$195.
Richard Widman.
19 Rooms. 19 Private Baths. 11 Fireplaces. Guest phone in room. TV in room. Beds: KQD. B&B. Jacuzzi. Handicap access. CCs: MC VISA AX. Historic tours, running trail, bicycling, golf, tennis, water sports.
Seen in: *Innsider.*

"200 years of American history in two nights; first class accommodations, great staff. John Rutledge should've had it so good!"

Kings Courtyard Inn
198 King St
Charleston SC 29401
(803) 723-7000 (800) 845-6119

Circa 1853. Architect Francis D. Lee designed this three-story build-

ing in the Greek Revival style with unusual touches of Egyptian detail. As Charleston's oldest structure originally built as an inn, it catered to plantation owners. The atmosphere has been authentically restored and some rooms have fireplaces, canopied beds and views of the two inner courtyards or the garden.
Location: In the historic district.
*Rates: $80-$120.
Laura Fox.
34 Rooms. 34 Private Baths. 9 Fireplaces. Guest phone in room. TV in room. Beds: KQT. Continental-plus breakfast. Jacuzzi. Handicap access. Conference room. CCs: MC VISA.

The Kitchen House

126 Tradd St
Charleston SC 29401
(803) 577-6362

Circa 1732. This elegantly restored and refurbished Georgian manor

was once the home of Dr. Peter Fayssoux, surgeon-general to the Continental army during the Revolutionary War. In the double drawing room an Adams-style mantel features molded swags and sunburst patterns. English antiques and flowered chintz draperies are enhanced by finely crafted moldings and exposed interior corner posts. In the walled garden colonial herbs grow just beyond the shade of an enormous magnolia tree. Guest rooms are in the separate Kitchen House with its four original fireplaces.

*Rates: $75-$135.
Lois Evans.
3 Rooms. 3 Private Baths. 4 Fireplaces. Guest phone in room. TV in room. Beds: QD. Full breakfast. CCs: MC VISA AX. Beach nearby.
Seen in: *New York Times, Colonial Homes.*

"By all comparisons, one of the very best."

Rutledge Museum Guest House

114 Rutledge Ave
Charleston SC 29401
(803) 722-7551

Circa 1889. This Victorian house is situated in the Charleston Historic District. It is distinquished by round decorative porches, columns and gingerbread. With 10-foot tall doors, the rooms are decorated in a quaint, antique decor and all are air conditioned. The focal point of this bed and breakfast is the front porch.

Rates: $35-$65.
B.J., Mike, Jean.
12 Rooms. 5 Private Baths. 10 Fireplaces. Guest phone available. TV in room. Beds: QD. Continental breakfast. Handicap access. Boat and carriage rides, beaches, plantations.

"Your friendliness and willingness to help is what they mean by 'southern hospitality.'"

Sword Gate Inn

111 Tradd St
Charleston SC 29401
(803) 723-8518

Circa 1800. This stately three-story inn is framed by a cobbled court-

yard filled with magnolia trees, jasmine and azalea bushes. The elegantly appointed interiors make it easy to visualize formally attired guests passing through a reception line when the house served as the British consulate. There is a finely carved Italian Carrara marble fireplace and two enormous rococo Revival mirrors in the ballroom. Some of the guest rooms are furnished with canopied beds and have fireplaces.

Location: In the historic district.
Rates: $89-$125.
Walter & Amanda Barton.
6 Rooms. 6 Private Baths. Beds: QD. Full breakfast. Conference room. CCs: MC VISA. Bicycles, sailing, boating, fishing.
Seen in: *Business Week.*

"As always, your hospitality is second to none."

Two Meeting Street Inn

2 Meeting St
Charleston SC 29401
(803) 723-7322

Circa 1890. Located directly on the Battery, horses and carriages carry visitors past the inn, perhaps the most photographed in Charleston. In the Queen Anne style, this Victorian has an unusual veranda graced by several ornate arches. The same family has owned and managed the inn since 1946 with no

lapse in gracious southern hospitality. Among the elegant amenities are original Tiffany stained-glass windows, English oak paneling and exquisite collections of silver and antiques. Although suffering considerable damage from hurricane Hugo in 1989, the inn reopened with an additional floor and much redecorating.

Location: On the Battery.
Rates: $95-$125.
Karen B. Spell.
9 Rooms. 9 Private Baths. Guest phone available. TV available. Beds: QD. Continental breakfast. Water sports, beaches, tennis.
Seen in: *Innsider, Southern Bride.*

"A magnificent Queen Anne mansion." Southern Bride.

Vendue Inn

19 Vendue Range
Charleston SC 29401
(803) 577-7970

Circa 1864. Built as a warehouse in the French Quarter, the inn is one short block from the historic waterfront. The bright lobby features fans and wicker furniture, and latticework screens, leather chairs, and writing tables fill the reading room. Afternoon wine and cheese and turn-down service are special features.

Location: In the historic district and near city market.
*Rates: $75-$145.
Evelyn & Morton Needle.
33 Rooms. 33 Private Baths. 8 Fireplaces. Guest phone in room. TV in room. Beds: KQDC. Continental-plus breakfast. Restaurant. Gourmet meals. Jacuzzi. CCs: MC VISA AX. Bicycles, tennis, golf.
Seen in: *Southern Living, Bon Appetit.*

"Delightful. Excellent service."

Columbia

Claussen's Inn
2003 Green St
Columbia SC 29205
(800) 622-3382

Circa 1928. The Claussen bakery building, a 25,000-square-foot brick building, has been renovated to accommodate 29 king-size guest rooms. The three-story atrium features skylights and a fountain. All the guest rooms contain traditional furnishings and some feature four-poster beds.

Location: In Five Points adjacent to the University.
✻Rates: $75-$95.
Dan Vance.
29 Rooms. 29 Private Baths. Guest phone in room. Beds: KQD. Continental breakfast. Jacuzzi. Handicap access. Conference room. CCs: MC VISA AX.
Seen in: *The State.*

Hilton Head

Fripp House Inn
See: Bluffton, SC

Mt Pleasant

Guilds Inn
101 Pitt St
Mt Pleasant SC 29464
(803) 881-0510

Circa 1888. The Guilds Inn is located six miles from Charleston in a

building that was purchased by the innkeeper's grandfather. The family businesses conducted here have included a hardware store and grocery. The house has been restored and appointed in 18th-century reproduction furnishings. Supper at Seven is the dining room, with gleaming mahogany tables, sterling silver, and gold-rimmed china. Each table has an old-fashioned bell pull.

✻Rates: $85-$125.
John & Amy Malik.
6 Rooms. 6 Private Baths. Guest phone in room. TV available. Beds: Q. EP. Restaurant. Jacuzzi. Conference room. CCs: MC VISA AX. Bicycles, tennis, both free.
Seen in: *Travelhost, Charleston News and Courier.*

"Supper at Seven is the most outstanding restaurant I have ever visited in South Carolina." Ruth Achermann, *Travelhost.*

Pendleton

Liberty Hall Inn
Pendleton SC 29670
(803) 646-7500

Circa 1840. On four acres of woods, lawns and gardens, this house is noted for the two-story columned verandas that stretch across the front. An elegant foyer with a polished staircase greets guests as they enter the inn. All the rooms are furnished with antiques

and original art, and there are wide-pine floorboards throughout. The Pendleton Historic District is one of the largest in the National Register and a short stroll brings guests to the town square.

Location: In the historic district.
✻Rates: $57-$67.
Tom & Susan Jonas.
10 Rooms. 10 Private Baths. Guest phone available. Beds: KDT. Continental-plus breakfast. Restaurant. Conference room. CCs: MC VISA AX DC CB DS.
Seen in: *Country Home, Anderson Independent-Mail.*

"Elegant surroundings and excellent food! Best job of innkeeping we've seen."

South Dakota

Canova

B&B at Skoglund Farm

Rt 1 Box 45
Canova SD 57321
(605) 247-3445

Circa 1927. This is a working farm on the South Dakota prairie. Ostriches and peacocks stroll around the farm along with cattle, chickens and horses. Guests can ride horses and enjoy an evening meal with the family.

Location: Southeast South Dakota.
*Rates: $25.
Alden & Delores.
6 Rooms. Guest phone available. TV available. Beds: QDT. Full breakfast. Horseback riding, buggy rides.

"Thanks for the down home hospitality and good food."

Tennessee

Chattanooga

Gordon-Lee Mansion B&B

See: Chickamauga, GA

Gatlinburg

Buckhorn Inn

Rt 3 Box 393
Gatlinburg TN 37738
(615) 436-4668

Circa 1937. Set high on a hilltop, Buckhorn is surrounded by more

than 30 acres of woodlands and green lawns. There are inspiring mountain views and a spring-fed lake on the grounds. Paintings by area artists enhance the antique-filled guest rooms, most with working fireplaces.

Location: One mile from the Great Smoky Mountains National Park.
Rates: $55-$95.
John & Connie Burns.
10 Rooms. 10 Private Baths. 5 Fireplaces. Guest phone available. TV available. Beds: KQDT. B&B. Gourmet meals. Handicap access. Conference room. Ski area nearby.
Seen in: *The Atlanta Journal and Constitution, Country.*

The Graustein Inn

See: Knoxville, TN

Greeneville

Big Spring Inn

315 N Main St
Greeneville TN 37743
(615) 638-2917

Circa 1905. This three-story brick manor house has huge porches, leaded and stained glass windows, a grand entrance hall and an upstairs library. Original wallpaper illustrating a park with willow trees and men, women and children strolling by is still in the dining room. The dining room is also graced with a 1790 Hepplewhite table. The house is in the Main Street Historical District of Greenville. The smallest state in the United States, Franklin, was formed here when local pioneers seceded from North Carolina. It later became a part of Tennessee, having lasted only three years.

*Rates: $55-$75.
Jeanne Driese & Cheryl Van Dyck.
5 Rooms. 3 Private Baths. TV available. Beds: KT. B&B. Swimming pool. Conference room. CCs: MC VISA AX.
Seen in: *Kingsport Times News.*

"We couldn't have chosen any place more perfect."

Knoxville

The Graustein Inn

8300 Nubbin Ridge Rd
Knoxville TN 37923
(615) 690-7007

Circa 1975. This enchanting European chateau, nestled on 20 wooded acres at the end of a quarter-mile driveway, is a reproduction of an 1870 German inn. Old World craftsmen used historic building methods and materials including 200 tons of limestone to create this gray stone estate. Tongue and groove walnut walls, and a circular three-story central staircase are features of the inn. The Great Smoky Mountain National Park is 30 minutes away.

Location: Twenty minutes west of downtown.
*Rates: $55-$98.
Darlene & Jim Lara, Vanessa Gwin.
5 Rooms. 3 Private Baths. 1 Fireplace. Guest phone available. TV available. Beds: QDT. B&B. Restaurant. Gourmet meals. Conference room. CCs: MC VISA AX. Hiking, water skiing.
Seen in: *Knoxville News.*

"Almost overwhelmingly wonderful." Vicki Davis, *Huntsville Times.*

Memphis

Lowenstein-Long House

217 N Waldran-1084 Poplar
Memphis TN 38105
(901) 527-7174

Circa 1899. Department store owner Abraham Lowenstein built this Victorian mansion and it later

became the Beethoven Music Club. In the Forties it was a boarding house, the Elizabeth Club for Girls, in the days before young ladies had their own apartments.

Rates: $50.
Samantha & Walter Long.
4 Rooms. 4 Private Baths. 4 Fireplaces. Guest phone available. TV in room. Beds: Q. Continental-plus breakfast. Conference room. CCs: MC VISA AX.

"We found it just lovely and enjoyed our stay very much."

Monteagle

Edgeworth Inn
PO Box 365
Monteagle TN 37356
(615) 924-2669

Circa 1896. Edgeworth is a three-story pale yellow Victorian situated on the Monteagle Assembly grounds, formed to provide a 19th

century program of lectures and entertainment in a resort setting (a chatauqua). Wide verandas are filled with white wicker furnishings and breezy hammocks. Guest rooms are decorated in floral prints with brass and iron beds. There are 96 acres of rolling hills with creeks and waterfalls, natural caves and scenic overlooks adjacent to the South Cumberland State Recreation Area.

Rates: $60-$90.
Merrily Teasley.
8 Rooms. 8 Private Baths. 1 Fireplace. Guest phone available. TV available. Beds: KDT. B&B. Swimming, hiking.
Seen in: *Country Inns.*

"Leaving totally rejuvenated."

Rogersville

Hale Springs Inn
110 W Main St
Rogersville TN 37857
(615) 272-5171

Circa 1824. On the town square, this is the oldest continually operating inn in the state. Presidents Andrew Jackson, James Polk, and Andrew Johnson stayed here. Mc-

Kinney Tavern, as it was known then, was Union headquarters during the Civil War. Canopy beds, working fireplaces, and an evening meal by candlelight in the elegant dining room all make for a romantic stay.

Location: Near Gatlinburg.
Rates: $35-$60.
Ed Pace, Capt. & Mrs. Carl Netherland-Brown.
10 Rooms. 10 Private Baths. 9 Fireplaces. Guest phone available. TV in room. Beds: KQT. EP. Restaurant. CCs: MC VISA AX. Swimming, tennis, golf.
Seen in: *The Miami Herald.*

Rugby

Newbury House at Historic Rugby
Hwy 52, PO Box 8
Rugby TN 37733
(615) 628-2430

Circa 1880. Mansard-roofed Newbury House first lodged visitors to

this English village when author and social reformer Thomas Huges, founded Rugby. Filled with authentic Victorian antiques, the inn includes some furnishings that are original to the colony. There is also a restored three-bedroom cottage on the property.

Rates: $50-$60.
Historic Rugby Staff.
5 Rooms. 3 Private Baths. 1 Fireplace. Guest phone available. Beds: D. Restaurant. Conference room. CCs: MC VISA. Hiking, white water rafting, canoeing.
Seen in: *New York Times, Americana, USA Weekend, The Tennessean.*

Sewanee

Edgeworth Inn
See: Monteagle, TN

Texas

Austin

The McCallum House

613 W 32nd
Austin TX 78705
(512) 451-6744

Circa 1907. This two-story Princess Anne Victorian was built by school

superintendent A.N. McCallum and designed by his wife Jane. As Mrs. McCallum raised her five children she assumed a leadership position in the women's suffrage movement and formed the "Petticoat Lobby" advancing human service reforms in Texas. In 1926 she became secretary of state for Texas. In addition to several rooms in the main house with private porches, there are two suites with kitchens. It is an eight block walk to the University of Texas.

Rates: $60-$70.
Nancy & Roger Danley.
5 Rooms. 5 Private Baths. Guest phone in room. TV available. Beds: QDT. Full breakfast. CCs: MC VISA. State Capitol Building, LBJ Library.
Seen in: *Austin American Statesman.*

"What a special home and history. It is lucky that you are bringing it back to life!"

Southard House

908 Blanco
Austin TX 78703
(512) 474-4731

Circa 1900. This house, an Austin historic landmark, originally had a

single story but was raised to accommodate an additional level at the turn of the century. There is an upper and lower parlor and 11-foot ceilings provide a background for antiques and paintings. A gazebo, porch and deck are popular spots. The University of Texas and the Capitol are a mile and a half away.

Location: Downtown.
*Rates: $49-$98.
The Southards.
5 Rooms. 5 Private Baths. 1 Fireplace. Guest phone available. TV available. Beds: QD. Continental-plus breakfast.

"A memory to be long cherished. We especially enjoyed the home atmosphere and the lovely breakfasts in the garden."

Dallas

B&B Texas Style

4224 W Red Bird Ln
Dallas TX 75237
(214) 298-8586

Circa 1925. The only state-wide bed and breakfast reservation service in Texas, this agency features more than 100 inspected homes throughout the state. One home in Dallas, for instance, is a large, Frank Lloyd Wright style, prairie home in an area of restored mansions. Its three floors include a music room and an upstairs sunroom. A historic marker notes its significance.

Rates: $35-$85.
2 Rooms. Beds: KD. Continental breakfast. Swimming pool. CCs: MC VISA. Each host home is individual and has special features.
Seen in: *Southern Bride.*

Raphael House

See: Ennis, TX

Tarlton House of 1895

See: Hillsboro, TX

El Paso

The Lodge

See: Cloudcroft, NM

Ennis

Raphael House

500 W Ennis Ave
Ennis TX 75119
(214) 875-1555

Circa 1906. Built and owned by the Raphael family for 82 years, this Greek Revival house is highlighted with a three-story porch. Century-old pecan trees border a gracious English Garden. Inside, the open foyer flows to a parlor, separated only by massive, polished, clear pine Doric columns. There are gleaming heart pine floors

throughout and many original furnishings. Spacious bedchambers include handsome antique bedsteads and canopied beds, all with down comforters. A carriage pulled by Belgian horses stops to pick up riders across the street from the inn.
*Rates: $55-$85.
Danna K. Cody.
6 Rooms. 6 Private Baths. Guest phone available. TV available. Beds: KQD. Full breakfast. Gourmet meals. Conference room. CCs: MC VISA. Water sports, carriage rides, fishing, nature trails.
Seen in: *Dallas Times Herald.*

"This house has been refurbished to a truly magnificent standard by a perfectionist."

Fort Davis

Sutler's Limpia Hotel
PO Box 822
Fort Davis TX 79734
(915) 426-3237

Circa 1912. Located on the town square, this hotel was constructed of pink limestone quarried nearby. It was restored in 1978. The parlor features a fireplace and over-stuffed furniture. All the guest rooms have period oak furnishings. High tin ceilings are found throughout. There is a sun porch and veranda, both with views of the mountains.
Rates: $42-$60.
Joan Stocks Nobles.
20 Rooms. 20 Private Baths. Guest phone available. TV in room. Beds: DT. Restaurant. CCs: MC VISA AX.
Seen in: *San Angelo Standard Times, Texas Monthly.*

"Not many like this one left. Great."

Fredericksburg

Country Cottage Inn
405 E Main St
Fredericksburg TX 78624
(512) 997-8549

Circa 1850. This beautifully preserved house was built by black-

smith and cutler Frederick Kiehne. With two-foot-thick walls, it was the first two-story limestone house in town. The Country Cottage holds a collection of Texas primitives and German country antiques, accentuated by Laura Ashley linens. Some of the baths include whirlpool tubs.
*Rates: $65-$95.
Jeffery Webb, Jean & Mike Sudderth.
5 Rooms. 5 Private Baths. 1 Fireplace. Guest phone in room. TV available. Beds: KC. Continental-plus breakfast. Jacuzzi. CCs: MC. Front porch swings, water sports.
Seen in: *Weekend Getaway, Dallas Morning News.*

"A step back in time in 1850 style."

Galveston Island

Gilded Thistle B&B
1805 Broadway
Galveston Island TX 77550
(713) 763-0194

Circa 1893. The Gilded Thistle is a fanciful Victorian with a double bay

and porches overlooking flower gardens. A gracious antique-filled parlor is dominated by a handsome fireplace and floor-to-ceiling windows. Wine and cheese is served in the evening.
Rates: $100-$135. Season: Jan. - Dec.
Helen L. Hanemann.
3 Rooms. 1 Private Bath. Guest phone available. TV in room. Beds: D. B&B. CCs: MC VISA.
Seen in: *House Beautiful, New York Times, Texas Monthly, PM Magazine.*

"Best B&B in Texas!"

Hillsboro

Tarlton House of 1895
211 N Pleasant St
Hillsboro TX 76645
(817) 582-7216

Circa 1895. Steeply pitched gables punctuate the roof line of this light

blue and white Queen Anne Victorian. A veranda curves around the front and side. The entrance door contains 123 pieces of beveled glass, and when the morning sunlight filters through, rainbows sparkle over the carved oak stairway and woodwork of the interior. There are seven coal fireplaces and twelve-foot ceilings. Original English antiques collected by the Rhoads, Girard, Goodwin, Wharton & Stockdill families of the inn's owners fill its 21 rooms.
*Rates: $68-$86.
Jean & Rudy Rhoads.
9 Rooms. 7 Private Baths. 3 Fireplaces. Guest phone available. TV in room. Beds: KQD. Full breakfast. Conference room. CCs: MC VISA AX. Water sports, tennis, golf, fishing.
Seen in: *Dallas Morning News, Dallas Downtowner.*

"We appreciated your warm hospitality, the beauty of your home and all that delicious food!"

Houston

Sara's B&B Inn
941 Heights Blvd
Houston TX 77008
(713) 868-1130

Circa 1898. This mauve and white, gingerbread Victorian is located in the Houston Heights, one of the first planned suburbs in Texas. A three-

story stairway winds up to a cupola and there are handsome bay windows and a turret. Antiques fill the rooms, named after Texas cities.
Location: Four miles from downtown.
Rates: $46-$96.
Donna & Tillman Arledge.
10 Rooms. 1 Private Bath. Guest phone available. TV available. Beds: KQDTC. Continental breakfast. Jacuzzi. CCs: MC VISA AX DC CB. Bicycles, jogging, walking.
Seen in: *Houston Chronicle.*

Jefferson

Hotel Jefferson
124 Austin St
Jefferson TX 75657
(214) 665-2631

Circa 1851. This building was originally a cotton warehouse and

was on the river front when Jefferson was an inland port. Victorian homes, antique shops, museums, and restaurants are nearby.
Rates: $45-$75.
J.B. Terry.
23 Rooms. 23 Private Baths. Guest phone available. TV in room. Beds: KQD. Restaurant. CCs: MC VISA AX DS.

McKay House
306 E Delta St
Jefferson TX 75657
(214) 665-7322 (214) 348-1929

Circa 1851. Both Lady Bird Johnson and Alex Haley have enjoyed the gracious southern

hospitality offered at the McKay House. Framed by a Williamsburg-style picket fence, the Greek Revival cottage features a pillared front porch. Heart-of-pine floors and 14-foot ceilings set off a collection of American and Scottish antiques. Cheese biscuits, strawberry bread and cream cheese, and shirred eggs are served on vintage china. Victorian nightshirts and gowns await guests in each of the bed chambers.
*Rates: $60-$85.
Peggy & Tom Taylor.
6 Rooms. 4 Private Baths. 6 Fireplaces. Guest phone available. Beds: D. B&B. CCs: MC VISA. Mule drawn buggy, trolley, train, museum.
Seen in: *Southern Accents, The Dallas Morning News.*

"The facilities of the McKay House are exceeded only by the service and dedication of the owners."

Marshall

Three Oaks
609 N Washington
Marshall TX 75670
(214) 938-6123

Circa 1895. Three towering bur oaks shade the lawn of this Colonial Revival house with a widow's walk atop a sculptured tin roof. A bay window and six-over-six windows attest to Queen Anne accents. Tall columns divide the entrance hall and music rooms highlighting the 13-foot ceilings. Beveled, cut-glass French doors open from the parlor to a conservatory. The house is furnished with period oak and walnut furnishings. Three Oaks is a seven-room suite designed for one family, a couple or a corporate group.
Rates: $65.
Sandra & Bob McCoy.
1 Room. 1 Private Bath. 1 Fireplace. Guest phone in room. TV in room. Beds: QD. B&B. Horseback riding, skiing, water sports, golf, tennis, museums, antique shops.

"The house is magnificent — with hosts to match!!"

Nacogdoches

The Wade House
See: San Augustine, TX

San Augustine

The Wade House
202 E Livingston St
San Augustine TX 75972
(409) 275-5489 (409) 275-2553

Circa 1940. The Wade House is a Mt. Vernon-style red brick house located two blocks from the old courthouse square. Guest rooms, decorated in a mix of contemporary and antique furnishings, are cooled by ceiling fans and air conditioning.
Rates: $40-$80.
Julia & Nelsyn Wade.
5 Rooms. 3 Private Baths. Guest phone available. Beds: KQD. B&B. Handicap access. Conference room. CCs: MC VISA. Golf nearby.
Seen in: *San Augustine Tribune.*

"The house is one of the most beautiful in the area. Each room is decorated to the utmost excellence."

Stephenville

The Oxford House
563 N Graham
Stephenville TX 76401
(817) 965-6885

Circa 1898. A $3,000 lawyer's fee provided funds for construction of

the Oxford House, and the silver was brought to town in a buckboard by W. J. Oxford, Esq. The house was built of cypress with porches three-quarters of the way around. Hand-turned gingerbread trim and a carved ridgerow are special features.
Rates: $60-$80.
Paula & Bill Oxford.
4 Rooms. 4 Private Baths. Guest phone available. TV available. Beds: QD. CCs: MC VISA. Antiquing.

"A perfect evening of serenity sitting on the front porch with such kind hosts."

Utah

Midway

The Homestead

700 N Homestead Dr
Midway UT 84049
(801) 654-1102 (800) 327-7220

Circa 1886. Originally Simon Schneitter built this two-story brick house for his parents and the family soon began taking in guests when travelers began to appreciate the site's mineral springs. In the Fifties it was redeveloped as the Homestead. The Virginia House is the most historic part of the lodge.

*Rates: $59-$165.
Britt Mathwich.
92 Rooms. 92 Private Baths. 8 Fireplaces. Guest phone in room. TV in room. Beds: KQTC. MAP. Restaurant. Gourmet meals. Jacuzzi. Sauna. Handicap access. Swimming pool. Conference room. CCs: MC VISA AX DS. Golf, hot air ballooning, tennis, horseback riding, cross-country skiing, sleigh & hay rides, trout fishing, mountain bikes, snowmobiling. Kid camp.
Seen in: *Express-News, Country Inns.*

"The Homestead is the most romantic place Nicole and I have ever been."

Park City

The Homestead

See: Midway, UT

The Old Miners' Lodge A B&B Inn

615 Woodside Ave, PO Box 2639
Park City UT 84060-2639
(801) 645-8068

Circa 1893. This was originally established as a miners' boarding house by E. P. Ferry, owner of the Woodside-Norfolk silver mines. A two-story Victorian with western flavor, the lodge is a significant structure in the Park City National

Historic District. Just on the edge of the woods beyond the house is a deck and a steaming hot tub.

Location: In the historic district.
*Rates: $40-$165.
Jeff Sadowsky, Susan Wynne & Hugh Daniels.
10 Rooms. 10 Private Baths. 1 Fireplace. Guest phone available. Beds: KQDTC. B&B. Gourmet meals. Jacuzzi. Conference room. CCs: MC VISA AX DS. Downhill & cross-country skiing, golf, tennis, ice skating, hiking.
Seen in: *Boston Herald, Los Angeles Times.*

"This is the creme de la creme. The most wonderful place I have stayed at bar none including ski country in the U.S. and Europe."

Washington School Inn

544 Park Ave, PO Box 536
Park City UT 84060
(801) 649-3800 (800) 824-1672

Circa 1889. Made of local limestone, this inn was the former school house for Park City children. With its classic belltower, the four-story building is listed in the National Register. The inn is noted for its luxuriously appointed guest rooms. An inviting jacuzzi and sauna are on the property.

Location: Park City Historic District.

*Rates: $75-$225.
Faye Evans & Delphine Covington.
15 Rooms. 15 Private Baths. 2 Fireplaces. Guest phone in room. TV available. Beds: KQT. Continental-plus breakfast. Jacuzzi. Sauna. Conference room. CCs: MC VISA AX.

Provo

The Homestead

See: Midway, UT

Salt Lake City

Brigham Street Inn

1135 E South Temple
Salt Lake City UT 84102
(801) 364-4461

Circa 1896. This turretted Victorian is one of many historic mansions

that dot South Temple Street (formerly Brigham Street). The for-

mal dining room features golden oak woodwork and a fireplace. With skylights, fireplaces or perhaps a jacuzzi, each of the nine rooms was created by a different designer for a showcase benefit for the Utah Heritage Foundation. The American Institute of Architects and several historic associations have presented the inn with architectural awards. The inn also holds a Triple A four-diamond award.
*Rates: $65-$140.
Nancy & John Pace.
9 Rooms. 9 Private Baths. 5 Fireplaces. Beds: QWC. Continental-plus breakfast. Jacuzzi. CCs: MC VISA. 40 minutes from 5 major ski areas.
Seen in: *Innsider.*

"Your managers, pleasant, courteous, and helpful, uphold the high standards exemplified throughout your elegantly designed inn."

The Homestead
See: Midway, UT

The Spruces B&B
6151 S 900 E
Salt Lake City UT 84121
(801) 268-8762

Circa 1903. This Gothic Victorian was built as a residence for cabinet-maker Martin Gunnerson and his family. It is set amidst 16 tall spruce trees transplanted in 1915 from Big Cottonwood Canyon. The house is decorated with folk art and south-western touches. The Cellar Suite includes a hydrobath and children

enjoy its fruit cellar bedroom. A quarter horse breeding farm is adjacent.
*Rates: $40-$80.
Glen & Lisa Dutton.
7 Rooms. 4 Private Baths. Beds: QDT. Continental-plus breakfast. Jacuzzi. Conference room. CCs: MC VISA. Skiing.

"We have never had a more peaceful, serene business trip. Thank you for your hospitality."

St George

Greene Gate Village Historic B&B Inn
76 W Tabernacle
St George UT 84770
(801) 628-6999

Circa 1876. This is a cluster of four restored pioneer homes all located within one block. The Bentley House has an elegant Victorian decor while the Supply Depot is decorated in a style reflective of its origin as a shop for wagoners on their way to California. The Orson Pratt house and the Carriage House are other choices, all carefully restored.
*Rates: $35-$75.
Mark & Barbara Greene.
15 Rooms. 12 Private Baths. 9 Fireplaces. Guest phone in room. TV in room. Beds: KQDTWC. B&B. Gourmet meals. Jacuzzi. Handicap access. Swimming pool. Conference room. CCs: MC VISA AX. Golf, hiking, boating, tennis.
Seen in: *Spectrum.*

"You not only provided me with rest, comfort and wonderful food, but you fed my soul."

Seven Wives Inn
217 N 100 W
St George UT 84770
(801) 628-3737

Circa 1873. The inn is named after the innkeeper's great-grandfather Benjamin Johnson who served Joseph Smith, founder of the Mormon Church, as private secretary. Mr. Johnson had seven wives. The Melissa room was named after his first wife and it features a fireplace and an oak-rimmed tin bathtub. The attic of the house, concealed by a secret door, is thought to have been a refuge for polygamists. It is now the Jane room and has a skylight and stenciling.
**Rates: $35-$65.
Donna & Jay Curtis; Alison & Jon Bowcutt.
13 Rooms. 13 Private Baths. 6 Fireplaces. Guest phone available. Beds: QTC. Full breakfast. Jacuzzi. Handicap access. Swimming pool. Conference room. CCs: MC VISA AX DS. Golf, horseback riding. , tennis.
Seen in: *Salt Lake Tribune.*

"This was great! We want to return."

Vermont

Arlington

The Arlington Inn
Historic Rt 7A
Arlington VT 05250
(802) 375-6532

Circa 1840. The Arlington Inn is one of Vermont's finest examples of

Greek Revival architecture. Set on lushly landscaped grounds, the inn boasts elegantly appointed guest rooms filled with period antiques. Norman Rockwell once used the carriage house as a studio.

Location: Intersection of Route 313.
*Rates: $70-$150.
Paul & Madeline Kruzel.
13 Rooms. 13 Private Baths. 1 Fireplace. Guest phone available. TV available. Beds: QDT. B&B. Game room. Conference room. CCs: MC VISA AX. Skiing, hiking, biking, canoeing, antiqueing.
Seen in: *New York, Bon Appetit.*

"What a romantic place and such outrageous food!!"

Hill Farm Inn
RR 2 Box 2015
Arlington VT 05250
(802) 375-2269

Circa 1790. One of Vermont's original land grant farmsteads, Hill Farm Inn has welcomed guests since 1905 when the widow Mettie Hill opened her home to summer vacationers. One section of the house was hauled by 40 yoke of oxen to its present location. The

farm has recently benefited from a community conservancy group's efforts to save it from subdivision.

Location: One half mile from Historic Route 7A.
*❀Rates: $65-$90.
George & Joanne Hardy.
13 Rooms. 7 Private Baths. Guest phone available. TV available. Beds: KQTC. MAP. CCs: MC VISA AX DS. Downhill and cross-country skiing, hiking, fishing, bicycles.
Seen in: *Providence Journal, Boston Globe, Innsider.*

"A superb location with lots to do indoors and out. Beautifully kept rooms and excellent home cooking."

Barre

The Inn at Montpelier
13 E St
Barre VT 05641
(802) 223-2727

Circa 1828. Two Federal-style homes compose the Inn at Montpelier. Ten fireplaces, Greek-style woodwork and glass-fronted china cupboards are original. A favorite guest room is number two with a lace-canopy bed. A few blocks from the inn are restaurants, business districts, and the 100-acre Hubbard Park. The inn holds a four-diamond award.

Rates: $75-$110.
Maureen Russell.
19 Rooms. 19 Private Baths. 6 Fireplaces. Guest phone in room. TV in room. Beds: KQT. B&B. Conference room. CCs: MC VISA AX. Downhill & cross-country skiing, hiking, horseback riding, fishing, swimming.
Seen in: *Glamour Magazine, The Times Argus.*

"My hunch that the Inn at Montpelier would be ideal was well founded."

Woodruff House
13 East St
Barre VT 05641
(802) 476-7745

Circa 1883. This blue Queen Anne Victorian with cranberry shutters

was built by an area granite manufacturer. (Barre is the Granite Center of the World and has the world's largest granite quarries.) The Woodruff House has an eclectic atmosphere and friendly family.

Location: Halfway between Boston & Montreal.

Rates: $45-$60.
Robert & Terry Somani.
2 Rooms. 1 Private Bath. Guest phone available. TV available. Beds: KQ. Full breakfast.

"Friendly and warm. Like going home to Grandma's."

Barton

Fox Hall B&B

Willoughby Lake Rd
Barton VT 05822
(802) 525-6930

Circa 1890. This whimsical Victorian was a former girl's camp, Camp Songadeewin of Keeweydin. The gambrel-roofed mid-section is flanked by round towers. There are spectacular views from the veranda of Willoughby Lake surrounded by granite cliffs and gentle mountains. Designated a Registered National Landmark, much of the lake area is protected parkland. The inn is decorated in a country-style with ruffled curtains and bed covers.

Rates: $65 & up.
The Pyden Family.
9 Rooms. 4 Private Baths. 2 Fireplaces. Beds: QDT. B&B. CCs: MC VISA. Golf, skiing, antiquing.
Seen in: *Toronto Globe & Mail.*

"A wonderful experience. What a beautiful room!"

Belmont

The Parmenter House

Church St
Belmont VT 05730
(802) 259-2009

Circa 1874. This twelve-room Victorian was the private home of three

generations of Parmenters. The living room is decorated in the Eastlake style amid paintings and screens by Alfred Rasmussen, Cynthia's grandfather. Belmont Village, a historic district of Rutland County, is noted for its pristine lake and mountain views.

Rates: $65-$95. Season: Mid June thru Oct.
Lester & Cynthia Firschein.
4 Rooms. 4 Private Baths. Guest phone available. Beds: D. EP. CCs: MC VISA. Horseback riding, water sports, summer theater.

It's the prettiest inn I've ever seen."

Bennington

Blantyre

See: Lenox, MA

Bethel

Greenhurst Inn

River St, RD 2, Box 60
Bethel VT 05032
(802) 234-9474

Circa 1890. Greenhurst is a gracious Victorian mansion built for the

Harringtons of Philadelphia. Overlooking the White River, the inn's opulent interiors include etched windows once featured on the cover of *Vermont Life.* There are eight masterpiece fireplaces and a north and south parlor.

Location: Route 107, 3 miles west of I-89.
*Rates: $50-$95.
Lyle & Claire Wolf.
13 Rooms. 7 Private Baths. 8 Fireplaces. Guest phone available. TV available. Beds: QDTC. Continental-plus breakfast. Conference room. CCs: MC VISA DS. Tennis, horseback riding, fishing, hiking, biking, canoeing.
Seen in: *Los Angeles Times, Time Magazine.*

"The inn is magnificent! The hospitality unforgettable."

Bolton

The Inn at Thatcher Brook Falls

See: Waterbury, VT

Brandon

The Arches

53 Park St
Brandon VT 05733
(802) 247-8200

Circa 1910. The facade of this unusual Colonial features five arches at the formal entrance. Built around a courtyard, the house was constructed in a U shape. The guest rooms are spacious and offer selections such as a canopy bed or a room with its own fireplace. Stencilled borders are featured. The breakfast room offers expansive views across manicured green lawns. Middlebury and Rutland are within 20 miles of the inn.

*Rates: $70-$95.
Ellen & Jack Scheffey.
7 Rooms. 7 Private Baths. 3 Fireplaces. Guest phone available. TV available. Beds: KDTC. B&B. Restaurant. Conference room. CCs: MC VISA AX. Fishing, golf, horseback riding, tennis, skiing, hiking, biking.
Seen in: *Early American Life.*

"Fantastic. We shall return."

The Churchill House Inn

RD 3 Rt 73 East
Brandon VT 05733
(802) 247-3300

Circa 1871. Caleb Churchill and his son Nathan first built a three-story lumber mill, a grist mill and a distillery here, all water powered. Later, with their milled lumber, they constructed this 20-room house. Because of its location it became a stagecoach stop and has served generations of travelers with comfortable accommodations.

Location: Four miles east of Brandon.
Rates: $70-$80.
Roy & Lois Jackson.
9 Rooms. 8 Private Baths. Guest phone available. Beds: KQT. Full breakfast. Sauna. Swimming pool. CCs: MC VISA. Hiking, cross-country skiing, fishing, bicycling.

"We felt the warm, welcoming, down-home appeal as we entered the front

hall. The food was uncommonly good - home cooking with a gourmet flair!"

Moffett House

69 Park St
Brandon VT 05733
(802) 247-3843

Circa 1860. This graceful French Second Empire house has a mansard

roof and a Queen Anne Victorian veranda that was added in 1880. Widow walks top the roof, and gingerbread trim adds to the street-side appeal of Moffett House. The inn was named after Hugh Moffett, Time-Life editor and Vermont legislator. A country breakfast is served in the kitchen. The Kellington-Pico ski area is nearby.
Rates: $60-$75.
Nancy & Elliot Phillips.
6 Rooms. 2 Private Baths. 1 Fireplace. Guest phone available. TV available. Beds: KQDTC. Full breakfast. Game room. Horseback riding, canoeing, water sports, fishing, golf, skiing, hiking.
Seen in: *Rutland Business Journal.*

"My mother, aunt, cousin and I were all delighted with the lovely accommodations and the delicious breakfasts."

Brownesville

Mill Brook B&B

PO Box 410, Rt 44
Brownesville VT 05037
(802) 484-7283

Circa 1860. Once known as the House of Seven Gables, Mill Brook has been in constant use as a family home and for a while, a boarding house for mill loggers. Old German Fraktur paintings decorate the woodwork and there are three sitting rooms for guests. Antique furnishings are found throughout. Popular activities in the area include

hang gliding, bike tours and canoeing.
Location: Fourteen miles from Woodstock, seven from Windsor.
*Rates: $40-$65.
Kay Carriere.
8 Rooms. 3 Private Baths. Guest phone available. TV available. Beds: QDT. CCs: MC VISA. Lawn games, hammock, fishing on premises. Nearby horseback riding. Midweek specials. Afternoon tea.

"Splendid hospitality. Your B&B was beyond our expectation."

Burlington

Swift House Inn

See: Middlebury, VT

The Inn at Thatcher Brook Falls

See: Waterbury, VT

Ye Olde England Inne

See: Stowe, VT

Chelsea

Shire Inn

PO Box 37
Chelsea VT 05038
(802) 685-3031

Circa 1832. This handsome Federal home is highlighted by massive

granite lintels over each window and the front door. Accentuated with a picket fence, the inn is on 17 acres of woods and fields, and a stream from the White River flows on the property. Wide-plank flooring is a fine backdrop for a collection of antiques and fireplaces.
Rates: $65-$95.
James & Mary Lee Papa.
6 Rooms. 6 Private Baths. 4 Fireplaces. Guest phone available. Beds: KQD. B&B. Gourmet meals. CCs: MC VISA. Swimming, bicycling, hiking, fishing, cross-country skiing.
Seen in: *Country Inn Review.*

"Max and I really enjoyed our stay in your wonderful inn and the meals were great."

Chester

Chester House

Main St, Box 708
Chester VT 05143
(802) 875-2205

Circa 1780. This beautifully restored Federal-style clapboard home

is listed in the National Registry of Historic Places. It is situated across from the village green in the quaint and historic village of Chester. The inn is tastefully furnished throughout with early American furniture and appointments.
Rates: $45-$70.
Irene & Norm Wright.
4 Rooms. 4 Private Baths. Guest phone available. TV available. Beds: KQTD. Full breakfast. Jacuzzi. Conference room. Downhill & cross-country skiing, bicycling, hiking, antiquing.

"The best hosts and the greatest of inns."

Greenleaf Inn

PO Box 188
Chester VT 05143
(802) 875-3171

Circa 1850. This Victorian has changed ownership only three times in 140 years. Set on a spacious lawn, the inn looks out to ancient apple trees and a babbling brook. It is furnished with antiques such as a Hepplewhite dining room set, and there is a gallery displaying Vermont artists' paintings of New England life. The innkeeper, Dan

Duffield, spent his summers here on the old Newton farm as a boy.
Rates: $60-$70.
Elizabeth & Dan Duffield.
5 Rooms. 5 Private Baths. Guest phone available. Beds: QT. B&B. Game room. Skiing. Rent-an-Inn.
Seen in: *Black River Tribune.*

"We found paradise! Your inn is a piece of heaven on earth! We'll be back!"

Henry Farm Inn

PO Box 646
Chester VT 05143
(802) 875-2674

Circa 1750. Fifty acres of scenic woodlands provide the setting for

this handsomely restored stagecoach stop in the Green Mountains. There are original wide pine floors, eight fireplaces, and carefully selected early American furnishings. A pond and river are nearby.
Rates: $70-$90.
Jean Bowman.
7 Rooms. 7 Private Baths. 8 Fireplaces. Guest phone available. TV available. Beds: TW. Full breakfast. CCs: MC VISA. Skating, antiquing, horseback riding, and skiing.

The Inn at Long Last

PO Box 589
Chester VT 05143
(802) 875-2444

Circa 1923. Located on the green, this renovated inn reflects the personality of the owner Jack Coleman, former college president and author. Fulfilling a dream, he has created an inn for all seasons with fine cuisine

and civilized surroundings. A library, tennis courts, fishing stream, and personally designed guest rooms contribute to the atmosphere.
*Rates: $85-$105.
Jack Coleman.
30 Rooms. 28 Private Baths. Guest phone available. TV available. Beds: QDTC. AP. Restaurant. Conference room. CCs: MC VISA. Skiing, golf, hiking, antiquing.
Seen in: *New York Times, Philadelphia Inquirer, Connoisseur.*

*"For ambience and food combined, I would choose the...Inn at Long Last in Chester (the rooms also look lovely)."*Carol Binzler, *Vogue*

Old Town Farm Inn

See: Gassets, VT

The Stone Hearth Inn

Rt 11 West
Chester VT 05143
(802) 875-2525

Circa 1810. Exposed beams, wide-pine floors and Vermont stone fireplaces are features of this re-

stored country inn near Chester's historic Stone Village. Guests can relax in the parlor, library or attached barn that has been converted into a comfortable common room with a fieldstone fireplace. There is a fully stocked pub on the property.
Location: One mile west of Chester.
*Rates: $30-$80.
Janet & Don Strohmeyer.
10 Rooms. 8 Private Baths. Guest phone available. TV available. Beds: KQTC. Full breakfast. Restaurant. Jacuzzi. Conference room. CCs: MC VISA. Bicycling, swimming, tennis, golf, fishing, skiing, snowmobiling.

"We love coming here and last time we brought the whole family. Good times, memories and friends were made here."

Chittenden

Mountain Top Inn

Box 493, Mountain Top Rd
Chittenden VT 05737
(800) 445-2100 (802)483-2311 VT & Canada

Circa 1880. This secluded inn is situated in the Green Mountains of

Central Vermont and affords a spectacular view of the lake and surrounding mountains. Room selections include a few cottages with fireplaces or rooms with a view.
Location: Ten miles northeast of Rutland.
*Rates: $159-$330.
William P. Wolfe.
39 Rooms. 39 Private Baths. 4 Fireplaces. Guest phone in room. TV available. Beds: KQDTC. MAP. Restaurant. Jacuzzi. Sauna. Handicap access. Swimming pool. Game room. Conference room. CCs: MC VISA AX. Sailing, fishing, tennis, golf, cross-country skiing, sleigh rides, ice skating.

"Twenty years ago we spent a very enjoyable week here with our daughter. The inn, the service and atmosphere were superior at that time and we are glad to report that it hasn't changed."

Tulip Tree Inn

Chittenden Dam Rd
Chittenden VT 05737
(802) 483-6213

Circa 1842. Thomas Edison was a regular guest here when the house

was the country home of William Barstow. The inn is surrounded by the Green Mountains on three sides with a stream flowing a few yards

away. The guest rooms feature an antique decor.
*Rates: $60-$100.
Ed & Rosemary McDowell.
8 Rooms. 8 Private Baths. Guest phone available. Beds: QT. AP. Jacuzzi. CCs: MC VISA. Hiking, bicycling, skiing, horseback riding.
Seen in: *New England Getaways.*

"Tulip Tree Inn is one of the warmest, friendliest & coziest country inns you'll find in New England." New England Getaways.

Craftsbury Common

Inn On The Common

Main St
Craftsbury Common VT 05827
(802) 586-9619

Circa 1795. The Inn On the Common, built by the Samuel French family, is an integral part of this pic-

turesque classic Vermont village. With its white picket fence and graceful white clapboard exterior, the inn provides a quietly elegant retreat. Pastoral views are framed by the inn's famous perennial gardens.
Rates: $180-$240 MAP.
Michael & Penny Schmitt.
18 Rooms. 18 Private Baths. Guest phone available. TV available. Beds: QTC. MAP. Swimming pool. Conference room. CCs: MC VISA. Tennis, hiking, croquet, golf.
Seen in: *The New York Times, Craftsbury Common.*

"The closest my wife and I came to fulfilling our fantasy of a country inn was at the Inn on the Common." Paul Grimes, "In Search of the Perfect Vermont Inn, *New York Times."*

Danby

Silas Griffith Inn

RR 1 Box 66F, S Main St
Danby VT 05739
(802) 293-5567

Circa 1891. Originally on 55,000 acres, this stately Queen Anne Vic-

torian mansion features solid cherry, oak, and bird's eye maple woodwork. Considered an architectural marvel, an eight-foot round solid cherry pocket door separates the original music room from the front parlor.
*Rates: $67-$82.
Paul & Lois Dansereau.
17 Rooms. 11 Private Baths. Guest phone available. TV available. Beds: QT. B&B. Restaurant. Swimming pool. Conference room. CCs: MC VISA AX. Hiking, bicycling, skiing.
Seen in: *The Vermont Weathervane, Rutland Business Journal.*

"The warm welcome of antiques and beautiful country surroundings made the inn an ideal place."

Dorset

Barrows House

Dorset VT 05251
(802) 867-4455

Circa 1784. The Barrows House is situated on six acres of lawns,

flowering gardens and cross-country ski trails in the heart of the village. The oldest section of the inn once served as the meeting room for Dorset's first church. A cluster of cottages and other guest quarters date from the 1800s to 1920. The foyer, salon, tavern and parlor feature hand-stenciled borders and comfortable, overstuffed furniture. The old stable on the property now serves as a bike and ski rental shop, depending on the season. Fresh raspberry pancakes are a favorite breakfast of the inn's highly regarded restaurant.
Rates: $155-$200.
Sally & Tim Brown.
30 Rooms. 28 Private Baths. 1 Fireplace. Guest phone available. TV in room. MAP. Restaurant. Gourmet meals. Sauna. Handicap access. Swimming pool. Conference room. CCs: AX. Horseback riding, downhill & cross-country skiing, fishing, hiking, quarry swimming, bicycling.
Seen in: *The Washingtonian, Sunday Times Union.*

"A classic meal, a perfect setting."

Cornucopia Of Dorset

Rt 30 Box 307
Dorset VT 05251
(802) 867-5751

Circa 1800. The newly renovated Cornucopia is a comely 19th century

colonial home set on a peaceful green lawn. All the inn's guest rooms have poster or canopy beds. A handsome cottage tucked in the trees has its own living room with a fireplace and cathedral ceiling. Dorset summer theater is within a five-minute walk.
Rates: $90-$145.
Bill & Linda Ley.
5 Rooms. 5 Private Baths. Guest phone available. TV available. Beds: KQT. Full breakfast. CCs: MC VISA. Skiing, hiking, swimming, biking, tennis.
Seen in: *West Hartford News.*

The Little Lodge at Dorset
Rt 30 Box 673
Dorset VT 05251
(802) 867-4040

Circa 1810. The Little Lodge at Dorset forms the northern boundary

of Dorset's historic district. The inn was built 16 miles away and was disassembled, moved and reassembled on a foundation of Dorset marble 60 years ago. Nestled against a backdrop of stately trees, it overlooks green lawns, a trout pond, and golf course.
Rates: $80-$110.
Allan & Nancy Norris.
5 Rooms. 5 Private Baths. Guest phone available. TV available. Beds: KTC. B&B. Handicap access.

"All my search for the perfect bed & breakfast paid off!"

East Burke

Burke Green
RR 1 Box 81
East Burke VT 05832
(802) 467-3472

Circa 1840. This modest farmhouse has been remodeled with large pic-

ture windows framing views of Burke Mountain. Original wood beams and a cozy fireplace remain. The village of East Burke is less than three miles away. Cross-country and downhill skiing are 10 minutes from the inn.
Location: Exit 23 I-91, 2.7 miles from village of East Burke.
Rates: $40-$44.
Harland & Beverly Lewin.
3 Rooms. 1 Private Bath. TV in room. Beds: DT. Continental breakfast. Handicap access. CCs: VISA. Water sports, biking, golf, snowmobiling.

East Middlebury

The Waybury Inn
Rt 125
East Middlebury VT 05740
(802) 388-4015

Circa 1810. This is the famous Bob Newhart inn featured in the TV series. (And yes, Larry Darryl and his brother Darryl have stayed here.) In continuous operation for more than 150 years, it was originally built as a stagecoach stop and tavern. There remains a fully licensed pub on the premises. Nearby, is the local swimming hole, a natural gorge in a rocky river.
Rates: $100-$115.
Kimberly Smith.
14 Rooms. 14 Private Baths. Guest phone available. TV available. Beds: KQD. Full breakfast. CCs: MC VISA AX.

Fair Haven

Maplewood Inn
Rt 22A, South
Fair Haven VT 05743
(802) 265-8039

Circa 1850. This beautifully restored Greek Revival house was once

the family home of the founder of Maplewood Dairy, Isaaac Wood. Period antiques and reproductions grace the inn's spacious rooms and suites. A collection of antique spinning wheels and yarn winders is displayed. A porch wing is thought to have been a tavern formerly located down the road. Overlooking three acres of lawn, garden, and stream, the inn offers an idyllic setting.
Location: One mile south of Fair Haven village.
Rates: $65-$95.
Cindy & Paul Soder.
5 Rooms. 5 Private Baths. 1 Fireplace. Guest phone available. TV available. Beds: QDT. B&B. CCs: MC VISA. Horseback riding, skiing, boating, waterskiing.

"Your inn is perfection. Leaving under protest."

Fairlee

Silver Maple Lodge & Cottages
S Main St, RR1, Box 8
Fairlee VT 05045
(802) 333-4326

Circa 1850. This old Victorian farmhouse became an inn in the Twenties when Elmer & Della

Batchelder opened their home to guests. It became so successful that several cottages, built from lumber on the property, were added and for 60 years the Batchelder family continued the operation. They misnamed the lodge, however, mistaking silver poplar trees on the property for what they thought were silver maples. Guest rooms are decorated with many of the inn's original furnishings and the new innkeepers have added antique sinks and wallpapers. A screened-in porch surrounds two sides of the house.
*Rates: $40-$50.
Scott & Sharon Wright.
14 Rooms. 12 Private Baths. Guest phone available. TV available. Beds: KDT. Continental breakfast. CCs: MC VISA AX. Golf, tennis, fishing, hiking, canoeing, hot air balloon flights, croquet, badminton.
Seen in: *Boston Globe, Vermont Country Sampler.*

"Your gracious hospitality and attractive home all add up to a pleasant experience."

Gassets

Old Town Farm Inn
Rt 10
Gassets VT 05143
(802) 875-2346

Circa 1861. This comfortable New England inn with its elegant spiral staircase was called the Town Farm

of Chester because anyone who needed food and lodging were provided for, in return for a day's work on the farm. Fred R. Smith, famous as "Uncle Sam" in the Twenties and Thirties resided here. Artists have been inspired by the scenic views, which include a pond and meadow and woodlands inhabited by deer and wild turkey. Maple syrup from surrounding trees is served, as is the family's popular "Country Inn Spring Water."

✻❀Rates: $60-$70.
Ruth & Dick Lewis.
10 Rooms. 3 Private Baths. Guest phone available. TV available. Beds: DTC. MAP. Game room. CCs: MC VISA. Skiing, hunting, fishing, hiking, golf, swimming, horses.
Seen in: *Yankee Magazine.*

"A warm haven! Very friendly and comfortable."

Gaysville

Cobble House Inn

PO Box 49
Gaysville VT 05746
(802) 234-5458

Circa 1864. This Victorian mansion is one of the grandest houses

around, and commands a breathtaking view of the Green Mountains. The White River flows just below the inn, enticing the sporting set to fish for salmon and trout. Canoeing and tubing also are popular.

✻Rates: $75-$95.
Beau, Phil & Sam Benson.
6 Rooms. 6 Private Baths. 1 Fireplace. Guest phone available. Beds: QD. B&B. Restaurant. Gourmet meals. Conference room. CCs: MC VISA. Cross-country skiing, swimming, fishing, hiking, White River tubing.

"My favorite place!"

Goshen

Blueberry Hill Inn

RD 3
Goshen VT 05733
(802) 247-6735

Circa 1813. Originally built for loggers, this colonial clapboard inn has

operated full-time since 1940. The *Blueberry Hill Cookbook* was written by a previous owner in the 1940s, and the current English innkeeper is known for "involving guests in things only mad dogs and Englishmen might ordinarily consider." *Chicago Tribune,* Andrew Nemethy.

Location: On the Goshen-Ripton Road. Surrounded by the Green Mountain National Forest.
Rates: $146-$196 MAP.
Tony Clark.
12 Rooms. 12 Private Baths. Guest phone available. Beds: QD. MAP. Sauna. Handicap access. Conference room. CCs: MC VISA. Cross-country, skiing, hiking.
Seen in: *Ski-XC, Chicago Tribune, Better Homes and Gardens, Self, Hideaway Report.*

Killington

The Inn at Long Trail

Rt 4 Box 267
Killington VT 05751
(802) 775-7181

Circa 1939. The inn was the first ski lodge in Vermont. It has a pub with a 22-foot log bar and an enormous boulder incorporated into the decor. The lobby features sofas and tables constructed from tree trunks. Most of the rooms are decorated in a country style and there are several fireplace suites.

Location: Nine miles east of Rutland.
✻Rates: $52 & up. Season: June - Sept.
Kyran & Rosemary McGrath.
20 Rooms. 20 Private Baths. 6 Fireplaces. Guest phone available. TV available. Beds: QT. B&B. Restaurant. Jacuzzi. Conference room. CCs: MC VISA. Skiing, hiking, golf, tennis, swimming.
Seen in: *The Mountain Times.*

"We enjoyed our honeymoon for five days at the inn and we loved your Guiness stew after a cold, snowy day."

The Vermont Inn

Rt 4
Killington VT 05751
(802) 775-0708

Circa 1840. Surrounded by mountain views, this rambling red and

white farmhouse has provided lodging for many years. Exposed beams add to the atmosphere in the living and game rooms. The inn boasts an indoor sauna and hot tub. The award-winning dining room provides candlelight tables beside a huge fieldstone fireplace.

✻Rates: $MAP.
Susan & Judd Levy.
16 Rooms. 12 Private Baths. Guest phone available. TV available. Beds: QC. Full breakfast. Jacuzzi. Sauna. Swimming pool. CCs: MC VISA. Tennis, shuffleboard. Canoeing and horseback riding nearby. The inn is closed April - May.

"We had a wonderful time. The inn is breathtaking. Hope to be back."

Lower Waterford

Rabbit Hill Inn
Pucker St
Lower Waterford VT 05848
(802) 748-5168

Circa 1825. Above the Connecticut River overlooking the White Mountains, Samuel Hodby opened this tavern and provided a general store and inn to travelers. As many as 100 horse teams a day traveled by the inn. The ballroom, constructed in 1855, was supported by bentwood construction that gave the dance floor a spring effect. The classic Greek Revival exterior features solid pine Doric columns.
*Rates: $140-$180.
John & Maureen Magee.
18 Rooms. 18 Private Baths. 5 Fireplaces. Guest phone available. TV available. Beds: KQT. MAP. Restaurant. Gourmet meals. Conference room. CCs: MC VISA. Swimming, fishing, hiking, cross-country skiing, sleigh rides, canoeing, golf.
Seen in: *New York Times, Los Angeles Herald Examiner, Today Show.*

"For the most loving, heartfelt service, I vote for Rabbit Hill Inn." C. Dragonwagon, *Uncommon Lodgings.*

Ludlow

The Andrie Rose Inn
13 Pleasant St
Ludlow VT 05149
(802) 228-4846

Circa 1829. This village Colonial has been named for Andrie Rose,

who operated a guest house, The Pleasant Lodge, here during the Fifties. Recently, the inn has been polished to a shine and lavishly appointed with antiques, wallpapers, down comforters and whirlpool tubs. A Vermont country breakfast is served buffet style. Dinners are available. This is the closest inn to the access road of Okemo Mountain.

Location: One block off Main St (Rte 103).
❀Rates: $95-$110.
Rick & Carolyn Bentzinger.
8 Rooms. 8 Private Baths. Guest phone available. Beds: D. B&B. Jacuzzi. Game room. CCs: MC VISA AX. Skiing, canoeing, horseback riding, hiking.

"You two are certainly experts. Our weekend was perfect."

The Governor's Inn
86 Main St
Ludlow VT 05149
(802) 228-8830

Circa 1890. Governor Stickney built this house for his bride, Elizabeth Lincoln, and it retains the

intimate feeling of an elegant country house furnished in the Victorian fashion. The Governor would have been pleased to know that *The Governor's Inn* has been elected to the prestigious Master Chefs Institute of America. It was also awarded first prize for "Best in American Country Inn Cooking" by Uncle Ben's Rice.
❀Rates: $170 MAP.
Charlie & Deedy Marble.
8 Rooms. 8 Private Baths. Guest phone available. AP. Gourmet meals. CCs: MC VISA. Skiing, golf, tennis, sleigh rides, horses, antiquing.
Seen in: *The Washington Post, Los Angeles Times, Mature Outlook, Gourmet Magazine.*

"As Rolls Royce is to cars... it is the standard by which all other inns can be judged." Ed Oakie.

Old Town Farm Inn
See: Gassets, VT

Manchester

The Arlington Inn
See: Arlington, VT

Birch Hill Inn
West Rd, Box 346
Manchester VT 05254
(802) 362-2761

Circa 1790. It's rare to meet a Vermont innkeeper actually from Ver-

mont but at Birch Hill the hostess is the fourth generation to live in this old farmhouse. The bedrooms are elegantly furnished, and some have mountain views and fireplaces. There are eight miles of groomed, picturesque cross-country trails that lead past a small pond and flowing brook.
Rates: $140.
Jim & Pat Lee.
6 Rooms. 6 Private Baths. 1 Fireplace. Guest phone available. Beds: KQT. AP. Swimming pool. CCs: MC VISA. Cross-country skiing, hiking, fishing.
Seen in: *The Rye Chronicle.*

"Without a doubt the loveliest country inn it has ever been my pleasure to stay in. I. Pastarnack, *Rye Chronicle.*

The Inn at Manchester
Box 41, Historic Rt 7A
Manchester VT 05254
(802) 362-1793

Circa 1880. This restored Victorian and its carriage house are in the National Register.

There is an extensive art collection of old prints and paintings. Guest rooms have French doors, bay win-

dows, and antiques re stored by the innkeepers.
*Rates: $55-$90.
Harriet & Stan Rosenberg.
21 Rooms. 13 Private Baths. Guest phone available. TV available. Beds: KQDT. Full breakfast. Swimming pool. Game room. Conference room. CCs: MC VISA AX. Skiing, golf, tennis, swimming, bicycling.
Seen in: *New York Times, Boston Globe, Travel & Leisure.*

"Spectacular! Bob Newhart - eat your heart out."

Manchester Highlands Inn
PO Box 1754, Highland Ave
Manchester VT 05255
(802) 362-4565

Circa 1898. From the three-story turret of this Victorian mansion

guests can look out over Mt. Equinox, the Green Mountains and the valley below. Guest rooms are homey and comfortable, and a large veranda is provided with rocking chairs.
*Rates: $80-$98.
Robert & Patricia Eichorn.
15 Rooms. 12 Private Baths. Guest phone available. TV available. Beds: KQDTC. B&B. Swimming pool. Game room. CCs: MC VISA AX. Downhill and cross-country skiing, golf, tennis, cycling, fishing, horseback riding, canoeing.
Seen in: *Toronto Sun.*

"We couldn't believe such a place existed. Now we can't wait to come again."

Reluctant Panther Inn
Box 678, West Rd
Manchester VT 05254
(802) 362-2568

Circa 1850. Elm trees line a street of manicured lawns and white clapboard estates. Suddenly, a muted purple clapboard house appears, the Reluctant Panther. Rooms have recently been renovated and some

include fireplaces, whirlpool tubs, and cable TV.
Rates: $95-$180.
Robert & Maye Bachofen.
14 Rooms. 14 Private Baths. Guest phone in room. Beds: KQDT. Full breakfast. Restaurant. Jacuzzi. Handicap access. CCs: MC VISA.
Seen in: *Vermont Summer, Sunday Republican.*

"We enjoyed our stay so much that now we want to make it our yearly romantic getaway."

White Rocks Inn
See: Wallingford, VT

Wilburton Inn
Box 468, River Rd
Manchester VT 05254
(802) 362-2500 (800) 648-4944

Circa 1902. Shaded by tall maples, this three-story brick mansion sits

high on a hill overlooking the Battenkill Valley set against a majestic mountain backdrop. Carved moldings, mahogany paneling, oriental carpets, and leaded-glass windows are complemented by carefully chosen antiques. The inn's 17 acres provide three tennis courts, a pool and green lawns and is popular for country weddings.
*Rates: $75-$155.
Georgette & Albert Levis, Stanley Holton.
32 Rooms. 32 Private Baths. 3 Fireplaces. Guest phone in room. TV available. Beds: KQDTC. AP. Restaurant. Gourmet meals. Swimming pool. Game room. Conference room. CCs: MC VISA AX. Horseback riding, downhill & cross-country skiing, golf, canoeing, hiking, biking. Specialize in country weddings.
Seen in: *Great Escapes TV, Travelhost, Getaways For Gourmets.*

"I have traveled extensively in Europe and the United States...if there is a more romantic and peaceful setting in the world, then I am not aware of its existence."

Manchester Village

1811 House
Historic Rt 7A
Manchester Village VT 05254
(802) 362-1811

Circa 1775. Since 1811, the historic Lincoln Home has been operated as an inn, except for one time. It was the private residence of Mary Lincoln Isham, granddaughter of President Lincoln. It has been authentically restored to the Federal period with antiques and canopy beds. The gardens look out over a golf course and it's just a short walk to tennis or swimming.
Location: Center of Manchester Village.
Rates: $100-$160.
John & Mary Hurst, Pat & Jeremy David.
14 Rooms. 14 Private Baths. Guest phone available. TV available. Beds: KQ. Full breakfast. CCs: MC VISA. Skiing, tennis, golf, hiking.
Seen in: *New York.*

Village Country Inn
PO Box 408
Manchester Village VT 05254
(802) 362-1792

Circa 1889. The Kellogg cereal family built this as a summer house.

The present owners have renovated and redecorated it in a French Colonial style, creating soft country vignettes in each room. A French country breakfast is served.
Location: Historic route 7A.
*Rates: $153-$175.
Anne & Jay Degen.
30 Rooms. 30 Private Baths. Guest phone available. TV in room. Beds: KDTW. MAP. Restaurant. Swimming pool. CCs: MC VISA AX. Tennis, golf, skiing, horseback riding.

Seen in: *Country Inn Magazine.*

"An inn for choosy guests." Albany Times Union.

Marlboro

Longwood A Country Inn at Marlboro

Rt 9 Box 86
Marlboro VT 05344
(802) 257-1545

Circa 1800. This rambling Colonial includes four studios in the Carriage House, each accommodating three to six people. The ice skating pond is stocked with rainbow trout (and bullfrogs) each spring. Activities vary with the season and include sleigh rides, skiing, horseback riding and walking through the woods.

Location: Nine miles west of Route 91.
Rates: $85-$175.
Andrea & Douglas Sauer.
15 Rooms. 13 Private Baths. Guest phone available. TV available. Beds: KQT. AP. Restaurant. Jacuzzi. Handicap access. CCs: MC VISA.
Seen in: *Boston Globe.*

Middlebury

Historic Brookside Farms

See: Orwell, VT

Moffett House

See: Brandon, VT

Swift House Inn

25 Stewart Lane
Middlebury VT 05753
(802) 388-9925

Circa 1815. Former governor of Vermont, John Stewart, bought the

elegant Swift House in 1875 from Jonathan Swift. The governor's daughter, philanthropist Jessica Swift, was born and lived in the mansion there for 110 years, till 1981. Elaborately carved walnut and marble fireplaces, and window seats grace the sitting rooms of the inn. The spacious lawns and formal gardens can be enjoyed from terraces and guest rooms.

Location: Corner of Rt. 7 and Stewart Lane.
Rates: $70-$150.
John & Andrea Nelson.
20 Rooms. 20 Private Baths. 8 Fireplaces. Guest phone in room. TV in room. Beds: KQDTC. B&B. Restaurant. Gourmet meals. Jacuzzi. Sauna. Handicap access. Exercise room. Conference room. CCs: MC VISA AX DC DS. Skiing, bicycling, swimming, golf, tennis, boating, horseback riding, museums.
Seen in: *Valley Voice, Uncommon Lodgings, Boston Magazine.*

"Fabulous wine list, great food, comfortable and relaxing atmosphere, friendly staff."

Middletown Springs

Middletown Springs Inn

Box 1068, On The Green
Middletown Springs VT 05757
(802) 235-2198

Circa 1879. This Italianate Victorian mansion on the green was built when the bubbling springs of

Middletown rivaled those of Saratoga. The inn is decorated in middle to late Victorian antiques, with mahogany and cherry furniture, rich wallpapers and lace curtains. A staircase with an ornate newel post sweeps upstairs to the guest rooms. There are additional rooms in the carriage house, once the village blacksmith shop.

Location: Fourteen miles from Rutland on Route 133.
*Rates: $40-$75.
Steve & Jane Sax.
10 Rooms. 8 Private Baths. TV available. Beds: QTD. AP. Conference room. CCs: MC VISA. Skiing, hiking, swimming, sailing, golf, bicycles, horses.
Seen in: *National Geographic Traveler, Cleveland Plain Dealer.*

"The charm of the inn, Steve's exquisite cuisine and the ambiance you both provide blend wonderfully."

Montgomery Village

Black Lantern Inn

Route 118
Montgomery Village VT 05470
(802) 326-4507

Circa 1803. This brick inn and restaurant originally served as a

stagecoach stop. There is a taproom with beamed ceilings, and two downstairs lounges. A large three-bedroom suite has its own jacuzzi. Vermont antiques fill all the guest rooms. A few minutes from the inn, skiers (novice and expert) can ride the tramway to the top of Jay Peak.

*Rates: $55-$75.
Rita & Allan Kalsmith.
11 Rooms. 11 Private Baths. 1 Fireplace. Guest phone available. TV available. Beds: KQDT. MAP. Gourmet meals. Jacuzzi. CCs: MC VISA AX. Downhill & cross-country skiing, hiking, biking.

"...one of the four or five great meals of your life." Jay Stone, *Ottawa Citizen.*

Montpelier

Shire Inn

See: Chelsea VT

North Hero

North Hero House

Rt 2 PO 106
North Hero VT 05474
(802) 372-8237

Circa 1891. This three-story inn stands on a slight rise overlooking Lake Champlain and Vermont's highest peak, Mt. Mansfield. Three other houses, including the Wadsworth store located at the City Dock, also provide accommodations for the inn's guests. Rooms hang over the water's edge and feature waterfront porches.

Rates: $41-$95. Season: June - Oct.

Apgar & Sherlock Families.
23 Rooms. 21 Private Baths. Guest phone available. TV available. Beds: TC. EP. Restaurant. Sauna. Handicap access. Fishing, swimming, tennis, canoeing, sailing, bicycling, boating.
Seen in: *Gourmet.*

"We have visited many inns and this house was by far the best, due mostly to the staff!"

Orleans

Valley House Inn

4 Memorial Sq
Orleans VT 05860
(802) 754-6665

Circa 1873. There has been a Valley House in existence since 1833,

though the present structure was built in 1873. A small dining room serves a hearty Vermont breakfast, and there is a tavern with live entertainment on the weekends.
Location: In the village on Route 58, off I-91, exit 26.
Rates: $28-$54.
David & Louise Bolduc.
21 Rooms. 9 Private Baths. Full breakfast. Restaurant. CCs: MC VISA. Golf, hiking, bicycling, fishing, hunting, antiquing.

Orwell

Historic Brookside Farms

Rt 22A Box 036
Orwell VT 05760
(802) 948-2727

Circa 1789. Nineteen stately Ionic columns grace the front of this neoclassical Greek Revival farmhouse,

redesigned by James Lamb. This is a working farm with Hereford cattle, Hampshire sheep, maple syrup production and poultry. There are 300 acres of lush country landscape including a 26-acre pond. Innkeeper Murray Korda is a concert violinist and speaks seven languages.
*Rates: $75-$150.
Joan & Murray Korda & Family.
8 Rooms. 4 Private Baths. Guest phone available. TV available. Beds: DTC. AP. Handicap access. Conference room. Cross-country skiing, fishing, hiking, tennis, golf, horses.
Seen in: *New York Times, Burlington Free Press.*

"A wonderful piece of living history."

Pittsfield

The Inn at Pittsfield

PO Box 526
Pittsfield VT 05762
(802) 746-8943

Circa 1830. The Inn at Pittsfield stands across from the Valley green

and just beyond the covered bridge. It was once a stagecoach stop providing both meals and lodging to travelers. A pot-bellied stove warms the common room where guests gather. A country decor is highlighted by old quilts, pull-back curtains, and floral arrangements. A four-course single sitting dinner is served.
*Rates: $130.
Barbara Morris, Vikki Budasi.
9 Rooms. 9 Private Baths. Guest phone available. Beds: DT. MAP. CCs: MC VISA AX. Horseback riding, hiking, mountain biking, fishing, downhill & cross-country skiing, snowmobiling.
Seen in: *The Discerning Traveler.*

"I am still savoring that great food, hospitality and help that you provided all of us...it was beyond our expectations."

Plymouth

Salt Ash Inn

Jct 100 & 100A
Plymouth VT 05056
(802) 672-3748

Circa 1830. In the mid-1800s, the Woodstock to Ludlow Stagecoach

stopped at the Union House, as the Salt Ash Inn was then known. Most of the antiques featured at Salt Ash were in use when the building was a post office, general store and inn. Pine beds piled with homemade quilts or plaid blankets provide pleasant comfort. An English pub and circular fireplace are welcome spots. This is the closest country inn to Killington Ski Resort.
*Rates: $68-$120.
Glen & Ann Stanford.
15 Rooms. 13 Private Baths. Guest phone available. TV available. Beds: QTC. Full breakfast. Jacuzzi. CCs: MC VISA. Skiing, bicycling, fishing, golf, hiking, antiquing.

Poultney

Stonebridge Inn

Rt 30
Poultney VT 05764
(802) 287-9849

Circa 1808. The inn's land was part of a grant from Lord Poultney, first

Earl of Bath. In 1841, an addition was added with a five-foot-thick foundation, designed as the vault of the First Bank of Poultney. The house was built in the Federal style and a later addition added the Greek Revival front.

*Rates: $64-$84.
Gail R. Turner.
5 Rooms. 2 Private Baths. 3 Fireplaces. Guest phone available. TV available. Beds: QD. Continental-plus breakfast. CCs: MC VISA. Boating, sailing, fishing, cross-country & downhill skiing, tennis, horseback riding, golf.

Proctorsville

Castle Inn
Rt 103 & 131, PO Box 157
Proctorsville VT 05153
(802) 226-7222

Circa 1904. The Fletcher family settled in the Ludlow area in the 1700s.

Allen Fletcher grew up in Indiana but returned to Vermont, tearing down a Victorian house to build this English-style mansion overlooking the Okemo valley. It features an oval dining room, a mahogany-paneled library, and spacious guest accommodations complete with individual sitting areas. In 1911, Mr. Fletcher became governor of Vermont.
Rates: $150-$180.
Michael & Sheryl Fratino.
13 Rooms. 9 Private Baths. Guest phone available. TV available. Beds: QD. MAP. Restaurant. Jacuzzi. Sauna. Swimming pool. Game room. Conference room. CCs: MC VISA AX. Bicycling, tennis, swimming, cross-country skiing.

"Castle Inn has to be the very best place in Vermont."

The Golden Stage Inn
Depot St, PO Box 218
Proctorsville VT 05153
(802) 226-7744

Circa 1780. The Golden Stage Inn was a stagecoach stop shortly after

Vermont's founding. It became a link in the Underground Railroad and the home of Cornelia Otis Skinner. Extensive gardens surround the wraparound porch as well as the swimming pool. The innkeepers were flavor experts for a New York company but now put their tasting skills to work for their guests.
Location: Near Ludlow.
Rates: $65-$75.
Kirsten Murphy & Marcel Perret.
10 Rooms. 6 Private Baths. Guest phone available. Beds: QT. AP. Swimming pool. CCs: VISA. Swimming, golf, bicycling, hiking, cross-country skiing, tennis.
Seen in: *Journal Inquirer.*

"The essence of a country inn!"

Putney

Hickory Ridge House
RFD 3 Box 1410
Putney VT 05346
(802) 387-5709

Circa 1808. This comely brick Federal house was built as an elegant farmhouse on a 500-acre

Merino sheep ranch. Palladian windows, and six Rumford fireplaces are original features. Rooms are painted in bright Federal colors, such as pink, salmon, blue and yellow. Weddings are popular here and innkeeper Steve Anderson often serves as Justice of the Peace.
Rates: $42-$75.
Jacquie Walker & Steve Anderson.
7 Rooms. 3 Private Baths. 4 Fireplaces. Guest phone available. TV available. Beds: QDTC. EP. Handicap access. Conference room. CCs: MC VISA. Cross-country skiing, swimming, boating, hiking.
Seen in: *Phildelphia Inquirer.*

"We love your serene and peaceful house and we thank you for your hospitality and warmth, good food and good company."

Quechee

Quechee Inn At Marshland Farm
Clubhouse Rd, Box 104
Quechee VT 05059
(802) 295-3133

Circa 1793. Colonel Joseph March, the first Lieutenant Governor of Ver-

mont, built this farm on the banks of the Ottauquechee River. The inn is decorated with traditional antiques, and guest rooms feature massive four-poster beds. Panoramic vistas of the lake, river, meadows and hills may be seen from many of the inn's rooms. A short walk rewards guests with views of Quechee Gorge, considered the Grand Canyon of the East. The inn is home to the Vermont Fly Fishing School.
Location: Central Vermont.
Rates: $108-$198.
Michael Maderia.
24 Rooms. 24 Private Baths. 7 Fireplaces. Guest phone available. TV in room. Beds: KQDTC. MAP. Restaurant. Conference room. CCs: MC VISA AX DC. Golf, tennis, swimming, squash, skiing, bicycles, canoeing.
Seen in: *Gourmet Magazine.*

"If I knew for sure that Heaven was like this, I'd work a little harder to get there."

Ripton

Chipman Inn
Rt 125
Ripton VT 05766
(802) 388-2390

Circa 1828. This was the home of Daniel Chipman, a prominent legislator and founder of Middlebury College. Chipman also managed the "Center Turnpike" (now Route 125) through the Green Mountains. A replica of the tariff board stands near the inn. The inn's lounge/bar is in the original kitchen, with its old fireplace and bread oven.

Rates: $78-$98. Season: Closed April & Dec.
Joyce Henderson & Bill Pierce.
9 Rooms. 9 Private Baths. Guest phone available. Beds: DT. MAP. Gourmet meals. CCs: MC VISA AX. Hiking trails, downhill & cross-country skiing, swimming, antique shops.

Rochester

Harvey's Mountain View Inn

Rochester VT 05767
(802) 767-4273

Circa 1809. The Harvey family has owned and operated this homestead

as a farm for more than 180 years. During the summer, guests of all ages enjoy gathering eggs and watching the milking when not in the pool. Sunset hayrides are popular, and there are rental horses nearby. A cottage is available for a weekly rate.
Rates: $38-$45.
Donald & Maggie Harvey.
9 Rooms. 2 Private Baths. Guest phone available. TV available. Beds: KQTDC. MAP. Handicap access. Golf, hiking, cross-country skiing, fishing, hunting.
Seen in: *The New York Times.*

"Children are right at home here. They don't fight. They don't fuss. They're too busy. And when the children are happy, the parents are happy."

Rutland

Moffett House

See: Brandon, VT

Swift House Inn

See: Middlebury, VT

Saint Johnsbury

Echo Ledge Farm Inn

Rt 2 Box 77
Saint Johnsbury VT 05838
(802) 748-4750

Circa 1793. Phineas Page settled here on the banks of the Moose River. Later, his son supervised the farm and made it a political meeting place where representatives to Congress were chosen. Today, guests enjoy the stenciled walls, fresh wallpapers and old maple floors polished to a high gloss.
Rates: $40-$65.
6 Rooms. 4 Private Baths. Guest phone available. Beds: DT.
Seen in: *Vermont Country Sampler.*

"Great. We'll come back again!"

Shrewsbury

Buckmaster Inn

Lincoln Hill Rd, RR 1 Box 118
Shrewsbury VT 05738
(802) 492-3485

Circa 1801. John Buckmaster's tavern was licensed in 1820, and the

inn soon became well known on the Woodstock Road. Standing majestically on a knoll, the Buckmaster overlooks a picturesque red barn and valley scene. Its center hall, grand staircase and wide-pine floors are accentuated with family heirlooms. There are wood-burning fireplaces, a library, and large porches.
Rates: $40-$60.
Sam & Grace Husselman.
4 Rooms. 1 Private Bath. Guest phone available. TV available. Beds: KQTD. B&B. Conference room. Hiking, swimming, fishing, skiing, horseback riding.

"I've been in many B&Bs but the accommodations and hospitality are best here."

South Londonderry

Londonderry Inn

PO Box 3018
South Londonderry VT 05155
(802) 824-5226

Circa 1826. For almost one hundred years the Melendy Homes-

tead, overlooking the West River and the village, was a dairy farm. In 1940, it became an inn. A tourist brochure promoting the area in 1881 said, "Are you overworked in the office, counting room or workshop and need invigorating influences? Come ramble over these hills and mountains and try the revivifying effects of Green Mountain oxygen."
Location: Route 100.
*Rates: $31-$75.
Jim & Jean Cavanagh.
25 Rooms. 20 Private Baths. Guest phone available. TV available. Beds: KQDTC. Full breakfast. Restaurant. Handicap access. Swimming pool. Conference room. Hiking, cross-country skiing.

"A weekend in a good country inn, such as the Londonderry, is on a par with a weekend on the ocean in Southern Maine, which is to say that it's as good as a full week nearly any place else." The Hornet.

South Strafford

Watercourse Way B&B

Rt 132 Box 101
South Strafford VT 05070
(802) 765-4314

Circa 1850. Watercourse Way is a traditional white clapboard Cape with classic post-and-beam construction solid to this day. A striking red barn and goat pasture are just beyond the house. During World War II, Strafford was the site of the

country's largest copper mine. Many geologists from Harvard and MIT made this house their home.
Location: North of White River Junction.
*Rates: $50-$60.
Anna & Lincoln Alden.
3 Rooms. 1 Fireplace. Guest phone available. Beds: QTC. Full breakfast. Bicycling, fishing, kayaking.
"A gem of a place in a beautiful surrounding, excellent breakfast too!"

South Wallingford

Green Mountain Tea Room

Rt 7 RR 1 Box 400
South Wallingford VT 05773
(802) 446-2611

Circa 1792. Originally a stagecoach stop, this Colonial house possessed a barn large enough to hold the 12 horses needed for a complete change on the journey from Bennington to Rutland. The three upstairs bedrooms were originally a ballroom that saw many a gala affair when the house was known as Miller's Hall.
Rates: $55-$65.
Ed & Candy Pino.
5 Rooms. 2 Private Baths. Guest phone available. TV available. Beds: D. Full breakfast. CCs: MC VISA. Hiking, fishing, hunting, cross-country & downhill skiing.
"A very relaxing atmosphere."

South Woodstock

Kedron Valley Inn

Rt 106 Box 145
South Woodstock VT 05071
(802) 457-1473

Circa 1822. This inn has served the traveling public for more than 150 years. One of the guest buildings has a secret attic passageway and is rumored to have been a stop on the Underground Railway during the

Civil War. There is a 32-piece quilt collection that includes 100-year-old quilts made by great grandmothers of the hostess. Outdoors are a white sand beach and swimming lake. A stable with horses for trail rides or inn-to-inn excursions is nearby.
*Rates: $138-$199.
Max & Merrily Comins.
28 Rooms. 28 Private Baths. 7 Fireplaces. Guest phone available. TV in room. Beds: KQDTC. MAP. Restaurant. Handicap access. Conference room. CCs: MC VISA AX. Horses, golf, tennis, cross-country & downhill skiing.
Seen in: *Oprah Winfrey Show, Good Housekeeping.*
"It's what you dream a Vermont country inn should be and the most impressive feature is the innkeepers...outgoing, warm and friendly."

St. Johnsbury

Rabbit Hill Inn

See: Lower Waterford, VT

Stowe

The 1860 House

School St, PO Box 276
Stowe VT 05672
(802) 253-7351

Circa 1860. This charming National Register house is an Italianate style

with an intersecting gable. All the windows are topped with peaked lintel boards, and paired scroll brackets adorn the roof cornices. The interior is furnished in period furnishings.
*Rates: $75-$100.
Richard M. Hubbard & Rose Marie Matulionis.
5 Rooms. 5 Private Baths. TV available. Beds: KQTC. Full breakfast. Jacuzzi. Sauna. Swimming pool. Conference room. CCs: MC VISA. Skiing, skating, hiking, fishing, golf, tennis, horseback riding.
"A memorable place to visit...You do a great job!"

Green Mountain Inn

PO Box 60
Stowe VT 05672
(802) 253-7301

Circa 1833. This rambling inn consists of several buildings, including

the main building and the old depot built for the Mt. Mansfield Electric Railroad. These two buildings are numbers 13 and 14 in the National Register. Early American reproductions furnish the inn, and there are Walton Blodgett original paintings of Stowe.
*Rates: $65-$115.
Darcy Curran.
57 Rooms. 57 Private Baths. 1 Fireplace. Guest phone in room. TV in room. Beds: QDTC. AP. Restaurant. Gourmet meals. Jacuzzi. Sauna. Handicap access. Exercise room. Swimming pool. Game room. Conference room. CCs: MC VISA AX. Tennis, horseback riding, golf, sking, fishing, ice skating.

The Inn at Thatcher Brook Falls

See: Waterbury, VT

Ye Olde England Inne

Mountain Rd
Stowe VT 05672
(802) 253-7558

Circa 1890. Originally a farmhouse, Ye Olde England Inne has acquired a Tudor facade, interior beams and stone work. Brass and copper pieces, Laura Ashley decor and English antiques add to the atmosphere. The inn sponsors polo events and features a polo package.

Gliding and golf packages are also available.
*Rates: $68-$95.
Christopher & Linda Francis.
21 Rooms. 21 Private Baths. 3 Fireplaces. Guest phone in room. TV in room. Beds: QDT. MAP. Restaurant. Gourmet meals. Jacuzzi. Swimming pool. CCs: MC VISA. Skiing, skating, antiquing.
Seen in: *National Geographic Traveler Magazine.*
"Even more perfect than we anticipated."

Sunderland

The Inn at Sunderland
Historic Rt 7A
Sunderland VT 05250
(802) 362-4213

Circa 1840. Farmer and merchant William Bradley built this house as

a wedding present for his wife. Heart medallions are incorporated into the roof trim and under each window. Chestnut trim and doors, and a polished walnut staircase are features of the interior where guests are surrounded with luxury and comfort.
Rates: $65-$95. Season: May - March.
Tom & Peggy Wall.
10 Rooms. 8 Private Baths. Beds: QDTC. Full breakfast. Handicap access. CCs: MC VISA. Fishing, golf, tennis, bicycling.
Seen in: *Country Living, Bennington Banner.*
"We've traveled many inns, this is the best!"

Waitsfield

Beaver Pond Farm Inn
See: Warren, VT

Lareau Farm Country Inn
PO Box 563, Rt 100
Waitsfield VT 05673
(802) 496-4949

Circa 1832. This Greek Revival house was built by Simeon Stoddard, the town's first physician. Old-fashioned roses, lilacs, del-

phiniums, iris and peonies fill the gardens. The inn sits in a wide meadow next to the crystal-clear Mad River. A canoe trip, or a refreshing swim are possibilities here.
Location: Central Vermont, Sugarbush Valley.
*Rates: $60-$90.
Dan & Susan Easley.
14 Rooms. 10 Private Baths. Guest phone available. TV available. Beds: QDT. B&B. Handicap access. CCs: MC VISA. Downhill & cross-country skiing, sleigh rides, hiking.
Seen in: *The Pittsburgh Press, The Philadelphia Inquirer.*
"Hospitality is a gift. Thank you for sharing your gift so freely with us."

Mad River Barn
Rt 17 Box 88
Waitsfield VT 05673
(802) 496-3310

Circa 1800. The inn consists of two farmhouses and a converted barn. One farmhouse was recently remodeled to contain a two-story lounge, game room, bar and restaurant. Guests may stay in the barn or the more luxurious farmhouse. Just beyond the barn is a path to the mountain. Old stone walls and lumber trails run through the property.
*Rates: $50-$110.
Betsy Pratt.
16 Rooms. 15 Private Baths. Guest phone available. Beds: QTC. AP. Restaurant. Conference room. CCs: MC VISA. Cross-country skiing, golf, tennis, hiking, swimming.
*"My favorite lounge, one with a massive stone fireplace and deep leather chairs."*Christina Tree, *Boston Globe.*

Millbrook
RFD Box 62
Waitsfield VT 05673
(802) 496-2405

Circa 1840. Guests enter Millbrook through the warming room, where an antique Glenwood parlor stove is usually roaring. This classic Cape-

style farmhouse is known for its individually stenciled guest rooms, Green Mountain views, and one of the valley's best dining rooms.
*Rates: $66-$90. Season: Closed May.
Joan & Thom Gorman.
7 Rooms. 4 Private Baths. Guest phone available. Beds: DT. AP. CCs: MC VISA DC. Skiing, horseback riding, golf, hiking, bicycling.
Seen in: *Boston Globe, Travel Today, Gourmet Magazine.*
"A weekend at your place is just what the doctor had in mind."

Wallingford

White Rocks Inn
RR 1 Box 297, Rt 7
Wallingford VT 05773
(802) 446-2077

Circa 1840. Both the barn and farmhouse are listed in the National

Register. The barn is a fine example of Gothic architecture. The house was built by Israel Munson whose name is still engraved on the front doorbell. Furnished with antiques, oriental rugs, and canopied beds, the inn provides views of White Rocks Mountain.
Location: Eleven miles south of Rutland.
*Rates: $60-$85.
June & Alfred Matthews.
5 Rooms. 5 Private Baths. Guest phone available. TV available. Beds: KQTDC. Full breakfast. CCs: MC VISA. Horseback riding, hiking, canoeing, skiing.

"Excellent on all counts! We enjoyed every minute. Breakfasts were delightful, as were our hosts."

Warren

Beaver Pond Farm Inn

RD Box 306, Golf Course Rd
Warren VT 05674
(802) 583-2861

Circa 1860. Formerly a working dairy and sheep farm, this Vermont

farmhouse is situated in a meadow overlooking several beaver ponds. It has been tastefully and graciously restored by its present owners, with antiques and Laura Ashley wallpapers adding to the decor. Mrs. Hansen holds cooking classes here.

*Rates: $32-$45.
Betty & Bob Hansen.
5 Rooms. 3 Private Baths. Guest phone available. TV available. Beds: QT. Full breakfast. Gourmet meals. Conference room. CCs: MC VISA AX. Skiing, golf, tennis, swimming, hiking.
Seen in: *Los Angeles Times, New Woman Magazine.*

"The inn is simply magnificent. I have not been in a nicer one on three continents. Breakfast was outrageous."

Waterbury

Inn at Blush Hill

Blush Hill Rd, Box 1266
Waterbury VT 05676
(802) 244-7529

Circa 1790. This shingled Cape-style house was once a stagecoach stop en route to Stowe. A 12-foot-long pine farm hand's table is set near the double fireplace and the kitchen window revealing views of the Worcester Mountains. A favorite summertime breakfast is pancakes with fresh blueberries.

*❀Rates: $60-$95.
Pamela & Gary Gosselin.
5 Rooms. 3 Private Baths. 1 Fireplace. Guest phone available. TV available. Beds: QD. B&B. CCs: MC VISA. Water sports, golf, cross-country & Alpine skiing, tennis.
Seen in: *Charlotte Observer.*

"Our room was wonderful - especially the fireplace. Everything was so cozy and warm."

The Inn at Thatcher Brook Falls

RD 2, Box 62
Waterbury VT 05676
(802) 244-5911

Circa 1899. Framed by tall trees, this Victorian belonged to Stedman

Wheeler, owner and operator of the local sawmill. Across the street, behind the Colby Mansion, are two beautiful waterfalls that powered the mill. Mr. Wheeler used bird's-eye maple, quarter-sawn maple, cherry, oak and birch in the house. The fireplace and stairway are hand-carved. There is a front porch gazebo, and Bailey's Fireside Tavern is in the oak room.

*Rates: $75-$145.
Peter Varty & Kelly Fenton.
24 Rooms. 24 Private Baths. 2 Fireplaces. Guest phone in room. TV available. Beds: KQDT. B&B. Restaurant. Gourmet meals. Jacuzzi. Handicap access. Game room. Conference room. CCs: MC VISA AX DS. Skiing, bicycling, hiking, swimming, canoeing, golf, tennis, boating.

"I'd have to put on a black tie in Long Island to find food as good as this and best of all it's in a relaxed country atmosphere. Meals are underpriced."

Waterbury Center

The Black Locust Inn

RR 1, Box 715
Waterbury Center VT 05677
(802) 244-7490

Circa 1830. Set on a hill graced with tall black locust trees native to the Southeast, is this three-gabled farmhouse. For more than a century the old house presided over a 90-acre dairy farm, looking out to the Green Mountain range and Camel's Hump. Antiques and brass beds decorate guest chambers now, while white wicker chairs are gathered on the front porch. Afternoon snacks are served, with wine and cheese in the evening.

Rates: $70-$85.
George & Anita Gajdos.
6 Rooms. 6 Private Baths. Guest phone available. TV available. Beds: QDT. Full breakfast. Handicap access. CCs: MC VISA. All winter & summer activities within five miles.

"Your inn is absolutely beautiful and your breakfast perfect."

Weathersfield

The Inn at Weathersfield

Rt 106, PO Box 165
Weathersfield VT 05151
(802) 263-9217 (802) 263-9219 (Fax)

Circa 1795. Built by Thomas Prentis, a Revolutionary War veteran,

this was originally a four-room farmhouse set on 237 acres of wilderness. Two rooms were added in 1796, and a carriage house in 1830. During the Civil War, the inn served as a station on the Underground Railroad. Six pillars give the inn a Southern Colonial look, and there are 11 fireplaces, a beehive oven, wide-plank floors and period antiques throughout.

*❀Rates: $150-$200.
Mary Louise & Ron Thorburn.
12 Rooms. 12 Private Baths. 7 Fireplaces. Guest phone available. TV available.

Beds: QDT. AP. Restaurant. Jacuzzi. Sauna. Handicap access. Conference room. CCs: MC VISA AX DS. Sleigh rides, cycling, hiking, skiing, horseback riding, canoeing, swimming pond. Thanksgiving in colonial dress, medieval banquets, mystery weekends.
Seen in: *The Boston Herald, Los Angeles Sunday Times, Country Inns.*

"There isn't one thing we didn't enjoy about our weekend with you and we are constantly reliving it with much happiness."

West Dover

Austin Hill Inn

Rt 100, Box 859
West Dover VT 05356
(802) 464-5281

Circa 1940. Situated in a quiet area on the edge of a mountain, this completely renovated inn has walls decorated with old barn board and floral Victorian wallpapers. Old antiques and family heirlooms include family photographs dating from 1845 in antique frames. Most rooms have balconies and four-poster or brass beds. A five-course, home-cooked candlelight dinner is available on weekends.

Location: Two miles from Mount Snow.
Rates: $100-$110.
Robbie Sweeney.
12 Rooms. 10 Private Baths. Guest phone available. TV available. Beds: KQDT. MAP. Restaurant. Gourmet meals. Swimming pool. CCs: MC VISA AX. Horseback riding, skiing, biking, golf.
Seen in: *Garden City Life.*

"A wonderful escape!"

Snow Den Inn

Rt 100
West Dover VT 05356
(802) 464-9355

Circa 1885. John Davis built his rambling home from lumber worked in his waterwheel mill. The interior is noted for its original wax-rubbed ash encasements. It was the last home to be built in the town, but it became the first guest inn in the Mt. Snow area in 1952. Several rooms have fireplaces and sitting areas. All have private baths.

*Rates: $75-$130. Season: June 15-April 15.
Andrew & Marjorie Trautwein.
8 Rooms. 8 Private Baths. 5 Fireplaces. Guest phone available. TV in room. Beds: QD. EP. CCs: MC VISA AX. Horseback riding, water sports, hiking, golf, skiing, antiquing, music festivals.
Seen in: *Inn Spots & Special Places, Southern Vermont Magazine.*

"No small details are overlooked."

West Rutland

The Silver Fox Inn

Rt 133 Box 1222
West Rutland VT 05777
(802) 438-5555

Circa 1768. One of the first houses built in the area, this was the home

of Captain John Smith. It was for Smith's head the governor of a neighboring state once offered the sum of 40 pounds. The inn is furnished with Queen Anne cherrywood and oak. The Clarendon River runs along the property.

*Rates: $105-$145. Season: May - March.
Pam & Gerry Bliss.
7 Rooms. 7 Private Baths. Guest phone available. TV available. Beds: QD. AP. Restaurant. Gourmet meals. Handicap access. Conference room. CCs: MC VISA. Bicycling, cross-country skiing, golf, tennis, fishing, hiking.
Seen in: *The Rutland Business Journal.*

"We never expected dinner could be so imaginative. We used to stay at a ski condo but breakfast in bed is my idea of a great getaway."

"A four-star inn. Everything we thought it would be."

West Townsend

Windham Hill Inn

RR 1 Box 44
West Townsend VT 05359
(802) 874-4080

Circa 1825. Windham Hill was originally a working dairy farm owned by William Lawrence. It was sold at auction but most of the existing furniture, silverware, rugs, and quilts belonged to the Lawrence

family. Surrounded by 175 acres in a secluded hillside setting, Windham Hill was selected by Uncle Ben's Rice Company and Innsider as one of the top 10 inns for 1988 and 1989.

Rates: $70-$105. Season: May - March.
Ken & Linda Busteed.
15 Rooms. 15 Private Baths. Guest phone available. TV available. Beds: KQTD. AP. Handicap access. CCs: MC VISA. Hiking, cross-country skiing.

"The inn lived up to the expectations of any New Yorker or Bostonian who conjures up a romantic vision of a Vermont country inn. It also lived up to a Vermonter's expectation of a country inn." Madeleine Kunin, Governor of Vermont.

Weston

1830 Inn on the Green

Rt 100 Box 104
Weston VT 05161
(802) 824-6789

Circa 1830. Originally a wheelwright's shop, the building was later a town hall and an undertaker's parlor. Moved to its present site, it became a private home graced with a beautiful curving staircase from the house of Hetty Green, "The Witch of Wall Street." Situated in the Weston Historic District and tucked in a hollow of the Green Mountains, the inn is across the village green from the oldest summer theater in the state.

Rates: $60-$80.
Sandy & Dave Granger.
4 Rooms. 2 Private Baths. Guest phone available. TV available. Beds: KQD. B&B. CCs: MC VISA. Skiing, bicycling, hiking, golf, tennis, fishing, canoeing, horseback riding.
Seen in: *Yankee Homes.*

Williamsville

The Country Inn Williamsville

Grimes Hill Rd, Box 166
Williamsville VT 05362
(802) 348-7148

Circa 1795. Overlooking 99 acres, this Federal-style house once

presided over a dairy and apple farm. The sugar house served as the village auction house. The inn is filled with English and Victorian antiques collected in London.

✻Rates: $76-$161.
Bill & Sandra Cassill.
6 Rooms. 6 Private Baths. Guest phone available. TV available. Beds: KQTD. AP. CCs: MC VISA. Hiking, skiing, bicycling, swimming, antiquing. Close to the Marlboro music festival.
Seen in: *Southern Vermont Magazine.*

"Four stars. Ideal setting, memorable dining and most gracious hosts."

Woodstock

The Charleston House

21 Pleasant St
Woodstock VT 05091
(802) 457-3843

Circa 1835. This authentically restored Greek Revival townhouse is listed in the National Register. It is furnished with antiques, an art collection and oriental rugs. The picturesque village of Woodstock has been called one of the most beautiful villages in America by *National Geographic Magazine.*

Rates: $100-$125.
Barbara & Bill Hough.
7 Rooms. 7 Private Baths. Guest phone available. TV available. Beds: QDT. Full breakfast. CCs: MC VISA. Cross-country skiing, tennis, fishing, hiking.

"I felt like I was a king, elegant but extremely comfortable."

Kedron Valley Inn

See: South Woodstock, VT

Shire Inn

See: Chelsea, VT

Virginia

Alexandria

Memory House
See: Arlington, VA

Arlington

Memory House
6404 N Washington Blvd
Arlington VA 22205
(703) 534-4607

Circa 1899. This vintage Victorian inn, built by a former mayor of Falls

Church, was restored by the owners over a period of several years. Terra-cotta, cream, and green highlight the gingerbread and shingled gables of the house. Inside are stenciled borders, polished hardwood floors, antique furnishings and collectibles. Restaurants are within eight blocks, and the East Falls Church subway station is one block away, making this a convenient base for exploring the nation's capitol.

Location: Two blocks from I-66 via exit 22.
*Rates: $65-$70.
John & Marlys McGrath.
2 Rooms. 1 Private Bath. Guest phone in room. TV in room. Beds: DT. Continental-plus breakfast. Tennis, bicycling, sightseeing.
Seen in: *The Washington Post.*

"It was a joy to stay in this beautiful home! Marlys and John were perfect hosts."

Burkeville

Hyde Park Farm
Rt 2 Box 38
Burkeville VA 23922
(804) 645-8431

Circa 1752. This is a three-story farmhouse, situated on 1,000 acres of farmland. It once served as a sanctuary for young Jewish people who escaped from Germany just prior to World War II. They planted a peach orchard, raised poultry and developed a dairy farm while awaiting naturalization as U.S. citizens. Now, the house has 14 guest rooms in its 8,000 square feet. The honeymoon suite features a fireplace, silk sheets, a Gay 90s wedding gown and walnut arches leading to a jacuzzi tub. The inn caters to those who prefer a casual, easy-going atmosphere. Pleasant streams wind through Hyde Park's pastures and woodlands.

*Rates: $60-$150.
Anne C. Scott.
14 Rooms. 12 Private Baths. 11 Fireplaces. Guest phone available. TV in room. Beds: QDTC. B&B. Gourmet meals. Jacuzzi. Game room. Conference room. Walking trails, outdoor games, fish pond.
Seen in: *The Richmond News Leader, The Amelia Bulletin Monitor.*

"Feels like Grandmother's arms."

Charles City

Edgewood Plantation
Rt 5 Historic
Charles City VA 23030
(804) 829-2962

Circa 1849. This Carpenter Gothic plantation was built by Northerner

Spencer Rowland. Romantic guest rooms are furnished with antiques and old-fashioned country artifacts. There are 10 fireplaces and a winding three-story staircase. A few yards from the inn is a three-story mill with an unusual inside mill wheel built in 1725.

Location: Halfway between Williamsburg and Richmond.
Rates: $88-$135.
Dot & Juilian Boulware.
6 Rooms. 2 Private Baths. Guest phone available. TV available. Beds: KQD. Full breakfast. Jacuzzi. Swimming pool. CCs: MC VISA. Hiking, bicycling, golf, fishing, antiquing. Complimentary refreshments at two nearby taverns.
Seen in: *Country Home Magazine, Unique Inns of Virginia.*

"A feast for the eyes."

North Bend Plantation

Rt 1 Box 13A
Charles City VA 23030
(804) 829-5176

Circa 1819. The Copland family lived here for three generations. The

present owner is twice great-grandson of noted agriculturist Edmund Ruffin, who is said to have fired the first shot of the Civil War at Fort Sumpter. Sheridan headquartered at North Bend. His desk is still here, one of many treasured family heirlooms.

Location: West of Colonial Williamsburg, 25 minutes.
Rates: $68-$79.
George & Ridgely Copland.
4 Rooms. 1 Private Bath. 3 Fireplaces. Guest phone available. TV available. Beds: QD. Full breakfast. Game room. Nature walks, croquet, horseshoes, volleyball, badminton.
Seen in: *The Washington Post, Travel Talk.*

"Your hospitality, friendship and history lessons were all priceless. Your love of life embraced us in a warmth I shall never forget."

Piney Grove Southall's Plantation

Rt 1 Box 148, Piney Grove
Charles City VA 23030-9735
(804) 829-2480

Circa 1800. The Gordineers welcome you to their two historic homes. Piney Grove is a rare Tidewater log building (circa 1800) located on Old Main Road among farms, plantations, country stores and quaint churches. Ladysmith House is a modest antebellum plantation home (circa 1857). Both homes are furnished with a unique collection of artifacts and antiques that illustrate their histories. Guests also enjoy meandering among the gardens and grounds.

Location: James River Plantation outside of Williamsburg.
Rates: $95-$125.
Brian E. Gordineer, Joseph & Joan Gordineer.
6 Rooms. 4 Private Baths. 5 Fireplaces. Guest phone available. TV available. Beds: DT. Full breakfast. Gourmet meals. Swimming pool. Conference room. Historic sightseeing, nature trail, bird-watching.
Seen in: *Richmond Times-Dispatch.*

Charlottesville

200 South Street Inn

200 South St
Charlottesville VA 22901
(804) 979-0200

Circa 1853. This house was built for Thomas Jefferson Wertenbaker, son of Thomas Jefferson's librarian at the University of Virginia. It is furnished with English and Belgian antiques. Guests may choose rooms with whirlpool baths, fireplaces and canopy beds.

Location: Downtown historic district of Charlottesville.
*Rates: $85-$160.
Donna Deibert.
20 Rooms. 20 Private Baths. TV available. Beds: QT. Continental-plus breakfast. Restaurant. Jacuzzi. Handicap access. Conference room. CCs: MC VISA.
Seen in: *New York Times, Gourmet, Vogue Magazine.*

"True hospitality abounds in this fine inn which is a neatly turned complement to the inspiring history surrounding it."

Chester

See: Scottsville, VA

Guesthouses

PO Box 5737
Charlottesville VA 22905
(804) 979-7264

Circa 1750. Guesthouses, America's first reservation service for bed and

breakfast accommodations, appropriately originated in an area with a centuries-old tradition of outstanding hospitality. Many of the homes are in the National Register. They are located in Charlottesville and throughout Albermarle County, and have been inspected carefully to assure a pleasant stay.

Rates: $50-$150.
CCs: MC VISA.
Seen in: *Roanoke Times & World-News, Good Housekeeping.*

High Meadows

See: Scottsville, VA

Mayhurst Inn

See: Orange, VA

Prospect Hill

See: Trevilians, VA

Silver Thatch Inn

3001 Hollymead Dr, PO Box 6370
Charlottesville VA 22901
(804) 978-4686

Circa 1780. This white clapboard inn, shaded by tall elms, was built for British officers by Hessian soldiers who were prisoners during the Revolutionary War. Before its current life as a country inn, Silver Thatch was a boys' school, a melon farm, a tobacco plantation, and more recently, the home of Dean Runk, former Dean of the School of Architecture of the University of Virginia. Many additions have been made to the original house, now called the Hessian Room, creating an antique-filled country inn. There are three intimate dining rooms.

Rates: $95-$115.
Joe & Mickey Geller.
7 Rooms. 7 Private Baths. 4 Fireplaces. Guest phone available. TV available. Beds: QD. Continental-plus breakfast. Restaurant. Conference room. CCs: MC VISA. Horseback riding, canoeing, hiking, golf, jogging trails, tennis.
Seen in: *Travel & Leisure, Washington Post, Los Angeles Times.*

"Everything was absolutely perfect! The room, the food, and above all, the people!"

Woodstock Hall

Rt 3 Box 40
Charlottesville VA 22901
(804) 293-8977

Circa 1757. After leaving Thomas Jefferson's Monticello, a French

duke who stayed at Woodstock Hall tavern wrote, "Mr. Woods Inn is so good and cleanly...I cannot forbear mentioning those circumstances with pleasure." These standards remain at this national historic landmark. The two-story clapboard house contains hand-blown windowpanes, a fireplace in each guest room, and many period antiques selected from the innkeeper's antique shop.
Location: On Route 637, 1.8 miles off I-64, Ivy exit.
Rates: $95-$130.
Jean Wheby & Mary Ann Elder.
4 Rooms. 4 Private Baths. Guest phone available. TV in room. Beds: KQ. B&B. Gourmet meals. Conference room. Golf, tennis, pool available in summer, walking trail and gazebo.

Chincoteague

Miss Molly's Inn

113 N Main St
Chincoteague VA 23336
(804) 336-6686

Circa 1886. This Victorian was built by J. T. Rowley, the "Clam King of the World." His daughter Miss Molly lived in it for 84 years. The house has been beautifully restored and furnished in period antiques. Marguerite Henry wrote *Misty of Chincoteague* here while rocking on the front porch with Miss Molly and Captain Jack.
Rates: $55-$105. Season: April - Dec.
Dr. & Mrs. James Stam.
7 Rooms. 1 Private Bath. 1 Fireplace. Guest phone available. TV available. Beds: KDT. B&B. Conference room. Swimming, fishing, clamming, crabbing, hiking, sailing, surfing.

"Your hospitality and warmth exuded with each guest and made all of us feel most at home."

Culpeper

Fountain Hall B&B

609 S East St
Culpeper VA 22701
(703) 825-8200

Circa 1859. Culpeper was first surveyed by George Washington. This

was Lot #3 of a subdivision of 33 acres. Fountain Hall was originally a Victorian house, but in the Twenties was remodeled as a Colonial Revival. Most of the rooms are named after historic families in the community. The Frey Drawing Room displays old prints and a library wall of books from the late 1800s.
*Rates: $55-$75.
Steve & Kathi Walker.
5 Rooms. 3 Private Baths. 3 Fireplaces. Guest phone in room. TV available. Beds: QDTC. B&B. Handicap access. Conference room. CCs: MC VISA AX. Horseback riding, skiing, basketball, tennis, golf.
Seen in: *Culpeper Exponent.*

"Liked the friendly greeting and atmosphere. Food was delicious."

Flint Hill

Caledonia Farm B&B

Rt 1 Box 2080
Flint Hill VA 22627
(703) 675-3693

Circa 1812. This Federal-style stone house is beautifully situated on 52 acres adjacent to Shenandoah National Park and was built by a Revolutionary War officer, Captain John Dearing. His musket is displayed over the mantel. The house has been restored and the colonial color scheme retained. The innkeeper is a retired broadcaster.
Location: Four miles north of Washington, Virginia.
*Rates: $70-$100.
Phil Irwin.
3 Rooms. 2 Private Baths. 3 Fireplaces. Guest phone available. TV available. Beds: D. Full breakfast. Handicap access. Conference room. CCs: MC VISA. Hiking, golf, tennis, swimming, fishing, canoeing, hay rides.
Seen in: *The Washington Post.*

"Our first bed & breakfast was a delight!"

Fredericksburg

Fredericksburg Colonial Inn

1707 Princess Anne St
Fredericksburg VA 22401
(703) 371-5666

Circa 1928. The modern streamlined facade of the Fredericksburg

Colonial Inn belies a treasure of antiques and hospitality found within. High four-poster beds with their

own step stools, Victorian sofas and carved tables fill each guest room. Best of all, innkeeper and storyteller, Jim Hirst, is knowledgeable about local history and keeps a mini-library on Fredericksburg on hand.
Rates: $45.
Jim Hirst.
33 Rooms. 33 Private Baths. Guest phone available. TV in room. Beds: KQDTC. Continental breakfast. Handicap access. Conference room. CCs: MC VISA. Golf, fishing, boating, swimming, tennis, racquet-ball.
Seen in: *The Philadelphia Inquirer, Travel Today.*
"Breathtaking!"

La Vista Plantation
4420 Guinea Station Rd
Fredericksburg VA 22401
(703) 898-8444

Circa 1838. La Vista has a long and unusual past rich in Civil War history. Both Confederate and Union armies camped here, and this is where the Ninth Calvary was sworn in. A classical Revival structure with high ceilings and pine floors, the house sits on 10 acres of pasture and woods. There is a pond stocked with sunfish.
Rates: $70.
Michele & Edward Schiesser.
2 Rooms. 2 Private Baths. 1 Fireplace. Beds: KQDC. Full breakfast. Conference room. CCs: MC VISA. Fishing, hiking, bicycles, horseback riding.
"Thanks for the best weekend we've ever had."

Front Royal

Chester House Inn
43 Chester St
Front Royal VA 22630
(703) 635-3937

Circa 1905. This stately Georgian estate rests on two acres of terraced gardens, which include vast plantings of boxwood, wisteria arbors, a fountain and brick walkways and walls. Elaborately carved marble mantels from London remain, and an original speaker tube extends from the second floor bedroom to the kitchen. Just down the street is the renovated village commons.
*Rates: $55-$95.
Bill & Ann Wilson.
6 Rooms. 1 Private Bath. Guest phone available. TV available. Beds: KQDT.

B&B. Conference room. CCs: MC VISA. Boating, hiking, horseback riding, golf, tennis, camping, wineries, antiquing.
Seen in: *Winchester Star, Northern Virginia Daily.*
"A home of greater charm would be hard to find."

Gordonsville

Sleepy Hollow Farm
Rt 3 Box 43 on VA 231
Gordonsville VA 22942
(703) 832-5555

Circa 1775. Many generations have added on to this brick farmhouse

with its 18th-century dining room and bedrooms. The pink and white room was frequently visited by a friendly ghost from Civil War days according to local stories. She hasn't been seen for several years since the innkeeper, a former missionary, had the house blessed. The grounds include an herb garden, a pond with gazebo, a chestnut slave cabin, terraces and abundant wildlife.
Location: Between Gordonsville & Somerset on Rt 231.
Rates: $55-$85.
Beverly Allison.
6 Rooms. 6 Private Baths. 1 Fireplace. Guest phone available. TV available. Beds: QTC. Full breakfast. Conference room. CCs: MC VISA. Horseback riding, golf, pond swimming, fishing, hiking.
Seen in: *The Orange County Review.*
"This house is truly blessed."

Hillsboro

Inn Between the Hills
RR 3, Rt 9, PO 68A
Hillsboro VA 22132
(703) 668-6162

Circa 1780. Happening upon Hillsborough and the Inn Between the Hills was a serendipitous

surprise. Picturesquely set in the gap of the Short Hills, the town boasts numerous stone houses from the 18th century. Many, like the inn, saw both Union and Confederate soldiers march to the battles of Bull Run and Manassas. During the John Brown uprising, the inn housed the Hillsboro Border Guards. Carefully restored, guest rooms offer feather beds, antiques and fine reproductions. The inn is only open weekends.
Rates: $60-$85.
Kathy & Josh Margolis.
3 Rooms. 1 Private Bath. 1 Fireplace. Guest phone available. Beds: QDT. B&B. Gourmet meals. Canoeing, kayaking, tubing, hiking, biking, antiquing.
Seen in: *Leesburg Today.*
"It's the little touches that you do so well."

Leesburg

Inn Between the Hills
See: Hillsboro, VA

Laurel Brigade Inn
20 W Market St
Leesburg VA 22075
(703) 777-1010

Circa 1759. This handsome Colonial stone house originally opened as an ordinary. Prices were set for lodging by the local parish justices of six shillings "on clean sheets, otherwise nothing." The long ell on the west side of the inn was

erected to entertain the Marquis de Lafayette when he visited James Monroe. The inn features marble mantle pieces from France, Swiss door fixtures and a well-known dining room. It has been operated since 1945 by the Flippo family.
Rates: $50-$90. Season: Feb. 14-Dec. 31
Ellen Flippo Wall.
6 Rooms. 6 Private Baths. 2 Fireplaces. Guest phone available. TV available. Beds: KDT. Restaurant. Hiking, horseback riding.
Seen in: *Saturday Evening Post, Southern Living, New York Times, Washington Post.*

Norris House Inn
108 Loudoun St SW
Leesburg VA 22075
(703) 777-1806

Circa 1806. The Norris brothers, Northern Virginia's foremost architects and builders, purchased this building in 1850 and began extensive renovations several years later. They used the finest wood and brick available, remodeling the exterior to an Eastlake style. Beautifully restored, the inn features built-in bookcases in the library and a cherry fireplace mantel.

Rates: $60-$125.
Laura Walton.
8 Rooms. 2 Private Baths. 4 Fireplaces. Guest phone available. Beds: QDT. Full breakfast.
Seen in: *New York Times, Better Homes and Gardens Country Home, Washingtonian Magazine.*

"Thank you for your gracious hospitality. We enjoyed everything about your lovely home, especially the extra little touches that really make the difference."

Lexington

Fassifern B&B
Rt 5 Box 87
Lexington VA 24450
(703) 463-1013

Circa 1867. Fassifern, which draws its name from the seat of the Cameron Clan in Scotland, was built on the site of an older dwelling just after the Civil War. Nestled in the Shenandoah Valley, the inn is on three-and-a-half acres, surrounded by stately trees and graced with a pond.

Location: Route 39, 3/4 miles from I-64, Exit 13.
Rates: $42-$65
Ann-Carol & Arthur Perry.
6 Rooms. 4 Private Baths. Guest phone available. Continental-plus breakfast. CCs: MC VISA. Horseback riding, swimming, canoeing, golf, tennis, hiking, fishing.

"Excellent - best B&B ever. Exquisite room, excellent hospitality."

Llewellyn Lodge at Lexington
603 S Main St
Lexington VA 24450
(703) 463-3235

Circa 1936. This brick Colonial shaded by tall trees, features three gables on the third story. It is decorated in antique and traditional furnishings. Nearby historic attractions include the home of Stonewall Jackson, the Natural Bridge and the Robert E. Lee house.

Location: Fifty miles north of Roanoke.
*Rates: $49-$68.
Ellen Thornber & John Roberts.
6 Rooms. 6 Private Baths. Guest phone available. TV available. Beds: KQDT. Full breakfast. Handicap access. Conference room. CCs: MC VISA AX. Swimming, golf, tennis, hiking, fishing, hunting.
Seen in: *The News-Gazette, The New York Times.*

"Like being at home! The breakfast was the best ever."

Luray

The Ruffner House
Rt 4 Box 620
Luray VA 22835
(703) 743-7855

Circa 1739. Situated on a farm nestled in the heart of the Shenandoah Valley, this stately manor was built by Peter Ruffner, the first settler of Page Valley and Luray. Ruffner family members discovered a cavern opposite the entrance to the Luray Caverns, which were found later. Pure bred Arabian horses graze in the pasture on this 18-acre estate.

Location: Shenandoah Valley, South of Hwys. 211 and 340.
*Rates: $55-$110.
Mrs. Roman.
7 Rooms. 5 Private Baths. Guest phone available. TV available. Beds: Q. Full breakfast. Swimming pool. Conference room. CCs: MC VISA. Swimming, golf, canoeing, rafting, horses, tennis, hiking.
Seen in: *Page News and Courier, The Virginian Pilot.*

"This is the loveliest inn we have ever stayed in. We were made to feel very welcome and at ease."

Mathews

Ravenswood Inn

PO Box 250
Mathews VA 23109
(804) 725-7272

Circa 1913. This intimate waterfront home is located on five acres along the banks of the East River, where passing boats still harvest crabs and oysters. A long screened porch captures river breezes. Most rooms feature a river view and are decorated in Victorian, country, nautical or wicker. The inn's speciality is its noted French and Mediterranean cuisine. Williamsburg, Jamestown and Yorktown are within an hour.

Rates: $150. Season: Feb. 12-Dec. 12.
Peter & Sally Preston.
4 Rooms. 4 Private Baths. Beds: KQT. MAP. Gourmet meals. Jacuzzi. Charter fishing, charter sailing, bicycles, sailboats, croquet, badminton.
Seen in: *The Virginian Pilot, Daily Press.*

"While Ravenswood is one of the most beautiful places we've ever been, it is your love, caring and friendship that has made it such a special place for us."

Riverfront House & Cottage

Rt 14 E, PO Box 310
Mathews VA 23109
(804) 725-9975

Circa 1840. This farmhouse and its waterfront cottage are situated on 10

acres along Put In Creek. The main house features a wraparound veranda. Guests use the dock for crabbing, boating, and sunbathing. Mathews County is surrounded by the Chesapeake and Mobjack Bays and dozens of creeks, harbors and inlets. The landscape includes old sawmills, churches, farmlands and oystering boats. Riverfront House makes a good base for daytrips to Williamsburg, Yorktown, Richmond and the James River Plantations.

*Rates: $60-$85. Season: May-November.
Annette Waldman Goldreyer.
8 Rooms. 8 Private Baths. Guest phone available. TV available. Beds: KQT. Full breakfast.

"A joyful relaxing experience."

Middleburg

Red Fox Inn & Mosby's Tavern

PO Box 385, 2 E Washington St
Middleburg VA 22117
(703) 687-6301

Circa 1728. Originally Chinn's Ordinary, the inn was a popular stop-

ping place for travelers between Winchester and Alexandria. During the Civil War, Colonel John Mosby and General Jeb Stuart met here. Guest rooms are furnished in 18th-century decor and most feature four-poster canopy beds.

Location: Two miles east of Washington on Route 50.
*Rates: $115-$200.
Dana & Turner Reuter, Jr.
27 Rooms. 27 Private Baths. 10 Fireplaces. Guest phone in room. TV in room. Beds: KQDTC. B&B. Restaurant. Gourmet meals. Handicap access. Conference room. CCs: MC VISA AX. Fox hunting, horseback riding by arrangement. Vineyard tours.

Welbourne

Middleburg VA 22117
(703) 687-3201

Circa 1775. This seventh-generation mansion once presided over 10,000 acres. With family members

starting their own estates, Welbourne now stands at 600 acres. Furnishings were collected during world travels over the past 200 years. Civil War stories fill the family history book, and in the 1930s, F. Scott Fitzgerald and Thomas Wolfe used the house as a setting for their writings.

Location: Fifty miles west of Washington, DC.
*Rates: $80-$100.
Mrs. N. H. Morison.
10 Rooms. 10 Private Baths. 7 Fireplaces. Guest phone available. TV available. Beds: QT. Full breakfast. Conference room. Fox hunting.

"...furnishings portray a house and home that's been around for a long, long time. And none of it is held back from guests. Life today at Welbourne is quiet and unobtrusive. It's genteel..." Philip Hayward, *Country Magazine.*

Mollusk

Greenvale Manor

Rt 354, PO Box 70
Mollusk VA 22517
(804) 462-5995

Circa 1840. Beautifully situated on the Rappahannock River and Greenvale Creek, Greenvale is a classic waterfront plantation. This land was patented to Anthony Stephens in 1651, but in 1607 Captain John Smith said of Virginia's Northern Neck, *"Heaven and earth never agreed better to frame a place for men's habitation... rivers and brooks all running most pleasantly...with fruitful and delightsome land."* The gracious manor lifestyle extends from tastefully furnished guest rooms to a licensed captain available for boat tours from the dock.

Location: Eight miles from Lancaster Courthouse off Route 3.
Rates: $60-$90.
Pam & Walt Smith.
9 Rooms. 7 Private Baths. 2 Fireplaces. Guest phone available. TV available. Beds: KQDT. Full breakfast. Swimming pool. Game room. Conference room. Boating, bicycling, golf, tennis, badminton. Private beach.
Seen in: *Rural Living, Conde Nast Traveler.*

"The inn and grounds are gorgeous, the water views breathtaking, but it's the innkeepers who make it really special."

Monterey

Highland Inn
PO Box 40
Monterey VA 24465
(703) 468-2143

Circa 1904. Listed in the National Register, this clapboard Victorian

hotel has outstanding Eastlake wraparound verandas. Small-town life may be viewed from rocking chairs and swings. Guest rooms are furnished in country fashion, with iron beds and antiques. Sheep outnumber people in a pastoral setting surrounded by three million acres of National Forest.

Location: Thirty-seven miles west of Staunton.
*Rates: $35-$55.
John & Joanne Crow.
17 Rooms. 17 Private Baths. Guest phone available. TV available. Beds: KQTWDC. Restaurant. Conference room. CCs: MC VISA. Hiking, cross-country skiing, fishing, golf.

Montross

The Inn at Montross
Courthouse Sq
Montross VA 22520
(804) 493-9097

Circa 1683. Montross was rebuilt in 1800 on the site of a 17th-century

tavern. Operating as an "ordinary" since 1683, parts of the structure have been in continuous use for more than 300 years. It was visited by burgesses and Justices of the Court (Washington, Lee and Jefferson). The guest rooms feature canopy beds and Colonial furnishings.

Location: Seven miles from Stratford Hall.
*Rates: $65-$75.
Eileen & Michael Longman.
6 Rooms. 6 Private Baths. Guest phone in room. TV in room. Beds: QDT, Continental-plus breakfast. Restaurant. Gourmet meals. Conference room. CCs: MC VISA AX DC CB DS. Tennis on premises.

Mount Jackson

The Widow Kip's Country Inn
Rt 1 Box 117
Mount Jackson VA 22842
(703) 477-2400

Circa 1830. This lovingly restored farmhouse with its sweeping view

of the Massanutten Mountains is situated on seven acres. It's a stone's throw from a fork of the Shenandoah River. Locally-crafted quilts enhance the four-poster, sleigh and hand-carved Victorian beds. Two restored cottages (the Silk Purse and Sow's Ear) as well as a gift shop, create a Williamsburg-style courtyard. Cows graze unexpectedly a few feet away from the swimming pool.

Location: I-81 to Mt. Jackson. Exit 69 to Route 11, south to 263.
*Rates: $60-$75.
Rosemary Kip.
7 Rooms. 7 Private Baths. 5 Fireplaces. Guest phone available. TV in room. Beds: QD. Full breakfast. Sauna. Swimming pool. CCs: VISA DS. Bicycling, skiing, horseback riding.
Seen in: *Country Inns, Mid Atlantic Country, Americana.*

"Everything sparkled. The rooms were decorated with flair and imagination."

New Market

A Touch of Country B&B
9329 Congress St
New Market VA 22844
(703) 740-8030

Circa 1873. This white clapboard Shenandoah Valley "I" frame house has a second-story pediment centered above the veranda entrance. It was built by Captain William Rice, commander of the New Market Calvary. Rice's unit was highly praised by General Lee for its efforts during the Civil War. Guest chambers are in the main house and in the handsome carriage house.

Rates: $55-$65.
Jean Schoellig & Dawn M. Kason.
6 Rooms. 2 Private Baths. Guest phone available. TV available. Beds: QD. B&B. CCs: MC VISA. Golf, swimming, skiing, hiking, canoeing.
Seen in: *USA Today Weekend.*

"Every morning should start with sunshine, bird song and Dawn's strawberry pancakes."

Orange

Hidden Inn
249 Caroline St
Orange VA 22960
(703) 672-3625

Circa 1880. Acres of huge, old trees can be seen from the wraparound

veranda of this Victorian inn nestled in the Virginia countryside. Meticulous attention has been given to every detail of the inn's restoration, right down to the white lace and fresh cut flowers. Montpelier, James Madison's famous estate, is just five miles from the inn. Civil War sites and many fine wineries are located nearby.

Location: Intersection of Rte 15 & Rte 20.

*Rates: $69-$129.
Barbary & Ray Lonick.
9 Rooms. 9 Private Baths. 2 Fireplaces. Guest phone available. TV in room. Beds: KQDT. EP. Restaurant. Gourmet meals. Jacuzzi. CCs: MC VISA. Fishing, waterskiing, tennis.

"It just doesn't get any better than this!"

Mayhurst Inn

US 15 South, PO Box 707
Orange VA 22960
(703) 672-5597

Circa 1859. An extravagant Italianate Victorian villa, Mayhurst

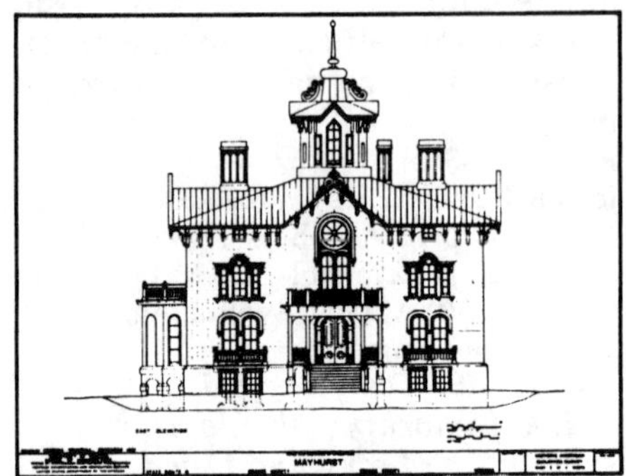

was built by the great-nephew of President James Madison, Col. John Willis. It is noted for its fanciful architecture and oval spiral staircase ascending four floors to a rooftop gazebo. It was once host to General Stonewall Jackson and during the Civil War served as the Northern Virginia army headquarters. Thirty-six acres of old oaks, cedars, and magnolias surround the inn.
Location: One mile south of Orange, 95 miles south of Washington, D.C.
*Rates: $85-$95.
Stephen & Shirley Ramsey.
7 Rooms. 7 Private Baths. 5 Fireplaces. Guest phone available. Beds: QDT. Full breakfast. Gourmet meals. Conference room. CCs: MC VISA. Horseback riding, a pond for fishing and swimming.
Seen in: *Lifestyle.*

"It's Victorian splendor at its highest."

Richmond

Abbie Hill B&B

PO Box 4503
Richmond VA 23220
(804) 355-5855

Circa 1909. Situated on a one-acre city lot in the historic district is this Federal-style bed and breakfast. It

once provided a third-story office for Realtor John Bagby, while his wife and five children filled the rooms downstairs. The host, an interior designer, has redecorated and furnished guest rooms with antiques such as four-poster beds. Birds and plants fill the bay window in the paneled dining room lit with a massive crystal chandelier. An afternoon tea and a full Virginia breakfast are house specialties.
Rates: $65-$95.
Barbara & Bill Fleming.
3 Rooms. 2 Private Baths. 2 Fireplaces. Guest phone available. TV in room. Beds: QDT. B&B. Walking tours, museums.

"Thanks for the relaxing stay and great breakfast!!"

Bensonhouse of Richmond at Monument

2036 Monument Ave
Richmond VA 23220
(804) 353-6900

Circa 1909. This graciously restored historic home is a showcase of brightly colored walls, fireplaces, and detailed windows. The innkeepers have renovated five Richmond homes and love collecting antiques, art and new friends.
Rates: $72-$115.
Lyn M. Benson.
3 Rooms. 2 Private Baths. Guest phone available. TV available. Beds: QT. Full breakfast. CCs: MC VISA.

"We loved the house and thoroughly enjoyed our stay. We have done quite a few B&Bs and your service rates a 10! Many thanks!"

The Catlin-Abbott House

2304 E Broad St
Richmond VA 23223
(804) 780-3746

Circa 1845. This house was built for William Catlin by a slave, Wil-

liam Mitchell, a noted brick mason of the time. During reconstruction, a six-room addition was built to accommodate boarders. It now serves as innkeeper's quarters. This richly appointed inn is one block from St. John's Church, site of Patrick Henry's famous *Liberty or Death* speech.
*Rates: $82-$140.
Dr. & Mrs. James L. Abbott.
3 Rooms. 3 Private Baths. Guest phone available. TV available. Beds: QT. Full breakfast. CCs: MC VISA.

"The accommodations were immaculate."

Fredericksburg Inn

See: Fredericksburg, VA

Mr. Patrick Henry's Inn

2300 E Broad St
Richmond VA 23223
(804) 644-1322

Circa 1858. Elegant Mr. Patrick Henry's is located in Richmond's oldest neighborhood, Church Hill, an area of gas-lit streets and beautifully restored town houses. The Greek Revival inn has a formal garden, carriage house, and an old bridal path. Most of the guest rooms have a fireplace, kitchenette and private porch.

Rates: $85-$125.
Jim & Lynn News.
4 Rooms. 4 Private Baths. 3 Fireplaces. Guest phone in room. TV in room. Beds: KQT. Full breakfast. Restaurant. Conference room. CCs: MC VISA DC.
Seen in: *Roanoke Times, Mid-Atlantic Country.*

North Bend Plantation B&B

See: Charles City, VA

Roanoke

Manor at Taylor's Store

See: Smith Mountain Lake, VA

The Mary Blandon House B&B

381 Washington Ave Old SW
Roanoke VA 24016
(703) 344-5361

Circa 1891. This Elizabethan Victorian, located in Roanoke's historic

area once served as a boarding house, operated by "Mother Bladon." There are several ornate fireplaces, and the home is furnished with antiques and local craft items. Spacious porches provide a spot to relax. The innkeeper's cats and dogs are said to be well behaved and kept from guest quarters.
Rates: $65.
Sally Pfister.
4 Rooms. 2 Private Baths. 2 Fireplaces. Guest phone available. TV available. Beds: D. Full breakfast. CCs: MC VISA.
Seen in: *Country Magazine, Roanoke Times.*

"You are doing a fabulous job."

Scottsville

High Meadows

Rt 4, Box 6
Scottsville VA 24590
(804) 286-2218

Circa 1832. Minutes from Charlottesville on the Constitution High-

way (Route 20), High Meadows stands on 22 acres of gardens, forests, ponds, a creek, and a vineyard. Listed in the National Register, it is actually two historic homes joined together by a breezeway. The inn is furnished in Federal and Victorian styles. Guests are treated to gracious Virginia hospitality in an elegant and peaceful setting.
Rates: $85.
Peter Sushka & Mary Jae Abbitt.
7 Rooms. 7 Private Baths. 4 Fireplaces. Beds: QDT. Gourmet meals. Conference room. Canoeing, fishing, hiking, croquet, horseshoes, skiing, wineries.
Seen in: *The Washington Times, The Cavalier Daily.*

"We have rarely encountered such a smooth blend of hospitality and expertise in a totally relaxed environment."

Smith Mountain Lake

Manor at Taylor's Store

Rt 1 Box 533
Smith Mountain Lake VA 24184
(703) 721-3951

Circa 1820. Situated on 105 acres of rolling countryside, this two-story, columned manor was built on the site of Taylor's Store, a trading post and ordinary just off the old Warwick Road. It served as the plantation house for a prosperous tobacco farmer, Moses Greer Booth. Guest rooms feature a variety of antiques and styles including traditional Colonial and English Country. From the solarium, a wildflower trail winds through the inn's green meadows where a canoe awaits those who wish to paddle across one of the five ponds studding the property.
Rates: $50-$80.
Lee & Mary Lynn Tucker.
5 Rooms. 5 Private Baths. 6 Fireplaces. Guest phone available. TV available. Beds: QD. B&B. Gourmet meals. Jacuzzi. Handicap access. Exercise room. Swimming pool. Game room. Conference room. CCs: MC VISA. Boating, fishing, golf, tennis, horses, hiking.
Seen in: *Franklin News-Post, Smith Mountain Eagle, Lake Country.*

"This B&B experience is a delightful one!"

Staunton

Frederick House

Frederick and New Streets
Staunton VA 24401
(703) 885-4220 (800)334-5575(outside VA)

Circa 1810. The three historic homes that comprise Frederick House appear as one. The oldest

structure is believed to be a copy of a home designed by Thomas Jefferson and built on the campus of the University of Virginia. Original staircases and woodwork are highlighted throughout.
Location: Downtown.
*Rates: $40-$70.
Joe & Evy Harman.
11 Rooms. 11 Private Baths. Guest phone in room. TV in room. Beds: KQTC. Continental breakfast. Restaurant. Jacuzzi. Sauna. Exercise room. Swimming pool. Conference room. CCs: MC VISA AX DC CB DS. Golf, tennis, skiing, hiking, horseback riding.
Seen in: *Richmond Times-Dispatch, The News Journal.*

"Thanks for making the room so squeaky clean and comfortable! I en-

joyed the Virginia hospitality. The furnishings and decor are beautiful."

Trevilians

Prospect Hill

Rt 613, RD 3 Box 430
Trevilians VA 23093
(703) 967-0844

Circa 1732. On a quarter of a mile of green lawn, nestled in the midst of an English garden, is the Manor House. Rare magnolias shade the inn, and nearby is an old log cabin dating to 1699, now one of the guest accommodations. During the Civil War, Mrs. Wilson stood on the landing and Union soldiers shot around her trying to discover where slaves were hidden. After the war, the owners began to take in guests and this hospitality has continued for more than 100 years.

Location: Fifteen miles east of Charlottesville near Zion Crossroads.
*Rates: $110-$160.
The Sheehan Family.
11 Rooms. 11 Private Baths. 10 Fireplaces. Guest phone available. Beds: QDT. AP. Jacuzzi. Swimming pool. Conference room. CCs: MC VISA. Swimming, Jogging, Walking.
Seen in: *The Washington Post, Americana Magazine, The Daily Progress.*

"We've been to many wonderful inns - this is the nicest!"

Wachapreague

The Burton House

11 Brooklyn St
Wachapreague VA 23480
(804) 787-4560

Circa 1883. Located one block from the waterfront, The Burton House is

a good point from which to take day trips to Tangier Island, Chincoteague, Assateague and the Barrier Islands. Recently restored, the inn has an inviting screened gazebo with gingerbread trim and posts salvaged from the old Wachapreague Hotel. Baskets of red geraniums, wicker furniture, and a gentle breeze off the water entice guests to relax awhile.

Location: Midway between Norfolk, Virginia and Salisbury, Maryland.
Rates: $60.
Pat, Tom & Mike Hart.
7 Rooms. 1 Private Bath. 1 Fireplace. Guest phone available. TV available. Beds: QT. Full breakfast. Bicycling, boating, tennis.
Seen in: *Virginia Pilot, Self Magazine.*

"Staying here is like visiting with a favorite cousin."

Warm Springs

The Inn at Gristmill Square

PO Box 359
Warm Springs VA 24484
(703) 839-2231

Circa 1800. The inn consists of five restored buildings. The old blacksmith shop and silo, the hardware store, the Steel House and the Miller House all contain guest rooms. (The old mill is now the Waterwheel Restaurant). A few antiques and old prints appear in some rooms while others are furnished in a contemporary style. There are tennis courts and a swimming pool at the inn. A short walk over Warm Springs Mill Stream and down the road brings travellers to historic Warm Springs Pools.

Rates: $85-$127.
The McWilliams Family.
14 Rooms. 14 Private Baths. 8 Fireplaces. Guest phone in room. TV in room. Beds: KQDTC. MAP. Restaurant. Sauna. Swimming pool. Conference room. CCs: MC VISA. Tennis, golf, skeet, skiing, ice skating, horseback riding, fishing, hunting, chamber music.
Seen in: *New York Times, Bon Appetit.*

Meadow Lane Lodge

Star Rt A Box 110
Warm Springs VA 24484
(703) 839-5959

Circa 1920. This lodge, the family home of the present innkeeper's parents, is situated on 1600 acres. It was part of a land grant made by King George III to Charles Lewis, a pioneer settler. Foundations of an old fort and large brick home are still visible, as is an ancient family cemetery. The lodge is decorated with comfortable furnishings and antiques. Two miles of the Jackson River that meanders through the estate are stocked with brown trout for guests. Walking trails pass hay fields, a swimming hole and a beaver bog against Allegheny ridgelines. A limestone spring provides a million gallons of delicious drinking water each day. Deer, fox, herons and osprey are often seen from a nearby cliffside deck.

Rates: $89-$220. Season: April - Jan.
Philip & Catherine Hirsh.
11 Rooms. 11 Private Baths. 3 Fireplaces. Guest phone in room. TV in room. Beds: KQDT. Full breakfast. Jacuzzi. Handicap access. Swimming pool. Conference room. CCs: MC VISA AX. Horseback riding, skiing, golf, bowling, natural warm springs pools, canoeing, croquet, tennis, mountain biking, farm animals.
Seen in: *The Washingtonian Magazine.*

"This was the cleanest, neatest and best done room we can remember having enjoyed anywhere."

Washington

Caledonia Farn

See: Flint Hill, VA

The Foster-Harris House

PO 333
Washington VA 22747
(703) 675-3757

Circa 1901. This Victorian stands on a lot laid out by George Washington and is situated at the

edge of the village. The streets of the town are exactly as surveyed 225 years ago and the town is the first of more than 28 Washingtons in the United States. The village has many galleries and craft shops as well as the Inn at Little Washington, a five-star restaurant. The innkeeper is known in the area for her flower beds and floral arrangements.

Location: Fifty miles north of Charlottesville.
Rates: $70-$105.
Camille Harris.
3 Rooms. 1 Private Bath. 1 Fireplace. Guest phone available. TV available. Beds: Q. Full breakfast. Conference room. CCs: MC VISA. Tennis, canoeing, fishing, cross-country skiing, horseback riding.
Seen in: *Culpeper News, Richmond Times Dispatch.*

"The View Room is charming, as are the hosts."

Heritage House B&B

Main St, PO Box 427
Washington VA 22747
(703) 675-3207

Circa 1837. This two-story columned house is situated in the heart of the historic district of

Washington, a town surveyed by George Washington in 1749. Furnished in antiques, the inn's new owners are of Scandinavian heritage and feature Swedish country breakfasts. Guests may easily walk to craft and antique shops, an art gallery and a restaurant.
Rates: $75-$95.
Polly & Al Erickson.
4 Rooms. 2 Private Baths. Guest phone available. Beds: QD. Full breakfast. Handicap access. CCs: MC VISA. Hiking, horseback riding, vineyards.
Seen in: *Country Almanac.*

"Having been to a number of bed & breakfasts, yours is #1 in its setting, the wonderful food and your hospitality.

The Inn at Little Washington

PO Box 300, Middle & Main Sts
Washington VA 22747
(703) 675-3800

Circa 1915. This two-story white clapboard inn was once a repair garage. With the assistance of English designer Joyce Conwy-Evans, fantasy and romance were created with lavish fabrics, faux woods and antiques. A garden courtyard includes a gazebo and reflecting pool. The restaurant and lodging is so notable that the Inn at Little Washington has been awarded five stars and five diamonds.
Rates: $240-$420.
Patrick O'Connell & Reinhardt Lynch.
10 Rooms. 10 Private Baths. Beds: KQ. Continental breakfast. Handicap access. CCs: MC VISA.
Seen in: *USA Today.*

"One of the most celebrated restaurants and inns in America." Bon Appetit.

White Post

L'Auberge Provencale

PO Box 119
White Post VA 22663
(703) 837-1375

Circa 1753. This stone farmhouse was built with fieldstones gathered

from the area. Hessian soldiers crafted the woodwork of the main house, Mt. Airy. It contains three of the inn's dining rooms. Guest rooms are decorated in Victorian antiques.
Location: One mile south of Route 50 on Route 340.
Rates: $100-$145. Season: Feb. - Dec.
Alain & Celeste Borel.
6 Rooms. 6 Private Baths. Guest phone available. Beds: QD. Conference room. CCs: MC VISA DC. Horseback riding, canoeing, golf, indoor tennis, racquetball, Skyline Drive.
Seen in: *Washington Dossier, The Washington Post.*

"Peaceful view and atmosphere, extraordinary food and wines. Honeymoon and heaven all in one!"

Williamsburg

Applewood Colonial B&B

605 Richmond Rd
Williamsburg VA 23185
(804) 229-0205

Circa 1921. This Flemish-bond brick home was built during the restoration of Colonial Williamsburg. The inn's parlor is decorated in a colonial style and features dentil crown molding. A crystal chandalier hangs above the dining table where breakfast is served. The Colonel Vaughn suite boasts a private entrance, a fireplace and queen-size canopy bed.
Rates: $65-$100.
Fred Strout
4 Rooms. 4 Private Baths. 1 Fireplace. Guest phone available. Beds: Q. Continental-plus breakfast. CCs: MC VISA. Pottery factory, outlet stores, shops. Afternoon tea.

"Our accommodations were the best and you were most kind."

Bensonhouse of Williamsburg

Contact Bensonhouse of Richmond
Williamsburg VA 23185
(804) 353-6900

Circa 1983. A copy of the 1760 Sheldon's Tavern in Litchfield, Connecticut, this home is located one mile from Colonial Williamsburg and the College of William and Mary in a quiet, wooded area. A Palladian-style window, antique heart-pine, wide-plank floors from Philadelphia, and oak paneling from an old Indiana church are special features. For reservations, contact Bensonhouse, 2036 Monument Avenue, Richmond, VA 23220.
Location: One block to Colonial Williamsburg.
Rates: $72-$85.
1 Room. 1 Private Bath. Guest phone available. Beds: QC. Full breakfast. Handicap access. CCs: MC VISA.

"You certainly chose wisely when you matched us with our hosts! You have a great thing going with the brochure, maps, and wonderful houses."

Liberty Rose Colonial B&B

1022 Jamestown Rd
Williamsburg VA 23185
(804) 253-1260

Circa 1929. This slate-roofed, two-story clapboard house is tucked

among tall trees a mile from Colonial Williamsburg. Constructed by the owner of Jamestown, much of the brick was brought from the Colony before it became a historic landmark. The entry porch is marked with the millstone from one of Williamsburg's old mills. The inn is lavishly decorated with antiques and collectables.
Rates: $75-$125.
Brad & Sandra Hirz.
4 Rooms. 3 Private Baths. Guest phone available. TV in room. Beds: QD. Full breakfast. CCs: MC VISA AX.

"More delightful than we could possibly have imagined."

Newport House

710 South Henry St
Williamsburg VA 23185
(804) 229-1775

Circa 1988. This neo-Palladian house is a 1756 design by Peter Harrison, architect of rebuilt Williamsburg. It features wooden rusticated siding. Colonial country dancing is held in the inn's ballroom on Tuesday evenings. Guests are welcome to participate. There are English and American antiques, and reproductions include canopy beds in all the guest rooms.

The host was a museum director and captain of a historic tall ship.
Location: Five minute walk from Colonial Williamsburg.
*Rates: $75-$90.
John & Cathy Millar.
2 Rooms. 2 Private Baths. 1 Fireplace. Guest phone available. TV available. Beds: QT. B&B. Conference room. CCs: DS. Scottish country dancing.

"Host and hostess were charming and warm."

North Bend Plantation B&B

See: Charles City, VA

Piney Grove at Southall's Plantation

See: Charles City, VA

Ravenswood Inn

See: Mathews, VA

Woodstock

Country Fare

402 N Main St, Rt 11
Woodstock VA 22664
(703) 459-4828

Circa 1772. Originally an American foursquare home, the front section of this inn has a log substructure. A tunnel originating at the Abraham Miller house across the street is accessed by a trap door in that house's study floor, which runs under the house. Local tradition says soldiers hid in the tunnel during the Civil War. Family keepsakes and hand-stenciled walls recapture the atmosphere of this authentic log home, set on an acre of magnolias and Japanese cherry.
Rates: $50-$60.
5ette Hallgren.
3 Rooms. 1 Private Bath. Beds: DT. Continental-plus breakfast. Hiking, fishing.
Seen in: *Valley-Herald, Woodstock House Tour.*

"Relaxing and pleasurable as always."

The Inn at Narrow Passage

PO Box 608
Woodstock VA 22664
(703) 459-8000

Circa 1740. This log inn has been welcoming travelers since the time

settlers took refuge here against the Indians. Later, it served as a stagecoach inn on the old Valley Turnpike, and in 1862, as Stonewall Jackson's headquarters. Many guest rooms feature fireplaces and views of the lawn as it slopes down to the Shenandoah River.
Location: On Shenandoah River and US 11, 2-1/2 miles south of Woodstock.
*Rates: $55-$80.
Ellen & Ed Markel.
12 Rooms. 8 Private Baths. Guest phone available. TV available. Beds: Q. Full breakfast. Conference room. CCs: MC VISA. Horseback riding, fishing, hiking, skiing, boating. Vineyards and historic sites nearby.
Seen in: *Capital Entertainment.*

"Just the setting I needed to unwind from my hectic civilized world."

Washington

Anacortes

Channel House

2902 Oakes Ave
Anacortes WA 98221
(206) 293-9382

Circa 1902. Built by an Italian count, the Channel House is desig-

nated the Krebs House by the Historical Home Tour. Guest rooms view Puget Sound and the San Juan Islands, and the ferry is minutes away. The inn has a Victorian flavor, with a library, three fireplaces, and a dining room with French doors leading out to the garden.
Location: 85 miles north of Seattle.
*Rates: $65-$80.
Dennis & Patricia McIntyre.
6 Rooms. 4 Private Baths. 2 Fireplaces. Guest phone available. Beds: QD. B&B. Jacuzzi. CCs: MC VISA. Boating, biking, swimming. Tulip festival.
Seen in: *Skagit Valley Herald.*

"The house is spectacular and your friendly thoughtfulness is the icing on the cake."

Hasty Pudding House

1312 8th Street
Anacortes WA 98221
(206) 293-5773

Circa 1913. This Edwardian Craftsman house is located in a

quiet neighborhood near historic downtown, the waterfront and Causland Park. The front porch solarium contains wicker furnishings, while the house is decorated with antiques, lace curtains and coordinated wallpapers.
Rates: $50-$75.
4 Rooms. 1 Private Bath. Beds: KQDT. Full breakfast. Boating, fishing, crabbing, hiking, rock climbing, kayaking, golf, tennis.

*"You and your beautiful bed and breakfast really made our trip."*D

Bainbridge Island

Bombay House

8490 Beck Rd NE
Bainbridge Island WA 98110
(206) 842-3926

Circa 1907. This Victorian captain's house is set atop Blakely Hill, amidst colorful, unstructured gardens. It boasts a quaint widow's walk and an old-fashioned gazebo overlooking picturesque sailboats and ferries cruising through Rich Passage. Take the scenic Seattle ferry ride six miles to Bainbridge.
❀Rates: $50-$78.
Bunny Cameron & Roger Kanchuk.
5 Rooms. 3 Private Baths. Guest phone available. TV available. Beds: KT. Continental-plus breakfast. Conference room.

"Your breakfast was marvelous! No lunch today!"

Bellingham

The Castle B&B

1103 15th & Knox Sts
Bellingham WA 98225
(206) 676-0974

Circa 1889. All the guest rooms of this Victorian mansion look out to Bellingham Bay and the San Juan Islands. The gables, steeply pitched turret, and bays are highlighted in mauve. The Cupola Room, with its panoramic water view, is the inn's honeymoon suite. Underneath the suite's castle-type furnishings is a red carpet. The Bayview Room opens to a veranda and has its own fireplace. Your hosts have an extensive lamp and clock collection sprinkled throughout the house's 21 rooms.
Rates: $45-$75.
Gloria & Larry Harriman.
4 Rooms. 1 Private Bath. 1 Fireplace. Guest phone in room. TV available. Beds: QT. B&B. CCs: MC VISA. Skiing, boating, hiking, golf.
Seen in: *Sunset Magazine, Daughters of the Painted Ladies.*

"Never have I seen a B&B with so many museum quality pieces of furniture."

North Garden Inn
1014 N Garden
Bellingham WA 98225
(206) 671-7828

Circa 1897. Listed in the National Register, this Queen Anne Victorian originally had bars on the basement windows to keep out the bears. Guest rooms feature views of Bellingham Bay and the surrounding islands. A mahogany Steinway piano is often played for guests. The inn is within walking distance to Western Washington University.
*Rates: $44-$54.
Frank & Barbara DeFreytas.
10 Rooms. 2 Private Baths. Guest phone available. Beds: KQD. Full breakfast. Conference room. CCs: MC VISA. Skiing, sailing, golfing.

Bremerton

Willcox House
2390 Tekiu Rd
Bremerton WA 98312
(206) 830-4492

Circa 1936. Colonel Julian Willcox and his family, once members of San

Francisco high society, selected Lionel Pries to build this home on a wooded bluff overlooking Hood Canal. Holding court thereafter, the family entertained fashionable Northwest personalities, including Clark Gable. The 7,800 square foot manse was constructed with a slate tile exterior, copper roofing and vast expanses of small-paned windows, affording views of the shimmering waters, the Olympic mountains and forested hillsides. There are five marble and copper fireplaces, silk wallpaper, oak floors, fine antiques and period pieces throughout. The Julian Room sports a double jacuzzi tub.
*Rates: $90-$150.
Cecilia & Phillip Hughes.
5 Rooms. 5 Private Baths. 1 Fireplace. Guest phone available. Beds: K. Full breakfast. Gourmet meals. Jacuzzi. Swimming pool. Game room. CCs: MC VISA. Water sports, hiking, fishing, antiquing, relaxing.
Seen in: *The Olympian, Journal American.*

"Diane & I and Clark love the place and delight in the knowledge that all Californians aren't bad - in fact some are down right wonderful."

Coupeville

Victorian House
PO Box 761, 602 N Main
Coupeville WA 98239
(206) 678-5305

Circa 1889. This graceful Italianate Victorian sits in the heart of one of the nation's few historic reserves. It was built for German immigrant Jacob Jenne, who became the proprietor of the Central Hotel on Front Street. Noted for having the first running water on the island, the house's old wooden water tower stands in the back garden. An old-fashioned store front, once the local dentist's office, sits demurely behind a picket fence, now a private hideaway for guests.
*Rates: $75-$95.
Dolores Colton Fresh.
3 Rooms. 3 Private Baths. Guest phone available. TV available. Beds: D. Full breakfast. CCs: MC VISA. Hiking, bicycling, sailing, fishing.
Seen in: *The Seattle Times.*

"If kindness and generosity are the precursors to success (and I certainly hope they are!), your success is assured."

Eatonville

Old Mill House B&B
PO Box 543
Eatonville WA 98328
(206) 832-6506

Circa 1925. Tucked behind huge elm trees, this is a 6,000 square-foot, three-story Colonial-style estate. It still retains its basement speakeasy, with both a bar and a dance floor. Old Mill House was the home of John Galbraith, mill owner and early Eatonville mayor. A Twenties decor prevails, and each room is named for a personality of that era. In the F. Scott Fitzgerald Room, an ongoing novel is being written by a

steady stream of guests. Some return just to add to the story.
*Rates: $55-$70.
Catharine & Michael Gallagher.
4 Rooms. 1 Private Bath. Guest phone available. Beds: KQDT. B&B. CCs: MC VISA. Cross-country skiing, water skiing, wildlife reserve.
Seen in: *Seattle Times, Tacoma News Tribune, Dispatch.*

Greenbank

Guest House B&B & Cottages
835 E Christenson Rd
Greenbank WA 98253
(206) 678-3115

Circa 1920. This cozy Whidbey Island home is located on 25 acres of forest and meadows, where deer wander by the wildlife pond and storybook cottages. Guest rooms have art deco touches. There is a log house with a free-form jacuzzi and a view over the pond to the sound. The Wildflower Suite and the Farm Guest Cottage are the most historic accommodations.
Location: On Whidbey Island.
*Rates: $75-$195.
Don & Mary Jane Creger.
6 Rooms. 6 Private Baths. 5 Fireplaces. Guest phone available. TV in room. Beds: KQDT. B&B. Jacuzzi. Exercise room. Swimming pool. CCs: MC VISA AX DS. Horseback riding, golf, fishing, hiking, clamming, boating. Exercise room, bathrobes provided.
Seen in: *Los Angeles Times, Woman's Day.*

"Best B&B experience on the West Coast." Lewis Green, *Los Angles Times.*

Kirkland

Shumway Mansion

11410 99th Place NE
Kirkland WA 98033
(206) 823-2303

Circa 1909. This resplendent 22-room, 10,000 square-foot mansion is

situated on more than two acres overlooking Juanita Bay. With a large ballroom and veranda with water views, few could guess that a short time ago, the building was hoisted on hydraulic lifts. It was then pulled three miles across town to its present site, near the beach.

Location: West of I-405 at Juanita Bay.
*Rates: $52-$72.
Richard & Salli Harris, & daughter Julie.
7 Rooms. 7 Private Baths. Guest phone available. TV available. Beds: Q. Full breakfast. Jacuzzi. Sauna. Exercise room. Swimming pool. Conference room. CCs: MC VISA. Skiing, tennis. Athletic club.
Seen in: *Northgate Journal, Journal American, Northwest Living.*

"Guests enjoy the mansion so much they don't want to leave." Northwest Living.

La Conner

Rainbow Inn

1075 Chilberg Rd, PO Box 1600
La Conner WA 98257
(206) 466-4578

Circa 1900. This Victorian farmhouse is situated peacefully among fields planted in tulips, daffodils, iris or sweet peas. An enclosed wraparound porch is the site for breakfast. Antiques and artistically arranged country collectibles gathered for several years decorate the inn. Old-fashioned wallpapers, period furnishings and claw-footed tubs add to the atmosphere. The village of La Conner is a half mile away.

Rates: $65-$95.
Marilyn Lee, Ray Degler.
8 Rooms. 5 Private Baths. Guest phone available. Beds: Q. Full breakfast. Jacuzzi. CCs: MC VISA.
Seen in: *Sunset, Eddie Bauer Catalog.*

"Lovely and generous service in a gracious country atmosphere. Super hideaway jacuzzi."

LaConner

White Swan Guest House

See: Mount Vernon, WA

Langley

Country Cottage of Langley

PO Box 459, 215 6th St
Langley WA 98260
(206) 221-8709

Circa 1926. Outstanding views of the Cascades, Saratoga Passage and the village can be seen from the three acres surrounding Country Cottage. Rooms are decorated with Laura Ashley prints and antiques for an elegant country style, and the guest sitting area has a fireplace. A newly built miniature farmhouse situated for extensive views of the Sound, contains two suites. An old creamery has been converted to another cottage. The garden has decking and a gazebo.

Rates: $75-$85.
Trudy & Whitney Martin.
5 Rooms. 5 Private Baths. Guest phone available. TV available. Beds: Q. Full breakfast. Handicap access. CCs: MC VISA. Sailing, boating, bicycling, hiking, fishing, horseback riding.

"Hospitality plus! Nicely decorated rooms. Beautiful breakfasts."

Mount Vernon

White Swan Guest House

1388 Moore Rd
Mount Vernon WA 98273
(206) 445-6805

Circa 1898. The turret of this Victorian farmhouse was once used as the lookout for the small ferry that crossed the Skaget River before the bridge was built. Refurbished by New York designer Peter Goldfarb, the inn was named after the white swans that flock to the corn fields

behind the house. A favorite choice is the Turret Room with its own window seat. In the morning, guests stroll to the kitchen to watch Innkeeper Peter Goldfarb prepare breakfast or to look out to the Cascade ridges framing the valley. La Conner is six miles away.

Rates: $55-$60.
Peter Goldfarb.
3 Rooms. Guest phone available. Beds: KQ. Continental-plus breakfast. CCs: MC VISA. Tulip Field Tours, Museums.
Seen in: *The Spokesman-Review Spokane Chronicle.*

"Like Grandma's house."

Mt. Rainier

Old Mill House B&B

See: Eatonville, WA

Orcas

Orcas Hotel

PO Box 155
Orcas WA 98280
(206) 376-4300

Circa 1900. Listed in the National Register, this three-story Victorian

inn across from the ferry landing has been a landmark to travelers and boaters since the early 1900s. An open porch stretches around three sides and is filled with white wicker furniture. From this vantage point, guests enjoy views of terraced lawns and flower beds of peonies, daffodils, iris and roses. A white

picket fence and a vista of sea and islands complete the picture.
Location: Overlooking the ferry landing on Orcas Island.
*Rates: $48-$125.
Barbara Jamieson.
12 Rooms. 3 Private Baths. Guest phone available. TV available. Beds: QTC. Continental breakfast. Restaurant. Gourmet meals. Jacuzzi. Handicap access. Conference room. CCs: MC VISA AX. Bicycling, sailing, golfing, horseback riding, fishing, hiking.
Seen in: *Los Angeles Times, Seattle Times, The New York Times.*
"Wonderful hospitality, super good food, pleasant surroundings, all provided a delightful experience."

Orcas Island

Turtleback Farm Inn
Rt 1 Box 650, Eastsound
Orcas Island WA 98245
(206) 376-4914

Circa 1890. This handsome farmhouse was considered one of the finest homes on Orcas Island in

the early 1900s. The inn was restored and expanded from the ground up in 1985, with particular attention to authenticity and detail, including bathroom fixtures purchased from the old Empress Hotel in Victoria. Cattle graze on the inn's 80 idyllic acres of meadows, pastures and woodlands.
Location: Six miles from ferry landing, 2 miles from Westsound.
*Rates: $65-$135.
William & Susan Fletcher.
7 Rooms. 7 Private Baths. Guest phone available. TV available. Beds: KQDT. B&B. CCs: MC VISA. Golf, kayaking, fishing, sailing, swimming.
Seen in: *Travel & Leisure, Contra Costa Sun.*

Port Angeles

Tudor Inn
1108 S Oak
Port Angeles WA 98362
(206) 452-3138

Circa 1910. This English Tudor inn has been tastefully restored to dis-

play its original woodwork and fir stairway. Guests enjoy stone fireplaces in the living room and study. A terraced garden with 100-foot oak trees graces the property.
Location: Eleven blocks south of the harbor with water & mountain views.
*Rates: $40-$70.
Jane & Jerry Glass.
5 Rooms. 1 Private Bath. Guest phone available. TV available. Beds: KQTD. Full breakfast. CCs: MC VISA.
"Delicious company and delicious food. Best in hospitality and warmth. Beautiful gardens!"

Port Townsend

Arcadia Country Inn
1891 S Jacob Miller Rd
Port Townsend WA 98368
(206) 385-5245

Circa 1878. This red and white Craftsman-style house is situated on 80 acres of woodland and pasture. It is owned by the Flying Karamazov Brothers who sometimes practice in the barn where dances and theater were once held. Guest rooms are decorated with antiques. One room features a view of the Olympic Mountains.
Location: Three-and-a-half miles north of town.
Rates: $50-$80.
Ande Grahn.
5 Rooms. 5 Private Baths. Guest phone available. Beds: QDT. Continental breakfast. Jacuzzi. Conference room. CCs: MC VISA.

Heritage House Inn
305 Pierce St
Port Townsend WA 98368
(206) 385-6800

Circa 1880. This stately Italianate listed in the National Register, was the home of Francis Pettygrove, a founder of Port Townsend and Portland, Oregon. (He flipped a coin to name it Portland or Boston. Portland won.) The innkeepers have collected an array of unusual antiques, including a fold-down bathtub on wheels. Because of the mild climate and low rainfall, half that of Seattle, the town's elegant houses have withstood the ravages of time, and contain the best examples of Victorian architecture north of San Francisco.
Location: Across the street from the water.
*Rates: $45-$79.
Pat & Jim Broughton, Bob & Carolyn Ellis.
6 Rooms. 3 Private Baths. Guest phone available. Beds: QD. B&B. Handicap access. CCs: MC VISA AX. Skiing, fishing, boating.
"You two provide the perfect balance between nurturing and unobtrusiveness. Difficult to do!"

James House
1238 Washington
Port Townsend WA 98368
(206) 385-1238

Circa 1889. This Queen Anne mansion built by Francis James over-

looks Puget Sound with views of the Cacades and Olympic mountain ranges. The three-story staircase was constructed of solid wild cherry brought around Cape Horn from Virginia. Parquet floors are comprised of oak, cherry, walnut and maple providing a suitable setting for the inn's collection of antiques.

Location: On the bluff overlooking Port Townsend Bay.
Rates: $60-$125.
Lowell & Barbara Bogart.
12 Rooms. 4 Private Baths. 3 Fireplaces. Guest phone available. TV available. Beds: QD. Continental-plus breakfast. Handicap access. Conference room. CCs: MC VISA. Fishing, tennis, golf, horseback riding, hiking, bicycling, swimming, boat charters.
Seen in: *Washington Magazine, The Seattle Weekly.*

"We were enchanted by Victorian splendor and delicious breakfasts."

Lincoln Inn

538 Lincoln
Port Townsend WA 98368
(206) 385-6677

Circa 1888. This Victorian was faced in brick with cornerstones by local mason Elias Devoe as a showplace for his brick company. The original kerosene chandeliers were converted to electric. The polished floors are covered with Persian rugs. Bicycles are available from the innkeeper for touring.

*Rates: $65-$75. Season: Feb. - Christmas.
Joan & Robert Allen.
5 Rooms. 5 Private Baths. Guest phone available. Beds: QD. Full breakfast. Gourmet meals. Jacuzzi. CCs: MC VISA. Hiking, rafting, wind surfing, cross-country skiing, boating.
Seen in: *Daughters of Painted Ladies.*

"Exceeded our expectations. Thanks for a great honeymoon!"

Lizzie's

731 Pierce St
Port Townsend WA 98368
(206) 385-4168

Circa 1887. Named for Lizzie Grant, a sea captain's wife, this Italianate Victorian is elegant and

airy. In addition to the gracious interiors, some rooms command an outstanding view of Port Townsend Bay, Puget Sound, and the Olympic and Cascade mountain ranges. Each room is filled with antiques dating from 1840 to the turn-of-the-century. The dog's house in the garden is a one-quarter scale replica of the original house. Lizzie's is known for its elaborate breakfasts, where guests are encouraged to help themselves to seconds.

Location: In uptown Historic District.
Rates: $49-$89.
Bill & Patti Wickline.
8 Rooms. 5 Private Baths. Guest phone available. Beds: KQ. Full breakfast. CCs: MC VISA. Hiking, boating, wind surfing, fishing, golf.
Seen in: *Travel & Leisure.*

"As they say in show biz, you're a hard act to follow."

Starrett House Inn

744 Clay St
Port Townsend WA 98368
(206) 385-3205

Circa 1889. George Starrett came from Maine to Port Townsend and

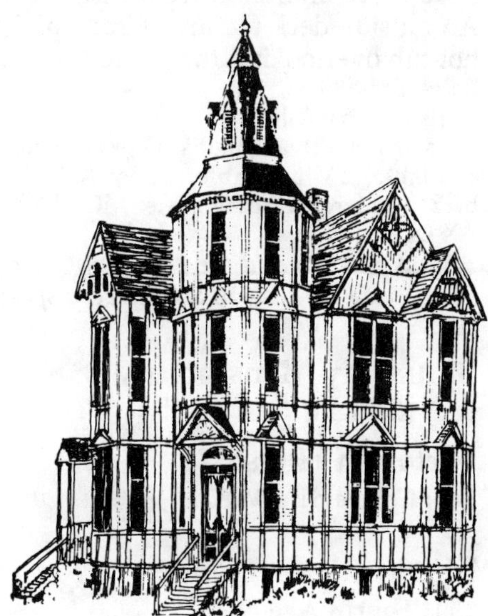

became the major residential builder. By 1889, he had constructed one house a week, totaling more than 350 houses. The Smithsonian believes the elaborate free-hung spiral staircase is the only one of its type in the United States. A frescoed dome atop the octagonal tower depicts four seasons and four virtues. On the first day of each season, the sun causes a ruby light to point toward the appropriate painting.

Location: Three blocks from the business district.
Rates: $55-$90.
Bob & Edel Sokol.
9 Rooms. 7 Private Baths. Guest phone available. Beds: Q. Continental-plus breakfast. CCs: MC VISA. Fishing, wind surfing, golf, cross-country skiing, tennis. Cruises.
Seen in: *Peninsula Magazine, New York Times.*

"The Grande Bonbon of them all." Jan Halliday, *Pacific Northwest."*

Quinault

Lake Quinault Lodge

PO Box 7, S Shore Rd
Quinault WA 98575
(206) 288-2571 (800) 562-6672 (WA only)

Circa 1926. After a devastating fire, Lake Quinault Lodge was rebuilt

from the ground up in 70 days. President Franklin Roosevelt stayed here in 1938, and signed the Olympic National Park into law. The lawn of the old lodge slopes to the water's edge. A quaint gazebo provides views of the wooded slopes beyond. Dominating the lobby, a huge brick fireplace attracts guests who often gather to plan an excursion out to the inn's 20 miles of trails through the rain forest. Under new management, the lodge was spiffed up and refurbished in 1989.

Location: Two miles East of US 101, on South shore of Lake Quinault.
*Rates: $60-$95.
Tom McFadden.
57 Rooms. 57 Private Baths. 16 Fireplaces. Guest phone available. TV available. Beds: QDTC. EP. Restaurant. Jacuzzi. Sauna. Swimming pool. Game room. Conference room. CCs: MC VISA. Hiking, canoeing, paddle boats, fishing.
Seen in: *Seattle Post-Intelligencer.*

Seattle

Chambered Nautilus B&B Inn

5005 22nd NE
Seattle WA 98105
(206) 522-2536

Circa 1915. This blue, Georgian Colonial was built by a British mis-

sionary, Dr. Herbert Gowen, who founded the Department of Oriental Studies at the University of Washington. Three dormers and Palladian doors grace the front of the house. Coved ceilings, fireplaces, fully stocked bookcases, Persian rugs, and English and American antiques compliment its gracious decor. Many of the guest rooms have French doors and balconies overlooking the gardens.
Location: In the University District.
Rates: $59-$89.
Bunny & Bill Hagemeyer.
6 Rooms. 2 Private Baths. Guest phone available. Beds: QD. Full breakfast. Conference room. CCs: MC VISA AX. Boating, skiing, bicycling and jogging trails, tennis, golf.
Seen in: *Innsider Magazine.*

"I think you've spoiled us for any other inn, anyplace. We felt like Royalty and family members all at the same time."

Chelsea Station B&B Inn

4915 Linden Ave N
Seattle WA 98103
(206) 547-6077

Circa 1920. This Federal Colonial home is one of Seattle's finest examples of the bricklayer's art. It is located in a tranquil wooded setting in the midst of the city. A secluded hot tub is tucked away in one of the carriage houses. The inn has 29 varieties of its own special roses, including a Mint Julep. The Woodland Park Zoo and Rose Gardens are only a few steps away.
Location: Just north from downtown. Near Greenlake & Seattle's Rose Gardens.
*Rates: $59-$85.
Dick & Marylou Jones.
5 Rooms. 5 Private Baths. 2 Fireplaces. Guest phone available. TV available. Beds: K. Full breakfast. Jacuzzi. CCs: MC VISA AX DC CB. Swimming, boating, tennis, biking, golf.
Seen in: *Seattle Post-Intelligencer.*

"What a wonderful fairyland room and hospitable hosts."

Galer Place

318 W Galer St
Seattle WA 98119
(206) 282-5339

Circa 1906. This two-story, shingled house is located in South Queen Anne Hill and is within walking distance to Seattle Center. The rooms are furnished in antiques and plants. The English innkeepers have made afternoon tea a tradition. An outside deck features a redwood hot tub overlooking the garden.
Rates: $85-$95.
Chris & Terry Giles.
4 Rooms. 4 Private Baths. Guest phone available. TV available. Beds: KQDT. B&B. Conference room. CCs: MC VISA AX DC.

"Your warmth and the charm of Galer Place made my visit to Seattle very special."

Shumway Mansion

See: Kirkland, WA

Victorian House

See: Coupeville, WA

The Williams House

1505 Fourth Ave N
Seattle WA 98109
(206) 285-0810

Circa 1905. Built by a mid-western cart builder, the inn features much original woodwork and gaslight fixtures, as well as an ornate gas fireplace. A formal parlor is accentuated with Victorian furnishings. Many of the rooms have commanding views of mountains, lakes, Puget Sound, and the downtown Seattle skyline.
Location: Queen Anne Hill.
*Rates: $70-$90.
Susan, Doug & Danielle Williams.
5 Rooms. 1 Private Bath. Guest phone available. TV available. Beds: KQDC. Continental-plus breakfast. Exercise room. Swimming pool. Conference room. CCs: MC VISA AX DC CB.

Seaview

Shelburne Inn

PO Box 250, Pacific Hwy 103 & 45th
Seaview WA 98644
(206) 642-2442

Circa 1896. The Shelburne is known as the oldest continuously operating hotel in the state of

Washington. The front desk at the hotel is a former church altar. Art nouveau stained-glass windows rescued from a church torn down in Morcambe, England, now shed light and color on the dining room. The guest rooms are appointed in antiques. In between the Columbia River and the Pacific Ocean, the inn is situated on Long Beach Peninsula, a 28-mile stretch of seacoast that includes bird sanctuaries and lighthouses.
Location: Southwest Washington State.
*Rates: $69-$135.
David Campiche & Laurie Anderson.
16 Rooms. 13 Private Baths. Guest phone available. Beds: QTDC. Full breakfast. Restaurant. Handicap access. Conference room. CCs: MC VISA. Horseback riding, fishing, beach walking, clamming. English-style pub.
Seen in: *Better Homes & Gardens, Bon Appetit, Washington Magazine, Esquire.*

"Homey but elegant atmosphere. Hospitable service, like being a guest in an elegant home."

South Cle Elum

Moore House B&B Country Inn

PO Box 2861
South Cle Elum WA 98943
(509) 674-5939

Circa 1909. Built by the Chicago, Milwaukee and Pacific railroads,

this bunk house was designed to house crew men on layover. At the 2,000 foot level, it is adjacent to Iron Horse State Park, where guests may cross-country ski, cycle or take a sleigh ride. Covered wagon rides are available and end at the inn for western barbecues on Wednesdays. The bunkhouse has been renovated and guest rooms are decorated with railroad memorabilia. The Mel Faudee caboose has been furnished for families of five or less. The town of Cle Elum is noted for its old bakery, whose brick oven is said to have been kept continuously hot since 1906.

*Rates: $39-$89.

Monty & Connie Moore.

11 Rooms. 5 Private Baths. Guest phone available. TV in room. Beds: QDT. B&B. Jacuzzi. Conference room. CCs: MC VISA AX. Horse trails, hiking, fishing, boating, covered-wagon rides. Halloween Murder Mystery.

Seen in: *Washington Magazine.*

"Great accommodations and host and hostess that are just plain fun to be with. I am looking forward to my second visit."

Vashon Island

The Old Tjomsland House

99 Ave SW & 171st St, Box 913
Vashon Island WA 98070
(206) 463-5275

Circa 1890. A. T. Tjomsland, builder of the Methodist Church and Parsonage, constructed this traditional farmhouse. It reflects the small-town America atmosphere of Vashon Island. The two guest rooms on the upper floor have a separate entrance. They share a common bath, large living room and kitchenette. A family-style dinner

may be arranged. Your hosts speak French and German.

Location: Twenty minutes by ferry from Seattle and Tacoma.

*Rates: $55.

Jan & Bill Morosoff.

2 Rooms. Guest phone available. TV available. Beds: QT. B&B. CCs: MC VISA. Bicycling, golf. Alcohol-free and smoke-free.

Seen in: *Vashon-Maury Island Beachcomber.*

"Your house is neat as a pin, spotless. We have been at B&Bs all over the world and yours is outstanding."

Washington DC

Washington

Adams Inn

1744 Lanier Pl NW
Washington DC 20009
(202) 745-3600

Circa 1908. This restored town house has fireplaces, a library, and parlor, all furnished home-style, as are the guest rooms. Former residents of this neighborhood were Tallulah Bankhead, Woodrow Wilson, and Al Jolson. The Adams-Morgan area is home to diplomats, radio and television personalities and government workers. A notable firehouse across the street holds the record for the fastest response of a horse-drawn fire apparatus.

Location: Two miles from the White House, walking distance to major hotels.
*Rates: $60-$95.
Gene & Nancy Thompson.
25 Rooms. 12 Private Baths. Guest phone available. TV available. Beds: DT. Continental-plus breakfast. CCs: MC VISA AX DC. Sightseeing, antiquing, shops.

"We enjoyed your friendly hospitality and the homelike atmosphere. Your suggestions on restaurants and helping plan our visit were appreciated."

Embassy Inn

1627 16 St NW
Washington DC 20009
(202) 234-7800 (800) 423-9111

Circa 1920. A sister inn to Windsor Inn, the Embassy is furnished in a Federalist style reminiscent of the days of Thomas Jefferson - designer of several of the town houses on 16th Street. The Embassy's philosophy of innkeeping was inspired by the small family hotels of Europe, noted for providing personal attention and cheerful hospitality. Because of its proximity to many of Washington's important government and business centers, the inn offers a separate boardroom for guests planning business meetings.

*Rates: $89.
Susan Araujo.
39 Rooms. 39 Private Baths. Guest phone in room. TV in room. Beds: DT. Continental breakfast. CCs: MC VISA AX. Carriage rides, theater, National zoo, museums.
Seen in: *The Business Review.*

"When I return to D.C., I'll be back at the Embassy."

Fredericksburg Inn

See: Fredericksburg, VA

Kalorama Guest House

1854 Mintwood Place NW
Washington DC 20009
(202) 667-6369

Circa 1900. This is a group of six Victorian townhouses decorated with period antiques and artwork. The inn features original wainscoting, fireplace mantles and claw-footed tubs. Brass beds, plush comforters, oriental rugs, and sunny bay windows add to the charm. Each house is hosted year round and sherry is served by the fireplace each afternoon. The subway is a short walk, as are the Chinese Embassy, the French Embassy, major hotels and stately Massachusetts Avenue diplomatic residences.

Location: Downtown residential area 10 minutes to the Mall and White House.
**Rates: $45-$95.
Tammi Wood.
31 Rooms. 12 Private Baths. Guest phone available. TV available. Beds: QDT. Continental breakfast. Conference room. CCs: MC VISA AX. Horseback riding, hiking, boating.
Seen in: *The Philadelphia Inquirer, The Washington Post.*

"The Kalorama is one of the friendliest and comfortable places that I have stayed in anywhere in the world."

Memory House

See: Arlington, VA

Norris House Inn

See: Leesburg, VA

Reeds B&B

PO Box 12011
Washington DC 20005
(202) 328-3510

Circa 1887. This three-story Victorian town house was built by John Shipman, who owned one of the first construction companies in the city. The turn-of-the-century revitalization of Washington began here in Logan Circle, considered to be

the city's first truly residential area. During the house's restoration, flower gardens, terraces and fountains were added. Victorian antiques, original wood paneling, stained glass, and chandeliers, as well as practical amenities such as air conditioning and laundry facilities make this a comfortable bed and breakfast experience.
*Rates: $65-$75.
Charles & Jackie Reed.
6 Rooms. 1 Private Bath. Guest phone in room. TV in room. Beds: QDTC. Continental breakfast. CCs: MC VISA AX DC.
Seen in: *Philadelphia Inquirer, Washington Gardner Magazine.*

"This home was the highlight of our stay in Washington!"

Swiss Inn

1204 Massachusetts Ave NW
Washington DC 20005
(202) 371-1816

Circa 1900. This turn-of-the-century Victorian is typical of the Washingtonian town house architecture of the day, with a four-story bay and high-ceiling interiors. Each of the inn's suites has been uniquely decorated and features individual climate control units. There are also kitchenettes and remote-control color televisions. Weekly and monthly rates are occasionally available.
*Rates: $58.
Ralph Nussbaumer.
6 Rooms. 6 Private Baths. Guest phone in room. TV in room. Beds: Q. CCs: MC VISA AX.

Windsor Inn

1842 16th St NW
Washington DC 20009
(202) 667-0300

Circa 1920. Originally operated from 1940 to 1963 by the Dadian family, this large town house-style inn was closed for over two decades. When the new owners entered, they found everything exactly as it had been 22 years before - including the soap in the bathrooms. Recently renovated, the inn has been reopened as a bed and breakfast inn. Carved, marble-top antiques are in abundance, and a private club atmosphere prevails. Complimentary cocktails are served each evening.
*Rates: $89.
Susan Araujo.
49 Rooms. 49 Private Baths. Guest phone in room. TV in room. Beds: QDT. Continental breakfast. CCs: MC VISA AX. Historical Washington sites and museums.
Seen in: *The InTowner.*

"Being here was like being home."

West Virginia

Charles Town

The Cottonwood Inn

Rt 2 Box 61 S
Charles Town WV 25414
(304) 725-3371

Circa 1800. The bucolic six-acres of Cottonwood Inn once belonged to

George Washington's 4,000-acre tract. The land is studded with cottonwood and maple trees. Creek trout are sometimes fished out of Bull Skin Run, a creek that flows across the inn's front lawn. Four-poster beds, porch rockers and pecan griddle cakes are specialities of the innkeepers. Addicted to nurturing, Eleanor and Calin were trained by the nine children they reared on the farm.

Rates: $75-$85.
Eleanor & Colin Simpson.
6 Rooms. 6 Private Baths. 1 Fireplace. Guest phone available. TV in room. Beds: QT. Full breakfast. Gourmet meals. Conference room. CCs: MC VISA. Horse racing, rafting, boating, fishing, auto racing.
Seen in: *The Washington Post, Country Inns.*

"The warmth of your home was only a reflection of the personalities you possess."

Gilbert House B&B

Rt 1 Box 160
Charles Town WV 25414
(304) 725-0637

Circa 1760. A magnificent greystone of early Georgian design, the

Gilbert House boasts the state's oldest flagstone sidewalk. During restoration, graffiti found on the upstairs bedroom walls included a drawing of President James Polk and a child's growth chart from the 1800s. The inn is elegantly appointed with fine oriental rugs, tasteful art and antique furnishings. Located in the village of Middleway which contains one of the country's most well-preserved collections of 18th-century log houses.

*Rates: $85-$125.
Jean & Bernie Heiler.
3 Rooms. 3 Private Baths. 2 Fireplaces. Guest phone available. TV available. Beds: QD. B&B. Conference room. CCs: MC VISA.

"We have stayed at inns for 15 years and yours is at the top of the list as best ever!"

Magnus Tate's Kitchen

201 E Washington St
Charles Town WV 25414
(304) 725-8052

Circa 1796. Magnus Tate, wealthy planter and business associate of

George Washington's brother Charles, built this town house with a separate two-story brick building as the kitchen and servant's quarters. It is this building that has been restored. Recently featured in the Spring House and Garden Tour, it reflects a gracious 18th-century lifestyle.

Rates: $75-$95.
Louis & Katherine Santucci.
2 Rooms. 2 Private Baths. 2 Fireplaces. Guest phone available. Beds: D. Full breakfast. CCs: MC VISA. Horse racing, white-water rafting, hiking, cross-country skiing.
Seen in: *Wonderful West Virginia Magazine.*

"Thank you for making our honeymoon so wonderful. We enjoyed staying at such a lovely place and the breakfasts were unbelievable."

Davis

Bright Morning
William Ave, Rt 32
Davis WV 26260
(304) 259-5119

Circa 1898. This was originally constructed as a lumberjack boarding house. Handmade nails, exposed beams and wooden overlaid water pipes are still in evidence. Early American antiques are complemented by locally handcrafted quilts and rugs. The innkeepers also manage Trans-Montane Outfitters across the road, offering expert guides for white-water rafting, skiing and spelunking.

Location: Thirty five miles from Elkins, 18 miles from Oakland.
*Rates: $55-$65.
George & Missy Bright.
11 Rooms. 8 Private Baths. Guest phone available. TV available. Beds: DT. AP. Restaurant. Handicap access. Conference room. Tennis, golf, hiking, rafting, canoeing. Two state parks nearby.

Gerrardstown

Prospect Hill Farm
PO Box 135
Gerrardstown WV 25420
(304) 229-3346

Circa 1789. An 18th-century gentleman's home, this Georgian mansion belonged to William Wilson, a member of Thomas Jefferson's cabinet. (He outfitted wagon trains going west.) A hand-painted wall mural of colonial scenes winds up the staircase to the third floor. There are 100 acres of woodlands, and an additional 125 acres of pasture, orchards, and vegetable and berry patches. The ponds are stocked for fly fishing.

Location: Three-and-a-half miles west of I-81 on Route 51.
Rates: $75-$85.
Hazel & Charles Hudock.
2 Rooms. 2 Private Baths. 2 Fireplaces. Guest phone available. TV in room. Beds: QD. EP. Restaurant. CCs: MC VISA. Hiking, fishing.
Seen in: *The Daily Mail, the Washington Post, West Virginia Magazine.*

"What a wonderful old house, full of history."

Harper's Ferry

Inn Between the Hills
See: Hillsboro, VA

Harpers Ferry

Fillmore Street B&B
Box 34
Harpers Ferry WV 25425
(301) 377-0070 (304) 535-2619

Circa 1890. This two-story clapboard Victorian was built on the

foundation of a Civil War structure on land deeded by Jefferson Davis, Secretary of War. The surrounding acreage was an encampment for both the Union and Confederate soldiers (at different times). Within walking distance to the inn are the national park, museums, shopping, and dining.

Rates: $64.
Alden and James Addy.
2 Rooms. 2 Private Baths. 2 Fireplaces. Guest phone available. Beds: Q. Full breakfast. Hiking, rafting, bicycling.

"Delightful! What superb hosts you two are. We enjoyed ourselves luxuriously."

Martinsburg

Boydville
The Inn at Martinsburg
601 S Queen St
Martinsburg WV 25401
(304) 263-1448

Circa 1812. This Georgian estate was saved from burning by Union

troops only by a specific proclamation from President Lincoln dated July 18, 1864. Tall maples line the long driveway leading up to the house. It is constructed of two-foot-thick stone walls covered with plaster. The entry hall retains the original wallpaper brought from England in 1812 and hand-painted murals, fireplaces, and antiques adorn the spacious guest rooms. Sunlight filters through tree tops onto estate-sized lawns and gardens.

*Rates: $75-$105.
Owen Sullivan & Ripley Hotch.
6 Rooms. 6 Private Baths. 2 Fireplaces. Guest phone available. Beds: Q. Full breakfast. Fishing, golf, hiking, skiing.
Seen in: *Washington Post, Mid-Atlantic Country.*

"Your gracious home, hospitality and excellent amenities were enjoyed so much. Such a fine job of innkeeping."

The Dunn Country Inn
Rt 3, Box 33J
Martinsburg WV 25401
(304) 263-8646

Circa 1805. This Federal-style country home was built of native

limestone and is surrounded by acres of farmlands and woods. In 1873, a new addition was constructed with Romanesque and Italianate features, including seven-foot windows and a porch. An ancient 1790 spring house is on the property, a favorite picnic spot. The inn is decorated with period furnishings and country accents.

Location: 90 miles W of Washington, DC & Baltimore.
Rates: $75-$100.
Prince & Dianna Dunn.
6 Rooms. 2 Private Baths. 2 Fireplaces. Guest phone available. Beds: QDT. Full breakfast. CCs: MC VISA. White water rafting, hiking, horseback riding, golf, tours of Civil War Battlefield.
Seen in: *Mid-Atlantic Country.*

"It felt like staying with old friends."

Pence Springs

The Pence Springs Hotel

Rt 3
Pence Springs WV 24962
(304) 445-2606

Circa 1913. The stately columns of this brick plantation-style hotel

remind guests of the days when it was one of the famous mineral spas. Known as West Virginia's most luxurious hotel, the Grand — as it was known, closed during the depression. During its heyday, 14 trains a day stopped to transport guests here. Sixteen of the original 60 rooms have been restored and are decorated in an art deco style reminiscent of the hotel's more flourishing era.
*Rates: $55-$65.
O. Ashby Berkley.
16 Rooms. 16 Private Baths. 2 Fireplaces. Guest phone in room. TV available. Beds: KDT. B&B. Restaurant. Gourmet meals. Handicap access. Game room. Conference room. CCs: MC VISA DC CB. Skiing, white-water rafting, golf, fishing, hunting, antiquing.
Seen in: *The Morgan Messenger, Berkley Post Herald.*

Shepherdstown

Stonebrake Cottage

PO Box 1612 Shepherd Grade Rd
Shepherdstown WV 25443
(304) 876-6607

Circa 1880. Pink farmer's roses nestle against a white fence marking the entrance to the 140-acre farm upon which Stonebrake Cottage rests. Thought to have been built for an aunt or grandmother, it has been

refurbished and decorated with antique country chests and four-poster beds. This completely private Victorian cottage contains three bedrooms, a living room and a kitchen stocked with the makings for a full country breakfast. A 10-acre woodland is nearby.
Rates: $85-$90.
Anne & Dennis Small.
3 Rooms. 2 Private Baths. Guest phone available. TV in room. Beds: QDTC. Full breakfast. CCs: VISA DS. Golf, white water rafting, canoeing.
Seen in: *The Washington Post, Martinsburg Journal.*

"Absolutely charming...food was wonderful."

Thomas Shepherd Inn

Box 1162, German & Duke St
Shepherdstown WV 25443
(304) 876-3715

Circa 1868. Spreading oaks and maples shade the cobbled streets outside this stately two-story brick house, once a Lutheran parsonage. It was built on land owned by Thomas Shepherd a founder of Shepherdstown, West Virginia's oldest town. Furnishings are American antiques.
Location: Eastern panhandle of West Virginia.
Rates: $70-$85.
Ed & Carol Ringoot.
6 Rooms. 4 Private Baths. 1 Fireplace. Guest phone available. TV available. Beds: QTD. Full breakfast. CCs: MC VISA. Golf, rafting, canoeing, biking, tennis, cross-country skiing.
Seen in: *The Baltimore Sun, Herald Mail, Travel & Leisure.*

"The elegance and tastefulness of the inn, the breakfast and the trip back into time that it affords can only be exceeded by the hospitality of Carol and Ed."

Wisconsin

Alma

The Gallery House

215 N Main St
Alma WI 54610
(608) 685-4975

Circa 1861. This quaint river town stretches along the bluffs of the Mississippi and is the setting for The Gallery House, an artist's gallery and home. Watercolors and prints decorate the inn, which is furnished in antiques and traditional furnishings.

Location: On the Great River Road.
Rates: $40.00
John & Joan Runions
3 Rooms. Beds: D. Full breakfast. CCs: MC VISA. Boat rental, swimming, tennis, golf.

Appleton

The Parkside B&B

402 E North St
Appleton WI 54911
(414) 733-0200

Circa 1906. This three-story Richardson Romanesque house features gables, bays and a partial center turret. The house is filled with sunlight, filtered through windows of decorative leaded glass. It is situated near downtown, and faces the park and Lawrence University campus, in the neighborhood that was once home to Harry Houdini and Edna Ferber.

Rates: $51-$62.
Bonnie Riley
1 Room. 1 Private Bath. Guest phone available. Beds: K. Full breakfast. Conference room. Swimming.
Seen in: *Sunday Post-Crescent.*

"Thank you for making our visit so delightful! Everything was perfect."

Baraboo

The Barrister's House

226 9th Ave
Baraboo WI 53913
(608) 356-3344

Circa 1932. Built by a prominent Baraboo attorney, this stately home was designed by architect Frank Riley (builder of the governor's mansion) to replicate the warmth and grace of colonial New England homes. The fireplaces, crystal chandeliers, library and veranda are favorites with guests.

Rates: $50-$60.
Glen & Mary Schulz.
4 Rooms. 4 Private Baths. Beds: QD. Continental-plus breakfast. Skiing, hiking, fishing, swimming, boating.
Seen in: *Country Inns.*

"Your home is simply wonderful and we've enjoyed every moment. Lovely rooms, gracious hosts, delicious food!"

Bayfield

Old Rittenhouse Inn

301 Rittenhouse Ave, PO Box 584-1
Bayfield WI 54814
(715) 779-5111

Circa 1890. This rambling Queen Anne Victorian was built by Civil War General Allen Fuller, using cedar shingles and the local brownstone for which Bayfield was famous. Antique furnishings abound throughout the inn, which has 12 working fireplaces. Underneath massive gables, a wraparound veranda is filled with geraniums, petunias, and white wicker furnishings. There is a spectacular view of Lake Superior.

Location: On Bayfield's main street, 5 blocks from Lake Superior shore.
Rates: $79-$159. Season: April - Nov.
Jerry & Mary Phillips.
11 Rooms. 11 Private Baths. 10 Fireplaces. Guest phone available. TV available. Beds: KQDC. B&B. Restaurant. Gourmet meals. Jacuzzi. Handicap access. Conference room. CCs: MC VISA. Cross-country skiing, sailing, swimming, Apostle Island National Lakeshore.

Seen in: *Wisconsin Trails, The Magazine of Good Living.*

"The whole decor, the room, the staff, and the food were superb! Your personalities and talents give a great warmth to the inn."

Cedarburg

Stagecoach Inn B&B

W 61 N 520 Washington Ave
Cedarburg WI 53012
(414) 375-0208

Circa 1853. Restored by historian Brook Brown, this stone Greek Revival house was originally used as a stagecoach stop between Milwaukee and Greenbay. Authentically decorated with antiques, all the suites feature king-size whirlpools. There is a pub, chocolate shop and bookstore on the first floor.

Location: Downtown Cedarburg.
Rates: $45-$85.
Brook & Liz Brown.
12 Rooms. 12 Private Baths. Guest phone available. TV available. Beds: QTDC. Continental-plus breakfast. Conference room. CCs: MC VISA. Cross-country skiing, bicycling, tennis, golf, horseback riding.
Seen in: *News Graphic Pilot, Midwest Living.*

The Washington House Inn

W 62 N 573 Washington Ave
Cedarburg WI 53012
(414) 375-3550

Circa 1886. Completely renovated, this original Cream-City-brick building is decorated in a light-hearted country Victorian style, featuring antiques, whirlpool baths and fireplaces. The original guest registry, more than one hundred years old, is displayed proudly in the lobby.

Location: In the heart of downtown Cedarburg.
*Rates: $59-$129.
Judith Drefahl.
29 Rooms. 29 Private Baths. 9 Fireplaces. Guest phone in room. TV in room. Beds: KQDC. B&B. Jacuzzi. Sauna. Handicap access. Conference room. CCs: MC VISA AX DC CB DS. Victorian interlude dinner package.
Seen in: *Country Home, Chicago Sun Times.*

"A piece of time lost to all but a fortunate few who will experience it. Please save it for my children."

Ellison Bay

The Griffin Inn

11976 Mink River Rd
Ellison Bay WI 54210
(414) 854-4306

Circa 1910. This New England-style country inn is situated on five

acres of rolling lawns and maple trees with a gazebo. There are verandas with porch swings, a gracious lobby with a stone fireplace, and a cozy library. Guest rooms are furnished with antique beds and dressers, and feature handmade quilts. In addition to the main house, there are four cottages.

Location: Two blocks east of Highway 42 on the Door County Peninsula.
Rates: $62 & up.
Jim & Laurie Roberts.
10 Rooms. Guest phone available. Beds: DT. B&B. Cross-country skiing, golf, hiking, fishing, swimming.
Seen in: *Ladies Circle.*

"A classic bed and breakfast inn." Travel and Leisure Magazine.

Fish Creek

Thorp House Inn & Cottages

4135 Bluff Rd, PO Box 90
Fish Creek WI 54212
(414) 868-2444

Circa 1902. Freeman Thorp picked the site for this home because of its

view of Green Bay and the village. Before his house was finished, however, he perished in the bay when the *Erie L. Hackley* sank. His wife completed it as a guest house. Each room has a view of the harbor, cedar forest, or village. A stone fireplace is the focal point of the parlor and two of the cottages on the property have fireplaces.

Location: Heart of Door County, in the village of Fish Creek.
Rates: $53-$66.
Christine & Sverre Falck-Pedersen.
4 Rooms. 4 Fireplaces. Guest phone available. Beds: QD. Continental-plus breakfast. Swimming, fishing, bicycling, hiking, golf, tennis, horses.
Seen in: *Green Bay Press-Gazette.*

"Amazing attention to detail from restoration to the furnishings. A very first class experience."

Janesville

Jackson Street Inn

210 S Jackson St
Janesville WI 53545
(608) 754-7250

Circa 1900. For more than 30 years the Sessler family has operated this

guest house. A stately American Foursquare home, it features massive carved oak woodwork. Beveled leaded-glass windows create rainbows and dancing prisms on the walls and ceilings when the sun shines through. Glass interior entrance doors and glass pocket doors add to the character of the house. Brass beds, air conditioning, antique rocking chairs and bowls of potpourri are additional features.

*Rates: $45-$60.
Ilah & Robert Sessler.
4 Rooms. 2 Private Baths. Guest phone available. TV in room. Beds: QT. B&B. CCs: MC VISA. Golf, ski trials, hiking, biking, pool, beach, shuffleboard, horseshoes.
Seen in: *Janesville Gazette, Milwaukee Journal.*

Kenosha

The Manor House
6536 3rd Ave
Kenosha WI 53140
(414) 658-0014

Circa 1928. This stately Georgian mansion overlooking Lake Michigan was built for the daughter of the Nash Motor Company founder. There are Chippendale furnishings and antiques from Rothchild's Mentmore Manor in Buckinghamshire, England. The grounds feature a sunken pool, water fountain and gazebo. Across the street is an 11-acre wooded park with tennis courts, an art gallery and fishing pier.

Location: Thirty minutes between Milwaukee & Chicago.
Rates: $80-$110.
Ron & Mary Rzeplinski.
4 Rooms. 4 Private Baths. Guest phone available. TV in room. Beds: KQT. Continental breakfast. Conference room. CCs: MC VISA AX. Tennis, bicycling, skiing nearby, fishing, swimming, golf.
Seen in: *Kenosha News*.

"Elegant, magnificent, beautiful beyond words. Absolutely superb."

La Crosse

Trillium
See: La Farge, WI

La Farge

Trillium
Rt 2, Box 121
La Farge WI 54639
(608) 625-4492

Circa 1929. This little cottage once provided for Grandma when she came to live with her children on the farm. Stones from the banks of nearby Kickapoo River were used to construct the fireplace and the chimney for the old cookstove. The cottage sleeps up to four adults and two children. In spring, a hammock sways beneath blossoming apple trees. A hearty country breakfast is served. Both children and adults enjoy watching deer, wild turkeys, and owls, or visiting the livestock.

Rates: $63.
Rosanne Boyett.
1 Room. 1 Private Bath. 1 Fireplace. Guest phone available. Beds: DTC. B&B. Horseback riding, canoeing, hiking, biking, fishing, skiing.

"It's a place to unwind, listen to the song birds, putter in the organic garden and orchard, stroll the long country lane, sit by the waterfall, or relax in the hammock."

"Cozy cottage and warm hospitality."

Madison

Plough Inn B&B
3402 Monroe St
Madison WI 53711
(608) 238-2981

Circa 1853. Originally constructed as a tavern and inn, this Greek

Revival building is adjacent to the University of Wisconsin Arboretum. The Arborview Room takes full advantage of this by providing a splendid tree-top view of the landscaped grounds. This room also has its own fireplace, wet bar and whirlpool tub. The original Tap Room is now outfitted as a guest room featuring brass fixtures and plaid decor.

Rates: $55-$89.
P. Katherine Naherny & Roger H. Ganser.
3 Rooms. 3 Private Baths. 1 Fireplace. Guest phone available. TV available. Beds: Q. B&B. CCs: MC VISA. Biking, cross-country skiing, golf, sailing, swimming, tennis.
Seen in: *Chicago Tribune, Milwaukee Journal*.

"This was exactly what we needed."

Milwaukee

The Manor House
See: Kenosha, WI

Ogden House
2237 N Lake Dr
Milwaukee WI 53202
(414) 272-2740

Circa 1916. Listed in the National Register, this white brick Federal house is located in the North Point-South Historic District. It was built for Miss Ogden, who lived to be 101 years old and was one of the founders of the Milwaukee County Historical Society. Guest rooms feature handmade quilts. There is a sunroom and sundeck with views of the garden. The house is set on a bluff overlooking Lake Michigan.

Location: One block from Lake Michigan, 1 mile north of downtown.
*Rates: $65-$75.
Mary Jane & John Moss.
2 Rooms. 2 Private Baths. Guest phone in room. TV in room. Beds: Q. Continental-plus breakfast.

"You made me feel as if I were staying with friends and at the same time added the details desired at a fine hotel. I'm ready to adopt my room."

The Washington House Inn
See: Cedarburg, WI

Mineral Point

Chesterfield Inn
20 Commerce St
Mineral Point WI 53565
(608) 987-3682

Circa 1834. Miners from Cornwall, England used cut stone to build the

Chesterfield Inn, originally a stage coach stop. A nearby guest cottage is in the Shake Rag Valley, (so named because Cornish wives shook a dishrag to signal to their husbands at the lead mines that dinner was ready). Rooms at both locations are furnished with antiques. The Chesterfield Inn is noted for its excellent Midwest cuisine. Wood carvers, sculptors, potters, weavers

and other crafts people have been drawn to Mineral Point.
Rates: $40-$60. Season: April - Nov.
V. Duane Rath.
80 Rooms. Guest phone available. Beds: QDT. Continental-plus breakfast. Restaurant. CCs: MC VISA. Cross-country & downhill skiing.

Wilson House Inn

110 Dodge St Hwy 151
Mineral Point WI 53565
(608) 987-3600

Circa 1853. One of Wisconsin's first attorney generals, Alexander Wil-

son, built this three-story red brick Federal house, now on the Mineral Point Historic Tour. It has a wraparound veranda and several Italianate features. Period wallpapers and Victorian furnishings are found throughout. One bed chamber boasts a highback Norwegian hand-painted bed and a marble-topped dresser. Spinning workshops are sometimes held in the winter near the marble fireplace in the parlor.
Rates: $50-$55.
Bev & Jim Harris.
4 Rooms. Guest phone available. Beds: T. Full breakfast. CCs: MC VISA. Fishing, swimming, skiing, bicycling.

"Your hospitality is second to none. It's invigorating to stay here."

Sturgeon Bay

Gray Goose B&B

4258 Bay Shore Dr
Sturgeon Bay WI 54235
(414) 743-9100

Circa 1862. Civil War veteran Alexander Templeton would have been proud of the transformation of his homestead to an intimate country inn. Surrounded by trees and an apple orchard, the Gray Goose overlooks Green Bay. Jessie, an inveterate antique collector, has

decorated the inn to reflect this passion. All shapes and sizes of old cookie cutters form a unique ceiling border in the Pewter room where there is a sunset view of the bay and authentic American pewter on display in the corner cupboard.
Rates: $55-$65.
Jack & Jessie Burkhardt.
4 Rooms. Guest phone available. TV available. Beds: QDT. Full breakfast. Game room. CCs: MC VISA AX. Tennis, fishing, golf, water sports, horseback riding, skiing, bicycling.
Seen in: *Door County Advocate.*

"Thanks for such charming and comfortable accommodations! It has been a delightful experience. Everything was just great."

Inn at Cedar Crossing

336 Louisiana St
Sturgeon Bay WI 54235
(414) 743-4200

Circa 1884. This historic hotel, in the National Register, is a

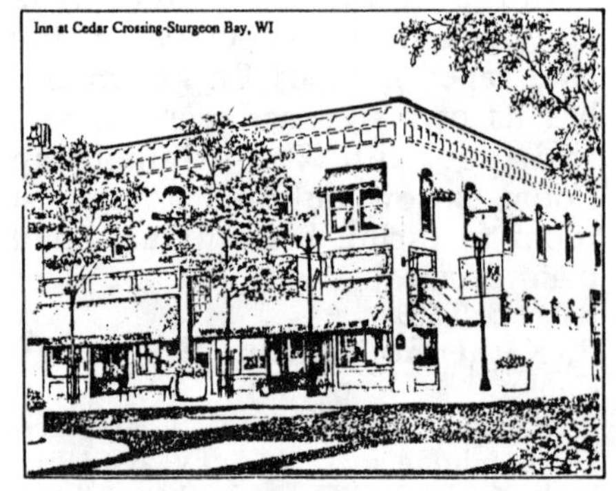

downtown three-story brick building, which once housed street-level shops with second floor apartments for the tailors, shop keepers and pharmacists who worked below. The upstairs, now guest rooms, are decorated with floral wallpapers, stenciling and antiques. The Anniversary Room, for instance, has a mahogany bed and a whirlpool tub. There are two dining rooms, both with fireplaces, on the lower level. The waterfront is three blocks away.
Rates: $65-$105.
Terry Wulf.
9 Rooms. 9 Private Baths. Guest phone available. TV available. Beds: KQ. B&B. Restaurant. Gourmet meals. Jacuzzi. CCs: MC VISA DS. Sailing, cross-country skiing, fishing, art galleries.
Seen in: *New Month Magazine.*

The Scofield House B&B

908 Michigan St, PO Box 761
Sturgeon Bay WI 54235
(414) 743-7727

Circa 1902. Mayor Herbert Scofield, prominent locally in the lumber and hardware business, built

this late Victorian house with a sturdy square tower and inlaid floors that feature intricate borders patterned in cherry, birch, maple, walnut, and red and white oak. Oak moldings throughout the house boast raised designs of bows, ribbons, swags and flowers. Equally lavish decor is featured in the guest rooms with fluffy flowered comforters and cabbage rose wallpapers highlighting romantic antique bedsteads. Door County cherry muffins are a house specialty.
Rates: $65-$105.
Bill & Fran Cecil.
4 Rooms. 4 Private Baths. 2 Fireplaces. Guest phone available. TV available. Beds: QD. B&B. Gourmet meals. Jacuzzi. Horseback riding, hiking, fishing, sailing, biking, cross-country skiing, ice skating, snowmobiling.
Seen in: *Innsider, Glamour, Country, Wisconsin Trails, Green Bay Press Gazette.*

"Lovely accommodations and warm hospitality."

White Lace Inn

16 N 5th Ave
Sturgeon Bay WI 54235
(414) 743-1105

Circa 1903. White Lace Inn is three Victorian houses, one an ornate

Queen Anne. It is adjacent to two districts listed in the National Register. Often the site for romantic wedding festivities, a favorite suite has a two-sided fireplace, magnificent walnut Eastlake Bed, English country fabrics, and a two-person whirlpool tub.
Location: Door County, Lake Michigan on one side, Green Bay on the other.
Rates: $58-$125.
Dennis & Bonnie Statz.
15 Rooms. 15 Private Baths. Guest phone available. Beds: Q. B&B. Jacuzzi. Handicap access. CCs: MC VISA. Cross-country skiing, beaches.
Seen in: *Wisconsin Trails, Milwaukee Sentinel, Brides Magazine.*

"Each guest room is such an overwhelming visual feast, such a dazzling fusion of colors, textures, and beautiful objects. It is one of these rare gems that established a tradition the day it opened." Wisconsin Trails.

Wisconsin Dells

Historic Bennett House

825 Oak St
Wisconsin Dells WI 53965
(608) 254-2500

Circa 1863. This handsomely restored Federal-style home, framed by a white picket fence, housed the Henry Bennetts whose family still operates the Bennett photographic studio, the oldest continuously operating studio in the country. Noted for the first stop-action photography, Mr. Bennett's work is displayed in the Smithsonian. Antiques and whimsical collectibles have been gathered to decorate the inn. A Victorian garden is highlighted with a gazebo.

❀Rates: $45-$89.
Gail & Rich Obermeyer.
4 Rooms. 1 Private Bath. Guest phone available. TV in room. Beds: KQD. B&B. Golf, water sports, skiing, state parks, museums.
Seen in: *Milwaukee Journal.*

"Special people with a very beautiful and special home."

Wyoming

Rawlins

Ferris Mansion

607 W Maple St
Rawlins WY 82301
(307) 324-3961

Circa 1903. This Queen Anne Victorian with its gables, steeply pitched turret, gazebo and veranda, was designed by a Knoxville, Tennessee architectural firm, Barber and Klutz. Julia Ferris built it after the death of her husband who was killed by a runaway team of horses when he was returning from his copper mine. An elegant Victorian decor takes full advantage of the house's fanciful design.

Rates: $45-$55.
Janice Lubbers.
4 Rooms. 4 Private Baths. 2 Fireplaces. Guest phone available. TV in room. Beds: QDT. Full breakfast.

Savery

Savery Creek Thoroughbred Ranch

PO Box 24
Savery WY 82332
(307) 383-7840

Circa 1889. This is a working sheep, cattle and horse ranch that has been taking in guests since the Twenties. In those days, visitors were met with horses at the top of the Continental Divide because cars couldn't make it. In addition to the rambling old ranch house, there are guest cabins, barns, a saddle house, blacksmith shop, and corrals nestled among the cottonwood trees. Savery Creek has popular swimming holes in the summer. The ranch is known for exceptional riding horses and delicious meals.

Location: 9 miles north of Savery (population 25).
*Rates: $55-$220.
Joyce B. Saer.
5 Rooms. 1 Private Bath. 1 Fireplace. Guest phone available. TV available. Beds: Q. AP. Gourmet meals. Conference room. Horseback riding, cross-country skiing, skating, fishing, tennis on the ranch. Rodeos, picnics, cookouts. Bald eagles and wildlife.
Seen in: *Sunset Magazine.*

"Marianne and I had a wonderful stay at your place (too short!)"

Puerto Rico

Condado, San Juan

El Canario Inn

1317 Ashford Ave
Condado, San Juan PR 00907
(809) 722-3861

Circa 1938. This three-story inn is close to white sandy beaches. All

rooms are air-conditioned, and there is a tropical patio with a swimming pool.

*Rates: $80-$85.
Judy & Keith Olson
25 Rooms. 25 Private Baths. Guest phone in room. TV available. Beds: DTC. Continental breakfast. Swimming pool. CCs: MC VISA AX DC DS. Beach, windsurfing, sailing, water skiing, jet ski, casinos, horse races.

Virgin Islands

Saint Thomas

Hotel 1829

PO Box 1567
Saint Thomas VI 00804-1567
(809) 776-1829 (800) 524-2002

Circa 1829. Designed by an Italian architect, this Spanish-style inn was built for a French sea captain and his bride. Old brick walls, Morracan tiles and iron gates add atmosphere to the stunning harbor views that may be enjoyed from many of the rooms. Tropical plants border the swimming pool and pink bougainvillea cascades down the stucco walls. The inn is next to the famous 99 steps, on Governor's Hill.

*Rates: $60-$280.
Mr. & Mrs. V. Vernon Ball.
15 Rooms. 15 Private Baths. Guest phone in room. TV in room. Beds: QDT. Continental breakfast. Swimming pool. CCs: MC VISA AX. Sailing, diving, water skiing, scuba diving, beaches.

Directory of American Historic Inns

The following directory contains the names, addresses, and phone numbers of Bed & Breakfast Inns, Country Inns, and guesthouses believed to be of historic significance. Every attempt has been made to be as comprehensive and as accurate as possible, however, there always remains the possibility of error, omission, or change. This list is presented for information purposes only and is offered without warranty of any kind. Additions, corrections or changes, if any, and if brought to our attention, will be made in subsequent editions.

Please note: although there are many fine inns in the list, inclusion does not constitute a recommendation nor does non-inclusion indicate a nonrecommendation.

Inns listed in **bold type** are described in more detail in the main body of the book.

We suggest that if you are interested in making reservations with any of these that you drop them a postcard or give them a call and request brochures or other information. Be sure to mention that you saw them in **The Official Guide to American Historic Inns**.

Alabama

Anniston
Victoria, 1604 Quintard Ave 36201 ....(205)236-0503
Birmingham
B&B Birmingham, Box 31328 35222 ....(205)933-2487
Decatur
Dancy-Polk House, 901 Railroad St NW 35601 ....(205)353-3579
Fairhope
Mershond Court, 203 Fairhope Ave 36532 ....(205)928-7398
Franklin
Rutherford Johnson House, PO Box 202 36444 ....(205)282-4423
Mentone
Mentone Inn, Highway 117, PO Box 284 35984 ....(205)634-4836
Millbrook
B&B Montgomery, Box 886 36054 ....(205)285-5421
Mobile
Malaga Inn, 359 Church St 36602 ....(205)438-4701
Vincent-Doan Home, 1664 Springhill Ave 36604 ....(205)433-7121
Montrose
Seven Gables 36559 ....(205)928-5454
Opelika
Under The Oaks, 707 Geneva St 36801 ....(205)745-2449
Scottsboro
Brunton House, PO Box 1006, 112 College Ave 35768 ....(205)259-1298

Alaska

Anchorage
A Log Home B&B, 2440 Sprucewood St 99508 ....(907)276-8527
Alaska Private Lodgings, PO Box 200047 99511 ....(907)248-2292
Green Bough Inn, 3832 Young St 99508 ....(907)562-4636
McCarthy Wilderness B&B, Box 111241 99511 ....(907)277-6867
Angoon
Favorite Bay Inn, PO Box 101 99820 ....(907)788-3123
Gustavus
Gustavus Inn, PO Box 31 99826 ....(907)697-3311
Haines
Fort William Seward B&B, House-1, PO Box 5 99827 ....(907)766-2856
Homer
Driftwood Inn, 135-T W Bunnell Ave 99603 ....(907)235-8019
Juneau
Fifth & Franklin B&B, 505-TN Franklin 99801
Mullins House, 526 Seward St 99802 ....(907)586-2959
Petersburg
Scandia Haus, PO Box 689, 206 Nordic Dr 99833 ....(907)772-4281
Skagway
Golden North Hotel, PO Box 431 99840 ....(907)983-2294
Irene's Inn, PO Box 543 99840 ....(907)983-2520
Skagway Inn, PO 292 99840 ....(907)983-2294
Talkeetna
Fairview Inn, PO Box 379 99676 ....(907)733-2423
Tenakee Springs
Tanakee Inn, 167 S Franklin 99801 ....(907)586-1000
Tok
1260 Inn, Mi 1260, Ak Hwy 99780 ....(907)778-2205

Arizona

Ajo
The Manager's House, One Greenway Dr 85321 ....(602)387-6505
Bisbee
Bisbee Inn, 45 OK St, PO Box 1855 85603 ....(602)432-5131
Inn At Castle Rock, Box 1161, 112 Tombstone Canyon 85603 ....(602)432-7195
Park Place B&B, 200 E Vista 85603 ....(602)432-5516
Carefree
Adobe Inn-Carefree, Box 1081, Elbow Bend & Sidewinder 85377 ....(602)488-4444
Cochise
Cochise Hotel, PO Box 27 85606 ....(602)384-3156
Flagstaff
Birch Tree Inn, 824 W Birch Ave 86001 ....(602)774-1042
Dierker House B&B, 423 W Cherry 86001 ....(602)774-3249
Rainbow Ranch, 2860 N Fremont 86001 ....(602)774-3724
Walking L Ranch, RR 4, Box 721B 86001 ....(602)779-2219
Fountain Hills
Villa Galleria B&B, 16650 E Hawk Dr 85268 ....(602)837-1400
Phoenix
Westways "Private" Resort, PO 41624 85080 ....(602)582-3868
Prescott
Marks House Inn, 203 E Union 86303 ....(602)778-4632
Prescott Pines Inn, 901 White Spar Rd 86303 ....(602)445-7270
Sasabe
Rancho De La Osa, PO Box 1 85633 ....(602)823-4257
Scottsdale
Valley 'O the Sun B&B, PO Box 2214 85252 ....(602)941-1281
Sedona
Garland's Oak Creek Lodge, PO Box 152, Hwy 89A 86336 ....(602)282-3343
Keyes' B&B, Box 1682, 2271 Roadrunner 86336 ....(602)282-6008
Moore's Music Museum B&B, 3085 W Hwy 89A 86336 ....(602)282-3419
Saddle Rock Ranch, 255 Rock Ridge Dr 86336 ....(602)282-7640
Tempe
Mi Casa-Su Casa B&B, PO Box 950 85281 ....(602)990-0682
Tucson
Casa Suecia B&B, PO Box 36883, Ste 181 86704
Desert Needlework Ranch, 1645 N Harrison Rd 85715 ....(602)885-6264
La Posada Del Valle, 1640 N Campbell Ave 85719 ....(602)795-3840
The Peppertrees B&B, 724 E University 85719 ....(602)622-7167
Wickenburg
Kay El Bar Ranch, PO Box 2480 85358 ....(602)684-7593
Rancho De Los Caballeros, Box 1148 85358 ....(602)684-5484

Arkansas

Brinkley
The Great Southern Hotel, 127 West Cedar 72021 ....(501)734-4955
Clarksville
May House, 101 Railroad Ave 72830 ....(501)754-6851
Des Arc
The 5-B's, 210 S 2nd St 72040 ....(501)256-4789
Eureka Springs
The Basin Park Hotel, Prospect St 72632
Bridgeford Cottage, 263 Spring St 72632
Brownstone Inn, 75 Hillside, PO Box 409 72632 ....(501)253-7505
Cabin On The Boardwalk, Box 492, 185 Spring St 72632
Coach House Inn, 140A S Main 72632 ....(501)253-8099
Crescent Cottage Inn, 211 Spring St 72632 ....(501)253-6022
Crescent Hotel, Prospect St 72632
Crescent Moon Townhouse, PO Box 429 72632 ....(501)253-9463
Dairy Hollow House, 515 Spring St 72632 ....(501)253-7444
The Inn on Depot Grade, 75 Hillside Ave 72632
Elmwood House, 110 Spring St #62b 72632
Heart of the Hills Inn, 5 Summit 72632 ....(501)253-7468
The Heartstone Inn & Cottages, 35 King's Hwy 72632 ....(501)253-8916
Johnson's Hilltop Cabin, Rt 1, Box 503 72632 ....(501)253-9537
Lake Lucerne Resort, PO Box 441 72632 ....(501)253-8085
Lookout Cottage, 12 Lookout Cir. 72632
Main Street Inn, 217 N. Main St 72632
Maplewood B&B, 4 Armstrong St 72632 ....(501)253-8053
New Orleans Hotel, 63 Spring St 72632 ....(501)253-8630
Oak Crest Cottages, Rt 2, Box 26 72632 ....(501)253-9493
The Old Homestead, 78-82 Armstrong St 72632
Palace Hotel, 135 Spring 72632 ....(501)253-7474
The Piedmont House, 165 Spring St 72632 ....(501)253-9258
Red Bud Valley Resort, RR 1, Box 500 72632 ....(502)253-9028
Redbud Manor, 7 Kings Hwy 72632
Riverview Resort, RR 2, Box 475 72632 ....(501)253-8367
Singleton House B&B, 11 Singleton 72632 ....(501)253-9111
Sunnyside Cottage, 5 Ridgeway 72632
Sweet Seasons Guest Cottages, 26 Spring St 72632 ....(501)253-7603
Tatman-Garrett House, Box 171 72632
White Flower Cottage, 62 Kings Hwy 72632 ....(501)253-9636
Everton
Corn Cob Inn, Rt 1 Box 183 72633 ....(501)429-6545

Fort Smith
McCartney House, 500 S 19th St 72901 ....(501)782-9057
Thomas Quinn Guest House, 815 N B St 72901 ....(501)782-0499
Gilbert
Anna's House, PO Box 58 72636 ....(501)439-2888
Heber Springs
Oak Tree Inn, Vinegar Hill & 110 W 72543 ....(501)362-8870
Helena
Edwardian Inn, 317 S Biscoe 72342 ....(501)338-9155
Hot Springs
Stillmeadow Farm Reproduction, Rt 1 Box 434-d 71913
Williams House Inn, 420 Quapaw St 71901 ....(501)624-4275
Hot Springs Natl Pk
Dogwood Manor B&B, 906 Malvern Ave 71901 ....(501)624-0896
Jasper
Cliff House Inn, Scenic Ark, Hwy 7 72641 ....(501)446-2292
Morrilton
Tanyard Springs, Rt 3, Box 335 72110 ....(501)727-5200
Mountain View
The Commercial Hotel, PO Box 72, Washington at Peabody St 72560 ....(501)269-4383
Romance
Hammons Chapel Farm, 1 Mi of Ark 5 72136 ....(501)849-2819
Washington
Old Country Jail, PO Box 157 71862 ....(501)983-2178
Yellville
Red Raven Inn, PO Box 160 72687 ....(501)449-5168

California

Alameda
Garratt Mansion, 900 Union St 94501 ....(415)521-4779
Albion
Fensalden B&B, PO Box 99 95410 ....(707)937-4042
Alleghany
Kenton Mine Lodge, Box 942 95910 ....(916)287-3212
Altadena
Eye Openers, PO Box 694 91003 ....(818)797-2055
Amador City
Mine House Inn, PO Box 245, S Hwy 49 95601 ....(209)267-5900
Anaheim
Anaheim Country Inn, 856 South Walnut St 92802 ....(714)778-0150
Angels Camp
Cooper House, 1184 Church St 95222 ....(209)736-2145
Aptos
Apple Lane Inn, 6265 Soquel Dr 95003 ....(408)475-6868
Bayview Hotel B&B Inn, 8041 Soquel Dr 95003 ....(408)688-8654
The Inn at Depot Hill, 134 Hyannis Ct 95003 ....(408)462-DEPO
Mangels House, 570 Aptos Creek Rd, PO Box 302 95001 ....(408)688-7982
Arcata
Lady Ann, 902 14th St 95521 ....(707)822-2797
Plough & the Stars Country Inn, 1800 27th St 95521 ......(707)822-8236
Arroyo Grande
Guest House, 120 Hart Ln 93420 ....(805)481-9304
Rose Victorian Inn, 789 Valley Rd 93420 ....(805)481-5566
Auburn
Power's Mansion Inn, 164 Cleveland Ave 95603 ....(916)885-1166
Avalon
Glenmore Plaza Hotel, 120 Sumner Ave 90704 ....(213)510-0017
The Inn On Mt. Ada, Box 2560, 207 Wrigley Rd 90704 .....(213)510-2030
Island Inn, PO Box 467, 125 Metropole 90704 ....(213)510-1623
The Old Turner Inn, PO Box 97 90704 ....(213)510-2236
Zane Grey Pueblo Hotel, PO Box 216 90704 ....(213)510-0966
Ben Lomond
Fairview Manor, 245 Fairview Ave 95005 ....(408)336-3355
Benicia
The Union Hotel, 401 First St 94510 ....(707)746-0100
Berkeley
Gramma's Inn, 2740 Telegraph 94705 ....(415)549-2145
Old Blue Hotel, 2740 Telegraph Ave 94705-1131 ....(415)549-9281

Big Bear City
Gold Mountain Manor, 1117 Anita, PO Box 2027 92314 ....(714)585-6997
Big Bear Lake
Knickerbocker Mansion, 869 S Knickerbocker Rd 92315 ....(714)866-8221
Big Sur
Deetjen's Big Sur Inn, Hwy One 93920 ....(408)667-2377
Bishop
Chalfant House, 213 Academy St 93514 ....(619)872-1790
Boonville
Toll House Inn, Box 268, 15301 Hwy 25 95415 ....(707)895-3630
Calistoga
Brannan Cottage Inn, 109 Wapoo Ave 94515 ....(707)942-4200
Calistoga's Wine Way Inn, 1009 Foothill Blvd 94515 ......(707)942-0680
Culver's, A Country Inn, 1805 Foothill Blvd 94515 ....(707)942-4535
Foothill House, 3037 Foothill Blvd 94515
Larkmead Country Inn, 1103 Larkmead Ln 94515
Mount View Hotel, 1457 Lincoln Ave 94515
The Pink Mansion, 1415 Foothill Blvd 94515 ....(707)942-0558
Scarlett's Country Inn, 3918 Silverado Trail N 94515 ......(707)942-6669
Trailside Inn, 4201 Silverado Tr 94515 ....(707)942-4106
Cambria
Olallieberry Inn, 2476 Main St 93428 ....(805)927-3222
Carlsbad
Pelican Cove Inn, 320 Walnut Ave 92008 ....(619)434-5995
Carmel
Cypress Inn, 7th & Lincoln Streets, PO Box 7 93921 ....(408)624-3871
Happy Landing Inn, Monte Verde between 5th & 6th 93921 ....(408)624-7917
Holiday House, Box 782, Camino Real At 7th Ave 93921
Martin House B&B, 26270 Dolores St 93921
Pine Inn, Ocean & Monte Verde St 93921
Sea View Inn, Box 4318 93921 ....(408)624-8778
The Stonehouse Inn, Box 2517 93921 ....(408)624-4569
Vagabond's House Inn, Box 2747 93921 ....(408)624-7738
Chico
Bullard House, 256 E First Ave 95926 ....(916)342-5912
Cloverdale
Abrams House Inn, 314 N Main St 95425 ....(707)894-2412
Vintage Towers Inn, 302 N Main St 95425 ....(707)894-4535
Ye Olde Shelford House, 29955 River Rd 95425 ....(707)894-5956
Colfax
Bear River Mountain Farm, 21725 Placer Hills Rd 95713
Coloma
Coloma Country Inn, PO Box 502, #2 High St 95613 ......(916)622-6919
Sierra Nevada House, PO Box 268 95613 ....(916)622-5856
Vineyard House, Cold Spring Rd, PO Box 176 95613 .....(916)622-2217
Columbia
City Hotel, PO Box 1870, Main St 95310 ....(209)532-1479
Fallon Hotel, PO Box 1870, Washington St 95310 ....(209)532-1470
Colusa
O'Rourke Mansion, 1765 Lurline Rd 95932 ....(916)458-5625
Coulterville
Jeffrey Hotel, PO Box 4 95311 ....(209)878-3400
Crowley Lake
Rainbow Tarns, PO Box 1097, Rt 1 93546 ....(619)935-4556
Davenport
New Davenport B&B, 31 Davenport Ave 95017 ....(408)425-1818
Davis
The Partridge Inn, 521 First St 95616 ....(916)753-1211
Del Mar
Rock Haus B&B Inn, 410 15th St 92014 ....(619)481-3764
Dinsmore
Dinsmore Lodge, Hwy 36 95526 ....(707)574-6466
Downieville
Sierra Shangri-la, PO Box 285 95936 ....(916)289-3455
Dulzura
Brookside Farm, 1373 Marron Valley Rd 92017 ....(619)468-3043
Elk
Elk Cove Inn, PO Box 367 95432 ....(707)877-3321
Green Dolphin Inn, PO Box 132, 6145 S Hwy 1 95432 ......(707)877-3342
Harbor House - Inn by the Sea, 5600 S Hwy 1 95432 ......(707)877-3203
Etna
Scott Valley Inn, PO Box 261, 642 Main St 96027 ....(916)467-3229

California (Continued)

Eureka

Carter House, 1033 Third St 95501 ....(707)445-1390
Eagle House, 139 Second St 95501 ....(707)442-2334
Heuer's Victorian Inn, 1302 E St 95501 ....(707)442-7334
Old Town B&B Inn, 1521 Third St 95501 ....(707)445-3951
Steven's House, 917 Third St 95501 ....(707)445-9080

Fairfield

Frietas House Inn, 744 Jackson St 94533 ....(707)425-1366

Ferndale

Ferndale Inn, PO Box 887, 619 Main St 95536 ....(707)786-4307
Shaw House Inn, PO Box 1125, 703 Main St 95536 ....(707)786-9958

Fish Camp

Narrow Gauge Inn, 48571 Hwy 41 93623 ....(209)683-7720

Fort Bragg

Avalon House, 561 Stewart St 95437 ....(707)964-5555
Captain Capps, 32980 Gibney Lane 95437 ....(707)964-1415
Colonial Inn, PO Box 565, 533 E Fir 95437 ....(707)964-9979
Country Inn, 632 N Main St 95437 ....(707)964-3737
Glass Beach B&B, 726 N Main St 95437 ....(707)964-6774
Grey Whale Inn, 615 N Main St 95437 ....(707)964-0640
Jughandle Beach Country B&B Inn, 32980 Gibney Ln 95437 ....(707)964-1415
Noyo River Lodge, 500 Casa Del Noyo Dr 95437 ....(707)964-8045
Pudding Creek Inn, 700 N Main St 95437 ....(707)964-9529

Freestone

Green Apple Inn, 520 Bohemian Hwy 95472 ....(707)874-2526

Fremont

Lord Bradley's Inn, 43344 Mission Blvd Mission San Jo 94539 ....(415)490-0520

Fresno

The Victorian, 1003 S Orange Ave 93702

Garberville

Benbow Inn, 445 Lake Benbow Dr 95440 ....(707)923-2124

Georgetown

American River Inn, Orleans St, PO Box 43 95634 ....(916)333-4499

Geyserville

Campbell Ranch, 1475 Canyon Rd 95441 ....(707)857-3476
Isis Oasis, 20889 Geyserville Ave 95441
The Hope-Bosworth House, Box 42, 21238 Geyserville Ave 95441
The Hope-Merrill House, Box 42, 21253 Geyserville Ave 95441

Glen Ellen

Stone Tree Ranch, PO Box 173, 7910 Sonoma Mtn Rd 95442 ....(707)996-8173

Goleta

Circle Bar B Ranch, 1800 Refugio Rd 93117 ....(805)968-1113

Grass Valley

Annie Horan's, 415 W Main St 95945 ....(916)272-2418
Domike's Inn, 220 Colfax Ave 95945 ....(916)273-9010
Golden Ore House B&B, 448 S Auburn 95945 ....(916)272-6870
Holbrooke Hotel & Purcell House, 212 W Main 95945 .....(916)273-1353
Murphy's Inn, 318 Neal St 95945 ....(916)273-6873
Swan-Levine House, 328 S Church St 95945 ....(916)272-1873

Groveland

Hotel Charlotte, PO Box 884 95321 ....(209)962-6455

Gualala

Gualala Hotel, PO Box 675 95445 ....(707)884-3441
The Old Milano Hotel & Restaurant, 38300 Hwy 1 95445 ....(707)884-3256
St. Orres, PO Box 523 95445 ....(707)884-3303
Whale Watch Inn, 35100 Hwy 1 95445 ....(707)884-3667

Guerneville

Creekside Inn, PO Box 2185 95446 ....(707)869-3623
Ridenhour Ranch, 12850 River Rd 95446 ....(707)887-1033
Santa Nella House, 12130 Hwy 116 95466 ....(707)869-9488

Half Moon Bay

Mill Rose Inn, 615 Mill St 94019 ....(415)726-9794
Old Thyme Inn, 779 Main St 94019 ....(415)726-1616
San Benito House, 356 Main St 94019 ....(415)726-3425

Hanford

The Irwin Street Inn, 522 North Irwin St 93230 ....(209)584-9286
Victorian Inn, 322 N Irwin St 93230 ....(209)584-9286

Healdsburg

Belle Du Jour Farm, 16276 Healdsburg Ave 95448 ....(707)433-7892
Calderwood, 25 West Grant St, PO Box 967 95448 ....(707)431-1110
Camellia Inn, 211 North St 95448 ....(707)433-8182
Grape Leaf Inn, 539 Johnson St 95448 ....(707)433-8140
Haydon House, 321 Haydon St 95448 ....(707)433-5228
Healdsburg Inn On The Plaza, 116 Matheson St, PO Box 1196 95448 ....(707)433-6991
Madrona Manor, A Country Inn, PO Box 818 1001 Westside Rd 95448 ....(707)433-4231
Raford House, 10630 Wohler Rd 95448 ....(707)887-9573

Homewood

Rockwood Lodge, 5295 W Lake Blvd, PO Box 544 95718 .(916)525-4663

Idyllwild

Wilkum Inn, 26770 Hwy 243, PO Box 1115 92349 ....(714)659-4087

Independence

Winnedumah Inn, PO Box 209, 211 N Edwards 93526 ......(619)878-2040

Inverness

Blackthorne Inn, PO Box 712 94937 ....(415)663-8621
Ten Inverness Way, 10 Inverness Way 94937 ....(415)669-1648

Ione

The Heirloom, 214 Shakeley Lane 95640 ....(209)274-4468

Jackson

Ann Marie's, 410 Stasal St 95642 ....(209)223-1452
Broadway Hotel, 225 Broadway 95642 ....(209)223-3503
Court Street Inn, 215 Court St 95642 ....(209)223-0416
Gate House Inn, 1330 Jackson Gate Rd 95642 ....(209)223-3500

Jamestown

National Hotel, Main Street, PO Box 502 95327 ....(209)984-3446

Jenner

Stillwater Cove Ranch 95450 ....(707)847-3227

Julian

Julian Gold Rush Hotel, 2032 Main St, PO Box 1856 92036 ....(619)765-0201
Julian Lodge, PO Box 1430 92036 ....(619)765-1420
Pine Hills Lodge, 2960 La Posada Way, PO Box 2260 92036 ....(619)765-1100

Kyburz

Strawberry Lodge, Hwy 50 95720 ....(916)659-7030

La Jolla

The B&B Inn at La Jolla, 7753 Draper Ave 92037 ....(619)456-2066

Laguna Beach

Carriage House, 1322 Catalina St 92651 ....(714)494-8945
Casa Laguna, 2510 S Coast Hwy 92651 ....(714)494-2996
Eiler's Inn, 741 S Coast Hwy 92651 ....(714)494-3004

Lake Arrowhead

Lakeview Lodge Victorian, Box 128 92352 ....(714)337-6633

Little River

Glendeven, 8221 N Hwy 1 95456 ....(707)937-0083
Heritage House 95456 ....(707)937-5885
Little River Inn 95456 ....(707)937-5942
The Victorian Farmhouse, 7001 N Hwy 1, PO Box 357 95456 ....(707)937-0697

Long Beach

Appleton Place, 935 Cedar Ave 90813 ....(213)432-2312
Lord Mayor's B&B Inn, 435 Cedar Ave 90802 ....(213)436-0324

Los Alamos

Union Hotel, PO Box 616, 362 Bell St 93440 ....(805)344-2744

Los Angeles

Eastlake Victorian Inn, 1442 Kellam Ave 90026 ....(213)250-1620
Salisbury House, 2273 W 20th St 90018 ....(213)737-7817
Terrace Manor, 1353 Alvarado Terrace 90006 ....(213)381-1478
West Adams B&B Inn, 1650 Westmoreland Blvd 90006 .(213)737-5041

Los Gatos

Los Gatos Hotel, 39 E. Main St #1 95030-6907 ....(408)354-4440

Mammoth Lakes

Snow Goose Inn, PO Box 946 93546 ....(619)934-2660

Mariposa

Granny's Garden, 7333 Hwy 49 N 95338 ....(209)377-8342
Meadow Creek Ranch B&B Inn, 2669 Triangle Rd 95338 ....(209)966-3843

McCloud

McCloud Guest House, PO Box 1510, 606 W Colombero Dr 96057 ....(916)964-3160

Mendocino

Agate Cove Inn, PO Box 1150 95460 ....(707)937-0551
Ames Lodge, PO Box 207 95460 ....(707)937-0811

B.G. Ranch & Inn, 9601 N Hwy 1 95460 ....(707)937-5322
Big River Lodge/Stanford Inn, PO Box 487, Hwy 1 95460 ....(707)937-4752
Blue Heron Inn, 390 Kasten St 95460 ....(707)937-4323
Brewery Gulch Inn, 9350 Hwy 1 95460 ....(707)937-4752
The Headlands Inn, PO Box 132, Howard & Albion Sts 95460 ....(707)937-4431
Joshua Grindle Inn, 44800 Little Lake Rd, PO Box 647 95460 ....(707)937-4143
Kelly's Attic, PO Box 858, 699 Ukiah St 95460 ....(707)937-5588
MacCallum House Inn, 45020 Albion St 95460 ....(707)937-0289
Main Street Guest House, PO Box 108, 1021 Main St 95460 ....(707)937-5150
Mendocino Bay Trading Co., PO Box 817, 750 Albion St 95460 ....(707)937-5266
Mendocino Hotel, PO Box 587, 45080 Main St 95460 ....(707)937-0511
Mendocino Village Inn, 44860 Main St, PO Box 626 95460 ....(707)937-0246
Sea Gull Inn, PO Box 317 95460 ....(707)937-5204
Sears House Inn, PO Box 844 95460 ....(707)937-4076
Whitegate Inn, PO Box 150, 499 Howard St 95460 ....(707)937-4892

Mill Valley
Mountain Home Inn, 810 Panoramic Hwy 94941 ....(415)381-9000

Mokelumne Hill
Hotel Leger, PO Box 50 95245 ....(209)286-1401

Montecito
San Ysidro Ranch, 900 San Ysidro Ln 93108

Monterey
The Jabberwock, 598 Laine St 93940 ....(408)372-4777
Merritt House, 386 Pacific St 93940 ....(408)646-9640
Old Monterey Inn, 500 Martin St 93940 ....(408)375-8284
The Spindrift Inn, Box 3196, 652 Cannery Row 93940

Muir Beach
Pelican Inn, 10 Pacific Way 94965 ....(415)383-6000

Murphys
Dunbar House, 1880, 271 Jones St, PO Box 1375 95247 ....(209)728-2897
Murphy's Hotel, 457 Main St 95247 ....(209)728-3444

Napa
Arbor Guest House, 1436 G St 94559 ....(707)252-8144
Beazley House, 1910 First St 94559 ....(707)257-1649
Churchill Manor, 485 Brown St 94559 ....(707)253-7733
Coombs Residence "Inn on the Park", 720 Seminary St 94559 ....(707)257-0789
Gallery Osgood B&B Inn, 2230 First St 94559 ....(707)224-0100
Goodman House, 1225 Division St 94558 ....(707)257-1166
Hennessey House B&B, 1727 Main St 94559 ....(707)226-3774
Magnolia Hotel, PO Box M, 6529 Yount St 94599 ....(707)944-2056
Napa Inn, 1137 Warren St 94559 ....(707)257-1444
Old World Inn, 1301 Jefferson 94559 ....(707)257-0112
Sybron House, 7400 St Helena Hwy 94559 ....(707)944-2785
Yesterhouse Inn, 643 Third St 94559 ....(707)257-0550

Napa Valley
Burgundy/Bordeaux House, PO Box 2776, 6600 Washington 94599 ....(707)944-2855

National City
Dickinson Boal Mansion, 1433 East 24th St 92050 ....(619)477-5363

Nevada City
Downey House, 517 West Broad St 95959 ....(916)265-2815
Grandmere's Inn, 449 Broad St 95959 ....(916)265-4660
National Hotel, 211 Broad St 95959 ....(916)263-4551
Piety Hill Inn, 523 Sacramento St 95959 ....(916)265-2245
The Red Castle Inn, 109 Prospect St 95959 ....(916)265-5135

Newport Beach
Doryman's Inn, 2102 W Ocean Front 92663 ....(714)675-7300

Nipomo
The Kaleidoscope Inn, Box 1297, 130 E Dana St 93444 ....(805)929-5444

Nipton
Hotel Nipton, Rt 1, Box 357 92364 ....(619)856-2335

North Fork
Ye Old South Fork Inn, 57665 Rd 225 93643 ....(209)877-7025

Oakland
Rockridge B&B, 5428 Thomas Ave 94618 ....(415)655-1223

Ojai
Ojai Manor Hotel, 210 E Matilija 93023 ....(805)646-0961
The Theodore Woolsey House, 1484 E Ojai Ave 93023 ....(805)646-9779
Wheeler Hot Springs, PO 250, 16825 Maricopa 93023

Olema
Bear Valley Inn, PO Box 33, 88 Bear Valley 94950 ....(415)663-1777
Point Reyes Seashore Lodge, 10021 Coastal Hwy 1, PO 39 94950 ....(415)663-9000

Olympic Valley
Christy Hill, 1650 Squaw Valley Rd Box 2449 95730 ....(916)583-8551

Orland
The Inn at Shallow Creek Farm, Rt 3, Box 3176 95963 ....(916)865-4093

Pacific Grove
Centrella Hotel, PO Box 884, 612 Central 93950 ....(408)372-3372
Gosby House Inn, 643 Lighthouse Ave 93950 ....(408)375-1287
Green Gables Inn, 104 5th St 93950 ....(408)375-2095
Martine Inn, 255 Ocean View Blvd. 93950 ....(408)373-3388
Old St Angela Inn, 321 Central Ave 93950 ....(408)372-3246
Roserox Country Inn By-The-Sea, 557 Ocean View Blvd 93950 ....(408)373-7673
Seven Gables Inn, 555 Ocean View Blvd 93950 ....(408)372-4341

Palm Springs
Ingleside Inn, 200 W Ramon Rd 92262 ....(619)325-0046

Palo Alto
The Victorian On Lytton, 555 Lytton Ave 94301 ....(415)322-8555

Pasadena
Donneymac Irish Inn, 119 N Meridith 91106 ....(818)440-0066

Philo
Philo Pottery Inn, PO Box 166, 8550 Rt 128 95466 ....(707)895-3069

Placerville
Chichester House B&B, 800 Spring St 95667 ....(916)626-1882
Fleming-Jones Homestead, 3170 Newton Rd 95667 ....(916)626-5840

Point Richmond
East Brother Light Station Inc., 117 Park Pt. 94801 ....(415)233-2385

Quincy
The Feather Bed, 542 Jackson St, PO Box 3200 95971 ....(916)283-0102

Rancho Cucamonga
Christmas House B&B Inn, 9240 Archibald Ave 91730 ....(714)980-6450

Red Bluff
Faulkner House, 1029 Jefferson St 96080 ....(916)529-0520

Redlands
Morey Mansion, 190 Terracina Blvd. 92373 ....(714)793-7970

Reedley
Hotel Burgess, 1726 11th St 93654 ....(209)638-6315

Rutherford
Rancho Caymus Inn, PO Box 78 94573 ....(707)963-1777

Sacramento
Amber House, 1315 22nd St 95816 ....(916)444-8085
Aunt Abigail's, 2120 G St 95816 ....(916)441-5007
Bear Flag Inn, 2814 I St 95816 ....(916)448-5417
Briggs House B&B, 2209 Capitol Ave 95816 ....(916)441-3214
Driver Mansion Inn, 2019 21st St 95818 ....(916)455-5243
Hartley House Inn, 700 22nd St 95816 ....(916)447-7829
Sterling Hotel, 1300 H St 95814 ....(916)448-1300

Saint Helena
Ambrose Bierce House, 1515 Main St 94574 ....(707)963-3003
Bell Creek B&B, 3220 Silverado Trail 94574 ....(707)963-2383
Chalet Bernensis, 225 St Helena Hwy 94574 ....(707)963-4423
Chestelson House, 1417 Kearny St 94574 ....(707)963-2238
Cornerstone B&B Inn, 1308 Main St 94574 ....(707)963-1891
Deer Run B&B, 3996 Spring Mtn Rd 94574 ....(707)963-3794
Hotel Saint Helena, 1309 Main St 94574 ....(707)963-4388
Ink House, 1575 St Helena Hwy 94574 ....(707)963-3890
Prager Winery B&B, 1281 Lewelling Ln. 94574 ....(707)963-3713
Shady Oaks Country Inn, 399 Zinfandel 94574 ....(707)963-1190
The Cinnamon Bear, 1407 Kearney 94574 ....(707)963-4653
White Ranch, 707 White Ln 94574 ....(707)963-4635
Wine Country Cottage, 400 Meadow Wood Ln. 94574 ....(707)963-4633

San Andreas
Black Bart Inn, PO Box 576, 55 St Charles 95249 ....(209)754-3808
Robin's Nest, PO Box 1408, 247 W St Charles 95249 ....(209)754-1076

San Diego
Britt House, 406 Maple St 92103 ....(619)234-2926
Carole's B&B, 3227 Grim Ave 92104 ....(619)280-5258
Heritage Park B&B Inn, 2470 Heritage Park Row 92110 (619)295-7088
Keating House Inn, 2331 Second Ave 92101 ....(619)239-8585
The Quince Street Trolley, PO Box 7654 92107 ....(619)226-8454
Surf Manor & Cottages, PO Box 7695 92107 ....(619)225-9765

California (Continued)

San Francisco

1818 California, 1818 California St 94109 ....(415)885-1818
Alamo Square Inn, 719 Scott St 94117 ....(415)922-2055
Andrews Hotel, 624 Post St 94109 ....(415)563-6877
Archbishop's Mansion, 1000 Fulton St 94117 ....(415)563-7872
Art Center/Wamsley Gallery & B&B, 1902 Filbert St 94123 ....(415)567-1526
B&B Near The Park, 1387 Sixth Ave 94122 ....(415)753-3574
Edward II Inn, 3155 Scott St 94123 ....(415)921-9776
El Drisco Hotel, 2901 Pacific Ave 94115 ....(415)346-2880
Golden Gate Hotel, 775 Bush St 94108 ....(415)392-3702
Grove Inn, 890 Grove St 94117 ....(415)929-0780
Hermitage House, 2224 Sacramento St 94115 ....(415)921-5515
Hotel Louise, 845 Bush St 94108 ....(415)928-6000
Inn At Union Square, 440 Post St 94102 ....(415)397-3510
Inn On Castro, 321 Castro St 94114 ....(415)861-0321
The Inn San Francisco, 943 S Van Ness 94110 ....(415)641-0188
Jackson Court, 2198 Jackson St 94115 ....(415)929-7670
Marina Inn B&B, 431 Hugo St 94123 ....(415)928-1000
Moffatt House, 431 Hugo St 94122 ....(415)661-6210
Monte Cristo, 600 Presidio Ave 94115 ....(415)931-1875
The Nolan House, 1071 Page St 94117 ....(415)863-0384
Pension San Francisco, 1668 Market St 94102 ....(415)864-1271
Petite Auberge, 863 Bush St 94108 ....(415)928-6000
Red Victorian B&B Inn, 1665 Haight St 94117 ....(415)864-1978
Riley's B&B, 1234 Sixth Ave 94122 ....(415)731-0788
Sherman House, 2160 Green St 94123 ....(415)563-3600
Spencer House, 1080 Haight St 94117 ....(415)626-9205
Spreckels Mansion, 737 Buena Vista West 94117 ....(415)861-3008
Stanyan Park Hotel, 750 Stanyan St 94117 ....(415)751-1000
The Mansion Hotel, 2220 Sacramento St 94115 ....(415)929-9444
The Monte Cristo, 600 Presidio Ave 94115 ....(415)931-1875
The Red Victorian, 1665 Haight St 94117 ....(415)864-1978
Union Street Inn, 2229 Union St 94123 ....(415)345-0424
Victorian Inn On The Park, 301 Lyon St 94117 ....(415)931-1830
White Swan Inn, 845 Bush St 94108 ....(415)775-1755

San Juan Bautista

B&B San Juan, PO Box 613 95045 ....(408)623-4101

San Juan Capistrano

Hospitality Plus, PO Box 388 92693 ....(714)496-6953

San Luis Obispo

Heritage Inn, 978 Olive St 93401 ....(805)544-7440

San Pedro

Grand Cottages, 809 S Grand Ave 90731 ....(213)548-1240

San Rafael

Casa Soldavini, 531 "C" St 94901 ....(415)454-3140
Panama Hotel, 4 Bayview St 94901 ....(415)457-3993

Santa Ana

The Craftsman, 2900 N Flower St 92706 ....(714)543-1168

Santa Barbara

Bath Street Inn, 1720 Bath St 93101 ....(805)682-9680
Blue Quail Inn, 1908 Bath St 93101 ....(805)687-2300
Cheshire Cat Inn, 36 W Valerio 93101 ....(805)569-1610
Glenborough Inn, 1327 Bath St 93101 ....(805)966-0589
Harbour Carriage House, 420 W Montecito St 93101 ....(805)962-8447
Hitchcock House, 431 Corona Del Mar 93103 ....(805)962-3989
Inn at Two Twenty Two, 222 W Valerio 93101 ....(805)687-7216
The Old Yacht Club Inn, 431 Corona Del Mar 93103 ....(805)962-1277
Olive House, 1604 Olive St 93101 ....(805)962-4902
The Parsonage, 1600 Olive St 93101 ....(805)962-9336
Red Rose Inn, 1416 Castillo St 93101 ....(805)966-1470
Simpson House Inn, 121 E Arrellaga St 93101 ....(805)963-7067
Tiffany Inn, 1323 De La Vina 93101 ....(805)963-2283
Upham Hotel, 1404 De La Vina St 93101 ....(805)962-0058
Villa d' Italia, 780 Mission Canyon Rd 93105 ....(805)687-6933
Villa Rosa, 15 Chapala St 93101 ....(805)966-0851

Santa Clara

Madison Street Inn, 1390 Madison St 95050 ....(408)249-5541

Santa Cruz

Babbling Brook B&B Inn, 1025 Laurel St 95060 ....(408)427-2437
Chateau Victorian, 118 First St 95060 ....(408)458-9458
Cliff Crest, 407 Cliff St 95060 ....(408)427-2609
Darling House, 314 W Cliff Dr 95060 ....(408)458-1958

Santa Monica

Channel Road Inn, 219 West Channel Road 90402 ....(213)459-1920
Sovereign at Santa Monica Bay, 205 Washington Ave 90403 ....(800)331-0163

Santa Paula

Glen Tavern Inn, 134 N Mill St 93060 ....(805)525-6658
The Lemon Tree Inn, 299 W Santa Paula St 93060

Santa Rosa

The Gables, 4257 Petaluma Hill Rd 95404 ....(707)585-7777
Inn At The Belvedere, 727 Mendocino Ave 95401 ....(707)575-1857
Melitta Station Inn, 5850 Melita Rd 95409 ....(707)538-7712
Pygmalion House, 331 Orange St 95407 ....(707)526-3407

Sausalito

Alta Mira Hotel, 125 Bulkley St 94965 ....(415)332-1350
Casa Madrona Hotel, 801 Bridgeway 94965 ....(415)332-0502
Sausalito Hotel, 16 El Portal 94965 ....(415)332-4155

Seal Beach

The Seal Beach Inn & Gardens, 212 5th St 90740 ....(213)493-2416

Sierra City

Busch & Heringlake Country Inn, PO Box 68 96125 ....(916)862-1501

Sierraville

Campbell Hot Springs Spiritual Retreat, Box 234 #1 Campbell Hot Springs Rd 96126 ....(916)994-3737

Sky Forest

Storybook Inn, PO Box 362 92385 ....(714)336-1483

Sonoma

The Hidden Oak, 214 E Napa St 95476 ....(707)996-9863
Overview Farm, 15650 Arnold Dr 95476 ....(707)938-8574
Sonoma Hotel, 110 W Spain St Box 1326 95476 ....(707)996-2996
Thistle Dew Inn, 171 W Spain St Box 1326 95476 ....(707)938-2909
Trojan Horse Inn, 19455 Sonoma Hwy 95476 ....(707)996-2430
Victorian Garden Inn, 316 E Napa St 95476 ....(707)996-5339

Sonora

Barretta Gardens Inn, 700 S Barretta St 95370 ....(209)532-6039
Gunn House, 286 S Washington St 95370 ....(209)532-3421
Llamahall Guest Ranch, 18170 Wards Ferry Rd 95370 ....(209)532-7264
Lulu Belle's, 85 Gold St 95370 ....(209)533-3455
The Ryan House B&B, 153 S Shepherd St 95370 ....(209)533-3445
Serenity, PO Box 3484 95370 ....(209)533-1441
Sonora Inn, 160 S. Washington 95370 ....(209)532-7468

Soulsbyville

Willow Springs Country Inn, 20599 Kings Ct. 95372 ....(209)533-2030

South Lake Tahoe

Christiana Inn, PO Box 18298 95706 ....(916)544-7337
Strawberry Lodge, Hwy 50 95720 ....(916)659-7030

Sutter Creek

Hanford House, PO Box 847 95685 ....(209)267-0747
Nancy & Bob's 9 Eureka Street Inn, 55 Eureka St, PO Box 386 95685 ....(209)267-0342
The Foxes, PO Box 159, 77 Main St 95685 ....(209)267-5882

Tahoe City

Mayfield House, 256 Grove St, PO Box 5999 95730 ....(916)583-1001
The Cottage Inn, PO Box 66 95730

Templeton

Country House Inn, 91 Main St 93465 ....(805)434-1598

Three Rivers

Cort Cottage, PO Box 245 93271 ....(209)501-4671

Timbercove

Timberhill Ranch, 35755 Hauser Bridge Rd 95421 ....(707)847-3477

Truckee

Alta Hotel, PO Box 2118 95734 ....(916)587-6668
Bradley House, PO Box 2011 95734 ....(916)587-5388
Mountain View Inn, PO Box 8579, Off Hwy 267 95737 ....(916)587-2545

Tuolumne

Oak Hill Ranche, Box 307 95379 ....(209)928-4717

Ukiah

Sanford House, 306 S Pine 95482 ....(707)462-1653
Vichy Springs Resort, 2605 Vichy Springs Rd 95482 ....(707)462-9515

Valley Ford

Inn At Valley Ford, PO Box 439, 14395 Hwy 1 94972 ....(707)876-3182

Venice

Venice Beach House, 15 30th Ave 90291 ....(213)823-1966

Ventura

Bella Maggiore Inn, 67 S California St 93001 ....(805)652-0277
La Mer, 411 Poli St 93001 ....(805)643-3600

California (Continued)

Volcano
St. George Hotel, PO Box 9 95689 ....(209)296-4458
Watsonville
Warner Embassy Inn, 24 Sunset Dr 95076-9651
Weaverville
Hocker-Bartlett House, PO Box 1511, 807 Main St 96093 .(916)623-4403
Westport
Bowen's Pelican Lodge & Inn, PO Box 35, 38921 N Hwy 1 95488 ....(707)964-5588
DeHaven Valley Farm, 39247 N Highway One 95488 ....(707)961-1660
Howard Creek Ranch, 40501 North Hwy, PO Box 121 95488 ....(707)964-6725
Williams
Wilbur Hot Springs 95987 ....(916)473-2306
Yosemite
Hotel Charlotte, Tr 120 95321 ....(209)962-6455
Yountville
Magnolia Hotel, Drawer M, 6529 Yount St 94599 ....(707)944-2056
Napa Valley Railway Inn, Box 2568, 6503 Washington 94599
The Webber Place, Box 2873 94599
Yuba City
Harkey House B&B, 212 C St 95991 ....(916)674-1942
The Wicks, 560 Cooper Ave 95991 ....(916)674-7951

Colorado

Allenspark
Lazy H Ranch, Box 248 80510
Aspen
Alpina Haus, 935 E Durant 81611 ....(800)242-7736
Aspen Ski Lodge, 101 W Main St 81611 ....(303)925-3434
Christmas Inn, 232 W Main St 81611 ....(303)925-3822
Copper Horse House, 328 W Main St 81611
Fireside Inn, 130 W Cooper 81661 ....(303)925-6000
Hearthstone House, 134 E Hyman St 81611
Innsbruck Inn, 233 W Main St 81611
Little Red Ski Haus, 118 E Cooper 81611
Molly Gibson Lodge, 120 W Hopkins 81611
Pomegranate Inn, Box 1368 81612 ....(800)525-4012
Sardy House, 128 E Main St 81611 ....(303)920-2525
Snow Queen Lodge, 124 E Cooper 81611
Tipple Inn, 747 S Galena St 81611
Ullr Lodge, 520 W Main St 81611
Bayfield
Deer Valley Resorts, PO Box 796 81122 ....(303)884-2600
Boulder
B&B Colorado, Ltd, PO Box 6061 80306 ....(303)442-6664
Briar Rose B&B, 2151 Arapahoe 80302 ....(303)442-3007
Pearl Street Inn, 1820 Pearl St 80302 ....(303)444-5584
Breckenridge
Fireside Inn, 212 Wellington PO Box 2252 80424
Buena Vista
Adobe Inn B&B, Hwy 24 #2 Sterling 81211 ....(303)395-6340
Blue Sky Inn, 719 Arizona St 81211 ....(303)395-8865
Carbondale
Crystal River Inn, Hell Roaring Ranch, 12954 Hwy 133. 81657 ....(303)963-3902
Central City
Golden Rose Hotel 80427 ....(303)582-5060
Two Ten Casey, PO Box 154 80427
Colorado Springs
Hearthstone Inn, 506 N Cascade Ave 80903 ....(719)473-4413
Holden House-1902, 1102 W Pikes Peak Ave 80904 ....(719)471-3980
Crested Butte
Claim Jumper Inn, 704 Whiterock, Box 1181 81224 ....(303)349-6471
Forest Queen Hotel, Box 127 2nd/Elk Ave 81224 ....(303)349-5336
Nordic Inn, PO Box 939 81224
Purple Mountain Lodge, PO Box 897, 714 Gothic Ave 81224 ....(303)349-5888
Cripple Creek
Imperial Hotel, 123 N Third St 80813 ....(719)689-2922
Del Norte
Balloon Ranch, Box 41 81132 ....(303)754-2533
The Windsor Hotel, 605 Grande Ave, Box 762 81132 ....(719)657-2668
Denver
The Oxford Alexis, 1600 17th St 80202 ....(800)228-5838
Queen Anne Inn, 2147 Tremont Place 80205 ....(303)296-6666
Sheets Residence, 577 High St 80218 ....(303)329-6170
The Merritt House, 941 E 17th Ave 80218 ....(303)861-5230
Victoria Oaks Inn, 1575 Race St 80218 ....(303)355-1818
Durango
B&B Durango, PO Box 544 81301 ....(303)247-2223
Tall Timber, Box 90G 81301 ....(303)259-4813
Victorian Inn, 2117 W Second Ave 81301
Eldora
Goldminer Hotel, 601 Klondyke Ave 80466 ....(303)258-7770
Empire
The Peck House, PO Box 428 80438 ....(303)569-9870
Estes Park
The Anniversary Inn, 1060 Mary's Lake Rd, Moraine Rt 80517 ....(303)586-6200
Aspen Lodge, Longs Peak Rte 80517 ....(303)586-4241
Fort Collins
Elizabeth Street Guesthouse, 202 E Elizabeth 80524 ....(303)493-2337
Georgetown
The Hardy House, 605 Brownell St, Box 0156 80444 ....(303)569-3388
Glenwood Springs
Hideout, 1293 117 Rd 81601 ....(303)945-5621
Talbott House, 928 Colorado Ave 81601 ....(303)945-1039
Golden
The Dove Inn, 711 14th St 80401 ....(303)278-2209
Granby
Drowsy Water Ranch, Box 147A 80446 ....(303)725-3456
Grand Junction
The Gatehouse, 2502 N 1st St 81501 ....(303)242-6105
Grant
Tumbling River Ranch 80448 ....(303)838-5981
Green Mountain Falls
Columbine Lodge, Box 267 80819
Outlook Lodge, Box 5 80819 ....(719)684-2303
Gunnison
Waunita Hot Springs Ranch, 8007 County Rd 877 81230 ....(303)641-1266
Gypsum
7-W Guest Ranch, 3412 County Rd 151 81637 ....(303)524-9328
Sweetwater Creek Guest Ranch, 2650 Sweetwater Rd 81637 ....(303)524-9301
Hesperus
Blue Lake Ranch, 16919 Hwy 140 81326 ....(303)385-4537
Ignacio
Ute Creek Ranch, 2192 County Rd 334 81137 ....(303)563-4464
La Veta
1899 B&B Inn, 314 S Main 81055 ....(303)742-3576
Lake City
Crystal Lodge 81235 ....(303)944-2201
Leadville
Hilltop House, 100 W 9th St 80461 ....(303)486-2362
The Leadville Country Inn, 127 East Eighth St 80461
Loveland
The Lovelander, 217 W 4th St 80537 ....(303)669-0798
Manitou Springs
Billy's Cottage, 117 Deer Path 80829 ....(303)685-1828
Sunnymede, 106 Spencer 80829
Meredith
Diamond J Guest Ranch, 26604 Frying Pan Rd 81642 ....(303)927-3222
Nathrop
Deer Valley Ranch, Box Y 81236 ....(303)395-2353
Ouray
Baker's Manor, 317 Second St 81427
House Of Yesteryear, Box 440 81427
St. Elmo Hotel, 426 Main St 81427
Weisbaden Spa & Lodge, Box 349 81427
Parshall
Bar Lazy J Guest Ranch, Box N 80468 ....(303)725-3437
Redstone
Avalanche Ranch, 12863 Highway 133 81623 ....(303)963-2846
Historic Redstone Inn, 82 Redstone Blvd 81623

Colorado (Continued)

Ridgway
MacTiernan's San Juan Ranch, 2882 Hwy 23 81432 ....(303)626-5360
Pueblo Hostel & Cantina, PO Box 346 81432 ....(303)626-5939
Rifle
Coulter Lake Guest Ranch, PO Box 906 81650 ....(303)625-1473
Salida
Poor Farm Country Inn, 8495 Co Rd 160 81201
Shawnee
North Fork Ranch, Box B 80475 ....(303)838-9873
Silver Plume
Brewery Inn, 246 Main St, PO Box 473 80476 ....(303)674-5565
Silverton
Alma House, PO Box 780 81433
Fool's Gold, 1069 Snowden 81433 ....(303)387-5879
Grand Imperial Hotel, 1219 Green St 81433 ....(303)387-5527
Teller House Hotel, 1250 Greene St 81433 ....(303)387-5423
Steamboat Springs
Bear Pole Ranch, Star Rt 1 Box Bb 80487
Crawford House, 1184 Crawford Ave, Box 775062 80477 .(303)879-1859
Inn at Steamboat, 3070 Columbine Dr 80477 ....(303)879-2600
The House On The Hill, PO Box 770598 80477
Steamboat Village
Scandinavian Lodge, Box 5040 80449 ....(303)879-0517
Telluride
Dahl House, PO Box 695 81435
Johnstone Inn, PO Box 546 81435
New Sheridan Hotel, 231 W Colorado Ave, PO Box 980 81435
The San sophia, 330 W Pacific Ave, PO 1825 81435 ....(303)728-3001
Skyline Guest Ranch, 7214 Hwy 145, PO Box 67 81435 ....(303)728-3757
Victorian Inn, PO Box 217 81435 ....(303)728-3684
Victor
The Portland Inn, 412 W Portland Ave, PO Box 32 80860 (303)689-2102
Woodland Park
Woodland Hills Lodge, PO Box 276 80863 ....(800)621-8386

Connecticut

Bolton
Jared Cone House, 25 Hebron Rd 06043 ....(203)643-8538
Bridgewater
Sanford/Pond House, PO Box 306 06752
Bristol
Chimney Crest Manor, 5 Founders Dr 06010 ....(203)582-4219
Brooklyn
Tannerbrook, 329 Pomfret Rd 06234
Chester
Inn At Chester, 318 W Main St 06412 ....(203)526-4961
Clinton
Captain Dibbell House, 21 Commerce St 06413 ....(203)669-1646
Cornwall Bridge
Turning Point Farm, Rt 45 06754
Cos Cob
Harbor House Inn, 50 River Rd 06807 ....(203)661-5845
Coventry
Maple Hill Farm B&B, 365 Goose Ln 06423 ....(203)742-0635
Deep River
Riverwind, 209 Main St 06417 ....(203)526-2014
Selden House, 20 Read Rd 06417
Durham
Durham B&B, Carriage Dr 06422 ....(203)344-2779
East Haddam
Bishop's Gate, Goodspeed Landing 06423 ....(203)873-1677
Gelston House,Inn At Goodspeed's Landing, Rt 9 Ex 7 06423
Stonecroft Inn, 17 Main St 06423
Whispering Winds Inn, 93 River Rd 06423 ....(203)526-3055
East Lyme
The Red House, 365 Boston Post Rd 06333
East Windsor
The Stephen Potwine House, 84 Scantic Rd 06088 ....(203)623-8722
Essex
Griswold Inn, 48 Main St 06426 ....(203)767-1812
Glastonbury
Butternut Farm, 1654 Main St 06033 ....(203)633-7197
Greenwich
Homestead Inn, 420 Field Point Rd 06830 ....(203)869-7500
Stanton House, 76 Maple Ave 06830 ....(203)869-2110
Groton Long Point
Shore Inne, 54 East Shore Rd 06340 ....(203)536-1180
Higganum
Simeon Platt B&B, 365 Old Saybrook Rd 06441
Ivoryton
Copper Beech Inn, 46 Main St 06442 ....(203)767-0330
Ivoryton Inn, Main St 06442 ....(203)767-0422
Kent
1741 Saltbox Inn, PO Box 677 06757
Constitution Oak Farm, Beardsley Rd 06757 ....(203)354-6495
The Country Goose B&B, RFD 1 Box 276 06757
The Sam Matson's B&B, Birch Hill Ln, Box 66 06757 ....(203)927-3643
Killingworth
Killingworth Inn, 249 Rt 81 06417
Lakeville
Wake Robin Inn, Rt 41 06039 ....(203)435-2515
Ledyard
Applewood Farms Inn, 528 Col Ledyard Hwy 06339 ......(203)536-2022
Litchfield
Tollgate Hill Inn, Route 202 and Tollgate Rd 06759 ....(203)567-4545
Madison
Dolly Madison Inn, 73 W Wharf Rd 06443 ....(203)245-7377
Madison Beach Hotel, 94 W Wharf Rd 06443 ....(203)245-1404
Middlebury
Tucker Hill Inn, 96 Tucker Hill Rd 06762 ....(203)758-8334
Montville
1841 House, 1851 Rt 32 06382
Moodus
Fowler House, PO Box 432 06469 ....(203)873-8906
Mystic
Adams House, 382 Cow Hill Road 06355
Comolli's Guest House, 36 Bruggeman Pl. 06355
Harbour Inne and Cottage, Edgemont Street 06355 ....(203)572-9253
The Inn at Mystic, Jct Rt 1 & 27 06355 ....(203)536-9604
Red Brook Inn, PO Box 237 06372 ....(203)572-0349
Whalers Inne, PO Box 488t 06355 ....(203)536-1506
Mystic - Noank
Palmer Inn, 25 Church St 06340 ....(203)572-9000
New Canaan
Maples Inn, 179 Oenoke Ridge 06840
Roger Sherman Inn, 195 Oenoke Ridge 06840 ....(203)955-4541
New Hartford
Cobble Hill Farm, Steele Rd 06057 ....(203)379-0057
Highland Farms B&B, Highland Ave 06057 ....(203)379-6029
New Haven
The Inn at Chapel West, 1201 Chapel St 06511 ....(203)777-1201
New London
Lighthouse Inn, 6 Guthrie Place 06320 ....(203)443-8411
Queen Anne Inn & Antique Gallery, 265 Williams St 06320 ....(203)447-2600
New Milford
Homestead Inn, 5 Elm St 06776 ....(203)354-4080
New Preston
Birches Inn, West Shore Rd 06777 ....(203)868-0229
Boulders Inn, Rt 45 06777 ....(203)868-7918
Hopkins Inn, Hopkins Rd 06777
Inn on Lake Waramaug, North Shore Rd 06777 ....(203)868-0563
Newton
Hawley Manor Inn, 19 Main St 06470 ....(203)426-4456
Norfolk
Blackberry River Inn, Rt 44 06058
Greenwoods Gate, Greenwoods Rd E 06058
Manor House, Maple Ave, Box 447 06058 ....(203)542-5690
Mountain View Inn, Rt 272 06058 ....(203)542-5595
Weaver's House, Rt 44 06058 ....(203)542-5108
North Stonington
Randall's Ordinary Inn, PO Box 243 06359
The Old Tavern Farm, Rt 184, Box 477 06359 ....(203)599-5264

Norwalk
Silvermine Tavern, Silvermine & Perry Aves 06850 .... (203)847-4558
Old Greenwich
Harbor House Inn, 165 Shore Rd 06850 .... (203)637-0145
Old Lyme
Bee And Thistle Inn, 100 Lyme St 06371
Old Lyme Inn, 85 Lyme St 06371 .... (203)434-2600
Old Mystic
The Old Mystic Inn, 58 Main St, Box 318 06372 .... (203)572-9422
Old Saybrook
Castle Inn-Cornfield Pointe, Hartland Dr 06475
Pomfret
Cobbscroft, Routes 169 & 44 06258
Grosvenor Place, Rt 97 06258
Wintergreen, Rt 44 & 169 06259 .... (203)928-5741
Pomfret Center
Colonel Angell House, Wrights Crossing Rd 06259
Inn at Gwyn Careg, Rt 44 06230 .... (203)928-9352
Selah Farm, Rt 44 & 169, PO Box 43 06259
Portland
The Croft B&B, 7 Penny Corner Road 06480
Putnam
Feishaw Tavern, Five Mile River Road 06260 .... (203)928-3467
Ridgefield
Butterfield B&B .... (203)438-1608
Epenetus Howe House .... (203)438-4693
Marley B&B .... (203)438-9486
Stonehenge, Rt 7 06877
The Elms Inn, 500 Main St 06877
West Lane Inn, 22 West Ln. 06877
Riverton
Old Riverton Inn, Rt 20 Box 6 06065
Salisbury
Ragamont Inn, Main St 06068 .... (203)435-2372
Under Mountain Inn, Rt 41 06068 .... (203)435-0242
White Hart Inn, Village Green 06068
Yesterday's Yankee B&B, Rt 44 E 06068 .... (203)435-9539
Sharon
The Cottage .... (203)364-0477
Simsbury
Simsbury House, 731 Hopmeadow St 06070
Somersville
The Old Mill Inn, 63 Maple St 06072 .... (203)763-1473
Southington
Chaffee's B&B, 28 Reussner Rd 06489 .... (203)628-2750
Stafford Springs
Winterbrook Farm, Beffa Rd 06076
Stonington
Farnan House, 10 Mcgrath Ct 06378
Stonington Village
Lasbury's B&B, 24 Orchard St 06378 .... (203)535-2681
Stony Creek
Cabin in the Woods, 80 Quarry Rd, PO Box 3291 06405 .... (203)488-5284
Storrs
Altnaveigh Inn, 957 Storrs Rd 06268 .... (203)429-4490
Farmhouse On The Hill, 418 Gurleyville Rd 06268
Thompson
Hedgerow House, 1020 Quaddick Rd 06277
Samuel Watson House, Rt 193 Box 86 06277 .... (203)923-2491
Tolland
Old Babcock Tavern, 484 Mile Hill Rd 06084
Tolland Inn, 63 Tolland Green, Box 717 06084 .... (203)872-0800
Uncasville
Hillcrest House, 2351 Norwich New London Tpke 06382
Washington
Mayflower Inn, Rt 47 06793 .... (203)868-0515
Waterbury
Boulevard B&B, 15 Columbia Blvd 06710 .... (203)755-0314
The House On The Hill, 92 Woodlawn Terrace 06710 .... (203)757-9901
The Parsonage, 18 Hewlett St 06710 .... (203)574-2855
Watertown
1849 House B&B, 249 Litchfield Rd 06795 .... (203)274-1917
The Clark's B&B, 97 Scott Ave 06795 .... (203)274-4866
West Woodstock
Ebenezer Stoddard House, Rt 171 & Perrin Rd 06267 .... (203)974-2552
Westbrook
Captain Stannard House, 138 S Main St 06498 .... (203)399-7565
Talcott House, 161 Seaside Ave, PO Box 1016 06498 .... (203)399-5020
Westport
Cotswold Inn, 76 Myrtle Ave 06880 .... (203)226-3766
Longshore Inn, 280 Compo Rd S 06883 .... (203)226-3316
Winsted
Provincial House, 151 Main St 06098
Woodbury
Curtis House, Main St 06798 .... (203)263-2101
Woodstock
The Inn at Woodstock Hill, Plaine Hill Rd 06267 .... (203)928-0528

Delaware

Bethany Beach
166 Ocean View, PO Box 275, 166 Ocean View Pkwy 19930
.... (302)539-3707
The Addy Sea, Box 275 19930
Homestead Guests, 721 Garfield Pkwy. 19930
Sea-Vista Villas, Box 62 19930
The Sandbox, Box 62 19930 .... (302)539-3354
Camden
Jonathan Wallace House, 9 South Main St 19934 .... (302)697-2921
Dover
Biddles B&B, 101 Wyoming Ave 19901 .... (302)736-1570
The Inn at Meeting House Square, 305 S Governors Ave 19901
.... (302)678-1242
Nobel Guest House, 33 S Bradford St 19901 .... (302)674-4048
Laurel
Spring Garden, Rt 1 Box 283-A 19956 .... (302)875-7015
Lewes
Savannah Inn, 330 Savannah Rd 19958 .... (302)645-5592
Milford
The Towers, 101 Northwest Front St 19963 .... (302)422-3814
New Castle
David Finney Inn, 216 Delaware St 19720 .... (302)322-6367
The Jefferson House B&B, The Strand at the Wharf 19720
.... (302)323-0999
William Penn Guest House, 206 Delaware St 19720 .... (302)328-7736
Odessa
Cantwell House, 107 High St 19730 .... (302)378-4179
Rehoboth Beach
The Abbey, 31 Maryland Ave 19971 .... (302)227-7023
Corner Cupboard Inn, 50 Park Ave 19971
Gladstone Inn, 3 Olive Ave 19971 .... (302)227-2641
Lord Baltimore Lodge, 16 Baltimore Ave 19971 .... (302)227-2855
Pleasant Inn Lodge, 31 Olive Ave 19971 .... (302)227-7311
Sea Lodge, 15 Hickman St 19971
Wilmington
The Boulevard B&B, 1909 Baynard Blvd. 19802 .... (302)656-9700

Florida

Amelia Island
The 1735 House, 584 S Fletcher Ave 32034 .... (904)261-5878
Apalachicola
Gibson Inn, PO Box 221 32320 .... (904)653-2191
Boca Grande
Gasparilla Inn 33921 .... (813)964-2201
Bokeelia
Cabbage Key Inn, PO Box 489 33922 .... (813)283-2278
Bradenton
Banyan House, 624 Fontana Ln. 33529
Cedar Key
Historic Island Hotel, Box 460 32625 .... (904)543-5111
Coral Gables
Hotel Place St. Michel, 162 Alcazar Ave 33134 .... (305)444-1666
Daytona Beach
St. Regis Hotel, 509 Seabreeze Blvd 32018 .... (904)252-8743

Florida (Continued)

Englewood
Lemon Bay B&B, 12 S Wind Dr 33533 ....(813)474-7571
Everglades City
Rod & Gun Club, PO Box G 33929
Fernandina Beach
Bailey House, PO Box 805 32034 ....(904)261-5390
Greyfield Inn, Box 878 Cumberland Isl. 32034
Seaside Inn, 1998 South Fletcher Ave 32034
Fort Myers
Wind Song Garden, 5570-4 Woodrose Ct 33907 ....(813)936-6378
Ft Lauderdale Beach
Casa Alhambra B&B Inn, 3029 Alhambra St 33304 ....(305)467-2262
Hawthorne
Yearling Cabins, Rt 3, Box 123 32640 ....(904)466-3033
Holmes Beach
Harrington House B&B, 5626 Gulf Dr 34217 ....(813)778-5444
Indianatown
Seminole Country Inn, 15885 Warfield 33456
Inverness
Crown Hotel, 109 N. Seminole Ave 32650
Jacksonville
House on Cherry St, 1844 cherry St 32205 ....(904)384-1999
Key West
Alexander's, 1118 Fleming St 33040 ....(305)294-9919
Artist House, 534 Eaton St 33040 ....(305)296-3977
Author's, 725 White At Petronia 33040 ....(305)294-7381
Chelsea House, 707 Truman 33040 ....(305)296-2211
Coconut Grove Guest House, 817 Fleming St 33040 ....(305)296-5107
Colours Key West - The Guest Mansion, 410 Fleming St 33040 ....(305)294-6977
Cypress House, 601 Caroline St 33040 ....(305)294-6969
Duval House, 815 Duval St 33040 ....(305)294-1666
Eaton Lodge, 511 Eaton St 33040 ....(305)294-3800
Eden House, 1015 Fleming 33040 ....(305)296-6868
Ellie's Nest, 1414 Newton St 33040 ....(305)296-5757
Garden House, 329 Elizabeth St 33040 ....(305)296-5368
Heron House, 512 Simonton St 33040 ....(305)294-9227
Island City House, 411 William St 33040 ....(305)294-5702
Island House, 1129 Fleming St 33040 ....(305)294-6284
Key West B&B, Popular House, 415 William St 33040 ....(305)296-7274
Marquesa Hotel, 600 Fleming St 33040 ....(305)292-1919
Merlinn Guest House, 811 Simonton St 33040 ....(305)296-3336
Oasis Guest House, 823 Fleming St 33040 ....(305)296-2131
Palms Of Key West, 820 White St 33040 ....(305)294-3146
Pines of Key West, 521 United St 33040 ....(305)296-7467
Simonton Court, 320 Simonton St 33040 ....(305)294-6386
Sunrise Sea House B&B, 39 Bay Dr 33040 ....(305)745-2875
Sweet Caroline Guest House, 529 Caroline St 33040 ....(305)296-5173
The Hollinsed House, 609-11 Southard St 33040 ....(305)296-8031
Walden Guest House, 223 Elizabeth 33040 ....(305)296-7161
The Watson House, 525 Simonton 33040 ....(305)294-6712
Whispers B&B Inn at Gideon Lowe House, 409 William St 33040 ....(305)294-5969
Wicker Guest House, 913 Duval St 33040 ....(305)296-4275
Kissimee
Beaumont House, 206 S Beaumont Ave 32741 ....(305)846-7916
Lake Wales
Chalet Suzanne, 319 W Starr Ave, Drawer AC 33859-9003 ....(813)676-6011
Mayo
Jim Hollis' River Rendezoux, Rt 2, Box 60 32066
Miami
B&B Company, PO Box 262 33243 ....(305)661-3270
Micanopy
Herlong Mansion, Cholakka Blvd. 32667
Mount Dora
Lakeside Inn, Box 1390 32757 ....(800)556-5016
Naples
Inn by the Sea, 287 Eleventh Ave S 33940 ....(813)649-4124
Ocala
Doll House B&B, 719 SE 4th St 32671 ....(904)351-1167
Ritz — Ocala's Historic Inn, 1205 E Silver Springs Rd 32670 ....(904)867-7700
Orange Springs
Orange Springs, 1 Main St, Box 550 32682 ....(904)546-2052
Orlando
Avonelle's, 4755 Anderson Rd 32806 ....(305)275-8733
Fugate House, Box 2009 32802 ....(305)423-8382
Meadow Marsh, 940 Tildenville School Rd 32787 ....(305)656-2064
Spencer Home B&B, 313 Spencer St 32809 ....(305)855-5603
The Norment-Parry Inn, 211 N Lucerne Circle E 32801 ....(305)648-5188
Pensacola
Sunshine, 508 Decatur Ave 32507 ....(904)455-6781
Saint Augustine
Carriage Way B&B, 70 Cuna St 32084 ....(904)829-2467
Casa de la Paz, 22 Avenida Menendez 32084 ....(904)829-2915
Casa de Solana, 21 Aviles St 32084 ....(904)824-3555
Kenwood Inn, 38 Marine St 32084 ....(904)824-2116
Sailor's Rest, 298 St George St 32084 ....(904)824-3817
St. Francis Inn, 279 St George St 32084 ....(904)824-6068
Victorian House B&B, 11 Cadiz St 32084 ....(904)824-5214
Westcott House, 146 Avenida Menendez 32084 ....(904)824-4301
Saint Petersburg
Bayboro House on Old Tampa Bay, 1719 Beach Dr, SE 33701 ....(813)823-4955
Siesta Key, Sarasota
Cresent House, 459 Beach Rd 34242 ....(813)346-0857
Tarpon Springs
Spring Bayou Inn, 32 W Tarpon Ave 34689 ....(813)938-9333
Wakulla Springs
Wakulla Springs Lodge & Conference Ctr, 1 Spring Dr 32305 ....(904)224-5950
West Palm Beach
Hibiscus House, PO Box 2612 33402

Georgia

Athens
The Serpentine Inn, 1416 S Milledge Ave 30606 ....(404)353-8548
Atlanta
Beverly Hills Inn, 65 Sheridan Dr NE 30305 ....(404)233-8520
Shellmont B&B Lodge, 821 Piedmont NE 30308 ....(404)872-9290
Augusta
Oglethorpe Inn, 836 Greene St 30901 ....(404)724-9774
Peach Blossom Inn, 1119 Green St 30901
Telfair Inn, 326 Greene St 30901 ....(404)724-3315
Barnesville
Bird In A Bush, 722 Thomaston St 30204
Blairsville
1880 Victorian Inn, Box 2901 Town Creek Rd 30512
Blakely
Layside, 611 River St 31723
Blue Ridge
Creekside Farm B&B ....(404)632-3851
Chickamauga
Gordon-Lee Mansion B&B, 217 Cove Rd 30707 ....(404)375-4728
Clarkesville
Burns-Sutton House, 124 S Washington St, Box 992 30523 ....(404)754-5565
Charm House Inn, Box 392, Hwy 441 30523 ....(404)754-9347
Glen-Ella Springs Hotel, Rt 3, Bear Gap Rd 30523 ....(404)754-7295
Laprade's, Rt 1, Hwy 197 30523
Clayton
The English Inn ....(404)782-4411
Kennett Home ....(404)782-3186
Cleveland
McCollum House, Rt 4 Box 309, Rt 255 30528
Ru Sharon, Box 273 30528
Columbus
De Loffre House, 812 Broadway 31901
Dahlonega
Forest Hills Mt. Resort, Rt 3 30533
Smith House, 202 S. Chestatee St 30533 ....(404)864-2348
Worley Homestead Inn, 410 W Main 30533 ....(404)864-7002

Dalton
Amy's Place, 217W Cuyler 30720
Dillard
Dillard House Inn, PO Box 10 30537 ....(404)746-5349
Forsyth
A Country Place, Route 3, Box 290 31019
Fort Oglethorpe
Captain's Quarters, Barnhardt Circle 30742 ....(404)858-0624
Gainesville
Dunlap House, 635 Green St 30501
Greenville
Samples Plantation, Rt 1 Box 735 30222
Hartwell
Hartwell Inn, 504 W Howell St 30643
Helen
Derdenhof Inn, PO Box 405 30545
Helendorf Inn, PO Box 305 30545 ....(404)878-2271
Lakemont
Anapauo Farm, Star Rt, Box 13C 30522 ....(404)782-6442
Lake Rabun Hotel, Rt 1 Box 101 30552 ....(404)782-4946
Macon
1842 Inn, 353 College St 31201 ....(912)741-1842
The Carriage Stop Inn, 1129 Georgia Ave 31201 ....(912)743-9740
Hutnick House, 273 Orange St 31201
La Petite Maison, 1165 Dures Ln 31201 ....(912)742-4674
Marietta
Arden Hall, 1052 Arden Dr SW 30060 ....(404)422-0780
The Marlow & Stanley House, 192 Church St 30060 ....(404)426-1887
Marshallville
Suite Revenge ....(912)967-2252
McDonough
D.P. Cook House, 69 Keys Ferry St 30253 ....(404)957-7562
Mountain City
The York House, Box 126 30562 ....(404)746-2068
Newnan
Parrott Camp Soucy House ....(404)253-4846
Plains
Plains B&B ....(912)824-7252
Plains Country Inn ....(912)824-4410
Rutledge
Jones Cottage ....(404)557-2516
Saint Mary's
Riverview Hotel, 105 Osborne St 31558 ....(912)882-3242
Saint Simons Island
Little St. Simons Island, PO Box 1078 G 31522 ....(912)638-7472
Sautee
Stovall House, Rt 1 Box 1476 30571 ....(404)878-3355
Woodhaven Chalet, Rt 1, Box 39 30571 ....(404)878-2580
Savannah
17 Hundred 90 Inn, 307 E. President 31401 ....(912)236-7122
417 The Haslam-Fort House, 417 East Charlton St 31401 ....(912)233-6380
B&B Inn, 117 W Gordon St 31401 ....(912)238-0518
Ballastone Inn, 14 E Oglethorpe Ave 31401 ....(912)236-1484
Barrister House, 25 W Perry St 31401
Charlton Court, 403 E. Charlton St 31401 ....(912)236-2895
Comer House, 2 East Taylor St 31401
East Bay Inn, 225 E Bay St 31401 ....(912)238-1225
Eliza Thompson House, 5 W. Jones St 31401
Foley House Inn, 14 W Hull St 31401 ....(912)232-6622
The Forsyth Park Inn, 102 W Hall St 31401 ....(912)233-6800
Gastonian, 220 E.gaston St 31401
Greystone Inn, 214 E. Jones St 31401
Haslam-Fort House, 417 E Charlton St 31401 ....(912)233-6380
Jesse Mount House, 209 W Jones St 31401 ....(912)236-1774
Liberty Inn 1834, 128 W Liberty St 31401 ....(912)233-1007
Magnolia Place Inn, 503 Whitaker St 31401 ....(912)236-7674
Mary Lee's House, PO Box 607 31402
Morel House, 117 W Perry St 31401 ....(912)234-4088
Mulberry Inn, 601 E. Bay St 31402
Olde Harbour Inn, 508 E Factors Walk 31401 ....(912)234-4100
Planters Inn ....(912)232-5678
Presidents' Quarters, 225 E President St 31401 ....(912)233-1600
Pulaski Square Inn, 203 W Charlton 31401
Remshart-Brooks House, 106 W Jones St 31401 ....(912)234-6928
Royal Colony Inn, 29 Abercorn St 31401 ....(912)232-5678
RSVP Savannah B&B Reservation Service, 417 E Charlton St 31401 ....(912)232-7787
Stoddard-Cooper House, 19 W Perry St 31401
Timmons House, 407 E Charlton St 31401 ....(912)233-4456
Senoia
Culpepper House, Corner of Broad & Morgan PO 462 30276 ....(404)599-8182
The Veranda - Hollberg Hotel, 252 Seavy St 30276-0177 (404)599-3905
St Simons Island
Country Hearth Inn ....(912)638-7805
Statesboro
Statesboro Inn B&B, 301 South 30458 ....(912)489-8628
Thomaston
The Guest House, 318 W Main St 30286 ....(404)647-1203
Thomasville
Neel House, 502 S Broad St 31792 ....(912)228-6000
Susina Plantation Inn, Rt 3 Box 1010 31792 ....(912)377-9644
Toccoa
Habersham Manor House, 326 Doyle St 30577
Washington
Liberty Street, 108 W Liberty St 30673
Water Oak Cottage, 211 S Jefferson St 30673
Winterville
Old Winterville Inn, 108 S Main St 30683 ....(404)742-7340

Hawaii

Aiea
Alohaland Guest House, 98-1003 Oliwa St 96701 ....(808)487-0482
Captain Cook
Manago Hotel, Box 145 96704 ....(808)323-2642
Haiku, Maui
Haikuleana B&B Inn, 69 Haiku Rd 96708 ....(808)575-2890
Hana
Heavenly Hana Inn, PO Box 146 96713 ....(808)248-8442
Kaia Ranch & Co, PO Box 404, Ulaino Rd 96713 ....(808)248-7725
Hawi
Aha Hui Hawaiian Plantation, PO Box 10 96719 ....(808)889-5523
Honolulu
B&B Waikiki Beach, PO Box 89080 96830 ....(808)923-5459
Hale O Kahala, 4614 Kilauea Ave #565 96816 ....(808)732-5889
Hawaii Kai, 876 Ka'ahue St 96825 ....(808)395-8153
The Manoa Valley Inn, 2001 Vancouver Dr 96822 ....(808)947-6019
Kaunakakai, Molokai
Pau Hana Inn, PO Box 546 96748 ....(800)367-8047
Lahaina
Plantation Inn, 174 Lahainaluna Rd 96761 ....(800)433-6815
Lahaina, Maui
The Lahaina Hotel, 127 Lahainaluna Rd 96761 ....(808)661-0577
Poipu Beach, Kauai
Poipu B&B Inn, 2720 Hoonani Rd 96756 ....(808)742-1146
Volcano
My Island B&B, Box 100 96785

Idaho

Boise
Sunrise, 2730 Sunrise Rim Rd 83705 ....(208)345-5260
Bonner's Ferry
Deep Creek Inn 83805 ....(208)267-2373
Coeur d'alene
Blackwell House, 820 Sherman Ave 83814 ....(208)664-0656
Coeur d'Alene
Greenbriar B&B, 315 Wallace 83814 ....(208)667-9660
Grangeville
Tulip House, 403 S Florence St 83530 ....(208)983-1034
Hailey
Comfort Inn, Box 984 83333 ....(208)788-2477
Horseshoe Bend
Old Riverside Depot, Rt 1 Box 14a 83629 ....(208)793-2408
Idaho City
Idaho City Hotel, PO Box 70 83631 ....(208)392-4290

Idaho (Continued)

Irwin
McBride's B&B, PO Box 166 83428 ....(208)483-4221
Kellogg
Dorsett House, 305 S Division 83837 ....(208)786-2311
Ketchum
Lift Haven Inn, Box 21, 100 Lloyd Dr 83340 ....(208)726-5601
Powderhorn Lodge, Box 3970 83340 ....(208)726-3107
Kooskia
Looking Glass Ranch, HC-75, Box 32 83539 ....(208)926-0855
Meridian
Home Place, 415 W Lake Hazel Rd 83642 ....(208)888-3857
Northfork
Indian Creek Ranch, Rt 2 Box 105 83466
Pocatello
Holmes Retreat, 178 N Mink Creek Rd 83204
Saint Mraies
Knoll Hus, PO Box 572 83861 ....(208)245-4137
Sandpoint
Whitaker House, 410 Railroad Ave #10 83466
Stanley
Idaho Rocky Mtn. Ranch, HC 64 Box 9934 83278
Redfish Lake Lodge, PO Box 9 83278 ....(208)774-3536
Wallace
Jameson B&B, 304 Sixth St 83873 ....(208)556-1554
Pine Tree Inn, 177 King St, Box 1023 83873 ....(208)752-4391

Illinois

Alton
Haagen House B&B, 617 State St 62002 ....(618)462-2419
Arcola
Curly's Corner B&B, RR 2, Box 85B 61910 ....(217)268-3352
Arthur
Favorite Brother Inn, 106 E Columbia 61911 ....(217)543-2938
Barrington Hills
The Old Cheese Factory, 90 Meadow Hill Rd 60010 ....(312)381-8840
Bishop Hill
Holden's Guest House, E Main & Sun-Up Ln 61419 ....(309)927-3500
Bushnell
The Old Smith Home & Breakfast, 287 W Hail St 61422 ....(309)772-3908
Carlinville
Courthouse Inn, 307 E First South St 62626 ....(217)854-6566
Carthage
Wright Farmhouse, RR3 62321 ....(217)357-2421
Casey
Cumberland Trail B&B, 201 W Main St 62420 ....(217)932-5522
Champaign
Davidson Place B&B, 1110 Davidson Dr 61820 ....(217)356-5915
Grandma Joan's Homestay, 2204 Brett Dr 61821 ....(217)356-5828
Chicago
Burton House B&B Inn, 1454 N Dearborn Pkwy 60610 .(312)787-9015
Heritage Homes, PO Box 409218 60640 ....(312)728-7935
Victorian, 2525 N Burling 60614 ....(312)327-0751
Cisco
Country House, Rt 1 Box 61 61803 ....(217)669-2291
Collinsville
Maggie's B&B, 2102 N Keebler Rd 62234 ....(618)344-8283
Dallas City
1850's Guest House, Rt 1 62330 ....(217)852-3652
Decatur
Hamilton House, 500 W Main St 62522 ....(217)429-1669
Dixon
Colonial Inn, Rt 3 Grand Detour 61021 ....(815)652-4422
River View Guest House, 507 E Everett 61021 ....(815)288-5974
Dunlap
Eagle's Nest, 11125 N Trigger Rd 61525 ....(309)243-7376
Duquoin
Francie's B&B, 104 S Line St 62832 ....(618)542-6686
Eldred
Hobson's Bluffdale, Rt 1, Hillview Rd 62027 ....(217)983-2854
Elsah
Corner Nest B&B, 3 Elm St, PO Box 22 62028 ....(618)374-1892
Green Tree Inn, 15 Mill St, Box 96 62028 ....(618)374-2821
Maple Leaf Cottage Inn, 12 Selma St, PO Box 156 62028 ..(618)374-1684
Evanston
Homestead, 1625 Hinman Ave 60201 ....(312)475-3300
Freeburg
The Westerfield House, RR 2, Box 34 62243 ....(618)539-5643
Galena
Aldrich Guest House, 900 Third St 61036
Amber Creek Farm, PO Box 5 61036 ....(815)598-3301
Avery Guest House, 606 S Prospect St 61036 ....(815)777-3883
Bedford Guest House, Rt 20 W 61036 ....(815)777-2043
Belle Aire Mansion, 11410 Rt 20 W 61036 ....(815)777-0893
Captain Harris Guest House, 713 S Bench St 61036
Chestnut Mountain Resort, 8700 W Chestnut Rd 61036 ...(800)435-2914
Colonial Guest House, 1004 Park Ave 61036 ....(815)777-0336
Comfort Guest House, 1000 Third St 61036
Country Valley Guest Home, 2690 Blackjack Rd 61036 ....(815)777-2322
DeSoto House Hotel, 230 S Main St 61036 ....(815)777-0090
Farmer's Home Hotel, 334 Spring St 61036 ....(815)777-3456
Farster's Executive Inn, 305 N Main St 61036
Felt Manor, 125 S Prospect St 61036 ....(815)777-9093
Four Oaks Guest House, 6594 Hwy Rt 84 N 61036 ....(815)777-9567
Gallery Guest Suite, 204 1/2 S Main St 61036 ....(815)777-1222
The Goldmoor, 9001 Sand Hill Rd 61036 ....(815)777-3921
Grandview Guest Home, 113 S Prospect St 61036 ....(815)777-1387
Hellman Guest House, 318 Hill St 61036 ....(815)777-3638
Log Cabin Guest House, 11661 W Chetlain Ln 61036
Mother's Country Inn, 349 Spring St 61036
Pat's Country Guest Home, 5148 Hwy 20 W 61036 ....(815)777-1030
Renaissance Vintage Suites, Box 291 61036
Robert Scribe Harris House, 713 S Bench St 61036 ....(815)777-1611
Ryan Mansion Inn, Rt 20 W 61036
Spring Street Guest House, 418 Spring S 61036
Stillman's Country Inn, 513 Bouthillier 61036 ....(815)777-0557
Stillwater's Country Inn, 7213 W Buckhill Rd 60613 ....(815)777-0223
The Homestead, 1022 Fourth St 61036
Victorian Mansion Guest House, 301 S High St 61036 ....(815)777-0675
Galva
Country Hills B&B, Rt 1 61434 ....(309)932-2886
Geneva
The Oscar Swan Country Inn, 1800 W State St 60134 ....(312)232-0173
Gibson City
Stolz Home, RR 2, Box 27 60936 ....(217)784-4502
Golconda
Heritage Haus, Main & Columbus, Box 562 62938 ....(618)683-3883
Riverview Mansion Hotel, Columbus Ave, PO Box 56 62938 ....(618)638-3001
The Mansion Of Golconda, 515 Columbus St, Box 339 62938 ....(618)683-4400
Goodfield
Brick House Inn, Box 301, Conklin Ct 61742 ....(309)965-2545
Grand Detour
Colonial Inn, Rock & Green Sts 61021 ....(815)652-4422
Grant Park
The Bennett Curtis House, 302 W Taylor....(815)465-6025
Harden
Wittmond Hotel, c/o Calhoun Herald 62017 ....(818)883-2345
Hillsboro
Hillsboro Hotel's Red Rooster Inn, 123 E Seward 62049 ...(217)532-6332
Jacksonville
The 258 Inn, 258 W Morton 62650 ....(217)245-2588
The Gable Inn, 258 W Monton 62650
Joliet
Stonegate Inn, 619 Cornelia St 60435 ....(815)723-6548
Lake Forest
Deer Path Inn, 255 E Illinois Rd 60045 ....(312)234-2280
Lanark
Standish House, 540 W Carroll St 61046 ....(815)493-2307
Leland
Our CountryHome, 4359 E 1950th Rd 60531 ....(815)495-9091
Watseka Farm, 4377 E 2551 Rd 60531 ....(815)498-9820
Lockport
Hotel President, 933 State St 60441
Marseilles
Annie Tique's Hotel, 378 Main St 61341 ....(815)795-5848

Mendota
Elizabeth's B&B, 1100 FifthSt 61432 ....(815)539-5555
Monmouth
Carr Mansion Guest House, 416 E Broadway 61462 ....(309)734-3654
Mt. Carroll
Country Palmer House, Rt 3, Box 254 61053 ....(815)244-2343
The Farm, Rt 1, Box 112 61053 ....(815)244-9885
Mt. Carroll Guest House, 111 N Main 61053 ....(815)244-9712
Prairie Path Guest House, RR 3, Box 223 61053 ....(815)244-3462
Mt. Pulaski
Dorsey's B&B, 318 N Belmont 62548 ....(217)792-3347
Mundelein
Round-Robin Guesthouse, 231 Maple Ave 60060 ....(312)566-7664
Naperville
Die Blaue Gans Guesthaus, 9S 265, Rt 59 60565 ....(312)355-0835
Harrison House, 26 N Eagle 60565 ....(312)420-1117
Nauvoo
Hotel Nauvoo, Rt 96 Town Center PO 398 62354 ....(217)453-2211
Mississippi Memories, Box 291, Riverview Hgts 62354 ....(217)453-2771
Oak Park
Toad Hall B&B House, 301 N Scoville 60302 ....(312)386-8623
Oakland
Inn On the Square, 3 Montgomery 61943 ....(217)346-2289
Oregon
LynDel Mansion, 400 N 3rd St 61061 ....(815)732-7313
Pinehill B&B, 400 Mix St 61061 ....(815)732-2061
Peoria
Wildlife Prairie Park, RR 2 61615 ....(309)676-0998
Petersburg
Carmody's Clare Inn, 207 S Twelfth St 62675 ....(217)632-2350
Luthringer House, 122 W Sheridan 62675 ....(217)893-0469
Pleasant Hill
Pleasant Haven, 201 E Quincy, PO Box 51 62366 ....(217)734-9357
Polo
Barber House Inn, 410 W Mason 61064 ....(815)946-2607
Port Byron
The Olde Brick House, 502 N High St 61275 ....(309)523-3236
Princeton
Yesterdays Memories B&B, 303 E Peru St 61356 ....(815)872-7753
Quincy
The Kaufmann House, 1641 Hampshire 62301 ....(217)223-2502
Rock Island
Potter House B&B, 1906-7 Ave 61201 ....(309)788-1906
Top O' The Morning, 1505 19th Ave 61201 ....(309)786-3513
Rockford
The Barn, 6786 Guilford Rd 61107 ....(815)399-5210
Victoria's B&B, 201 N 6th St 61107
Somonauk
Watseka Farm, PO Box 272 60552 ....(815)498-9820
Springfield
Corinne's B&B Inn, 1001 S Sixth St 62703 ....(217)527-1400
Mischler House, 718 S 8th St 62703 ....(217)523-3714
St. Charles
Charleston Guest House, 612 W Main St 60174 ....(312)377-1277
Stage Coach Inn, 41 W 278 Whitney Rd 60174 ....(312)584-1263
Stockton
Herrings Maple Lane Farm, 3114 Rush Creek Rd 61085
Maple Lane Country Inn, 3114 S Rush Creek Rd 61085 ....(815)947-3773
Memory Lane Lodge, 409 N Canyon Park Rd 61085 ....(815)947-2726
Sycamore
Country Charm B&B, Rt 2 Box 154 60178
Stratford Inn, 355 W State 60178 ....(815)895-6789
Tolono
Aunt Zelma's Country Guest House, RR 1, Box 129 61880
....(217)485-5101
Warren
Noni's B&B, 516 W Main, Hwy 78 61087 ....(815)745-2045
West Salem
Thelma's B&B, 201 S Broadway 62476 ....(618)456-8401
Wheaton
Wheaton Inn, Roosevelt Rd & Wheaton Ave 60187 ....(312)690-2600
Winnetka
Chateau des Fleurs, 552 Ridge Rd 60093 ....(312)256-7272
Woodstock
The Bundling Board Inn, 220 E South St 60098 ....(815)338-7054
Wuincy
The Kaufman House, 1641 Hampshire 62301 ....(217)223-2502

Indiana

Auburn
Auburn Inn, 225 Touring Dr 46707 ....(219)925-6363
Batesville
Sherman House Restaurant & Inn, 35 S Main St 47006 .(812)934-2407
Berne
Schug House Inn, 206 W Main St 46711 ....(219)589-2303
Beverly Shores
Dunes Shore Inn, Box 807, Lakeshore County Rd 46301 ..(219)879-9029
Bloomingdale
Ewbank-Loudermilk House, RR 1, Box 104 47832 ....(317)597-2579
Bloomington
The Bauer House B&B, 4595 N Maple Grove Rd 47401 ....(812)336-4383
Bristol
Open Hearth B&B, 56782 SR 15 46507 ....(219)825-2417
Chesterton
Wingfield's Inn B&B, 526 Indian Oak Mall 46304 ....(702)348-0766
Columbus
The Columbus Inn, 445 Fifth St 47501 ....(812)378-4289
Lafayette Street B&B, 723 Lafayette St 47201 ....(812)372-7245
Corydon
Kintner House Inn, 101 S Capital 47112 ....(812)738-2020
Crawfordsville
Davis House, 1010 W Wabash Ave 47933 ....(317)364-0461
Yount's Mill Inn, 3729 Old SR 32 W 47933 ....(317)362-5864
Decatur
Cragwood Inn, 303 N Second St 46733 ....(219)728-2000
Evansville
Brigadoon B&B Inn, 1201 SE Second St 47713 ....(812)422-9635
Fort Wayne
The Candlewyck B&B, 331 W Washington Blvd 46802 .....(219)424-2643
Roebuck Inn, 2727 Canterbury Blvd 46835 ....(219)485-9619
Goshen
Checkerberry Inn, 62644 Country Rd 37 46526
Greencastle
Walden Inn, 2 Seminary Sq 46135 ....(317)653-2761
Hagerstown
Teetor House, 300 W Main St 47346 ....(317)489-4422
Hartford City
De'Coy's B&B, 1546 W 100 N 47348 ....(317)348-2164
Indianapolis
Barn House, 10656 E 63rd St 46236
Hollingsworth House Inn, 6054 Hollingsworth Road 46254
....(317)299-6700
Le Chateau Delaware, 1456 N Delaware St 46202 ....(317)636-9156
Osborne House, 1911 N Delaware 46202 ....(317)924-1777
Pairadux Inn, 6363 N Guilford Ave 46220 ....(317)259-8005
Stewart Manor, 612 E 13th St 46202 ....(317)634-1711
Knightstown
Old Hoosier House, Rt 2 Box 299-I 46148 ....(317)345-2969
La Grange
The 1886 Inn, PO Box 5, 212 W Factory St 46761 ....(219)463-4227
Leavenworth
Ye Olde Scotts Inn, RR 1, Box 5 47137 ....(812)739-4747
Madison
Main Street B&B, 739 W Main St 47250 ....(812)265-3539
Millwood House, 512 West St 47250 ....(812)265-6780
The Cliff House, 122 Fairmount Dr 47250 ....(812)265-5272
Metamora
The Publick House, PO Box 219 47030 ....(317)647-6235
The Thorpe House, Clayborne St 47030 ....(317)647-5425
Michigan City
Creekwood Inn, Rt 20-35 46460 ....(219)872-8357
Duneland Beach Inn, 3311 Potawatomi 46360
Nutcracker Inn, 220 W 10th St 46360 ....(219)872-3237
Plantation Inn, RR 2 Box 296-s 46360 ....(219)874-2418

Indiana (Continued)

Middlebury
Bee Hive B&B, PO Box 1191 46540 ....(219)825-5023
Essenhaus Country Inn, 240 US 20 E 46540 ....(317)472-7151
Patchwork Quilt, 11748 Cr 2 46540
Mishawaka
The Beiger Mansion Inn, 317 Lincoln Way E 46544 ....(219)256-0365
Morgantown
The Rock House, 380 W Washington St 46160 ....(812)597-5100
Muncie
Old Franklin House, 704 East Washington St 47305 ....(317)286-0277
Nappanee
East 253 Market Guest House, 253 E Market 46550 ....(219)773-2261
Indiana Amish Country B&B, 1600 W Market St 46550 ....(219)773-4188
The Victorian Guest House, 302 E Market St 46550 ....(219)773-4383
Nashville
Allison House, 90 S Jefferson St 47448 ....(812)988-6664
McGinley's Cabins, Rt 3, Box 332 47448 ....(812)988-7337
Seasons, PO Box 187 47448 ....(812)988-2284
Story Inn, PO Box 64 47448 ....(812)988-2273
Sunset House, RR 3, Box 127 47448 ....(812)988-6118
New Harmony
New Harmony Inn, North St 47631 ....(812)682-4491
Newburgh
Phelps Mansion Inn, 208 N State St 47630 ....(812)853-7766
Paoli
Braxtan House Inn B&B, 210 N Gospel St 47454 ....(812)723-4677
Plymouth
Driftwood, PO Box 16 46563 ....(219)546-2274
Richland
Country Homestead, Rt 1, Box 353 47634 ....(812)359-4870
Rising Sun
Jelly House Country Inn, 222 S Walnut St 47404 ....(812)438-2319
Roachdale
Victorian House, RR 1 Box 27 46172
Rockport
The Rockport Inn, Third At Walnut 47635 ....(812)649-2664
Shipshewana
Green Meadow, Rt 2 Box 592, State Rd 5 46565
Old Davis Hotel, 228 W Main St, PO Box 545 46565 ....(219)768-7300
South Bend
Jamison Inn, 1404 N Ivy Rd 46637 ....(219)277-9682
Queen Anne Inn, 420 W Washington 46601 ....(219)234-5959
Story
Story Inn, State Rd 135 S 47448 ....(812)988-2273
Vincennes
Mayor Wilhelm's Villa, 428 N Fifth St 47591 ....(812)882-9487
Wabash
Hilltop House B&B, 88 W Sinclair St 46992 ....(219)563-7726
Wappanee
Amish Acres, Inc., 160 W Market 46550 ....(219)773-4188
Warsaw
Candlelight Inn, 503 E Fort Wayne St 46580 ....(219)267-2906
Westfield
Camel Lot, 4512 W 131st St 46074 ....(317)873-4370
Country Roads Guesthouse, 2731 W 146th St 46074 ....(317)846-2376

Iowa

Adair
Stagecoach Inn 50002 ....(515)742-3658
Adel
Walden Acres B&B, RR 1, Box 30 50003 ....(515)987-1567
Amana Colonies
Die Heimat Country Inn, Main St 52236 ....(319)622-3937
Avoca
Victorian B&B Inn, 425 Walnut St 51521 ....(712)343-6336
Bellvue
Mont Rest, 300 Spring St 52031 ....(319)872-4220
Bentonsport
Mason House Inn, RR 2 52565 ....(319)592-3133
Brooklyn
Hotel Brooklyn, 154 Front St 52211 ....(515)522-9229
Burlington
Roads-Gardner House, 521 Court St 52601 ....(319)689-4222
Calmar
Calmar Guesthouse, RR 1 Box 206 52132 ....(319)562-3851
Carroll
Knit & Pearl, 1520 Salinger 51401 ....(712)792-3921
Centerville
Paint 'n Primitives, 107 E Washington 52544 ....(515)856-8811
Clear Lake
"Norsk Hus" - By The Shore, 3611 N Shore Dr 50428 ....(515)357-8368
Budget Inn, Box 102 50428
Larch Pine Inn, 401 N Third St 50428 ....(515)357-7854
Clermont
Bushman Cozy Ranch, R #2, Box 100 52135 ....(319)423-7369
Corning
Pheasants Galore, 616 Davis Ave 50841 ....(515)322-3749
Council Bluffs
Robin's Nest Inn B&B, 327 9th Ave 50501 ....(712)323-1649
Davenport
River Oaks Inn, 1234 E River Dr 52803 ....(319)326-2629
Village B&B, 2017 E 13 St 52803 ....(319)322-4905
Decorah
Bruvold Farm, RR #1 52101 ....(319)382-4729
Montgomery Mansion, 812 Maple Ave 52101 ....(319)382-5088
Orval & Diane Bruvold, Rt 1 52101 ....(319)382-4729
Des Moines
Brownwood B&B, 5938 SW 48th Ave 50321 ....(515)382-2949
Dubuque
Collier Mansion, 1072 W Third St 52001 ....(319)588-2130
Redstone Inn, 504 Bluff St 52001 ....(800)331-5454
The Richards House, 1492 Locust St 52001 ....(319)557-1492
Stout House, 1105 Locust 52001 ....(800)331-5454
The Hancock House, 1105 Grove Terrace 52001 ....(319)582-5421
Elgin
Country Swiss Guest House, R #2, Box 55 52141 ....(319)426-5712
Elk Horn
Rainbow H. Lodging House, RR 1, Box 89 51531 ....(712)764-8272
The Travelling Companion B&B, 4314 Main St 51531 ....(712)764-8932
Elkader
Little House Vacations 52043 ....(319)783-7774
Estherville
Hoffman Guest House, 221 N Eight St 51334 ....(712)362-5994
Fort Atkinson
Cloverleaf Farm, Rt 2, Box 140A 52144 ....(319)534-7061
Fort Madison
The Morton House, 7 Highpoint 52627 ....(319)372-9517
Galva
Pioneer Farm B&B, RR #1, Box 96 51020 ....(712)282-4670
Homestead
Die Heimat Country Inn, Main St 52236 ....(319)622-3937
Keosauqua
Hotel Manning, 100 Van Buren St 52565 ....(319)293-3232
Mason House Inn, RR 2 - Bentonsport 52565 ....(319)592-3133
Keota
Elmhurst, RR 1, Box 3 52248 ....(515)636-3001
Lansing
Fitzgerald's Inn, 106 3rd St 52151 ....(319)538-4872
Lansing House, Box 97, 291 N Front St 52151 ....(319)538-4263
Le Claire
Mohrhaus, 2450 Great River Rd N 52753 ....(319)289-4503
The Monarch B&B, 303 2nd St 52753 ....(319)289-3011
Leighton
Heritage House, RR 1 50143 ....(515)626-3092
Maquoketa
Decker Hotel, 128 N Main 52060 ....(319)652-6654
Marion
Martin Farm - L-Mar, 1777 Austin Rd, RR #3 52302 ....(319)377-2055
Massena
Amdor's Evergreen Inn, RR 1, Box 65 50853 ....(712)779-3521
Maynard
Westside B&B, 125 7th St N 50655 ....(319)637-2711

McGregor
Little Switzerland Inn, 126 Main St 52157 ....(319)873-3670
McGregor Riverton Inn, 424 Main St 52157 ....(319)873-2385
Missouri Valley
Apple Orchard Inn, RR 3, Box 129 51555 ....(712)642-2418
Morengo
Loy's B&B, RR 1 52301 ....(319)642-7787
Muscatine
Alexander 6 Clark House, 205 W 3rd St 52761
Newton
La Corsette Maison Inn, 629 First Ave East 50208 ....(515)792-6833
Pella
Strawtown Inn, Llll Washington St 50219 ....(515)628-2681
Prescott
Maple Hill Farms, RR #2, Box 83 50859 ....(515)369-4874
Preston
B&B in Iowa, Ltd., Box 430 52069 ....(319)689-4222
Red Oak
Ushers, 7110 Corning St 51566 ....(712)829-2214
Rockwell City
Spring Brook Farm, RR 2, PO Box 160 50579 ....(712)466-255
Spencer
The Hannah Marie
Country Inn, Rt 1, Hwy 71 S 51301 ....(712)262-1286
Spillville
Old World Inn, 331 S Main St 52168 ....(319)562-3739
Stuart
Summit Grove Inn, 1427 S 7th 50250 ....(515)523-2147
Swisher
Terra Verde Farm, Rt 1, Box 86 52338 ....(319)846-2478
Tipton
Victorian House Tipton, 508 E 4th St 52772 ....(319)886-2633
Titonka
Mile-Away Farm, Box 368 50480 ....(515)928-2447
Our Country Place, RR Box 207 50480 ....(515)928-2502
Washington
Antiques and Old Lace, 403 W Main 52353 ....(319)653-6486
Waukon
Allamakee B&B, 700 Allamakee St 52170 ....(319)568-3103
Webster City
Centennial Farm, RR 2 50595 ....(515)832-3050
West Branch
Cross Country Traveler, Box 578 52358 ....(319)643-2433
Williamsburg
Lucille's Country Inn, RR 2, Box 55 52361 ....(319)668-1185

Kansas

Ashland
Hardesty House, 712 Main St 67831 ....(316)635-2911
Cimarron
The Cimarron Hotel, 203 N Main 67835 ....(316)855-2244
Council Grove
The Cottage House Hotel, 25 N Neosho 66846 ....(316)767-6828
Fort Scott
Country Quarters, Rt 5, Box 80 66701 ....(316)223-2889
Lawrence
Halcyon House, 1000 Ohio 66044 ....(913)841-0314
Manhattan
Kimble Cliff, Rt 1 Box 139 66502
Melvern
Schoolhouse Inn, 106 E Beck, PO Box 175 66510 ....(913)549-3473
Peabody
Jones Sheep Farm B&B, RR 2 66866 ....(316)983-2815
Rogersville
Anchor Hill Lodge, Rt 1 65742
Tonganoxie
Almeda's B&B, 220 S Main 66086 ....(913)845-2295
Topeka
Heritage House, 3535 SW 6th St 66606 ....(913)233-3800
Valley Falls
The Barn B&B, RR 2 Box 87 66088 ....(913)945-3303
Wakefield
B&B On Our Farm, Rt 1 Box 132 67487 ....(913)461-5596
Wichita
Inn at the Park, 3751 E Douglas 67208 ....(316)652-0500

Kentucky

Bardstown
Bruntwood 1802, Mrs. Bare, 714 N 3 St 40004
Jailer's Inn, 111 W Stephen Foster Ave 40004 ....(502)348-5551
Old Talbott Tavern, Court Square, 107 W Stephen Foster 40004
....................(502)348-3494
Berea
Boone Tavern Hotel, Main St CPO 2345 40403 ....(606)986-9358
Bowling Green
Bowling Green B&B, 659 E 14th Ave 42101 ....(502)781-3861
Brandenburg
Doe Run Inn, Rt 2 40108 ....(502)422-2982
Covington
Amos Shinkle Townhouse, 215 Garrard St 41011 ....(606)431-2118
Cynthiana
Broadwell Acres, Rt 6 Box 58 41031 ....(606)234-4255
Frankfort
Olde Kentucke, 210 E Fourth St 40601 ....(502)227-7389
Georgetown
Log Cabin B&B, 350 N Broadway 40324 ....(502)863-3514
Harrodsburg
Beaumont Inn, 638 Beaumont Dr 40330 ....(606)734-3381
Canaan Land Farm B&B, 4355 Lexington Rd ....(606)734-3984
Shakertown At Pleasant Hill, Rt 4 40330 ....(606)734-5411
Independence
Ohio Valley B&B Service, 6876 Taylor Mill Rd 41051 ....(606)356-7865
Lexington
547 B&B, 547 N Broadway 40508 ....(606)255-4152
Rokeby Hall, 318 S Mill St 40508 ....(606)252-2368
Middlesborough
The RidgeRunner B&B, 208 Arthur Heights 40965 ....(606)248-4299
Murray
The Diuguid House, 603 Main St 42071 ....(502)753-5470
Paducah
Ehrhardts B&B, 285 Springwell Dr 42001 ....(502)554-0644
Richmond
Jordan Hill Farm, 722 Walker Parks Rd 40475 ....(606)623-8114
Simpsonville
The Old Stone Inn, Rt 5 40065 ....(502)722-8882
Versailles
Bluegrass B&B, Rt 1 Box 263 40383 ....(606)873-3208
Peacham, Rt 1 Box 263 40383
Springdale, Rt 1 Box 263 40383
Welcome Hall, Rt 1 Box 263 40383

Louisiana

Baton Rouge
Mount Hope Plantation, 8151 Highland Rd 70808 ....(504)766-8600
Brittany
Rosewood Manor, 10254 Hwy 431, Box 127 70718 ....(504)675-5781
Clinton
Brame-Bennet House, 227 S Baton Rouge St 70722 ....(504)683-5241
Convent
Tezcuco Plantation, Rt 1 Box 157 70723
Covington
Plantation Bell Guest House, 204 W 24th Ave 70433
Jackson
Asphodel Plantation, Rt 2 Box 89 70748 ....(504)654-6868
Milbank, 102 Bank St 70748 ....(504)634-5901
Jeanerette
Patout's Guest House, Rt 1, Box 288 70544 ....(318)364-0644

Louisiana (Continued)

Lafayette
Ti Frere's House, 1905 Verot School Rd 70508
Napoleonville
Madewood Plantation, Rt 2 Box 478 70390 ....(504)369-7151
New Iberia
Mintmere Plantation, 1400 E Main 70560
New Orleans
A Creole House, 1013 St Ann St 70116 ....(504)524-8076
A Hotel, the Frenchman, 417 Frenchman St 70116 ....(504)948-2166
Andrew Jackson Hotel, 919 Royal St 70166 ....(504)561-5881
Burgundy Inn, 911 Burgundy St 70116 ....(504)524-0141
Chimes Cottages, 1360 Moss St, Box 52257 70152 ....(504)525-4640
Club La Pension, 501 Canal St 70130
Columns Hotel, 3811 St Clarles Ave 70115 ....(504)899-9308
The Cornstalk Hotel, 915 Royal St 70116 ....(504)523-1515
Dauzat House, 337 Burgandy St 70130 ....(504)524-2075
Dusty Mansion, 2231 General Pershing 70115 ....(504)891-6061
French Quarter Maisons, 1130 Chartres St 70116
Grenoble House, 329 Dauphine 70112 ....(504)522-1331
Hotel Maison De Ville, 727 Rue Toulouse 70130 ....(504)561-5858
Hotel Ste. Helene, 508 Rue Chartres St 70130 ....(504)522-5014
Hotel Villa Convento, 616 Ursulines St 70116
Jensen's B&B, 1631 Seventh St 70115 ....(504)897-1895
Josephine Guest House, 1450 Josephine St 70130 ....(504)524-6361
Lafitte Guest House, 1003 Bourbon St 70116 ....(504)581-2678
Lamothe House, 621 Esplanade Ave 70116 ....(504)947-1161
Longpre Garden's Guest House, 1726 Prytania 70130 ....(504)561-0654
Maison De Ville, 727 Toulouse St 70130 ....(504)561-5858
Marquette Hostel, 2253 Carondelet St 70130
Mazant Street Guest House, 906 Mazant St 70117 ....(504)944-2662
Nine-O-Five Royal Hotel, 905 Rue Royal St 70116 ....(504)523-4068
Noble Arms Inn, 1006 Royal St 70116
Old World Inn, 1330 Prytania 70130
Park View, 7004 St Charles St 70118
Prince Conti Hotel, 830 Conti St 70112 ....(504)529-4172
Prytania Inn, 1415 Prytania St 70130 ....(504)566-1515
The Prytania Park Hotel, 1525 Prytania St 70130 ....(800)862-1984
Soniat House, 1133 Chartres St 70116 ....(504)522-0570
St. Charles Guest House, 1748 Prytania St 70130 ....(504)523-6556
St. Peter House, 1005 St Peter St 70116 ....(504)524-9232
The Stone Manor Hotel, 3800 St Charles Ave 70115 ....(504)899-9600
Terrell House Mansion, 1441 Magazine St 70130 ....(504)524-9859
The Columns Hotel, 3811 St Charles Ave 70115 ....(504)899-9308
New Roads
Bondy House & Claiborne House, Box 386, 304 Court St 70760
Pointe Coupee B&B, 605 E Main St 70760 ....(504)638-6254
Opelousas
Estorge House, 427 N. Market St 70570
Ruston
Twin Gables, 711 N Vienna St 71270 ....(318)255-4452
Saint Francisville
Barrow House, 524 Royal St 70775 ....(504)635-4791
Cottage Plantation, Rt 5 Box 425 70775 ....(504)635-3674
Myrtles Plantation, PO Box 1100 70775 ....(504)635-6277
St. Francisville Inn, 118 N Commerce St, PO 1369 70775 ..(504)635-6502
Saint Martinville
Evangeline Oak Corner, 215 Evangeline Blvd 70582 ....(318)394-7675
Shreveport
The Columns on Jordan, 615 Jordan 71101 ....(318)222-5912
Fairfield Place, 2221 Fairfield Ave 71104 ....(318)222-0048
Vacherie
Oak Alley Plantation, Rt 2 Box 10 Hwy 18 70090
Vinton
Old Lyons House, 1335 Horridge St 70668
Viroqua
Viroqua Heritage Inn, 220 E Jefferson Inn 54665 ....(608)637-3306
Wakefield
Wakefield Plantation, PO Box 41 70784
White Castle
Nottoway, PO Box 160, Mississippi River Rd 70788 ....(504)545-2409
Wilson
Glencoe Plantation, PO Box 178 70789

Maine

Alfred
The Olde Berry Inn, Kennebunk Rd 04002 ....(207)324-0603
Annaolis
Jonah Williams House, 101 Severn Ave 21403 ....(301)267-7005
Ashville
Green Hill Farm, RFD #1, Box 328 04607 ....(207)422-3273
Augusta
Crosby's B&B, 51 Green St 04330
Bailey Island
Cloverleaf Cottage B&B, RFD 1 Box 326 04003
Driftwood Inn 04003
The Lady & The Loon, PO Box 98 04003 ....(207)833-6871
Bar Harbor
The Atlantean Inn, 11 Atlantic Ave 04609 ....(207)288-3270
Bayview Inn & Hotel, 111 Eden St 04609
Black Friar Inn, 10 Summer St 04609 ....(207)288-5091
The Inn at Canoe Point, Rt 3 Box 216A - Hull's Cove 04644
..(207)288-9511
Canterbury Cottage, 12 Roberts Ave 04609 ....(207)288-2112
Castlemaine Inn, 39 Holland Ave 04609 ....(207)288-4563
Central House, 60 Cottage St 04609
Clefstone Manor, 92 Eden St 04609
Cottage Inns of Bar Harbor, 16 Roberta Ave 04609 ....(207)288-3443
Dow Cottage Inn, 227 Main St 04609
Graycote Inn, 40 Holland Ave 04609 ....(207)288-3044
Hearthside Inn B&B, 7 High St 04609 ....(207)288-4533
Holbrook House, 74 Mount Desert St 04609 ....(207)288-4970
Ledgelawn Inn, 66 Mount Desert 04609 ....(207)288-4596
Manor House Inn, W St Historic District 04609 ....(207)288-3759
The Maples, 16 Roberts Ave 04609 ....(207)288-3443
Mira Monte Inn, 69 Mt Desert St 04609 ....(207)288-4263
Primrose Cottage Inn, 73 Mt Desert St 04609 ....(207)288-4031
Ridgeway Manor, 11 High St 04609 ....(207)288-9682
Shady Maples, RD 1 Box 360 04609
Stratford House Inn, 45 Mount Desert St 04609 ....(207)288-5189
The Inn On High, 15 High St 04609
The Tides, 119 West St 04609 ....(207)288-4968
Thornhedge, 47 Mt. Desert St 04609
Town Guest House, 12 Atlantic Ave 04609
Bar Mills
Royal Brewster B&B, Box 307, Corner Rt 202 & 112 04004
..(207)929-3012
Bass Harbor
Bass Harbor Inn, Shore Rd 04653 ....(207)244-5157
Pointy Head Inn, Rt 102A 04653
Bath
Elizabeth's B&B, 360 Front St 04530 ....(207)443-1146
Fairhaven Inn, RR 2 Box 85, N Bath Rd 04530 ....(207)443-4391
Glad II, 60 Pearl St 04530
Levitt Family B&B, 50 Pearl St 04530
Packard House, 45 Pearl St 04530 ....(207)443-6069
Pine Hill B&B, HC 31 Box 85 04530 ....(207)443-2143
Belfast
Fiddler's Green Farm, RFD #1, Box 656 04915 ....(207)338-3568
Hiram Alden Inn, 19 Church St 04915 ....(703)338-2151
Horatio Johnson House, 36 Church St 04915 ....(207)338-5153
The Jeweled Turret Inn, 16 Pearl St 04915 ....(207)338-2304
Londonderry Inn, Rt 3, Belmont Ave 04915 ....(207)338-3988
Northport House B&B, City One, Mounted Rt, US Rt. 1 04915
..(207)338-1422
Penobscot Meadows, Rt 1 04915
The Palmer House, 7 Franklin St 04915 ....(207)338-5790
Bethel
Bakers B&B, RFD 2 Box 2090 04217
Bethel Inn & Court, PO Box 26 04217 ....(800)654-0125
Chapman Inn, PO Box 206 04217
Douglass Place, Rt 2, Box 9 04217 ....(207)824-2229
Four Seasons Inn, Upper Main St 04217 ....(207)824-2755
Hammons House, Broad St 04217 ....(207)824-3170
L'Auberge Country Inn, PO Box 21 04217 ....(207)824-2774
Norseman Inn, Rt 2 Rumford Rd 04217 ....(207)824-2002
Sudbury Inn, Lower Main St 04217 ....(207)824-2174

Sunday River Inn, Sunday River Rd 04217 ....(207)824-2410
The Pointed Fir, PO Box 745 04217 ....(207)824-2251

Biddefordpool

Lodge, 19 Yates 04006 ....(617)284-7148

Blue Hill

Altenhofen House, Peters Point 04614
Arcady Down East, South St 04614 ....(207)374-5576
Blue Hill Farm Country Inn, Rt 15 Box 437 04614 ....(207)374-5126
John Peters Inn, PO Box 916 04614 ....(207)374-2116

Boothbay

Kenniston Hill Inn, Rt 27 04537 ....(207)633-2159

Boothbay Harbor

Admiral's Quarters, 105 Commercial St 04538 ....(207)633-2474
The Anchor Watch, PO Box 04538 ....(207)366-2284
The Atlantic Ark Inn, 64 Atlantic Ave 04538 ....(207)633-5690
Boothbay Harbor Inn, 37 Atlantic Ave, Box 446 04538 ....(207)633-6302
Captain Sawyer's Place, 87 Commercial St 04538 ....(207)633-2290
Green Shutters Inn, PO Box 543 04538
Harbour Towne Inn, 71 Townsend Ave 04538 ....(207)633-4300
Hilltop House, 44 Mckown Hill 04538
Howard House, Route 27 04538
Seafarer Guest House, 38 Union St 04538
Thistle Inn, PO Box 176 04538
Topside, Mckown Hill 04538
Welch House, 36 Mckown St 04538
Westgate Guest House, 18 West St 04538

Bowdoinham

The Maples, RR 1 Box 75 04008 ....(207)666-3012

Bridgton

The 1859 Guest House, 60 S High St 04009 ....(207)647-2508
Mountainside B&B, PO Box 290 04009
Noble House, PO Box 180 04009 ....(207)647-3733
North Woods B&B, 55 N High St 04009
Tarry-a-While Resort, Box A 04009 ....(207)647-2522

Bristol

Middlefield Farm, PO Box 4 04539
The Bristol Inn, Upper Round Pond Rd, PO Box 130 04539 ....(207)563-1125

Brunswick

Aaron Dunning House, 76 Federal St 04011 ....(207)729-4486
Brunswick B&B, 165 Park Row 04011 ....(207)729-4914
Harborgate B&B, RD 2-2260 04011 ....(207)725-5894
Harriet Beecher Stowe House, 63 Federal St 04011 ....(207)725-5543
Samuel Newman House, 7 South St 04011 ....(207)729-6959

Bryant Pond

The Glen Mountain House, PO Box 176 04219

Bucksport

Jed Prouty Tavern, Box 550 04416
L'ermitage, 219 Main St 04416 ....(207)469-3361
The Old Parsonage Inn, PO Box 1577, 190 Franklin St 04416 ....(207)469-6477
The River Inn, 210 Main St 04416 ....(207)469-3783

Camden

Blackberry Inn, 82 Elm St 04843 ....(207)236-6060
Blue Harbor House, 67 Elm St, Rt 1 04843 ....(207)236-3196
Camden Harbour Inn, 83 Bayview St 04843 ....(207)236-4200
Chestnut House, 69 Chestnut St 04843
Edgecombe-Coles House, 64 High St, HCR 60 Box 3010 04843 ....(207)236-2336
The Elms, 84 Elm St, Rt 1 04843 ....(207)236-6250
Hartstone Inn, 41 Elm St 04843 ....(207)236-4259
Hawthorn Inn, 9 High St 04843 ....(207)236-8842
Lord Camden Inn, 24 Main St 04843
Maine Stay B&B, 22 High St 04843 ....(207)236-9636
Mansard Manor, 5 High St 04843 ....(207)236-3291
Norumbega Inn, 61 High St 04843 ....(207)236-4646
Owl And The Turtle, 8 Bay View 04843 ....(207)235-4769
Park Street Inn, 90 Mechanic St 04843
The Swan House, 49 Mountain St 04843 ....(207)236-8275
Whitehall Inn, 52 High St 04843

Cape Elizabeth

Crescent Beach Inn, Rt 77 04107

Cape Neddick

Cape Neddick House, Rt 1 Box 70 03902
Sea Chimes B&B, Shore Rd 03902
Wooden Goose Inn, Rt 1 Box 195 03902

Cape Newagen

Newagen Seaside Inn, Box H 04552 ....(207)633-5242

Cape Porpoise

Cove House, S Maine St, PO Box 115 04014 ....(207)967-3704

Carrabassett Valley

Sugarloaf Inn, Carrabasset Vly 04947 ....(207)237-2701

Casco

Maplewood Inn, Rt 302 Box 627 04015 ....(207)655-7586

Castine

Castine Inn, PO Box 41 04421 ....(207)326-4365
The Manor, Battle Ave, PO Box 276 04421 ....(207)326-4861
Pentagoet Inn, PO Box 4 04421 ....(207)326-8616

Center Lovell

Center Lovell Inn, Rt 5 04016 ....(207)925-1575
Westways On Kezar Lake, Rt 5 04016

Chebeague Island

Chebeague Island Inn, Box 492-MBB 04107 ....(207)846-5155
Chebeague Inn 04017 ....(207)967-3118

Cherryfield

Ricker House, Box 256 04622

Clark Island

Craignair Inn, Clark Island Rd 04859 ....(207)594-7644

Coopers Mills

Claryknoll Farm, Rt 215, Box 751 04341 ....(207)549-5250

Cornish

Cornish Country Inn, Box 206 04020
The Cornish Inn, Rt 25 Box 266 04020 ....(207)625-8501

Cutler

Little River Lodge, Rt 191 04626 ....(207)259-4437

Damariscotta

The Brannon Bunker, PO Box 045, HCR 64 04543 ....(207)563-5941
Yellow House B&B, Water St, Box 732 04543 ....(207)563-1388

Deer Isle

Eggemoggin Inn, RFD Box 324 04650 ....(207)348-2540
Pilgrim's Inn, Main St 04627

Deer Isle Village

Laphroaig B&B, Rte 15, PO Box 67 04627 ....(207)348-6088

Dennysville

Lincoln House Country Inn, Rts 1 & 86 04628 ....(207)726-3953

Dixmont

Ben-loch Inn, RFD 1 Box 1020 04932 ....(207)257-4768

Dover-Foxcroft

The Foxcroft, 25 W Main St 04426

East Boothbay

Linekin Village B&B, Ocean Point Rd, Rt 96 04544 ....(207)633-3681
Ocean Point Inn, Shore Rd 04544 ....(207)633-4200

East Machias

East River B&B, PO Box 205, High St 04630 ....(207)255-8467

East Waterford

Waterford Inne, Box 49 04233

Eastport

Artists Retreat, 29 Washington St 04631 ....(207)853-4239
The Inn At Eastport, 13 Washington St 04631 ....(207)853-4307
Todd House, Todd's Head 04631 ....(207)853-2328
Weston House, 26 Boynton St 04631 ....(207)853-2907

Eliot

Ewenicorn Farm B&B, 116 Goodwin Rd, Rt 101 03903 ....(207)439-1337
High Meadows B&B, Rt 101 03903 ....(207)439-0590

Ellsworth

Victoria's B&B, 58 Pine St 04605

Five Islands

Grey Havens Inn, Box 82 04546

Freeport

181 Main St, 181 Main St 04032 ....(207)865-1226
The Bagley House, RR 3 Box 269C 04032 ....(207)865-6566
Captain Josiah Mitchell House, 188 Main St 04032 ....(207)865-3289
Harraseeket Inn, 162 Main St 04032 ....(207)865-9377
Holbrook Inn, 7 Holbrook St 04032 ....(207)865-6693
Isaac Randall House, Independence Drive 04032 ....(207)865-9295
Maple Hill B&B, 18 Maple Ave 04032 ....(207)865-3730
Nathan Nye Inn, 11 Nathan Nye St 04032 ....(207)865-9606
Old Red Farm, Rr2 Box 242 Desert Rd 04032 ....(207)865-4550

Fryeburg

The Oxford House Inn, 105 Main St 04037

Maine (Continued)

Gorham
Country Squire B&B, Box 178 Mighty St Rt1 04038
Gouldsboro
Sunset House, HCR #60, Box 62 04607 ....(207)963-7156
Greenville
Greenville Inn, Norris St, PO Box 1194 04441 ....(207)695-2206
Guilford
Trebor Inn, PO Box 299 04443
Hancock
Apple Store B&B, HCR 77 Box 480 04640 ....(207)422-9959
Harpswell
Lookout Point House, 141 Lookout Point Rd 04079 ....(207)833-5509
Harrison
Tolman House Inn, PO Box 551, Tolman Rd 04040 ....(207)583-4445
Houlton
The Mallard Inn, 48 North St 04730 ....(207)532-4377
Isle Au Haut
The Keeper's House, PO Box 26 04645 ....(207)367-2261
Islesboro
Dark Harbor House Inn, Box 185 04848
Islesboro Inn 04848 ....(207)734-2222
Islesford
Island B&B, Box 275 04646 ....(207)244-9283
Jonesboro
Chandler River Lodge, Rt 1 04648 ....(201)679-2778
Jonesport
Tootsie's B&B, Trynor Sq, RFD 1, Box 252 04649
Kennebunk
Alewife House, 1917 Alewive Rd, Rt 35 04043 ....(207)985-2118
Captain Littlefield Inn, 26 Fletcher St 04043
Kennebunk Inn 1799, 45 Main St 04043
Kennebunk Beach
Sundial Inn, PO Box 1147 04043 ....(207)967-3850
Kennebunkport
1802 House, Box 646A Locke St 04046 ....(207)967-5632
Breakwater, PO Box 1160 04046
Captain Fairfield House, PO Box 202 04046
Captain Jefferds Inn, Box 691 04046
Captain Lord Mansion, Pleasant & Green, PO Box 800 04046 ....(207)967-3141
Chetwynd House, PO Box 130 04046
Dock Square Inn, PO Box 1123 04046
English Meadows, Rt 35 04046
English Robin, Rt 1 Box 194 04046
Farm House, RR 1, Box 656 04046 ....(207)967-4169
Flakeyard Farm, RFD 2 04046
Green Heron Inn, Drawer 151 04046 ....(207)967-3315
The Inn at Harbor Head, Pier Rd, RFD #2 Box 1180 04046 ....(207)967-5564
Harbor Inn, PO Box 538A 04046 ....(207)967-2074
Kennebunkport Inn, Box 111, Dock Sq 04046 ....(207)967-2621
Kylemere House 1818, South Street, PO Box 1333 04046 ....(207)967-2780
Maine Stay Inn and Cottages, Maine St, PO Box 500A 04046 ....(207)967-2117
North Street Guest House, Box 1229 04046
Old Fort Inn, Old Fort Ave, PO Box M 24 04046 ....(207)967-5353
Port Gallery Inn, PO Box 1367 04046 ....(207)967-3728
Seaside Inn, Gooch's Beach 04046
The Inn on South Street, PO Box 478A, South St 04046 .(207)967-5151
The Green Heron Inn, Ocean Ave 04046
Tides Inn By The Sea, Goose Rock Beach 04046
Village Cove Inn, PO Box 650 04046 ....(207)967-3993
The Welby Inn, Ocean Ave, PO Box 774 04046 ....(207)967-4655
The White Barn Inn, Beach St, RR 3 Box 387 04046 ....(207)967-2321
Kingfield
Herbert Inn, PO Box 67 04947 ....(800)533-INNS
Three Stanley Avenue, PO Box 169 04947
The Inn on Winter's Inn, Box 587 04947 ....(207)265-5421
Kittery
Melfair Farm B&B, 365 Wilson Rd 03904
Kittery Point
Harbor's Watch, RFD 1 Box 42 03905
Whaleback Inn, Pepperrell Rd, Box 162 03905 ....(207)439-9570
Lincolnville
Green Woods, RFD #2 04849 ....(207)338-3187
Longville, PO Box 75 04849 ....(207)236-3785
Red House, HC 60, Box 540 04849 ....(207)236-4621
Sign of the Owl, Rt 1, Box 85 04849 ....(207)338-4669
Youngtown Inn, Rt 52 04849 ....(207)763-3037
Lincolnville Beach
North House 1792, Box 165 04849
Litchfield
Old Tavern Inn, PO Box 445 04350
Lubec
Bayviews, 6 Monument St 04652 ....(207)733-2181
Breakers-by-the-Bay, 37 Washington 04652 ....(207)733-2487
Due East, Bailey's Mistake 04652 ....(207)733-2413
Home Port Inn, 45 Main Street 04652 ....(207)733-2077
Hugel Haus B&B, 55 Main St 04652 ....(207)733-4965
Overview, RD 2, Box 106 04652 ....(207)733-2005
Machias
Clark Perry House, 59 Court St 04654 ....(207)255-8458
Manset
The Moorings 04679
Matinicus
Tuckanuck Lodge, Shag Hollow Rd, PO Box 217 04851 ....(207)366-3830
Milbridge
Birch Point Cottage, Wyman Rd, Rte 1, Box 73 04658 ....(207)546-2955
Monhegan
Monhegan House 04852 ....(207)594-7983
Monhegan Island
Island Inn, Shore Rd 04852
Shinning Sails Inc, Box 44 04852 ....(207)596-0041
Mount Desert
The Collier House, Rt 102 PO Box 198 04660 ....(207)288-3162
Mount Vernon
Feather Bed Inn, Box 65 04352
Naples
The Augustus Bove House, RR 1 Box 501 04055 ....(207)693-6365
The Inn at Long Lake, Lake House Rd, PO Box 806 04055 ....(207)693-6226
Songo B&B, Songon Locks Rd 04055 ....(207)693-3960
The Epicurean Inn, PO Box Aq 04055 ....(207)693-3839
New Harbor
Bradley Inn, 361 Pemaquid Pt. 04554
Gosnold Arms, Northside Rd, Rt 32 04554 ....(207)677-3727
Southside-By The Harbor, Southside Rd 04554 ....(207)677-2991
Newcastle
Elfinhill, 20 River Rd, PO Box 497 04553 ....(207)563-1886
Glidden House, Glidden St, RR 1 Box 740 04553 ....(207)563-1859
Hearthside Inn B&B, 20 River Rd 04553 ....(207)563-8885
Mill Pond Inn, RFD 1 Box 245 04553 ....(207)563-8014
The Newcastle Inn, River Rd 04553 ....(207)563-5685
The Captain's House, PO Box 516 04553 ....(207)563-1482
The Markert House, PO Box 224, Glidden St 04553 ....(207)563-1309
Nobleboro
Oliver Farm Inn, Old Rt 1, Box 136 04555 ....(207)563-1527
Norridgewock
Norridgewock Colonial Inn, RFD 1 Box 1190 04957
North Edgecomb
Channelridge Farm, 358 Cross Pt Rd 04556
North Haven
Pulpit Harbor Inn, Crabtree Point Rd 04853
North Waterford
Olde Rowley Inn, Rt 35 N 04267 ....(207)583-4143
Northeast Harbor
Grey Rock Inn 04662
Harbourside Inn 04662
Ogunquit
Berwick, Box 261 03907 ....(207)646-4062
Blue Shutters, 6 Beachmere Pl. 03907
Blue Water Inn, Beach St 03907
Channing Hall, 3 Pine Hill Rd 03907
Clipper Ship Guest House, 46 N Main St 03907
Gazebo, Rt 1 Box 668 03907
Hillcrest Inn Resort, Shore Rd 03907 ....(207)646-7776
Inn At 77 Shore Road, 77 Shore Rd 03907

Juniper Hill Inn, Rt 1 N 03907 ....(207)646-4501
Leisure Inn, 19 School St 03907 ....(207)646-2737
Marimor Motor Inn, 66 Shore Rd 03907 ....(207)646-7397
Morning Dove B&B, 5 Bourne Ln, PO Box 1940 03907 ..(207)646-3891
Ogunquit House, PO Box 1883 03907
Old Village Inn, 30 Main St 03907 ....(207)646-7088
Sea Chambers-The Sea Bell, 37 Shore Rd 03907 ....(207)646-9311
Seafair Inn, 24 Shore Rd Box 1221 03907
Strauss Haus, Shore Rd 03907 ....(207)646-7756
Terrace By the Sea, 11 Wharf Ln 03907 ....(207)646-3232
Trellis House, Box 2229, 2 Bearhmere Pl 03907 ....(207)646-7909
Yardarm Village Inn, PO Box 773 03907
Yellow Monkey Guest House, 44 Main St 03907 ....(207)646-9056

Oquossoc
Oquossoc's Own B&B, PO Box 27 04964 ....(207)864-5584

Otisfield
The Birches B&B, Christian Ridge Rd, PO Box 38 04271 ..(207)743-9315

Oxford
Claibern's B&B, Rt 121 PO Box B 04270 ....(207)539-2352

Peaks Island
Moonshell Inn, Island Ave 04081 ....(207)766-2331

Pemaquid
Little River Inn, Rt 130 04588

Phippsburg
Riverview, Church Ln, Box 29 04562 ....(207)389-1124

Phippsburg Center
The Captain Drummond House, PO Box 72 04562 ....(207)289-1394

Port Clyde
Copper Light, PO Box 67 04855 ....(207)372-8510
Ocean House, Box 66 04855

Portland
Carleton Gardens, 43 Carleton St 04102 ....(207)772-3458
Inn At Carleton, 46 Carleton St 04102
Inn at Parkspring, 135 Spring St 04101 ....(207)774-1059
Pomegranate Inn, 49 Neal St 04102 ....(207)772-1006
The Inn At Park Spring, 135 Spring St 04101 ....(207)774-1059
York Harbor Inn, York Harbor, ME

Prospect Harbor
Oceanside Meadows Inn, Box 85 04669 ....(207)963-5557

Rangeley
Farmhouse Inn, PO Box 173 04970

Raymond
North Pines Health Resort 04071 ....(207)655-7624

Robinhood
Benjamin Riggs House, PO Box 440 04530 ....(207)371-2256

Rockport
Bread & Roses B&B, Corner US Rt 1 & Beech St 04856 ....(207)236-6116
Rosemary Cottage, Russell Ave 04856 ....(207)236-3513
Sign Of The Unicorn, 191 Beauchamp Ave 04856

Round Pond
The Briar Rose B&B, Rt 32 Box 27 04564 ....(207)529-5478

Sanford
Allen's Inn, 279 Main St 04073

Sargentville
Oakland House, Herricks Rd 04673 ....(207)359-8521

Searsport
Carriage House Inn, Rt 1 E Main St 04974
Homeport Inn, Rt 1 E Main St 04974 ....(207)548-2259
House Of Three Chimneys, Rt 1 Box 397 04974 ....(207)548-6117
McGilvery House, PO Box 588 04974 ....(207)548-6289
Sunrise Lodge B&B, PO Box 330 04974 ....(207)548-6575
The Hannah Nickels House, Rt 1 Box 38 04974 ....(207)548-6691

Sebasco Estates
Rock Gardens Inn 04565 ....(207)389-1161

Skowhegan
Brick Farm B&B, RFD 1, Box 1500 04976 ....(207)474-3949

Small Point
Edgewater Farm, Small Point Rd, Rt 216, Box 464 04565 .(207)389-1322

South Berwick
Tatnic B&B, Tatnic Rd, RFD #1, Box 518A 03908 ....(207)676-2209

South Brooksville
Buck's Harbor Inn, Rt 176 Box 268 04617

South Casco
Migis Lodge, Rt 302 04077 ....(207)655-4524
Thomas Inn & Playhouse, PO Box 128 04077

South Harpswell
Alfred M. Senter B&B, Box 830 04079 ....(207)833-2874
Senter B&B, Rt 123 04079 ....(207)833-2874

South Thomaston
The Weskeag Inn, PO Box 213 04858 ....(207)596-6676

Southport
Albonegon Inn, Capitol Island 04538

Southwest Harbor
Claremont 04676 ....(207)244-9828
Harbor Lights Home, Rt 102 04679
The Island House, Box 1006 04679 ....(207)244-5180
Island Watch B&B, Box 1359, Freeman Ridge Rd 04679 ....(207)244-7229
Lindenwood Inn, PO Box 1328 04679 ....(207)244-5335
Penury Hall, Main St Box 68 04679 ....(207)244-7102

Stonington
Rosehip, Box 346 04681

Stratton
Widow's Walk, Box 150 04982

Sullivan Harbor
Sullivan Harbor Inn, Rt 1 04689 ....(207)422-3591

Sunset
Goose Cove Lodge, Deer Isle 04683

Surry
Surry Inn, PO Box 25, Rte 172 04684 ....(207)667-5091

Tenants Harbor
Church Hill B&B, Box 126 04860 ....(207)372-6256
East Wind Inn & Meeting House, PO Box 149 04680
Mill Pond House, Box 640 04860 ....(207)372-6209

The Forks
Crab Apple Acres, Rt 201 04985

Thomaston
Bedside Manor Guest House, HCR 35, Box 100 04861 ....(207)354-8862
The Belvedere, 163 Main St 04861
Captain Frost's B&B, 241 W Main St 04861 ....(207)354-8217
Gracie's B&B, 52 Main St 04861
River House B&B, HCR 35, Box 119 04861 ....(207)354-8936

Topsham
Captain Purinton House, 64 Elm St 04086 ....(207)729-3603
Middaugh B&B, 36 Elm St 04086 ....(207)725-2562
The Walker Wilson House, 2 Melcher Place 04086

Union
Shepard Hill B&B, PO Box 338 04862

Vinalhaven
Fox Island Inn, Carver St 04863
Old Granite Inn, PO Box 570 04863-0570

Waldoboro
Broad Bay Inn & Gallery, Main St, PO Box 607 04572 ....(207)832-6668
Le Vatout, Rt 32, Box 375 04572 ....(207)832-4552
Letteney Farm Vacations, RFD 2, Box 166A 04572 ....(207)832-5143
Medomark House, PO Box 663, Friendship St 04572 ....(207)832-4971
The Roaring Lion, Box 756 04572
Tide Watch Inn, PO Box 94, Pine St 04572 ....(207)832-4987

Walpole
The Bittersweet Inn, Hcr 64, PO Box 013 04573 ....(207)563-5552

Washington
Windward Farm, Young's Hill Rd 04574

Waterford
Artemus Ward House 04088
Kedarburn Inn, Rt 35 Box A-1 04088
Lake House, Rts 35 & 37 04088 ....(207)583-4182

Waterville
The Inn at Silver Grove, 184 Silver St 04901 ....(207)873-7724

Weld
Kawanhee Inn Lakeside Lodge, Lake Webb 04285 ....(207)585-2243
Weld Inn, Box 8 04285

Wells
Bayview Inn B&B, Rt 1-2131 04090
Grey Gull Inn, 321 Webhannet Dr 04090
Purple Sandpiper Guest House, RR 3, Box 226 04090 ....(207)646-7990

Wells Beach
The Haven, Church St 04090 ....(207)646-4194

West Bath
Bakke B&B, RD 1, Box 505A 04530 ....(207)442-7185
New Meadows Inn, Bath Rd 04530 ....(207)443-3921

Maine (Continued)

West Bethel
King's Inn, PO Box 92 04286
Winter Harbor
Main Stay Inn, PO Box 459 04693 ....(207)963-5561
Wiscasset
The Squire Tarbox Inn, RR 2 Box 620 04578 ....(207)882-7693
The Stacked Arms, RR 2 Box 146 04578 ....(207)882-5436
Twenty-Two Federal B&B, PO Box 57 04578
York
A Summer Place, D 1 Box 196 03909
Dockside Guest Quarters, PO Box 205, Harris Island 03909 ....(207)363-2868
Hannah's Loft, Chases Pond Rd, RFD #2, Box 117 03909 .(207)363-7244
Hutchins House, 173 Organug Rd 03909 ....(207)363-3058
Summer Place, RFD 1 Box 196 03909 ....(207)363-5233
The Wild Rose Of York, 78 Long Sands Rd 03909 ....(207)363-2532
York Beach
Lighthouse Inn, Box 249, Nubble Rd 03910 ....(207)363-6072
Lilac Inn, Box 1325 3 Ridge Rd 03910 ....(207)363-3930
Nautilus B&B, 7 Willow Ave, Box 916 03910 ....(207)363-6496
The Katahdin Inn "on The Ocean", PO Box 193 03910 ....(207)363-2759
York Harbor
Edwards' Harborside Inn, Stage Neck Rd 03911 ....(207)363-3037
The Inn At Harmon Park, York St 03911
York Harbor Inn, Rt 1A Box 573 03911 ....(207)363-5119

Maryland

Annapolis
Charles Inn, 74 Charles St 21401 ....(301)268-1451
Gibson's Lodgings, 110-114 Prince George 21401 ....(301)268-5555
Green Street B&B, 161 Green St 21401 ....(301)268-9549
Historic Inns of Annapolis, 16 Chruch Circle 21401 ....(301)263-2641
Maryland Inn, 16 Church Circle 21401 ....(301)263-2641
Prince George Inn, 232 Prince George St 21401 ....(301)263-6418
Reynolds Tavern, 4 Church Circle 21401 ....(301)263-2641
State House Inn, 15 State Circle 21401 ....(301)263-2641
William Page Inn B&B, 8 Martin St 21401 ....(301)626-1506
Baltimore
Admiral Fell Inn, 888 S Broadway 21231 ....(301)522-7377
Betsy's B&B, 1428 Park Ave 21217 ....(301)383-1274
Bolton Hill B&B, 1534 Bolton St 21217 ....(301)669-5356
Eagles Mere B&B, 102 E Montgomery 21230 ....(301)332-1618
Harborview, 112 E Montgomery St 21230 ....(301)528-8692
Mulberry House, 111 West Mulberry St 21201 ....(301)576-0111
The Shirley-Madison Inn, 205 W Madison St 21201 ....(301)728-6550
Society Hill Hotel, 58 W Biddle St 21201 ....(301)837-3630
Society Hill Hopkins, 3404 St Paul St 21218 ....(301)235-8600
Society Hill Government House, 1125 N Calvert St 21202 ....(301)752-7722
Twin Gates, 308 Morris Ave 21093 ....(301)252-3131
Bethesda
Winslow Home, 8217 Caraway St 20818
Betterton
Ye Lantern Inn, PO Box 310 21610 ....(301)348-5809
Buckeystown
Inn At Buckeystown, 3521 Buckeystown Pike 21717
Cabin John
Winslow Home, 8217 Caraway St 20818 ....(301)229-4654
Cambridge
Glasgow Inn, 1500 Hambrooks Blvd 21613 ....(301)228-0575
Sarke Plantation, Rt 3 Box 139 21613
Cascade
Inwood Guest House, Box 378, Rt 1 21719 ....(301)241-3467
Chestertown
Brampton, RR2, Box 107 21620 ....(301)778-1860
Flyway Lodge, Rt 1, Box 660 21620 ....(301)778-5557
Great Oak Manor, Rt 2 Box 608 21620 ....(301)778-5796
Hill's Inn, 114 Washington Ave 21620 ....(301)778-4667
Imperial Hotel, 208 High St 21620 ....(301)778-5000
Inn At Mitchell House, RD 2 Box 329, Rt 21 21620 ....(301)778-6500
Radcliffe Cross, Quaker Neck Rd, Rt 3 Box 360 21620 ....(301)778-5540
White Swan Tavern, 231 High St 21620 ....(301)778-2300
Denton
Sophie Kerr House, Rt 3 Box 7-B, Kerr & 5th Aves 21629 ....(301)479-3421
Easton
Hynson Tourist Home, 804 Dover Rd 21601 ....(301)822-2777
Tidewater Inn, Dover & Harrison St 21601 ....(301)822-1300
Ellicott City
Hayland Farm, 500 Sheppard Ln 21043 ....(301)531-5593
Frederick
Spring Bank Inn, 7945 Worman's Mill Rd 21701 ....(301)694-0440
Tran Crossing, 121 E Patrick St 21701 ....(301)663-8449
Turning Point Inn, 3406 Urbana Pike 21701 ....(301)874-2421
Freeland
Freeland Farm, 21616 Middletown Rd 21053 ....(301)357-5364
Georgetown
Kitty Knight House, Rt 213 21930 ....(301)648-5305
Hagerstown
Lewrene Farm B&B, RD 3 Box 150 21740 ....(301)582-1735
Harwood
Oakwood, 4566 Solomons Island Rd 20776 ....(301)261-5338
Havre De Grace
Vandiver House, 301 S Union Ave 21078 ....(301)939-5055
Manokin
Hunters Cove, Box 4 21836 ....(301)651-9664
Middletown
Fountaindale Inn, 4253 Old National Pike 21769
Mount Savage
Castle, PO Box 578, Rt 36 21545 ....(301)759-5946
New Market
National Pike Inn, 9-11 W Main St, PO Box 299 21774 ....(301)865-5055
Strawberry Inn, 17 Main St, PO Box 237 21774 ....(301)865-3318
Oakland
Red Run Inn, Rt 5, Box 268 21550 ....(301)387-6606
Oxford
1876 House, 110 N Morris St 21654 ....(301)226-5496
The Robert Morris Inn, Box 70, On The Tred Avon 21654 ....(301)226-5111
Princess Anne
Elmwood C. 1770 B&B, Locust Point, PO Box 220 21853 ..(301)651-1066
Washington Hotel & Inn, Somerset Ave 21853
Rising Sun
Chandlee House, 168 Chandlee Rd 21911 ....(301)658-6958
Saint Leonard
Matoaka Cottages, PO Box 124 20685 ....(301)586-0269
Saint Michaels
Hambleton Inn/Harbor, 202 Cherry St, Box 299 21663 ....(301)245-3350
Kemp House Inn, 412 S Talbot St 21663 ....(301)745-2243
Parsonage Inn, 210 N Talbot St 21663 ....(301)745-5519
The Inn At Perry Cabin 21663
Two Swan Inn, PO Box 727 21663 ....(301)745-2929
Scotland
St Michael's Manor B&B, St Michael's Manor 20687 ....(301)872-4025
Sharpsburg
The Inn at Antietam, PO Box 119 21782 ....(301)432-6601
Piper House On Antietam Battlefield, Box 100 21782 ....(301)797-1862
Snow Hill
Snow Hill Inn, 104 E Market St 21863 ....(301)632-2102
Solomons
Capt. & Ms. J's Guest House, Calvert & A St 20688
Locust Inn, Box 254 20688
Solomons Island
Davis House, PO Box 759 20688 ....(301)326-4811
Stevenson
Mensana Inn, 1718 Greenspring Valley Rd 21153 ....(301)653-2403
Sykesville
Long Way Hill, 7406 Springfield Ave 21782 ....(301)795-8129
Taneytown
Glenburn, 3515 Runnymede Rd 21787
Tilghman
Harrison's Country Inn, PO Box 310 21671 ....(301)886-2123
Vienna
Governor's Ordinary, Church & Water Box 156 21869

Nanticoke Manor House, Church St & Water Box 248 21869
Tavern House, 111 Water St, PO Box 98 21869 ....(301)376-3347
Westminster
Judge Thomas House, 195 Willis St 21157 ....(301)876-6686
The Winchester Country Inn, 430 S Bishop St 21157 ......(301)876-7373
Woodsboro
Rosebud Inn, 4 N. Main St 21798

Massachusetts

Adams
Butternut Inn, 6 East St 01220 ....(413)743-9394
Amherst
The Amity House, 194 Amity St 01002 ....(413)549-6446
Ashfield
Ashfield Inn, Main St, PO Box 129 01330 ....(413)628-4571
Bull Frog B&B, Box 210, Star Rt 01330 ....(413)628-4493
Gold Leaf Inn, Box 477 01330 ....(413)628-3392
Attleboro
Colonel Blackinton Inn, 203 N Main St 02703 ....(617)222-6022
Auburn
Captain Samuel Eddy House Inn, 609 Oxford St S 01501 ....(508)832-5282
Barnstable
Ashley Manor, 3660 Olde Kings Hwy PO Box 856 02630 ....(508)362-8044
Cobbs Cove, PO Box 208, Rt 6a 02630 ....(508)362-9356
Goss House B&B, 61 Pine Ln 02630 ....(617)362-8559
Thomas Huckins House, 2701 Main St, Rt 6A 02630 ......(508)362-6379
Barnstable Village
Beechwood, 2839 Main St 02630 ....(508)362-6618
Charles Hinckley House, Olde Kings Hwy, PO Box 723 02630 ....(508)362-9924
Barre Common
Olde Jenkins Guest House, Rt 122 01005 ....(508)355-6444
Bass River
Anchorage, 122 S Shore Dr 02664 ....(617)398-8265
The Anchorage, 122 South Shore Dr 02664 ....(508)398-8265
Belvedere B&B Inn, 167 Main St 02664 ....(508)398-6674
Captain Isaiah's House, 33 Pleasant St 02664
Old Cape Inn, 108 Old Main St 02664
Becket
Canterbury Farm, Fred Snow Rd 01223 ....(413)623-8765
Long House B&B, High St 01223 ....(413)623-8360
Berlin
Stonehedge, 119 Sawyer Hill Rd 01503 ....(617)838-2574
Bernardston
Bernardston Inn, Church St 01337 ....(413)648-9282
Blandford
Tirnanoag-McKenna Place, Chester Rd 01008 ....(413)848-2083
Boston
Beacon Hill B&B, 27 Brimmer, Box 638 02108 ....(617)523-7376
The Federal House, 48 Fayette 02116 ....(617)350-6657
Host Homes of Boston, PO Box 117, Waban Branch 02168 ....(617)244-1308
The Terrace Townhouse, 60 Chandler St 02116 ....(617)350-6520
Victorian B&B, 35 Greenwich Park 02118 ....(617)247-1599
Boylston
Frenches' B&B, 5 Scar Hill Rd 01505
Brewster
Bramble Inn, Rt 6a 2019 Main St 02631 ....(508)896-7644
Isaiah Clark House, 1187 Old King's Hwy 02631 ....(508)896-2223
Old Manse Inn, 1861 Main St, PO 839 02631 ....(508)896-3149
Old Sea Pines Inn, 2553 Main St 02631 ....(508)896-6114
Brookline
Beacon Plaza, 1459 Beacon St 02146 ....(617)232-6550
Beacon Street Guest House, 1047 Beacon St 02146 ....(800)872-7211
Brookline Manor House, 32 Centre St 02146 ....(617)232-0003
Buckland
1797 House, Charlemont Rd 01338 ....(413)625-2975
Scott House, Hawley Rd 01338 ....(413)625-6624
Cambridge
A Cambridge House
B&B Inn, 2218 Massachusetts Ave 02140 ....(617)491-6300
Harvard Square B&B Of Cambridge, Box 211 02140 ....(617)491-6300
Cape Cod-Eastham
Over Look Inn, PO Box 771 02642 ....(508)255-1886
Centerville
Carver House, 638 Main St 02632 ....(617)775-9414
Copper Beech Inn, 497 Main St 02632 ....(508)771-5488
Eagar's B&B, 101 Lietrim Circle 02632 ....(508)428-8439
The Inn at Fernbrook, 481 Main St 02632 ....(508)775-4334
Old Hundred House, 1211 Craigville Beach Rd 02632 ......(508)775-6166
Terrace Gardens Inn, 539 Main St 02632 ....(617)775-4707
Charlemont
Forest Way Farm, Rt 8a (heath) 01339 ....(413)337-8321
Charlton
The Mower Homestead, RR Box 86 01507
Chatham
Bow Roof House, 59 Queen Anne Rd 02633 ....(617)945-1346
Captain Moses Nickerson's, PO Box 468 02659 ....(617)945-5859
Chatham Bars Inn, Shore Rd 02633 ....(617)945-0096
The Cranberry Inn at Chatham, 359 Main St, Cape Cod 02633 ....(508)945-9232
Cyrus Kent House, 63 Cross St 02633
Queen Anne Inn, 70 Queen Anne Rd 02633 ....(617)945-0394
Seafarer Motel, Main St 02633 ....(617)432-1739
Chatham, Cape Cod
Chatham Town House Inn, 11 Library Ln 02633 ....(508)945-2180
Chestnut Hill
The Pleasant Pheasant, 296 Heath St 02167 ....(617)566-4178
Chilmark
Breakfast at Tiasquam, PO Box 578 02535 ....(508)645-3685
Colrain
Grandmother's House, Rt 1 Box 37 Rte 112n 01340 ....(413)624-3771
Concord
Anderson-Wheeler Homestead, 154 Fitchburg Turnpike 01742 ....(508)369-3756
Colonel Roger Brown House, 1694 Main St 01742 ....(508)369-9119
Colonial Inn, 48 Monument Sq 01742 ....(617)369-9200
Hawthorne Inn, 462 Lexington Rd 01742 ....(508)369-5610
Conway
Hilltop B&B, Truce Rd 01341 ....(413)369-4928
Poundsworth B&B, Old Cricket Hill Rd 01341
Cotuit
Allen's B&B, 60 Nickerson Ln Box 222 02635 ....(617)428-5702
Milestones B&B, 90 Piney Rd, PO Box 496 02635 ....(508)428-6764
Salty Dog B&B, 451 Main St 02635 ....(617)428-5228
Cummington
Hill Gallery, Cole St 01026 ....(413)238-5914
Windfields Farm, Rt 1 Box 170 Bush Rd 01026 ....(413)684-3786
Dalton
Dalton House, 955 Main St 01226 ....(413)684-3854
Danvers
Salem Village B&B, 34 Centre St 01923 ....(617)774-7851
Deerfield
Deerfield Inn, The Street 01342 ....(413)774-5587
Dennis
Bed & Breakfast, 16 Bay View Rd, Box 789 02638 ....(508)385-9256
Four Chimneys Inn, 946 Main St, Rt 6A 02638 ....(508)385-6317
Isaiah Hall B&B Inn, 152 Whig St 02638 ....(508)385-9928
Dennisport
By-the-Sea Guests, 57 Chase Ave, Box 507 02639 ....(617)398-8685
Dorchester
The Emma James House, 47 Ocean St 02124 ....(617)288-8867
Thomas Jones, 373 Adams St 02122 ....(617)825-7676
Duxbury
Black Friar Brook Farm, 636 Union St 02332 ....(617)834-8528
Campbell's Country B&B, 68 Alden St 02332 ....(617)934-0862
Winsor House Inn, PO Box 387 Shs 390 Washington St 02331
East Brewster
Ocean Gold Cape Cod B&B, 74 Locust Lane Rt 2 02631 ....(617)255-7045
East Orleans
The Parsonage, 202 Main St, PO Box 1016 02643 ....(508)255-8217
Ships Knees Inn, Beach Rd 02643 ....(508)255-1312
The Farmhouse At Nauset Beach, 163 Beach Rd 02653 ......(508)255-6654
The Nauset House Inn, Box 774 02643
East Sandwich
Wingscorton Farm Inn, 11 Wing Blvd 02537 ....(508)888-0534

Massachusetts (Continued)

Eastham
Kingsbury House, Rt 6, Box 262 02642 ....(508)255-6026
Whalewalk Inn, 169 Bridge Rd 02642

Edgartown
The Arbor, 222 Upper Main St 02539 ....(508)627-8137
Ashley Inn, 129 Main St 02539 ....(508)627-9655
Captain Dexter House
of Edgartown, 35 Pease's Point Way 02539 ....(508)627-7289
Chadwick Inn, 67 Winter St 02539 ....(508)627-4435
Charlotte Inn, S Summer St 02539 ....(508)627-4751
Colonial Inn, Box 668 02539 ....(617)627-4711
Daggat House, PO 1333 59 N. Water St 02539
Dr. Shiverick House, Pent Lane, PO Box 640 02539 ....(508)627-8497
Edgartown Inn, 56 N Water 02539 ....(508)627-4794
Governor Bradford Inn, 128 Main St 02539 ....(508)627-9510
The Harbor View Hotel, Box 7 N Water St 02539 ....(508)627-4333
Harborside Inn, Box 67 02539 ....(617)627-4321
Katama Guest House, RFD 108, 166 Katama Rd 02539 ....(617)627-5158
Kelly House, PO Box 37 02539 ....(508)627-4394
Point Way Inn, 104 Main St, Box 128 02539 ....(508)627-8633
Shiretown Inn, N Water St, Box 921 02539 ....(800)541-0090
Victorian Inn, S Water St, PO Box 947 02539 ....(508)627-4784

Fairhaven
Edgewater B&B, 2 Oxford St 02719 ....(508)997-5512

Falmouth
Amherst, 30 Amherst Ave 02540 ....(617)548-2781
Captain Tom Lawrence House, 75 Locust St 02540 ....(508)540-1445
Elm Arch Inn, Elm Arch Way 02540 ....(617)548-0133
Gladstone Inn, 219 Grand Ave S 02540 ....(617)548-9851
Grafton Inn, 261 Grand Ave S 02540
Grandview Guest House, 197 Grand Ave S 02540 ....(508)548-4025
Hastings By the Sea, 28 Worcester Ave 02540 ....(617)548-1628
Mostly Hall B&B Inn, 27 Main St 02540 ....(508)548-3786
Palmer House Inn, 81 Palmer Ave 02540 ....(508)548-1230
The Moorings Lodge, 207 Grand Ave 02540 ....(508)540-2370
The Worcester House, 9 Worcester Ave 02540 ....(508)540-1592
Village Green Inn, 40 W Main St 02540 ....(508)548-5621
Woods Hole Passage, 186 Woods Hole Rd 02540 ....(508)540-7469
Wyndemere House at Sippewissett, 718 Palmer Ave 02193 ....(508)540-7069

Fiskdale
Commonwealth Inn, PO Box 251 01518 ....(617)347-7603

Gardner
Hawke B&B, 162 Pearl St 01440 ....(508)632-5909

Gloucester
Blue Shutters Inn, 1 Nautilus Rd 01930 ....(617)281-2706
Gray Manor, 14 Atlantic Rd 01930 ....(617)283-5409
Williams Guest House, 136 Bass Ave 01930

Goshen
The Whale Inn, Rt 9, Main St 01032 ....(413)268-7246

Great Barrington
Bread And Roses, Star Rt 65 Box 50 01230 ....(413)528-1099
Littlejohn Manor, Newsboy Monument Rt 23 01230 ....(413)528-2882
Seekonk Pines Inn, 142 Seekonk Cross Rd 01230 ....(413)528-4192
Thornewood, Rt. 7 & Rt. 183 01230
Turning Point Inn, RD 2 Box 140 3 Lake Buel Rd 01230
Windflower Inn, Egremont Star Rt, PO 25 Rt 23 01230 ....(413)528-2720

Groton
Hunt Family B&B, 83 Champney St 01450 ....(508)448-5552

Harwich
The Larches, 97 Chatham Rd 02645 ....(508)432-0150

Harwich Center
Victorian Inn At Harwich, Box 340 102 Parallel St 02645 (508)432-8335

Harwich Port
Captain's Quarters, 85 Bank St 02646 ....(508)432-0337
Country Inn Acres, 86 Sisson Rd 02646 ....(508)432-2769
Dunscroft By the Sea, 24 Pilgrim Rd 02646 ....(508)432-0810
Harbor Breeze, 326 Lower County Rd 02646 ....(508)432-0337
Harbor Walk, 6 Freeman St 02646 ....(617)432-1675
The Coach House, 74 Sisson Rd 02646 ....(508)432-9452
The Inn On Bank Street, 88 Bank St 02646 ....(508)432-3206

Heath
Pen y Bryn, Jacksonville Stage Rd 01339 ....(413)376-683

Holland
Alpine Haus, Mashapaung Rd, Box 782 01550 ....(413)245-9082

Holyoke
Yankee Pedler Inn, 1866 Northampton St 01040 ....(413)532-9494

Hopkinton
The Laurels, 18 Ash St 01748 ....(617)435-5410

Huntington
Paulson B&B, Allen Coit Rd 01050 ....(413)667-3208

Hyannis
Acorn House, 240 Sea St 02601 ....(617)771-4071
Captain Sylvester Baxter House, Park Square Village, 156 Main St 02601 ....(508)775-5611
Cranberry Cove, Rosetta St, Box 362 02601 ....(508)775-5049
Elegance By-The-Sea, 162 Sea St 02601 ....(617)775-3595
Inn on Sea Street, 358 Sea St 02601 ....(617)775-8030
Park Square Village, 156 Main St 02601 ....(617)775-5611
Sea Breeze By The Beach, 397 Sea St Cape Cod 02601

Lanesboro
Bascom Lodge, PO Box 686 01237 ....(413)743-1591
The Tuckered Turkey, Old Cheshire Rd, PO Box 638 01237 ....(413)442-0260

Lee
1777 Greylock House, 58 Greylock St 01238
Haus Andreas, RR 1 Box 605 B 01238
Morgan House, 33 Main St 01238 ....(413)243-0181
Ramsey House, 203 W Park St 01238 ....(413)243-1598

Lenox
Amity House, 15 Cliffwood St 01240 ....(413)637-0005
Apple Tree Inn, 224 West St 01240 ....(413)637-1477
Birchwood Inn, 7 Hubbard St, Box 2020 01240 ....(413)637-2600
Blantyre, Rt 20 01240 ....(413)637-3556
Brook Farm Inn, 15 Hawthorne St 01240 ....(413)637-3013
Candlelight Inn, 53 Walker St 01240 ....(413)637-1555
Cliffwood Inn, 25 Cliffwood St 01240 ....(413)637-3330
Cornell House, 197 Main St 01240 ....(413)637-0562
East Country Berry Farm, 830 East St 01240 ....(413)442-2057
The Gables Inn, 103 Walker St, Rt 183 01240 ....(413)637-3416
Garden Gables Inn, 141 Main St 01240 ....(413)637-0193
Rookwood Inn, 19 Stockbridge Rd 02140 ....(413)637-9750
Strawberry Hill, PO Box 718 01240 ....(413)637-3381
The Quincy Lodge, 19 Stockbridge Rd 01240 ....(413)637-9750
Underledge Inn, 76 Cliffwood St 01240 ....(413)637-0236
Village Inn, 16 Church St 01240 ....(413)637-0020
Walker House, 74 Walker St 01240 ....(413)637-1271
Wheatleigh, PO Box 824 01240 ....(413)637-0610
Whistler's Inn, 5 Greenwood St 01240 ....(413)637-0975

Lexington
Ashley's B&B, 6 Moon Hill Rd 02173 ....(617)862-6488
Halewood House, 2 Larchmont Ln 02173 ....(617)862-5404
Red Cape B&B, 61 Williams Rd 02173 ....(617)862-4913

Lowell
Sherman-Berry House, 163 Dartmouth St 01851 ....(508)459-4760

Lynn
Caron House, 142 Ocean St 01902 ....(617)599-4470

Manchester
Old Corner Inn, 2 Harbor St 01944 ....(617)526-4996

Marblehead
10 Mugford Street B&B, 10 Mugford St 01945 ....(508)631-5642
The Garden House, 3 Oak Circle 01945 ....(508)631-2324
Harbor Light Inn, 58 Washington St 01945 ....(617)631-2186
Harborside House, 23 Gregory St 01945 ....(508)631-1032
Lindsey's Garrett, 38 High St 01945 ....(508)631-2653
Spray Cliff on the Ocean, 25 Spray Ave 01945 ....(508)741-0680
Tidecrest, Spray Ave 01945 ....(508)631-4515

Martha's Vineyard
Captain Dexter House
of Vineyard Haven, 100 Main St, PO Box 2457 02568 ....(508)693-6564
Farmhouse, State Rd 02568 ....(617)693-5354

Mashpee
The Blackwood's, 11 Weather Crescent 02649 ....(508)477-9252

Mattapoisett
Tall Pines B&B, 135 N St 02739 ....(508)758-2076

Menemsha
Beach Plum Inn, Box 98 02552 ....(617)645-9454

Middlefield
Strawberry Banke Farm, Skyline Tr 01243 ....(413)623-6481

Monument Beach
Bay Breeze, PO 307 02553
Nantucket
76 Main Street, 76 Main St Box E 02554 ....(508)228-2533
Anchor Inn, 66 Centre St 02554 ....(508)228-0072
Beachside Resort, 31 N Beach St 02554 ....(800)322-4433
Beachway Guests, 3 N Beach St 02554 ....(508)228-1324
Brass Lantern Inn, 11 N Water St 02554 ....(508)228-4064
The Carlisle House Inn, 26 N Water St 02554 ....(508)228-0720
Centerboard, 8 Chester St 02584 ....(508)228-9696
Century House, 10 Cliff Rd Box 603 02554 ....(508)228-0530
Cliff House, 34 Cliff Rd 02554 ....(508)228-2154
Cliffside Beach Club, PO Box 449 02554 ....(508)228-0618
Cobblestone Inn, 5 Ash St 02554 ....(508)228-1987
Easton House, 17 N Water St 02554 ....(508)228-2759
Eighteen Gardner Street, 18 Gardner St 02554
Fair Gardens, 27 Fair St 02554 ....(508)228-4258
Fair Winds, 4 Ash St 02554 ....(508)228-4899
The Folger Hotel & Cottages, Easton St 02554 ....(508)228-0313
Four Ash Street, 4 Ash St 02554
Great Harbor Inn, 31 India St 02554 ....(508)228-6609
The Grey Goose, 24 Hussey St 02554 ....(508)228-6597
Halliday's Nantucket House, Box 165 02554 ....(508)228-9450
Hawthorn House, 2 Chestnut St 02554 ....(508)228-0326
Hawthorne House, 2 Chestnut St 02554 ....(508)228-1468
The House At Ten Gay Street, 10 Gay St 02554 ....(508)228-4425
The House of Orange, 25 Orange St 02554 ....(508)228-9287
House of Seven Gables, 32 Cliff Rd 02554 ....(508)228-4706
Hussey House, 15 N Water St 02554 ....(508)228-0747
India House, 37 India St 02554 ....(508)228-9043
The Island Reef, 20 N Water St 02554 ....(508)228-2156
Ivy Lodge, 2 Chester St 02554 ....(508)228-0305
Jared Coffin House, 29 Broad St 02554 ....(508)228-2400
Le Languedoc Inn, 24 Broad St 02554 ....(508)228-2552
Nantucket Landfall, 4 Harbor View Way 02554 ....(508)228-0500
The Nantucket Whaler, 8 N Water St 02554 ....(508)228-6597
The Nesbitt Inn, 21 Broad St 02554 ....(508)228-0156
Parker Guest House, 4 East Chestnut St 02554 ....(508)228-4625
Paul West House, 5 Liberty St 02554 ....(508)228-2495
Periwinkle Guest House, 9 N Water St 02554
Phillips House, 54 Fair St 02554 ....(508)228-9217
Quaker House, 5 Chestnut St 02554 ....(508)228-0400
Roberts House, 11 India St 02554 ....(508)228-9009
Ruben Joy Homestead, 107 Main St 02554 ....(508)228-1703
Ships Inn, 13 Fair St 02554 ....(508)228-0040
Stumble Inne, 109 Orange St 02554 ....(508)228-4482
Ten Hussey, 10 Hussey St 02554 ....(508)228-9552
Ten Lyon Street Inn, 10 Lyon St 02554 ....(508)228-0072
The White House, 48 Centre St 02554 ....(508)228-0405
Union Street Inn, 7 Union St 02554 ....(508)228-9222
The Wauwinet, An Inn by the Sea, PO Box 2580 02584 ....(800)426-8718
West Moor Inn, Off Cliff Rd 02554 ....(508)228-0877
The Woodbox, 29 Fair St 02554 ....(508)228-0587
Nantucket Island
Brant Plantation Inn, 6 N Beach St 02554 ....(508)228-5442
Chestnut House, 3 Chestnut St 02554 ....(508)228-0049
Corner House, 49 Centre St, PO Box 1828 02554 ....(508)228-1530
Four Chimneys, 38 Orange St 02554 ....(508)228-1912
Martin's Guest House, 61 Centre St 02554 ....(508)228-0678
Wharf Cottages, New Whale St 02554 ....(508)228-4620
Needham
Brock's B&B, 60 Stevens Rd 02192 ....(617)444-6573
New Bedford
Durant Sail Loft Inn, 1 Merrill's Wharf 02740 ....(508)999-2700
Melville House, 100 Madison St 02740 ....(508)990-1566
New Marlborough
Old Inn On The Green, Star Rt 70 01230
Red Bird Inn, Rt 57 & Grosby Rd 01230 ....(413)229-2433
Newburyport
Benjamin Choate House, 25 Tyng St 01950
Essex Street Inn, 7 Essex St 01950 ....(617)465-3145
Garrison Inn, On Brown Square 01950 ....(617)465-0910
Morrill Place Inn, 209 High St 01950
Windsor House, 38 Federal St 01950
North Billrtivs
Ted Barbour, 88 Rogers St 01862 ....(617)667-7317

North Eastham
The Penny House, Rt 6 Box 238 02651 ....(508)255-6632
North Falmouth
Wingate Crossing, R 28a/190 N Falmouth Hwy 02556 ....(508)540-8723
North Scituate
Rasberry Ink, 748 Country Way 02060 ....(617)545-6629
Northampton
Autumn Inn, 259 Elm St 01060 ....(413)584-7660
The Knoll, 230 N Main 01060 ....(413)584-8164
Northfield
Centennial House, 94 Main St 01360 ....(413)498-5921
Northfield Country House, School St RR 1 Box 79a 01360
Oak Bluffs
Attleboro House, 11 Lake Ave Box 1564 02557 ....(508)693-4346
Circuit House, Box 2422, 150 Circuit Ave 02557 ....(508)693-5033
Dockside Inn, Box 1206 02557 ....(508)693-2966
Narragansett House, 62 Narragansett Ave 02557 ....(508)693-3627
Nashua House, 30 Kennebec Ave, PO Box 803 02557 ....(508)693-0043
Oak House, Box 299 02557 ....(508)693-4187
Orleans
The Captain Doane House, 1 Captain Doane Rd 02653 ....(508)255-0652
Osterville
East Bay Lodge, East Bay Rd PO Box N 02655 ....(508)428-6961
Village B&B, PO Box 785 02655 ....(508)428-7004
Peru
Chalet d'Alicia, E Windsor Rd 01235 ....(413)655-8292
Petersham
Winterwood at Petersham, North Main St 01366 ....(508)724-8885
Pittsfield
Greer B&B, 193 Wendell Ave 01201 ....(413)443-3669
Plymouth
Another Place Inn, 240 Sandwich St 02360 ....(617)746-0126
Colonial House Inn, 207 Sandwich St 02360
Princeton
Country Inn At Princeton, 30 Mountain Rd 01540
Harrington Farm, 178 Westminster Rd 01541 ....(617)464-5600
Hill House, PO Box 276, 105 Merriam Rd 01541 ....(617)464-2061
Provincetown
1807 House, 54 Commercial St 02657
Asheton House, 3 Cook St 02657 ....(508)487-9966
Bradford Gardens Inn, 178 Bradford St 02657 ....(508)487-1616
Cape Codder Guest House, 570 Commercial St 02657 ....(508)487-0131
Captain Lysander Inn, 96 Commercial St 02657 ....(508)487-2253
Elephant Walk Inn, 156 Bradford St 02657 ....(508)487-2543
Fairbanks Inn, 90 Bradford St 02657 ....(508)487-0386
Fiddle Leaf, 186 Commercial St 02657 ....(508)487-1443
Hargood House, 493 Commercial St 02657 ....(508)487-1324
Lamplighter Guest House, 26 Bradford St 02657 ....(508)487-2529
Land's End Inn, 22 Commercial St 02657 ....(508)487-0706
Ocean's Inn, 386 Commercial St 02657 ....(508)487-0358
Red Inn, 15 Commercial St 02657 ....(508)487-0050
Rose And Crown, 158 Commercial St 02657 ....(508)487-3332
Somerset House, 378 Commercial St 02657 ....(508)487-0383
Sunset Inn, 142 Bradford St 02657 ....(508)487-9810
Twelve Center Guest House, 12 Center St 02657 ....(508)487-0381
Victoria House, 5 Standish St 02657 ....(508)487-1319
Watership Inn, 7 Winthrop St 02657 ....(508)487-0094
Wave's Landing Guest House, 158 Bradford St 02657 ....(508)487-9198
White Wind Inn, 174 Commercial St 02657 ....(508)487-1526
Windamar House, 568 Commercial St 02657 ....(508)487-0599
Rehoboth
Perryville Inn, 157 Perryville Rd 02769 ....(508)252-9239
Richmond
Cogswell Guest House, Rt 41 01254 ....(413)698-2750
Pierson Place, Rt 41 01254 ....(617)698-2750
Westgate, Rt 295 01254 ....(413)698-2657
Rockport
Addison Choate Inn, 49 Broadway 01966 ....(508)546-7543
Cable House, Norwood Ave 01966 ....(508)546-6383
Captain's House, 109 Marmion Way 01966 ....(508)546-3825
The Inn on Cove Hill, 37 Mt Pleasant St 01966 ....(508)546-2701
Eden Pines Inn, Eden Rd 01966 ....(508)546-2505
Lantana House, 22 Broadway 01966 ....(617)546-3535
Mooringstone Guesthouse, 12 Norwood Ave 01966 ....(508)546-2479
Old Farm Inn, 291 Granite St 01966 ....(508)546-3237
Pleasant Street Inn, 17 Pleasant St 01966 ....(508)546-3915

Massachusetts (Continued)

Ralph Waldo Emerson Inn, Phillips Ave 01966 ....(508)546-6321
Rocky Shores Inn, Eden Rd 01966 ....(508)546-2823
Sally Webster Inn, 34 Mt Pleasant St 01966 ....(508)546-9251
Seacrest Manor, 131 Marmion Way 01966 ....(508)546-2211
Seafarer Inn, 86 Marmion Way 01966 ....(508)546-6248
Seaward Inn, 62 Marmion Way 01966 ....(508)546-3471
Seven South Street Inn, 7 S St 01966 ....(508)546-6708
Tuck Inn, 17 High St 01966 ....(508)546-6252
Yankee Clipper Inn, Box 2399, 99 Granite St 01966

Sagamore Beach

Bed & Breakfast, One Hawes Rd, Box 205 02562 ....(617)888-1559

Salem

Amelia Payson Guest House, 16 Winter St 01970 ....(508)744-8304
Coach House Inn, 284 Lafayette St 01970 ....(508)744-4092
The Salem Inn, 7 Summer St 01970 ....(508)741-0680
Stephen Daniels House, 1 Daniels St 01970 ....(508)744-5709
Suzannah Flint House, 98 Essex St 01970 ....(508)744-5281

Sandisfield

New Boston Inn, Jct Rt 8 & 57 01255-0120 ....(413)258-4477

Sandwich

Academy Hill B&B, 4 Academy Rd 02563 ....(508)888-8083
Captain Ezra Nye House, 152 Main St 02563 ....(800)388-2278
The Dan'l Webster Inn, 149 Main St 02563 ....(508)888-3622
Isaiah Jones Homestead, 165 Main St 02563 ....(508)888-9115
Quince Tree, 164 Main St 02563
Sandwich B&B, 13 School St 02563 ....(508)888-4542
Six Water Street, 6 Water St, Rt 130 02563 ....(508)888-6808
The Summer House, 158 Main St 02563 ....(508)888-4991

Seekonk

Simeon's Mansion House, 940 County St 02771 ....(508)336-6674

Sheffield

Centuryhurst B&B, Box 486 Main St 01257 ....(413)229-8131
Colonel Ashley Inn, Bow Wow Rd, PO Box 142 01257 .....(413)229-2929
Ivanhoe House, Rt 41 Undermountain Rd 01257 ....(413)229-2143
Stagecoach Hill Inn, Rt 41 01257 ....(413)229-8585
Staveleigh House, PO 608, S Main St 01257 ....(413)229-2129
Unique B&B, Under Mountain Rd 01257 ....(413)229-3363

Shelburne Falls

Country Comfort, 15 Masonic Ave 01370 ....(413)625-9877
Parson Hubbard House, Old Village Rd 01370 ....(413)625-9730
The Elmer House, Bray Rd, RFD #1 Box 224 01370 ....(413)625-9590

Siasconset

Summer House, Bocx 313 02564 ....(617)257-9976

South Chatham

Ye Olde Nantucket House, Box 468, 2647 Main St 02659 .(508)432-5641

South Dartmouth

Salt Marsh Farm, 322 Smith Neck Rd 02748 ....(508)992-0980

South Deerfield

The Yellow Gabled House, 307 N Main St 01373 ....(413)665-4922

South Egremont

Egremont Inn, Old Sheffield Rd 01258 ....(413)528-2111
Weathervane Inn, PO Box 388 01258 ....(413)528-9580

South Harwich

House on the Hill, PO Box 51, 968 Main St 02661 ....(617)432-4321

South Lancaster

Deershorn Manor B&B, 357 Sterling Rd, Box 805 01561 ....(508)365-9022

South Lee

Federal House Inn, Rt 102 Main St 01260 ....(413)243-1824
Merrell Tavern Inn, Rt 102 Main St 01260 ....(413)243-1794

South Orleans

Hilbourne House, Rt 28, O Box 190 02662 ....(508)255-0780

South Sudbury

Longfellow's Wayside Inn, Wayside Inn Rd 01776 ....(617)443-8846

South Yarmouth

Four Winds B&B, 345 High Bank Rd 02664 ....(508)394-4182
River Street Guest House, 9 River St 02664 ....(508)398-8946

Southfield

Langhaar House, PO Box 191 01259 ....(413)229-2007

Sterling

Sterling Inn, Rt 12 Box 609 01564
Sterling Orchards B&B, 60 Kendall Hill Rd 01564 ....(508)422-6595

Stockbridge

Broad Meadows, N Main St, Box 485 01262 ....(413)298-4972
Inn At Stockbridge, Rt 7 Box 2033 01262 ....(413)298-3337
The Red Lion Inn 01262 ....(413)298-5545

Sturbridge

Chamberlain House, PO Box 187 01566 ....(617)347-3313
Colonel Ebenezer Craft's, PO 187 01566
Commonwealth Inn, 11 Summit Ave 01566 ....(508)347-7603
Country Motor Lodge, PO Box 187 01566 ....(617)347-3313
Publick House Historic Inn, On The Common 01566 ....(617)347-3313
Sturbridge Country Inn, 530 Main St 01566 ....(508)347-5503

Sudbury

Checkerberry Corner, 5 Checkerberry Circle 01776 ....(617)443-8660
Sudbury B&B, 3 Drum Ln 01776 ....(617)443-2860

Townsend

B&B At Wood Farm, 40 Worchester Rd 01469 ....(617)597-5019
Wood Farm, 40 Worcester Rd 01469

Truro

Parker House B&B, Rt 6A, Box 114 02666 ....(617)349-3358

Tyringham

Golden Goose, Main Rd 01254 ....(413)243-3008

Uxbridge

Capron House, 2 Capron St 01569 ....(617)278-2214

Vineyard Haven

Gazebo B&B, Edgartown Rd 02568 ....(617)693-6955
Hanover House, Box 2107 02568 ....(617)693-1066
High Haven House, Box 289, Summer St 02568 ....(617)693-9204
Lothrop Merry House, Owen Park Box 1939 02568 ....(508)693-1646
Ocean Side Inn, Main St, Box 2700 02568 ....(617)693-1296
South Wind, Box 810 02568 ....(617)693-5031
Thorncroft Inn, 278 Main St, PO Box 1022 02568 ....(508)693-3333
Tuckerman House, 45 William St Box 194 02568 ....(508)693-0417

Ware

Wildwood Inn, 121 Church St 01082
The Wildwood Inn, 121 Church St 01082 ....(413)967-7798

Wareham

Little Harbor Guest House, 20 Stockton Shortcut 02571 ...(508)295-6329
Mulberry B&B, 257 High St 02571 ....(508)295-0684

Wellfleet

Holden Inn, Commercial St, PO Box 816 02667 ....(508)349-3450
Inn At Duck Creeke, PO Box 364 02667

West Barnstable

Honeysuckle Hill, 591 Main St 02668 ....(508)362-8418

West Boylston

The Old Rose Cottage, 24 Worcester St 01583 ....(617)835-4034

West Brookfield

Deer Meadow Farm, Bragg Rd, RFD #1 01585 ....(413)436-7129

West Dennis

The Beach House, 61 Uncle Stephen's Rd 02670
Beach Side Lodge, The Edwards, 140 Lower County Rd 02670
The Lighthouse Inn 02670

West Falmouth

Elms, PO 895 02574
Old Silver Beach B&B, 3 Cliffwood Ln, PO Box 642 02574 ....(508)540-5446
Sjoholm B&B Inn, 17 Chase Rd Box 430 02574 ....(508)540-5706
Sunset Hill B&B, 90 Fox Ln, PO Box 539 02574 ....(508)540-1763

West Harwich

Barnaby Inn, PO Box 151 02671 ....(508)432-6789
Lion's Head Inn, 186 Belmont Rd PO 444 02671 ....(508)432-7766
Sunny Pines B&B Inn, 77 Main St, PO Box 667 02671 ....(508)432-9628
The Gingerbread House, 141 Division St, Box 226 02671 ..(508)432-1901
The Tern Inn, 91 Chase St 02671 ....(508)432-3714

West Hawley

Stump Sprouts Guest Lodge, W Hill Rd 01339 ....(413)339-4265

West Hyannisport

B&B Cape Cod, Box 341 02672 ....(508)775-2772

West Newton

Sears-Withington House, 274 Otis St 02165 ....(617)332-8422

West Stockbridge

Westbridge Inn, Main St PO Box 378 01266 ....(413)232-7120
Williamsville Inn, Rt 41 01266 ....(413)274-6118

West Tisbury

Old Parsonage B&B, Box 137 State Rd 02575 ....(508)693-4289

West Yarmouth

Manor House, 57 Maine Ave 02673

Westborough
Heywood House, 207 W Main St 01581 ....(617)366-2161
Westhampton
Outlook Farm, Rt 66 01027 ....(413)527-0633
Whately
Sunnyside Farm, 11 River Rd 01093 ....(413)665-3113
Whitinsville
The Victorian, 583 Linwood Ave 01588 ....(617)234-2500
Williamsburg
Twin Maples B&B, 106 South St 01096 ....(413)268-7925
Williamstown
Le Jardin, 777 Coldspring Rd 01267 ....(413)458-8032
River Bend Farm, 643 Simonds Rd 01267 ....(413)458-5504
Steep Acres Farm, 520 White Oaks Rd 01267 ....(413)458-3774
Woods Hole
Grey Whale Inn, 565 Woods Hole Rd 02543 ....(508)548-7692
Marlborough, 320 Woods Hole 02543 ....(508)548-6218
Worcester-Rutland
The General Rufus Putnam House, 344 Main St 01543 ..(508)886-4256
Worthington
Franklin Burrs, Kinne Brook Rd 01098 ....(413)238-5826
Inn Yesterday, Rt 112, Huntington Rd 01098 ....(413)238-5529
Worthington Inn At Four Corners Farm, Rt 143 01098 ....(413)238-4441
Yarmouth Port
Crook' Jaw Inn, 186 Main St, Rt 6A 02675 ....(508)362-6111
Lane's End Cottage, 268 Main St 02675 ....(508)362-5298
Liberty Hill Inn, 77 Main St, Rt 6A 02675 ....(508)362-3976
Old Yarmouth Inn, 223 Main St 02675 ....(508)362-3191
Olde Captain's Inn, 101 Main St 02675 ....(508)362-4496
One Centre Street Inn, 1 Centre St Yarmouth Port 02675
Village Inn, 92 Main, Rt 6a, PO Box 1 02675 ....(508)362-3182

Michigan

Adrian
Briaroaks Inn, 2980 N Adrian Hwy 49221 ....(517)263-1659
Rosewood Country Inn, 3325 S Adrian Hwy (M-52) 49221 ....(517)263-5085
Albion
Smith-White House, 401 E Porter St 49224 ....(517)629-2220
Alden
Torch Lake B&B, Box 165 49612 ....(616)331-6424
Allegan
DeLano Inn, 302 Cutler St 49010 ....(616)673-2609
Winchester Inn, 524 Marshall St 49010 ....(616)673-3621
Allen
The Olde Bricke House, 231 E Chicago Rd, PO Box 211 49227 ....(517)869-2349
Alma
Granny's Garrett Guest Rooms, 910 Vassar St 48801 ....(517)463-3961
Alpena
Fireside Inn, 18730 Fireside Hwy 49707 ....(517)595-6369
Ann Arbor
Wood's Inn, 2887 Newport Rd 48103 ....(313)665-8394
Arcadia
Watervale Inn, Watervale Rd 49613 ....(616)352-9083
Au Gres
Point Au Gres Hotel, 3279 S Point Ln 48703 ....(517)876-7217
Battle Creek
Old Lamplighter's Home, 276 Capital Ave NE 49017 ....(616)963-2603
Bay City
Stonehedge Inn, 924 Center Ave 48708 ....(517)894-4342
William Clements Inn, 1712 Center Ave 48708 ....(517)894-4600
Bay View
Terrace Inn, 216 Fairview Ave 49770 ....(616)347-2410
The Florence 49770 ....(616)348-3322
The Gingerbread House, 205 Bluff, PO Box 1273 49770 ....(616)348-2829
Belding
The Rose Garden B&B, 322 E Washington St 48809 ....(616)794-3844
Bellaire
Bellaire B&B, 212 Park St 49615 ....(616)533-6077
Benton Harbor
Bolins' B&B, 576 Colfax Ave 49022 ....(616)925-9068
Beulah
Brookside Inn, 115 N Michigan 49617 ....(616)882-7271
Windermere Inn, 747 Crystal Dr 49617 ....(616)882-7264
Big Bay
The Big Bay Point Lighthouse B&B, 3 Lighthouse Rd 49808 ....(906)345-9957
Big Rapids
Taggart House, 371 Maple St 49307 ....(616)796-1713
Black River
Silver Creek, 4361 US-23 S 48721 ....(517)471-2198
Blaney Park
Celibeth House, Rt 1 Box 58A, M-77 Blaney Park Rd 49836
Blissfield
H. D. Ellis Inn, 415 W Adrian St 49228 ....(517)486-3155
Hathaway House, U.S. 223 49228 ....(517)486-2141
Hiram D. Ellis Inn, 415 W Adrian St (US 223) 49228 ....(517)486-3155
Boyne Falls
The Arman House, PO Box 195 49713 ....(616)549-2764
Brooklyn
Chicago Street Inn, 219 Chicago St, PO Box 546 49230 ....(517)592-3888
Buckley
A Wicklow House, 9270 M-37 49620 ....(616)269-4212
Calumet
The Calumet House, 1159 Calumet Ave 49913 ....(903)337-1936
Caseville
Carkner House, 6766 Pine St, PO Box 843 48725 ....(517)856-3456
Country Charm Farm, 5048 Conkey Rd 48725 ....(517)856-3110
Cedar
Hillside B&B, Rt 1-A W Lakeshore Rd 49621 ....(616)228-6106
Center Line
The Meares House, 8250 Warren Blvd 48015 ....(313)756-8250
Central Lake
Bridgewalk B&B, 2287 S Main, PO Box 577 49622 ....(616)544-8122
Darmon Street B&B, 7900 Darmon St, PO Box 284 49622 .(616)544-3931
Lamplight Inn, 2535 Main St, PO Box 778 49622 ....(616)544-6443
Charlevoix
Aaron's Windy Hill Guest Lodge, 202 Michigan 49720 ....(616)547-2804
Bay B&B, Rt 1, Box 136-A 49720 ....(616)599-2570
Belvedere House, 306 Belvedere Ave 49720 ....(616)547-4501
Boar's Head Inn, 306 Belvedere Ave 49720 ....(616)547-2251
Bridge Street Inn, 113 Michigan Ave 49720 ....(616)547-6606
Channelview Inn, 217 Park Ave 49720 ....(616)547-6180
Charlevoix Country Inn, 106 W Dixon Ave 49720 ....(616)547-5134
Patchwork Parlour B&B, 109 Petoskey Ave 49720 ....(616)547-5788
Clare
Doherty Hotel, 604 McEwan 48617 ....(800)525-4115
Clio
Chandelier Guest House, 1567 Morgan Rd 48420 ....(313)687-6061
Coldwater
Chicago Pike Inn, 215 E Chicago St 49036 ....(517)279-8744
Woodland Manor, 163 Marshall St 49036 ....(517)278-8057
Columbiaville
Redwing, 3176 Shady Oak Dr 48421 ....(313)793-4301
Conklin
Miller School Inn, 2959 Roosevelt Rd 49403 ....(616)677-1026
Davison
Oakbrook Inn, 7256 E Court St 48423 ....(313)653-1744
De Tour Village
Hubbard's Boonevue Lodge, 206 S Huron Box 65 49725 ..(906)297-2391
Dearborn
The Dearborn Inn, 20301 Oakwood Blvd 48124 ....(313)271-2700
Detroit
B&B in Michigan ....(313)561-6041
The Blanch House Inn, 506 Parkview Dr 48214 ....(313)822-7090
The Blanche House Inn, 506 Parkview Dr 48214 ....(313)822-7090
Dimondale
Bannicks B&B, 4608 Michigan Rd (M-99) 48821 ....(517)646-0224
Douglas
Rosemont Inn, 83 Lake Shore Dr 49406 ....(616)857-2637
Eagle Harbor
The Lake Breeze, Lake Breeze Rd 49950 ....(906)289-4514
East Jordan
Easterly Inn, 209 Easterly, PO Box 0366 49727 ....(616)536-3434
Jordan Inn, 228 Main St, PO Box 687 49727 ....(616)536-2631

Michigan (Continued)

East Lansing
Coleman Corners B&B, 7733 M-78 48823 ....(517)339-9360
East Troy
Pine Ridge B&B, 1152 Scout Rd 53120 ....(414)594-3269
Eastmanville
The Eastman House, 6754 W Leonard 49404 ....(616)837-6474
Eastport
Sunrise B&B, PO Box 52 49627 ....(616)599-2706
Edwardsburg
Glenda's B&B, 68699 M-62 49112 ....(616)663-7905
Egg Harbor
Country Gardens B&B, 6421 Hwy 42 54209 ....(414)743-7434
Elberta
Summer Inn, 809 Frankfort Ave 49628 ....(616)352-7279
Elk Rapids
Cairn House, 8160 Cairn Hwy 49629 ....(616)264-8994
Widows Walk, 603 River St 49629 ....(616)264-5767
Ellsworth
The House On The Hill, Lake St Box 206 49729 ....(616)588-6304
Empire
Clipper House Inn, 10085 Front St, PO Box 35 49630 ....(616)326-5518
Escanaba
The House of Ludington, 223 Ludington St 49829 ....(906)786-4000
Evart
B&B at Lynch's Dream, 22177 80th Ave 49631 ....(616)734-5989
Farmington Hills
The Botsford Inn, 28000 Grand River 48024 ....(313)474-4800
Fennville
"Porches", 2297 70th St 49408 ....(616)543-4162
Crane House & Cider Mill, 6051 124th Ave 49408 ....(616)561-6931
Heritage Manor, 2253 Blue Star Hwy 49408 ....(616)543-4384
Hiatus House, 2125 Lakeshore Dr 49408 ....(616)543-4530
J. Paules' Fenn Inn, 2254 S 58th St 49408 ....(616)561-2836
The Kingsley House, 626 W Main St 49408 ....(616)561-6425
The Porches B&B, 2297-70th St 49408 ....(616)543-4162
Fenton
Pine Ridge, N-10345 Old US-23 48430 ....(313)629-8911
Flint
Avon House, 518 Avon St 48503
Frankenmuth
B&B at the Pines, 327 Ardussi St 48734 ....(517)652-9019
Bavarian Town B&B, 206 Beyerlein St 48734 ....(517)652-8057
Bender Haus, 337 Trinklein St 48734 ....(517)652-8897
Home Away Lodgings, 176 Parker St 48734 ....(517)652-6839
Johnson Haus B&B, 242 S Franklin 48734 ....(517)652-8870
Kueffner's Haus, 176 Parker 48734 ....(517)652-8897
Lewis Haus, 337 Trinklein St 48734 ....(517)652-3133
Parlberg's Place, 8180 Roedel 48734 ....(517)652-8134
Frankfort
Chimney Corners, 1602 Crystal Dr 49635 ....(616)352-7522
Hotel Frankfort, Main St 49635 ....(616)882-7271
Galesburg
Old Memories Farm, PO Box 98 49053 ....(616)665-9516
Gaylord
Heritage House, 521 E Main St 49735 ....(517)732-1199
Norden Hem, PO Box 623 49735 ....(517)732-6794
Gladwin
Sullivan's B&B, PO Box 585 48624 ....(517)426-6426
The Riverside B&B, 66 Lockwood Dr 48624 ....(517)426-1206
Glen Arbor
The Sylvan Inn, PO Box 309 49636 ....(616)334-4333
White Gull Inn, PO Box 351 49636 ....(616)334-4486
Glenn
The Matteson House, Blue Star Hwy 494 ....(616)227-3918
Grand Blanc
The Country Inn, 6136 S Belsay Rd 48439 ....(313)694-6749
Grand Haven
Harbor House Inn, Harbor & Clinton 49417 ....(616)846-0610
Highland Park Hotel B&B, 1414 Lake St 49417 ....(616)842-6483
Washington Street Inn, 608 Washington St 49417 ....(616)842-1075
Grand Marais
Lakeview Inn, PO Box 297 49839 ....(906)494-2612
Grand Rapids
B&B of Grand Rapids, 455 College Ave SE 49503 ....(616)451-4849
Downtown B&B, 311 Lyon St NE 49503 ....(616)454-6622
Fountain Hill, 222 Fountain NE 49503 ....(616)458-6621
Urban Retreat B&B, 1330 Knapp NE 49505 ....(616)363-1125
Greenville
The Gibson House, 311 W Washington 48838 ....(616)754-6691
Winter Inn, 100 N Lafayette 48838 ....(616)754-7108
Harbor Beach
Wellock Inn, 404 S Huron Ave 48441 ....(517)479-3645
Harbor Springs
Harbour Inn, Beach Dr 49740 ....(616)526-2107
Main Street B&B, 403 E Main St 49740 ....(616)526-7782
Harrisville
Red Geranium Inn, 508 E Main St, Box 613 48740 ....(517)724-6153
Widow's Watch B&B, 401 Lake St, Box 271 48740 ....(517)724-5465
Hart
Rooms at "The Inn", 515 State St, PO Box 214 49420 ....(616)873-2448
Holland
Dutch Colonial Inn, 560 Central Ave 49423 ....(616)396-3664
McIntyre B&B House, 13 E 13th St 49423 ....(616)392-9886
The Old Holland Inn, 133 W 11th St 49423 ....(616)396-6601
The Parsonage, 6 E 24th St 49423 ....(616)396-1316
Homer
Grist Mill Inn, 310 E Main 49245 ....(517)568-4063
Hudson
The Sutton-Weed Farm, 18736 Quaker Rd 49247 ....(517)547-6302
Indian River
Tuscarora Historical Society B&B, 6024 Prospect St, PO Box 807 49749 ....(616)238-9072
Ionia
The Union Hill Inn, 306 Union 48846 ....(616)527-0955
Ithaca
Chaffin Farms B&B, 3239 W St Charles Rd 48847 ....(617)463-4081
Jonesville
Munro House B&B, 202 Maumee St 49250 ....(517)849-9292
Kalamazoo
Bartlett-Upjohn House, 229 Stuart Ave 49007 ....(616)342-0230
Hall House, 106 Thompson St 49007 ....(616)343-2500
Stuart Avenue Inn, 405 Stuart Ave 49007 ....(616)342-0230
The Touch of Dutch, 7062 S Sixth St 49009 ....(616)375-4527
Laingsburg
Seven Oaks Farm, 7891 Hollister Rd 48848 ....(517)651-5598
Lakeside
The Pebble House, 15093 Lakeshore Rd 49116 ....(616)469-1416
Lamont
The Stagecoach Stop B&B, 4819 Leonard Rd W Box 18 49430 ....(616)677-3940
Lansing
Cherry Hill B&B, 306 E Lenawee St 48933 ....(517)372-9545
Maplewood, 15945 Wood St 48906 ....(517)485-1426
Lawrence
Oak Cove Resort, 58881 46th St 49064 ....(616)674-8228
Lawton
Springbrook B&B, 8143 Springbrook Dr 49065 ....(616)624-6359
Leland
Manitou Manor, PO Box 864 49654 ....(616)256-7712
Riverside Inn, 302 River St 49654 ....(616)256-9971
Snowbird Inn, PO Box 1021 49653 ....(616)256-9462
The Highlands, 612 N Lake St 49654 ....(616)256-7632
Leslie
Hampton's Guest House, 112 Washington St, PO Box 123 49251 ....(517)589-9929
Lewiston
LakeView Hills B&B, Lakeview Dr, Fleming Rd, PO Box 365 49756 ....(517)786-2000
Lexington
Governor's Inn, 7277 Simons St 48450 ....(313)359-5770
The Crow's Nest, 5696 Main 48450 ....(313)359-8500
Vickie Van's B&B, 5076 S Lakeshore Rd 48450 ....(313)359-5533
West Wind B&B, 7156 Huron Ave 48450 ....(313)359-5772
Ludington
1880 Inn on the Hill, 716 E Ludington Ave 49431 ....(616)845-6458
The Ludington House, 501 E Ludington Ave 49431 ....(616)845-7769
Victorian Inn, 701 E Ludington Ave 49431 ....(616)845-7055

Mackinac Island
Bogan Lake Inn, Box 482 49757 ....(906)847-3439
Chippewa Hotel, PO Box 250 49757 ....(906)847-3341
Grand Hotel 49757 ....(906)847-3331
Haan's 1830 Inn, Box 123 49757 ....(906)847-3403
Iroquois Hotel-On-the-Beach 49757 ....(906)847-3321
Lake View Hotel 49757 ....(906)847-3384
Metivier Inn, Box 285 49757 ....(906)847-6234
Murray Hotel, Main St 49757 ....(906)847-3361
Pine Cottage, PO Box 519 49757 ....(906)847-3820
The Island House 49757 ....(906)847-3347
Thuya B&B Cottage, Box 459 49757 ....(906)847-3400

Manistee
E. E. Douville House, 111 Pine St 49660 ....(616)723-8654
Inn Wick-A-Te-Wah, 3813 Lakeshore Dr 49660 ....(616)889-4396
Manistee Country House, 1130 Lake Shore Rd 49660 ....(616)723-2367

Manistique
Margaret's B&B, 230 Arbutus, PO Box 344 49854 ....(906)341-5147

Maple City
Leelanau Country Inn, 149 E Harbor Hwy 49664 ....(616)228-5060

Marquette
Greenwood Estates, 18 Oakridge Dr 49855 ....(906)249-9246

Marshall
The National House Inn, 102 S Parkview 49068 ....(616)781-7374

McMillan
Helmer House Inn, Rt 3 Country Rd 417 49853 ....(906)586-3204

Mears
Duneland Inn-Foster's B&B, PO Box 53 49436 ....(616)873-5128

Mecosta
Blue Lake Lodge, 9765 Blue Lake Lodge Ln Box 1 48823 .(616)972-8391

Mendon
The Mendon Country Inn, 440 W Main St 49072 ....(616)496-8132

Midland
Jay's B&B, 4429 Bay City Rd 48640 ....(517)496-2498

Mio
Kilby House B&B, 405 Morenci Ave 48647 ....(517)826-3066

Montague
Country Haven B&B, 9691 Sikkenga Rd 49437 ....(616)894-4977
Old Channel Inn, 6905 Old Channel Tr 49437 ....(616)893-3805

Mount Pleasant
Country Chalet, 723 S Meridian Rd 48858 ....(517)772-9259

Muskegon
Blue Country B&B, 1415 Holton Rd 49445 ....(616)744-2555

New Buffalo
Little Bohemia, 115 S Whittaker 49117 ....(616)469-1440
Sans Souci B&B, 19265 S Lakeside Rd 49117 ....(616)756-7206
Tall Oaks Inn B&B, Box 6, Grand Beach 49117 ....(616)469-0097

Niles
Woods & Hearth B&B, 950 S Third St 49120 ....(616)683-0876
Yesterday's Inn, 518 N 4th 49120 ....(616)683-6079

Northport
Apple Beach Inn, 617 Shabwasung, PO Box 2 49670 ....(616)386-5022
Hutchinson's Garden, Box 661, 215 N High St 49670 ....(616)386-5534
North Shore Inn, 12794 Country Rd 640 49670 ....(616)386-7111
Old Mill Pond Inn, 202 W Third St 49670 ....(616)386-7341
Plum Lane Inn, Box 74 49670 ....(616)386-5774
Vintage House B&B, Box 424, 102 Shabwasung 49670 ....(616)386-7228
Wood How Lodge, Rt 1 Box 44 49670

Northville
The Atchison House, 501 W Dunlap 48167 ....(313)349-3340

Nunica
Stonegate Inn, 10831 Cleveland 49448 ....(616)837-9267

Olivet
Ackerman's B&B Inn, 243 Kalamo St 49076 ....(616)749-9422

Omena
Haus Austrian, 4626 Omena Point Rd 49674 ....(616)386-7338
Omena B&B, PO Box 75 49674 ....(616)386-7274

Owosso
Archer's Castle, 203 E King 48867 ....(517)723-2572
Merkel Manor, 623 N Park St 48867 ....(517)725-5600
Mulberry House, 1251 N Shiawassee St 48867 ....(517)723-4890
R & R Farm-ranch, 308 E Hibbard Rd 48867 ....(517)723-2553
Sylverlynd, 3452 McBride Rd 48867 ....(517)723-1267
Victorian Splendor B&B, 426 N Washington St 48867 ....(517)725-5168

Paw Paw
Carrington's Country House, 43799 Sixtieth Ave 49079 ....(616)657-5321

Pentwater
Pentwater Inn, 180 E Lowell Box 98 49449 ....(616)869-5909
Pentwater Abbey, PO Box 735, 85 W First St 49449 ....(616)869-4094

Petoskey
Apple Tree Inn, 915 Spring St, PO Box 574 49770 ....(616)347-2900
Bear & The Bay, 421 Charlevoix Ave 49770 ....(616)347-6077
Bed 'N' Breakfast, 212 Arlington 49770 ....(616)347-6145
Gull's Way, 118 Boulder Ln 49770 ....(616)347-9891
Perry Hotel, Bay & Lewis Sts 49770 ....(616)347-2516
Stafford's Bay View Inn, Box 3 49770 ....(616)347-2771
The Chapman House, 618 E Lake St 49770 ....(616)347-1338
The Cozy Spot, 1145 Kalamazoo 49770 ....(616)347-3869

Plymouth
52 Stafford, PO Box 217 53073 ....(414)893-0552
Mayflower B&B Hotel, Main & Ann Arbor Tr 48170 ....(313)453-1620

Port Austin
Garfield Inn, 8544 Lake St 48467 ....(517)738-5254
Lake Street Manor, 8569 Lake St 49467 ....(517)738-7720

Port Huron
Victorian Inn, 1229 Seventh St 48060 ....(313)984-1437

Port Sanilac
Raymond House Inn, M-25, 111 S Ridge St 48469 ....(313)622-8800

Portland
Webber House, 527 James St 48875 ....(517)647-4671

Prudenville
Spring Brook Inn, PO 390, 565 E West Branch Rd 48651 ..(517)366-6347

Reed City
Osceola Inn, 110 E Upton 49677 ....(616)832-5537

Romeo
Country Heritage B&B, 64707 Mound Rd 48065 ....(313)752-2879

Roscommon
Tall Trees, Rt 2, 323 Birch Rd 48653 ....(517)821-5592

Saginaw
Brockway House, 1631 Brockway 48602 ....(517)792-0746
Montague Inn, 1581 S Washington Ave 48601 ....(517)752-3939
The Heart House, 419 N Michigan 48602 ....(517)753-3145

Saint Clair
Murphy Inn, 505 Clinton 48079 ....(313)329-7118

Saint Ignace
Colonial House Inn, 90 N State St 49781

Saint James
McCann House B&B, PO Box (Beaver Island) 49782 ....(616)448-2387

Saint Joseph
South Cliff Inn, 1900 Lakeshore Dr 49055 ....(616)983-4881

Saline
The Homestead B&B, 9279 Macon Rd 48176 ....(313)429-9625

Saugatuck
Fairchild House, 606 Butler St 49453 ....(616)857-5985
Jann's Guest House, 132 Mason St 49453 ....(616)857-8851
Kemah Guest House, 633 Pleasant St 49453 ....(616)857-2919
The Kirby House, 294 W Center St, PO Box 1174 49453 .(616)857-2904
Maplewood Hotel, 428 Butler St Box 1059 49453 ....(616)857-1771
Newnham Inn, Box 1106, 131 Griffith St 49453 ....(616)857-4249
The Park House, 888 Holland St 49453 ....(616)857-4535
Twin Gables Country Inn, Box 881 49453 ....(616)857-4346
Wickwood Inn, 510 Butler St 49453 ....(616)857-1097

Sault Saint Marie
Ojibway Hotel, 240 W Portage St 49783 ....(906)632-4100

Schoolcraft
Grand Street B&B, 330 S Grand St, PO Box 454 49087 ....(616)679-5697

Sebewaing
Rummel's Tree Haven, 41 N Beck St 48759 ....(517)883-2450

South Haven
A Country Place B&B, Rt 5, Box 43 49090 ....(616)637-5523
The Last Resort, 86 N Shore Dr 49090 ....(616)637-8943
North Beach Inn & Restaurant, 51 North Shore Dr 49090 (616)637-6738
The Ross, 229 Michigan Ave 49090 ....(616)637-2256
Victoria Resort, 241 Oak 49090
Yelton Manor, 140 N Shore Dr 49090 ....(616)637-5220

Sparta
Morton House, 11 Pleasant St 49345 ....(616)887-7073

Spring Lake
Alberties Waterfront B&B, 18470 Main St 49456 ....(616)846-4016

Michigan (Continued)

Seascape B&B, 20009 Breton 49456 ....(616)842-8409
Shifting Sands, 19343 N Shore Dr 49456 ....(616)842-3594

Stanton

Clifford Lake Hotel, 561 Clifford Lake Dr 48888 ....(517)831-5151

Stockbridge

Ballacraine B&B, E Cooper Rd 49285 ....(517)851-7437

Suttons Bay

The Cottage B&B, 503 St. Joseph Ave 49682 ....(616)271-6348
Garthe Guest House, 504 St Joseph, PO Box 82 49682 ....(616)271-3776

Swartz Creek

Pink Palace Farms, 6095 Baldwin Rd 48473 ....(313)655-4076

Tecumseh

Boulevard Inn, 904 W Chicago Blvd 49286 ....(517)423-5169

Traverse City

Bowers Harbor B&B, 13972 Peninsula Dr 49684 ....(616)223-7869
Cedar Creek, 12666 W Bayshore Dr 49684 ....(616)947-5643
Cherry Knoll Farm, 2856 Hammond Rd East 49684 ....(616)947-9806
Cider House B&B, 5515 Barney Rd 49684 ....(616)947-2833
Hannah Beach House, 743 Munson Ave 49684 ....(616)947-8778
L'DA RU B&B, 4370 N Spider Lake Rd 49684 ....(616)946-8999
Linden Lea, 279 S Long Lake Rd 49684 ....(616)943-9182
Neahtawanta Inn, 1308 Neahtawanta Rd 49684 ....(616)223-7315
Painted Pony Inn, 8392 W M-72 49684 ....(616)947-9117
Queen Anne's Castle, 500 Webster 49684 ....(616)946-1459
Rafael's B&B, 325 Wellington 49684 ....(616)946-4106
The Stonewall Inn, 17898 Smokey Hollow Rd 49684 ....(616)223-7800
The Wooden Spool, 316 W Seventh St 49684 ....(616)947-0357
Thomas' Broadbrick Inn, 6369 Secor Rd 40794 ....(616)946-0650
The Victoriana, 622 Washington St 49684 ....(616)929-1009
Warwickshire Inn, 5037 Barney Rd 49684 ....(616)946-7176

Trenton

Bear Haven, 2947 4th St 48183 ....(313)675-4844

Union City

Victorian Villa, 601 N Broadway 49094 ....(517)741-7383

Union Pier

Gordon Beach Inn, 16240 Lakeshore Rd 49129
The Inn at Union Pier, 9708 Berrien, PO Box 222 49129 ....(616)469-4700

Walloon Lake Village

Walloon Lake Inn, PO Box 85 49796 ....(616)535-2999

West Branch

Green Inn, 4045 W M-76 48661 ....(517)345-0334
The Rose Brick Inn, 124 East Houghton Ave 48661 ....(517)345-3702

White Pigeon

River Haven, 9222 St Joseph River Rd 49099 ....(616)483-9104

Whitehall

Bunk 'N' Galley B&B, 1411 Mears Ave 49461 ....(616)894-9851

Williamston

Williamston B&B, 3169 S Williamston Rd 48895 ....(517)655-1061

Minnesota

Afton

The Afton House Inn, 3291 St Croix Tr Ave S 55001 ....(612)436-8883

Annandale

Thayer Hotel, Highway 55 55302 ....(612)274-3371

Askov

The Governor's House, Box 252 55704 ....(612)838-3296

Baudette

Rainy River Lodge 56623 ....(218)634-2730

Bloomington

Fitger's Inn, 1500 E 79th St 55420 ....(612)854-2906

Brainerd

Grand View Lodge, Rt 6 Box 22 56401
Pleasant Acres, Rt 6 Box 313 56401 ....(218)963-2482
Woods of Interlachen B&B, 7505 Interlachen Rd 56401 ....(218)963-7880

Caledonia

The Inn on the Green, Rt 1, Box 205 55921 ....(507)724-2818

Cannon Falls

Quill & Quilt, 615 W Hoffman St 55009 ....(507)263-5507

Chaska

Bluff Creek Inn, 1161 Bluff Creek Dr 55318 ....(612)445-2735

Chatfield

Lund's Guest House, 500 Winona St SE 55923 ....(507)867-4003

Crookston

Wilkinson-Thorson B&B, 327 Houston Ave 56716 ....(218)281-1601

Dodge Center

Eden B&B, Rt 1 Box 215 55927 ....(507)527-2311

Duluth

The Ellery House, 28 S 21st Ave E 55812 ....(218)724-7639
Fitger's Inn, 600 E Superior St 55082 ....(218)722-8826
The Mansion, 3600 London Rd 55804 ....(218)724-0739
Stanford Inn, 1415 E Superior St 55805 ....(218)724-3044

Elmare

Kuchenbecker Farm, PO Box 107 56027

Ely

Our Mom's B&B Inn, 323 E Sheridan St 55731 ....(218)365-6510
Three Deer Haven B&B, Star Rt 2, Box 5086 55731 ....(218)365-6464

Excelsior

Christopher Inn, 201 Mill St 55331 ....(612)474-6816

Faribault

Hutchinson House B&B, 305 NW Second St 55021 ....(507)332-7519

Garvin

Glenview B&B, RR 1 56132 ....(507)629-4808

Glenwood

Peters' Sunset Beach Hotel, Rt 2, Box 118 56334 ....(612)634-4501

Good Thunder

Cedar Knoll Farm, Rt 2, Box 147 56037 ....(507)524-3813

Graceville

Lakeside B&B, 113 W 2nd St 56240 ....(612)748-7657

Grand Marais

Cascade Lodge, PO Box 693 55604 ....(218)387-1112
Clearwater Lodge, Gunflint Tr (CR31B) 55604 ....(218)388-2254
East Bay Hotel 55604 ....(218)387-2800
Gunflint Lodge, PO 100 Gt 55604 ....(218)388-4487
Naniboujou Lodge, HC 1 Box 505 55604 ....(218)387-2688
Young's Island B&B, Gunflint Trail 67-1 55604 ....(218)388-4487

Harmony

Michel Farm Vacations, Rt 1 Box 914 55939 ....(507)886-5392

Hastings

Hazelwood, 705 Vermillion 55033 ....(612)437-3297
The River Rose, 620 Ramsey 55033 ....(612)437-3297
Thorwood, 4th & Pine 55033

Hendricks

Triple L Farm, Rt 1, Box 141 56136 ....(507)275-3740

Herman

Lawndale Farm, Rt 2 Box 50 56248

Hibbing

The Adams House, 201 E 23rd St 55746 ....(218)263-9742

Hinckley

Bed & Breakfast Lodge, Rt 3, Box 84A 55037 ....(612)384-6052

Kellogg

PJ's B&B, 132 Winona Ave 55945 ....(507)767-2203

Lake City

Evergreen Knoll Acres, Rt 1 Box 145 55041 ....(612)345-2257
The Rahilly House, 304 S Oak St 55041 ....(612)345-2257
Red Gables Inn, 403 N High St 55041 ....(612)345-2605
The Victorian B&B, 620 S High St 55041 ....(612)345-2167

Lanesboro

Carrolton Country Inn, RR 2 Box 139 55949 ....(507)467-2257
Mrs. B's Historic Lanesboro Inn, 101 Pkwy 55949 ....(507)467-2154
Scanlan House, 708 Park Ave S 55949 ....(507)467-2158

LeSueur

The Cosgrove, 228 S Second St 56058 ....(612)665-2763

Little Falls

Pine Edge Inn, 308 First St SE 56345

Lutsen

Lindgren's B&B, PO Box 56 (Co Rd 35) 55612 ....(218)663-7450

Mantorville

Grand Old Mansion, 501 Clay St 55955 ....(507)635-3231

Marine On St Croix

Asa Parker House, 17500 St Croix Tr N 55047 ....(612)433-5248

Marshall

Blanchford Inn B&B, 600 W Redwood St 56250 ....(507)532-5071

Miltona

The Country House, Rt 3, Box 110 56354 ....(218)943-2928

Minneapolis
Evelo's B&B, 2301 Bryant Ave S 55405
Linne' B&B, 2645 Fremont Ave S 55408 ....(612)377-4418
Nicollet Island Inn, 95 Merriam 55401 ....(612)331-1800
Whitney Hotel, 150 Portland 55401
Morris
The American House, 410 E Third St 56267 ....(612)589-4054
North Branch
Red Pine B&B, 15140 400th St 55056 ....(612)583-3326
Northfield
Archer House, 212 Division St 55057
Old Frontenac
Lowell House B&B, 531 Wood St 55026
Olivia
Sheep Shedde Inn, Hwy 212 & 71 W 56277
Orr
The Kettle Falls Hotel, Ash River Tr 55771 ....(218)374-3511
Owatonna
The Northrop House, 358 E Main St 55060 ....(507)451-4040
Park Rapids
Dickson Viking Huss B&B, 202 E Fourth 56470 ....(218)732-8089
Dorset Schoolhouse, PO Box 201 56470 ....(218)732-1377
Pipestone
The Calumet, PO Box 111 56164 ....(507)825-5658
Princeton
The Farm Inn, RR 6, Box 114 55371 ....(612)389-2679
Ray
Bunt's B&B, Lake Kabetogama 56669 ....(218)875-3904
Red Wing
Pratt-Taber Inn, 706 W Fourth 55066 ....(612)388-5945
The Sprague House, 1008 W Third St 55066 ....(612)388-3115
St. James Hotel, 406 Main St 55066 ....(612)388-2846
Rochester
Canterbury Inn B&B, 723 2nd St SW 55902 ....(507)289-5553
Rush City
Grant House, Fourth & Bremer (Box 87) 55069 ....(612)358-3661
Saint Joseph
Lamb's B&B, 29738 Island Lake Rd 56374 ....(612)363-7924
Saint Paul
Chatsworth B&B, 984 Ashland 55104 ....(612)227-4288
University Club of St. Paul, 420 Summit Ave 55102 ....(612)222-1751
Yoerg House, 215 W Isabel 55107
Sauk Centre
Palmer House Hotel, 500 Sinclair Lewis Ave 56378
Shafer
Country B&B, 32030 Ranch Tr. 55074 ....(612)257-4773
Shakopee
Sunny Morning Manor, 314 S Scott St 55379 ....(612)496-1482
Silver Bay
Guest House B&B, 299 Outer Dr 55614 ....(218)226-4201
Sleepy Eye
The Woodland Inn, Rt 4, Box 68 56085 ....(507)794-5981
Spicer
Spicer Castle, 11600 Indian Beach Rd 56288 ....(612)796-5870
Spring Grove
Touch of the Past, 102 Third Ave SE 55974 ....(507)498-5146
Spring Lake
Anchor Inn, Hwy 4, RR 56680 ....(218)798-2718
Spring Valley
Chase's, 508 N Huron Ave 55975 ....(507)346-2850
Stacy
Kings Oakdale Park Guest House, 6933 232nd Ave NE 55029 ....(612)462-5598
Stillwater
Driscolls For Guests, 1103 South 3rd St 55082 ....(612)439-7486
Lowell Inn, 102 N Second St 55082 ....(612)439-1100
The Overlook Inn, 210 E Laurel 55082 ....(612)439-3409
Rivertown Inn, 306 W Olive St 55082 ....(612)430-2955
Taylors Falls
Old Taylors Falls Jail, 102 Government Rd 55084 ....(612)465-3112
Wabasha
Anderson House, 333 Main St, PO Box 262 55981 ....(612)565-4524
The Parsonage House, 100 Coulee Way 55981 ....(612)565-2128
Walker
Chase On The Lake Lodge & Motor Inn, PO Box 206 56484 ....(218)547-1531
Weaver
Noble Studio & Galleries, Rt 1 Box 28 55910 ....(507)767-2244
Winona
Carriage House B&B, 420 Main St 55987 ....(507)452-8256
The Hotel, 129 W Third St 55987 ....(507)452-5460

Mississippi

Aberdeen
Rosemont, 407 S Meridian 39730 ....(601)369-9434
Brookhaven
Edgewood, 412 Storm Ave 39601 ....(601)833-2001
Chatham
Mount Holly, Box 140 38731 ....(601)827-2652
Columbus
Alexander's Inn, 408 7th S 39701 ....(601)327-4259
Antebellum Homes, 906 3rd Ave 39701 ....(601)327-4064
Cartney-Hunt House, 408 S 7th St 39701 ....(601)327-4259
Temple Heights, 515 9 St N 39701
Fayette
Historic Springfield Plantation, Hwy 553 39069 ....(601)786-3802
Fillmore
Generals Quarters, 924 Fillmore St 38834 ....(601)286-3325
Holly Springs
Hamilton Place, 105 E Mason Ave 38635 ....(601)252-4368
Jackson
Fairview, 734 Fairview St 39202
Judy Fenter, 1851 Drecon Dr 39211
Millsaps-Buie House, 628 N State St 39202 ....(601)352-0221
Lorman
Rosswood Plantation, Hwy 552 39096 ....(601)437-4215
Meridian
Lincoln, Ltd. B&B, PO Box 3479 39303 ....(601)482-5483
Nantucket
1806 Anchor Inn, 66 Centre St 02554 ....(508)228-0072
Natchez
The Burn, 712 N Union St 39120 ....(601)442-1344
Dixie, 211 S Wall St 39120 ....(601)442-2525
Dunleith, 84 Homochitto 39120 ....(601)446-8500
Guest House Of Natchez, 210 N Pearl St 39120 ....(601)445-6000
Hope Farm, 147 Homochitto St 39120
Linden, 1 Linden Place 39120 ....(601)445-5472
Monmouth Plantation, 36 Melrose 39120 ....(800)828-4531
Ravennaside, 601 S. Union St 39120
Silver Street Inn, 1 Silver St 39120
Texada, 212 S. Wall St 39120 ....(601)445-4283
Oxford
ISOM Place, 1003 Jefferson Ave 39655
Oliver-Britt House, 512 Van Buren Ave 38655
Port Gibson
Oak Square Plantation, 1207 Church St 39150 ....(601)437-4350
Vicksburg
Anchuca, 1010 First East 39180 ....(601)636-4931
Balfour House, 1002 Crawford St 39180
Cedar Grove Mansion Inn, 2300 Washington St 39180 ....(800)862-1300
The Corners, 601 Klein St 39180 ....(800)444-7421
The Duff Green Mansion, 1114 First East St 39180 ....(601)636-6968
Gray Oaks, 4142 Rifle Range Rd 39180
Old Feld Home, 2108 Cherry St 39180
Tomil Manor, 2430 Drummond St 39180 ....(601)638-8893
Woodville
Square Ten Inn, 242 Depot St 39669 ....(601)888-3993

Missouri

Arrow Rock
Borgman's B&B, Van Buren St 65320 ....(816)837-3350
Down Over Holdings, 602 Main St 65320 ....(816)837-3268
Bonne Terre
Mansion Hill Country Inn, Mansion Hill Dr 63628 ....(314)358-5311
The Lamplight Inn, 207 E School St 63628 ....(314)358-4222
Branson
Branson House, 120 4th St 65616 ....(417)334-0959
Ozark Mountain Country B&B, PO Box 295 65616 ....(417)334-4720
Carthage
Brewer's Maple Lane Farms, RR 1 64836 ....(417)358-6312
Cedar Grove
By Hammer & Hand Antiques & B&B 65320 ....(816)837-3441
Clayton
Seven Gables Inn, 26 N Meramec 63105 ....(314)863-8400
Gallatin
Gallatin B&B Inn, 200 E Grand 64640
Hannibal
Bordello House, 111 Bird 63401 ....(314)221-6111
The Fifth Street Mansion B&B, 213 S Fifth St 63401 ....(314)221-0445
Garth Woodside Mansion, RR 1 63401 ....(314)221-2789
Victorian Guest House, 3 Stillwell 63401
Hartville
Frisco House, PO Box 118 65667 ....(417)741-7304
Hermann
Birk's Goethe St Gauthaus, 700 Goethe St 65041 ....(314)486-2911
Captain Wohlt Inn, 123 E Third St 65041 ....(314)486-3357
Der Klingerbau Inn, 108 E 2nd St 65041 ....(314)486-2030
Seven Sisters B&B Cottage, 108 Schiller St 65041 ....(314)486-3717
William Klinger Inn, 108 E 2nd St 65041 ....(314)486-3528
Historic Weston
Benner House B&B, 645 Main St 64098 ....(816)386-2616
Jamesport
Richardson House B&B, PO 227 64648 ....(816)684-6664
Kansas City
Doanleigh Wallagh, 217 E 37th St 64111 ....(816)753-2667
Lathrop
Parkview Farm, RR 1, Box 54 64465 ....(816)664-2744
Lebanon
Historic Oakland Mansion, Rt 1 Box 179 65536 ....(417)588-3291
Lesterville
Wilderness Lodge, Box 90 63654 ....(314)637-2295
Macon
Wardell Guest House, 1 Wardell Rd 63552
New Haven
Augustine River Bluff Farm, RR 1, Box 42 63068 ....(314)237-3198
Rocheport
School House B&B, Third And Clark St 65279 ....(314)698-2022
Saint Charles
Boone's Lick Trail Inn, 1000 South Main St 63301 ....(314)947-7000
Saint Genevieve
Hotel Saint Genevieve, Main & Merchant St 63670 ....(314)883-2737
The Southern Hotel, 146 S Third St 63670 ....(314)883-3493
The Inn St. Gemme Beauvais, 78 N Main, PO Box 231 63670 ....(314)883-5744
Saint Joseph
Harding House, 219 N 20th St 64501 ....(816)232-7020
McNally House B&B, 1105 S 15 64503
Schuster-Rader Mansion, 703 Hall St 64501
Saint Louis
The Coachlight B&B, 1 Grandview Heights 63131 ....(314)965-4328
Lafayette House, 2156 Lafayette Ave 63104 ....(314)772-4429
Springfield
Walnut Street B&B, 900 E Walnut St 65806 ....(417)864-6346
St. Louis
Falicon Inn, 1 Grandview Hgts 63131 ....(314)965-4328
Washington
Schwegmann House, 438 West Front Street 63090 ....(314)239-5025
Washington House B&B Inn, PO Box 527 63090 ....(314)239-2417
Zachariah Foss Guest House, 4 Lafayette 63090 ....(314)239-6499

Montana

Big Fork
Schwartz's B&B, 890 McCaffery Rd 59911 ....(406)837-5463
Big Sky
Lazy K Bar Ranch, Box 550 59011 ....(406)537-4404
Lone Mountain Ranch, PO Box 145 59716 ....(406)995-4644
Billings
PJ's B&B, 722 N 29th St 59101 ....(406)259-3300
Bozeman
Hillard's Guest House, 11521 Axtell Gateway Rd 59715 ....(406)463-4696
Lehrkind Mansion, 719 N Wallace 59715
Silver Forest Inn, 15325 Bridger Canyon Rd 59715
Voss Inn, 319 S Willson 59715 ....(406)587-0982
Butte
Copper King Mansion, 219 West Granite 59701 ....(406)782-7580
Essex
Izaak Walton Inn, PO Box 653 59916 ....(406)888-5700
Eureka
Grave Creek B&B, PO Box 551 59917 ....(406)882-4658
Gallatin Gateway
Gallatin Gateway 59730 ....(406)763-4672
Great Falls
The Chalet B&B Inn, 1204 4th Ave, N 59401 ....(406)452-9001
Three Pheasant Inn, 626 5th Ave N 59401 ....(406)453-0519
Helena
Sanders Inn, 328 Ewing 59601 ....(406)442-3309
Huson
Whispering Pines, Box 36 59846 ....(406)626-5664
Nevada City
Nevada City Hotel 59755 ....(406)843-5377
Red Lodge
Pitcher Guest House, 2 S Platt PO 1148 59068 ....(406)446-2859
Willows Inn, 224 S. Platt Ave, PO Box 886 59068 ....(406)446-3913
St Ignatius
Mission Mountain B&B, RR Box 183-A 59865 ....(406)745-4331
Stevensville
Country Caboose, 852 Willoughby Rd 59870 ....(406)777-3145
Townsend
Hidden Hollow Hideaway, Box 233 59644 ....(406)266-3322
White Sulphur Spring
Foxwood Inn, Box 404 59645
Whitefish
Duck Inn, 1305 Columbia Ave 59937 ....(406)862-3825
Kandahar Lodge, PO Box 1659 59937 ....(406)862-6098

Nebraska

Alliance
Prairie House, 602 Box Butte 69301 ....(308)762-1461
Bartley
Pheasant Hill, HC 68 Box 12 69020 ....(308)692-3278
Crawford
Fort Robinson Inn, Box 392 69339
Dixon
The Georges, Rt 1 Box 50 68732 ....(402)584-2625
Lincoln
Rogers House, 2145 B St 68502 ....(402)476-6961
North Platte
Watson Manor Inn, 410 S Sycamore, PO Box 458 69103 ....(308)532-1124
Omaha
Offutt House, 140 N 39th St 68131 ....(402)553-0951

Nevada

Genoa
Genoa House Inn, PO Box 141, 180 Nixon St 89411 ....(702)782-7075
Orchard House, Box 77 89411
Imlay
Old Pioneer Garden, Star Rt, Unionville #79 89418 ....(702)538-7585
Lamoille
Breitenstein House 89828 ....(702)753-6356

Silver City
Hardwicke House, Box 96 89429
Smith
Windybrush Ranch, Box 85 89430 ....(702)465-2481
Sparks
Blue Fountain B&B, 1590 B St 89431 ....(702)359-0359
Unionville
Old Pioneer Garden Guest Ranch B&B 89418 ....(702)538-7585
Virginia City
Edith Palmer's Country Inn, South B Street, PO Box 756 89440 ....(702)847-0707
Gold Hill Hotel, Main St, PO Box 304 89440 ....(702)847-0111
Winnemucca
Robin's Nest Inn, 130 E Winnemucca 89445 ....(702)623-2410
Stauffer House, 82 Lay St 89445
Yerington
Robric Ranch, Box 2 89447

New Hampshire

Alexandria
Stone Rest B&B, 652 Fowler River Rd 03222 ....(603)744-6066
Alstead
Darby Brook Farm, Hill Rd 03602 ....(603)835-6624
Alton Bay
Oak Birch Inn, Rt 28a (23) 03810
Andover
Andover Arms Guest House, Main St, PO Box 256 03216 (603)735-5953
The English House, PO Box 162 03216
Antrim
Breezy Point Inn, RD 1 Box 302 03440 ....(603)478-5201
Maplehurst Inn, Rt 202 03440
Steele Homestead Inn, RR 1 Box 78, Rt 9 03440
Uplands Inn, Miltimore Rd 03440 ....(603)588-6349
Ashland
Cheney House, PO Box 683 03217
Country Options, PO 443 03217
Glynn House Victorian Inn, 43 Highland St, PO Box 819 03217 ....(603)968-3775
Bartlett
The Country Inn at Bartlett, Rt 302, PO Box 327 03812 ..(603)374-2353
Bedford
Bedford Village Inn, 2 Old Bedford Rd 03102 ....(603)472-2001
Bennington
David's Inn, Bennington Sq. 03442
Bethlehem
The Bells, Strawberry Hill, PO Box 276 03574 ....(603)869-2647
The Mulburn Inn, Main St 03574 ....(603)869-3389
Shepherd's Inn, PO Box 70 03574 ....(603)823-8777
The Highlands Inn, PO 118 C 03574
Bradford
Andrew Brook Lodge, RFD 1 Box 62 03221
The Bradford Inn, Main St 03221 ....(603)938-5309
Mountain Lake Inn, Rt 114 03221 ....(603)938-2136
Bridgewater
Pasquaney Inn On Newfound Lake, Star Rt 1 Box 1066 03222 ....(603)744-9111
Bristol
Victorian, 16 Summer St 03222 ....(603)744-6157
Campton
Mountain Fare Inn, Mad River Rd 03223 ....(603)726-4283
The Campton Inn, Rt 175 N Box 282 03223 ....(603)726-4449
Village Guest House, PO Box 222 03223 ....(603)726-4449
Canaan
Inn On Canaan Street, The Kremzners 03741 ....(603)523-7310
The Towerhouse Inn, 1 Parker St 03741 ....(603)523-7244
Canterbury
Sleepy Hollow B&B, RR 1, Baptist Hill Rd 03223 ....(603)267-6055
Center Harbor
Dearborn Place, Box 997 03226 ....(603)253-6711
Kona Mansion Inn, Box 458 03226 ....(603)253-4900
Center Ossipee
Hitching Post Inn, Old Rt 16 03814 ....(603)539-4482
Center Sandwich
Corner House Inn, Main St PO 204 03227
Centre Harbor
Red Hill Inn, RD 1 Box 99M 03226 ....(603)279-7001
Charlestown
Indian Shutters Inn, Rt 12 03603 ....(603)826-4445
Chichester
Hitching Post B&B, Dover Rd #2, Box 790 03263 ....(603)798-4951
Chocorua
Staffords-in-the-Field 03817
The Farmhouse, PO 14 Page Hill Rd 03817 ....(603)323-8707
Claremont
Goddard Mansion B&B, 25 Hillstead Rd 03743 ....(603)543-0603
The Poplars, 13 Grandview St 03743 ....(603)543-0858
Colebrook
Monadnock B&B, 1 Monadnock St 03576 ....(603)237-8216
Concord
Hitching Post-B&B, Dover Rd, RD #2 03263 ....(603)798-4951
Wyman Farm, Rt 8 Box 437 03301 ....(603)783-4467
Conway
The Darby Field Inn, Bald Hill, PO Box D 03818 ....(603)447-2181
Merrill Farm Resort, PO Box 2070 03818 ....(603)447-3866
Mountain Valley Manner, 148 Washington St 03818 ....(603)447-3988
Cornish
Chase House B&B, Rt 12 A, RR 2 Box 909 03745 ....(603)675-5391
Home Hill Country Inn, RFD 2 03781 ....(603)675-6165
Danbury
Inn At Danbury, Rt 104 03230
Dover
Pinky's Place, 38 Rutland St 03820 ....(603)742-8789
Silver Street Inn 03820 ....(603)749-6524
Dublin
Hidden Brooks B&B, Main St, Box 402 03444 ....(603)563-8452
Trinitarian Parsonage, Main St 03444 ....(603)563-8889
Durham
Country House, 2 Stagecoach Rd 03824
Hannah House B&B, Packers Falls Rd 03824 ....(603)659-5500
East Hebron
Six Chimneys, Star Rt Box 114 03232 ....(603)744-2029
East Sullivan
Delford Inn, Centre St 03445
Easton
Bangay Jar, PO Box 15, Rt 116 03850 ....(603)823-7775
Blanche's B&B, Rt 116 03580 ....(603)823-7061
Eaton Center
Inn At Crystal Lake, Rt 163 03832
Palmer House Inn, Rt 153 03832
Rockhouse Mountain Farm 03832 ....(603)447-2880
Elkins
Limner Haus, Box 126 03233
Enfield
Kluge's Sunset Hill Inn, Masacoma Lake 03748 ....(603)632-4335
Epping
Haley House Farm, N River Rd 03042
Etna
Moose Mountain Lodge, Moose Mountain Rd 03750 .....(603)643-3529
Exeter
The "G" Clef, Ashbrook Rd 03833 ....(603)772-8850
Exeter Inn, 90 Front St 03833 ....(603)772-5901
Fitzwilliam
Amos Parker House, 119 West 03447 ....(603)585-6540
Barntique, Sugar Hill Rd 03447
Fern Hill, PO Box 13 03447 ....(603)585-6672
Fitzwilliam Inn 03447 ....(603)585-9000
Francestown
Inn At Crotched Mountain, Mountain Rd 03043 ....(603)588-6840
Francestown Village
The Francestown B&B, Box 236 03043
Franconia
Bungay Jar B&B, PO Box 15 03580 ....(603)823-7775
Cannon Mountain Inn & Cottage, Easton Rd, Rt 116 03580 ....(603)823-9574
Franconia Inn, Easton Rd 03580 ....(603)823-5542

New Hampshire (Continued)

Lovett's Inn, Rt 18, Profile Rd 03580 ....(603)823-7761
Pinestead Farm Lodge, Rt 116 RD 1 03580
Sugar Hill Inn, Rt 117 03580

Franklin
Webster Lake Inn, Webster Ave 03235 ....(603)934-4050

Freedom
Freedom House, PO Box 338, 1 Maple St 03836 ....(603)539-4815
Knob Hill B&B, Rt 153 03836 ....(603)539-6576

Gilford
Cartway House Inn, 83 Old Lake Shore Rd 03246 ....(603)528-1172
Gunstock Inn, Rt 11A 03246 ....(603)293-2021
Hall's Hillside B&B, RD #4, BoxGA372 03246 ....(603)293-7290
Kings Grant Inn, RD 5 Box 385 03246 ....(603)293-4431

Gilmonton
The Historic Tavern Inn, Box 365 03237 ....(603)267-7349

Glen
Bernerhof Inn, Box 381 Rt 302 03838 ....(603)383-4414

Gorham
The Gables, 139 Main St 03581 ....(603)466-2875
The Gorham House Inn, 55 Main St 03581 ....(603)466-2271

Goshen
Cutter's Loft, Rt 31 03752 ....(603)863-5306

Grafton
Grafton Inn, Rt 4 Box 445 03240

Greenfield
The Greenfield Inn, Box 156 03047 ....(603)547-6327

Hampstead
Stillmeadow B&B at Hampstead, 545 Main St, PO Box 565 03841 ....(603)329-8381

Hampton
Blue Heron Inn, 124 Landing Rd 03842 ....(603)926-9666
The Inn at Elmwood Corners, 252 Winnacunnet Rd 03842 ....(603)929-0443
Friendly Persuasion Inn, 636 Exeter Rd 03842 ....(603)929-0002
The Curtis Field House, 735 Exeter Rd 03842 ....(603)929-0082

Hampton Beach
Boar's Head, 12 Dumas 03842 ....(603)926-3911
Century House, 552 Ocean Blvd. 03842
The Grayhurst, 11 F St 03842

Hancock
John Hancock Inn, Main St 03449 ....(603)525-3318
Westwinds of Hancock, Rt 137, RFD #1, Box 635 03449 ....(603)525-6600

Hanover
The Trumbull House, Box C29 03755 ....(603)643-1400

Harrisville
Harrisville Squire's Inn, Box 19, Keene Rd 03450 ....(603)827-3925

Haverhill
Haverhill Inn, Box 95 03765 ....(603)989-5961
Westgate House, 7 Court St, Box 178A 03765 ....(603)989-3311

Hebron
Six Chimneys, US Rt 3A, SRB 114 E 03232 ....(603)744-2029

Henniker
Colby Hill Inn, Box 778 03242
Hanscom House B&B 03242
The Meeting House Inn & Restaurant, 35 Flanders Rd 03242 ....(603)428-3228

Hillsborough
Stonebridge Inn, Rt 9 Box 82 03244

Holderness
The Inn on Golden Pond, Rt 3 Box 680 03245 ....(603)968-7269
Manor On Golden Pond, Rt 3 Box T 03245 ....(603)968-3348

Intervale
Mountain Vale Inn, Rt 16A, Box 482 03845 ....(603)356-9880
New England Inn, Rte. 16a 03845 ....(603)356-5541
Riverside, An Elegant Country Inn, Rt 16A 03845 ....(603)356-9060
The Forest-A Country Inn, PO Box 37 03845 ....(603)356-9772

Jackson
Blake House, Pinkham Notch Rd, PO Box 246 03846 ....(603)383-9057
Christmas Farm Inn, Rt 16 Box 176 03846
Ellis River House, Rt 16 Box 656 03846 ....(603)383-9339
The Inn at Jackson, PO Box H 03846 ....(603)383-4321
The Inn at Thorn Hill, PO Box A, Thorn Hill Rd 03846 (603)383-4242
Village House, Rt 16A Box 359 03846 ....(603)383-6666
Whitney's Village Inn, Rt 16B Box W 03846 ....(603)383-6886
Wildcat Inn, Main St, PO Box T 03846 ....(603)383-4245

Jackson Village
Nestlenook Inn, PO Box Q 03846

Jaffrey
B&B on Board, Old Peterboro Rd 03452 ....(603)532-8083
The Benjamin Prescott Inn, Rt 124 East 03452 ....(603)532-6637
Galway House B&B, Old Peterborough Rd 03452 ....(603)532-8083
Gould Farm, PO Box 27 03452 ....(603)532-6996
Jaffrey Manor Inn, 13 Stratton Rd 03452 ....(603)532-8069
Lilac Hill Farm, 5 Ingalls Rd 03452 ....(603)532-7278
Mill Pond Inn, 50 Prescott Rd 03452 ....(603)532-7687
Woodbound Inn, Woodbound Rd 03452 ....(603)532-8341

Jaffrey Center
Monadnock Inn, Main St Box 103 03454

Jefferson
The Jefferson Inn, Rt 2 03583 ....(603)586-7998
The Country Inn On Jefferson Hill, Rt 2 03583 ....(603)586-7998

Keene
289 Court, 289 Court St 03431 ....(603)357-3195
Carriage Barn Guest-House, 358 Main St 03431

Laconia
Ferry Point House, Rt 1 Box 335 03246 ....(603)524-0087
Hickory Stick Farm, RFD 2 03246
Mackissock House, 1047 Union Ave 03246
Parade Rest Inn, Parade Rd 03269 ....(603)524-3152
Perry Point House, Lower Bay Rd 03269 ....(603)524-0087
The Tin Whistle Inn, 1047 Union Ave 03246 ....(603)528-4185

Lancaster
A Touch of Home, 43 N Main St, Rt 3 03584 ....(603)788-4540

Lincoln
Charpentier B&B, Box 562 03251 ....(603)745-8517

Lisbon
Ammonoosuc Inn, Bishops Rd 03585 ....(603)838-6118

Littleton
1895 House, 74 Pleasant St 03561
Beal House Inn, 247 West Main St 03561 ....(603)444-2661
Edencroft Manor, Rt 135 03561 ....(603)444-6776
Thayers Inn, 136 Main St 03561 ....(603)444-6469

Lyme
Loch Lyme Lodge, Rt 10 RFD 278 03768 ....(603)795-2141
Lyme Inn, Route 10 03768
The The Dowds' Country Inn, On the Common 03768 .....(603)795-4712

Marlborough
Thatcher Hill Inn, Thatcher Hill Rd 03455
Tolman Pond, PO RFD 03455

Milford
Ram In The Thicket, Off Rt 101, Maple St 03055
Victoria Place, 88 Nashua St Rt 101-a 03055

Milton
Thirteen Colonies Farm, RFD Rt 16 03887 ....(603)652-4458

Moultonboro
Olde Orchard Inn, Box 256 03254 ....(603)476-5004

Mount Sunapee
Backside Inn, PO Box 171 03772 ....(603)863-5161
Blue Goose Inn, Rt 103B, PO Box 182 03772 ....(603)763-5519

Munsonville
The Old Mill House, Rt 9, Box 224 03457 ....(603)847-3224

New London
Maple Hill Farm, RR 1 Box 1620 03257
New London Inn, Box 8 Main St 03257 ....(603)526-2791
Pleasant Lake Inn, PO Box 1030, N Pleasant St 03257 ....(603)526-6271

Newmarket
Haley House Farm, Rt 1 N River 03857 ....(603)679-8713

Newport
The Inn at Coit Mountain, HCR 63, PO 3 Rt 10 03773 ....(603)863-3583

North Charlestown
Indian Shutters Inn, Rt 12 03603 ....(603)826-4445

North Conway
The 1785 Inn, Rt 16 at The Scenic Vista 03860 ....(603)356-9025
The Buttonwood Inn, Mt Surprise Rd, PO Box 1817A 03860 ....(603)356-2625
Cranmore Inn, PO Box 885 03860 ....(603)356-5502
Cranmore Mt Lodge, Kearsarge Rd, PO Box 1194 03860 (603)356-2044
Eastman Inn, Main St, Box 882 03860 ....(603)356-6707

Nereledge Inn & White Horse Pub, River Rd Off Main St 03860
Old Red Inn & Cottages, Rt 16 Box 467 03860
Peacock Inn, PO Box 1012 03860 ....(603)356-9041
Stonehurst Manor, Rt 16 03860 ....(603)356-3271
Wildflowers Guest House, Box 597 03860

North Sutton
Follansbee Inn, PO Box 92, Keyser St 03260 ....(603)927-4221

North Woodstock
The Birches B&B, Rt 175, PO Box 59 03262 ....(603)745-6603
Cascade Lodge, 222 Main St 03262 ....(603)745-2722
Mt. Adams Inn, Rt 3, South Main St 03262 ....(603)745-2711
Woodstock Inn, Rt 3 Box 118, Main St 03262 ....(603)745-3951

Northfield
Haus Alpenrose, 28 Summer St 03276

Northwood
Aviary, Bow Lake, Box 268 03261 ....(603)942-7755
Lake Shore Farm, Jeness Pond Rd 03261 ....(603)942-5521
Meadow Farm B&B, Jenness Pond Rd 03261 ....(603)942-8619

Ossipee
Acorn Lodge, PO Box 144, Duncan Lake 03864 ....(603)539-2151
Flag Gate Farm B&B, Rt 28, RFD #1, Box 238 03864 ....(603)539-2231
Kimberwick Farm 03864

Oxford
White Goose Inn, PO Box 17 03777 ....(603)353-4812

Peterborough
Salzburg Inn, Gov. Steele Estate 03458
Willows Inn, PO Box 527 03458

Pittsfield
Appleview Orchard B&B, Upper City Rd, PO Box 104 03263 ....(603)435-6867

Plymouth
Colonel Spencer Inn, Rt 3S, RFD #1, Box 50 03264 ....(603)536-3438
Crab Apple Inn, RR 4 Box 1955 03264 ....(603)536-4476
Northway House, RFD 1 US Rt 3 North 03264 ....(603)536-2838

Portsmouth
Inn At Christian Shore, 335 Maplewood, PO Box 1474 03801 ....(603)431-6770
Leighton Inn, 69 Richards Ave 03801 ....(603)433-2188
Martin Hill Inn, 404 Islington St 03801 ....(603)436-2287
Sheafe Street Inn, 3 Sheafe St 03801 ....(603)436-9104
Sise Inn, 40 Court St 03801 ....(603)433-1200
The Inn at Strawberry Banke, 314 Court St 03801 ....(603)436-7242

Rindge
Grassy Pond House 03461

Rye
Rock Ledge Manor B&B, 1413 Ocean 03870 ....(603)431-1413

Sanbornton
Ferry Point House, Lower Bay Road 03269

Seabrook Beach
The Bellingham by-the-Bay B&B, 16 Portsmouth Ave 03874 ....(603)474-2112

Shelburne
Philbrook Farm Inn, North Rd 03581 ....(603)466-3831

Snowville
Snowvillage Inn, Box 83, Foss Mt. Rd 03849 ....(603)447-2818

Strafford
Province Inn, PO Box 309, Bow Lake 03884 ....(603)664-2457

Stratham
The B's, 73 Union Rd, PO Box 138 03885 ....(603)772-5196
Maple Lodge B&B, 68 Depot Rd 03885 ....(603)778-9833
Stratham Hill Farm, 273 Portsmouth Ave 03885 ....(603)772-3999

Sugar Hill
Hilltop Inn, Main Street (Rt 117) 03585 ....(603)823-5695
The Homestead 03585 ....(603)823-5564
Ledgeland Inn & Cottages 03585 ....(603)823-5341
Sunset Hill House, Sunset Rd 03585 ....(603)823-5522

Sunapee
Dexter's Inn, Stagecoach Rd, PO Box 5 03782 ....(603)763-5571
Haus Edelweiss, Box 609 03782 ....(603)763-2100
Inn At Sunapee, Box 336 03782 ....(603)763-4444
Old Governor's House, Lower Main & Myrtle 03782 ....(603)763-9918
Seven Hearths Inn, Old Rt 11 03782 ....(603)763-5657
Times Ten Inn, Rt 103b, PO Box 572 03782 ....(603)763-5120

Suncook
Suncook House, 62 Main St 03275 ....(603)485-8141

Sutton Mills
Village House At Sutton Mills, Box 151 03221 ....(603)927-4765

Tamworth
Tamworth Inn, Main St 03886 ....(603)323-7721

Temple
Birchwood Inn, Rt 45 03084 ....(603)878-3285

Tilton
The Black Swan Inn, 308 W Main St 03276 ....(603)286-4524
Country Place, RD 2 Box 342, Rt 132 N. 03276 ....(603)286-8551
Tilton Manor, 28 Chestnut St 03276 ....(603)268-3457

Twin Mountain
Partridge House Inn, Profile Rd, PO Box 231 03595 ....(603)846-2277

Union
Thirteen Colonies Farm, RFD Rt 16 03887 ....(603)652-4458

Wakefield
Wakefield Inn, Mountain Laurel Rd, Rt 1 Box 2185 03872 ....(603)522-8272

Walpole
The 1801 House, Box 35 03608
The Josiah Bellows House, N Main St 03608 ....(603)756-4250

Warren
The Black Iris B&B, PO Box 83 03279 ....(603)764-9366

Waterville Valley
Silver Squirrel Inn, PO Box 363, Show's Brook Rd 03223 .(603)236-8325
Snowy Owl Inn, Waterville Valley Resort 03215 ....(603)236-8371

Wentworth
Hobson House, Town Common 03282 ....(603)764-9460
Wentworth Inn, Ellsworth Hill Rd, Off Rt 25 03282 ....(603)764-9923

West Chesterfield
Chesterfield Inn 03466 ....(603)256-3211

West Franklin
Maria Atwood Inn, RFD 2, Rt 3a 03235 ....(603)934-3666

Westmoreland
Partridge Brook Inn, Hatt Rd, PO Box 151 03467 ....(603)399-4994

Whitefield
The 1875 Mountain Inn, The Dieterichs 03598 ....(603)837-2220
Kimball Hill Inn, Kimball Hill Rd, PO Box 03264 03598 ...(603)837-2284

Wilmont Flat
Limner Haus, Box 126 03233 ....(603)526-6451

Wilton Center
Stepping Stones, RFD #1, Box 208 03086 ....(603)654-9048

Wolfeboro
Lakeview Inn, Rt 109 N Main St 03894
Tuc'Me Inn, PO 657 03894 ....(603)569-5702

Woodsville
Green Pastures Farm, RFD #1, Box 42 03785 ....(603)747-2802

New Jersey

Andover
Hudson Guide Farm 07821 ....(201)398-2679

Avon-By-The-Sea
Cashelmara Inn, 22 Lakeside Ave 07717 ....(201)776-8727

Avon-by-the-Sea
Sands Of Avon, 42 Sylvania Ave 07717 ....(201)776-8386

Basking Ridge
Old Mill Inn, PO Box 423 07920 ....(201)221-1100

Bay Head
Bay Head Sands, 2 Twilight Rd 08742 ....(201)899-7016
Conover's Bay Head Inn, 646 Main Ave 08742 ....(201)892-4664

Beach Haven
Barque, 117 Centre St 08008 ....(609)492-5539
Green Gables, 212 Centre St 08008 ....(609)492-3553
Magnolia House, 215 Centre St 08008 ....(609)492-0398
St. Rita Hotel, 127 Engleside 08008 ....(609)492-9192

Cape May
The Abbey, Columbia Ave & Gurney St 08204 ....(609)884-4506
Abigail Adams B&B, 12 Jackson St 08204 ....(609)884-1371
Albert G. Stevens Inn, 127 Myrtle Ave 08204 ....(609)884-4717
Alexander's Inn, 653 Washington St 08204 ....(609)884-2555
Barnard-Good House, 238 Perry St 08204 ....(609)884-5381
Bell Shields House, 501 Hughes St 08204 ....(609)884-8512

New Jersey (Continued)

Brass Bed Inn, 719 Columbia Ave 08204 ....(609)884-8075
Captain Mey's Inn, 202 Ocean St 08204 ....(609)884-7793
The Chalfonte, 301 Howard St 08204 ....(609)884-8409
COLVMNS by the Sea, 1513 Beach Dr 08204 ....(609)884-2228
Delsea, 621 Columbia Ave 08204 ....(609)884-8540
Dormer House, International, 800 Columbia Ave 08204 (609)884-7446
Duke of Windsor Inn, 817 Washington St 08204 ....(609)884-1355
Gingerbread House, 28 Gurney St 08204 ....(609)884-0211
Hanson House, 111 Ocean St 08204
Heirloom B&B, 601 Columbia Ave 08204 ....(609)884-1666
Holly House, 20 Jackson St 08204 ....(609)884-7365
Humphrey Hughes House, 29 Ocean St 08204 ....(609)884-4428
John F. Craig House, 609 Columbia Ave 08204 ....(609)884-0100
Mainstay Inn & Cottage, 635 Columbia Ave 08204 ....(609)884-8690
Manse Inn, 510 Hughes St 08204 ....(609)884-0116
The Mason Cottage, 625 Columbia Ave 08204 ....(609)884-3358
Mooring, 801 Stockton Ave 08204 ....(609)884-5425
Perry Street Inn, 29 Perry St 08204 ....(609)884-4590
Poor Richard's Inn, 17 Jackson St 08204 ....(609)884-3536
The Queen Victoria, 102 Ocean St 08204 ....(609)884-8702
Sand Castle Guest House, 829 Stockton Ave 08204 ....(609)884-5451
Seventh Sister Guesthouse, 10 Jackson St 08204 ....(609)884-2280
Springside, 18 Jackson St 08204 ....(609)884-2654
Summer Cottage Inn, 613 Columbia Ave 08204 ....(609)884-4948
The Manor House, 612 Hughes St 08204 ....(609)884-4710
Victorian Rose, 719 Columbia Ave 08204 ....(609)884-2497
Victorian Lace Inn, 901 Stockton Ave 08204 ....(609)884-1772
White House Inn, 831 Beach Dr 08204 ....(609)884-5329
Windward House, 24 Jackson St 08204 ....(609)884-3368
The Wooden Rabbit, 609 Hughes St 08204 ....(609)884-7293
Woodleigh House, 808 Washington St 08204 ....(609)884-7123

Chester
Publick House Inn, 111 Main St 07930 ....(201)879-6878

Dennisville
Henry Ludlum Inn, RD 3 Box 298 08270 ....(609)861-5847

Flemington
Jerica Hill B&B Inn, 96 Broad St 08822 ....(201)782-8234

Frenchtown
National Hotel, 31 Race St 08825 ....(201)996-4871
Old Hunterdon House, 12 Bridge St 08825 ....(201)996-3632

Island Heights
Studio Of John F. Peto, 102 Cedar Ave 08732 ....(201)270-6058

Lambertville
Chimney Hill Farm 08530 ....(609)397-1516
Coryell House, 44 Coryell St 08530 ....(609)397-2750
York Street House, 42 York St 08530

Longport
Winchester Hotel, 1 S 24 St 08403 ....(609)822-0623

Lyndhurst
The Jeremiah J. Yereance House, 410 Riverside 07071 ....(201)438-9457

Milford
Chesnut Hill, PO Box N, 63 Church St 08848 ....(201)995-9761

Montclair
Marboro Inn, 334 Grove St 07042 ....(201)783-5300

Ocean Grove
Cordova, 26 Webb Ave 07756 ....(201)774-3084
Keswick Inn, 32 Embury Ave 07756 ....(201)775-7506
Pine Tree Inn, 10 Main Ave 07756 ....(201)775-3264

Ocean View
Major Gandy's, 180 Shore Rd 08230

Red Bank
Shaloum Guest House, 119 Tower Hill 07701 ....(201)530-7759

Seagirt
Holly Harbor Guest House, 112 Baltimore Blvd. 08750 ....(201)449-9731

Spring Lake
Ashling Cottage, 106 Sussex Ave 07762 ....(201)449-3553
Chateau, 500 Warren Ave 07762 ....(201)974-2000
Johnson House, 25 Tuttle Ave 07762 ....(201)449-1860
Kenilworth, 1505 Ocean Ave 07762 ....(201)449-5327
The Normandy Inn, 21 Tuttle Ave 07762 ....(201)449-7172
Sandpiper Hotel, 7 Atlantic Ave 07762 ....(201)449-6060
Sea Crest-Spring Lake, 19 Tuttle Ave 07762 ....(201)449-9031
Stone Post Inn, 115 Washington Ave 07762 ....(201)449-1212
Victoria House, 214 Monmouth Ave 07762 ....(201)974-1882
Warren Hotel, 901 Ocean Ave 07762 ....(201)449-8800

Stanhope
Whistling Swan Inn, Box 791, 110 Main Street 07874 ....(201)347-6369

Stockton
Colligan's Stockton Inn, Rt 29 08559 ....(609)397-1250
Woolverton Inn, 6 Woolverton Rd 08559 ....(609)397-0802

Woodbine
Henry Ludlam Inn, 124 S Delsea Dr, RD 3 Box 298 08270 ....(609)861-5847

New Mexico

Albuquerque
Adobe and Roses B&B, 1011 Ortega NW 87114 ....(505)898-0654
Casita Chamisa, 850 Chamisal Rd NW 87107 ....(505)897-4644
W.E. Mauger Estate, 701 Roma Ave NW 87102 ....(505)242-8755

Alcalde
Hacienda de Los Luceros, PO Box 489 87511 ....(505)852-4717

Chimayo
Hacienda Rancho De Chimayo, Box 11 State Rd 520 87522 ....(505)351-2222
La Posada De Chimayo, Box 463 87522 ....(505)351-4605

Cloudcroft
The Lodge, PO Box 497 88317 ....(505)682-2566

Galisteo
Galisteo Inn, Box 4 87540 ....(505)982-1506

Glenwood
La Casita, Rt 10, Box 440 88039
Los Olmos Guest Ranch, PO Box 127 88039 ....(505)539-2311

Kingston
Black Range Lodge, Star Rt 2, Box 119 88042 ....(505)895-5652

Las Cruces
Inn Of The Arts, 618 S Alameda Blvd 88005 ....(505)526-3327
Llewellyn House, 618 S Alameda 88005 ....(505)526-3327

Lincoln
Wortley Hotel, Box 96 88338 ....(505)653-4500

Los Alamos
Los Alamos B&B, PO Box 1212 87544 ....(505)662-6041
Walnut Executive Suite, PO Box 777 87544 ....(505)662-9392

Mesilla
Meson de Mesilla, PO Box 1212 88046 ....(505)525-9212

Mesilla Park
Elms, PO Box 1176 88001 ....(505)524-1513

Nogal
Monjeau Shadows Inn, Bonito Rt 88341 ....(505)336-4191

Pilar
The Plum Tree, Box 1-a, Rt 68 87571 ....(505)758-4696

Placitas
Hacienda de Las Munecas, PO Box 564 87043 ....(505)867-3255

Ranchos de Taos
Ranchos Ritz B&B, PO Box 669 87557 ....(505)758-2640
Two Pipes, Box 52, Talpa Rt 87557 ....(505)758-4770

Red River
El Western Lodge, Box 301, Gilt Edge Tr 87558 ....(505)754-2272

Santa Fe
Adobe Guest House, PO Box 266 87504 ....(505)983-9481
El Paradero, 220 W Manhattan 87501 ....(505)988-1177
Grant Corner Inn, 122 Grant Ave 87501 ....(505)983-6678
Hotel St. Francis, 210 Don Gaspar Ave 87501 ....(505)983-5700
Inn of the Animal Tracks, 707 Paseo de Peralta 87501 ....(505)988-1546
Inn on the Alameda, 303 E Alameda 87501
La Posada de Santa Fe, 330 E Palace Ave 87501 ....(800)621-7231
Polly's Guest House, 410 Camino Don Miguel 87501
Preston House, 106 Faithway St 87501 ....(505)982-3465
Pueblo Bonito, 138 W Manhattan 87501 ....(505)984-8001
The Rim House, Box 1537 87501

Talpa
Blue Door B&B, La Maranda Rd, Box 1168 87571 ....(505)758-8360

Taos
American Artists Guest House, PO Box 584 87571 ....(505)758-4446
Dasburg House & Studio, Box 2764 87571 ....(505)758-9513

Gallery House West, E Kit Carson Rd, PO Box 2983 87571 ....(505)758-8001
Hacienda del Sol, 109 Mabel Dodge Ln, Box 177 87571 .(505)758-0287
Hotel Edelweiss, PO Box 83 87571 ....(505)776-2301
La Posada De Taos, 309 Juanita Ln, PO Box 1118 87571 .(505)758-8164
Las Palomas Conf. Center, Box 6689 87571 ....(505)758-9456
Mabel Dodge Lujan House, PO Box 3400 87571 ....(505)758-9456
Silvertree Inn, PO Box 1528 87571 ....(505)758-3071
The Taos Inn, 125 Paseo del Pueblo Norte 87571 ....(505)758-2233

Taos Ski Valley
Amizette Inn, PO Box 756 87571 ....(505)265-6777

Truchas
Rancho Arriba B&B, PO Box 338 87578 ....(505)689-2374

New York

Afton
Jericho Farm Inn, 155 E Main St 13730

Albany
Mansion Hill Inn & Restaurant, 115 Philip St 12202 ....(518)465-2038

Altamont
Appel Inn, Rte 146 12009 ....(518)861-6557

Amagansett
Mill Garth Mews, PO Box 700 11930 ....(516)267-3757

Amenia
Troutbeck, Box 26, Leedsville Rd 12501 ....(914)373-9681

Auburn
Springside Inn, Box 520 13021 ....(315)252-7247

Averill Park
Ananas Hus B&B, Rt 3 Box 301 12018 ....(518)766-5035
The Gregory House, PO Box 401 12018 ....(518)674-3774

Avon
Mulligan Farm, 5403 Barber Rd 14414

Bainbridge
Berry Hill Farm, Box 128, RD #1 13733

Bath
Wheeler B&B, RD 2 Box 455 14810 ....(607)776-6756

Bellport, Long Islan
The Great South Bay Inn, 160 S County Rd 11713 ....(516)286-8588

Boonville
Greenmeadow, RD 3 13309

Branchport
Four Seasons B&B, 470 W Lake Rd 14418 ....(607)868-4686

Brookfield
Gates Hill Homestead, Dugway Rd, Box 96 13314 ....(315)899-5837

Buffalo
Linwood House, 242 Linwood 14209 ....(716)882-6116

Burdett
The Red House Country Inn, Picnic Area Rd 14818 ....(607)546-8566

Cadyville
Martins' B&B, PO Box 84 12918 ....(518)293-7006

Cairo
Glen Durham, Rt 2 Box 816 12413

Cambridge
Lillybrook Manor, 9 Ave A 12816 ....(518)677-5028

Canaan
Inn At Shaker Mill Farm, Cherry Ln 12029 ....(518)794-9345
The Lace House, Rt 22 At Tunnel Hill Rd 12029 ....(518)781-4669

Canandaigua
Cricket Club Tearoom, 4510 Bristol Valley Rd 14424 ....(716)229-5343
Inn At Still Woode, 131 East St 14424 ....(716)394-0504
Nottingham Lodge B&B, 5741 Bristol Valley Rd 14424 ....(716)374-5355
Oliver Phelps Country Inn, 252 N Main St 14424 ....(716)396-1650
Wilder Tavern B&B, 5648 N Bloomfield Rd 14424 ....(716)394-8132

Canaseraga
The Country House, 37 Mill St 14822 ....(607)545-6439

Candor
Edge Of Thyme, 6 Main St 13743 ....(607)659-5155

Cazenovia
Brae Loch Inn, 5 Albany St, US Rt 20 13035 ....(315)655-3431
Lincklaen House, 79 Albany St 13035 ....(315)655-8171

Central Valley
Gasho Inn, Rt 32 10917

Chautauqua
Longfellow Inn, 11 Roberts Ave Box Y 14722 ....(716)357-2285

Chestertown
Balsam House Inn, Atateka Dr,rr1,box 365 12817 ....(518)494-2828
The Friends Lake Inn, Friends Lake Rd 12817 ....(518)494-4251

Clarence
Asa Ransom House, 10529 Main St 14031 ....(716)759-2315

Clayton
Thousand Islands Inn, 335 Riverside Dr 13624 ....(315)686-3030

Clinton
Lewago Hall, 68 College St 13323
Victorian Carriage House, 46 Williams St 13323

Cobleskill
The Gables, 62 W Main 12043

Cold Brook
Grand Inn, Stormy Hill Rd 13324 ....(315)826-7677

Cold Spring
Hudson House, 2 Main St 10516 ....(914)265-9355
One Market Street, 1 Market St 10516
The Old Post Inn, 43 Main St 10516

Cooperstown
Angelholm, PO Box 705, 14 Elm St 13326 ....(607)547-2483
Cooper Inn, PO Box 311 13326 ....(607)547-2567
The Inn at Cooperstown, 16 Chestnut St 13326 ....(607)547-5756
Creekside B&B, RD 1 Box 206 13326 ....(607)547-8203
Hickory Grove Inn, Rt 80 At Six Mile Pt 13326 ....(607)547-8100
Inn at Brook Willow Farm, Rt 33, RD2, Box 514 13326
The Inn at Mill Pond, PO Box 167 13326 ....(315)858-1654
The J. P. Sillhouse, 63 Chestnut St 13326

Corning
Cecce Guest House, 166 Chemung St 14830 ....(607)962-5682
Rosewood Inn, 134 E First St 14830 ....(607)962-3253
Victoria House, 222 Pine St 14830 ....(607)962-3413
White Birch, 69 E First 14830 ....(607)962-6355

Craryville
The Crary House, Rt 23, Box 209 12521 ....(518)325-5888

Cuba
33 South, 33 South St 14727 ....(716)968-1387

Davenport
The Davenport Inn, Main St 13750 ....(607)278-5068

Dolgeville
Adrianna B&B, 44 Stewart St 13329 ....(315)429-3249

Dryden
Margaret Thacher's Spruce Haven B&B, 9 James St, PO Box 119 13053 ....(607)844-8052
Sarah's Dream, 49 W Main St, PO Box 970 13053 ....(607)844-4321

Dundee
1819 Red Brick Inn, Box 57A 14837 ....(607)243-8844
Country Manor B&B, 4798 Dundee-Himrod Rd 14837 ....(607)243-8628
Lakeside Terrace B&B, 660 E Waneta Lake Rd 14837 ....(607)292-6606
Willow Cove, 77 South Glenora Rd, RD 1 Box 8 14837 ....(607)243-8482

East Aurora
Roycroft Inn, 40 S Grove St 14052 ....(716)652-9030

East Hampton
1770 House, 143 Main St 11937 ....(516)324-1770
Huntting Inn, 94 Main St 11937 ....(516)324-0410
Maidstone Arms, 207 Main St 11937 ....(516)324-5006
Mill House Inn, 33 N Main St 11937 ....(516)324-9766

Elka Park
Redcoat's Return, Dale Ln 12427 ....(518)589-6379
Windswept, County Rd 16 12427 ....(518)589-6275

Fleischmanns
Runaway Inn, Main St 12430 ....(914)254-5660

Fly Creek
Breezy Knoll, RFD #1 Box 18 13337 ....(607)547-8362

Forestburgh
The Inn at Lake Joseph, PO Box 81 12777 ....(914)791-9506

Frankfort
B&B Leatherstocking, 399 Brockway Rd 13340
Blueberry Hill, 389 Brockway Rd 13340 ....(315)733-0040

Fredonia
1865 Vintage Inn, 435 E Main St 14063 ....(716)673-1865

New York (Continued)

Fulton
Battle Island Inn, RD 1 Box 176 13069 ....(315)598-3985
Garrison
Bird & Bottle Inn, Rt 9 10524 ....(914)424-3000
Garrison Landing
The Golden Eagle Inn 10524
Geneseo
American House, 39 Main St 14454 ....(716)243-5483
Geneva
The Inn at Belhurst Castle, PO 609 14456 ....(315)781-0201
Geneva On The Lake, 1001 Lochland Rd 14456 ....(315)789-7190
The Cobblestones, Rt 2 14456
Gilbertsville
Leatherstocking Trails, RD 1 Box 40 13776 ....(607)783-2757
Gilboa
Windy Ridge B&B, S Gilboa Rd, Start Rd 01276 ....(607)588-6039
Glens Falls
The Crislip's B&B, RD 1 Box 57, Ridge Rd 12801 ....(518)793-6869
Gowanda
The Teepee, RFD #1 Box 543 14070 ....(716)532-2168
Greenport
Randy Wade, Box 5 11944
Greenville
Greenville Arms, South St 12083 ....(518)966-5219
Groton
Benn Conger Inn, 206 W Cortland 13073 ....(607)898-5817
Hadley
Highclere Inn, PO Box 179 12835 ....(518)696-2861
Halcottsville
Lake Wawaka Guest House, Old River Rd 12438 ....(607)326-4694
Hammondsport
Bowman's B&B, 61 Lake St, PO Box 586 14840 ....(607)569-2516
Laufersweller, 11 William St 14840 ....(607)569-3402
Hempstead
Duvall B&B, 237 Cathedral Ave 11550 ....(516)292-9219
Tara II B&B, 16 St Pauls Pl 11550 ....(516)292-0332
Henderson Harbor
Gill House Inn 13651
Herkimer
Bellinger Woods, 611 W German St 13350
Heuvelton
Oswegatchie B&B, Box 322 13654 ....(315)393-0780
High Falls
Captain Schoonmaker's House, Rt 2 Box 37 12440 ....(914)687-7946
House On The Hill, Box 86 12440
Highland
Monica Hunter, Pancake Hollow Rd, RD 2 Box 561 12528
Hillsdale
L'hostellerie Bressane, Corner Rts 22 & 23 12529
Howes Cave
Cavern View, RD #1 Box 23 12092
Hyde Park
Fala B&B, E Market St 12538 ....(914)229-5937
Ilion
Chesham Place, 317 W Main St 13357 ....(315)894-3552
Irvington-on-Hudson
Shadowbrook B&B, 821 N Broadway 10533 ....(914)591-9291
Ithaca
Buttermilk Falls, 110 E Buttermilk Falls Rd 14850 ....(607)273-3947
Falconer Inn, 140 College Ave 14850 ....(607)272-0919
Glendale Farm, 224 Bostwick Rd 14850 ....(607)272-8756
Rose Inn, Rt 34 N, Box 6576 14851-6576 ....(607)533-7905
Keene
The Bark Eater, Alstead Mill Rd 12942 ....(518)576-2221
Keeseville
Bosworth Tavern, Rt 9/Mace Chasm Rd Box 177 12944 ....(518)834-5401
Kingston
Rondout B&B, 88 W Chester St 12401
Lake Luzerne
Lamplight Inn, PO Box 70, 2129 Lake Ave (9N) 12846 ....(518)696-5294
Lake Placid
Highland House Inn, 3 Highland Pl 12946 ....(518)523-2377
The Stagecoach Inn, Old Military Rd 12946
Lansing
The Bay Horse B&B, 813 Ridge Rd 14882 ....(607)533-4612
The Federal House B&B, 175 Ludlowville Rd 14882
Leroy
Edson House, 7856 Griswold Circle 14482 ....(716)768-2340
Lewiston
The Peter House, 175 S Fourth St 14092 ....(716)754-8877
Little Valley
Napoli Stagecoach Inn 14755
Livingston Manor
Lanza's Country Inn, RD 2 Box 446, Shandelee Rd 12758 ....(914)439-5070
Lockport
Chestnut Ridge Inn, 7205 Chestnut Ridge 14094 ....(716)439-9124
Lowville
Hill Top B&B, RFD #1, Box 14 13367 ....(315)376-6364
Macedon
Iris Farm, 162 Hook Rd 14502 ....(315)986-4536
Margaretville
Margaretville Mountain Inn, Margaretville Mountain Rd 12455 ....(914)586-3933
Mattituck
Mattituck B&B, 795 Pike St 11952 ....(516)298-8785
North Fork B&B, 7015 Wickham Ave, PO Box 2 11952 ....(516)298-8293
Mayville
Plumbush B&B at Chautauqua, Chautauqua - Stedman Rd, Box 332 14757 ....(716)789-5309
The Village Inn, 111 S Erie St 14757 ....(716)753-3583
Mcgraw
Tinell's Hathaway House, Rt 41, Box 621 Solon 13101
Milford
Maple Shade B&B, Rt 1 Box 105 13807
Millerton
Simmon's Way Village Inn, Main St, Route 44 12546 ....(518)789-6235
Montauk
Greenhedges Oceanside Villa, Essex St, PO 122 11954 ....(516)668-5013
Mount Tremper
Mt. Tremper Inn, Rt 212 & Wittenberg Rd 12457 ....(914)688-5329
Mumford
Genesee Country Inn, 948 George St 14511 ....(716)538-2500
Naples
Maxfield Inn, 105 N Main 14512
Nelliston
The Historian, Rt 5, Box 224 13410
New Lebanon
New Lebanon Guest House, Rt 20 12125
New Paltz
Ujjala's B&B, 2 Forest Glen 12561 ....(914)255-6360
White House Farm, 211 Phillies Bridge Rd 12561
New York
Adobe B&B, PO Box 20022 10028
Chelsea Inn, 46 W 17th St 10011 ....(212)645-8989
Incentra Village House, 32 8th Ave 10014 ....(212)206-0007
Newfield
The Historic Cook House B&B, 167 Main St 14867 ....(607)564-9926
Newport
Roesler's B&B, RD #1 13416
Nicholville
Chateau L'Esperance, Hwy 11B 12965 ....(315)328-4669
North Hudson
Pine Tree Inn, PO Box 555 12855 ....(518)532-9255
Olcott
Bayside Guest House, Box 34 14126
Oneida
The Pollyanna, 302 Main St 13421 ....(315)363-0524
Ontario
The Tummonds House, 5392 Walworth/Ontario Rd 14519 ....(315)524-5381
Owego
Thompson Park House, 118 Front St 13827 ....(607)687-4323
Painted Post
Dannfield, 50 Canada Rd 14870

Palenville
Arlington House B&B, Main St Box 1 12463 ....(518)678-9081
Palmyra
Canaltown, 119 Canandaigua St 14522
Penn Yan
Finton's Landing, 661 E Lake Rd 14527 ....(315)536-3146
Fox Run Vineyards B&B, 670 Rte 14 RD 1 14527
On the Beach, 191 W Lake Rd 14527 ....(315)536-4646
The Wagener Estate B&B, 351 Elm St 14527 ....(315)536-4591
Pine Bush
Jane Whiteman B&B, RFD #3, Box 455 12566 ....(914)733-1324
Pittsford
Oliver Loud's Inn, 1474 Marsh Rd 14534 ....(716)248-5200
Plattsburgh
Sunny Side Up B&B, Butler Rd, Box 58 12901 ....(518)563-5677
Port Henry
Elk Inn, HCR #1 Box 87 12974 ....(518)546-7024
Port Jervis
Educators Inn East, 23 Hudson St 12771 ....(914)856-5543
Portageville
Genesee Falls Hotel, Rt 436 14536 ....(716)493-2484
Poughkeepsie
Inn At The Falls, 50 Red Oaks Mill Rd 12603
Pulaski
The Way Inn, 7377 Salina St 13142 ....(315)298-6073
Purling
Shepherd's Croft, HC Box 263 12470
Red Hook
The Red Hook Inn, 31 S Broadway 12571 ....(914)758-8445
Rensselaer
The Tibbitts House, 100 Columbia Turnpike 12144
Rensselaerville
Sweet Meadow Farm, HC-1 Box 4 12147 ....(518)797-3158
Rhinebeck
Beekman Arms, Rt 9, 4 Mill St 12572 ....(914)876-7077
The Jacob Kip
River House B&B, Long Dock Rd 12572 ....(914)876-8330
Kipp River House, Long Dock Rd 12572
Village Victorian Inn, 31 Center St 12572 ....(914)876-8345
Richfield Springs
Country Manor B&B, 50 E Main St, Rt 20 13439 ....(315)858-2561
Jonathan House, 39 E Main 13439
Summerwood B&B, PO Box 388 13439 ....(315)858-2024
Riverhead
The Libby House, Box 343 11901
Rochester
Strawberry Castle B&B, 1883 Penfield Rd, Rt 441 14526 (716)385-3266
The Rose Mansion & Gardens, 625 Mt Hope Ave 14620
Rock City Falls
The Mansion, Rt 29 Box 77 12863 ....(518)885-1607
Rock Stream
Vintage View B&B, 3975 Rt 14A Box 87 14878 ....(607)535-7909
Rome
Maplecrest B&B, 6480 Williams Rd 13440 ....(315)337-0070
Rosendale
Astoria Hotel, 25 Main St 12472 ....(914)658-8201
Roxbury
Scudder Hill House, Scudder Hill Rd 12474 ....(607)326-4215
Rushford
Klartag Farms B&B, West Branch Rd, PO Box 98 14777-0098
....................(716)437-2946
Sandy Creek
Pink House Inn, 9125 S Main St 13145 ....(315)387-3276
Saranac Lake
The Point, Star Route 12983 ....(518)891-5674
Saratoga Springs
Adelphi Hotel, 365 Broadway 12866 ....(518)587-4688
The Westchester House, 102 Lincoln Ave, PO Box 944 12866
....................(518)587-7613
Saugerties
High Woods Inn, 7472 Glasco Turnpike 12477 ....(914)246-8655
Schuylerville
Inn on Bacon Hill, 200 Wall Street 12871 ....(518)695-3693
Seneca Falls
Locustwood Country Inn, 3568 Rt 89 13148
Shandaken
Two Brooks B&B, Rt 42 12480
Shelter Island
Chequit Inn, 23 Grand Ave 11965 ....(516)749-0018
The Bowditch House, 166 N Ferry Rd 11965
Skaneateles
Sherwood Inn, 26 W Genesee St 13152 ....(315)685-3405
Sodus
Maxwell Creek Inn, 7563 Lake Rd 14551 ....(315)483-2222
Sodus Point
Carriage House Inn, 8375 Wickham Blvd 14555 ....(315)483-2100
South Dayton
Town & Country B&B, Pine St, PO Box 208 14138 ....(716)988-3340
Southampton
Country Inn, 200 Hill St 11968
The Old Post House Inn, 136 Main St 11968 ....(516)283-1717
Village Latch, 101 Hill St 11968 ....(503)283-2160
Southold
Goose Creek Guesthouse, 1475 Waterview Dr 11971 ....(516)765-3356
Spencertown
Spencertown Guests, Box 122, Elm St & Rt 203 12165 ....(518)392-2358
Stephentown
Kirkmead, Box 169A 12168 ....(518)733-5420
Millhof Inn, Rt 43 12168
Stone Ridge
Baker's B&B, Rt 2 Box 80 12484
Hasbrouck House Inn, PO Box 76 12484 ....(914)687-0055
Stony Brook
Three Village Inn, 150 Main St 11790 ....(516)751-0555
Tannersville
The Eggery Inn, County Rd 16 12485 ....(518)589-5363
Ticonderoga
Bonnie View Acres B&B, Canfield Rd 12883 ....(518)585-6098
Troy
Diane's B&B, 108 Second St 12180 ....(518)474-0345
Trumansburg
Sage Cottage, Box 121 14886
Turin
Towpath Inn, Box E 13473 ....(315)348-8122
Vernon
Lavender Inn, RD #1, Box 325 13476
Wappingers Falls
Castle Hill B&B, Box 325 12590 ....(914)298-8000
Warrensburg
White House Lodge, 53 Main St 12885 ....(518)623-3640
Waterloo
The Historic James R. Webster Mansion, 115 E Main St - Rts 5 & 20
13165 ....(315)539-3032
The Front Porch Antiques B&B, 1248 Rts 5/20 13165 ....(315)539-8325
Waterville
B&B in Waterville, 211 White St 13480 ....(315)841-8295
Watkins Glen
The Victorian, 216 N Madison Ave 14891 ....(607)535-6582
Webster
Country Schoolhouse, 336 Basket Rd 14580 ....(716)265-0963
Westfield
Westfield House, E Main Rd, PO Box 505 14787 ....(716)326-6262
The William Seward Inn, RD 2, S Portage Rd, Rt 394 14787
....................(716)326-4151
Westhampton Beach
1880 Seafield House, 2 Seafield Lane 11978 ....(516)288-1559
Windham
Albergo Allegria B&B, Rt 296 12496 ....(518)734-5560

North Carolina

Andrews
Walker Inn, 39 Junaluska Rd 28901 ....(704)321-5019
Asheville
Albemarle Inn, 86 Edgemont Rd 28801 ....(704)255-0027
Cedar Crest Victorian Inn, 674 Biltmore Ave 28803 ....(704)252-1389
Cornerstone Inn, 230 Pearson Dr 28801 ....(704)253-5644
Flint Street Inn, 100 & 116 Flint St 28801 ....(704)253-6723

North Carolina (Continued)

Heritage Hill, 64 Linden Ave 28801 ....(704)254-9336
The Old Reynolds Mansion, 100 Reynolds Hgts 28804 ..(704)254-0496
Ray House, 83 Hillside St 28801 ....(704)252-0106
Reed House B&B, 119 Dodge St 28803 ....(704)274-1604
Richmond Hill Inn
& Conference Center, 87 Richmond Hill Dr 28806 ....(704)252-7313
The Grove Park Inn & Country Club, 290 Macon Ave 28804
....................(704)252-2711
The Lion & The Rose, 276 Montford Ave 28801 ....(704)255-7673

Balsam
Balsam Lodge, Box 279, Valley Dr 28707 ....(704)456-6528

Banner Elk
Archers Inn, Rt 2 Box 56-a 28604 ....(704)898-9004
Mountain Chateau, Rt 1, Box 426 28604 ....(704)963-6593

Bat Cave
Old Mill Inn, PO Box 252, Hwy 64/74 28710 ....(701)625-4256
Original Hickory Nut Gap Inn, PO Box 246 28710 ....(704)625-9108
Stonehearth Inn, Rte 74, PO Box 9 28710 ....(704)625-9990

Bath
Bath Guest House, S Main St 27808 ....(919)923-6811

Beaufort
Belford House B&B, 129 Craven St 28516 ....(919)728-6031
Captains' Quarters
Bed & Biscuit, 315 Ann St 28516 ....(919)728-7711
Cedars at Beaufort, 305 Front St 28516 ....(919)728-7036
Inlet Inn, 601 Front at Queen St 28516 ....(919)728-3600
Langdon House, 135 Craven St 28516 ....(919)728-5499
The Shotgun House, 406 Ann St, Box 833 28516

Belhaven
River Forest Manor, 600 E Main St 28710 ....(919)943-2151

Black Mountain
The Blackberry Inn, Box 965 28711 ....(704)669-8303
Over Yonder B&B, 269 N Fork Rd 28711 ....(704)669-6762
Red Rocker Inn, 3888 40 Way S. 28711

Blowing Rock
Hound Ears Lodge & Club, PO Box 188 28605 ....(704)963-4321
Maple Lodge, PO Box 66, Sunset Drive 28605 ....(704)295-3331
Meadowbrook Inn, Box 2005 28605 ....(704)295-9341
Ragged Garden B&B, Box 1927 28605 ....(704)295-9703
Sunshine Inn, Box 528 28605

Brevard
Pines Country Inn, 719 Hart Rd 28768 ....(704)877-3131
Red House Inn, 412 W Probart St 28712 ....(704)884-9349
The Inn At Brevard, 410 E Main St 28712 ....(704)884-2105
Womble Inn, 301 W Main St 28712 ....(704)884-4770

Bryson City
Folkestone Inn, 767 W Deep Creek Rd 28713 ....(704)488-2730
Fryemont Inn, PO Box 459 28713 ....(704)488-2159
Nantahala Village, PO Drawer J 28713 ....(704)488-2826
Randolph House, PO Box 816 28713 ....(704)488-3472

Burnsville
Nu-Wray Inn, PO Box 156 28714 ....(704)682-2329

Chapel Hill
Caroline Inn, Box 1110 27514 ....(919)933-2001
Hillcrest House, 209 Hillcrest Rd 27514 ....(919)942-2369
Pineview Inn & Conference Center, Rt 10, Box 265 27514 (919)967-7166
The Inn At Bingham School, PO Box 267 27514

Charlotte
Fourth Ward B&B, 523 N Poplar St 28226 ....(704)334-1485
Hampton Manor, 3327 Carmel Rd 28211
The Homeplace B&B, 5901 Sardis Rd 28226 ....(704)365-1936
Inn On Providence, 6700 Providence Rd 28105 ....(704)366-6700
Morehead Inn, 1122 E Morehead St 28204 ....(704)376-3357
Overcarsh House, 326 W Eighth St 28202 ....(704)334-8477

Chimney Rock
Esmeralda Inn, Box 57 28720 ....(704)625-9105
Gingerbread Inn, PO Box 187, Hwy 74 28720 ....(704)625-4038

Clemmons
Tanglewood Manor, PO Box 1040 27012 ....(919)766-0591

Clinton
The Shield House, 216 Sampson St 28328 ....(919)592-2634

Dillsboro
Jarrett House, PO Box 219 28725 ....(704)586-9964
Squire Watkins Inn, Haywood Road, Box 430 28725 ....(704)586-5244

duck
Sanderling Inn, SR Box 319Y 27949 ....(919)261-4111

Durham
Arrowhead Inn, 106 Mason Rd 27712 ....(919)477-8430
The Blooming Garden, 513 Holloway St 27701

Edenton
The Lords Proprietors' Inn, 300 N Broad St 27932 ....(919)482-3641
Mulberry Hill, R7 D4 27923 ....(919)482-4175
Trestle House Inn, Rt 4 Box 370 27932 ....(919)482-2282

Flat Rock
Woodfield Inn, PO Box 98 28731 ....(704)693-6016

Franklin
Buttonwood Inn, 190 Georgia Road 28734 ....(704)369-8985
Franklin Terrace, 67 Harrison Ave 28734 ....(704)524-7907
Lullwater Farmhouse Inn, Rt 5, Box 540 28734 ....(704)524-6532
Poor Richards Summit Inn, PO Box 511 28734 ....(704)524-2006

Glendale Springs
Glendale Springs Inn 28629 ....(919)982-2102

Glenville
Mountain High, Big Ridge Rd 28736 ....(704)743-3094

Graham
Leftwich House, 215 E Harden St 27253 ....(919)226-5978

Greensboro
College Hill B&B, 922 Carr St 27403 ....(919)274-6829
Greenwich Inn, 111 W Washington 27401 ....(919)272-3474
Greenwood B&B, 205 N Park Dr 27401 ....(919)274-6350
Powhatan Condominiums, 906 W Market St 27401
The Erwin & Clark House, 214 S Mendenhall St 27401

Henderson
La Grange Plantation Inn, Rt 3 Box 610 27536 ....(919)438-2421

Hendersonville
Claddagh Inn at Hendersonville, 755 N Main St 28739 .(800)225-4700
Echo Mountain Inn, 2849 Laurel Park Hwy 28739
The Waverly Inn, 783 N Main St 28739 ....(800)537-8195

Hertford
Gingerbread Inn, 103 S Church St 27944 ....(919)426-5809

Hickory
The Hickory B&B, 464 7th St Sw 28602 ....(704)324-0548

High Point
Premier B&B Inn, 1001 Johnson St 27262 ....(919)889-8349

Highlands
Colonial Pines Inn, Hickory St, PO Box 2309 28741 ....(704)526-2060
Highlands Inn, PO Box 1030 28741 ....(704)526-9380
Old Edwards Inn, 4th & Main St 28741 ....(704)526-5036
Phelp's House, Main St, Rt 1, Box 55 28741

Hillsborough
Colonial Inn, 153 W King St 27278 ....(919)732-2461
Inn At Teardrop, West King St 27278 ....(919)732-1120

Kill Devil Hills
Ye Olde Cherokee Inn, 500 N Virginia Dare Trail 27948 (919)441-6127

Lake Junaluska
Brookside Lodge, 7 Lakeshore Dr 28745 ....(704)456-8897
Providence Lodge, 1 Atkins Loop 28745 ....(704)456-6486
Sunset Inn, 21 N. Lakeshore Dr 28745 ....(704)456-6114

Lake Lure
Fairfield Mountains, Rt 1, Buffalo Rd 28746 ....(704)625-9111
Lodge On Lake Lure, Rt 1 Box 529 28746 ....(704)625-2789

Lake Toxaway
Greystone Inn, Greystone Lane 28747 ....(704)966-4700

Lexington
Lawrences, Rt 1, Box 641 27292 ....(704)249-1114

Maggie Valley
Cataloochee Ranch, Rt 1 Box 500 28751 ....(704)926-1401
Mountainbrook Inn, PO Box 565, Hwy 19 28751 ....(704)926-3962

Mars Hill
Baird House, 121 S Main St 28754 ....(704)689-5722

Marshall
Marshall House, Box 865 28753 ....(704)649-9205

Milton
Woodside Inn, Box 197 28305 ....(919)234-8646

Mooresville
Oak Ridge Farm B&B, Rt 5, Box 111 28115 ....(704)663-7085

Morehead
Morehead Manor, 107 North 10th Street 28557

Mount Airy
Pine Ridge Inn, 2893 W Pine St 27030 .... (919)789-5034
Nags Head
First Colony Inn, Route 1, Box 748 27959 .... (919)441-2343
New Bern
The Aerie, 509 Pollock St 28560 .... (919)636-5553
Harmony House Inn, 215 Pollock St 28560 .... (919)636-3810
King's Arms Inn, 212 Pollock St 28560 .... (919)638-4409
New Berne House, 709 Broad St 28560 .... (800)842-7688
Ocracoke
The Beach House, Box 443 27960
The Berkley Center
Country Inn, Box 220 27960 .... (919)928-5911
Blackbeard's Lodge, PO Box 37 27960 .... (919)928-3421
Boyette House, PO Box 39 27960 .... (919)928-4261
Island Inn, Box 9 27960
Ships Timbers B&B, Box 10 27960 .... (919)928-6141
Ocracoke Island
Oscar's House, Box 206 27960 .... (919)928-1311
Old Fort
Inn at Old Fort, W Main St, Box 1116 28762 .... (704)668-9384
Oriental
The Tar Heel Inn, 205 Church Street 28571 .... (919)325-2592
Penland
Chinquapin Inn, PO Box 145 28765 .... (704)765-0064
Pilot Mountain
Pilot Knob-A B&B Inn, PO Box 1280 27041 .... (919)325-2502
Pinehurst
Magnolia Inn, Box 266 28374 .... (919)295-6900
Pittsboro
The Fearrington House, Fearrington Village Ctr 27312 .. (919)542-2121
Raleigh
The Oakwood Inn, 411 N Bloodworth St 27604 .... (919)832-9712
Robbinsville
Wilsons Tourist Home, PO Box 47 28771 .... (704)479-8679
Rosman
Red Lion Inn, Star Rt, Box 47 28772 .... (704)884-6868
Salisbury
Rowan Oak House, 208 S.fulton St 28144 .... (704)633-2086
Saluda
Bear Creek Lodge, Rt 1, Box 335 28773 .... (704)749-2272
Orchard Inn, PO Box 725 28773 .... (704)749-5471
Smithfield
Eli Olive's, 3719 US 70 W 27577 .... (919)934-9823
Southern Pines
Jefferson Inn, 150 W New Hampshire Ave 28387 .... (919)692-6400
Southport
Dosher Plantation House B&B, Rt 5 Box 100 28461 .... (919)457-5554
Sparta
Turby Villa, E Whitehead St 28675 .... (919)372-8490
Spruce Pine
The Richmond Inn, 101 Pine Ave 28777 .... (704)765-6993
Tarboro
Little Warren, 304 E Park Ave 27886 .... (919)823-1314
Tryon
L'Auberge of Tryon, PO Box 1251 28782 .... (704)859-6992
Pine Crest Inn, PO Box 1030, 200 Pine Crest Ln 28982 ... (704)859-9135
Stone Hedge Inn, Howard Gap Road, PO Box 366 28782 (704)859-9114
Valle Crucis
Mountainview Chateau, PO Box 723 28691 .... (704)963-6593
Wanchese
C.W. Pugh's B&B, PO Box 427 27981 .... (919)473-5466
Warsaw
The Squire's Vintage Inn, Rt 2 Box 130r 28398 .... (919)473-5466
Washington
Pamlico House, 400 E Main St 27889 .... (919)946-7184
Waynesville
Grandview Lodge, 809 Valley View Cir Rd 28786 .... (704)456-5212
Hallcrest Inn, 299 Halltop Cir 28786 .... (704)456-6457
Haywood Street Inn, 409 Haywood St 28786
The Palmer House B&B, 108 Pigeon St 28786 .... (704)456-7521
Piedmont Inn, 630 Eagle's Nest Rd 28786
The Swag, Rt 2 Box 280-a 28786 .... (704)926-0430
Weaverville
Dry Ridge Inn, 26 Brown St 28787 .... (704)658-3899
Wilmington
Anderson Guest House, 520 Orange St 28401 .... (919)343-8128
Five Star Guest House, 14 N 7th St 28401 .... (919)763-7581
Grayston Guesthouse, 100 S Third St 28401
Inn on Orange, 410 Orange 28401 .... (919)251-0863
James Place B&B, 9 S Fourth St 28401 .... (919)251-0999
Worth House
A Victorian Inn, 412 S Third St 28401 .... (919)762-8562
Wilson
Pilgrims Rest, 600 W Nash St 27893 .... (919)243-4447
Winston-Salem
Brookstown Inn B&B, 200 Brookstown Ave 27101 .... (919)725-1120
Colonel Ludlow Inn, Summit & W 5th 27101 .... (919)777-1887
Salem Inn, 1168 Burke St 27101 .... (919)722-8022

North Dakota

Grand Forks
Lord Bryon, 521 S Fifth 58201 .... (701)775-0194
Kemare
Farm Comfort 58746 .... (701)848-2433
Medora
The Rough Riders 58645 .... (701)623-4444
Stanley
Triple T Ranch, Rt 1, Box 93 58784 .... (701)628-2418

Ohio

Akron
Helen's Hospitality House, 1096 Palmetto Ave 44306 .... (216)724-7151
Portage House, 601 Copley Rd 44320 .... (216)535-9236
Albany
Albany House, 9 Clinton St 45710
Alliance
Aleida's B&B, 119 East College 44601 .... (216)823-1470
Archbold
Murbach House, 504 N Defiance St 43502 .... (419)445-5195
Ashtabula
Michael Cahill B&B, PO Box 3024, 1106 Walnut Blvd 44004
Bellefontaine
Whitmore House, 3985 SR 47W 43311
Bellville
Frederick Fitting House, 72 Fitting Ave 44813 .... (419)886-4283
Rockledge Manor, Rt 3, Possum Run Rd 44813 .... (419)892-3329
Belmont
Victorian B&B, 121 West Main St, Box 233 43718 .... (614)484-4872
Blue Rock
McNutt Farm/Outdoors Lodge, 6120 Cutler Lake Rd 43720
.... (614)674-4555
Centerburg
Otter Fork Hills, 6642 Bennington Chapel Rd 43011 .... (614)893-2467
Centerville
Yesterday B&B, 39 S Main St 45458 .... (513)433-0785
Chillicothe
Chillicothe B&B, 202 S Paint St 45601 .... (614)772-6848
Old McDill-Anderson Place, 3656 Polk Hollow Rd 45601
Vanmeter B&B, 178 Church St 45601 .... (614)774-3510
Cincinnati
Ohio Valley B&B, 7301 Nodding Way 45243
Circleville
The Castle B&B, 610 S Court St 43113 .... (614)477-3986
Cleveland
The Baricelli Inn, 2203 Cornell Rd 44106 .... (216)791-6500
Glidden House, 1901 Ford Dr 44106 .... (216)231-8900
Private Lodging, PO Box 18590 44118 .... (216)321-3213
Tudor House, PO Box 18590 44118 .... (216)321-3213
Clyde
Pine Rose Inn, 137 S Main St 43410

Ohio (Continued)

Columbus
Fifty Lincoln, 50 E Lincoln St 43215
Slavka's B&B, 180 Reinhard Ave 43206 ....(614)443-6076
Victorian B&B, 78 Smith Place 43201
Conesville
Log House B&B, PO Box 30 43811 ....(614)829-2757
Coshocton
1890 B&B, 663 N Whitewoman St 43812
Roscoe Village Inn, 200 N Whitewoman St 43812 ....(614)622-2222
Danville
The White Oak Inn, 29683 Walhonding Rd 43014 ....(614)599-6107
Dayton
Steamboat House B&B, 6 Josie St 45403
Degraff
Rollicking Hills B&B, 2 Rollicking Hills Ln 43318
Dellroy
Litt's Country Inn, 2196 Lodge Rd, Box 41 44620 ....(216)735-2035
Pleasant Journey Inn, 4247 Roswell Rd SW 44460 ....(216)735-2987
East Fultonham
Hill View Acres B&B, 7320 Old Town Rd 43735 ....(614)849-2728
Granville
Buxton Inn, 313 E Broadway 43023 ....(614)587-0001
Granville Inn, 314 E Broadway 43023 ....(614)587-3333
Hanoverton
Crystal Springs B&B, 12471 Bethesda Rd 44423
Hiram
The Lily Ponds, Box 322 44234 ....(800)325-5087
Huron
Captain Montague's Guests, 229 Center St 44839 ....(419)433-4756
Johnstown
The Pudding House, 60 N Main St 43021 ....(614)967-6060
Kelleys Island
The Beatty House, South Shore Dr, PO Box 402 43438 ....(419)746-2379
Cricket Lodge, Lakeshore Dr Box 323 43438 ....(419)746-2263
Southaven, PO Box 442 43438 ....(419)746-2784
Sweet Valley Inn, PO Box 733, Division St 43438 ....(419)746-2750
The Inn On Kelleys Island, Box 11 43438 ....(419)746-2258
Kent
Eidson House B&B, 141 Columbus St 44240
Lakeside
Rothenbuler's Guest House, 310 Walnut Ave 43440
Lakeville
Quite Country, 14758 Tr 453 44638 ....(216)378-3882
Lancaster
Barbara's Country Retreat, 3705 Crumley Rd 43130
Lebanon
Burl Manor, 230 S Mechanic St 45231 ....(513)932-1266
Golden Lamb, 27 South Broadway 45036 ....(513)932-5065
White Tor, 1620 Oregonia Rd 45036
Lewisville
Grandma Betty's B&B, 35226 SR 78 43754
Lexington
The White Fence Inn, 8842 Denman Rd 44904 ....(419)884-2356
Lodi
Squirrel's Run B&B, 9388 Kennard Rd 44254 ....(216)948-3026
Logan
B&B of Hocking County 43138 ....(614)385-4941
Bartholomew, 7657 Twp Rd, 234 43138 ....(614)385-8363
Bells, Downtown Logan 43138 ....(614)385-4384
The Inn at Cedar Falls, 21190 State Rt 374 43138 ....(614)385-7489
Log Cabin, 7657 TWP Rd 234 43138 ....(614)385-8363
Rainbow's End, 10671 Ellinger Rd 43138
Loudonville
Blackfork Inn, 303 North Water St, PO Box 149 44842 ....(419)994-3252
Lucas
Pleasant Valley Lodge, Pleasant Valley Rd, Rt 1 44843 ....(419)892-2443
Marblehead
Old Stone House Inn, 133 Clemons St 43440 ....(419)798-5922
Marietta
House Of Seven Porches, 331 Fifth St 45750 ....(614)373-1767
Larchmont B&B, 524 Second St 45750
Medina
Oakwood B&B, 226 N Broadway 44256 ....(216)723-1162
Millersburg
Inn At Honey Run, 6920 Country Rd 203 44654 ....(216)674-0011
Morrow
Country Manor B&B, 6315 Zoar Rd 45152
Locust Hill, 1659 East US 22-3 45152 ....(513)899-2749
Mount Gilead
Holiday House, 88 E High St 43338
Mount Vernon
Mount Vernon House, 304 Martinsburg Rd 43050
Oak Hill B&B, 16720 Park Rd 43050 ....(614)393-2912
The Russell-Cooper House, 115 E Gambier St 43050 ....(614)397-8638
Nashport
Bed and Breakfast 43830 ....(614)454-8289
New Richmond
Hollyhock B&B of New Richmond, 1610 N Altman 45157 ....(513)553-6585
Newark
Pitzer-Cooper House B&B, 6019 White Chapel Rd SE 43056
Wehrle Mansion B&B, 444 Hudson Ave 43055
Newtown
Wind's Way B&B, 3851 Edwards Rd 45244 ....(513)561-1933
Norwalk
Old Inn B&B, 1060 Peru Olena Rd 44857
Old Washington
Zane Trace B&B, Main St, PO Box 115 43768 ....(614)489-5970
Oxford
The Alexander House, 22 N College 45056 ....(513)523-1200
Duck Pond, 6391 Morning Sun Rd 45056
Peebles
The Bayberry Inn, 25675 State Rt 41 N 45660 ....(513)587-2221
Peninsula
Centennial House, 5995 Center St 44264 ....(216)657-2506
Fleder's B&B, 5964 Center St 44264 ....(216)657-2284
Pettisville
Tudor Country Inn, Box 113 43553
Pickerington
Central House, 27 W Columbus St, Old Village 43147 ....(614)837-0932
Piqua
Pickwinn B&B, 707 N Downing St 45356
Poland
The Inn at the Green, 500 S Main St 44514 ....(216)758-4688
Pomeroy
Holly Hill Inn, 114 Butternut Ave 45769 ....(614)992-5657
Port Clinton
Old Island House Inn, Box K, 102 Madison St 43452
Powell
Buckeye B&B, PO Box 130 43065 ....(614)548-4555
Put-In-Bay
Le Vent Passant, 1539 Langram Rd 43456 ....(419)285-5511
Put-in-bay
The Vineyard, Box 283 43456 ....(419)285-6181
Sagamore Hills
The Inn at Brandywine Falls, 8230 Brandywine Rd 44067 ....(216)467-1812
Sandusky
Cottage Rose, 210 W Adams St 44870
Pipe Creek, 2719 Columbus Ave 44870 ....(419)626-2067
Wagner's 1844 Inn, 230 E Washington St 44870 ....(419)626-1726
Sharon Center
Hart & Mather B&B, 1343 Sharon-Copley Rd, PO 93 44274
Somerset
Somer Tea B&B, 200 S Columbus St 43783
South Amherst
Birchway Villa, 111 White Birch Way 44001
South Bloomingville
Deep Woods, 24830 SR 56 43152
Spring Valley
3 B's B&B, 103 Race St 45370 ....(513)862-4241
Thornville
Wal-Mec Farm B&B, 5663 SR 204 NW 43076
Tiffin
Zelkovia Inn, 131 Main St 44883

Tipp City
Willowtree Inn, 1900 W State, Rt 571 45371 ....(513)667-2957
Toledo
Mansion View, 2035 Collingwood Blvd 43620 ....(419)244-5676
Troy
H.W. Allen Villa B&B, 434 S Market St 45373 ....(513)335-1181
Vermilion
Village Square Annex B&B, 720 Main St ....(216)967-1950
Walnut Creek
Indiantree Farm, PO Box 103 44687
Waynesville
Waynesville Guest, 117 Main St, PO Box 592 45068 ....(513)897-3811
West Milton
Locust Lane Farm, 5590 Kessler Cowlesville Rd 45383 .....(513)698-4743
West Union
Murphin Ridge Inn, 750 Murphin Ridge 45693
Westerville
Cornelia's Corner B&B, 93 W College Ave 43081
Priscilla's B&B, 5 S West St 43081
Sweet Apple Inn, 61 S Vine St 43081
Winchester
Kitty's Corner B&B, 18877 SR 136 45697
Wooster
The Howey House, 340 N Bever St 44691 ....(216)264-8231
The Wooster Inn, Wayne Ave & Gasche St 44691 ....(216)264-2341
Worthington
Worthington Inn, 649 High St 43085 ....(614)885-2600
Xenia
Hattle House, 502 N King St 45385 ....(513)372-2315
Zanesfield
Myeerah's Inn B&B, Sandusky St 43360
Zoar
Cider Mill, PO Box 441 44697 ....(216)874-3133
Cowger House #9, 9 Fourth St 44697 ....(216)874-3542
Haven at 4th & Park, PO Box 467 44697 ....(216)874-4672
Weaving Haus, c/o Zoar Community Assoc Box 621 44697
....(216)874-2646
Zoar Village
Cobbler Shop Inn, Corner of 2nd and Main St 44697 ....(216)874-2600

Oklahoma

Aline
Heritage Manor, RR1, Box 33 73716 ....(405)463-2563
Clayton
Clayton Country Inn, Rt 1 Box 8 74536
Grove
Edgewater B&B, Box 1746 74344
Guthrie
Harrison House, 124 W Harrison 73044 ....(405)282-1000
Stone Lion Inn, 1016 W Warner 73044
Oklahoma City
Chisolm Springs, 824 Evan Hale Rd 73127 ....(405)942-5193
The Grandison, 1841 NW 15th 73106 ....(405)521-0011
Tulsa
Holloway House, PO Box 52423 74152-0423 ....(918)582-8607

Oregon

Albany
Farm "Mini Barn" Guest House, 7070 Springhill Dr NW 97321
....(503)928-9089
Ashland
Ashland Guest Villa, 643 Iowa St 97520 ....(503)488-1508
Ashland's Main Street Inn, 142 W Main St 97520 ....(503)488-0969
Auburn Street Cottage, 549 Auburn St 97520 ....(503)482-3004
Chanticleer B&B Inn, 120 Gresham St 97520 ....(503)482-1919
Coach House Inn, 70 Coolidge St 97520 ....(503)482-2257
Columbia Hotel, 262 1/2 E Main 97520 ....(503)482-3726
Country Walrus Inn, 2785 E Main St 97520 ....(503)488-1134
Country Willows Inn, 1313 Clay St 97520 ....(503)488-1590
Cowslip's Belle, 159 N Main St 97520 ....(503)488-2901
Edinburgh Lodge B&B, 586 E Main St 97520 ....(503)488-1050
Hersey House, 451 N Main St 97520 ....(503)482-4563
Highland Acres, 1350 E Nevada St 97520 ....(502)482-2170
Iris Inn, 59 Manzanita St 97520
Lithia Rose Lodging, 163 Granite St 97520 ....(503)482-1882
McCall House, 153 Oak St 97520 ....(503)482-9296
Morical House, 688 N Main St 97520
Neil Creek House, 341 Mowetza Dr 97520 ....(503)482-1334
Oak Street Station, 239 Oak St 97520 ....(503)482-1726
Parkside, 171 Granite St 97520 ....(503)482-2320
Queen Ann, 125 N Main St 97520 ....(503)482-0220
Royal Carter House, 514 Siskiyou Blvd 97520 ....(503)482-5623
Scenic View B&B, 467 Scenic Dr 97520 ....(503)482-2315
Shutes Lazy S, 200 Mowetza Dr 97520 ....(503)482-5498
Stone House, 80 Hargadine St 97520 ....(503)482-9233
Treon's Country Homestay, 1819 Colestin Rd 97520 ....(503)482-0746
Winchester Inn, 35 S 2nd St 97520
Astoria
Franklin Street Station, 1140 Franklin 97103 ....(503)325-4314
Rosebriar Inn, 636 14th St 97103 ....(503)325-7427
The Collins House, 682 34th St 97103 ....(503)325-3292
Baker
Powder River B&B, HCR 87, Box 500 97814 ....(503)523-7143
Bend
Lara House B&B, 640 NW Congress 97701 ....(503)388-4064
Mirror Pond House, 1054 NW Harmon Blvd 97701 ....(503)389-1680
Brookings
Holmes Sea Cove, 17350 Holmes Dr 97415 ....(503)469-3025
Sea Dreamer Inn, 15167 Mcvay Ln 97415 ....(503)469-6629
Ward House B&B Inn, 516 Redwood St, Box 86 97415 ......(503)469-5557
Cave Junction
Oregon Caves Chateau, PO Box 128 97523 ....(503)592-3400
Cloverdale
Sandlake Country Inn, 8505 Galloway Rd 97112 ....(503)965-6745
The Hudson House, 37700 Hwy 101 S 97112 ....(503)472-4814
Coburg
Wheeler's B&B, Box 8201, 404 E McKinzy 97401 ....(503)344-1366
Coos Bay
Captain's Quarters B&B, PO Box 3231 97420 ....(503)888-6895
This Olde House B&B, 202 Alder St 97420 ....(503)267-5224
Corvallis
Huntington Manor, 3555 NW Harrison Blvd 97330 ....(503)753-3735
Madison Inn, 660 SW Madison Ave 97333
Cottage Grove
Ivanoffs' Inn, 3101 Bennett Creek Rd 97424
Lea House Inn, 433 Pacific Hwy 97424 ....(503)942-0933
Elmira
McGillivay's Log Home B&B, 88680 Evers Rd 97437 ....(503)935-3564
Eugene
Backroads B&B, 85269 Lorane Hwy 97405 ....(503)484-4602
Campus Cottage, 1136 E 19th Ave 97403 ....(503)342-5346
Country Lane, 31180 Lane's Turn Rd 97401 ....(503)686-1967
House in the Woods, 814 Lorane Hwy 97405 ....(503)343-3234
Shelley's Guest House, 1546 Charnelton St 97401 ....(503)683-2062
Florence
The Johnson House, 216 Maple St, PO 1892 97439 ....(503)997-8000
Frenchglen
Frenchglen Hotel 97736 ....(503)493-2565
Gardiner
Gardiner by Sea, 401 Front St, Box 222 97441 ....(503)271-4005
Gold Beach
Bien Venue B&B, 95629 Jerry Flat Rd 97444 ....(503)247-2335
Fair Winds B&B, PO Box 1274 97444 ....(503)247-6753
Grants Pass
Ahlf House, 762 NW 6th St 97526 ....(503)474-1374
Handmaidens' Inn, 230 Red Spur Dr 97527 ....(503)476-2932
Lawnridge House, 1304 NW Lawnridge 97526 ....(503)479-5186
Mt Baldy B&B, 678 Troll View Rd 97527 ....(503)479-7998
The Washington Inn, 1002 Washington Blvd. 97526 ....(503)476-1131
Halfway
Clear Creek Farm B&B, Rt Box 138 97834 ....(503)742-2238
Hood River
Barkheimer House, 3820 Westcliff Dr 97031 ....(503)386-5918
Columbia Gorge Hotel, 4000 W Cliff Dr 97031 ....(503)386-5566
Hackett House, 922 State St 97031 ....(503)386-1014
State Street Inn, 1005 State St 97031 ....(503)386-1899
Independence
Davidson House, 887 Monmouth St 97351 ....(503)838-3280
Out of the Blue B&B, 386 Monmouth St 97351 ....(503)838-3636

Oregon (Continued)

Jacksonville
Farmhouse B&B, 755 E California St 97530
Jacksonville Inn, 175 E California 97530 ....(503)899-1900
Livingston Mansion, 4132 Livingston Rd, PO 1476 97530 (503)899-7107
McCully House Inn, 240 E California 97530 ....(503)899-1656
Joseph
Chandler's Bed & Trail Inn, Box 639, 700 E Main 97846 ...(503)432-9765
Wallowa Lake Lodge, Rt 1 Box 320 97846 ....(503)432-4082
Kimberly
Lands End B&B, Star Rt #1 97848 ....(503)934-2485
La Grande
Stange Manor, 1612 Walnut 97850 ....(503)963-2400
Lakeside
Country Lane B&B, PO Box Y-177, Country Ln 97449 ....(503)759-3869
Lowell
Lakeside Cottage, 234 Pioneer S, Box 263 97452 ....(503)937-2443
Madras
Madras, 343 C Street At Hwy 26 97741 ....(503)475-2345
McMinnville
Mattey House, 10221 NE Mattey Ln 97128 ....(503)434-5058
Medford
Reuthlinger's B&B, 770 Griffin Creek Rd 97501
Under the Greenwood Tree, 3045 Bellinger Ln 97501 ....(503)776-0000
Merlin
Morrison's Rogue River Lodge, 8500 Galice Rd 97532 ....(503)476-3825
Milton-Freewater
Birch Tree Manor, 615 S Main St 97862 ....(503)938-6455
Newberg
Secluded B&B, 19719 NE Williamson Rd 97132 ....(503)538-2635
Newport
Oar House, 520 SW 2nd St 97365 ....(503)265-9571
Sylvia Beach Hotel, 267 NW Cliff St 97365 ....(503)265-5428
North Bend
Highlands, 608 Ridge Rd 97459 ....(503)756-0300
Sherman House B&B, 2380 Sherman Ave 97459 ....(503)756-3496
Oakland
Pringle House, Locust & 7th Sts 97462 ....(503)459-5038
Oceanside
Three Capes B&B, 1685 Maxwell Mountain Rd 97134 ....(503)842-6126
Pine Creek
Pine Creek Guest House, Star Rt, Box 65 97834 ....(503)785-3320
Port Orford
Gwendolyn's B&B, 735 8th, Box 913 97465 ....(503)332-4373
Home by the Sea, PO Box 606, 444 Jackson St 97465 ....(503)332-2855
Portland
Allenhouse B&B, 2606 NW Lorejoy St 97210 ....(503)227-6841
Corbett House B&B, 7533 SW Corbett 97219 ....(503)245-2580
General Hooker's House, 125 SW Hooker 97201 ....(503)222-4435
Heron Haus, 2545 NW Westover Rd 97210 ....(503)274-1846
John Palmer House, 4314 N Mississippi Ave, Ste AA 97217 ....(503)284-5893
Old Portland Estate, 1870 SE Exeter Dr 97202 ....(503)236-6533
Portland's White House, 1914 NE 22 97212 ....(503)287-7131
Salem
Harbison House, 1845 Commercial St 97302 ....(503)581-8118
State House B&B, 2146 State St 97301 ....(503)588-1340
Seal Rock
Blackberry Inn, 6575 NW Pacific Coast Hwy 97376 ....(503)563-2259
Seaside
Riverside Inn, 430 S Holladay St 97138 ....(503)738-8254
The Boarding House, 208 N Holladay Dr 97138 ....(503)738-9055
The Gilbert House, 341 Beach Dr 97138 ....(503)738-9770
Sisters
Lake Creek Lodge, Star Rt 97759 ....(503)595-6331
Spray
Pioneer B&B, Star Rt 97874 ....(503)462-3934
The Dalles
Bigelow B&B, 606 Washington 97058 ....(503)298-8239
Williams House Inn, 608 W 6th St 97058 ....(503)296-2889
Tillamook
Blue Haven Inn, Box 1034 97141 ....(503)842-2265
Vida
McKenzie River Inn, 49164 McKenzie Hwy 97488 ....(503)822-6260
Welches
Mountain Shadows B&B, Box 147 97067 ....(503)622-4746
Westport
King Salmon Lodge, Ferry Rd 97016
Wilsonville
Key's B&B, 5025 SW Homesteader Rd 97070 ....(503)638-3722
Wolf Creek
Wolf Creek Tavern, PO Box 97 97497 ....(503)866-2474
Yachats
Adobe 97498 ....(503)547-3141
Oceanaire Rest B&B, 95354 Hwy 101 97498 ....(503)547-3782
Oregon House Inn, 94288 Hwy 101 97498 ....(503)547-3329

Pennsylvania

Airville
Spring House, Muddy Creek Forks 17302 ....(717)927-6906
Allentown
Coachaus, 107-111 N 8th St 18102
Annville
Horseshoe Farm, Rt 1 Box 228 17003
Atglen
Umble Rest, RD 1 Box 79 19310 ....(215)593-2274
Avondale
Springs Valley Inn, RD 1 Box 532 19311 ....(215)268-2597
Beach Lake
Beach Lake Hotel, PO Box 144 18405 ....(717)729-8239
East Shore House B&B, Box 12 18405
Bear Creek
Bischwind, Box 7, One Coach Rd 18602 ....(717)472-3820
Bedford
Jean Bonnet Tavern, Rt 2 Box 188 15522 ....(814)623-2250
Bendersville
Historic Paul Sourss Plantation House, PO Box 238 17306 ....(717)677-6688
Benton
Grandmaws, Rt 3 Box 239 17814 ....(717)925-2630
Berlin
Ogline's B&B, 1001 E Main St 15530 ....(814)267-3696
Bernville
Sunday's Mill Farm, Rt 2 Box 419 19506 ....(215)488-7821
Bethlehem
Salisbury House, 910 East Emmaus Ave 18103 ....(215)791-4225
Bird-in-hand
Greystone Manor B&B, 2658 Old Philadelphia Pike POB 270 17505 ....(717)393-4233
Bloomsburg
The Inn at Turkey Hill, 991 Central Rd 17815 ....(717)387-1500
Boiling Springs
The Garmanhaus, 217 Front St 17007 ....(717)258-3980
Buck Hill Falls
Buck Hill Inn 18232 ....(800)233-8113
Buffalo Mills
Buffalo Lodge, RD 1, Box 277 15534 ....(814)623-2207
Canadensis
Brookview Manor B&B Inn, Rt 1 Box 365 18325 ....(717)595-2451
Dreamy Acres, PO Box 7, Seese Hill Rd & Rt 44 18325 ....(717)595-7115
Laurel Grove, Pocono Vacationland 18325 ....(717)595-7262
Nearbrook 81325 ....(717)595-3152
Overlook Inn, Dutch Hill Rd 18325
Pine Knob, Rt 447 18325 ....(717)595-2532
Pump House Inn, Sky Top Rd 18325
Cedar Run
Cedar Run Inn, Rt 414 17727 ....(717)353-6241
Central City
Noah's Ark, Rt 1 Box 425 15926
Chadds Ford
Hill House, Creek Rd 19317
Charlestown
King Tom Farm, PO Box 1440 02807 ....(401)364-3371

Christiana
Winding Glen Farm, PO Box 160 17509 ....(215)593-5535
Churchtown
Churchtown Inn, Rt 23 17555 ....(215)445-7794
The Foreman House B&B, 2129 Main St, Rt 23 17555 ....(215)445-6713
Clark
Tara, Box 475, 3665 Valley View 16113 ....(412)962-3535
Cooksburg
Gateway Lodge & Cabins, Rt 36 PO Box 125 16217 ....(814)744-8017
Cowansville
Garrott's B&B, RD 1 Box 73 16218 ....(412)545-2432
Cresco
La Anna Guest House, RD 2 Box 1051 18326 ....(717)676-4225
Danville
The Pine Barn Inn, 1 Pine Barn Place 17821 ....(717)275-2071
Delaware Water Gap
Mountain House, Mountain Rd 18327 ....(717)424-2254
Downington
Duck Hill Farm, Rt 1 19335
Doylestown
Doylestown Inn, 18 W State St 18901 ....(215)345-6610
Pear & PatridgeInn, Dept NT, Old Easton Rd 18901 ....(215)345-7800
Doylestown, Bucks Co
The Inn at Fordhook Farm, 105 New Britain Rd 18901 ..(215)345-1766
Dushore
Cherry Mills Lodge, PO 6525 19610 ....(717)928-8978
Eagles Mere
Eagles Mere Inn, PO Box 356 17731 ....(717)525-3273
Shady Lane Lodge, Allegheny Ave 17731 ....(717)525-3394
East Berlin
The Bechtel Mansion Inn, 400 West King St 17316 ....(717)259-7760
Ebensburg
Noon-Collins Inn, 114 E High St 15931 ....(814)472-4311
Elm
Elm Country Inn, Box 37 17521 ....(717)664-3623
Elverson
Rocky Side Farm, RD 1 19520 ....(215)286-5362
Emigsville
Emig Mansion, Box 486, 3342 N George St 17318 ....(717)764-2226
Ephrata
Covered Bridge Inn, 990 Rettew Mill Rd 17522 ....(717)733-1592
Gerhart House B&B, 287 Duke St 17522 ....(717)733-0263
Hackman's Country Inn, 140 Hackman Rd 17522 ....(717)733-3498
Smithton Inn, 900 W Main St 17522 ....(717)733-6094
Erie
Royal Acre Retreat, 5131 Lancaster Rd 16506 ....(814)838-7928
Erwinna
Evermay-on-the-Delaware, River Rd 18920 ....(215)294-9100
Golden Pheasant Inn, River Rd 18920 ....(215)294-9595
Isaac Stover House, River Road, PO Box 68 18920 ....(215)294-8044
Everett
Newry Manor, Rt 1 Box 475 15537 ....(814)623-1250
Exton
Duling Kurtz House, 146 S Whitford Rd 19341 ....(215)524-1830
Fairfield
Historic Fairfield Inn, Box 96 17320 ....(717)642-5410
Fayetteville
Herb Cottage Inn, Lincoln Hwy E, Rt 30 17222 ....(717)352-7733
Fogelsville
Glasbern, RD 1 Box 250 18051-9743 ....(215)285-4723
Freeport
Hobby House B&B, 174 Srader Grove Rd 16229
Gardners
Goose Chase, 200 Blueberry Rd 17324 ....(717)528-8877
Germantown
Germantown B&B, 5925 Wayne Ave 19144 ....(215)848-1375
Gettysburg
Abraham Spangler Inn, 264 Baltimore St 17325 ....(717)337-3997
Cozy Comfort Inn, 264 Baltimore St 17325 ....(717)337-3997
Dobbin House Tavern, 89 Steinwehr Ave 17325 ....(717)334-2100
The Doubleday Inn, 104 Doubleday Ave 17325 ....(717)334-9119
Gettystown Inn, 89 Steinwehr Ave 17325
Keystone Inn B&B, 231 Hanover St 17325 ....(717)337-3888
Swinn's Lodging, 31 E Lincoln Ave 17325
The Old Appleford Inn, 218 Carlisle St 17325
Twin Elms, 228 Buford Ave 17325 ....(717)334-4520
Glen Mills
Sweetwater Farm, PO Box 86, Sweetwater Rd 19342 ....(215)459-4711
Glen Moore
Conestoga Horse B&B, Hollow Rd, PO Box 256 19343 ....(215)458-8535
Gordonville
The Osceola Mill House, 313 Osceola Mill Rd 17529 ....(717)768-3758
Hallstead
Log Cabin B&B, Rt 11 Box 393 18822 ....(717)879-4167
The Corner Inn, Box 777 18822
Hanover
Beechmont Inn, 315 Broadway 17331 ....(717)632-3013
Country View Acres, 676 Beaver Creek Road 17331 ....(717)637-8992
Hawley
Academy Street B&B, 528 Academy St 18428 ....(717)226-3430
Settlers Inn, 4 Main Ave 18428 ....(717)226-2993
Hershey
Gibson's B&B, 141 W Caracas Ave 17033 ....(717)534-1035
Horetsky's Tourist Home, 217 Cocoa Ave 17033 ....(800)533-5783
Hesston
Aunt Susie's Country Vacations, Rt 1 Box 225 16647
Hickory
Shady Elms Farm B&B, Rt 1 Box 188 15340 ....(412)356-7755
Holicong
Ash Mill Farm, PO Box 202 18928 ....(215)794-5373
Barley Sheaf Farm, Rt 202 Box 10 18928 ....(215)794-5104
Hollidaysburg
Brun Run Estate, 132 Logan Blvd. 16648
Honesdale
Hotel Wayne, 1202 Main St 18431 ....(717)253-3290
Huntingdon
Yoder's B&B, RD 1, Box 312 16652 ....(814)643-3221
Jamestown
Das Tannen-Lied, Rt 1 16134 ....(412)932-5029
Jersey Shore
Ye Olde Library B&B, 310 S Main St 17740
Jim Thorpe
Harry Packer Mansion, Packer Hill 18229 ....(717)325-8566
Kane
Kane Manor Country Inn, 230 Clay St 16735 ....(814)837-6522
Kennett Square
Buttonwood Farm, 231 Pemberton Rd 19348 ....(215)444-0278
Longwood Inn, 815 E Baltimore Pike 19348 ....(215)444-3515
Meadow Spring Farm, 201 E St Rd 19348 ....(215)444-3903
Kintnersville
Bucksville House, Rt 2 Box 146 18930 ....(215)847-8948
Kinzer
Bethania Farm, PO Box 228 17535 ....(717)442-4939
Groff Tourist Farm, RD 1 Box 36 17353 ....(717)442-8223
Lahaska
Golden Plough Inn, Rt 263-Rt 202, Box 218 18931 ....(215)794-7438
The Buttonwood Inn, Rt 202 18931 ....(215)794-7438
Lampeter
Walkabout Inn, 837 Village Rd 17537 ....(717)464-0707
Lancaster
Buena Kotte B&B, 2020 Marietta Ave 17603
Hollinger House, 2336 Hollinger Rd 17602 ....(717)464-3050
Landyshade Farms, 1801 Colebrook Rd 17601 ....(717)898-7689
The Foreman House B&B, Churchtown, PA
Witmer's Tavern - Historic 1725 Inn, 2014 Old Philadelphia Pike 17602 ....(717)299-5305
Langhorne
The Waln House, 1242 Brownsville Rd 19047 ....(215)757-2921
Laughlintown
Ligonier Country Inn, PO Box 46 Rt 30 E 15655 ....(412)238-3651
Leesport
The Loom Room, RD 1 PO Box 1420 19533 ....(215)926-3217
Leola
Turtle Hill Road B&B, Rt 1, 111 Turtle Hill Rd 17540
Lewisburg
Pineapple Inn, 439 Market St 17837
Ligonier
Grant House B&B, 244 W Church St 15658 ....(412)238-5135

Pennsylvania (Continued)

Lincoln University
Royalview Dairy Farm, Box 93 19352
Lititz
The Alden House, 62 E Main St 17543 ....(717)627-3363
General Sutter Inn, 14 E Main St 17543 ....(717)626-2115
Swiss Woods B&B, 500 Blantz Rd 17543 ....(717)627-3358
Loganville
Country Spun Farm B&B, Box 117 17342 ....(717)428-1162
Lumberville
1740 House, River Rd 18933 ....(215)297-5661
Black Bass Hotel, River Rd 18933 ....(215)297-5770
Malvern
The Great Valley House, 110 Swedesford Rd 3 19355 ....(215)644-6759
Manheim
Herr Farmhouse Inn, 2256 Huber Dr 17545 ....(717)653-9852
Maytown
Three Center Square Inn, PO Box 428 17550 ....(717)653-4338
Mcelhatten
Restless Oak B&B, Box 241 17748
McKeesport
Guest Home, 1040 Lincoln Way 15132 ....(412)751-7143
Mcknightstown
New Salem House, 275 Old Rt 30, PO Box 24 17343 ....(717)337-3520
Mercer
Magoffin Guest House B&B, 129 S Pitt St 16137 ....(412)662-4611
Stranahan House B&B, 117 E Market St 16137
Mercerburg
The Mercerburg Inn, 405 S Main St 17236 ....(717)328-5231
Mertztown
Blair Creek Inn & Lodging 19539 ....(215)682-6700
Longswamp B&B, RD 2 PO Box 26 19539 ....(215)682-6197
Middletown
Finnegan's Inn, 120 Miantonomi Ave 02840 ....(401)847-0902
Milford
Black Walnut Inn, 509 Fire Tower Rd 18337
Cliff Park Inn, Cliff Park Rd 18337 ....(717)296-6491
The Vines, 107 E Ann St 18337 ....(717)296-6775
Millersville
Walnut Hill B&B, Rt 1 Box 113 17551 ....(717)872-2283
Montoursville
The Carriage House at Stonegate, RD 1 Box 11A 17754 ....(717)433-4340
Mount Bethel
Elvern Country Lodge, Box 177 18343 ....(215)588-7922
Mount Gretna
Mt Gretna Inn, Kaufman & Pine 17064 ....(717)964-3234
Mount Joy
Brenneman Farm B&B, Rt 1, Box 310 17552 ....(717)653-4213
Cameron Estate Inn, RD 1 Box 305 17552 ....(717)653-1773
Nolt Farm Guest Home, S Jacob St Farm 17552 ....(717)653-4192
Rocky Acre Farm, RD 3 17552 ....(717)653-4449
Mountville
Mountville Antique B&B, 407 E Main St, Rt 462 17554 ....(717)285-5956
Muncy
The Bodine House B&B, 307 S Main St 17756
Myerstown
Tulpehocken Manor Inn, 650 W Lincoln Ave 17067
New Albany
Waltman's B&B, Rt 1 Box 87 18833 ....(717)363-2295
New Hope
Backstreet Inn, 144 Old York Rd 18939 ....(215)862-9571
Centre Bridge Inn, Rts. 32 & 263 18938
Hacienda Inn, 36 W Mechanics St 18938 ....(215)862-2078
Hotel Du Village, N River Rd 18938 ....(215)862-9911
Inn At Phillips Mill, N River Rd 18938 ....(215)862-2984
Logan Inn, Main & Ferry Sts 18938 ....(215)862-2300
Pineapple Hill, 1324 River Rd 18938 ....(717)524-6200
The Wedgwood Inn, 111 W Bridge 18938 ....(215)862-2570
Whitehall Inn, Pineville Rd, RD 2 Box 250 18938 ....(215)598-7945
New Wilmington
Tavern, Box 153 On the Square 16142 ....(412)946-2020
Newfoundland
White Cloud Sylvan Retreat, RD 1 Box 215 18445 ....(717)676-3162
North East
Brown's Village Inn, 51 E Main St 16428 ....(814)725-5522
Windward Inn, 51 Freeport Rd 16428 ....(814)725-5336
North Wales
Joseph Ambler Inn, 1005 Horsham Rd 19454 ....(215)362-7500
Orbisonia
Salvino's Guest House, PO Box 116 17243 ....(814)447-5616
Orrtanna
Hickory Bridge Farm, 96 Hickory Bridge Rd 17353 ....(717)642-5261
Paradise
Maple Lane Farm, 505 Paradise Ln 17562 ....(717)687-7479
Neffdale Farm, 604 Strasburg Rd 17562 ....(717)687-7837
Rayba Acres Farm, 183 Black Horse Rd 17562 ....(717)687-6729
The Rose And Crown, 44 Frogtown Rd 17562 ....(717)768-7684
Peach Bottom
Lofty Acres, RD 1 Box 331 17563 ....(717)548-3052
Pleasant Grove Farm, Rt 1 Box 132 17563
Perkasie
The Benfield Mill #302, 624 E Walnut St 18944
Philadelphia
B&B of Valley Forge, PO Box 562, Valley Forge ....(215)783-7838
Germantown B&B, 5925 Wayne Ave 19144 ....(215)848-1375
La Reserve, 1804 Pine St 19103 ....(215)735-0582
Society Hill Hotel, 301 Chestnut St 19106 ....(215)925-1919
The Independence Park Inn, 235 Chestnut St 19106 ....(215)922-4443
Pittsburgh
Oakwood, 235 Johnston Rd 15241 ....(412)835-9565
The Priory, 614 Pressley St 15212 ....(412)231-3338
Plumsteadville
Plumsteadville Inn, Box 40 18949 ....(215)766-7500
Point Pleasant
Tattersall Inn, PO Box 569 18950
Pottstown
Coventry Forge Inn, RD 2 19464 ....(215)469-6222
Fairway Farm B&B, Vaughn Rd 19464 ....(215)326-1315
Quakertown
Sign Of Sorrel Horse, RD 3 18951 ....(215)536-4651
Reading
El Shaddai, 229 Madison Ave, Hyde Villa 19605 ....(215)929-1341
Red Lion
Red Lion B&B, 101 S Franklin St 17356 ....(717)244-4739
Ridgway
The Bogert House, 140 Main St 15853
Riegelsville
Riegelsville Hotel, 10-12 Delaware Rd 18077
Ronks
Candlelite Inn B&B, 2574 Lincoln Hwy E 17572 ....(717)299-6005
Scenery Hill
Century Inn, Rt 40 15360
Schellsburg
Millstone Inn, PO Box 279 15559 ....(814)733-4864
Scottdale
Pine Wood Acre, Rt 1 Box 278 15683-9567 ....(412)887-5404
Selinsgrove
The Blue Lion Inn, 350 S Market St 17870
Shartlesville
Haag's Hotel, Main St 19554 ....(215)488-6692
Shawnee-on-Delaware
Eagle Rock Lodge, River Rd, Box 265 18354 ....(717)421-2139
Shippensburg
Field & Pine B&B, RD 5 Box 161 17257 ....(717)776-7179
Siegel
Discoveries B&B, RD #1, Box 42 15680 ....(814)752-2632
Smoketown
Smoketown Village Tourist Home, 2495 Old Phila. Pike 17576
Solebury
Holly Hedge Estate, PO Box 213 18963 ....(215)862-3136
South Sterling
Sterling Inn, Rt 191 18460 ....(717)676-3311
The French Manor Inn, PO Box 39 18460 ....(717)676-3244
Spring House
Charles Bauerlein, Box 369 19477

Starlight
The Inn at Starlight Lake 18461 ....(717)798-2519
Strasburg
Limestone Inn B&B, 33 E Main St 17579 ....(717)687-8392
Siloan, Village Rd Box 82 17579 ....(717)687-6231
Strasburg Village Inn, 1 W Main St 17579 ....(717)687-0900
Sumneytown
Kaufman House, Box 183, Rt 63 18084 ....(215)234-4181
Thompson
Jefferson Inn, Rt 2 Box 36 18465
Thornton
Pace One Restaurant and Country Inn, Thornton Rd 19373 ....(215)459-9784
Towanda
Victorian Guest House, 118 York Ave 18848 ....(717)265-6972
Tyler Hill
Tyler Hill B&B, Rt 371, PO Box 62 18469 ....(717)224-6418
Upper Black Eddy
Bridgeton House, PO Box 167 18972 ....(215)982-5856
Tara, 1 Bridgeton Hill 18972 ....(215)982-5457
Upper Black Eddy Inn, Rt 32 River Rd 18972 ....(215)982-5554
Valley Forge
B&B of Valley Forge, PO Box 562 19481-0562 ....(215)783-7838
Warren
Willows, 40 Kinzua Rd 16365
Washington Crossing
Woodhill Farms Inn, 130 Glenwood Dr 18977
Waterford
Altheim B&B, Box 2081, 104 Walnut St 16441
Waterville
The Point House, Church St 17776 ....(717)299-5305
Wellsboro
Jesse Robinson Manor, 141 Main St 16901
West Chester
The Barn, 1131 Grove Rd 19380 ....(215)436-4544
Crooked Winsor, 409 S Church St 19382 ....(215)692-4896
Highland Manor B&B, 855 Hillsdale Rd 19382 ....(215)686-6251
Quarry House, RD 5, Street Rd 19382 ....(215)793-1725
Wexford
The Coreys, 2522 Wexford Run Rd 15090
Williamsport
Reighard House, 1323 E Third St 17701 ....(717)326-3593
Willow Street
Green Gables B&B, 2532 Willow St Pike 17584 ....(717)464-5546
Woodward
Woodward Inn, Box 177 16882 ....(814)349-8118
Wrightsville
Roundtop B&B, RD #2, Box 258 17368 ....(717)252-3169
Wycombe
Wycombe Inn, PO Box 204 18980
York
Inn At Mundis Mill, Rt 1 Box 15, Mundis Race Rd 17402 (717)755-2002

Rhode Island

Block Island
1661 Inn, PO Box 1 02807 ....(401)466-2421
Atlantic Inn, Box 188 02807 ....(401)466-2005
The Barrington Inn, Beach & Queen Ave, PO Box 397Y 02807 ....(401)466-5510
Bellevue, High St 02807 ....(401)466-2389
Blue Dory Inn, Dodge St 02807 ....(401)466-2254
Driftwind Guests, High St 02807 ....(401)466-5548
Gables Inn, PO Box 516 02807 ....(401)466-2213
Gothic Cottage/Ocean Villa, PO Box 876 02807 ....(401)466-2918
Guest House, PO Box 24, Center Rd 02807 ....(401)466-2676
Hotel Manisses, PO Box 1 02807 ....(401)466-2836
Island Manor Resort, Chapel St 02807 ....(401)466-5567
Mill Pond Cottages, Old Town Rd 02807 ....(401)466-2423
New Shoreham House, PO Box 356, Water St 02807 ....(401)466-2651
The Inn at Old Harbour, Water St, Box 994 02807 ....(401)466-2212
Old Town Inn, Old Town Rd, Box 35 02807 ....(401)466-5958
Rose Farm Inn, Roselyn Rd 02807 ....(401)466-2021
Sea Breeze Inn, Spring St, Box 141 02807 ....(401)466-2275
Seacrest Inn, 207 High St 02807 ....(401)466-2882
Sheffield House, PO Box 836 02807 ....(401)466-2494
The White House, Box 447 02807 ....(401)466-2653
Willow Grove, Corn Neck Rd PO Box 156 02807 ....(401)466-2896
Bristol
The Joseph Reynolds House, 956 Hope St, PO Box 5 02809 ....(401)254-0230
Charlestown
General Stanton Inn, Rt 1 Box 222 02813 ....(401)364-8888
Windswept Farm Inn, Rt 1, Post Rd, Box 1540 02807 ....(401)364-6292
East Providence
The Last Resort, 330 Sea View Ave 02915 ....(401)433-1577
Green Hill
Fairfield-by-the-Sea, 527 Green Hill Beach Rd 02879 ....(401)789-4717
Hopkinton City
The General Thurston House-1763, Main St 02833 ....(401)377-9049
Jamestown
Bay Voyage Inn 02835 ....(401)423-2100
Calico Cat Guest House, 14 Union St 02835 ....(401)423-2641
Little Compton
Ballyvoreen, Stone Church Rd 02837 ....(401)635-4396
Middletown
Lindsey's Guest House, 6 James St 02840 ....(401)846-9386
Peckham's Guest Home, 272 Paradise Ave 02840 ....(401)846-2382
Stone Towers, 152 Tuckerman Ave 02840 ....(401)846-3227
Whimsey Cottage, 42 Briarwood Ave 02840 ....(401)841-5824
Misquamicut
Andrea Hotel, 89 Atlantic Ave 02891 ....(401)348-8788
Atlantic Inn, Crandall Ave 02891 ....(401)596-7737
Misquamicut Beach
Ocean View, Atlantic Ave 02891 ....(401)596-7170
Narragansett
Chestnut House, 11 Chestnut St 02882 ....(401)789-5335
Duck Harbor, 295 Boston Neck Rd 02882 ....(401)783-3495
Four Gables, 12 S Pier Rd 02882 ....(401)789-6948
Going My Way, 75 Kingstown Rd 02882 ....(401)789-3479
Grinnel Inn, 83 Narragansett Ave 02882
Ilverthorpe Cottage, 41 Robinson St 02882 ....(401)789-2392
Kenyon Farms, PO Box 648 02882 ....(401)783-7123
Louis Sherry Cottage, 59 Gibson Ave 02882 ....(401)783-8626
Mon Reve, 41 Gibson Ave 02882 ....(401)783-2846
Murphy's B&B, 43 S Pier Rd 02882 ....(401)789-1824
Phoenix House, 29 Gibson Ave 02882 ....(401)783-2846
Sea Gull Guest House, 50 Narragansett Ave 02882 ....(401)783-4636
Southwest Wind Acres, 8 Lindsley Rd 02882 ....(401)783-5860
Starr Cottage, 68 Caswell St 02882 ....(401)783-2411
Stone Lea, 40 Newton Ave 02882 ....(401)783-9546
Summer House Inn, 87 Narragansett Ave 02882 ....(401)783-0123
The House Of Snee, 191 Ocean Rd 02882 ....(401)783-9494
Newport
Admiral Benbow Inn, 93 Pelham St 02840 ....(401)846-4256
Admiral Farragut Inn, 31 Clarke St 02840 ....(401)846-4256
The Admiral Fitzroy, 398 Thames St 02840 ....(401)846-4256
Beachstone, 14 Kay Blvd 02840 ....(401)849-3839
Bellevue House, 14 Catherine St 02840 ....(401)847-1355
Blue Stone, 33 Russell Ave 02840 ....(401)846-5408
Bluestone B&B, 33 Russell Ave 02840 ....(401)846-5408
The Brinley Victorian Inn, 23 Brinley St 02840 ....(401)849-7645
The Inn at Castle Hill, Ocean Dr 02840 ....(401)849-3800
Castle Keep, 44 Everett 02840 ....(401)846-0362
Cliff View Guest House, 4 Cliff Terrace 02840 ....(401)846-0885
Cliff Walk Manor, 82 Memorial Blvd 02840 ....(401)847-1300
Cliffside Inn, 2 Seaview Ave 02840 ....(401)847-1811
Covell Guest House, 43 Farewell St 02840 ....(401)847-8872
Easton's Inn On The Beach, 30 Wave Ave 02840 ....(401)846-0310
Ellery Park House, 44 Farewell St 02840 ....(401)847-6320
The Elliott Boss House, 20 Second St 02840 ....(401)849-9425
Flower Garden Guests, 1 Kyle Terrace 02840 ....(401)846-3119
Gingerbread B&B, 16 Park St 02840-2104 ....(401)846-3037
Harborside Inn, Christie's Landing 02840 ....(401)846-6600
Inn of Jonathan Bowen, 29 Pelham St 02840 ....(401)846-3324
Inntowne, 6 Mary St 02840 ....(401)846-9200
Ivy Lodge, 12 Clay St 02840 ....(401)849-6865
Jail House Inn, 13 Marlborough St 02840 ....(401)847-4638
The John Banister House, 626 Thames St 02840 ....(401)846-0050
La Forge Cottage, 96 Pelham St 02840 ....(401)847-4400
Ma Gallagher's, 348 Thames St 02840 ....(401)849-3975

Rhode Island (Continued)

The Melville House, 39 Clarke St 02840 ....(401)847-0640
Merritt House Guest, 57 2nd St 02840 ....(401)847-4289
Mill Street Inn, 75 Mill St 02840 ....(401)849-9500
Moulton-Weaver House, 4 Training Station Rd 02840 ....(401)847-0133
Oceancliff, Ocean Dr 02840 ....(401)847-7777
The Old Dennis House, 59 Washington St 02840 ....(401)846-1324
The Pilgrim House, 123 Spring St 02846 ....(401)846-0040
Queen Anne Inn, 16 Clarke St 02840 ....(401)846-5676
Sea Quest, 9 Cliff Ter 02840 ....(401)846-0227
Serendipity Cottage, 35 Carey St 02840 ....(401)847-7080
Spring Street Inn, 353 Spring St 02840 ....(401)847-4767
Sunnyside Mansion, 25 Old Beach Rd 02840 ....(401)849-3114
Tripp Southwick B&B, 71 Washington St 02840 ....(401)849-2862
The Victorian Ladies, 63 Memorialblvd 02840 ....(401)849-9960
The Wallett House, 91 Second St 02840 ....(401)849-5177
Wayside, Bellevue Ave 02840
William Fludder House, 30 Bellevue Ave 02840 ....(401)849-4220
Yankee Peddler Inn, 113 Touro St 02840 ....(401)846-1323
Yellow Cottage, 82 Gibbs Ave 02840 ....(401)847-6568

North Kingstown
Meadowland, 765 Old Baptist Rd 02852 ....(401)294-4168
The John Updike House, 19 Pleasant St 02852 ....(401)294-4905

Portsmouth
Sunset Cabins, 1172 W Main Rd 02871 ....(401)683-1874
Twin Spruce Tourist House, 515 Turnpike Ave 02871 ....(401)682-0673

Providence
Charles Hodges House, 19 Pratt St, PO Box 2591 02906 ....(401)861-7244
Old Court B&B, 144 Benefit St 02903 ....(401)751-2002

Snug Harbor
Gooseberry Marina B&B, 500 Gooseberry Rd 02879 ....(401)789-5431

Wakefield
B&B At Highland Farm, 4145 Tower Hill Rd 02879 ....(401)783-2408
Blueberry Bush B&B, 128 South Rd 02879 ....(401)783-0907
Highland Farm, 4145 Tower Hill Rd, Rt 1 02879 ....(401)783-2408
Larchwood Inn, 176 Main St 02879 ....(401)783-1709

Warren
Weatherside B&B, 12 Leonard St 02885 ....(401)245-6665

Warwick
Ope Gat Motel, 840 Quaker Ln 02886 ....(401)884-4490

Watch Hill
Hartley's Guest House, Larkin Rd 02891

Weekapaug
J. Livingston's Guest House By The Sea, 39 Weekapaug Rd 02891 ....(401)322-0249
Weekapaug Inn 02891 ....(401)322-0301

Westerly
Inn On The Hill, 29 Summer St 02891 ....(401)596-3791
Longvue Guest House, 311 Shore Rt 1 02891 ....(401)322-0465
Shelter Harbor Inn, Rt 1 02891 ....(401)322-8883
The Shore Inn at Misquamicut, Shore Rd 02891 ....(401)348-8637
Woody Hill Guest House, Woody Hill Rd, Box 676E 02891 ....(401)322-0452

Wickford
Sparrow's Nest, 470 Annaquatucket Rd 02852 ....(401)295-1142

South Carolina

Abbeville
Belmont Inn, 106 E Pickens St 29620 ....(803)459-9625

Aiken
Hair Residence, 544 Magnolia Lane SE 29801
Holley Inn, 235 Richland Ave 29801 ....(803)648-4265
Pine Knoll Inn, 305 Lancaster St 29801 ....(803)649-5939
The Brodie Residence, 422 York St 29801 ....(803)648-1445
Willcox Inn, 100 Colleton Ave at Whiskey Rd 29801 ....(803)649-1377

Anderson
Evergreen Inn, 1109 S Main 29621 ....(803)225-1109

Beaufort
Bay Street Inn, 601 Bay St 29902 ....(803)524-7720
Old Point Inn, 212 New St 29902 ....(803)524-3177
The Rhett House Inn, 1009 Craven St 29902 ....(803)524-9030
Twelve Oaks Inn, PO Box 4126, Rt 2 Box 293 29902 ....(803)525-1371

Beech Island
The Cedars B&B Inn, Box 117 1325 Williston Rd 29841 ...(803)827-0248

Bluffton
Fripp House Inn, Bridge & Boundary, Box 857 29910 ....(803)757-2139

Camden
Aberdeen, 1409 Broad St 29020 ....(803)432-2524
The Carriage House, 1413 Lyttleton St 29020 ....(803)432-2430
Inn on Broad, 1308/10 Broad St 29020 ....(803)425-1806
The Inn, 1308 19 Broad St 29020 ....(803)425-1806

Charleston
1837 B&B & Tea Room, 126 Wentworth St 29401 ....(803)723-7166
Ann Harper's B&B, 56 Smith St 29401 ....(803)723-3947
Ansonborough Inn, 21 Hasell St 29401 ....(803)732-1655
B&B, 36 Meeting St 29401 ....(803)722-1034
Barksdale House Inn, 27 George St 29401 ....(803)577-4800
Battery Carriage House, 20 S Battery St 29401 ....(803)723-9881
Belvedere B&B, 40 Rutledge Ave 29401 ....(803)722-0973
Cannonboro Inn, 184 Ashley Ave 29403 ....(803)723-8572
Charleston Society B&B, 84 Murray Blvd 29401 ....(803)723-4948
Church Street Inn, 177 Church St 29401 ....(800)845-7638
Coach House, 39 E Battery Pl 29401 ....(803)722-8145
Elliott House Inn, 78 Queen St 29401 ....(803)723-1855
Hayne House, 30 King St 29401 ....(803)577-2633
Historic Charleston B&B, 43 Legare St 29401 ....(803)722-6606
Jasmine House, 64 Hasell St 29401 ....(803)577-5900
John Rutledge House Inn, 116 Broad St 29401 ....(803)723-7999
Kings Courtyard Inn, 198 King St 29401 ....(803)723-7000
The Kitchen House, 126 Tradd St 29401 ....(803)577-6362
Maison Du Pre, 317 E Bay St 29401 ....(803)723-8691
Meeting Street Inn, 173 Meeting St 29401 ....(803)723-9881
Palmer Home, 5 East Battery 29401 ....(803)723-1574
Planters Inn, 112 N Market St 29401 ....(803)722-2345
Rutledge Museum
Guest House, 114 Rutledge Ave 29401 ....(803)722-7551
Sweet Grass Inn, 23 Vendue Range 29401 ....(803)723-9980
Sword Gate Inn, 111 Tradd St 29401 ....(803)723-8518
The Lodge Alley Inn, 195 E Bay St 29401 ....(803)722-1611
Two Meeting Street Inn, 2 Meeting St 29401 ....(803)723-7322
Vendue Inn, 19 Vendue Range 29401 ....(803)577-7970

Cheraw
Spears B&B, 501 Kershaw St 29520 ....(803)537-7733

Columbia
Claussen's Inn, 2003 Green St 29205 ....(800)622-3382

Dale
Coosaw Plantation 29401 ....(803)846-8225

Edgefield
Adams House, 212 Augusta Rd 29824
The Village Inn, Court House Sq 29824 ....(803)637-3789

Estill
The John Lawton House, 159 Third St E 29918 ....(803)625-3240

Fort Mill
Pleasant Valley B&B, 160 East At Blackweider 29715 ....(803)548-5671

Georgetown
1790 House, 630 Highmarket St 29440 ....(803)546-4821
Shaw House, 8 Cypress Ct 29440 ....(801)546-9663
Walton House, 530 Prince St 29440 ....(803)527-4330

Greenwood
The Inn On The Square, 104 Court St 29646 ....(803)223-4488

Hilton Head Island
Halcyon, Harbormaster 604 29928 ....(803)785-7912

Johnston
The Cox House Inn, 602 Lee St, PO Box 486 29832 ....(803)275-3234

Landrum
Holly Hill, Rt 1, Box 223 29356 ....(803)457-4010

McClellanville
Laurel Hill Plantation, 8913 N Hwy 17, PO Box 182 29458 ....(803)765-0440

Montmorenci
Annie's Inn, PO Box 311 29839 ....(803)649-6836

Mt Pleasant
Guilds Inn, 101 Pitt St 29464 ....(803)881-0510

Mullins
Webster Manor, 115 E James St 29574 ....(803)464-9632

Myrtle Beach
Serendipity, An Inn, 407 71st Ave N 29577 ....(803)449-5268

Pendleton
Liberty Hall Inn 29670 ....(803)646-7500
Sullivan's Island
The Palmettos, 2014 Middle St, PO Box 706 29482 ....(803)883-3389
Summerville
Gadsden Manor Inn, Box 1710 29483 ....(803)875-1710
Switzer
Nicholls-Crook Plantation House, PO Box 5812 29304 ....(803)583-7337
Union
Forest Hill Manor, Rt 2 Box 725 29379 ....(803)427-4525

South Dakota

Canova
B&B at Skoglund Farm, Rt 1 Box 45 57321 ....(605)247-3445
Custer
State Game Lodge 57730 ....(605)255-4541
Sylvan Lake Lodge, Box 752 57730 ....(605)574-2561
Hill City
Heart of the Hills B&B, 517 Main St 57745 ....(605)574-2704
Slyvan Lake Resort, Box 1000 57745 ....(605)574-2561
Milesville
Fitch Farms, Box 8 57553 ....(605)544-3227
Yankton
The Mulberry Inn, 512 Mulberry St 57078 ....(605)665-7116

Tennessee

Allardt
Charlo B&B, Box 69 38504 ....(615)879-8056
Bolivar
Magnolia Manor, 418 N Main St 38008
Brentwood
Herbert's B&B, Box 2166, Old Smyrna 37027 ....(615)373-9300
Sunny Hill Farm B&B, 6112 Murray Ln 37027 ....(615)373-1514
Chattanooga
Alford House, 2501 Lookout Mtn Pkwy 37419 ....(615)821-7625
The Chattanooga Choo-Choo Inn, 1400 Market St 37402 .(615)266-5000
Lookout Mountain Guest House, 4415 Guild Tr 37409 ....(615)821-8307
Clarksville
Hachland Hill Inn, 1601 Madison St 37040 ....(615)255-1727
Clifton
Hidden Hollow Farm-Log Cabin, Beech Creek Rd, Hwy 228 38424
....(615)676-5295
Cookeville
"Dun Movin" B&B Log House, Rt 4, Box 279 37501 ....(615)526-1734
Scarecrow Country Inn, 1720 E Spring St 38501 ....(615)526-3434
Fayetteville
Old Cowan Plantation B&B, Box 17, Rt 2 37334 ....(615)433-0225
The Magnolias, Box 806 37334 ....(615)433-3351
Franklin
Windsong Farm, Rt 3, Sweeney Hollow Rd 37064 ....(615)794-6162
Gatlinburg
Buckhorn Inn, Rt 3 Box 393 37738 ....(615)436-4668
Leconte Lodge, PO Box 350 37738 ....(615)436-4473
Moon Mountain Lodge, 964 River Rd 37738 ....(615)436-2131
Wonderland Hotel, Rt 2 37738 ....(615)436-5490
Greeneville
Big Spring Inn, 315 N Main St 37743 ....(615)638-2917
The Inn at Pigeon Creek Farm, Pigeon Creek Rd, PO 816 37744
....(615)638-7990
Hendersonville
Monthaven, 1154 W Main 37075 ....(615)824-6319
Jonesborough
Jonesborough, 100 Woodrow Ave 37659 ....(615)753-9223
Knoxville
The Graustein Inn, 8300 Nubbin Ridge Rd 37923 ....(615)690-7007
Mountain Breeze B&B, 501 Mtn Breeze Ln 37922 ....(615)966-3917
Three Chimneys, 1302 White Ave 37916 ....(615)521-4970
Windy Hill B&B, 1031 W Park Dr 37909 ....(615)690-1488
Limestone
Snapp Inn B&B, Rt 3 Box 102 37681 ....(615)257-2482
Loudon
River Road Inn, River Road, PO Box 372 37774 ....(615)458-4861
Lyles
Silver Leaf 1815-Country Inn, Rt 1 Box 122 37098 ....(615)670-3048
Lynchburg
Lynchburg B&B, PO Box 34 37532 ....(615)759-7158
Memphis
B&B in Memphis, PO Box 41621 38174 ....(901)726-5920
Lowenstein-Long House, 217 N Waldran-1084 Poplar 38105
....(901)527-7174
The Peabody, 149 Union Ave 38103
Monteagle
Edgeworth Inn, PO Box 365 37356 ....(615)924-2669
Monterey
Walnut House, Rt 2 38574
Murfreesboro
The Black Gnat House, Beesley Rd, Rt 2, Box 209 37130 ..(615)890-0263
Clardy's Guest House, 435 E Main St 37130 ....(615)893-6030
Nashville
B&B Host Homes of Tennessee, PO Box 110227 37222-0227
....(615)331-5244
Hachland Hill Vineyard, 5396 Rawlings Rd 37080 ....(615)255-1727
Host Homes Of Tennessee, Box 110227 37222-0227 ....(615)331-5244
Miss Anne's B&B, 3033 Windemere Cir 37214 ....(615)885-1899
Paris
The Oaks, 1001 Memorial Dr 38242
Pickwick Dam
Homestead House Inn, Box 79 38365 ....(901)689-5500
Pickwick Dam, Box 76 38365 ....(901)689-5500
Pigeon Forge
Mountain Home Inn & Cottage, 200 Two View Rd, PO Box 10 37863
....(615)453-6465
Red Boiling Springs
Donoho Hotel, Box 36 37150 ....(615)699-3141
Red Boiling Inn, Box 40 37150 ....(615)699-2180
Rogersville
Hale Springs Inn, 110 W Main St 37857 ....(615)272-5171
Rugby
Historic Rugby British Colony, Hwy 52, PO Box 8 37733 .(615)628-2441
Newbury House at Historic Rugby, Hwy 52, PO Box 8 37733
....(615)628-2430
Sevierville
Blue Mountain Mist Country Inn, Rt 3 Box 490 37862 ....(615)428-2335
Kero Mountain Resort, Rt 11, Box 380 37862 ....(615)453-7514
Seymour
Country Inn, Rt 3, Chris Haven Dr 37865 ....(615)573-7170
Shiloh
Leawood-Williams Estate, PO Box 24 38376 ....(901)689-5106
Somerville
Magnolia Place, 408 S Main St 38068 ....(901)465-3906
Sweetwater
Flow Blue Inn, PO Box 495 37874 ....(615)442-2964
Vonore
Edna's B&B Home, Rt 1, Box 353A 37885 ....(615)295-2354
Wartrace
Ledford Mill & Museum, Rt 2 Box 152 37183 ....(615)298-5674
Walking Horse Hotel & Restaurant, PO Box 266 37183 ....(615)389-6407
Waverly
Nolan House Inn, Rt 4 Box 164 37185 ....(615)296-2511

Texas

Austin
Brook House, 609 W 33rd St 78705 ....(512)459-0534
The McCallum House, 613 W 32nd 78705 ....(512)451-6744
Southard House, 908 Blanco 78703 ....(512)474-4731
Bastrop
Pfeiffer House, 1802 Main St 78602 ....(512)321-2100
Pink Lady Inn, 1307 Main St 78602 ....(512)321-6273
Bellville
High Cotton Inn, 214 S Live Oak 77419 ....(409)865-9796
Ben Wheeler
Wild Briar, PO Box 21 75754 ....(214)852-3975

Texas (Continued)

Big Sandy
Annie's B&B, 106 N Tyler, PO Box 928 75755 ....(214)636-4307
Buchanan Dam
Knittel House, PO Box 261 78639 ....(512)793-6408
Castroville
Landmark Inn Historic Site, Box 577 78009 ....(512)538-2133
Center
Pine Colony Inn, 500 Shelbyville St 75935 ....(409)598-7700
Cleburne
Cleburne House, 201 N Anglin 76031 ....(817)641-0085
Comfort
Gast Haus Lodge, 944 High St 78013 ....(512)995-2304
Corpus Christi
Sand Dollar Hospitality, 3605 Mendenhall 78415 ....(512)853-1222
Cuero
Reiffert-Mugge Inn, 304 W Prairie 77954 ....(512)275-2626
Dallas
B&B Texas Style, 4224 W Red Bird Ln 75237 ....(214)298-8586
Eagle Lake
Farris 1912, 201 N McCarty 77434 ....(409)234-2546
Edom
Red Rooster Square, Rt 3, Box 3387 75756 ....(214)852-6774
El Paso
Gardner Hotel, 311 E Franklin Ave 79901 ....(915)532-3661
Room with a View, 821 Rim Rd 79902 ....(915)534-4400
Ennis
Raphael House, 500 W Ennis Ave 75119 ....(214)875-1555
Fort Davis
Indian Lodge, PO Box 786 79734 ....(915)426-3254
Sutler's Limpia Hotel, PO Box 822 79734 ....(915)426-3237
Fort Worth
Medford House, 2344 Medford Court East 76109 ....(817)924-2765
Stockyards Hotel, Main & Exchange St 76106 ....(817)625-6427
Fredericksburg
B&B Fredericksburg, 407 S Cherry 78624 ....(512)997-4712
Baron's Creek Inn, 110 E Creek St 78624 ....(512)997-9398
Be My Guest, 330 W Main 78624 ....(512)997-7227
Country Cottage Inn, 405 E Main St 78624 ....(512)997-8549
Gastehaus Schmidt, 501 W Main St 78624 ....(512)997-5612
Hoerster Bldg, Chemist Loft, 242 W Main St 78624 ....(512)997-8615
J Bar K Ranch B&B, Mason Rt Box 53-A 78624 ....(512)669-2471
Pape-Dangers Guest House, 242 W Main St 78624 ....(512)997-8615
River View Farm, 145 E Main 78624 ....(512)997-7227
Schmidt Barn, 501 West Main 78624 ....(512)997-5612
The Historic Hotel Association of Texas ....(512)997-5616
Victorian House, 619 W Main 78624 ....(512)997-4937
Galveston
Hazelwood House, 1127 Church 77550 ....(713)762-1668
Key Largo, 5400 Seawall Blvd 77550 ....(800)833-0120
La Quinta Inn, 1402 Seawall Blvd 77550 ....(800)531-5900
Mather-Root Home, 1816 Winnie 77550 ....(713)439-6253
Michael's, 1715-35th St 77550 ....(409)763-3760
Tremont House, 2300 Ship's Mechanic Row 77550 ....(409)763-0300
Victorian Inn, 511 17th St 77550 ....(409)762-3235
Galveston Island
Gilded Thistle B&B, 1805 Broadway 77550 ....(713)763-0194
Matali B&B Inn, 1727 Sealy 77550 ....(409)763-4526
Glen Rose
Inn on the River, PO Box 1417 76043 ....(817)897-2101
Goliad
White House Inn, PO Box 922 77963 ....(512)645-2701
Graham
Louise Witkowski, 800 Third St 76046
Granbury
Nutt House, Town Square 76048 ....(817)573-5612
Hillsboro
Tarlton House of 1895, 211 N Pleasant St 76645 ....(817)582-7216
Houston
La Colombe D'or, 3410 Montrose Blvd 77006 ....(713)524-7999
Sara's B&B Inn, 941 Heights Blvd 77008 ....(713)868-1130
Woodlake House, 2100 Tanglewilde #371 77063
Jefferson
Austin Cottage, 402 W Austin St 75657 ....(214)938-5941
Excelsior House, 211 W Austin 75657 ....(214)665-2513
Gingerbread House, 601 E Jefferson 75657 ....(214)665-8994
Gone With the Wind Inn, 412 Soda St 75657
Hale House, 702 South Lee 75657
Hotel Jefferson, 124 Austin St 75657 ....(214)665-2631
Magnolias Inn, 209 E Broadway 75657 ....(214)665-2754
McKay House, 306 E Delta St 75657 ....(214)665-7322
Pride House, 409 Broadway 75657 ....(214)665-2675
Queen Anne's Lace, 304 N Alley 75657 ....(214)665-2483
Stillwater Inn, 203 E Broadway 75657 ....(214)665-8415
The Cottage in Jefferson, 307 Soda 75657 ....(214)665-8572
The Magnolias, 209 Broadway 75657 ....(214)665-2754
William Clark House, 201 W Henderson 75657 ....(214)665-8880
Wise Manor, 312 Houston St 75657 ....(214)665-2386
Llano
Badu House, 601 Bessemer 78643 ....(915)247-4304
Marble Falls
Harlyn House, 508 Main St 78654 ....(512)693-7651
Marshall
Cotten's Patch, 703 E Rusk 75670 ....(214)938-8756
Ginocchio Hotel, 707 N Washington 75670 ....(214)935-7635
La Maison Malfacon, 70 E Rusk 75670 ....(214)935-6039
Meredith House, 410 E Meredith St 75670 ....(214)935-7147
Three Oaks, 609 N Washington 75670 ....(214)938-6123
Weisman-Hirsch-Beil Home, 313 S Washington 75670 ....(214)938-5504
Mcallen
La Posada, 100 N Main 78501 ....(800)292-5659
Mount Vernon
Dutton-Teague B&B Inn, 110 Roach St 75457 ....(214)537-2603
Nacogdoches
Haden Edwards Inn, 106 N Nanana 75961 ....(409)564-9999
Tol Barret House, Rt 4, Box 9400 75961 ....(409)569-1249
Navasota
The Castle, 1403 E Washington 77868 ....(409)825-8051
New Braunfels
Comfort Common, 240 S Seguin Ave 78130 ....(512)995-3030
Prince Solms Inn, 295 E San Antonio 78130 ....(512)625-9169
Rio Grande City
La Borde House, 601 E Main St 78582 ....(512)487-5101
Rusk
Thomas J. Rusk Hotel, 105 E Sixth St 75785 ....(214)683-2556
Salado
Inn At Salado, N Main At Pace Park 76571 ....(817)947-8200
San Antonio
Belle Of Monte Vista, 505 Belknap Pl 78212 ....(512)732-4006
The Bullis House Inn, PO 8059, 621 Pierce St 78208 ....(512)223-9426
Bullis House Inn, PO Box 8059 78208 ....(512)223-9426
Menger Hotel, 204 Alamo Plaza 78205 ....(512)223-4361
Terrell Castle, 950 E Grayson St 78208 ....(512)271-9145
San Augustine
The Wade House, 202 E Livingston St 75972 ....(409)275-5489
San Marcos
Aquarena Springs Inn, 1 Aquarena Dr 78666 ....(512)396-8901
Crystal River Inn, 326 West Hopkins 78666 ....(512)396-3739
Stephenville
The Oxford House, 563 N Graham 76401 ....(817)965-6885
Terlingua
Lajitas on Rio Grande, Box 400 79852 ....(915)424-3471
Village Mills
Big Thicket Guest House, Box 91 77663 ....(409)834-2875
Weimar
Weimar Country Inn, Jackson Sq 78962 ....(409)725-8888
Weslaco
Rio Grande B&B, PO Box 16 78596 ....(512)968-9646
Wimberley
Southwind B&B, Rt 2, Box 15 78676 ....(512)847-5277
Yorktown
Hygeia Health Retreat, 439 Main St 78164 ....(512)564-3670

Utah

Bluff
Recapture Lodge, Box 36 84512 ....(801)672-2281

Cedar City
Paxman's Summer House, 170 N 400 W 84720 ....(801)586-3755
Woodbury Guest House, 237 S 300 W 84720 ....(801)586-6696
Logan
The Birch Trees B&B, 315 Blvd 84321 ....(801)753-1331
Center Street B&B, 169 E Center St 84321 ....(801)752-3443
Manti
Manti House Inn, 401 N Main St 84642 ....(801)835-0161
Yardley's Inn, 190 W 200 S 84642 ....(801)835-1861
Midway
The Homestead, 700 N Homestead Dr 84049 ....(801)654-1102
Moab
Cedar Breaks Condos B&B, Center & 4th E 84532 ....(801)259-7830
Mt Pleasant
Mansion House B&B, 298 S State St 84647 ....(801)462-3031
Park City
505 Woodside, Box 2446 84060 ....(801)649-4841
Claimjumper Hotel, 573 Main St 84060 ....(801)649-8051
The Old Miners' Lodge
A B&B Inn, 615 Woodside Ave, PO Box 2639 84060-2639
....(801)645-8068
Star Hotel, 227 Main St 84060 ....(801)649-8333
The Imperial Hotel, 221 Main St, PO Box 1628 84060 ....(801)649-1904
Washington School Inn, 544 Park Ave, PO Box 536 84060
....(801)649-3800
Provo
Chez Fontaine B&B, 45 N 300 E 84601 ....(801)375-8484
Sundance, PO Box 837 84601 ....(801)225-4100
The Pullman, 415 S University Ave 84601 ....(801)374-8141
Salina
Burr House, 195 W Main St 84654 ....(801)529-7320
Salt Lake City
Brigham Street Inn, 1135 E South Temple 84102 ....(801)364-4461
Eller B&B, 123 2nd Ave #202 84103-4712 ....(802)375-2272
Pinecrest B&B Inn, 6211 Emigration Canyon Rd 84108 ....(801)583-6663
Saltair B&B, 164 S 9th E 84102 ....(801)533-8184
The Spruces B&B, 6151 S 900 E 84121 ....(801)268-8762
The National Historic B&B, 936 E 1700 South 84105 ....(801)485-3535
Westminister B&B, 1156 Blain Ave 84105 ....(801)467-4114
Sandy
Quail Hills B&B, 3744 E N Little Cottonwood 84092 ....(801)942-2858
St George
Greene Gate Village
Historic B&B Inn, 76 W Tabernacle 84770 ....(801)628-6999
Seven Wives Inn, 217 N 100 W 84770 ....(801)628-3737

Vermont

Alburg
Auberge Alburg, RD 1, Box 3 05440 ....(802)796-3169
Arlington
The Arlington Inn, Historic Rt 7A 05250 ....(802)375-6532
Arlington's West Mountain Inn, PO Box 481 05250 ....(802)375-6516
Evergreen, Sandgate, Box 2480 05250 ....(802)375-2272
Four Winds Country Inn, River Rd 05250 ....(802)375-6734
Hill Farm Inn, RR 2 Box 2015 05250 ....(802)375-2269
Inn at Sunderland, RR 2 Box 2440 05250 ....(802)362-4213
Inn on Covered Bridge Green, RD 1 3550, River Rd 05250
....(802)375-9489
Shenandoah Farm, Rt 313, Battenkill Rd 05250 ....(802)375-6372
Sycamore Inn, Rt 7 Box 2485 05250 ....(802)362-2284
The Evergreen, Sandgate Rd 05250 ....(802)375-2272
Barnard
The Silver Lake House, PO Box 13, North Rd 05081 ....(802)234-9957
Barnet
Innwood Manor, Lower Waterford Rd 05821 ....(802)633-4047
Old Homestead Inn, PO Box 35 05821 ....(802)633-4100
Barre
The Inn at Montpelier, 13 E St 05641 ....(802)223-2727
Woodruff House, 13 East St 05641 ....(802)476-7745
Barton
The Barton Inn, PO Box 67, Main St 05822 ....(802)525-4721
Fox Hall B&B, Willoughby Lake Rd 05822 ....(802)525-6930
Lafont's Dairy Farm B&B, RFD #3, Box 90 05822 ....(802)755-6127
Paupers Manse B&B, Willoughby Lake Rd, 96A 05822 ....(802)525-3222
Bellows Falls
Horsefeathers B&B, 16 Webb Terr 05101 ....(802)463-9776
Belmont
The Parmenter House, Church St 05730 ....(802)259-2009
Bennington
Bennington Hus, 208 Washington Ave 05201 ....(802)447-7972
Four Chimneys Inn, 21 West Rd 05201 ....(802)447-3500
Mt. Anthony Guest House, 226 Main St 05201 ....(802)447-7396
Safford Manor B&B, 722 Main St 05201 ....(802)442-5934
South Shire Inn, 124 Elm St 05201 ....(802)447-3839
Bethel
Eastwood House, Rt 2 Rt 107 05032 ....(802)234-9686
Greenhurst Inn, River St, RD 2, Box 60 05032 ....(802)234-9474
Poplar Manor, Rt 2 05032 ....(802)234-5426
Bondville
Alpenrose Inn, Winhall Hollow Rd 05340 ....(802)297-2750
Bradford
Merry Meadow Farm, Lower Plain, Rt 5 05033 ....(802)222-4412
Village Inn, PO Box 354 05033 ....(802)222-9303
Brandon
The Arches, 53 Park St 05733 ....(802)247-8200
Brandon Inn, 20 Park Green 05733 ....(802)247-5766
The Churchill House Inn, RD 3 Rt 73 East 05733 ....(802)247-3300
Fort Vengeance, Rt 7, RFD #1 05733 ....(802)483-2136
Inn at Tiffany Corner, RD3, Blof Course Rd 05733 ....(802)247-6571
Moffett House, 69 Park St 05733 ....(802)247-3843
Norlo Inn, 25 Grove St 05733 ....(802)247-3235
Old Mill Inn 05773 ....(802)247-8002
Brattleboro
Green River Homespun, Jacksonville Stage Rd 05301 ....(802)257-7275
Bridgewater
Clay Gates Farm, N Bridgewater Rd 05034 ....(802)672-5294
Bridgewater Corners
October Country Inn, PO Box 66 05035 ....(802)672-3412
Bristol
Long Run Inn, RD 1, Box 560 05443 ....(802)453-3233
Maplewood Farm B&B, Rt 17, RD2, Box 520 05443 ....(802)453-2992
Brookfield
Green Trails Country Inn, Pond Village 05036 ....(802)276-3412
Maggie York House, PO Box 228, Rt 1 05036 ....(802)276-3437
Brookline
Massey Farm, 340 Grassy Brook Rd 05345 ....(802)365-4716
Brownesville
Inn At Mt. Ascutney, Brook Rd 05037 ....(802)484-7725
Mill Brook B&B, PO Box 410, Rt 44 05037 ....(802)484-7283
Burlington
Howden Cottage B&B, 32 N Champlain St 05401 ....(802)864-7198
Charlotte
Green Meadows B&B, Mt. Philo Rd, Box 1300 05445 ....(802)425-3059
Chelsea
Shire Inn, PO Box 37 05038 ....(802)685-3031
Chester
Chester House, Main St, Box 708 05143 ....(802)875-2205
Greenleaf Inn, PO Box 188 05143 ....(802)875-3171
Henry Farm Inn, PO Box 646 05143 ....(802)875-2674
Hugging Bear Inn & Shoppe, Main St, Box 32 05143 ....(802)875-2412
The Inn at Long Last, PO Box 589 05143 ....(802)875-2444
Old Town Farm Inn, RD 4, Box 383B 05143 ....(802)875-2346
Rowell's Inn, RR 1, Box 269 05143 ....(802)875-3658
The Stone Hearth Inn, Rt 11 West 05143 ....(802)875-2525
Chittenden
Mountain Top Inn, Box 493, Mountain Top Rd 05737 ....(800)445-2100
Tulip Tree Inn, Chittenden Dam Rd 05737 ....(802)483-6213
Colchester
On the Lamb B&B, 60 Depot Rd 05446 ....(802)862-2144
Craftsbury
Craftsbury Inn 05826 ....(802)586-2848
Gary Meadow Dairy Farm, RR 1 Box 11 05826 ....(802)586-2536
Craftsbury Common
Craftsbury B&B 05827 ....(802)586-2206
Inn On The Common, Main St 05827 ....(802)586-9619
Cuttingsville
Maple Crest Farm, Box 120 05738 ....(802)492-3367

Vermont (Continued)

Danby
Quail's Nest B&B, PO Box 221, Main St 05739 ....(802)293-5099
Silas Griffith Inn, RR 1 Box 66F, S Main St 05739 ....(802)293-5567
Derby Line
Derby Village Inn, 46 Main St 05830 ....(802)873-3604
Dorset
Barrows House 05251 ....(802)867-4455
Cornucopia Of Dorset, Rt 30 Box 307 05251 ....(802)867-5751
Dorset Hollow B&B, Dorset Hollow Rd, Box 655 05251 ....(802)867-5993
Dorset Inn 05251 ....(802)867-5500
Dovetail Inn, Rt 30 Box 976 05251 ....(802)867-5747
The Little Lodge at Dorset, Rt 30 Box 673 05251 ....(802)867-4040
Maplewood Colonial Inn, Rt 30 Box 1019 05251 ....(802)867-4470
Marble West Inn, PO Box 22 05251 ....(802)867-4155
Village Auberge, Rt 30 Box 970 05251 ....(802)867-5715
Duxbury
Schneider Haus, Rt 100 05676 ....(802)244-7726
East Barnet
Inwood Manor, Lower Waterford Rd 05821 ....(802)633-4047
East Burke
Burke Green, RR 1 Box 81 05832 ....(802)467-3472
Old Cutter Inn, Burke Mt Access Rd 05832 ....(802)626-5152
East Calais
Lake House B&B, RFD #1, Box 142 05650 ....(802)456-8186
East Hardwick
Brick House Guests, Box 128, Brick House Rd 05836 ....(802)472-5512
East Middlebury
The Waybury Inn, Rt 125 05740 ....(802)388-4015
East Poultney
Eagle Tavern, PO Box 587 05741 ....(802)287-9498
East Wallington
White Rocks Inn 05733 ....(802)446-2077
East Warren
The Soft Landing, Airport Rd, Box 116-G 05674 ....(802)496-6531
Enosburg Falls
Berkson Farms 05450 ....(802)933-2522
Essex Junction
Varnum's, 143 Weed Rd 05452 ....(802)899-4577
Fair Haven
Fair Haven Inn, 5 Adams St 05743 ....(802)254-4907
Maplewood Inn, Rt 22A, South 05743 ....(802)265-8039
Vermont Marble Inn, 12 W Park Dr 05743 ....(802)265-8383
Fairfax
Foggy Hollow Farm, Rt 104 05454
Fairfield
Hillside View Farm, South Rd 05455 ....(802)827-4480
Fairlee
Aloha Manor, Lake Morey 05045 ....(802)333-4478
Silver Maple Lodge
& Cottages, S Main St, RR1, Box 8 05045 ....(802)333-4326
Franklin
Fair Meadow Dairy Farm, Rt 235 Box 430 05457 ....(802)285-2132
Gassets
Old Town Farm Inn, Rt 10 05143 ....(802)875-2346
Gaysville
Cobble House Inn, PO Box 49 05746 ....(802)234-5458
Goshen
Blueberry Hill Inn, RD 3 05733 ....(802)247-6735
Grafton
Old Tavern at Grafton, Main St 05146 ....(802)843-2231
Stronghold Inn, HCR 40 Rt 121 05146 ....(802)843-2203
The Hayes House 05146 ....(802)843-2461
Woodchuck Hill Farm, Middletown Rd 05146 ....(802)843-2398
Greensboro
Highland Lodge, Caspian Lake 05841 ....(802)533-2647
Guildhall
Guildhall Inn, Box 129 05905 ....(802)676-3720
Hancock
Kincraft Inn, Rt 100 Box 96 05748 ....(802)767-3734
Hardwick
Carolyn's B&B, 15 Church St 05843 ....(802)472-6338
Kahagon At Nichols Pond, Box 728, Nichols Pond 05843 (802)472-6446

Hartford
House of Seven Gables, 221 Main St, Box 526 05047 ....(802)295-1200
Highgate Springs
Tyler Place 05460 ....(802)868-3301
Hyde Park
Fitch Hill Inn, RFD 1 Box 1879 05655 ....(802)888-5941
Jamaica
Three Mountain Inn, Box 180 Bbi 05343 ....(802)874-4140
Jay
Jay Village Inn, Rt 242 05859 ....(802)988-2643
Woodshed Lodge 05859 ....(802)988-4444
Jeffersonville
Jefferson House, PO Box 288, Main St 05464 ....(802)644-2030
Windridge Inn, Main St 05464 ....(802)644-8281
Jericho
Eatonhouse, Browns Trace Box 139 05465 ....(802)899-2354
Milliken's, RD 2 Box 397 05465 ....(802)899-3993
Killington
Grey Bonnet Inn 05751 ....(800)342-2086
The Inn at Long Trail, Rt 4 Box 267 05751 ....(802)775-7181
Mountain Meadows Lodge, Rt 1 Box 3 05751 ....(802)775-1010
Mountain Morgans, RFD #1, Box 138-A 05751 ....(802)422-3096
Sherburne Valley Inn, Rt 4 05751 ....(802)422-9888
Troutbrook Lodge, PO Box 212 05751 ....(802)672-3716
The Vermont Inn, Rt 4 05751 ....(802)775-0708
Londonderry
The Highland House, RR 1 Box 107 05148 ....(802)842-3019
The Village Inn At Londgrove, RD Box 215, Landgrove 05148
....................(802)824-6673
Lower Waterford
Rabbit Hill Inn, Pucker St 05848 ....(802)748-5168
Ludlow
The Andrie Rose Inn, 13 Pleasant St 05149 ....(802)228-4846
Black River Inn, 100 Main St 05149 ....(802)228-5585
Combes Family Inn, RFD 1 Box 275 05149 ....(802)228-8799
Echo Lake, PO Box 142 05149 ....(802)228-8602
The Governor's Inn, 86 Main St 05149 ....(802)228-8830
Jewell Brook Inn, 82 Andover St, Rt 100 05149 ....(802)228-8926
Okemo Inn, RFD 1 Box 133 05149 ....(802)228-8834
Lyndonville
The Wildflower Inn, Star Rt 05851 ....(802)626-8310
Manchester
Birch Hill Inn, West Rd, Box 346 05254 ....(802)362-2761
Butternut Country House, Butternut Ln, PO Box 2043 05255
....................(802)362-3371
Inn at Willow Pond, Box 1429, Rt 7 05255 ....(802)362-4733
The Inn at Manchester, Box 41, Historic Rt 7A 05254 .....(802)362-1793
Manchester Highlands Inn, PO Box 1754, Highland Ave 05255
....................(802)362-4565
Reluctant Panther Inn, Box 678, West Rd 05254 ....(802)362-2568
River Meadow Farm, PO Box 822 05255 ....(802)362-3700
Sky Line Inn, Box 325 05254 ....(802)362-1113
Wilburton Inn, Box 468, River Rd 05254 ....(802)362-2500
Manchester Village
1811 House, Historic Rt 7A 05254 ....(802)362-1811
Village Country Inn, PO Box 408 05254 ....(802)362-1792
Marlboro
Four-in-Hand, PO Box 70, Rt 9W 05344 ....(802)254-2894
Longwood
A Country Inn at Marlboro, Rt 9 Box 86 05344 ....(802)257-1545
Whetstone Inn 05344
Mendon
Red Clover Inn, Woodward Rd 05701 ....(802)775-2290
Middlebury
Middlebury Inn, Courthouse Sq 05753 ....(800)842-4666
Stevenson House, RFD #4, Box 300 05753 ....(802)462-2866
Swift House Inn, 25 Stewart Lane 05753 ....(802)388-9925
Middletown Springs
Middletown Springs Inn, Box 1068, On The Green 05757
....................(802)235-2198
Montgomery
Eagle Lodge, Box 900 05471 ....(802)326-4518
Montgomery Center
Inn On Trout River, The Main St 05471 ....(802)326-4391
Seven Bridges inn, Main St, Box 346 05471 ....(802)326-4661

Montgomery Village
Black Lantern Inn, Route 118 05470 ....(802)326-4507
Moretown
Camel's Hump View Farm, Rt 100B 05660 ....(802)496-3614
Schultzes' Village Inn, PO Box 465 05660 ....(802)496-2366
Morgan
Seymour Lake Lodge, Rt 111 05853 ....(802)895-2752
Morrisville
Inn By The Brook, PO Box 27 05661 ....(802)888-5862
Mount Holly
Hortonville Inn, RD 1 Box 14 05758 ....(802)259-2587
Hound's Folly, Box 591 05758 ....(802)259-2718
New Haven
Horn Farnsworth B&B, Rt 7 & River Rd, Box 170A 05472 ....(802)388-2300
Newbury
Century Past, Rt 5 Box 186 05051 ....(802)266-3358
Newfane
Four Columns Inn 05345 ....(802)365-7713
Old Newfane Inn, PO Box 101 05345 ....(802)365-4427
West River Lodge, RR 1 Box 693 05354 ....(802)365-7745
North Hero
Charlie's Northland Lodge, Box 88 05474 ....(802)372-8822
North Hero House, Rt 2 PO 106 05474 ....(802)372-8237
North Thetford
Stone House Inn, Rt 5 Box 47 05054 ....(802)333-9124
North Troy
Rose Apple Acres Farm, Box 300, E Hill Rd 05859 ....(802)988-4300
Norwich
Inn At Norwich, 225 Main St 05055 ....(802)649-1143
Orleans
Valley House Inn, 4 Memorial Sq 05860 ....(802)754-6665
Orwell
Historic Brookside Farms, Rt 22A Box 036 05760 ....(802)948-2727
Perkinsville
Peregrine's Rest, Upper Falls Rd 05151 ....(802)263-5784
Peru
Russell Inn 05152 ....(802)824-6631
Wiley Inn, PO Box 37 05152 ....(802)842-6600
Pittsfield
The Inn at Pittsfield, PO Box 526 05762 ....(802)746-8943
Swiss Farm Lodge, Rt 100N 05762 ....(802)746-8341
Pittsford
Fox Brothers Farm, Corn Hill Rd 05763 ....(802)483-2870
Ironmasters Inn, Furnace Rd, RFD #1, Box 101 05763 ....(802)483-2318
Plainview
Northview, RD #2 05667 ....(802)454-7191
Plymouth
Salt Ash Inn, Jct 100 & 100A 05056 ....(802)672-3748
The Hawk Inn, Rt 100 05056 ....(802)672-3811
Post Mills
Lake House Inn, Rt 244, PO Box 65 05058 ....(802)333-4025
Poultney
Lake St. Catherine Inn, PO Box 129 05764 ....(802)287-9347
Stonebridge Inn, Rt 30 05764 ....(802)287-9849
Tower Hall B&B, 2 Bentley Ave 05764 ....(802)287-4004
Proctorsville
Allens' Inn of Proctorsville, Depot St, PO 78 05153 ....(802)226-7970
Castle Inn, Rt 103 & 131, PO Box 157 05153 ....(802)226-7222
The Golden Stage Inn, Depot St, PO Box 218 05153 ....(802)226-7744
Okemo Lantern Lodge, PO Box 247 05153 ....(802)226-7770
Putney
Hickory Ridge House, RFD 3 Box 1410 05346 ....(802)387-5709
Mapleton Farm B&B, RD 2, Box 510 05346 ....(802)257-5252
Putney Inn, Depot Rd 05346 ....(802)387-6617
Quechee
Parker House, 16 Main St, Box 0780 05059 ....(802)295-6077
Quechee B&B, Rt 4 Box 0080 05059 ....(802)295-1776
Quechee Inn
At Marshland Farm, Clubhouse Rd, Box 104 05059 ....(802)295-3133
Randolph
The Three Stallion Inn, RD 2, Stock Farm Rd 05060 ....(802)728-5575
Reading
Hapgood Cottage, Bailey's Mills Rd 05062 ....(802)484-5540
The Peeping Cow B&B, Rt 106 Box 47 05062 ....(802)484-5036

Readsboro
Old Coach Inn, RR 1 Box 260 05350 ....(802)423-5394
Richmond
Rich Mound Acres B&B, Williams Hill Rd, Box 272 05477 ....(802)434-2454
Ripton
Chipman Inn, Rt 125 05766 ....(802)388-2390
Peaceful Acres, PO Box 114 05466 ....(802)388-2076
Rochester
Harvey's Mountain View Inn 05767 ....(802)767-4273
Liberty Hill Farm 05767 ....(802)767-3926
The New Homestead, PO Box 25 05767 ....(802)767-4751
Tupper Farm Lodge, RR 1 Box 149 05767 ....(802)767-4243
Royalton
Fox Stand Inn & Restaurant, Rt 14 05068 ....(802)763-8437
Rutland
Hillcrest Guest House, RR 1 Box 4459 05701 ....(802)775-1670
Saint Albans
Bellevue, 9 Parsons Ln 05478 ....(802)527-1115
Saint Johnsbury
Broadview Farm B&B, RFD #2, Box 153 05819 ....(802)748-9902
Echo Ledge Farm Inn, Rt 2 Box 77 05838 ....(802)748-4750
Looking Glass Inn, Rt 18 Box 199 05819 ....(802)748-3052
Saxtons River
Red Barn Guest House, Hatfield Ln 05154 ....(802)869-2566
Saxtons River Inn, Main St 05154 ....(802)869-2110
Shaftsbury
Munro Hawkins House, Historic Rt 7A 05262 ....(802)447-2286
Shoreham Village
Shoreham Inn, On The Village Green 05770 ....(802)897-5081
Shrewsbury
Buckmaster Inn, Lincoln Hill Rd, RR 1 Box 118 05738 ....(802)492-3485
South Burlington
Lindenwood, 916 Shelburne Rd 05404 ....(802)862-2144
South Londonderry
Londonderry Inn, PO Box 3018 05155 ....(802)824-5226
South Newfane
Inn At South Newfane, Dover Rd 05351 ....(802)348-7191
South Strafford
Watercourse Way B&B, Rt 132 Box 101 05070 ....(802)765-4314
South Wallingford
Green Mountain Tea Room, Rt 7 RR 1 Box 400 05773 ....(802)446-2611
South Woodstock
Kedron Valley Inn, Rt 106 Box 145 05071 ....(802)457-1473
Springfield
Hartness House Inn, 30 Orchard St 05156 ....(802)885-2115
Starksboro
North Country B&B, Rt 116, PO Box 1 05487 ....(802)453-3911
Stockbridge
Scarborough Inn, Rt 100 HC65 #23 05772 ....(802)746-8141
Stowe
The 1860 House, School St, PO Box 276 05672 ....(802)253-7351
Bittersweet Inn, Rt 100 S 05672 ....(802)253-7787
Edson Hill Manor, RR 1 Box 2480 05672 ....(802)253-7371
Fiddler's Green Inn, Mountain Rd Rt 108 05672 ....(802)253-8124
Fountain House, RR2, Box 2480 05672 ....(802)253-9285
Foxfire Inn, RD 2 Rt 100 05672 ....(802)253-4887
Gables Inn, Mountain Rd 05672 ....(802)253-7730
Golden Kitz Lodge, RD 1 Box 2980 05672 ....(802)253-4217
Green Mountain Inn, PO Box 60 05672 ....(802)253-7301
Grey Fox Inn, Route 108 05672 ....(802)253-8921
Innsbruck Inn, RR1, Box 1570 05672 ....(802)253-8582
Mountain Brook Inn, 1505 Mountain Rd 05672 ....(800)553-3035
Nichols Lodge, Box 1098 05672 ....(802)253-7683
Siebeness Lodge 05672 ....(802)253-8942
Ski Inn, Rt 108, Mountain Rd 05672 ....(802)253-4050
Spruce Pond Inn 05672 ....(802)253-4828
Stowe-Away Lodge, RR 1 Box 1360 05672 ....(802)253-7574
Stowe-Bound Lodge, RR 2 Box 2890 05672 ....(802)253-4515
The Inn at the Brass Lantern, RR2, Box 2610 05672 ....(802)253-2229
The Yodler, Rt 1 Box 10 05672 ....(802)253-4836
Wood Chip Inn, RR 1, Box 1618 05672 ....(802)253-9080
Ye Olde England Inne, Mountain Rd 05672 ....(802)253-7558
Sunderland
Eastbrook B&B, River Rd 05250 ....(802)375-6509

Vermont (Continued)

The Inn at Sunderland, Historic Rt 7A 05250 .... (802)362-4213

Townshend

Boardman House, On the Green 05353 .... (802)365-4086
Townshend Country Inn, RR 1, Box 3100 05353 .... (802)365-4141

Tunbridge

Mill Pond B&B, Rt 110 Spring Rd, Box 1 05077 .... (802)889-9441

Vergennes

Basin Harbor Club, Basin Harbor Rd 05491 .... (802)475-2311
Emersons' Guest House, 82 Main St 05491 .... (802)877-3293
Strong House Inn, RD 1 Box 9, Rt 22A 05491 .... (802)877-3337

Waitsfield

Finchingfield Farm, Rt 100, Box 159 05673 .... (802)496-7555
Honeysuckles Inn, PO Box 828 05673 .... (802)469-6200
Hyde Away, Rt 17 05673 .... (802)496-2322
Knoll Farm Country Inn, Bragg Hill Rd 05673 .... (802)496-3939
Lareau Farm Country Inn, PO Box 563, Rt 100 05673 ...... (802)496-4949
Mad River Barn, Rt 17 Box 88 05673 .... (802)496-3310
Millbrook, RFD Box 62 05673 .... (802)496-2405
Mountain View Inn, Rt 17 RFD Box 69 05673 .... (802)496-2426
Olde Tymes Inn, Rt 100, PO Box 165 05673 .... (802)196-3875
Round Barn Farm, RR Box 247 05673 .... (802)496-2276
Snuggery Inn, Box 65, RR #1 05673 .... (802)496-2322
The Valley Inn, Rt 100 Box 8 05673 .... (802)496-3450
Tucker Hill Lodge, RFD1, Box 147, Rt 17 05673 .... (802)496-3983

Wallingford

Dunham House, 7 S Main St 05773 .... (802)446-2600
Wallingford Inn, Box 404 05773 .... (802)446-2849
White Rocks Inn, RR 1 Box 297, Rt 7 05773 .... (802)446-2077

Warren

Beaver Pond Farm Inn, RD Box 306, Golf Course Rd 05674 .... (802)583-2861
Pitcher Inn, PO Box 408 05674 .... (802)496-3831
South Hollow Farm, RR1, Box 287 05674 .... (802)496-5627

Waterbury

Inn at Blush Hill, Blush Hill Rd, Box 1266 05676 .... (802)244-7529
The Inn at Thatcher Brook Falls, RD 2, Box 62 05676 ..... (802)244-5911

Waterbury Center

The Black Locust Inn, RR 1, Box 715 05677 .... (802)244-7490

Weathersfield

The Inn at Weathersfield, Rt 106, PO Box 165 05151 .... (802)263-9217

West Charleston

Hunts' Hideaway, RR1, Box 570 05872 .... (802)895-4432

West Dover

Austin Hill Inn, Rt 100, Box 859 05356 .... (802)464-5281
Deerhill Inn, PO Box 397 05356 .... (802)464-3100
Doveberry Inn, Rt 100 05356 .... (802)464-5652
Inn At Sawmill Farm, Box 8 05356 .... (802)464-8131
Snow Den Inn, Rt 100 05356 .... (802)464-9355
West Dover Inn, Rt 100 Box 506 05356 .... (802)464-5207

West Rutland

The Silver Fox Inn, Rt 133 Box 1222 05777 .... (802)438-5555

West Townsend

Windham Hill Inn, RR 1 Box 44 05359 .... (802)874-4080

Weston

1830 Inn on the Green, Rt 100 Box 104 05161 .... (802)824-6789
Darling Family Inn, Rt 100 05161 .... (802)824-6286
Inn At Weston, Rt 100 Box 56 05161 .... (802)824-5804
The Colonial House, Rt 100 Box 138 05161 .... (802)824-6286
Wilder Homestead Inn, RR 1 Box 106D 05161 .... (802)842-8172

White River Junction

Serenity Hill Farm, Center of Town Rd 05001 .... (802)295-9075

Williamstown

Autumn Crest Inn, Clark Rd 05679 .... (802)433-6627
Rosewood Inn, Rt 14 Box 31 05679 .... (802)433-5822

Williamsville

The Country Inn
Williamsville, Grimes Hill Rd, Box 166 05362 .... (802)348-7148

Wilmington

Brook Bound Bldg/Hermitage, Coldbrook Rd 05363 .... (802)464-3511
Darcroft's Schoolhouse, Rt 100 05363 .... (802)464-2631
Hermitage Inn, Coldbrook Rd 05363 .... (802)464-3511
Misty Mountain Lodge, Stowe Hill Rd, Box 114 05363 ..... (802)464-3961
Nordic Hills Lodge, 179 Coldbrook Rd 05363 .... (802)464-5130
Nutmeg Inn, Rt 9W, Molly Starke Tr 05363 .... (802)464-3351
On the Rocks Lodge 05363 .... (802)464-8364
Slalom Lodge, Shafter St 05363 .... (802)464-3783
The Red Shutter Inn, Box 636, Rt 9 05363 .... (802)464-3768
The White House, Rt 9 05363 .... (802)464-2136

Windsor

Juniper Hill Inn, Juniper Hill Rd, RR 1 Box 79 05089 .... (802)464-2135

Woodstock

Carriage House, Rt 4 W 05091 .... (802)457-4322
The Charleston House, 21 Pleasant St 05091 .... (802)457-3843
Deer Brook Inn, HCR 35, Box 189 05091 .... (802)672-3713
Jackson House, Rt 4 W 05091
Lincoln Covered Bridge Inn, RR 2, Box 40 05091 .... (802)457-3312
The Winslow House, #38, Rt 4 W 05091 .... (802)457-1820
The Woodstock Inn, Fourteen The Green 05091 .... (802)457-1000
Three Church Street, 3 Church St 05091 .... (802)457-1925
Village Inn Of Woodstock, 41 Pleasant St 05091 .... (802)457-1255

Virginia

Abingdon

Litchfield Hall, 247 E Valley St 24210 .... (703)628-9317
Maplewood Farm, Rt 7, Box 272 24210
Martha Washington Inn, 150 W Main St 24210 .... (703)628-3161
Mason Place B&B, 243 Mason Place, NW 24210 .... (703)628-2887
Summerfield Inn, 101 W Valley St 24210 .... (703)628-5905

Aldie

Little River Inn, PO Box 116 22001 .... (703)327-6742

Alexandria

Alexandria Lodgings, PO Box 416 22313 .... (703)836-5575
Princely B&B, Ltd., 819 Prince St 22314 .... (703)683-2159

Arlington

Memory House, 6404 N Washington Blvd 22205 .... (703)534-4607

Banco

Olive Mill B&B, Rt 231 22711 .... (703)923-4664

Bassett

Annie's Country Inn, Rt 5 Box 562 24055 .... (703)629-1517

Bedford

Elmo's Rest, Rt 2 Box 198 24523 .... (703)586-3707
Peaks of Otter Lodge, PO Box 489 24523 .... (703)586-1081

Bowling Green

The Old Mansion 22427

Bridgewater

Bear & Dragon B&B, 401 N Main St 22812 .... (703)828-2807

Burkeville

Hyde Park Farm, Rt 2 Box 38 23922 .... (804)645-8431

Charles City

Edgewood Plantation, Rt 5 Historic 23030 .... (804)829-2962
North Bend Plantation, Rt 1 Box 13A 23030 .... (804)829-5176
Piney Grove
Southall's Plantation, Rt 1 Box 148, Piney Grove 23030-9735 .... (804)829-2480

Charleston

Benedict Haid Farm, N 8 Hale St 25301 .... (804)346-1054

Charlottesville

200 South Street Inn, 200 South St 22901 .... (804)979-0200
Carrsbrook, Guesthouses, PO Box 5737 22905 .... (804)979-7264
English Inn, 316 14th St NW 22903 .... (804)295-7707
Guesthouses, PO Box 5737 22905 .... (804)979-7264
Silver Thatch Inn, 3001 Hollymead Dr, PO Box 6370 22901 .... (804)978-4686
Westbury, Guesthouses, PO Box 5737 22905 .... (804)979-8327
Woodstock Hall, Rt 3 Box 40 22901 .... (804)293-8977

Chatham

Sims Mitchell House, Box 846, 242 Whittle St SW 24531

Chincoteague

Channel Bass Inn, 100 Church St 23336 .... (804)336-6148
Miss Molly's Inn, 113 N Main St 23336 .... (804)336-6686
The Victorian Inn, 105 Clark St 23336 .... (804)336-1161
Year Of The Horse Inn, 600 S Main St 23336

Christiansburg

The The Oaks, 311 E Main St 24073 .... (703)381-1500

Churchville
Buckhorn Inn, Star Rt Box 139 24421 ....(703)337-6900
Culpeper
Fountain Hall B&B, 609 S East St 22701 ....(703)825-8200
Fairfax
Bailiwick Inn, 4023 Chain Bridge Rd 22030 ....(703)691-2266
Flint Hill
Caledonia Farm B&B, Rt 1 Box 2080 22627 ....(703)675-3693
Floyd
Brookfield Inn B&B, PO Box 341 24091 ....(703)763-3363
Fredericksburg
Fredericksburg Colonial Inn, 1707 Princess Anne St 22401 ....(703)371-5666
Kenmore Inn, 1200 Princess Anne St 22401 ....(703)371-7622
La Vista Plantation, 4420 Guinea Station Rd 22401 ....(703)898-8444
The Richard Johnston Inn, 711 Caroline St 22401 ....(703)899-7606
The McGrath House, 225 Princess Anne St 22401 ....(703)371-4363
Front Royal
Chester House Inn, 43 Chester St 22630 ....(703)635-3937
Gordonsville
Sleepy Hollow Farm, Rt 3 Box 43 on VA 231 22942 ....(703)832-5555
Hamilton
Hamilton Garden Inn, 353 W Colonial Hwy 22068 ....(703)338-3693
Harrisonburg
Joshua Wilton House, 412 S Main St 22801 ....(703)434-4464
Haywood
Shenandoah Springs Country Inn 22722 ....(703)923-4300
Hillsboro
Inn Between the Hills, RR 3, Rt 9, PO 68A 22132 ....(703)668-6162
Hot Springs
Vine Cottage Inn, Rt 220 24445 ....(703)839-2422
Irvington
King Carter Inn, PO Box 425 22480 ....(804)438-6053
Lancaster
The Inn at Levelfields, Star Rt 3 Box 216 22503 ....(804)435-6887
Leesburg
Laurel Brigade Inn, 20 W Market St 22075 ....(703)777-1010
Norris House Inn, 108 Loudoun St SW 22075 ....(703)777-1806
Lexington
Alexander-Withrow House, 3 W Washington 24450 ....(703)463-2044
Fassifern B&B, Rt 5 Box 87 24450 ....(703)463-1013
Historic Country Inn, 11 N Main St 24450 ....(703)463-2044
Llewellyn Lodge at Lexington, 603 S Main St 24450 ....(703)463-3235
Maple Hall, 11 N Main St 24450
McCampbell Inn, 11 N Main St 24450 ....(703)463-2044
Luray
Mountain View House B&B, 151 S Court St 22835 ....(703)743-3723
The Ruffner House, Rt 4 Box 620 22835 ....(703)743-7855
Shenandoah Countryside B&B, Rt 2 Box 377 22835 ....(703)743-6434
Lynchburg
Sojourners B&B, PO Box 3587 24503
Mathews
Ravenswood Inn, PO Box 250 23109 ....(804)725-7272
Riverfront House & Cottage, Rt 14 E, PO Box 310 23109 ....(804)725-9975
McGaheysville
Shenandoah Valley Farm & Inn, Rt 1 Box 142 22840 ....(703)289-5402
Middleburg
Briar Path At Middleburg, PO Box 803 22117 ....(703)327-4455
Red Fox Inn
& Mosby's Tavern, PO Box 385, 2 E Washington St 22117 ....(703)687-6301
Welbourne 22117 ....(703)687-3201
Middletown
Wayside Inn Since 1797, 7783 Main St 22645 ....(703)869-1797
Millwood
Brookside 22646 ....(703)837-1780
Mollusk
Greenvale Manor, Rt 354, PO Box 70 22517 ....(804)462-5995
Monterey
Highland Inn, PO Box 40 24465 ....(703)468-2143
Montross
The Inn at Montross, Courthouse Sq 22520 ....(804)493-9097
Mount Jackson
Sky Chalet, Star Rd, Box 28 22842 ....(703)856-2147

The Widow Kip's
Country Inn, Rt 1 Box 117 22842 ....(703)477-2400
Natural Bridge
Burger's County Inn B&B, Rt 1 Box 564 24578 ....(703)291-2464
Nellysford
The Meander Inn at Penny Lane Farm, Routes 612 & 613, Box 443 22958 ....(804)361-1121
New Market
A Touch of Country B&B, 9329 Congress St 22844 ....(703)740-8030
Occoquan
Rockledge B&B, 410 Mill St 22125 ....(703)690-3377
Onacock
Colonial Manor Inn, PO Box 94, Market St 23417 ....(804)787-3521
Orange
Hidden Inn, 249 Caroline St 22960 ....(703)672-3625
Mayhurst Inn, US 15 South, PO Box 707 22960 ....(703)672-5597
Paris
The Ashby Inn, Rt 1 Box 2A 22130 ....(703)592-3900
Petersburg
Mayfield Inn, W Washington PO Box 2265 23803 ....(804)733-0866
The High Street Inn, 405 High St 23803 ....(804)733-0505
Raphine
Oak Spring Farm & Vineyard, Rt 1, Box 356 24472 ....(703)377-2398
Rappahannock
Bunree, PO Box 53 22002 ....(703)937-4133
Richmond
Abbie Hill B&B, PO Box 4503 23220 ....(804)355-5855
B&B On The Hill, 2304 E Broad St 23223 ....(804)780-3746
Bensonhouse of Richmond at Monument, 2036 Monument Ave 23220 ....(804)353-6900
The Catlin-Abbott House, 2304 E Broad St 23223 ....(804)780-3746
Duncan Lee House, PO Box 15131 22314 ....(804)321-6277
Mr. Patrick Henry's Inn, 2300 E Broad St 23223 ....(804)644-1322
The Carrington Row Inn, 2309 E Broad St 23223 ....(804)343-7005
The Leonine Experience, PO Box 4772 23220 ....(804)349-1952
Roanoke
The Mary Blandon House B&B, 381 Washington Ave Old SW 24016 ....(703)344-5361
Scottsville
Chester, Rt 4, PO Box 57 24590 ....(804)286-3960
High Meadows, Rt 4, Box 6 24590 ....(804)286-2218
Smith Mountain Lake
Holland-Duncan House, Rt 3 Box 681 24121 ....(703)721-8510
Manor at Taylor's Store, Rt 1 Box 533 24184 ....(703)721-3951
Sperryville
Conyers House, Slate Mills Rd 22740 ....(703)987-8025
Nethers Mill, Rt 1, Box 62 22740 ....(703)987-8625
Staunton
Belle Grae Inn, 515 W Frederick St 24401 ....(703)886-5151
Frederick House, Frederick and New Streets 24401 ....(703)885-4220
Thornrose House At Gypsy Hill, 531 Thornrose Ave 24401 ....(703)885-7026
Steele's Tavern
The Osceola Mill Country Inn 24476 ....(703)377-6455
Strasburg
Hotel Strasburg, 201 Holliday St 22657 ....(703)465-9191
Surrey
Surrey House 23883 ....(804)294-3191
Swoope
Lambsgate B&B, Rt 1 Box 63 24479 ....(703)337-6929
Syria
Grave's Mountain Lodge 22743 ....(703)923-4231
Tangier
Sunset Inn, Box 156 23440 ....(804)891-2535
Trevilians
Prospect Hill, Rt 613, RD 3 Box 430 23093 ....(703)967-0844
Upperville
1763 Inn, Rt 1 Box 19 22176 ....(703)592-3848
Urbanna
The Town House, 1880 Prince George St, Box 757 23175 ....(804)758-3521
Virginia Beach
The Picket Fence, 209 43rd St 23451 ....(804)428-8861
Wachapreague
The Burton House, 11 Brooklyn St 23480 ....(804)787-4560

Virginia (Continued)

Warenton
Rosemont Farm Inn, Rt 3 Box 240 22186 ....(703)347-5422
Warm Springs
The Inn at Gristmill Square, PO Box 359 24484 ....(703)839-2231
Meadow Lane Lodge, Star Rt A Box 110 24484 ....(703)839-5959
Three Hills Inn, PO Box 99 24484 ....(703)839-5381
Washington
The Foster-Harris House, PO 333 22747 ....(703)675-3757
Heritage House B&B, Main St, PO Box 427 22747 ....(703)675-3207
Inn at Little Washington, Box 300 22747 ....(703)675-3800
The Inn at Little Washington, PO Box 300, Middle & Main Sts 22747 ....(703)675-3800
Waterford
The Pink House 22190 ....(703)882-3453
White Post
L'Auberge Provencale, PO Box 119 22663 ....(703)837-1375
Williamsburg
Applewood Colonial B&B, 605 Richmond Rd 23185 ......(804)229-0205
Brass Lantern Lodge, 1782 Jamestown Rd 23185 ....(804)229-4320
The Cedars, 616 Jamestown Rd 23185 ....(804)229-3591
Fox Grape Of Williamsburg, 701 Monumental Ave 23185 (804)229-6914
Governor's Trace, 303 Capitol Landing Rd 23185 ....(804)229-7552
Liberty Rose Colonial B&B, 1022 Jamestown Rd 23185 .(804)253-1260
Newport House, 710 South Henry St 23185 ....(804)229-1775
War Hill Inn, 4560 Long Hill Rd 23185 ....(804)565-0248
Wood's Guest Home, 1208 Stewart Dr 23185 ....(804)229-3376
Wirtz
Manor at Taylor's Store, Rt 1, Box 533 24184 ....(703)721-3951
Woodstock
Country Fare, 402 N Main St, Rt 11 22664 ....(703)459-4828
The Inn at Narrow Passage, PO Box 608 22664 ....(703)459-8000
Schlisselsmith 22664 ....(703)459-5369
The Candlewick Inn, 127 N Church St 22664 ....(703)459-8008

Washington

Acme
River Valley B&B, Box 158 98220 ....(206)595-2686
Anacortes
Channel House, 2902 Oakes Ave 98221 ....(206)293-9382
Hasty Pudding House, 1312 8th Street 98221 ....(206)293-5773
Lowman House, 701 "K" Ave 98221 ....(206)293-0590
Nantucket Inn, 3402 Commercial Ave 98221 ....(206)293-6007
White Gull, 420 Commercia 98221 ....(206)293-7011
Anohomish
Countryman B&B, 11 Cedar 98290 ....(206)568-9622
Ashford
Alexander's Country Inn, Highway 706 98304 ....(206)569-2300
Ashford Mansion, Box G 98304 ....(206)569-2739
Growly Bear, PO Box 103 98304 ....(206)569-2339
National Park Inn, Mt Ranier Guest Services, Star Rt 98304 ....(206)569-2563
Bainbridge Island
Beach Cottage, 5831 Ward Ave NE 98110 ....(206)842-6081
Bombay House, 8490 Beck Rd NE 98110 ....(206)842-3926
Olympic View B&B, 15415 Harvey Rd NE 98110 ....(206)842-4671
Bellevue
Bellevue B&B, 830-100th Ave SE 98004 ....(206)453-1048
Petersen B&B, 10228 SE 8th 98004 ....(206)454-9334
Bellingham
The Castle B&B, 1103 15th & Knox Sts 98225 ....(206)676-0974
De Cann House, 2610 Eldridge Ave 98225 ....(206)734-9172
North Garden Inn, 1014 N Garden 98225 ....(206)671-7828
Schnauzer Crossing, 4421 Lakeway Dr 98226 ....(206)733-0055
Bingen
The Grand Old House, Hwy 14 PO Box 667 98605 ....(509)493-2838
Bremerton
Willcox House, 2390 Tekiu Rd 98312 ....(206)830-4492
Carson
Carson Hot Springs Hotel, PO Box 370 98610 ....(509)427-8292
Cathlamet
Country Keeper B&B Inn, 61 Main St, PO Box 35 98612 ..(206)795-3030
Chelan
Em's B&B, PO Box 206, 304 Wapato 98816 ....(509)682-4149
Mary Kay's Whaley Mansion, Rt 1, Box 693 98816 ....(509)682-5735
North Cascades Lodge, PO Box W 98816 ....(509)682-4711
Chimacum
Summer House, 2603 Center Rd 98325 ....(206)732-4017
Colville
Lake Side Manor, Tiger Star Rt, Box 194 99114 ....(509)684-8741
Concrete Birdsview
Cascade Mountain Inn, 3840 Pioneer Ln 98237 ....(206)826-4333
Coupeville
Captain Whidbey, 2072 W Captain Whidbey Inn Rd 98239 ....(206)678-4097
Colonel Crockett Farm, 1012 S Ft. Casey Rd 98239 ....(206)466-3207
Victorian House, PO Box 761, 602 N Main 98239 ....(206)678-5305
Eastsound
Kangaroo House, 5 North Beach Rd, Orcas Island 98245 .(206)376-2175
Outlook Inn, Box 210 Main St 98245 ....(206)376-2200
Rosario Resort Hotel 88245 ....(206)376-2222
Eatonville
Old Mill House B&B, PO Box 543 98328 ....(206)832-6506
Edmonds
Heather House, 1011 "B" Ave 98020 ....(206)778-7233
Hudgrens Haven, 9313-190th SW 98020 ....(206)776-2202
Maple Tree B&B, 18313 Olympic View Dr 98020 ....(206)774-8420
Pinkham's Pillow, Dayton St & 3rd Ave 98020 ....(206)774-3406
Ferndale
Anderson House B&B, 2140 Main St 98248 ....(206)384-3450
Hill Top B&B, 5832 Church Rd 98248 ....(206)384-3619
Forks
Miller Tree Inn, PO Box 953 98331 ....(206)374-6806
Freeland
Cliff House, 5440 S Grigware Rd 98249 ....(206)321-1566
Pillars By The Sea, 1367 E Bayview 98249 ....(205)221-7736
Friday Harbor
Blair House B&B, 345 Blair Ave 98250 ....(206)378-5907
Collins House, 225 A St 98250 ....(206)378-5834
Moon & Six Pence, 3021 Beaverton Valley Rd 98250 ....(206)378-4138
Olympic Lights, 4531A Cattle Point Rd 98250 ....(206)378-3186
San Juan Inn, PO Box 776 98250 ....(206)378-2070
Tucker House B&B, 260 B St 98250 ....(206)378-2783
Wharfside B&B, PO Box 1212 98250 ....(206)378-5661
Gig Harbor
American Hearth B&B, 7506 Soundview Dr 98335 ....(206)851-2196
Olde Glencove Hotel, 9418 Glencove Rd 98335 ....(206)884-2835
Gold Bar
Bush House, PO Box 863, 5th & Index Aves 98251 ....(206)363-1244
Goldendale
Three Creeks Lodge, 2120 Hwy 97 Satus Pas 98620 ....(509)773-4026
Goose Prarie
Hopkinson House, 862 Bumping River Rd 98929 ....(509)248-2264
Greenbank
Guest House B&B & Cottages, 835 E Christenson Rd 98253 ....(206)678-3115
Ilwaco
The Inn at Ilwaco, 120 Williams St, NE 98624 ....(206)642-8686
Index
Bush House, PO Box 58 98256 ....(206)793-2312
Issaquah
Wildflower Inn, 25237 Issaquah-Fall City 98027 ....(206)392-1196
Kirkland
Shumway Mansion, 11410 99th Place NE 98033 ....(206)823-2303
La Conner
Downey House, 1880 Chilberg Rd 98257 ....(206)678-3115
Heron in La Conner, Box 716, 117 Maple St 98257 ....(206)466-4626
Katy's Inn, PO Box 304, 503 S 3rd 98257 ....(206)466-3366
La Conner Country Inn, PO Box 573 98257 ....(206)466-3101
Rainbow Inn, 1075 Chilberg Rd, PO Box 1600 98257 ......(206)466-4578
Langley
Country Cottage of Langley, PO Box 459, 215 6th St 98260 ....(206)221-8709
Lone Lake B&B, 5206 S Bayview 98260 ....(206)321-5325
The Orchard, 619 3rd St 98260 ....(206)221-7880
Whidbey House, PO Box 156, 106 First St 98260 ....(206)221-7115

Leavenworth
Bavarian Meadows B&B, 11099 Eagle Creek Rd 98826 ..... (509)548-4449
Edel Haus B&B, 320 Ninth St 98826 ..... (509)548-4412
Haus Lorelei Inn, 347 Division St 98826 ..... (509)548-5726
Haus Rohrback, 12882 Ranger Rd 98826 ..... (206)548-7024
Hotel Europa, 833 Front St 98826 ..... (509)548-5221
Mc Clain's B&B, 1226 Front St 98826 ..... (509)548-7755
Old Blewett Pass B&B, 3470 Hwy 97 98826 ..... (509)548-4475
Longmire
National Park Inn 98398 ..... (206)569-2565
Lopez Island
Inn at Swifts Bay, Rt 2 Box 3402 98261 ..... (206)468-3636
Lummi Island
The Willows, 2579 W Shore Dr 98262 ..... (206)758-2620
West Shore Farm, 2781 W Shore Dr 98262 ..... (206)754-2600
Lynden
Le Cocq House, 719 W Edson 98264 ..... (206)354-3032
Maple Valley
Maple Valley B&B, 20020 SE 228th 98038 ..... (206)432-1409
Mazawa
Mazawa Country Inn 98833 ..... (509)996-2681
Montesano
Sylvan Haus, Box 416, 417 Wilder Hill Rd 98563 ..... (206)249-3453
Morton
St. Helen's Manorhouse, 7476 US Hwy 12 98356 ..... (206)498-5243
Mount Vernon
Downey House, 1880 Chilberg Rd 98272 ..... (206)466-3207
White Swan Guest House, 1388 Moore Rd 98273 ..... (206)445-6805
Nordland
Ecologic Place, 10 Beach Dr 98358 ..... (206)385-3077
North Bend
Apple Tree Inn, 43317 S North Bend Way 98045 ..... (206)888-3672
Hillwood Gardens, 41812 SE 142nd St 98045 ..... (206)888-0799
Olympia
Harbinger Inn, 1136 E Bay Dr 98506 ..... (206)754-0389
Puget View Guesthouse, 7924 61st NE 98506 ..... (206)459-1676
Sylvester House, 1803 Capitol Way 98501 ..... (206)786-8582
Unicorn's Rest, 316 E Tenth St 98501 ..... (206)754-9613
Orcas
Orcas Hotel, PO Box 155 98280 ..... (206)376-4300
Woodsong B&B, PO Box 32 98280 ..... (206)376-2340
Orcas Island
Turtleback Farm Inn, Rt 1 Box 650, Eastsound 98245 ..... (206)376-4914
Packwood
Packwood Hotel, Rt 256 98361 ..... (206)494-5431
Pateros
Amy's Manor B&B, PO Box 411 98846 ..... (509)923-2334
French House B&B, 206 W Warren 98846 ..... (509)923-2626
Point Roberts
Old House, 674 Kendor Rd 98281 ..... (206)945-5210
The Olde House, 674 Kendor Rd 98281 ..... (206)945-5210
Port Angeles
Bennett House B&B, 325 E 6th 98362 ..... (206)457-0870
Glen Mar By the Sea, 318 N Eunice 98362 ..... (206)457-3424
Harbour House, 139 W 14th 98362 ..... (206)457-3424
Lake Crescent Lodge, Star Rt 1 98362 ..... (206)928-3211
Tudor Inn, 1108 S Oak 98362 ..... (206)452-3138
Port Orchard
Ogle's B&B, 1307 Dogwood Hills SW 98366 ..... (206)876-9170
Port Townsend
Arcadia Country Inn, 1891 S Jacob Miller Rd 98368 ..... (206)385-5245
Bishop Victorian Suites, 714 Washington St 98368 ..... (206)385-6122
Hastings House, 313 Walker St 98368 ..... (206)385-3553
Heritage House Inn, 305 Pierce St 98368 ..... (206)385-6800
James House, 1238 Washington 98368 ..... (206)385-1238
Lincoln Inn, 538 Lincoln 98368 ..... (206)385-6677
Lizzie's, 731 Pierce St 98368 ..... (206)385-4168
Manresa Castle, PO Box 564, 7th & Sheridan 98368 ..... (206)385-5750
Palace Hotel, 1004 Water St 98368 ..... (206)385-0773
Starrett House Inn, 744 Clay St 98368 ..... (206)385-3205
Poulsbo
Manor Farm Inn, 26069 Big Valley Rd 98370 ..... (206)779-4628
Quinault
Lake Quinault Lodge, PO Box 7, S Shore Rd 98575 ..... (206)288-2571

Randle
Hampton House B&B, 409 Silverboork Rd 98377
Redmond
A Colonial B&B, 1011-240th Ave NE 98053 ..... (206)868-4159
Roche Harbor
Hotel De Haro, PO Box 1 98250 ..... (206)378-2155
Roche Harbor Resort 98250 ..... (206)378-2155
Seattle
Beech Tree Manor, 1405 Queen Anne Ave N 98109 ..... (206)281-7037
Burton House, PO Box 9902 98109 ..... (206)285-5945
Challenger, 809 Fairview Place N 98109 ..... (206)340-1201
Chambered Nautilus B&B Inn, 5005 22nd NE 98105 ..... (206)522-2536
Chelsea Station B&B Inn, 4915 Linden Ave N 98103 ..... (206)547-6077
College Inn Guest House, 4000 University Way NE 98105 ..... (206)633-4441
Galer Place, 318 W Galer St 98119 ..... (206)282-5339
Hanson House, 1526 Palm Ave SW 98116 ..... (206)937-4157
Marit's B&B, 6208 Palatine Ave N 98103 ..... (206)782-7900
Mildred's B&B, 1202 15th Ave E 98112 ..... (206)325-6072
Roberta's B&B, 1147 16th Ave E 98112 ..... (206)329-3326
Shafer Mansion, 907-14th Ave 98112 ..... (206)823-2303
The Williams House, 1505 Fourth Ave N 98109 ..... (206)285-0810
Seaview
Shelburne Inn, PO Box 250, Pacific Hwy 103 & 45th 98644 ..... (206)642-2442
Shelton
Twin River Ranch, E 5730 Hwy 3 98584 ..... (206)426-1023
Snohomish
Country Manner B&B, 1120 First St 98290 ..... (206)568-8254
Countryman's B&B, 119 Cedar St 98290 ..... (206)568-9622
Snoqualmie
Old Honey Farm, 8910-384th Ave SE 98065 ..... (206)329-4628
South Cle Elum
Moore House B&B
Country Inn, PO Box 2861 98943 ..... (509)674-5939
Spokane
Durocher House B&B, W 4000 Randolph Rd 99204 ..... (509)325-4739
Fotheringham House, 2128 W 2nd Ave 99204 ..... (509)838-4363
Tacoma
Keenan House, 2610 N Warner 98407 ..... (206)752-0702
Tokeland
Tokeland Hotel, PO Box 1504 98590 ..... (206)267-7700
Trout Lake
Mio Amore Pensione, PO Box 208 98650 ..... (509)395-2264
Usk
River Bend Inn, Rt 2 Box 943 99180 ..... (509)445-1476
Vashon Island
Island Inn B&B, Rt 1, Box 950 98070 ..... (206)567-4832
The Old Tjomsland House, 99 Ave SW & 171st St, Box 913 98070 ..... (206)463-5275
Walla Walla
Rees Mansion Inn, 260 E Birch St 99362 ..... (509)529-7845
White Salmon
Inn of the White Salmon, PO 1446, 172 SE Jewett 98672 ..... (509)493-2335
Orchard Hill Inn, Rt 2 Box 130 98672 ..... (509)493-3024

Washington DC

Washington
Adams Inn, 1744 Lanier Pl NW 20009 ..... (202)745-3600
Connecticut-Woodley, 2647 Woodley Rd NW 20008 ..... (202)667-0218
Embassy Inn, 1627 16 St NW 20009 ..... (202)234-7800
Kalorama Guest House, 1854 Mintwood Place NW 20009 ..... (202)667-6369
Meg's International Guest House, 1315 Euclid St NW 20009 ..... (202)232-5837
Morrison-Clark Inn, Massachusetts & 11 St NW 20001 ..... (202)898-1200
Reeds B&B, PO Box 12011 20005 ..... (202)328-3510
Tabard Inn, 1739 N St NW 20036 ..... (202)785-1277
Victorian Accommodations, 1309 Rhode Island Ave NW 20005 ..... (202)234-6292
Windsor Inn, 1842 16th St NW 20009 ..... (202)667-0300

West Virginia

Athens
Concord Church Inn, 304 Vermillion St 24712 ....(304)384-5084
Aurora
Cabin Lodge, Box 355, Rt 50 26705 ....(304)735-3563
Berkeley Springs
Country Inn, 207 S Washington St 25411 ....(304)258-2210
Folkestone B&B, Rt 2 Box 404 25411 ....(304)258-3743
Highlawn Inn, 304 Market St 25411 ....(304)258-5700
Manor, PO Box 342 25411 ....(304)258-1552
Maria's Garden & Inn, 201 Independence St 25411 ....(304)258-2021
Oak Lee B&B, 501 Johnson Mill Rd 25411
The Country Inn 25411 ....(304)258-2210
The Manor, 415 Fairfax St 25411 ....(304)258-1552
Bramwell
The Bluestone Inn, 1 Main St 24715 ....(304)248-7402
Three Oaks & A Quilt, Duhring St 24715 ....(304)248-8316
Burlington
Shelly's Homestead, Rt 1, Box 1-A 26710 ....(304)289-3941
Cass
Shay Inn, General Delivery 24927 ....(304)456-4652
Charles Town
Carriage Inn, 417 E Washington St 25414 ....(304)728-8003
The Cottonwood Inn, Rt 2 Box 61 S 25414 ....(304)725-3371
Gilbert House B&B, Rt 1 Box 160 25414 ....(304)725-0637
Hillbrook Inn, Rt 2 Box 152 25414
Magnus Tate's Kitchen, 201 E Washington St 25414 ....(304)725-8052
Chloe
Pennbrooke Farm B&B, Granny-she Run 25235 ....(304)655-7367
Crawley
Oak Knoll B&B, General Delivery 24931 ....(304)392-6903
Davis
Bright Morning, William Ave, Rt 32 26260 ....(304)259-5119
Twisted Thistle B&B, Box 480 26260 ....(304)259-5389
Elkins
Cheat River Lodge, Rt 1, Box 116 26241 ....(304)636-2301
Lincoln Crest B&B, Box 408 26241 ....(304)636-8460
Marian's Guest House, 731 Harrison Ave 26241 ....(304)636-9883
The Retreat, 214 Harpertown Rd 26241 ....(304)636-2960
The Wayside Inn, 201 Sycamore St 26241 ....(304)636-1985
Fairmont
Tichnell's Tourist Home, 1367 Locust Ave 26554 ....(304)366-3811
Gauley Bridge
Three Rivers Inn, PO Box 231 25085 ....(304)632-2121
Gerrardstown
Prospect Hill Farm, PO Box 135 25420 ....(304)229-3346
Glen Ferris
Glen Ferris Inn 25090 ....(304)632-1111
Greenbrier County
Oak Knoll B&B, Crawley 24931 ....(304)392-6903
Harpers Ferry
Fillmore Street B&B, Box 34 25425 ....(301)377-0070
Spangler Manor, 55 High St, Rt 3 Box 1402 25425
The View B&B, Box 286 25425 ....(304)535-2688
Helvetia
Beekeeper Inn 26224 ....(304)924-6435
Hillsboro
The Current, Box 135 25945
Huntington
Heritage Station, 11th St & Veterans Mem Blvd 25701 ....(304)523-6373
Jane Lew
West Fork Inn, Rt 2 Box 212 26378 ....(304)745-4893
Lewisburg
The General Lewis, 301 E Washington St 24901 ....(304)645-2600
Lynn's Inn B&B, Rt 4 Box 40 24901 ....(304)645-2003
Minnie Manor, 403 E Washington St 24901 ....(304)647-4096
Lost Creek
Country Corner, Box 112 26385 ....(304)745-3017
Lost River
Guest House, Low-Gap 26811 ....(304)897-5707
Martinsburg
Boydville
The Inn at Martinsburg, 601 S Queen St 25401 ....(304)263-1448
The Dunn Country Inn, Rt 3, Box 33J 25401 ....(304)263-8646
Mathias
Valley View Farm, PO Box 467 26812 ....(304)897-5229
Moorefield
Hickory Hill Farm, Rt 1 Box 355 26836 ....(304)538-2511
McMechen House Inn, 109 N Main St 26836 ....(304)538-2417
Morgantown
Chestnut Ridge School, 1000 Stewartstown Rd 26505 ....(304)598-2262
Maxwell B&B, Rt 12, Box 197 26505 ....(304)594-3041
Orlando
Kilmarnock Farms, Rt 1 Box 91 26412 ....(304)452-8319
Pence Springs
The Pence Springs Hotel, Rt 3 24962 ....(304)445-2606
Prosperity
Prosperity Farmhouse, Box 393 25909 ....(304)255-4245
Quicksburg
Mccoy's Mill, Rt 1 Box 94 22847 ....(304)358-7893
Romney
Hampshire House 1884, 165 N Grafton St 26757 ....(304)822-7171
Saint Albans
The Chilton House, 2 Sixth Ave 25177 ....(304)722-2918
Shepherdstown
Bavarian Inn & Lodge, Rt 1 Box 30 25443 ....(304)876-2551
Fuss 'N Feathers, Box 1088, 210 W German 25443 ....(304)876-6469
The Little Inn, PO 219, Princess At German St 25443 ....(304)876-2208
Mecklenburg Inn, 128 E German St 25443 ....(304)876-2126
Shang-Ra-La B&B, Rt 1, Box 156 25443 ....(304)876-2391
Stonebrake Cottage, PO Box 1612 Shepherd Grade Rd 25443 ....(304)876-6607
Thomas Shepherd Inn, Box 1162, German & Duke St 25443 ....(304)876-3715
Sinks Grove
Morgan Orchard, Rt 2 Box 114 24976 ....(304)772-3638
Sistersville
Cobblestone Inn B&B, 103 Charles St 25175 ....(304)652-1206
Wells Inn, 316 Charles St 26175 ....(304)652-3111
Slatyfork
Elk River Touring Center 26291 ....(304)572-3771
Fassiferns Farms, Rt 219 N 26291 ....(304)572-4645
Willis Farm, Rt 219 26291 ....(304)572-3771
Snowshoe
Whistlepunk Inn, Box 70 26209 ....(800)624-2757
Summerville
Old Wilderness Inn, 1 Old Wilderness Rd 26651 ....(304)872-3481
Summit Point
Countryside, PO Box 57 25446 ....(304)725-2614
Wellburg
Dovers Inn, 1001 Washington Pike 26070 ....(304)737-0188
Wheeling
Yesterdays, Ltd., 614 Main St 26003 ....(304)232-0864
White Sulphur Spring
The Greenbrier 24986 ....(304)536-1110
Winona
Garvey House, Box 98 25942 ....(304)574-3235

Wisconsin

Albany
Albany Guest House, 405 S Mill St 53502 ....(608)862-3636
Algoma
B&B Guesthomes, 698 County Rt 2 54201 ....(414)743-9742
Alma
The Gallery House, 215 N Main St 54610 ....(608)685-4975
Laue House, 1111 S Main 54610 ....(608)685-4923
Appleton
The Parkside B&B, 402 E North St 54911 ....(414)733-0200
The Queen Anne, 837 E College Ave 54911 ....(414)739-7966
Ashland
Hotel Chequamegon, 101 W Front St 54806 ....(715)682-9095
Baraboo
The Barrister's House, 226 9th Ave 53913 ....(608)356-3344

Frantiques Showplace, 704 Ash St 53913 .... (608)356-5273
House Of Seven Gables, PO 204, 215 6th St 53913 .... (608)356-8387

Bayfield

Chez Joliet, PO Box 768, Bayfield 54814 .... (715)779-5480
Cooper Hill House, 33 S Sixth St Box 5 54814 .... (715)779-5060
Greunke's Inn, 17 Rittenhouse 54184 .... (715)779-5480
Grey Oak Guest House, 7th & Manypenny 54814 .... (715)779-5111
Le Chateau Boutin, PO Box 584 54814 .... (715)779-5111
Old Rittenhouse Inn, 301 Rittenhouse Ave, PO Box 584-1 54814
... (715)779-5111
Pinehurst Inn, Hwy 13, PO Box 222 54814 .... (715)779-3676

Belleville

Abendruh B&B Swisstyle, 7019 Gehin Rd 53508 .... (608)424-3808
B&B Swiss Style, 7019 Cehin Rd 53508 .... (608)424-3808

Beloit

Richardson House, 829 Church St 53511 .... (608)365-1627

Burlington

Hillcrest B&B, 540 Storle Ave 53105 .... (414)763-4706
Hillcrest B&B, 540 Storle Ave 53105 .... (414)763-4706

Campbellsport

Mielke-Mauk House, 994 County Hwy F 53010 .... (414)533-8602

Cashton

The Convent House, Rt 1, Box 160 54619 .... (608)823-7906

Cassville

The Geiger House, 401 Denniston 53806 .... (608)725-5419

Cedarburg

Stagecoach Inn B&B, W 61 N 520 Washington Ave 53012
... (414)375-0208
The Washington House Inn, W 62 N 573 Washington Ave 53012
... (414)375-3550

Chippewa Falls

Wilson House, 320 Superior St 54729 .... (715)723-0055

Colfax

ClearView Hills B&B, Rt 2, Box 87 54730 .... (608)255-4230
Farm B&B, Rt 1 Box 132 54730 .... (715)962-4342
Son-ne-vale Farm B&B, Rt 1, Box 132 54730 .... (715)962-4343

Columbus

"By the Okeag", 446 Wisconsin St 53925 .... (414)623-3007

Curtiss

Thompson's Inn, PO Box 128, County Hwy E 54422 .... (715)223-6041

Dane

Dunroven House, 7809 Dunroven Rd 53529 .... (608)592-4560

De Pere

Birch Creek Inn, 2263 Birch Creek Rd 54415 .... (414)336-7084

DeForest

Circle B B&B, 3804 Vinburn Rd 53532 .... (608)846-3481

Delevan

Allyn House Inn, 511 E Walworth Ave 53115 .... (414)728-9090

DePere

R&R Homestead, 803 Morning Glory Ln 54115 .... (414)336-8244

Downsville

Creamery, Box 22 54735 .... (715)664-8354

East Troy

Greystone Farms, 770 Adams Rd 53120 .... (414)495-8485

Eau Claire

Fanny Hill Inn, 3919 Crescent Ave 54703 .... (715)836-8184
Otter Creek Inn, 2536 Hwy 12 54701 .... (715)832-2945
Westlin Winds, 3508 Halsey St 54701 .... (715)832-1110

Egg Harbor

Country Gardens B&B, 6421 Hwy 42 54209 .... (414)743-7434

Elkhart Lake

Siebken's, 284 S Lake St 53020 .... (414)876-2600

Elkhorn

Ye Olde Manor House, Rt 5, Box 390 53121 .... (414)742-2450

Ellison Bay

"Haus Zur Gemutlichkeit", 1052 Berry Ln N 54210 .... (414)854-4848
The Griffin Inn, 11976 Mink River Rd 54210 .... (414)854-4306
The Nelson Farm, 1526 Ranch Ln 54210 .... (414)854-5224

Elm Grove

The Krupp Farm Homestead, 1030 Terrace Dr 53122 .... (414)894-3216

Elton

Glacier Wilderness B&B, Box 12 54430 .... (715)882-5262

Ephraim

Eagle Harbor Inn, PO Box 72 B 54211 .... (414)854-2121
The Ephraim Inn, Rt 42, PO Box 247 54211 .... (414)854-4515
French Country Inn of Ephraim, Box 129, 3052 Spruce Ln 54211
.... (414)854-4001
Hillside Hotel, PO Box 17 54211 .... (414)854-2417

Fish Creek

Proud Mary, PO Box 193 54212 .... (414)868-3442
Thorp House Inn & Cottages, 4135 Bluff Rd, PO Box 90 54212
... (414)868-2444
Whistling Swan Inn, Main St Box 193 54212 .... (414)868-3442
White Gull Inn, PO Box 175 54212 .... (414)868-3517

Fontana-On-Geneva Lk

Emerald View House, PO Box 322 53125 .... (414)275-2266

Gills Rock

Harbor House Inn, 12666 Hwy 42 54210 .... (414)854-5196

Glen Haven

The Parson's Inn B&B, Rock School Rd 53810 .... (608)794-2491

Green Bay

La Baye House, 803 Oregon 54303 .... (414)437-5081

Green Lake

McConnell Inn, 497 S Lawson Dr, Box 639 54941 .... (414)294-6430
Oakwood Lodge, 365 Lake St 54941 .... (414)294-6580
Strawberry Hill B&B, Rt 1 Box 524-d 54941 .... (414)294-3450

Hartford

Jordan House, 81 S Main St 53027 .... (414)673-5643

Hartland

Monches Mill House, W 301 N 9430 Hwy E 53029 .... (414)966-7546

Hayward

Mustard Seed, 205 California, Box 262 54843 .... (715)634-2908
The Open Window B&B, Rt 5, Box 5194 54843 .... (715)462-3033

Hazel Green

De Winters of Hazel Green, 22nd at Main St 53811 .... (608)854-2768
Stagecoach Inn, 2105 Main 53811 .... (608)854-2233

Hazelhurst

Hazelhurst Inn, 6941 Hwy 51 54531 .... (715)356-6571

Hillsboro

Mascione's Hidden Valley, Rt 2, Box 74 54634 .... (608)489-3443

Horicon

The Charly House, 111 N Cedar St 53032 .... (414)485-3144

Hudson

Jefferson-Day House, 1109 Third St 54016 .... (715)386-7111

Iola

Taylor House B&B, 210 E Iola St 54945 .... (715)445-2204

Jamesville

Sessler's Guest House, 210 S Jackson St 53545

Kendall

Dusk to Dawn B&B, Rt 1, Box 191 54638 .... (608)463-7547

Kenosha

Library Square B&B, 6003-7th Ave 53140 .... (414)656-0207
The Manor House, 6536 3rd Ave 53140 .... (414)658-0014

Kewaunee

Duvall House, 815 Milwaukee St 54216 .... (414)388-0501
The Gables, 821 Dodge St 54216 .... (414)388-0220

Kohler

The American Club, Highland Dr 53044 .... (414)457-8000

La Farge

Trillium, Rt 2, Box 121 54639 .... (608)625-4492

La Pointe

Woods Manor, 165 Front St, PO Box 7 54850 .... (715)747-3102

Lac du Flambeau

Chippewa Lodge B&B, 3525 Chippewa Lodge Tr 54538 .... (715)588-3297
Ty-Bach, 3104 Simpson Ln 54538 .... (715)588-7851

Lake Delton

OJ's Victorian Village, Box 98, Hwy 12 53940 .... (608)254-6568
The Swallow's Nest, 141 Sarrington, PO 418 53940 .... (608)254-6900

Lake Geneva

Eleven Gables Inn, 493 Wrigley Dr 53147 .... (414)248-8393
Elizabethian Inn, 463 Wrigley Dr 53147 .... (414)248-9131
French Country Inn, Hwy 50 W, Rt 4, Box 690 53147 .... (414)245-5520
T.C. Smith Inn B&B, 865 Main St 53147 .... (414)248-1097

Lake Mills

The Bayberry Inn, 265 S Main St 53551 .... (414)648-3654
Fargo Mansion Inn, 406 Mulberry St 53551 .... (414)648-3654

Lewis

Seven Pines Lodge 54851 .... (715)653-2323

Livingston

Oak Hill Farm, 9850 Hwy 80 53554 .... (608)943-6006

Wisconsin (Continued)

Lodi
Victorian Treasure B&B, 115 Prairie St 53555 ....(608)592-5199
Madison
Annie's Hill House B&B, 2117 Sheridan Dr ....(608)244-2224
Mansion Hill Inn, 424 N Pinckney 53703 ....(608)255-3999
Plough Inn B&B, 3402 Monroe St 53711 ....(608)238-2981
The Collins House, 704 E Gorham 53703 ....(608)255-4230
Maiden Rock
Harrisburg Inn, Great River Rd, Box 15 54740 ....(715)448-4500
Marinette
Lauerman Guest House, 1975 Riverside Ave 54143
Mauston
Edward's Estates, N4775 22nd Ave 53948 ....(608)847-5246
Menomonee Falls
Dorshel's B&B Guest House, N7616 Lilly Rd 53051 ....(414)255-7866
Menomonie
Cedar Trail Guesthouse, Rt 4, Box 175 54751 ....(715)664-8828
Katy May House, 2013 Wilson St 54751 ....(715)235-1792
Mequon
American Country Farm, 12112 N Wauwatosa Rd 53092 .(414)242-0194
The Homestead, 1916 W Donges Bay Rd 53092 ....(414)242-4174
Sonnenhof Inn, 13907 N Port Washington 53092 ....(414)375-4294
Merrill
The Brick House, 108 S Cleveland St 54452 ....(715)536-3230
Candlewick Inn, 700 W Main St 54452 ....(715)536-7744
Milwaukee
B&B of Milwaukee, Inc., PO Box 20715 53220-0715 ....(414)327-1338
Guest House of 819, 819 N Cass St 53202 ....(414)271-1979
Ogden House, 2237 N Lake Dr 53202 ....(414)272-2740
Pfister Hotel, 424 E Wisconsin Ave 53202 ....(414)273-8222
Mineral Point
Chesterfield Inn, 20 Commerce St 53565
Chesterfield Inn, 20 Commerce St 53565 ....(608)987-3682
Duke Guest House B&B, 618 Maiden St 53565 ....(608)987-2821
General Store, 262 High St 53565 ....(608)987-2799
Jones House, 215 Ridge St, Hwy 151 53565 ....(608)987-2337
Wilson House Inn, 110 Dodge St Hwy 151 53565 ....(608)987-3600
Minocqua
Phoenix House B&B, 1075 Hwy F 54548 ....(715)356-3535
Monona
The Lake House on Monona, 4027 Monona Dr 53716 ....(608)222-4601
Montello
Country Peddler Guest House, Rt 2, Box 188 53949 ....(414)295-0100
Westmont Farms, Rt 3, Box 556 53959 ....(414)293-4456
Montreal
Inn, 30 Wisconsin Ave 54550 ....(715)561-5180
Mount Horeb
H.B. Dahle House, 200 N 2nd St 53572
Neillsville
Bluebell Inn, 122 Hewett St 54456 ....(715)743-2929
New Holstein
The Farm Homestead, W1982 Kiel Rd, Rt 2 53061 ....(414)782-5421
New Lisbon
The Evansen House, Rt 1 Box 18 53950
Newton
Rambling Hills Tree Farm, 8825 Willever Ln 53063 ....(414)726-4388
Norwalk
Lonesome Jake's Devil's Hole Ranch, Rt 1, 104 54648 ....(608)823-7585
Oconomowoc
Inn at Pine Terrace, 351 Lisbon Rd 53066 ....(414)567-7463
Oneida
Stonewood Haus, 894 Riverdale Dr 54155 ....(414)499-3786
Ontario
Downings' B&B, Hwy 33 54651 ....(608)337-4352
The Inn at Wildcat Mountain - B&B, Hwy 33, PO Box 112 54651 ....(608)337-4352
Oshkosh
Marybrooke Inn, 705 W New York Ave 54901 ....(414)426-4761
Oxford
Halfway House, Rt 2 Box 80 53952 ....(608)586-5489
Phelps
Limberlost Inn, 2483 Hwy 17 54554 ....(715)545-2685
Plain
Bettinger House B&B, Hwy 23 53577 ....(608)546-2951
The Kraemer House, 1190 Spruce St 53577 ....(608)546-3161
Platteville
The Cunningham House, 110 Market St 53818 ....(608)348-5532
Plymouth
52 Stafford, 52 Stafford St 53073 ....(414)893-0552
Irish Guest House, 52 Staffrord 53073
Silver Springs Inn & Resort, PO Box 562 53073 ....(414)893-0969
Yankee Hill B&B, 315 Collins St 53073 ....(414)892-2222
Portage
Bonnie Oaks Estate, 3rd Ave, RR 3, Box 147 53901 ....(608)981-2057
Breese Waye B&B, 816 Macfarlane Rd 53901 ....(608)742-5281
Country Aire, Rt 2, Box 175 53901 ....(608)742-5716
Potosi
O'Reilly House, 7509 Stiger Rd 53820 ....(608)763-2386
Poynette
Jamieson House, 407 N Franklin 53955 ....(608)635-4100
Prairie du Chien
Newmann House B&B, 121 N Michigan St 53821 ....(608)326-8104
Prescott
Yankee Bugler Inn, 506 Oak St 54021 ....(715)262-3019
Racine
Locknaiar Inn, 1121 Lake Ave 53043 ....(414)633-3300
Reedsburg
Parkview B&B, 211 N Park St 53959 ....(608)534-4333
Rhinelander
Cranberry Hill B&B, 209 E Frederick St 54501 ....(715)369-3504
Richland Center
Mansion, 323 S Central 53581 ....(608)647-2808
Ripon
The Farmer's Daughter Inn, Rt 1, Box 37 54971 ....(414)748-2146
River Falls
Knollwood House, Rt 1, Box 4 Knollwood Dr 54022 ....(715)425-1040
Saint Germain
Saint Germain B&B, 6255 Hwy 70 E, PO Box 6 54558 ....(715)479-8007
Sister Bay
Church Hill Inn, 425 Gateway Dr 54234 ....(414)854-4885
Renaissance Inn, 414 Maple Dr 54234 ....(414)854-5107
Soldiers Grove
Page's Old Oak Inn, Hwy 131 S 54655 ....(608)624-5217
Sparta
Just-N-Trails B&B, Rt 1, Box 263 54656 ....(608)269-4522
The Franklin Victorian, 220 East Franklin St 54656
Spring Green
Hardyns House, 250 N Winstead 53588 ....(608)588-7007
Hill Street B&B, 353 W Hill St 53588 ....(608)588-7751
Springbrook
The Stout Trout, Rt 1, Box 1630 54875 ....(715)466-2790
Stevens Point
Victorian Swan on Water, 1716 Water St 54481 ....(715)345-0595
Stockholm
Great River Farm, General Delivery 54769 ....(715)442-5656
Stoughton
Stokstad's Century Farm B&B, 305 Hwy 51 53589 ....(608)884-4941
Strum
Lake House, RR 2 Box 217 54770 ....(715)693-3519
Sturgeon Bay
The Barbican, 132 N Second Ave 54235 ....(414)743-4854
Bay Shore Inn, 4205 Bay Shore Dr 54235 ....(414)743-4551
Country Comforts, 5031 County TT 54235 ....(414)743-6317
Gandt's Haus, 2962 Lake Forest Park Rd 54235 ....(414)743-1238
Gray Goose B&B, 4258 Bay Shore Dr 54235 ....(414)743-9100
The Gray Goose B&B, 4258 Bay Shore Dr 54235 ....(414)743-9100
Inn at Cedar Crossing, 336 Louisiana St 54235 ....(414)743-4200
The Scofield House B&B, 908 Michigan St, PO Box 761 54235 ....(414)743-7727
White Lace Inn, 16 N 5th Ave 54235 ....(414)743-1105
Tomahawk
Frenchtown B&B Inn, 822 S Tomahawk Ave 54487 ....(715)453-3499
Verona
Riley B&B Inn, 8205 Klevenville-Riley Rd 53593 ....(608)845-9150
Viroqua
The Dyson Mansion, 217 E Jefferson St 54665
Serendipity Farm, Rt 3, Box 162 54665 ....(608)637-7708

Viroqua Heritage Inn, 220 E Jefferson St 54665 .... (608)637-3306
Waupaca
Crystal River B&B, E1369 Rural Rd 54981 .... (715)258-5333
Wausau
Rosenberry Inn, 511 Franklin St 54401 .... (715)842-5733
Wautoma
Kristine Ann's Inn, Rt 1, Box 10, 303 E Main 54982 .... (414)787-4901
West Salem
Wolfway Farm, RR 1, Box 18 54669 .... (608)486-2686
Westby
Westby House, State St 54667 .... (608)634-4112
Westfield
Martha's Ethnic B&B, 226-2nd St 53964 .... (608)296-3361
White Lake
Wolf River Lodge 54491 .... (715)882-2182
Whitewater
The Greene House B&B, Rt 2, Box 214, Hwy 12 53190 ..... (414)495-8771
Wilmot
Foxmoor B&B, Fox River Rd 53192 .... (414)862-6161
Wisconsin Dells
Historic Bennett House, 825 Oak St 53965 .... (608)254-2500
House On River Road, 922 River Rd 53965 .... (608)253-5573
Sherman House, 930 River Rd, Box 397 53965 .... (608)253-2721
Wisconsin Rapids
Nash House, 1020 Oak St 54494 .... (715)424-2001

Wyoming

Buffalo
Paradise Guest Ranch, PO Box 790 82834 .... (307)684-7876
Cody
Hidden Valley Ranch, 153 Rd, 6MF, S Fork Rd 82414 .... (307)587-5090
The Lockhart Inn, 109 W Yellowstone Ave 82414 .... (307)587-6074
Shoshone Lodge Resort, PO Box 790bb 82414 .... (307)587-4044
Valley Ranch, 100 Valley Ranch Rd 82414 .... (307)587-4661
Douglas
Akers Ranch, 81 Inez Rd, Rt 1 82633 .... (307)358-3741
Evanston
Pine Gables B&B, 1049 Center St 82930 .... (307)789-2069
Glenrock
Hotel Higgins, 416 W Birch 82637 .... (307)436-9212
Jackson
Spring Creek Ranch, Box 3154 83001 .... (307)733-8833
Jackson Hole
Buckrail Lodge, Box 23, 110 E Karns Ave 83001 .... (307)733-2079
Captain Bob Morris, PO Box 261 Teton Village 83025 .... (307)733-4413
Powderhorn Ranch, PO Box 7400 83001 .... (307)733-3845
Lander
Miner's Delight Inn, Atlantic City Rt, PO Box 205 82520 . (307)332-3513
Laramie
Annie Moore's Guest House, 819 University 82070 .... (307)721-4177
Moose
Bunkhouse, PO Box 384 83012 .... (307)733-7283
Moran
Box K Ranch B&B, Box 110 83013 .... (307)543-2407
Fir Creek Ranch, PO Box 190 83013416 .... (307)543-2416
Jenny Lake Lodge, PO Box 240 83013 .... (307)733-4677
Rawlins
Ferris Mansion, 607 W Maple St 82301 .... (307)324-3961
Saratoga
Wolf Hotel, PO Box 1298, 101 E Bridge 82331 .... (307)326-5525
Savery
Savery Creek
Thoroughbred Ranch, PO Box 24 82332 .... (307)383-7840
Wapita
Mountain Shadows Ranch, Box 110BB 82450 .... (307)587-2143
Wilson
Heck Of A Hill Homestead, PO Box 105 83014 .... (307)733-8023
Snow Job, PO Box 371 83014 .... (307)739-9695

U. S. Territories

Puerto Rico

Condado, San Juan
El Canario Inn, 1317 Ashford Ave 00907 .... (809)722-3861
Culebra
Posada La Hamaca, 68 Castelar St 00645 .... (809)742-3516
Culebra Island
Villa Boheme, PO Box 218 00645 .... (809)742-3508
Island Verde
La Casa Mathlesen, 14 Calle Uno Villamar 00913 .... (809)727-3223
La Playa, 6 Amapola 00630 .... (809)791-1115
Luquillo
Parador Martorell, PO Box 384 00673 .... (809)889-2710
Maricao
Parador Hacienda Juanita, PO Box 838 00706 .... (809)838-2550
Ocean Park
Beach House, 1957 Italia 00913 .... (809)727-5482
Buena Vista by-Sea, 2218 Gen Del Valle 00913 .... (809)726-2796
Patillas
Caribe Playa Resort, B. 2730 Guardamaya 00723
Rincon
Horned Dorset Primavera, Apartado 1132 00743
San German
Parador Oasis, PO Box 144 00753 .... (809)892-1175
San Juan
El Prado Inn, 1350 Luchetti St. Condado 00907 .... (809)728-5526
Green Isle Inn, 36 Calle Uno-Villamar 00913 .... (809)726-4330
Hosteria del Mar, 5 Cervantes St Condado 00907 .... (809)724-8203
Jewel's by the Sea, Seaview 1125-Condado 00907 .... (809)725-5313
San Antonio Guesthouse, 1 Tapia, Ocean Park 00752 .... (914)727-3302
Vieques
Bananas Guesthouse, Box 1300 Esperanza 00765 .... (809)741-8700
La Casa Del Frances, PO Box 458, Esperanza 00765 .... (809)741-3751
Sea Gate Guest House, Barriada Fuerts 00765 .... (809)741-4661

Virgin Islands

Saint Croix
Pink Fancy, 27 Prince St, Christiansted 00820 .... (809)773-8460
Saint John
Cruz Inn, Box 566, Cruz Bay 00830 .... (809)776-7688
Gallows Point, Box 58 00830 .... (809)776-6434
Intimate Inn of St. John, POB 432, Cruz Bay 00830 .... (809)776-6133
Raintree Inn, Box 566 00830 .... (809)776-7449
Saint Thomas
Galleon House, PO Box 6577 00801 .... (809)774-6952
Hotel 1829, PO Box 1567 00804-1567 .... (809)776-1829
Inn at Mandahl, PO Box 2483 00801 .... (809)775-2100
Limestone Reef Terraces, Water Island .... (809)774-2148
Mafolie Hotel, PO Box 1506 00801 .... (809)774-2790
Pavillions & Pools Hotel, Rt 6 00802 .... (800)524-2001
Pelican Beach Club, Box 8387 00801 .... (809)775-6855
Twins Guest House, 5 Garden St, Charlotte Ama 00801 ... (809)776-0131
Villa Elaine, 66 Water Island 00802 .... (809)774-0290

State Tourism Information

- Alabama Bureau of Tourism & Travel, 532 S Perry St, Montgomery AL 36104 ....(800) 252-2262
- Alaska Division of Tourism, PO Box E-445, Juneau AK 99811(907) 465-2010
- Arkansas Dept of Parks & Tourism, 1 Capitol Mall, Little Rock AR 72201 ....(501) 682-1511
- Arizona Office of Tourism, 1100 W Washington St, Phoenix AZ 85007 ....(602) 542-3618
- California Office of Tourism, Box 9278, Dept T-72, Van Nuys CA 91409 ....(800) 862-2543
- Colorado Board of Tourism, 1625 Broadway, Ste 1700, Denver CO 80202 ....(800) 255-5550
- State of Connecticut Economic Develop, 210 Washington St, Hartfort CT 06106 ....(800) 282-6863
- Delaware Tourism Office, 99 Kings Hwy, PO Box 1401, Dover DE 19903 ....(800) 441-8846
- Florida Dept of Commerce, 107 W Gaines St, Ste 410D, Tallahassee FL 32399 ....(904) 488-4141
- Georgia Dept of Industry, PO Box 1776, Atlanta GA 30301(404) 656-3590
- Hawaii Visitors Bureau, 3440 Wilshire Blvd, Ste 502, Los Angeles CA 90010 ....(213) 385-5301
- Dept of Commerce, 700 W State St, Boise ID 83720 ....(208) 334-2470
- Illinois Tourist Information Center, 310 S Michigan Ave, Ste 108, Chicago IL 60604 ....(312) 793-2094
- Indiana Dept of Commerce, 1 N Capitol Ave, Ste 700, Indianapolis IN 46204 ....(317) 232-8860
- Iowa Dept of Economic Development, 200 E Grand Ave, Ste A, Des Moines IA 50309 ....(800) 345-4692
- Kansas Dept of Commerce, 400 SW 8th St, 5th Floor, Topeka KS 66603 ....(913) 296-3481
- Kentucky Dept of Travel, Capitol Plaza Tower, 22nd Floor, Frankfort KY 40601 ....(800) 225-8747
- Louisiana Office of Tourism, PO Box 44291, Baton Rouge LA 70804 ....(800) 334-8626
- Maine Publicity Bureau, 97 Winthrop St, Hallowell ME 04347(800) 533-9595
- Maryland Office of Tourism, 217 E Redwood St, Baltimore MD 21202 ....(800) 543-1036
- Massachusetts Office of Travel & Tourism, 100 Cambridge St, 13th Floor, Boston MA 02202 ....(617) 727-3201
- Michigan Travel Bureau, Box 30226, Lansing MI 48909 (800) 543-2937
- Minnesota Office of Tourism, 250 Skyway Level, 375 Jackson St, St Paul MN 55101 ....(800) 328-1461
- Mississippi Dept of Economic, Po Box 22825, Jackson MS 39205 ....(800) 647-2290
- Missouri Division of Tourism, PO Box 1055, Jefferson City MO 65102 ....(314) 751-4133
- Travel Montana, 1424 9th Ave, Helena MT 59620 ....(800) 541-1447
- Travel & Tourism, State Dept of, PO Box 94666, Lincoln NE 68509 ....(800) 228-4307
- Nevada Commission on Tourism, Capitol Complex, Carson City NV 89710 ....(702) 885-4322
- Office of Vacation Travel, PO Box 856, Concord NH 03301(603) 271-2666
- Dept of Commerce & Economic Development, CN 826, 20 W State St, Trenton NJ 08625 ....(609) 292-2470
- New Mexico Tourism & Travel, 1100 St Francis Dr, Joe Montoya Bld, Santa Fe NM 87503 ....(800) 545-2040
- Division of Tourism, 1 Commerce Plaza, Albany NY 12245(800) 225-5697
- North Carolina Division of Travel, 430 N Salisbury St, 6th Floor, Raleigh NC 27611 ....(800) 847-4862
- Tourism Promotion Division, State Capitol Grounds, Bismark ND 58505 ....(800) 437-2077
- Ohio Division of Travel & Trouism, Po Box 1001, Columbus OH 43266 ....(800) 282-5393
- Tourism & Recreation Dept, 500 Will Rogers Bldg, Oklahoma City OK 73105 ....(405) 521-2406
- Tourism Division, Oregon Economic Devel, 595 Cottage St, NE, Salem OR 97310 ....(800) 547-7842
- Travel Development Bureau, 416 Forum Bldg, Harrisburg PA 17120 ....(800) 847-4872
- Rhode Island Dept of Economic Develop, 7 Jackson Walkway, Providence RI 02903 ....(800) 556-2484
- South Carolina Department of, PO Box 71, Inquiry Sections, Columbia SC 29202 ....(803) 734-0122
- Tourism, PO Box 1000, Pierre SD 57501
- Tennessee Tourist Development, PO Box 23170, Nashville TN 37202 ....(615) 741-2158
- Texas Dept of Commerce, PO Box 12008, Austin TX 78711(512) 462-9191
- Utah Travel Council, Capitol Hill, Salt Lake City UT 84114(801) 538-1030
- Travel Division Development Affairs, 134 State St, Montpelier VT 05602 ....(800) 634-8984
- Division of Tourism, 202 N 9th St, Ste 500, Richmond VA 23219 ....(800) 847-4882
- Washington State Tourism, 101 General Admin Bldg, Olympia WA 98504 ....(206) 586-2088
- Washington Convention & Visitors Assn, 1212 New York Ave NW, 6th Floor, Washington DC 20005 ....(202) 789-7000
- West Virginia Travel, 1900 Washington St E, Bldg 6, Charleston WV 25305 ....(800) 225-5982
- Wisconsin Division of Tourism, PO Box 7606, Madison WI 53707 ....(608) 266-2161
- Wyoming Travel Commission, I-12 & College Dr, Cheyenne WY 82002 ....(800) 225-5996

Reservation Services

Alabama

B&B Montgomery, PO Box 886, Milbrook 36054 .... (205)285-5421

Alaska

Stay With a Friend, 43605 Arctic Blvd #173, Anchorage 99503 .... (907)344-4006
Alaska B&B, 526 Seward St, Juneau 99801 .... (907)586-2959

Arizona

B&B in Arizona, 8433 N Black Canyon, Ste 160, Phoenix 85021 .... (602)995-2831
B&B-Scottsdale, PO Box 624, Scottsdale 85252 .... (602)998-7044
Mi Casa Su Casa, 1456 N Scottsdale Rd, #110, Tempe 85281 .... (602)990-0682
Old Pueblo Homestays, PO Box 13603, Tucson 85732 .... (602)790-2399

Arkansas

B&B Arkansas Ozarks, Rt1 Box 38, Calico Rock 72519 .... (501)297-8764
B&B Eureka Springs, Box 27, Eureka Springs 72632 .... (501)253-6767
B&B Reservations, 11 Singleton, Eureka Springs 72632 .... (501)253-9111

California

Eye Openers B&B, Box 694, Altadena 91001 .... (818)797-2055
B&B Homestay, Box 326, Cambria 93428 .... (805)927-4613
B&B Southern California, Box 218, Fullerton 92632 .... (714)738-8361
Rent-A-Room, 11531 Varna St, Garden Grove 92640 .... (714)638-1406
B&B International, 151 Ardmore, Kensington 94707 .... (415)525-4569
Napa Valley's Finest Lodging, 1834 First St, Napa 94559 .... (707)224-4667
America Family Inn B&B, Box 349, San Francisco 94101 .... (415)931-3083
Hospitality Plus, Box 388, San Juan Capistrano 92693 .... (714)496-7050
Megan's Friends, Box 4835, San Luis Obispo CA 93403 .... (805)544-4406
Educators' Vacation Alternatives, 317 Piedmont Rd, Santa Barbara CA 93105 .... (805)687-2947
Wine Country B&B, Box 3211, Santa Rosa 95403 .... (707)578-1661
California Houseguests, 6051 Lindley Ave #6, Tarzana 91356 .... (818)344-7878
B&B Los Angeles, 32127 Harborview Ln, Westlake Village 91361 .... (818)889-7325
Co-Host B&B, 11715 S Circle Dr, Whittier 90601 .... (213)699-8427

Colorado

B&B Rocky Mountains, Box 804, Colorado Springs 80901 (719)630-3433
Vail B&B, Box 491, Vail 81658 .... (303)949-1212

Connecticut

Nutmeg B&B, 222 Girard Ave, Hartford 06105 .... (203)236-6698
B&B in New Haven, Box 216, New Haven CT 06518 .... (203)469-3260
Covered Bridge B&B, Box 447, Norfolk CT 06058 .... (203)542-5944

Delaware

B&B of Delaware, 1804 Breen Ln, Wilmington 19810 .... (302)479-9500

Florida

B&B of the Keys, 5 Man-O-War Dr, Marathon 33050 .... (305)743-4118
B&B of the Palm Beaches, 5 Man-O-War, Marathon 33050 (305)743-4118
B&B Company, Box 262, S Miami 33243 .... (305)661-3270
B&B Suncoast, 8690 Gulf Blvd, St Petersburg 33706 .... (813)360-1753

Georgia

Atlanta Home Hospitality, 2472 Lauderdale Dr NE, Atlanta 30345 .... (404)493-1930
B&B Atlanta, 1801 Piedmont Ave NE #208, Atlanta 30324 (404)875-0525
RSVP Savannah, 417 E Charlton St, Savannah 31401 .... (912)232-7787
Savannah Historic Inns, 1900 Lincoln St, Savannah 31401 .... (912)226-7218
Quail Country B&B, 1104 Old Monticello, Thomasville 31792 .... (912)226-6882

Hawaii

B&B Honolulu, 3242 Kaohinani Dr, Honolulu 96817 .... (808)595-7533
Pacific-Hawaii B&B, 19 Kai Nani Place, Kailua, Oahu 96734 .... (808)262-6026
B&B Hawaii, Box 449, Kapaa 96746 .... (808)822-7771

Idaho

B&B of Idaho, 109 West Idaho, Boise ID 83702 .... (208)342-8066

Illinois

B&B Chicago, PO Box 14088, Chicago 60614 .... (312)951-0085
Heritage B&B, PO Box 409218, Chicago 60640 .... (312)728-7935

Indiana

Indiana Amish Country B&B, 1660 W Market St, Nappanee 46550 .... (219)773-4188
B&B Indiana, PO Box 481, Nashville 47448 .... (812)988-0733

Iowa

Pheasants Galore, 616 Davis Ave, Corning 50841 .... (515)322-3749
Midlands B&B, RR3 Box 129, Missouri Valley 51555 .... (712)642-2418
B&B in Iowa, Box 430, Preston 52069 .... (319)689-4222
Cross Country Traveler, Box 578, West Branch 52358 .... (319)643-2433

Kansas

B&B Kansas City, Box 14781, Lenexa 66215 ....(913)888-3636

Kentucky

Ohio Valley B&B, 6876 Taylor Mill Rd, Independence 41051 ....(606)356-7865
Kentucky Homes B&B, 1431 St James Ct, Louisville 40208 ....(502)635-7341
Bluegrass B&B, Rt 1, Box 263, Versailles 40383 ....(606)873-3208

Louisiana

Southern Comfort 2856 Hundred Oaks, Baton Rouge 70808 ....(504)346-1928
B&B Inc, 1360 Moss St, New Orleans 70152-2257 ....(504)525-4640
New Orleans B&B, PO Box 8128, New Orleans 70182 ....(504)822-5038
Peggy Lindsay Bed, Bath & Breakfast, Box 15843, New Orleans 70175 ....(504)897-3867

Maine

B&B Down East, Box 547, Eastbrook 04634 ....(207)565-3517
B&B of Maine, 32 Colonial Village, Falmouth 04105 ....(207)781-4528
Maine Publicity Bureau, 97 Winthrop, Hallowell 04347 ....(800)533-9595

Maryland

Traveller in Maryland, 33 West St, Annapolis 21401 ....(301)269-6232
Armanda's B&B, 1428 Park Ave, Baltimore 21217-4230 ....(301)225-0001

Massachusetts

B&B of Boston, 47 Commercial Wharf, Boston 02110 ....(617)720-3540
B&B Associates, Box 166 Babson Park, Boston 02157 ....(617)449-5302
Folkstone B&B, PO Box 931, Boylston 01505 ....(508)943-7118
A B&B Above the Rest, Box 732, Brookline 02146 ....(617)277-2292
Greater Boston Hospitality, Box 1142, Brookline 02146 ....(617)277-5430
B&B Cambridge & Greater Boston, Box 665 Kirkland St, Cambridge 02140 ....(617)576-1492
B&B Minuteman Country, Box 665, Cambridge 02140 ....(617)576-2112
Pineapple Hospitality, 47 N Second St, #3A, New Bedford 02740 ....(508)990-1696
Host Homes of Boston, Box 117, Newton 02158 ....(617)244-1308
New England B&B, 1045 Centre St, Newton Centre 02159(617)244-2112
Orleans B&B Associates, Box 1312, Orleans 02653 ....(508)255-3824
Be Our Guest B&B, Box 1333, Plymouth 02360 ....(617)837-9867
B&B Cape Cod, Box 341, West Hyannisport 02672 ....(508)775-2772
B&B Folks, 73 Providence Rd, Westford 01886 ....(508)692-3232
Berkshire B&B, Box 211, Main St, Williamsburg 01096 ....(413)268-7244

Michigan

Betsy Ross B&B, Box 1731, Dearborn 48121 ....(313)561-6041
Frankenmuth B&B, 337 Trinklein St, Frankenmuth 48734 .(517)652-8897
B&B Connection, PO Box 2201, Traverse City 49685 ....(616)943-9182

Minnesota

B&B of the Great Plains, PO Box 2333, Lincoln NE 68502 .(402)423-3480

Mississippi

Lincoln, Ltd, B&B, PO Box 3479, Meridian 39303 ....(601)482-5483
Natchez Pilgrimage Tours, Box 347, Natchez MS 39120 ....(800)647-6742

Missouri

Ozark Country B&B, Box 295, Branson 65616 ....(417)334-4720
B&B River Country, #1 Grandview Heights, St Louis 63131 ....(314)965-4328
B&B of St Louis, 1900 Wyoming, St Louis 63118 ....(314)965-4328
B&B St Louis, 4418 West Pine St, St Louis 63108 ....(314)533-9299

Montana

B&B Western Adventure, Box 20972, Billings 59104 ....(406)259-7993

Nebraska

Swede Hospitality B&B, 1617 Ave A, Gothenburg 69138 ...(308)537-2680
B&B of the Great Plains, Box 2333, Lincoln 68502 ....(402)423-3480

Nevada

Hospitality Plus, Box 388, San Juan Capistrano 92693 ....(714)496-7050

New Hampshire

New Hampshire B&B, RFD 3, Box 53, Lanconia 03246 ....(603)279-8348

New Jersey

Northern NJ B&B, 11 Sunset Trail, Denville 07834 ....(201)625-5129
B&B of New Jersey, #132, 103 Godwin Ave, Midland Park 07432 ....(201)444-7409
B&B of Princeton, PO Box 571, Princeton 08540 ....(609)924-3189

New Mexico

B&B Santa Fe, 218 E Buena Vista, Santa Fe 87501 ....(505)982-3332

New York

B&B, USA, PO Box 606, Croton-on-Hudson 10520 ....(914)271-6228
Alternate Lodgings, Box 1782, East Hampton 11937 ....(516)324-9449
Hampton B&B, PO Box 378, East Moriches 11940 ....(516)928-4034
B&B Rochester, Box 444, Fairport 14450 ....(716)223-8510
..........(716)223-8877
Leatherstocking B&B, 389 Brockway, Frankfort 13340 ....(315)733-0040
Cherry Valley Ventures, 6119 Cherry Valley Turnpike, Lafayette NY 13084 ....(315)677-9723
New World B&B, 150 Fifth Ave, #711, New York 10011 ....(212)675-5600
Urban Ventures, PO Box 426, New York 10024 ....(212)594-5650
Rainbow Hospitality, 9348 Hennepin, Niagara Falls 14304 ....(716)283-4794
Elaine's B&B & Inns, Box 392, Old Westbury 11568 ....(516)334-6231
A Reasonable Alternative, 117 Spring St, Port Jefferson 11777 ....(516)928-4034
American Country Collection, 984 Gloucester Place, Schenectady 12309 ....(518)370-4948
B&B of Greater Syracuse, 143 Didama St, Syracuse 13224 ....(315)446-4199

North Carolina

Charlotte B&B, 1700-2 Delane Ave, Charlotte 28211
B&B in the Albemarle, PO Box 248, Everetts 27825 ....(919)792-4584

North Dakota

The Old West B&B, Box 211, Regent 58650 ....(701)563-4542

Ohio

Private Lodging, PO Box 18590, Cleveland 44118 ....(216)321-3213
Columbus B&B, 769 S Third St, Columbus 43206 ....(614)443-3680
Buckeye B&B, PO Box 130, Powell 43065 ....(614)548-4555

Oklahoma

B&B Texas Style, 4224 W Red Bird Ln, Dallas TX 75237 ....(214)298-5433
..........(214)298-8586

Oregon

B&B Accommodations, 5733 SW Dickinson, Portland 97219 .... (503)287-4704
Northwest B&B Travel, 610 SW Broadway, Portland 97205 .... (503)243-7616

Pennsylvania

B&B Philadelphia, Box 630, Chester Springs 19425 .... (215)783-7838
The B&B Traveler, PO Box 21, Devon 19333 .... (215)687-3565
Hershey B&B, PO Box 208, Hershey 17033-0208 .... (717)533-2928
B&B Chester County, Box 825, Kennett Square 19348 .... (215)444-1367
B&B Lancaster County, Box 19, Mountville PA .... (717)285-5956
B&B Center City, 1804 Pine St, Philadelphia 19103 .... (215)735-1137
Rest & Repast, PO Box 126, Pine Grove Mills 16868 .... (814)238-1484
Pittsburgh B&B, Pittsburgh PA .... (412)934-1212
All About Town, PO Box 562, Valley Forge 19481 .... (215)783-7838
B&B of Valley Forge, Valley Forge 19481-0562 .... (215)783-7838
Brandywine Valley, PO Box 562, Valley Forge 19481 .... (215)783-7838
Guesthouses B&B, RD 9, West Chester 19380 .... (215)692-4575

Rhode Island

B&B of Rhode Island, PO Box 3291, Newport 02840 .... (401)849-1298
Castle Keep B&B, 44 Everett St, Newport RI 02804 .... (401)846-0362
Guest House Association, 23 Brinley St, Newport RI 02840 .... (401)849-7645

South Carolina

Bay Street Accommodations, 601 Bay St, Beaufort 29902 .. (803)524-7720
Charleston Society B&B, 84 Murray Blvd, Charleston 29401 .... (803)723-4948
Historic Charleston B&B, 43 Legare St, Charleston 29401 .... (803)722-6606

South Dakota

South Dakota B&B, PO Box 80137, Sioux Falls 57116 .... (605)987-2834

Tennessee

B&B in Memphis, PO Box 41621, Memphis 38174 .... (901)726-5920

Texas

Sand Dollar Hospitality B&B, 3605 Mendenhall, Corpus Christi 78415 .... (512)853-1222
B&B Texas Style, 4224 W Red Bird Ln, Dallas 75237 .... (214)298-5433
.... (214)298-8586
Gasthaus B&B, 330 W Main St, Fredericksburg 78624 .... (512)997-4712
B&B Society of Texas, 921 Heights Blvd, Houston 77008 ... (713)868-4654
B&B Hosts of San Antonio, 166 Rockhill, San Antonio 78209 .... (512)824-8036

Utah

B&B Rocky Mountains, PO Box 804, Colorado Springs CO 80901 .... (719)630-3433

Vermont

Vermont B&B, Box 1, East Fairfield 05448 .... (802)827-3827
American B&B in New England, Box 983, St Albans 05478 .... (802)524-4731

Virginia

Princely B&B, Ltd, 819 Prince St, Alexandria 22314 .... (703)683-2159
Blue Ridge B&B, Rt 2, Box 3895, Berryville 22611 .... (703)955-1246
Rockbridge Reservations, Box 76, Brownsburg 24415 .... (703)348-5698
Guesthouses B&B, Box 5737, Charlottesville 22905 .... (804)979-7264
Sojourners B&B, PO Box 3587, Lynchburg 24503 .... (804)384-1655
B&B of Tidewater, PO Box 3343, Norfolk 23514 .... (804)627-1983
Bensonhouse of Richmond and Williamsburg, 2036 Monument Ave, Richmond 23220 .... (804)648-7560
The Travel Tree, PO Box 838, Williamsburg 23187 .... (804)253-1571

Washington

(BABS)B&B Service, PO Box 5025, Bellingham 98227 .... (206)733-8642
Travellers' B&B, PO Box 492, Mercer Island 98040 .... (206)232-2345
Pacific B&B, 701 WN 60th St, Seattle 98107 .... (206)784-0539
INNterlodging Co-op, PO Box 7044, Tacoma 98407 .... (206)756-0343

Washington DC

The B&B League, PO Box 9490, Washington DC 20005 ...... (202)363-7767
Bed 'n Breakfast of Washington DC, PO Box 12011, Washington DC 20005 .... (202)328-3510

West Virginia

Blue Ridge B&B, Rocks & Rills, R 2, Box 3895, Berryville VA 22611 .... (703)955-1246

Wisconsin

B&B Guest-Homes, Rt 2, Algoma 54201 .... (414)743-9742
B&B Milwaukee, 320 E Buffalo St, Milwaukee 53202 .... (414)242-9680

Wyoming

B&B Western Adventure, Box 20972, Billings MT 59104 .... (406)259-7993

Awards

Each year the Association of American Historic Inns presents Outstanding Achievement Awards to innkeepers who have made significant contributions to the preservation of historic properties. These individuals go beyond the confines of their own inn and reach out to the community encouraging historic preservation and restoration locally, statewide and even nationally. Nominations for future awards should be sent to **The Association of American Historic Inns, PO Box 336, Dana Point, CA 92629.**

We congratulate the winners and are pleased to honor them with these awards.

Past recipients of the award:

Kit Sargent, Casita Chamisa, Albuquerque, New Mexico
Tom Carroll, Mainstay Inn, Cape May, New Jersey
Tim Tyler, Russell-Cooper House B&B, Mount Vernon, Ohio

Association of American Historic Inns
Outstanding Achievement Award for 1990
Ruth Keyes
Red Brook Inn
Old Mystic, Connecticut

Two years after settling into the historic Crary Homestead Ruth Keyes embarked on major restoration project. In 1984 the state of Connecticut announced that the Haley Tavern, circa 1740, would have to be moved to accommodate a road widening project. Ruth was awarded the bid, and in 1985 supervised the disassembly of the tavern. Each beam, board and stone was numbered and moved to a site prepared just above the existing Crary Homestead, now known as the Red Brook Inn. Here the colonial building was meticulously restored and reassembled. Today it is open to the public for viewing at no charge and on a daily basis Ruth converts many inn guests to avid preservationists. In the winter she demonstrates early colonial open-hearth cooking. In recognition of Ms. Keyes contributions to historic preservation, she has been awarded a lifetime membership in the Mystic River Historic Society and has been appointed as a Historic District Commissioner for the Mystic Historic District.

Association of American Historic Inns
Outstanding Achievement Award for 1990
Chuck & Ann Hillestad
Queen Anne Inn
Denver, Colorado

In the mid-Seventies Chuck and Ann Hillestad moved to a crumbling historic neighborhood that was scheduled for demolition. They restored two homes here (including the Queen Anne Inn) and turned their immediate neighborhood into a preservation showcase. They initiated the creation of a historic designation for the Clements Historic District. In addition they helped create the adjoining Benedict Fountain Park, worked to restore the historic fountain in the park, helped obtain historic street lights and signs for the district, helped organize historic fund-raising tours, and helped landscape the public areas. Mr. Hillestad has brought together several agencies as sponsors of "Denver Historic! A Self-Guided Walking Tour." Over 25,000 tour brochures have been published and through the Hillestad's efforts Denver's historic areas have been spotlighted in a wide variety of regional and national publications. The Hillestads are the recipients of the Colorado Company of the Year Special Judge's Award and the Award of Honor for "Most notable contributions to quality and vitality of Downtown Denver."

Inns of Interest

Oldest Continuously Operating Inns

Curtis House .... Woodbury CT
York House .... Mountain City GA
Village Inn .... Lenox MA
Century House .... Nantucket MA
Inn at Gristmill Square ..... Warm Springs VA
Seafarer Inn .... Rockport MA
Colligan's .... Stockton NJ
Woodfield Inn .... Flat Rock NC
Colonial Inn .... Hillborough NC
Pasquaney Inn .... Bridgewater NH
Mt. Adams Inn .... North Woodstock NH
Inn at Montross .... Montross VA
Wakefield Inn .... Wakefield NH
Cranberry Inn .... Chatham MA
Maryland Inn .... Historic Inns of Annapolis MD
Hale Springs Inn .... Rogersville TN
Burton Inn .... Granville OH
Fitzwilliam Inn .... Fitzwilliam NH
Logan Inn .... New Hope PA

Old Taverns

Tollgate Hill Inn .... Litchfield CT
Silvermine Tavern .... Norwalk CT
David Finney Inn .... New Castle DE
White Swan Tavern .... Chestertown MD
Tavern House .... Vienna MD
Birchwood Inn .... Lenox MA
Historic Merrell Tavern Inn .... South Lee MA
Longfellow's Wayside Inn .... South Sudbury MA
Red Fox Inn .... Middlebury VA
Plough Inn .... Madison WI
Six Chimneys .... East Hebron NH
American House .... Geneseo NY
Bird & Bottle Inn .... Garrison NY
Rabbit Hill Inn .... Lower Waterford VT
Reynolds Tavern .... Historic Inns of Annapolis MD
Laurel Brigade .... Leesburg VA

Old Mills

Old Mill Inn .... Somersville CT
Inn at Mill Pond .... Cooperstown NY
Osceola Mill House .... Gordonville PA
Edgewood Plantation .... Charles City VA
The Inn at Gristmill Square .... Warm Springs VA

Train Stations

Inn at Depot Hill .... Aptos CA
Moore House .... South Cle Elum WA
Green Mountain Inn .... Stowe VT

Jail Houses

Jailer's Inn .... Bardstown KY
Jail House Inn .... Newport RI

Lighthouses

Richmond Brothers .... San Francisco CA
Lighthouse Inn .... Dennis MA
Big Bay Lighthouse .... Big Bay MI
The Keeper's House .... Isle Au Haut ME

Barns

The Barn B&B .... Valley Falls KS
Bedford Village Inn .... Bedford NH
Woods Hole Passage .... Falmouth MA
Round Hill Farm .... Great Barrington MA
Pine Barn Inn .... Danville PA

Archaeological Sites

Casita Chamisa .... Albuquerque NM
White Oak Inn .... Danville OH

Inns Prior to 1776

1637 York Harbor Inn .... York Harbor ME
1660 The Taos Inn .... Taos NM
1667 Stephen Daniels House .... Salem MA
1680 William Penn Guest House .... New Castle DE
1683 The Inn at Montross .... Montross VA
1692 The Dan'l Webster Inn ... Sandwich MA
1692 B&B of Valley Forge ..... Valley Forge PA
1693 The Joseph Reynolds House .. Bristol RI
1696 Old Yarmouth Inn ... Yarmouth Port MA
1699 Ashley Manor .... Barnstable MA
1700 Country Inn Acres ..... Harwich Port MA
1700 Historic Inns of Annapolis .... Annapolis MD
1702 Admiral Farragut Inn .... Newport RI
1705 Thomas Huckins House Barnstable MA
1708 Black Friar Brook Farm .... Duxbury MA
1708 The Jacob Kip River House B&B .... Rhinebeck NY
1709 The Woodbox .... Nantucket MA
1709 B&B Cape Cod ... West Hyannisport MA
1710 Colligan's Stockton Inn ...... Stockton NJ
1710 The Robert Morris Inn .... Oxford MD
1712 Harbor Light Inn .... Marblehead MA
1713 Historic Charleston B&B Charleston SC
1720 Butternut Farm .... Glastonbury CT
1720 Admiral Fell Inn .... Baltimore MD
1722 Logan Inn .... New Hope PA
1723 Corner House ...... Nantucket Island MA
1725 Witmer's Tavern .... Lancaster PA
1728 Red Fox Inn & Mosby's Tavern .... Middleburg VA
1730 White Swan Tavern .... Chestertown MD
1731 Maple Hill Farm B&B .... Coventry CT
1732 The Kitchen House .... Charleston SC
1732 Prospect Hill .... Trevilians VA
1733 Langdon House .... Beaufort NC
1734 Joseph Ambler Inn .... North Wales PA
1734 Fairway Farm B&B .... Pottstown PA
1735 Churchtown Inn .... Churchtown PA
1736 High Meadows B&B .... Eliot ME
1738 Herr Farmhouse Inn .... Manheim PA
1739 The Ruffner House .... Luray VA
1740 The Old Dennis House .... Newport RI
1740 Under Mountain Inn .... Salisbury CT
1740 Red Brook Inn .... Mystic CT
1740 Evermay-on-the-Delaware .. Erwinna PA
1740 Barley Sheaf Farm .... Holicong PA
1740 The Inn at Narrow Passage .... Woodstock VA
1740 Sterling Orchards B&B .... Sterling MA
1742 Kelly House .... Edgartown MA
1744 Yesterday's Yankee B&B ... Salisbury CT
1745 Black Bass Hotel .... Lumberville PA
1750 The General Rufus Putnam House .... Worcester-Rutland MA
1750 The Melville House .... Newport RI
1750 Henry Farm Inn .... Chester VT
1750 Hickory Bridge Farm .... Orrtanna PA

1750 Golden Plough Inn ....Lahaska PA
1750 Backstreet Inn ....New Hope PA
1750 Guesthouses ....Charlottesville VA
1750 Galisteo Inn ....Galisteo NM
1751 The Penny House ... North Eastham MA
1751 Three Village Inn ....Stony Brook NY
1752 Hyde Park Farm ....Burkeville VA
1753 L'Auberge Provencale..... White Post VA
1754 Curtis House .... Woodbury CT
1755 Hayne House ....Charleston SC
1757 Wingscorton Farm Inn ....East Sandwich MA
1757 Woodstock Hall.........Charlottesville VA
1759 Laurel Brigade Inn .... Leesburg VA
1759 Colonial Inn ....Hillsborough NC
1760 Edgewater B&B ....Fairhaven MA
1760 Mountain Lake Inn ....Bradford NH
1760 Henry Ludlam Inn .... Woodbine NJ
1760 The Inn at Fordhook Farm .... Doylestown, Bucks Co PA
1760 Gilbert House B&B .. Charles Town WV
1760 The Winchester Country Inn ....Westminster MD
1761 Bird & Bottle Inn ....Garrison NY
1761 Lookout Point House...... Harpswell ME
1762 Goose Chase ....Gardners PA
1763 Smithton Inn ....Ephrata PA
1763 Casa de Solana .... Saint Augustine FL
1763 John Rutledge House Inn ....Charleston SC
1764 Birchwood Inn ....Lenox MA
1765 Captain Samuel Eddy House Inn ....Auburn MA
1765 The Squire Tarbox Inn .....Wiscasset ME
1765 Appel Inn ....Altamont NY
1765 The Carlisle House Inn..Nantucket MA
1766 Beekman Arms .... Rhinebeck NY
1766 The Osceola Mill House ....Gordonville PA
1768 The Silver Fox Inn ..... West Rutland VT
1770 Garden Gables Inn ....Lenox MA
1770 The Parsonage ....East Orleans MA
1770 Guesthouse and 1777 House at Doneckers ....Ephrata PA
1771 Village Inn ....Lenox MA
1771 Cartway House Inn ....Gilford NH
1772 Jail House Inn .... Newport RI
1772 The Bagley House .... Freeport ME
1772 Country Fare ....Woodstock VA
1773 Peacock Inn ....North Conway NH
1775 Colonel Roger Brown House ....Concord MA
1775 Chase House B&B ....Cornish NH
1775 Todd House ....Eastport ME
1775 1811 House .... Manchester Village VT
1775 Jared Cone House .... Bolton CT
1775 Welbourne ....Middleburg VA
1775 Sleepy Hollow Farm ... Gordonsville VA
1775 Arrowhead Inn ....Durham NC
1775 Salt Marsh Farm South Dartmouth MA
1776 Griswold Inn ....Essex CT

Revolutionary War

Ashley Manor .... Barnstable MA
The Village Green..................... Falmouth MA
Spring House .... Airville PA
Churchtown Inn ....Churchtown PA
Pace One Restaurant and Country Inn ....Thornton PA
B&B of Valley Forge............ Valley Forge PA
Melville House .... Newport RI
The Silver Thatch Inn.......Charlottesville VA
Caledonia Farm ....Flint Hill VA
The Inn at Weathersfield .. Weathersfield VT
Robert Morris................................. Oxford MD
John Rutledge House .... Charleston SC
Magnolia Place Inn.................. Savannah GA
Lincoln House Country Inn Dennysville ME
Colonel Roger Brown House .... Concord MA
Dan'l Webster Inn.....................Sandwich MA

Literary Figures

Robert Louis Stevenson
Brannan Cottage ....Calistoga CA

Pearl Buck
Historic Island Hotel................Cedar Key FL

Ralph Waldo Emerson
Island House .... Southwest Harbor FL

Harriet Beecher Stowe Uncle Tom's Cabin
Cornstalk Hotel ....New Orleans LA

Harriet Beecher Stowe
Harriet Beeacher Stowe House ....Brunswick ME

Replica of Shakespeare's birthplace (built by the publisher of Little Women)
Stratford House Inn ....Bar Harbor ME

Longfellow's The Courtship of Miles Standish
Isaac Randall House ....Freeport ME

Sophie Kerr
Sophie Kerr House ....Denton MD

Ralph Waldo Emerson, Louisa Mae Alcott, Nathaniel Hawthorne
Hawthorne Inn ....Concord MA

Nathaniel Hawthorne
Edgartown Inn ....Edgartown MA

Edith Wharton
The Gables Inn ....Lenox MA

The Yankee Bodleys Naomi Babson
Old Farm Inn ....Rockport MA

Henry Wadsworth Longfellow
Longfellow's Wayside Inn .... South Sudbury MA

F. Scott Fitzgerald
University Club .... St Paul MN

Mark Twain
Garth Woodside Mansion .... Hannibal MO

Becky Thatcher
The Fifth Street Mansion .... Hannibal MO

Marguerite Henry Misty of Chincoteague
Miss Molly's Inn ....Chincoteague VA

F. Scott Fitzgerald, Thomas Wolfe
Welbourne ....Middleburg VA

Who Slept Here

Wrigley chewing gum family
The Inn on Mt. Ada .... Avalon, Santa Catalina CA

Scripps family
Britt House .... San Diego CA

Spreckels Sugar Family
Spreckels Mansion .... San Francisco CA

Marilyn Monroe, Arthur Miller
Homestead Inn......................New Milford CT

George Washington
David Finney Inn ....New Castle DE

William Penn
William Penn Guest House ...New Castle DE

George Washington
Jacob Kip ....Rhinebeck NY

Susan B. Anthony
The Park House ....Saugatuck MI

John Phillip Souza
The B&B Inn at La Jolla ....La Jolla CA

Jefferson Davis, Henry Clay, Governor of Mexico & Mississippi
Monmouth Plantation .... Natchez MS

Samuel Clemens
Garth Woodside Mansion ....Hannibal MO

The Woolworth family, Barbara Hutton, Cary Grant
The Mulburn Inn .... Bethlehem NH

Salmon Chase chief justice and on Lincoln's cabinet
Chase House B&B .... Cornish NH

Architect Stanford White
The Inn at Jackson ....Jackson NH

Pillsbury family
Ferry Point House ....Laconia NH

Babe Ruth
Cranmore Mountain Lodge ....North Conway NH

Bigelow family
Stonehurst Manor ....North Conway NH

Robert E. Lee
The Wooden Rabbit....................Cape May NJ

Presidents Wilson, Cleveland, and Roosevelt
Cordova ....Ocean Grove NJ

Judy Garland, Pancho Villa, Clark Gable
The Lodge .... Cloudcroft NM

Betty Davis
Blackberry Inn .... Camden ME

Georgia O'Keefe
Hacienda del Sol .... Taos NM

Teddy Roosevelt
Troutbeck .... Amenia NY

Newberry family
Shadowbrook B&B .... Irvington-on-Hudson NY

Aaron Burr, William Jennings Bryan, Horace Greeley, Franklin Roosevelt
Beekman Arms .... Rhinebeck NY

William Rockefeller
The Point .... Saranac Lake NY

William Seward
William Seward Inn .... Westfield NY

Cornwallis Aaron Burr
Colonial Inn .... Hillsborough NC

Charles Dickens
Golden Lamb .... Lebanon OH

Burpee family
The Inn at Fordhook Farm .... Doylestown PA

Marx Brothers Lillian Hellman S. J. Perlman
Barley Sheaf Farm .... Holicong PA

General Lafayette
Joseph Reynolds House .... Bristol RI

"Bob Newhart" Inn
The Waybury Inn .... East Middlebury VT

Kellogg family
Village Country Inn .. Manchester Village VT

Cornelia Otis Skinner
The Golden Stage .... Proctorsville VT

General Stonewall Jackson
Mayhurst Inn .... Orange VA
Inn at Narrow Passage .... Woodstock VA

Robert E. Lee and President Van Buren
The Greenbrier River Inn Caldwell West VA

Norman Rockwell
The Inn on Covered Bridge Green .... West Arlington VT

Susan B. Anthony
Park House .... Saugatuck MI

Margaret Mitchell (Gone With the Wind)
The Veranda .... Senoia GA

Abraham Lincoln, Ulysses S. Grant
DeSoto House .... Galena IL

Thomas Edison
Tulip Tree Inn .... Chittenden VT

Still in the Family

Standish House .... Lanark IL
The Homestead .... Sugar Hill NH
General Hooker's House .... Portland OR
The Inn at Fordhook Farm .... Doylestown Bucks Co PA
Historic Charleston B&B .... Charleston SC
North Bend Plantation .... Charles City VA
Welbourne .... Middleburg VA
Birch Hill Inn .... Manchester VT
Inn at Fordhook Farm .... Doylestown PA
Waunita Hot Springs .... Gunnison CO
Chalfonte .... Cape May NJ
Millsaps-Buie House .... Jackson MS

Tunnels & Secret Passageways

Ashley Manor .... Barnstable MA
Historic Inns of Annapolis MD
Sterling Orchards .... Sterling MA
Wingscorton Farm .... East Sandwich MA
7 Wives Inn .... St George UT
Reed House .... Asheville NC
B&B of Valley Forge PA
Country Fare .... Woodstock VA
Kedron Valley Inn .... South Woodstock VT

Black History

A Hotel the Frenchman .... New Orleans LA
Cornstalk Hotel .... New Orleans LA
Dauzat House .... New Orleans LA
Isaac Randall .... Freeport ME
Old Manse Inn .... Brewster MA
Wingscorton Farm Inn .... East Sandwich MA
Ships Inn .... Nantucket MA
Colonel Ashley Inn .... Sheffield MA
Rosswood Plantation .... Lorman MS
The Wooden Rabbit .... Cape May NJ
Troutbeck .... Amenia NY
B&B Valley Forge .... Valley Forge PA
Sleepy Hollow Farm .... Gordonsville VA
The Catlin-Abbott House .... Richmond VA
Prospect Hill .... Trevilians VA
Kedron Valley Inn .... South Woodstock VT
The Inn at Weathersfield ... Weathersfield VT
The Golden Stage Inn .... Proctorsville VT
Jacob Kip .... Rhinebeck NY
Twin Gates .... Baltimore MD

Civil War

Gordon Lee Mansion .... Chickamauga GA
Historic Island Hotel .... Cedar Key FL
Culpepper House .... Senoia GA
Cornstalk Hotel .... New Orleans LA
Elmwood C. 1770 .... Princess Anne MD
Rosswood Plantation .... Lorman MS
Dunleith .... Natchez MS
Oak Square .... Port Gibson MS
Cedar Grove Mansion Inn .... Vicksburg MS
Langdon House .... Beaufort NC
Dry Ridge Inn .... Weaverville NC
The Russell-Cooper House .... Mount Vernon OH
Churchtown Inn .... Churchtown PA
The Doubleday Inn .... Gettysburg PA
Beechmont Inn .... Hanover PA
Kane Manor Country Inn .... Kane PA
Bay Street Inn .... Beaufort SC
Hale Springs Inn .... Rogersville TN
North Bend Plantation .... Charles City VA
La Vista Plantation .... Fredericksburg VA
Red Fox Inn & Tavern .... Middleburg VA
Welbourne .... Middleburg VA
The Widow Kip's Country Inn .... Mt Jackson VA
Mayhurst Inn .... Orange VA
Prospect Hill .... Trevilians VA
Old Rittenhouse Inn .... Bayfield WI
The Greenbrier River Inn .... Caldwell WV
Prospect Hill .... Gerrardstown WV
Fillmore St B&B .... Harpers Ferry WV
Boydville - The Inn at Martinsburg .... Martinsburg WV

Inns by Name

The following is a list of inns by name. It lists only those described in the main body of this book.

Red Brook Inn	Mystic CT
The Red Castle Inn	Nevada City CA
Red Fox Inn & Mosby's Tavern	Middleburg VA
Red Hill Inn	Centre Harbor NH
The Red House Country Inn	Burdett NY
Red House Inn	Brevard NC
Redstone Inn	Dubuque IA
Reed House B&B	Asheville NC
Reeds B&B	Washington DC
Reluctant Panther Inn	Manchester VT
Remshart-Brooks House	Savannah GA
The Rhett House Inn	Beaufort SC
The Richards House	Dubuque IA
Richardson House B&B	Jamesport MO
Richmond Hill Inn & Conference Center	Asheville NC
River Forest Manor	Belhaven NC
Riverfront House & Cottage	Mathews VA
Rivertown Inn	Stillwater MN
Riverview Hotel	Saint Mary's GA
Riverwind	Deep River CT
The Robert Morris Inn	Oxford MD
Rock Haus B&B Inn	Del Mar CA
The Rock House	Morgantown IN
Rocky Shores Inn	Rockport MA
Rogers House	Lincoln NE
Rose And Crown	Provincetown MA
Rose Inn	Ithaca NY
Rose Victorian Inn	Arroyo Grande CA
Rosebriar Inn	Astoria OR
Rosemont	Aberdeen MS
Roserox Country Inn By-The-Sea	Pacific Grove CA
Rosewood Inn	Corning NY
Rosswood Plantation	Lorman MS
The Rough Riders	Medora ND
Round Hill Farm	Great Barrington MA
Royal Brewster B&B	Bar Mills ME
Royal Carter House	Ashland OR
RSVP Savannah B&B Reservation Service	Savannah GA
The Ruffner House	Luray VA
The Russell-Cooper House	Mount Vernon OH
Rutledge Museum Guest House	Charleston SC
The Ryan House B&B	Sonora CA
Saddle Rock Ranch	Sedona AZ
The Salem Inn	Salem MA
Salisbury House	Bethlehem PA
Salisbury House	Los Angeles CA
Salt Ash Inn	Plymouth VT
Salt Marsh Farm	South Dartmouth MA
San Benito House	Half Moon Bay CA
Sand Castle Guest House	Cape May NJ
Sandlake Country Inn	Cloverdale OR
Sandpiper Hotel	Spring Lake NJ
Sara's B&B Inn	Houston TX
Sarah's Dream	Dryden NY
Sardy House	Aspen CO
Sausalito Hotel	Sausalito CA
Savery Creek Thoroughbred Ranch	Savery WY
Scanlan House	Lanesboro MN
Scarlett's Country Inn	Calistoga CA
Schwegmann House	Washington MO
The Scofield House B&B	Sturgeon Bay WI
Seafarer Inn	Rockport MA
The Seal Beach Inn & Gardens	Seal Beach CA
Sears-Withington House	West Newton MA
Seekonk Pines Inn	Great Barrington MA
Settlers Inn	Hawley PA
Seven Gables Inn	Pacific Grove CA
Seven Wives Inn	St George UT
Seventh Sister Guesthouse	Cape May NJ
Shady Oaks Country Inn	Saint Helena CA
Shakertown At Pleasant Hill	Harrodsburg KY
The Inn at Shallow Creek Farm	Orland CA
Shaw House Inn	Ferndale CA
Shelburne Inn	Seaview WA
Shellmont B&B Lodge	Atlanta GA
Shelter Harbor Inn	Westerly RI
Sherman House Restaurant & Inn	Batesville IN
Sherman-Berry House	Lowell MA
Sherwood Inn	Skaneateles NY
The Shield House	Clinton NC
Ships Inn	Nantucket MA
Ships Knees Inn	East Orleans MA
Shire Inn	Chelsea VT
The Shirley-Madison Inn	Baltimore MD
Shumway Mansion	Kirkland WA
Silas Griffith Inn	Danby VT
The Silver Fox Inn	West Rutland VT
Silver Maple Lodge & Cottages	Fairlee VT
Silver Thatch Inn	Charlottesville VA
Silvermine Tavern	Norwalk CT
Simpson House Inn	Santa Barbara CA
Six Chimneys	East Hebron NH
Sleepy Hollow Farm	Gordonsville VA
Smithton Inn	Ephrata PA
Snow Den Inn	West Dover VT
Snowvillage Inn	Snowville NH
Society Hill Government House	Baltimore MD
Society Hill Hopkins	Baltimore MD
Society Hill Hotel	Baltimore MD
Society Hill Hotel	Philadelphia PA
Sonoma Hotel	Sonoma CA
Sophie Kerr House	Denton MD
Sorensen's Resort	Hope Valley CA
The Inn on South Street	Kennebunkport ME
Southard House	Austin TX
Spencer House	San Francisco CA
Spray Cliff on the Ocean	Marblehead MA
Spreckels Mansion	San Francisco CA
Spring Bank Inn	Frederick MD
Spring Bayou Inn	Tarpon Springs FL
Spring Garden	Laurel DE
Spring House	Airville PA
Springside	Cape May NJ
The Spruces B&B	Salt Lake City UT
The Squire Tarbox Inn	Wiscasset ME
St Michael's Manor B&B	Scotland MD
St. Charles Guest House	New Orleans LA
St. Francis Inn	Saint Augustine FL
Stagecoach Inn B&B	Cedarburg WI
Standish House	Lanark IL
Stanyan Park Hotel	San Francisco CA
The Inn at Starlight Lake	Starlight PA
Starrett House Inn	Port Townsend WA
State House B&B	Salem OR
State Street Inn	Hood River OR
Staveleigh House	Sheffield MA
Stephen Daniels House	Salem MA
The Stephen Potwine House	East Windsor CT
Sterling Hotel	Sacramento CA
Sterling Orchards B&B	Sterling MA
Stillman's Country Inn	Galena IL
Stillmeadow B&B at Hampstead	Hampstead NH
The Stone Hearth Inn	Chester VT
Stone Lea	Narragansett RI
Stone Post Inn	Spring Lake NJ
Stonebrake Cottage	Shepherdstown WV
Stonebridge Inn	Poultney VT
The Stonehouse Inn	Carmel CA
Stonehurst Manor	North Conway NH
Story Inn	Nashville IN
Storybook Inn	Sky Forest CA
Stout House	Dubuque IA
Stovall House	Sautee GA
Strawberry Castle B&B	Rochester NY
Strawberry Lodge	Kyburz CA
Sturbridge Country Inn	Sturbridge MA
The Summer House	Sandwich MA
The Inn at Sunderland	Sunderland VT
Sundial Inn	Kennebunk Beach ME
Sunny Pines B&B Inn	West Harwich MA
Sunny Side Inn	North Conway NH
Surf Manor & Cottages	San Diego CA
Surry Inn	Surry ME
Susina Plantation Inn	Thomasville GA
Sutler's Limpia Hotel	Fort Davis TX
The Sutton-Weed Farm	Hudson MI

Association of American Historic Inns

Discount Certificates

These are offered by innkeepers listed in this book to help promote historic inns. These are not paid advertisments. Note: DO NOT REMOVE. These are only valid when presented with and attached to this book. Advance reservations are required. All offers are subject to availability.

The Official Guide to American Historic Inns

Save 20% on a Sunday through Thursday midweek stay. Excluding Holidays. Relax and unwind in our charming rooms while enjoying the quaint village of La Jolla.

The B&B Inn at La Jolla
7753 Draper Ave
La Jolla CA 92037
(619)456-2066

Valid thru 12/91
Void if detached

The Official Guide to American Historic Inns

Stay two nights, third night is free. Valid November through April, excluding Holidays.

Howard Creek Ranch
40501 North Hwy, PO Box 121
Westport CA 95488
(707)964-6725

Valid thru 12/91
Void if detached

The Official Guide to American Historic Inns

30% off per night, Sunday through Thursday. 10% discount Friday & Saturday. Excludes holidays.

Casa Laguna
2510 S Coast Hwy
Laguna Beach CA 92651
(714)494-2996

Valid thru 12/91
Void if detached

The Official Guide to American Historic Inns

25% discount. Reservations cannot be made more than 7 days prior to arrivel. Must I.D. discount at time of reservation request. Not applicable with any other discounts.

Westways "Private" Resort
PO Box 41624
Phoenix AZ 85080
(602)582-3868

Valid thru 12/91
Void if detached

The Official Guide to American Historic Inns

10% discount good anytime.

The Kaleidoscope Inn
Box 1297, 130 E Dana St
Nipomo CA 93444
(805)929-5444

Valid thru 12/91
Void if detached

The Official Guide to American Historic Inns

$10 off mid-week rates, Sunday through Thursday except Holidays. Two night minimum.

Knickerbocker Mansion
869 S Knickerbocker Rd
Big Bear Lake CA 92315
(714)866-8221

Valid thru 12/91
Void if detached

The Official Guide to American Historic Inns

20% off a Sunday through Thursday midweek stay. Excluding Holiday periods. Includes full breakfast and high tea.

Britt House
406 Maple St
San Diego CA 92103
(619)234-2926

Valid thru 12/91
Void if detached

The Official Guide to American Historic Inns

20% discount Monday through Thursday, October 15 through April 15.

Simpson House Inn
121 E Arrellaga St
Santa Barbara CA 93101
(805)963-7067

Valid thru 4/15/91
Void if detached

The Official Guide to American Historic Inns

10% off Sunday through Thursday. Includes lavish breakfast - Honeymoon packages available. Rates from $88-$145.

The Seal Beach Inn & Gardens
212 5th St
Seal Beach CA 90740
(213)493-2416

Valid thru 12/91
Void if detached

The Official Guide to American Historic Inns

10% discount anytime.

Queen Anne Inn
2147 Tremont Place
Denver CO 80205
(303)296-6666
Valid thru 12/91
Void if detached

The Official Guide to American Historic Inns

10% discount good anytime.

Greenbriar B&B
315 Wallace
Coeur d'Alene ID 83814
(208)667-9660
Valid thru 12/91
Void if detached

The Official Guide to American Historic Inns

15% off regular rates for your first visit, anytime. 20% off regular rates Sunday through Thursday, May-October. 30% off regular rates Sunday through Thursday, November-April.

Queen Anne Inn & Antique Gallery
265 Williams St
New London CT 06320
(203)447-2600
Valid thru 11/91
Void if detached

The Official Guide to American Historic Inns

Relax in a wicker rocker on our veranda while you save 20% on your guest room Monday through Thursday, from March to August.

Braxtan House Inn B&B
210 N Gospel St
Paoli IN 47454
(812)723-4677
Valid thru 8/91
Void if detached

The Official Guide to American Historic Inns

10% discount midweek.

Manor House
Maple Ave, Box 447
Norfolk CT 06058
(203)542-5690
Valid thru 12/91
Void if detached

The Official Guide to American Historic Inns

20% discount weekday 10% discount weekends

Lafitte Guest House
1003 Bourbon St
New Orleans LA 70116
(504)581-2678
Valid thru 12/91
Void if detached

The Official Guide to American Historic Inns

10% discount good anytime (if space available)

Kalorama Guest House
1854 Mintwood Place NW
Washington DC 20009
(202)667-6369
Valid thru 12/91
Void if detached

The Official Guide to American Historic Inns

Second night half price (November '90 - April '91)

Captain Dexter House of Edgartown
35 Pease's Point Way
Edgartown MA 02539
(508)627-7289
Valid thru 4/91
Void if detached

The Official Guide to American Historic Inns

Guided walking tour of "Old Dover Historic District" (guided tour by Dover Heritage Trail, Inc.).

The Inn at Meeting House Square
305 S Governors Ave
Dover DE 19901
(302)678-1242
Valid thru 12/91
Void if detached

The Official Guide to American Historic Inns

Second night half price (November '90 - April '91)

Captain Dexter House of Vineyard Haven
100 Main St, PO Box 2457
Martha's Vineyard MA 02568
(508)693-6564
Valid thru 4/91
Void if detached

The Official Guide to American Historic Inns

Extend your stay and save 15%. (Applies after first night is paid at full rate. Certain holidays excluded.)

Amelia Payson Guest House
16 Winter St
Salem MA 01970 — Valid thru 12/91
(508)744-8304 — Void if detached

The Official Guide to American Historic Inns

20% off regular rates midweek (Sunday through Thursday) July, August, January & February. Based upon availability.

Admiral Fell Inn
888 S Broadway
Baltimore MD 21231 — Valid thru 8/91
(301)522-7377 (800)292-INNS — Void if detached

The Official Guide to American Historic Inns

15% discount midweek.

Staveleigh House
PO 608, S Main St
Sheffield MA 01257 — Valid thru 12/91
(413)229-2129 — Void if detached

The Official Guide to American Historic Inns

20% discount good anytime (if space available)

The Shirley-Madison Inn
205 W Madison St
Baltimore MD 21201 — Valid thru 12/91
(301)728-6550 — Void if detached

The Official Guide to American Historic Inns

Champagne for two.

Broad Bay Inn & Gallery
Main St, PO Box 607
Waldoboro ME 04572 — Valid thru 12/91
(207)832-6668 — Void if detached

The Official Guide to American Historic Inns

Half price discount on second consecutive night stay from Nov. 15 to March 31.

The Fifth Street Mansion B&B
213 S Fifth St
Hannibal MO 63401 — Valid thru 3/91
(314)221-0445 — Void if detached

The Official Guide to American Historic Inns

10% discount, Monday through Thursday.

Kemah Guest House
633 Pleasant St
Saugatuck MI 49453 — Valid thru 12/91
(616)857-2919 — Void if detached

The Official Guide to American Historic Inns

Nightshirts to wear, plus $10 off two night stay (Monday through Thursday).

Garth Woodside Mansion
RR 1
Hannibal MO 63401 — Valid thru 12/91
(314)221-2789 — Void if detached

The Official Guide to American Historic Inns

10% discount and glass of wine, Monday through Wednesday.

Red House Inn
412 W Probart St
Brevard NC 28712 — Valid thru 12/91
(704)884-9349 — Void if detached

The Official Guide to American Historic Inns

Two nights lodging, full breakfast, dinner for two - $120 Sunday through Thursday, $135 Friday and Saturday. Valid June 19 through September 30. (Lobster dinner and alcohol not included).

Chase On The Lake Lodge & Motor Inn
PO Box 206
Walker MN 56484 — Valid thru 9/90
(218)547-1531 (800)533-2083 — Void if detached

The Official Guide to American Historic Inns

Getaway Package. Room, gourmet dinner & breakfast. $60 per person first night, $40 per person second night, $20 per person third night! (Excludes holiday weekends.)

Tamworth Inn
Main St
Tamworth NH 03886
(603)323-7721
Valid thru 12/90
Void if detached

The Official Guide to American Historic Inns

Stay in the White Oak Inn, rooms furnished with antiques, one night and receive a 10% discount Monday through Thursday.

The White Oak Inn
29683 Walhonding Rd
Danville OH 43014
(614)599-6107
Valid thru 12/91
Void if detached

The Official Guide to American Historic Inns

Breakfast by candlelight and classical music. 10% discount subject to availability.

Captain Mey's Inn
202 Ocean St
Cape May NJ 08204
(609)884-7793
Valid thru 12/91
Void if detached

The Official Guide to American Historic Inns

Stay in a Victorian ambiance Monday through Thursday and receive a 10% discount.

The Russell-Cooper House
115 E Gambier St
Mount Vernon OH 43050
(614)397-8638
Valid thru 12/91
Void if detached

The Official Guide to American Historic Inns

Your country place is available for dreams at 10% discount Sunday through Thursday.

Henry Ludlam Inn
124 S Delsea Dr, RD 3 Box 298
Woodbine NJ 08270
(609)861-5847
Valid thru 12/91
Void if detached

The Official Guide to American Historic Inns

$10 off room price Sunday through Thursday.

Willowtree Inn
1900 W State, Rt 571
Tipp City OH 45371
(513)667-2957
Valid thru 12/91
Void if detached

The Official Guide to American Historic Inns

Getaway Package. Any dinner selection, bottle of wine, one night's lodging, full breakfast. $120-$135 w/fireplace. February 4-April 30, 1990, November 1-December 21, 1990.

Asa Ransom House
10529 Main St
Clarence NY 14031
(716)759-2315
Valid thru 12/21/90
Void if detached

The Official Guide to American Historic Inns

Return to Grandma's Victorian Bedroom and receive a 10% discount good Monday through Thursday.

John Palmer House
4314 N Mississippi Ave, Ste AA
Portland OR 97217
(503)284-5893 Ext. 400
Valid thru 12/91
Void if detached

The Official Guide to American Historic Inns

10% discount Monday through Thursday.

Rose Inn
Rt 34 N, Box 6576
Ithaca NY 14851-6576
(607)533-7905
Valid thru 12/91
Void if detached

The Official Guide to American Historic Inns

Celebrating something special, receive a special gift.

Backstreet Inn
144 Old York Rd
New Hope PA 18939
(215)862-9571
Valid thru 12/91
Void if detached

The Official Guide to American Historic Inns

$10 off two night stay (Monday through Thursday).

The Rhett House Inn
1009 Craven St
Beaufort SC 29902
(803)524-9030

Valid thru 12/91
Void if detached

The Official Guide to American Historic Inns

Victorian Rates: $2.00 on your birthday! Present this certificate on your birthday and you will be charged $2.00. (The person sharing your room will be charged the current single rate.)

The Governor's Inn
86 Main St
Ludlow VT 05149
(802)228-8830

Valid thru 12/91
Void if detached

The Official Guide to American Historic Inns

10% discount good anytime on Melissa's Room with the secret door.

Seven Wives Inn
217 N 100 W
St George UT 84770
(801)628-3737

Valid thru 12/91
Void if detached

The Official Guide to American Historic Inns

Stay two nights and the third night is free. Not Valid Holidays or Foliage Season.

Inn at Blush Hill
Blush Hill Rd, Box 1266
Waterbury VT 05676
(802)244-7529

Valid thru 12/91
Void if detached

The Official Guide to American Historic Inns

Complimentary copy of recipes from the kitchen of Hill Farm Inn.

Hill Farm Inn
RR 2 Box 2015
Arlington VT 05250
(802)375-2269

Valid thru 12/91
Void if detached

The Official Guide to American Historic Inns

MAKING WHOOPIE! Innkeeper will sing his rendition on demand with this coupon. Complimentary bottle of champagne for honeymooners and those celebrating anniversaries and birthdays.

The Inn at Weathersfield
Rt 106, PO Box 165
Weathersfield VT 05151
(802)263-9217 (802)263-9219 (Fax)

Valid thru 12/91
Void if detached

The Official Guide to American Historic Inns

10% discount on two night stay.

Old Town Farm Inn
Rt 10
Gassets VT 05143
(802)875-2346

Valid thru 12/91
Void if detached

The Official Guide to American Historic Inns

10% discount Sunday through Thursday, excluding June through September and holidays.

Bombay House
8490 Beck Rd NE
Bainbridge Island WA 98110
(206)842-3926

Valid thru 12/91
Void if detached

The Official Guide to American Historic Inns

10% discount off two-night midweek stay. (Excluding foilage and holidays.)

The Andrie Rose Inn
13 Pleasant St
Ludlow VT 05149
(802)228-4846

Valid thru 12/91
Void if detached

The Official Guide to American Historic Inns

10% discount Monday through Thursday.

Historic Bennett House
825 Oak St
Wisconsin Dells WI 53965
(608)254-2500

Valid thru 12/91
Void if detached

Association of American Historic Inns
PO Box 336 Dana Point CA 92629 (714) 496-6953

Inn Evaluation Form

The Inn we visited: ______________________________

	A	B	C	D	F
Location for our needs					
Cleanliness					
Bathroom facilities					
Beds					
Attitude & Friendliness of host					
Food & Presentation					
Worth the price					

A = Outstanding
B = Good
C = Average
D = Needs to be improved
F = Disaster

Any comments on the above: ______________________________

____

I especially appreciated: ______________________________

____

Suggestions for improvement: ______________________________

____

Name (optional): ______________________________

Date of stay: ______________________________

Please COPY and complete this form for each stay and mail to the address above. Since 1981 we have maintained files that include thousands of evaluations by inn goers. We value your comments which help us to keep abreast of the hundreds of new inns that open each year and to follow the changes in established inns.

Thank you.